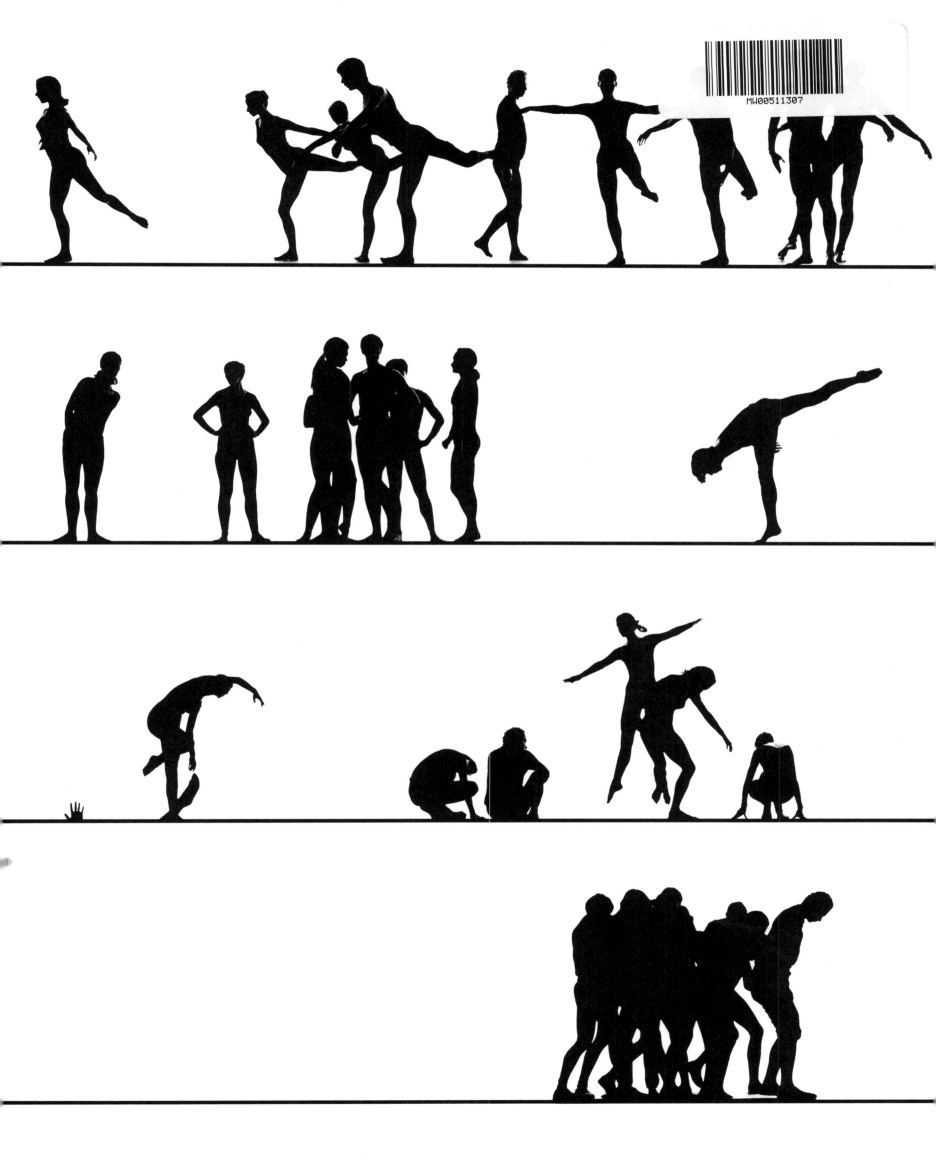

MERCE CUNNINGHAM REDUX

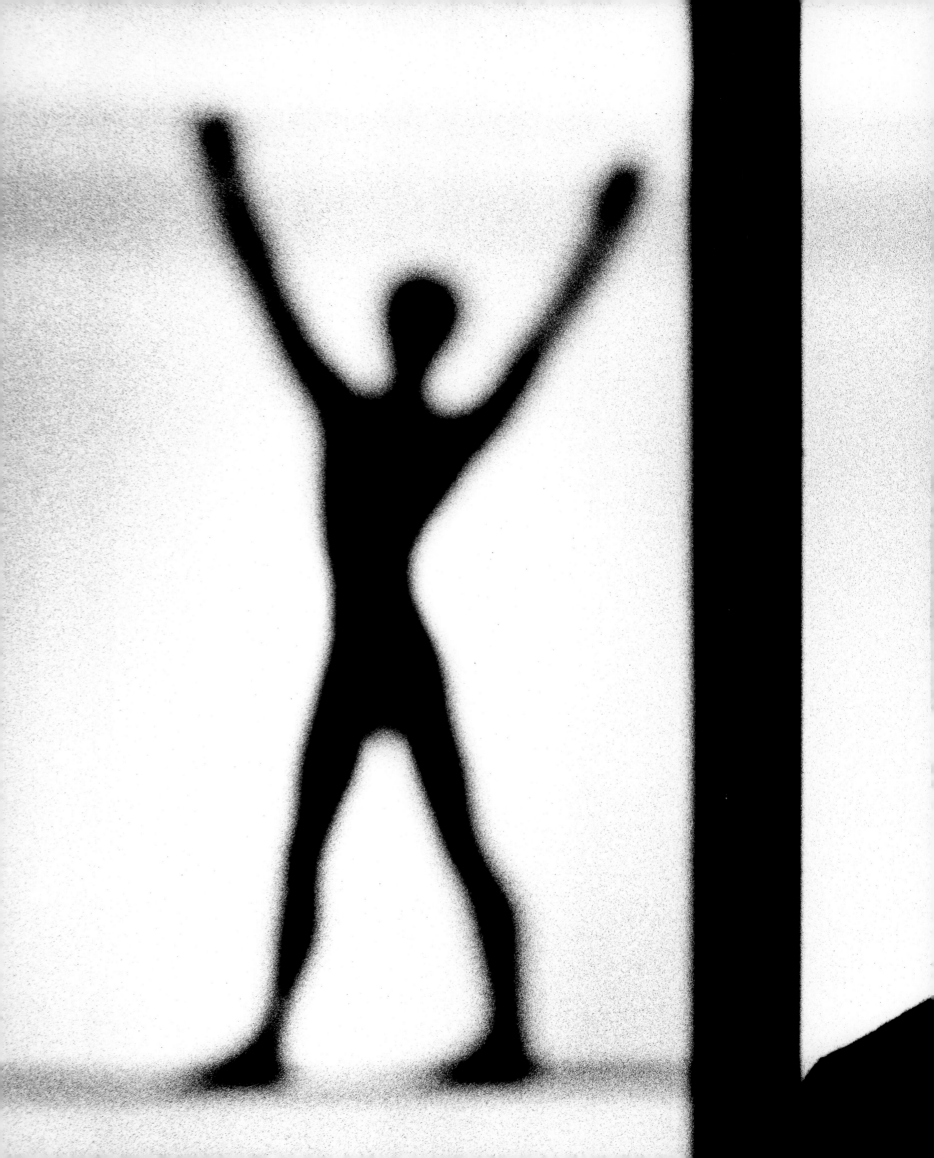

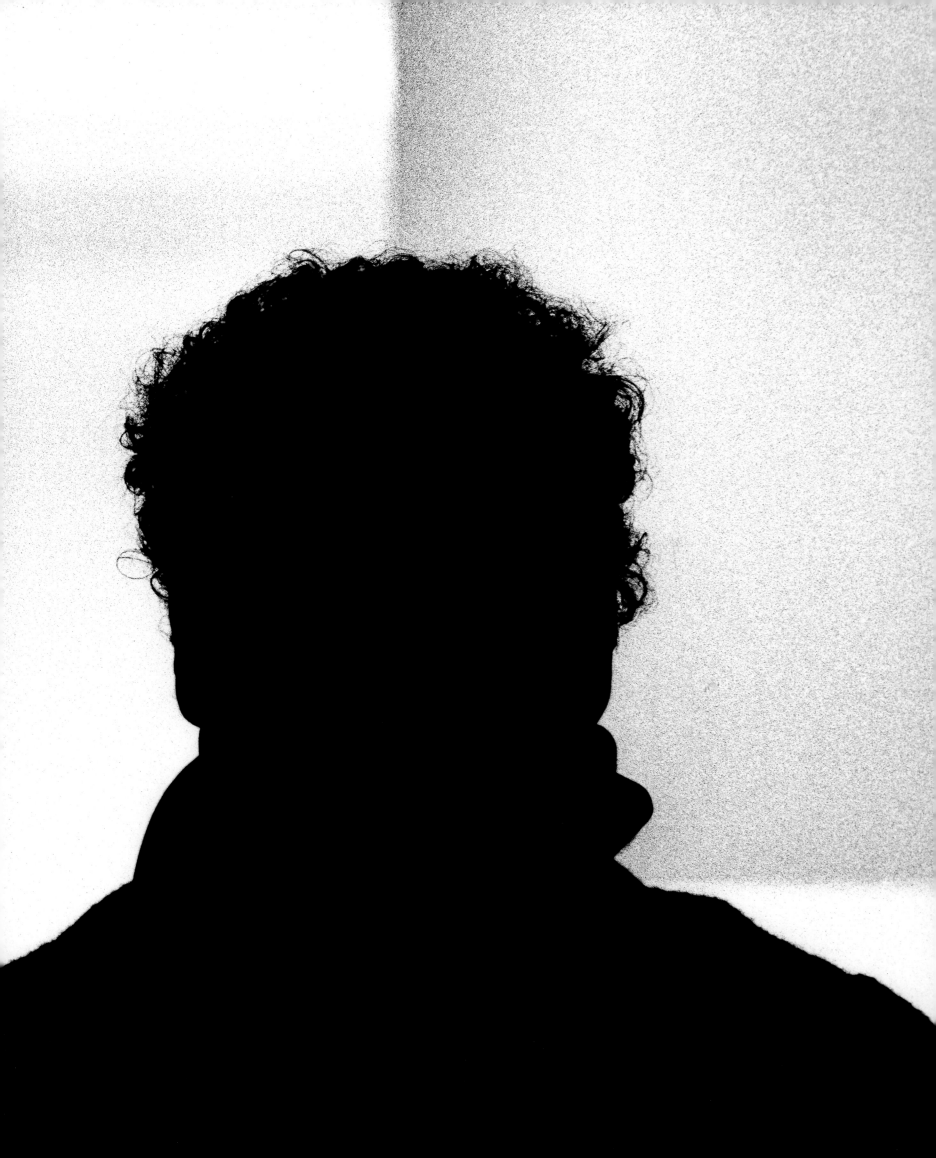

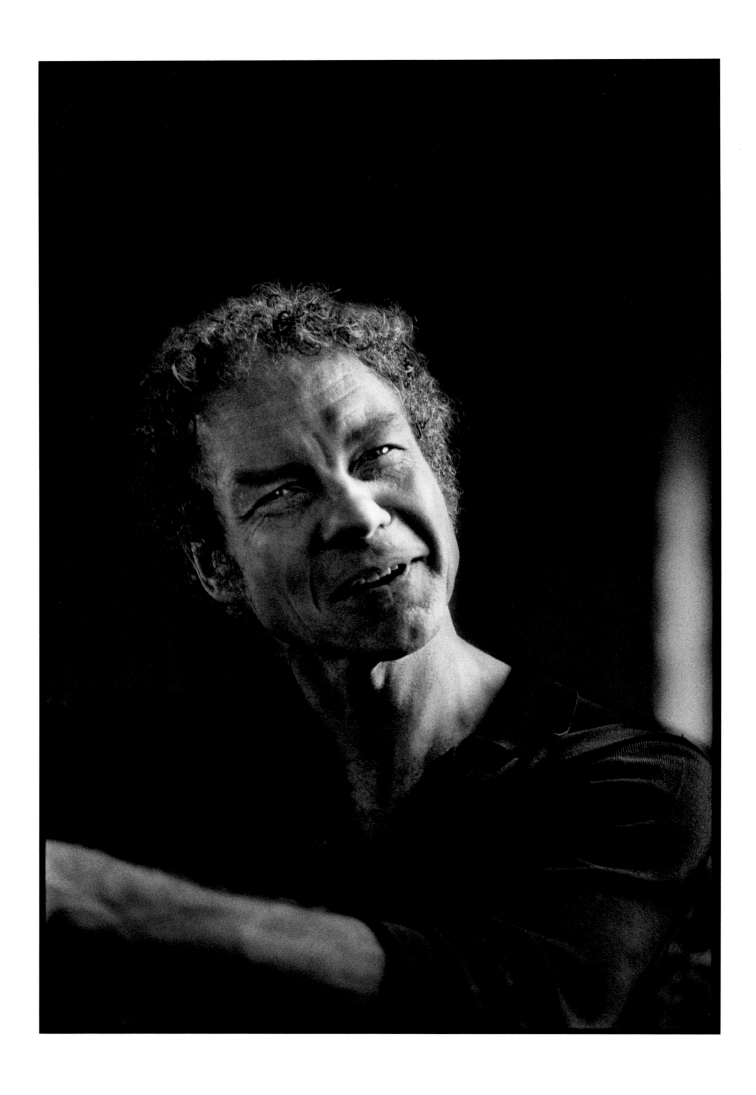

MERCE CUNNINGHAM REDUX

JAMES KLOSTY

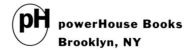

powerHouse Books
Brooklyn, NY

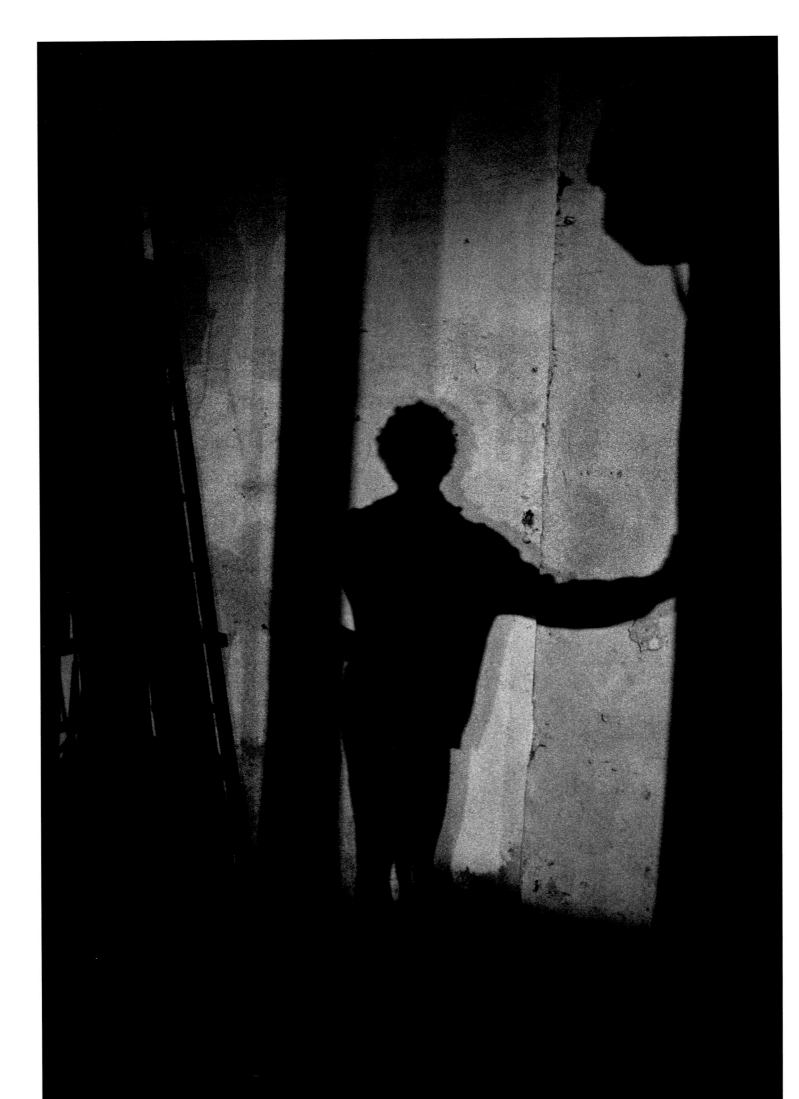

CONTENTS

*Bolded entries refer to dance titles

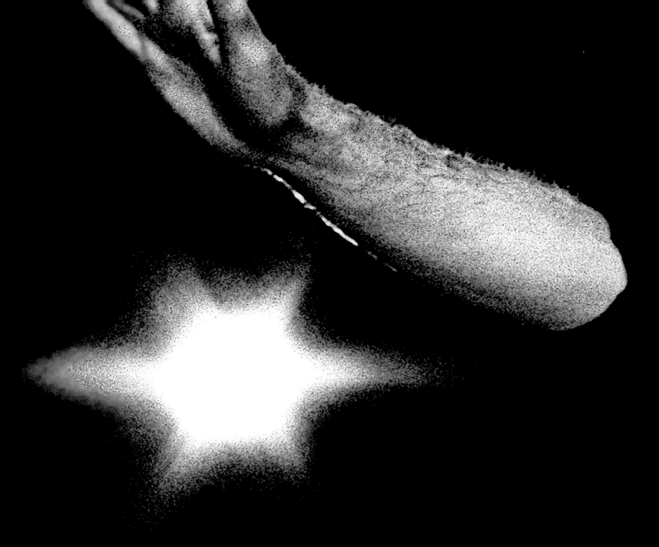

FOREWORD

I waited until April 16, Merce Cunningham's 100th birthday, to write this foreword to *Merce Cunningham: Redux*, but awoke to find the world shaken by images of Notre Dame ablaze. Why mention it? Cunningham's oft-quoted statement that dance "gives you nothing but that single fleeting moment when you feel alive" could not be more irreconcilably distant from that massive edifice of dour medieval stone. And yet . . .

And yet. Although we live in an age when knowledge of how to reconstruct such structures may be extinct, on this very night a reconstruction no less arcane takes place simultaneously in London, New York, and Los Angeles. Incorporeal movement is the only mortar but its battle against extinction is no less weighty. The *Night of 100 Solos*. One hundred dancers in three cities simultaneously grasping hold of Cunningham's phrases and presenting them via livestreaming to the world. It would seem Cunningham and Notre Dame do share something, something implausible but hardly unimportant. It has nothing to do with stone and everything to do with the continuation of spirit.

What I stated in my 1975 introduction—"this is not a dance book,"—cannot be said of *Merce Cunningham: Redux*. Images of Merce's dances performed when he was in his prime have acquired a poignancy and power I didn't anticipate forty-five years ago. Merce, sadly, has proven to be an unreplicatable dancer. In crucial ways, while he was still dancing, the key to his private realm was his own body and the doors that key unlocked more often than not led to dark places . . . dramas, despite the common belief his dances were abstract. Arthur Penn, director of *Bonnie and Clyde* and *The Miracle Worker*, worked with Cunningham at Black Mountain College and is reported to have found his sense of the stage almost miraculous, saying "he really existed up there—in a way that very few people I'd ever seen had."

So, far more than the original edition, *Merce Cunningham: Redux* is a dance book, one in which I emphasize dances particularly important to me, especially *Second Hand*, *Winterbranch*, *Place*, and *Canfield*. And I admit it should contain many more photographs of John Cage, Merce's partner in life as in art. To those regretting his absence I grant myself the privilege of pointing out that in 2014 I published *John Cage Was*, a full-fathom-five celebration of Cage's unique and uniquely camera-friendly persona. Feel free to seek him there.

—*James Klosty*
Millbrook, New York, April 16, 2019

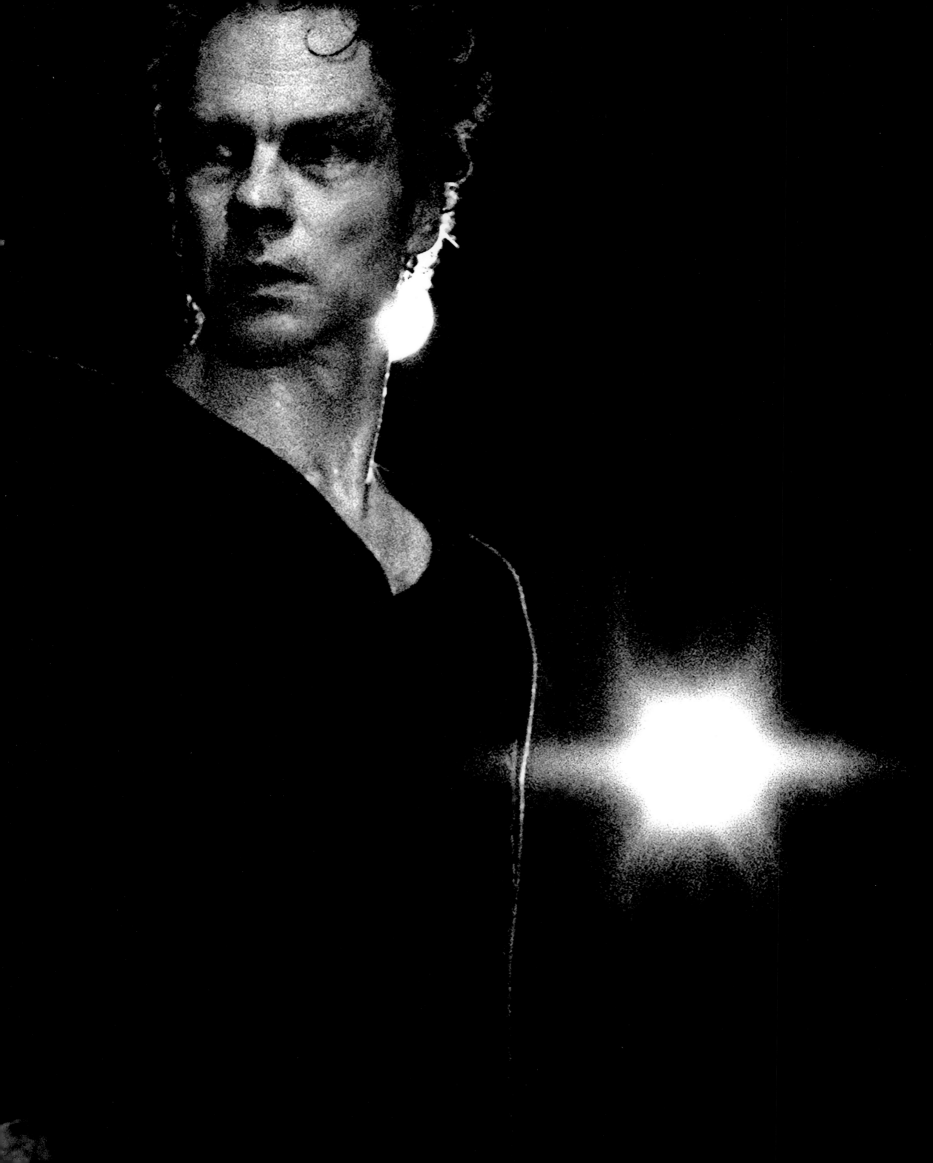

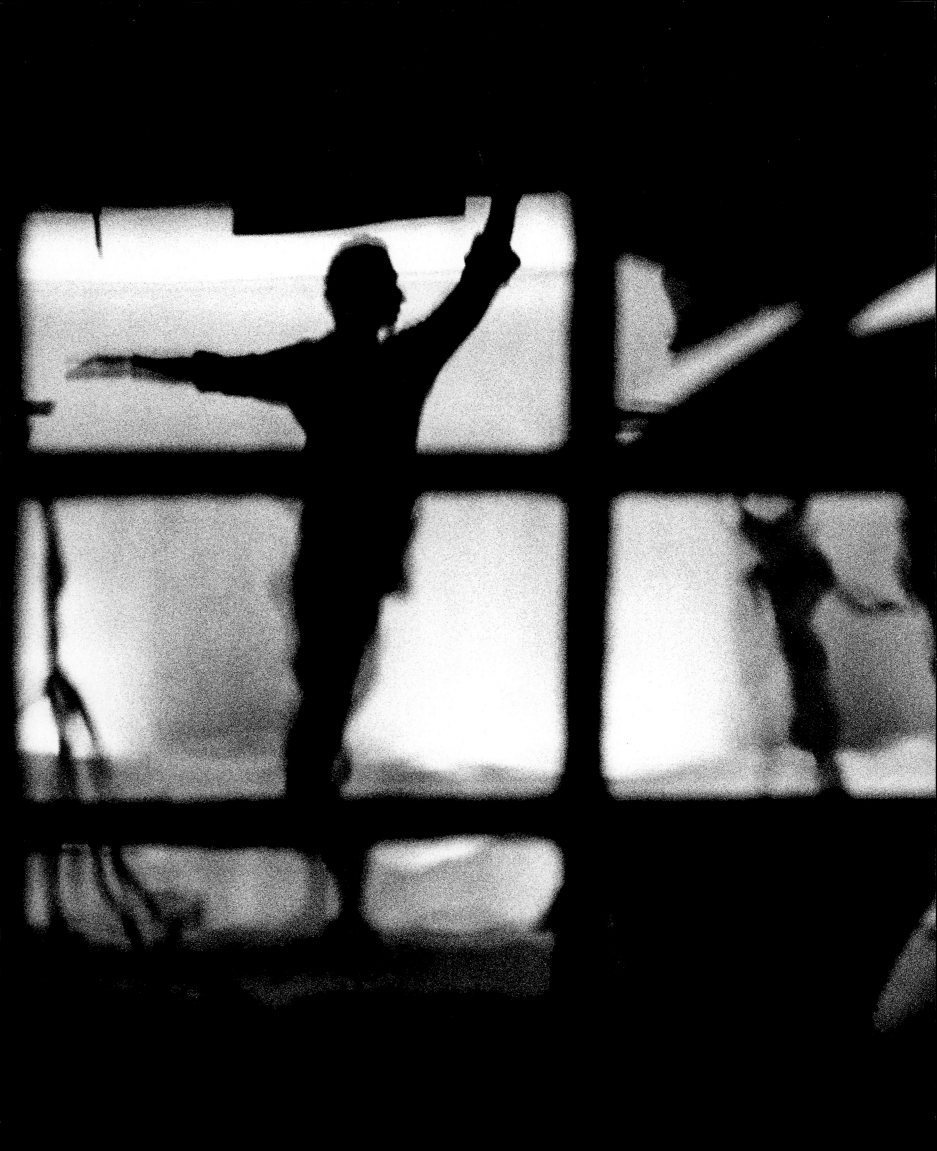

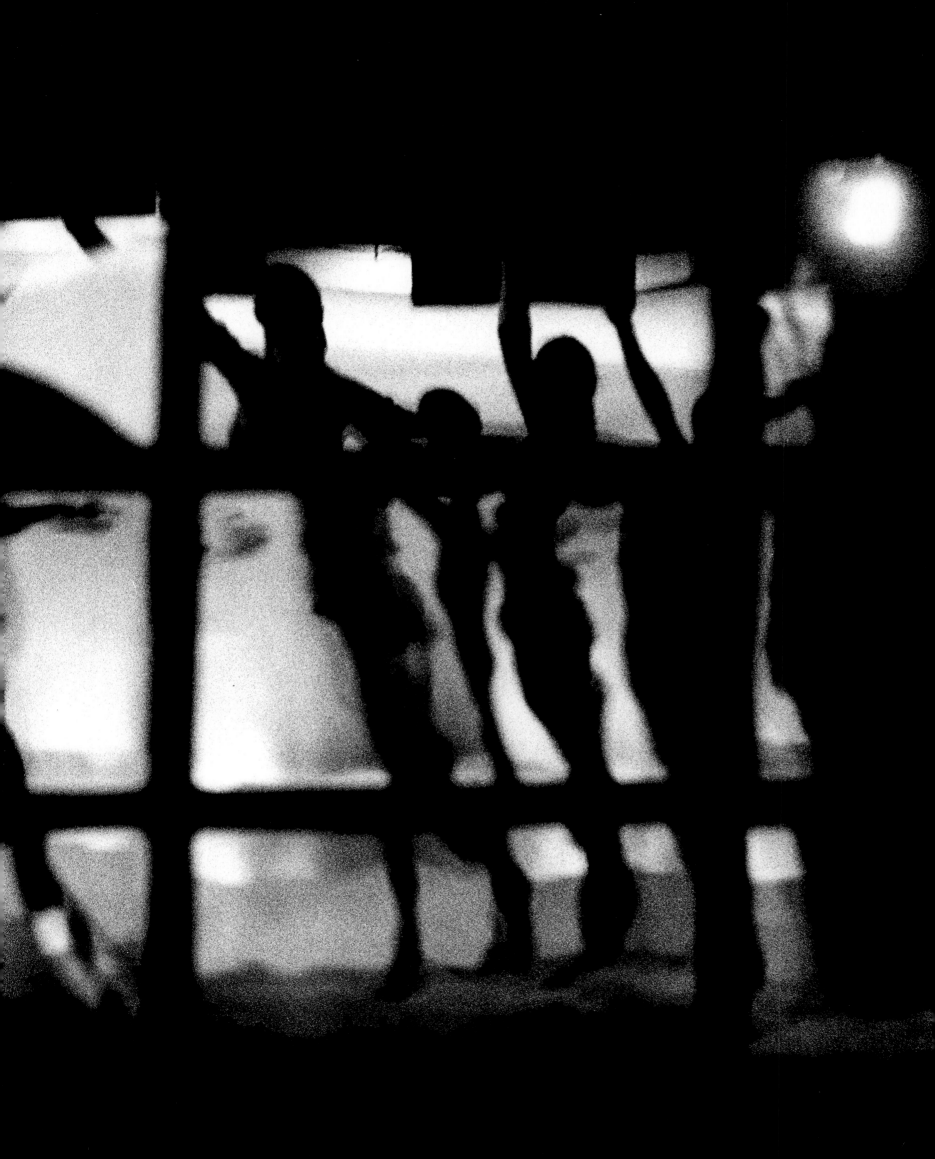

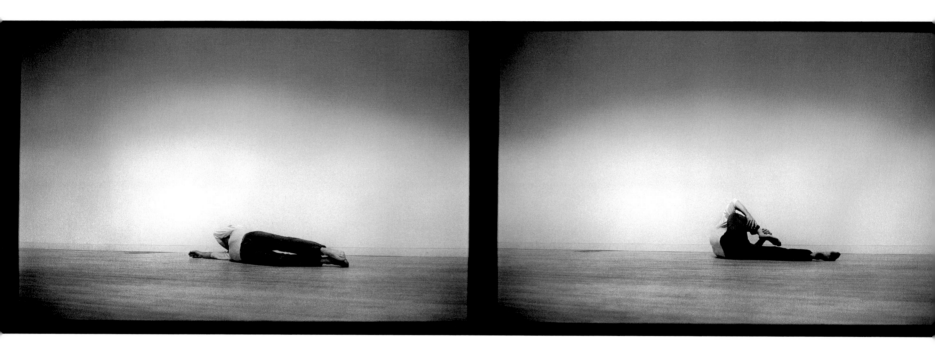

"Dialogue" Event, Walker Arts Center, 1972

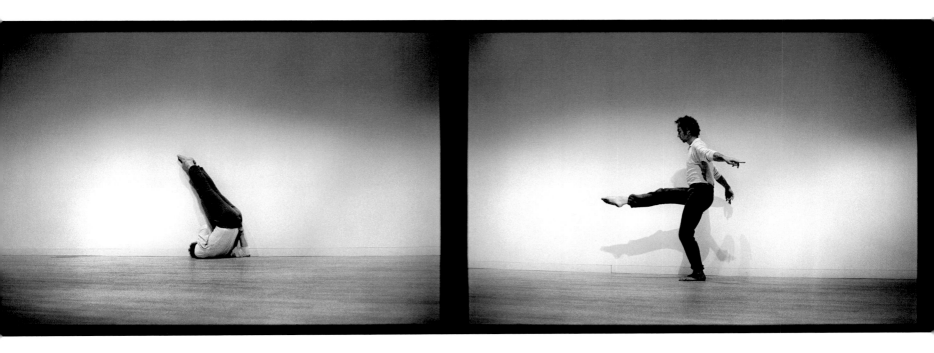

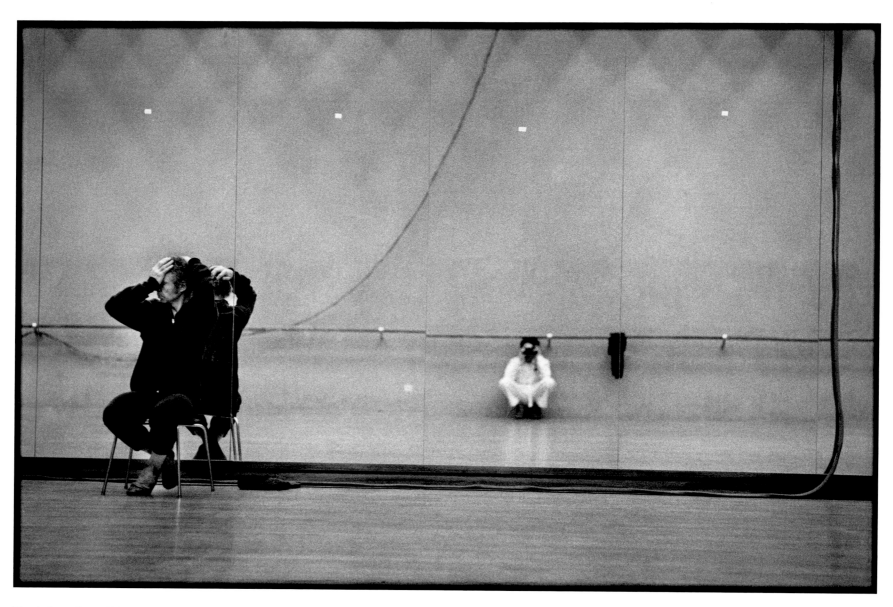

The photographer and his subject, Grenoble, France, 1972

INTRODUCTION BY JAMES KLOSTY

—From the 1975 edition

This is not a dance book. It is what I know, as a photographer, about a singular man, the dancers, composers, painters, and designers who work with him, and the life they share as Merce Cunningham and Dance Company. Almost all the contributors to this book have worked directly with Merce Cunningham. Thus most of them are artists and none—save Edwin Denby—are dance critics. Should any readers feel seriously deprived by this exclusion, I would ask them to consider a remark by the late Igor Stravinsky:

> What a reviewer says may
> be inconsequential,
> even in the short run.
> What I object to
> Is his right to say it.

Merce Cunningham. Dancer. Choreographer. Teacher. Born in Centralia, Washington, an obscure number of years before the stock market crashed. Draws careful studies of plants for pleasure. Charming in public. Fierce in self-discipline. At ease in motion. At home in secrecy. By example and accomplishment has done more to generate and influence the contemporary arts than any other choreographer.

Cunningham's revolution, begun in the early 1950s, was undertaken not to startle or to scandalize, but to discover a way of working comfortable for his personality and compatible with his personal vision. His ideas were not unique. They were shared by friends; composers (John Cage, Earle Brown, Morton Feldman, Christian Wolff); and painters (Robert Rauschenberg, Jasper Johns, etc.). But the ideas were not shared by his compatriots in the world of dance. In fact, Cunningham's ideas were *antithetical* to commonly held concepts of serious dancing, to many ideals of classical ballet, and particularly to the aesthetic of Martha Graham, in whose company Cunningham's career had begun.

Cunningham was urged to leave Graham by John Cage, soon to become America's most controversial composer, as well as a respected poet, philosopher, graphic artist, and mycologist. The two men gave several concerts together in the 1940s, and when Cunningham began to assemble his own company of dancers, Cage did whatever had to be done to keep the company going. At one time or another he has been its program designer, agent, pianist, composer, chauffeur, food gatherer, impresario, apologist, fund-raiser, chef de cuisine, comedian, and spiritual mentor.

Cunningham's association with Cage was as much an idea as it was a fact. Their working together brought forth a new aesthetic holding that dance is dance and music is music—an aesthetic so simple that few were able to accept it with equanimity. Both men shared the belief that neither dance nor music need function as a dependent of the other, that the two have nothing arbitrarily in common but custom, that their combination is less necessity than reflex, and that they can be advantageously freed of one another's syntax.

Cunningham proceeded to develop a choreography and a technique based on the kinetic integrity of the body unconstrained by the rhythmic, melodic, or formal proposals of an external music. It was a concept of dance quite beyond plotless Balanchine or Ashton's *Symphonic Variations*, those highly refined examples of an art that has always been subsumed in implied or explicit musical structures. Cunningham chose to begin at the root. He turned dance back upon itself, focusing on its primary component: each movement as an atomic gesture in time. He felt that dancing need not concern Itself with narrative nor with philosophical, psychological, or mythic pretensions. Presumably, if one danced, and danced well, that ought to be enough—both for the dancer and for his audience. Martha Graham and José Limón were clearly of another mind. True, for modern dance's Doris Humphrey and certain ballet choreographers nonnarrative dancing was quite respectable, but the whitest of "white" ballets was still about music in some sense, still about the great ongoing affair between dancer and orchestra or dancer and piano. If ballet-goers couldn't *name* the steps they nonetheless could *hum* them. But the music at Cunningham performances was new and usually experimental. It was difficult enough to listen to, no less to hum. And Cunningham's dancers, as an ultimate insult, attempted to do neither! Ballet without meanings was one thing, since music helped to underline the dancing for one's eyes through one's ears. But an enterprise in which music was as irrelevent as narrative? Thus are anarchists and *enfants terribles* born! Dionysiacs too—to use the epithet for Cunningham one critic preferred.

But the cries of "anarchy" were far-fetched, as outlandish as the reference to Dionysus. Far from Bacchic abandon, the rule for Cunningham's dancers is absolute definition. Traditional ballet is a far more Dionysian enterprise, for the dancer can ride the musical pulse, using it as a kind of surrogate heartbeat on which bodily functions play without consciousness. Absence of metrical accompaniment only intensifies the mental effort needed to establish the strict order that supports each dancer's part. Cunningham dancing is a rigorously Apollonian activity: it is the dancer, not the music, who recreates the spatial and temporal structure that is each dance. To perform a work of several sections, each several minutes in duration, with one's muscular memory the only "clock," and to come within seconds of a required time at each performance, is a task no Dionysian would contemplate—nor attempt—nor accomplish.

Cunningham inherited a stage space bound by the proscenium arch and held together by a system of gravity derived from a formula of perspective unchanged since the Renaissance. Center stage was the center of gravity, and the eye was coaxed there by the architecture of the theater and by every means of symmetry and asymmetry at the choreographer's disposal. As a result, stage space implied a class society in which center stage was regal, the exclusive sanctuary of soloist and star. The sides, the back and corners? Strictly plebeian, home of the brave corps.

By choice Cunningham decentralized stage space through chance, transforming central focus into field perspective. There is no best spot on a Cunningham stage. In dances that permit the dancers to choose where they will move, there is no crush of bodies at stage center. In fact, the most characteristic quality of the use of the stage in Cunningham is that no matter how few dancers are on stage the space always appears to be full. When they are in two-, three-, or four-sided arenas, some dancers are assigned different "stage-fronts" from others, and these directions alternate throughout the evening. Thus, the stage is not merely decentralized, it is demagnetized. True north is simultaneously north, east, south, and west.

Both Cage and Cunningham have chosen methods of composition that rely, to varying degrees, on chance procedures. Their reasons for using chance, like their methods, vary. For Cage chance is a way to disarm the power of individual will and elude the dictates of personal taste. For Cunningham, it is less a philosophical choice than a pragmatic, potent tool. Cunningham uses chance much as he might use a magnet, to draw possibilities to him from beyond his reach, and to arrange his materials, like iron filings, into relationships he might not otherwise have seen.

The play of bodies in space and time. When I choreograph a piece by tossing pennies—by chance, that is—I am finding my resources in that play, which is not the product of *my will*, but which is an energy and a law which I too obey. Some people think it is inhuman and mechanistic to toss pennies in creating a dance instead of chewing the nails or beating the head against a wall or thumbing through old notebooks for ideas. But the feeling I have when I compose in this way is that I am in touch with a natural resource far greater than my own personal inventiveness could ever be, much more universally human than the particular habits of my own practice, and organically rising out of common pools of motor impulses.

Cunningham began to use chance when ordering a work made up of solos, duets, trios, and quartets, *Sixteen Dances for Soloist and Company of Three* (1951). "I remember one arrangement," he told me, "where I looked at it, tried it, and realized it didn't really matter; I could just toss a coin. I don't know if that's *exactly* what I said, but it was something about chance. So I did that . . . *within a very strict arrangement, of course.*" In 1953 Cunningham made *Suite By Chance.* This was the first dance in which "all the elements as much as possible" were made with the aid of chance methods. Since then he has used chance procedures in every dance he has made, although they have often played a very minor role in the creative process.

How does one make a dance by chance? Cunningham began by throwing coins to assemble his materials. His procedures require hours of arduous manual labor drawing up charts—charts to determine the number of dancers, charts for their spacing, charts for sequences, charts for movements for certain parts of the body, charts for whatever element of a work he wishes to submit to chance procedures. He may use chance, but chance ". . . within a very strict arrangement, of course."

When I asked whether *the way* he used chance in making each dance was also a matter of chance, his reply was hardly that of the wild-eyed anarchist:

> Well you see, one of the difficulties about making pieces is the amount of time I have. If I am involved with a lot of things like teaching, or doing this and doing that, then I don't have time to sit down ahead of working with the dancers and think about a chance operation which would have a great deal of detailed paper work in it. I would still like to, but I don't have the time. I may get to the dancers with some ideas about chance but

as we work I see "Well, I'm got going to have enough time to do that." So I have to eliminate that chance possibility or whittle it down and see what others there might be.

Open form, a central concern of the music of Earle Brown, is a concept Cunningham has applied to choreography in a variation of his own, the latest development of which he calls "Events." As conceived by Brown and Morton Feldman, open form music, or *music indeterminate of its performance*, is quite different in nature from music composed by chance processes, but because there are chance elements in both the concepts are often confused. John Cage first developed chance methods of composing music in the early 1950s, using simple imperfections in pieces of paper and more complex operations involving the *I Ching*. The compositions that resulted were set down in a definitive form, like any composition by Mozart or Beethoven, and they remained unchanged from performance to performance. Brown's and Feldman's concerns were somewhat different. Brown, in particular, was interested in developing a means of writing music that gave the instrumentalist creative responsibility, allowed him spontaneous choices effecting realization of the score, but at the same time preserved Brown's role as composer. A work like *Four Systems* (1954), the music for Cunningham's *Galaxy*, is traditionally composed and fully notated, but it is not given a definitive form. The material is all there, but the manner in which it is presented (which sections are played, in what order, for what durations, in what combinations, etc.) differs in each performance. It is a work whose form is discovered anew at every presentation, and although its materials do not change they exhibit different qualities from one hearing to the next much as Calder's mobiles—Brown's favorite analogy—present different aspects at different times.

Cunningham tentatively approached the concept of open form in 1953 with *Dime A Dance*. Like his earlier *Sixteen Dances*, it was made up of a number of small sections. Unlike *Sixteen Dances*, though, the sections of *Dime A Dance* were never given a definitive order. When the piece was first presented, members of the audience paid a dime to pick cards from a deck, thus determining the evening's sequence. *Galaxy* (1956), four solos for four dancers, was a more thorough experimentation with open form. A performance in which the solos were densely overlapped could be followed by one in which they were sparsely separated in time and space. Any combination was possible, and the presentation differed at each performance. Of Cunningham dances to date, *Rune* (1959), *Story* (1963), *Field Dances* (1963), *Scramble* (1967), *Canfield* (1969), *Signals* (1970), *Landrover* (1972), *TV Rerun* (1972), and *Changing Steps* (1973) possess elements of open form. In *Scramble* and *Landrover* these are rudimentary: the order of major sections is rearrangeable. In *Field Dances*, *Story*, and *TV Rerun* they are complex: dancers choose spontaneously what material to perform, and how long, where on stage, and with whom to perform it. Even the choice of performing *none* of the material is possible.

But the majority of Cunningham dances do *not* grant such freedoms. And the dances that do use chance do *not* permit the dancers to improvise their material on the spot. Whatever material appears on stage has been choreographed and rehearsed—rehearsed at length.

Cunningham's own unique contribution to the concept of open form is his ongoing series of "Events." These programs originated as solutions to problems that arose in nontheatrical, nonproscenium spaces: museums, gymnasiums, open squares, etc. They evolved into intermissionless performances in which the entire repertory of the company is available as a vast, pooled resource from which single details and sections may be extracted out of context and reassembled into an unforeseen and novel unity. It is not unusual for an audience to be confronted with excerpts from two or three completely different works at the same moment. Ordinarily, an Event is prepared and rehearsed on the day of its performance. Its organization is transcribed onto paper and posted around the performance space like choreographic shopping lists to which the dancers refer throughout the performance to keep the evening's order clear in their minds. By forcing both audience and performer to experience known material differently, these events have redefined the meaning of the word "repertory." Today's younger choreographers, who think nothing of performing in unusual spaces, are following a precedent Cunningham tested in Viennese and Swedish museums in 1964 and perfected over a decade in nontheatrical spaces throughout the world.

Many other ideas for which Cunningham has at one time or another been attacked, revered, or even ridiculed have quietly filtered down to become unquestioned tools of the new generation of choreographers and dancers. But for all the changes he has brought to dance's composition process, its formal and structural concepts, and its ability to utilize traditional and untraditional space, these innovations are probably less obvious to the casual dance observer than the movement resources he has rehabilitated: just as Cage burst open music's definitions to include a whole world of sound, Cunningham enlarged the physical vocabulary we use to describe "dance." Cunningham is a virtuoso dancer, and his interests as a choreographer have honored—but transcended—virtuosity. To the specialized technique that ballet refined over the centuries he added the commonplace movement of daily life: movement seen every day—everyone is capable of it, but few of us pay real attention to it. To ballet's virtuosity and grace, to Graham's implosive intensity, he added the possibility of awkwardness—a quality that has always intrigued him—and his choreography is the first to honor equally the arabesque and the limp.

From the start, Cunningham wanted a theater capable of reconciling Precision and the Unpredictable. He achieved this goal by extending the aesthetic developed early in his association with Cage—the independence of dance and music—to include the theatrical disciplines of lighting and stage design. Eventually, the mutual independence of *all* disciplines became this untraditional company's one inviolable tradition. I have more than once seen Cunningham refuse to alter aspects of performances that have displeased him, in strict practice of his faith in independence. But it is during the creation of new works that he applies the principle most stringently. Those who design the decor and compose the music have almost no contact with the secreted gentleman who choreographs the movement. Even his dancers do not know who will or won't be in a work until time makes the cast obvious to all, nor are they ever told the nature of the dance that they are learning. There are no detailed consultations between choreographer and composer, no stormy confrontations between choreographer and designer, nothing that would be called a "collaboration" in the commonly understood sense of the word. When Frank Stella was asked to design the decor for *Scramble* there was no discussion of the nature of the dance. "Merce just asked me for something the dancers could move around the stage." That may be the most specific request Cunningham has ever made of a designer. And composers know little more. When necessary, Cunningham tells them the length of time his dance will inhabit, and they proceed with that as their sole guideline.

Clearly, such noncollaborative collaborations are cannily suited to the requirements of Cunningham's reclusive personality. Nevertheless, artists who might have remained aloof from the theater under other circumstances have been attracted by his hands-off attitude, and the result has been an association of dancers, composers, painters, musicians, and designers unique in the history of the American theater. Some have called it a baffling and self-destructive exercise in anarchy. Others have called it the only modern-day successor to the heritage of Diaghilev's Ballets Russes. In reality, it is neither. Cunningham is no Diaghilev. He does not use dance, music, lighting, and decor to achieve *his* purposes, but leaves them free to achieve *their* purposes within the time and space of a given performance. He is far more an ecologist than an impresario. It is hardly chance

that next to dancing plants, animals, and the workings of nature fascinate him most, and his theater echoes that preoccupation by imitating nature in its manner of operation.

The number of contemporary composers whose music Cunningham has presented is remarkable. He was the first choreographer to use *musique concréte*, making *Collage* in conjunction with excerpts from Pierre Schaeffer's *Symphonie Pour Un Homme Seul* in 1952. Since then his repertory has included dances with music by John Cage, Morton Feldman, Igor Stravinsky, Christian Wolff, Pierre Boulez, Earle Brown, Josef Matthias Hauer, Bo Nilsson, Chou Wen-Chung, Ben Johnston, Conlon Nancarrow, Toshi Ichiayanagi, Serge Garrant, LaMonte Young, Gordon Mumma, David Behrman, David Tudor, Pauline Oliveros, Alvin Lucier, and others, not to mention his repeated use of the perennially iconoclastic music of Erik Satie. With only a few exceptions, the music that accompanies Cunningham dances is presented in live, rather than taped, performances.

If one considers the meager financial history of the company, the number of contemporary painters presented by Cunnningham puts other dance companies to shame. When I asked him about this Cunningham replied:

> I was always interested, and eager, to work with visual artists and set out from the beginning to not get in their way, to allow for separateness, as had happened with the music. In the early dances, these were in simple ways, true—David Hare for the solo *Mysterious Adventure*, Sonja Sekula with the painted costume for *Dromenon*, Richard Lippold's gold wire tail for the *Monkey Dances*. Then a few years later I asked Robert Rauschenberg if he would make something for *Minutiae* that could be put in the middle of the stage, and through which and around which we could move. He said yes, and a few days later showed a strange and beautiful object that delighted me, but I knew it wouldn't work. It had to be hung from the flies, and at that time we rarely played in theaters with them. I explained. He understood immediately, and shortly after presented me with another equally strange and beautiful object which stood on its own seven feet. It was the beginning of ten years of collaboration that were full of beautiful objects, costumes, and ideas.

Throughout the 1950s Rauschenberg and Remy Charlip designed the vast majority of the company's costumes. (Charlip, choreographer, director, and award-winning author of children's books, danced with Cunningham from 1950 to 1961.) For four years, from 1961 until the end of the 1964 world tour, Rauschenberg and the company were inseparable. As the company's stage manager he traversed the floors of countless filthy stages on hands and knees, pulling out exposed nails, removing splinters, taping cracks, and mopping up before rehearsals and performances. During the same period he designed and executed all the company's lighting, most of its costumes, and all its decors. Of the latter, his muted, pointillist design for *Summerspace* is best known.

In 1966 Jasper Johns became the company's "artistic director," a position intentionally less active than Rauschenberg's, for Johns's personal inclinations were not the same as his predecessor's. "Jasper doesn't really like to involve himself in the theater that much," Cunningham told me. "He's willing to do the costumes and the coloring, but that overall thing, being involved in the theater in the way Bob was, he's not that kind of person." But Johns initiated the practice of inviting other artists to contribute ideas and decors. For Rauschenberg's singular, multifaceted involvement he substituted both his own personal vision and the concepts of Marcel Duchamp, Frank Stella, Andy Warhol, Robert Morris, Bruce Nauman, and Niels Jenny. It was Johns who hit upon the idea of using Duchamp's major work, *The Large Glass*, otherwise known as *The Bride Stripped Bare By Her Bachelors, Even*, as a decor. He transcribed *The Glass*, by hand, onto seven vinyl boxes of varying shapes and sizes. The dance, named *Walkaround Time* (1968), included an unchoreographed entr'acte Cunningham describes as "straight out of *Relache*. . . . Duchamp was in *Relache*, of course" and one of the most exquisite decors ever set within a proscenium arch.

Johns, Rauschenberg, Cage. Alluring names. Often they dominate the publicity accorded this company. But none of the three, not even Cage, is Cunningham's most important associate. That distinction of course belongs to his dancers. They are Cunningham's only true collaborators, his one indispensable resource, self-reliant and totally self-sufficient. Given adequate space, sufficient time, and goodly amounts of energy, they have no need of music, lighting, costumes, or decor. But their reliability is a Damoclean sword, and can be something of a liability whenever they perform. An Event, for example, posits no restrictions on the musicians and lighting designer, but by doing so weighs the dancers with greater responsibilities. The musicians are free to conjure up whatever their imaginations dictate. The lighting designer is as free as they within the limitations of the theater's capabilities. The dancers however, are far from free. They must execute precise, always taxing material—material whose considerable virtuosity is rarely perceived, which they have rehearsed that afternoon in silence under a simple work light. And they must perform it as they rehearsed it regardless of what occurs around them; the situation is duplicated when each new dance

is premiered. This virtuosity-in-adversity is self-concealing and underappreciated. Cunningham's dancers have no stories to act out, no thirty-two fouettes to toss off (or not toss off), no flashy tours de force that are great fun to describe (though there are many unflashy ones quite difficult to describe). Consequently they are rarely mentioned in reviews and receive little public notice.

The principal compensation? They are doing work they believe in. Until very recently, choosing Merce meant choosing work so much believed in that poverty was irrelevant. In the beginning even the opportunity of performing, of being applauded, or of being booed with any regularity was rare. There was only the work: weeks, even months of rehearsals in studios where the roof leaked and there was no central heating in preparation for the occasional performance that might—or might not—be arranged. In the fifties and early sixties Merce's dancers worked with him out of total dedication. There can't be any other word for it. Their only pay was ten dollars—somewhat later twenty-five—per performance, out of Merce's pocket. There was no rehearsal pay. Not until 1964 did Cunningham's dancers begin to earn enough money to support themselves, and then only because they were guaranteed enough weeks of paid employment to qualify for unemployment insurance all those other weeks in which they worked for nothing. In the year 1970/71, Carolyn Brown's nineteenth year with Cunningham, the year in which she received the prestigious *Dance Magazine* award along with Frederick Ashton and Ted Shawn, she was earning less money than a first year debutante in the New York City Ballet corps.

Under these circumstances, what sort of person would want to dance with Merce Cunningham? (You can learn a lot, they say, from the company a man keeps.) His dancers have had but one thing in common: diversity. If that elusive phenomenon "a dancer's mentality" actually exists, Cunningham's company is the wrong place to look for it. Cunningham formed his company in 1953. Since that time he has asked forty-one dancers to work with him and has seen thirty-one of them eventually go on to other things. Of those thirty-one, twenty-three have since produced their own creative work in the fields of choreography, painting, directing, etc. Perhaps that remarkable fact is the best insight into the Cunningham dancer, and by extension into Cunningham himself. All thirty-one past members of the Cunningham Dance Company are listed below:

Shareen Blair
Carolyn Brown
William Burdick
Louise Burns
Remy Charlip
William Davis

Anita Dencks
Ulysses Dove
Douglas Dunn
Judith Dunn
Viola Farber
Nanette Hassall
Deborah Hay
Bruce King
Barbara Lias
Barbara Lloyd
Jo Anne Melsher
Sandra Neels
Steve Paxton
Marianne Preger
Albert Reid
Yseult Riopelle
Chase Robinson
Peter Saul
Jeff Slayton
Gus Solomons Jr.
Cynthia Stone
Paul Taylor
Dan Wagoner
Mel Wong
Marilyn Wood

As of this writing the Cunningham Company consists of:
Ellen Cornfield
Meg Harper
Susana Hayman-Chaffey
Cathy Kerr
Chris Komar
Robert Kovich
Brynar Mehl
Charles Moulton
Julie Roess-Smith
Valda Setterfield

Shortly after I finished taking the photographs for this book Merce Cunningham went to Paris and choreographed *Un Jour ou Deux*, an evening-length work, on the Paris Opera Ballet. In the fall of 1974 he will mount two of his dances, *Summerspace* and *Winterbranch*, on the Boston Ballet. Traditional repertory for his own company doesn't interest him at the moment. He presents events. Only events. Television is beginning to intrigue him and he is planning work specifically for the possibilities that medium presents. It would be appropriate to anticipate here what Cunningham will be doing in the coming years, but I think I had better abstain. Where this man is concerned predictions are useless.

Finally, concerning the photographs. Why is a book about a dance company not a "dance book"? It is a question of intention. Mine has not been to document or "illustrate" Cunningham's dances. The union of dancing and photography has always seemed to me an ill-fated marriage of opposites. The images it spawns are often of rare beauty, but I question what one can learn from them about either dancing or choreography. We consider dance photography successful when it destroys time at precisely the right moment, forcing an eternal extension upon exquisitely transient shape. But dancing is a process far less understandable—infinitely more mysterious—than the arresting, gracious, somehow comprehensible form the dancer's body assumes upon a piece of paper for our leisurely and careful admiration. Dancing is about something beyond the syntactical ability of graphic images to describe. It is about qualities of movement. Not the shape of movement but the quality of movement. While photography is literally a timeless art—what's left when time is taken away—dancing's very being is time. The essence of its art is the linking of seconds into a language, and without time it is as meaningless as sculpture without density or poetry without words. By removing continuity even the finest photographs of dancing falsify its reality and subvert its truth. By lighting the cocoon they kill the animating life within.

For this reason my focus is not dancing but an association of artists . . . whose focus is dancing. To the extent that dancing is part of their lives it is part of this book. But what has absorbed me most since I began this book in 1968—what to some extent absorbs all those in contact with Merce Cunningham—is the current almost palpably surrounding the man, charging his work, informing every aspect of that world which, by his presence, he defines. Merce Cunningham has remained a subject of conjecture, a mystery, not only to critics, other artists and the public, but to the company he calls his own. For over twenty years his energy has been dichotomous, distinct in nature and in purpose: partly radiant—catalyzing ideas and practices within the arts, and partly insular—sequestering a private man, even from those few with whom he works intimately day by day. Lines I wrote over four years ago questioned Dionysus ("old purple-foot") about that hidden, enigmatic man. Even out of context, they continue to express my deepest feelings about Merce Cunningham and about his work:

Old purple-foot, you sot!
Is this your jealousy: that he
Has made more than wine of panic
And from labyrinthine silence
Managed form that keeps the maze?

—James Klosty, Milbrook, New York, Summer 1974

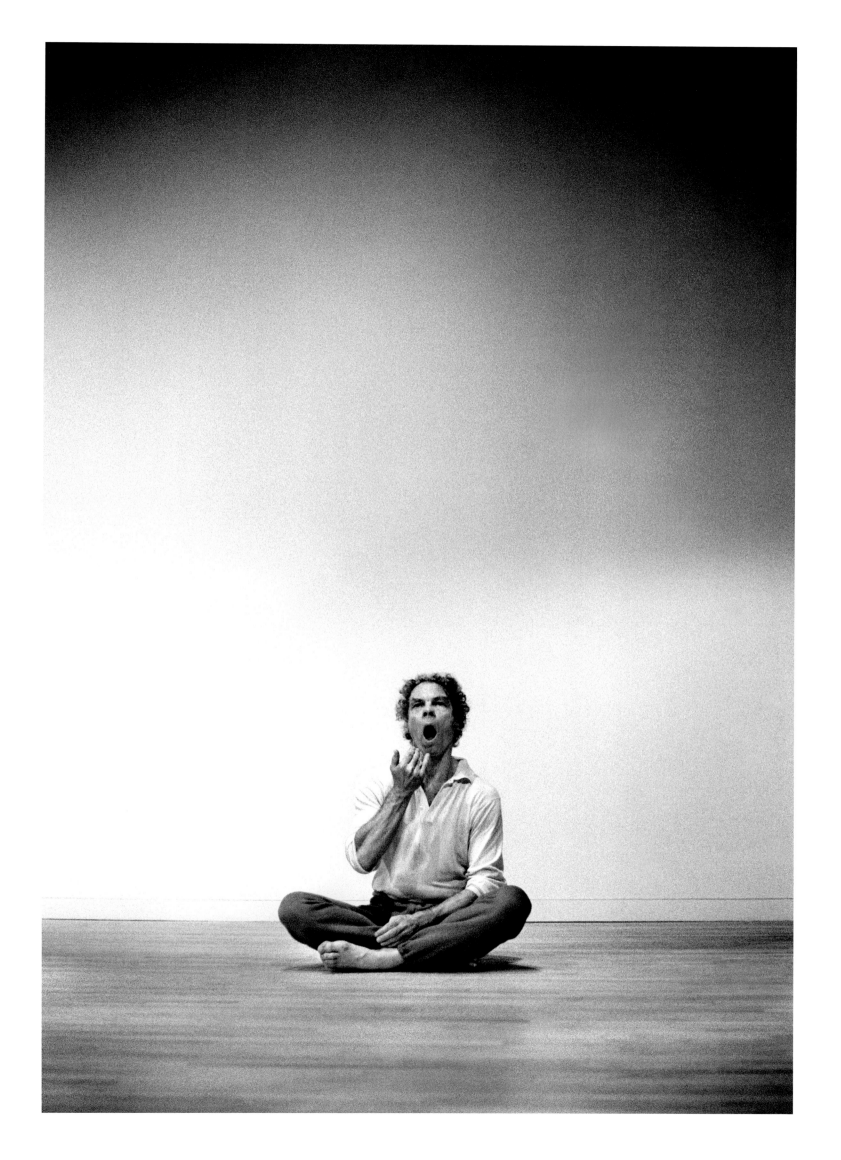

498 THIRD AVENUE

This was the first Cunningham studio I knew. The Cunningham Company had previously been in residence above the Living Theater at 61 West 14th Street and moved into 498 Third Avenue during the summer of 1966. A few months later, my beloved Sunbeam Alpine and I were driving north on Third Avenue when we were struck, outside 498, by a car ineptly trying to parallel park. I was not happy. I got out. It was John Cage! I asked him to sign the dent. He happily agreed. I still have the door.

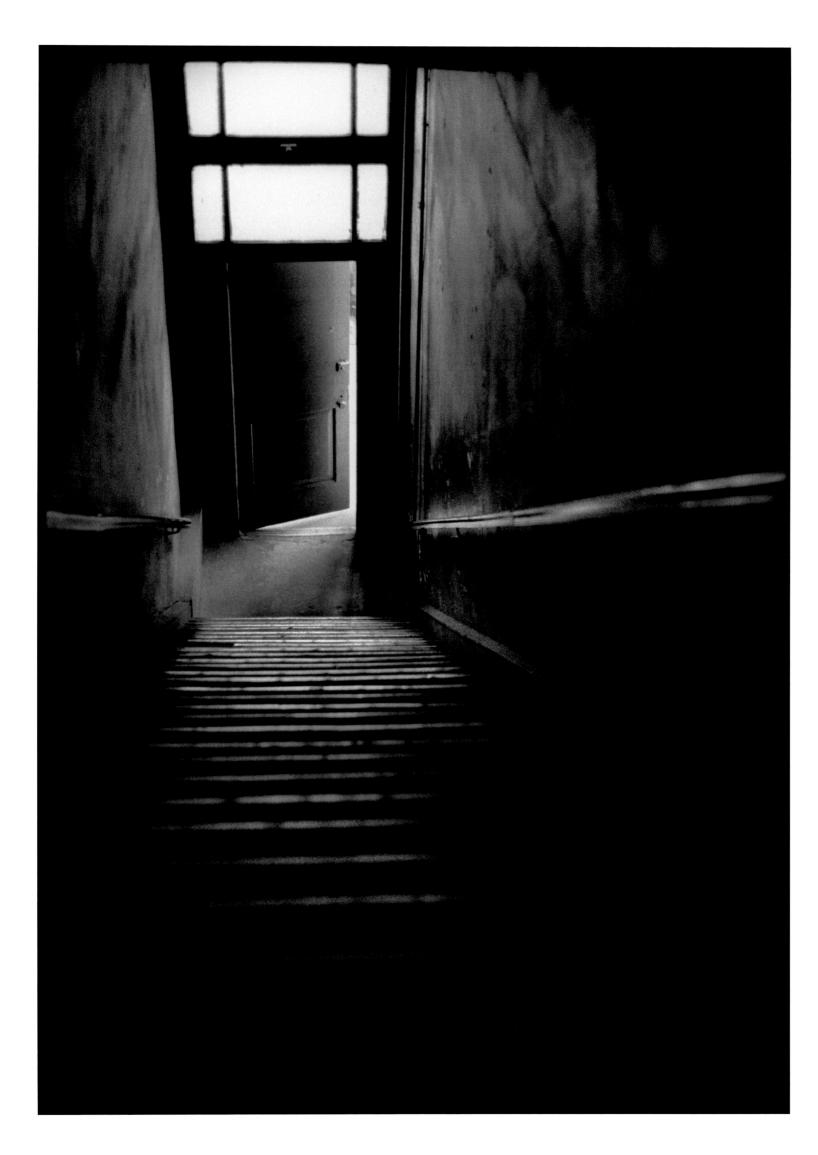

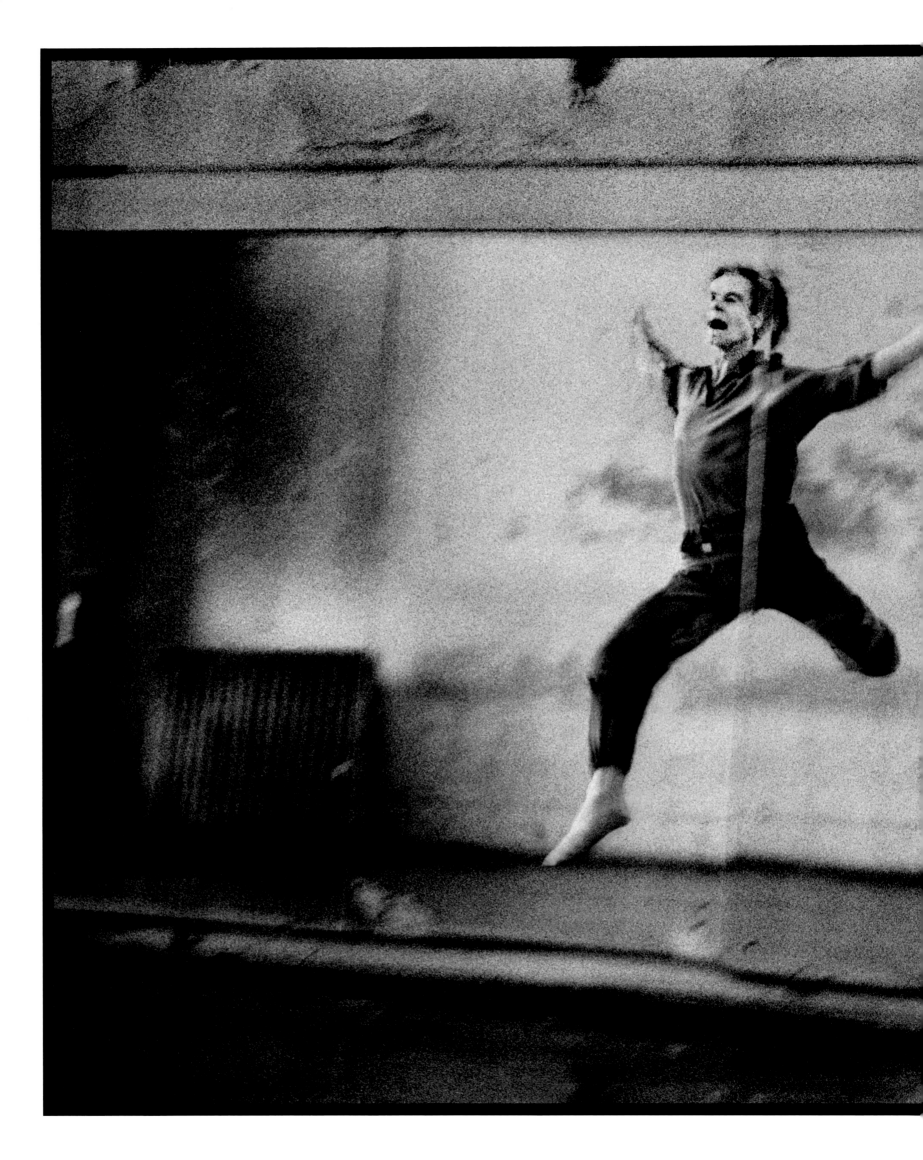

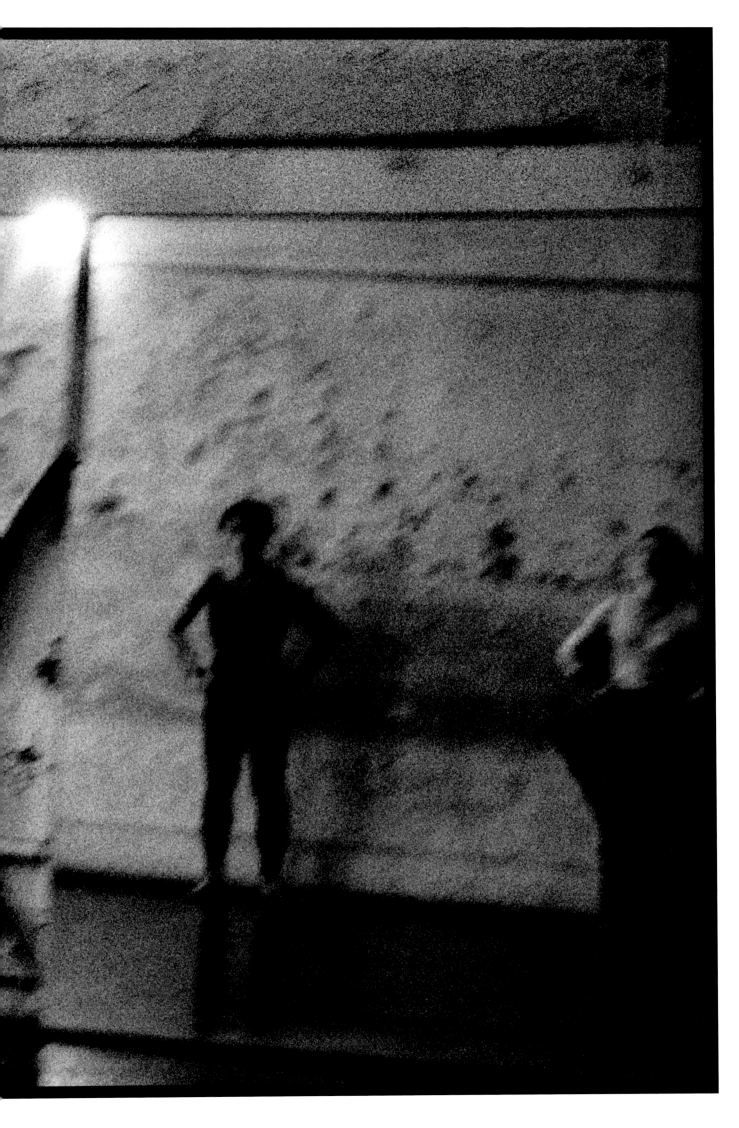

Merce Cunningham
in rehearsal

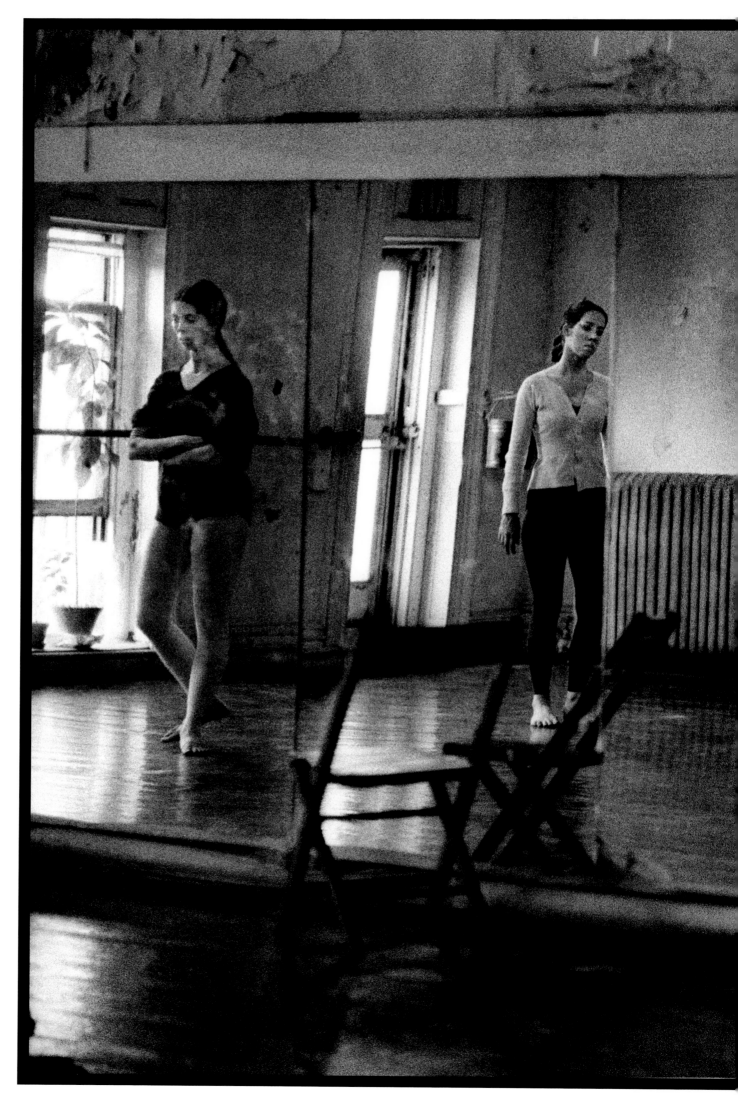

Sandra Neels, Susana Hayman-Chaffey, Merce Cunningham, Valda Setterfield, and Mel Wong

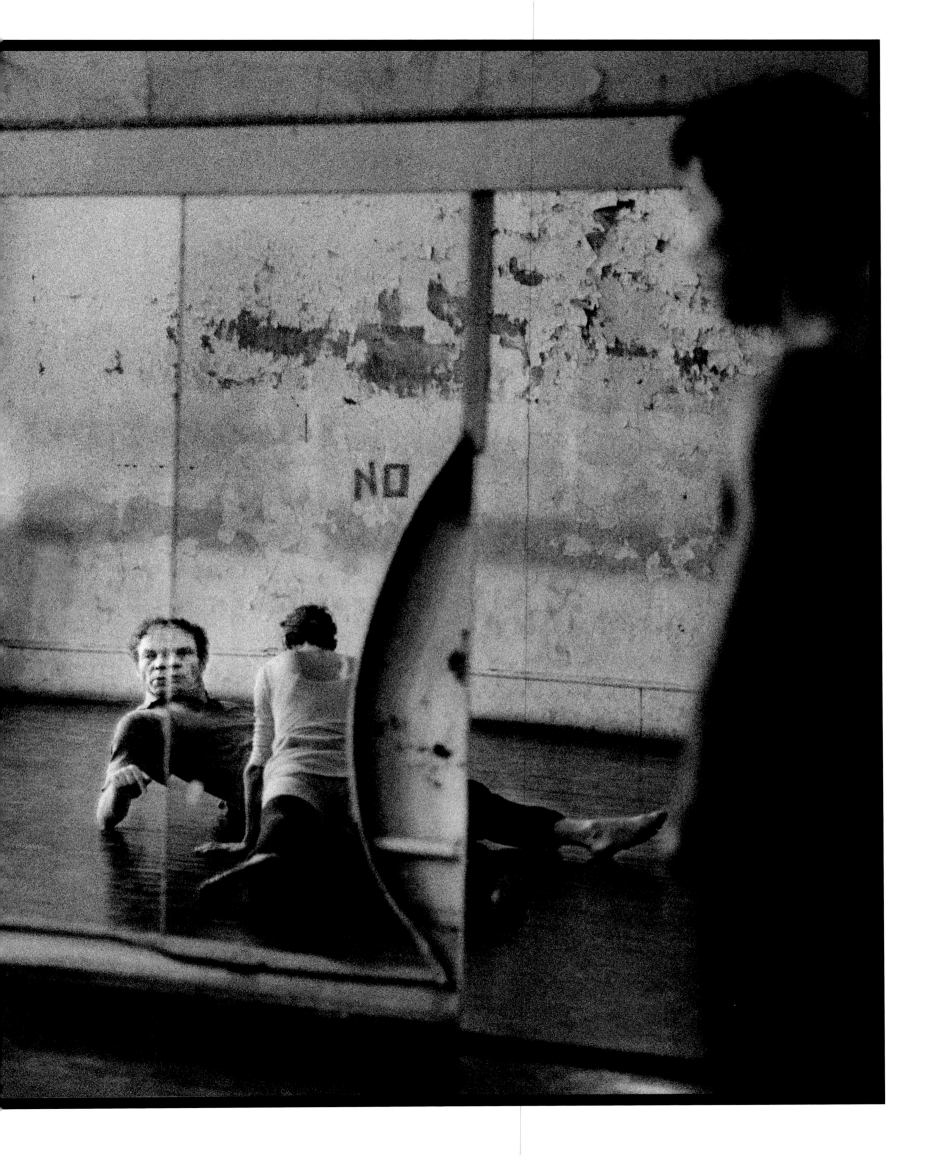

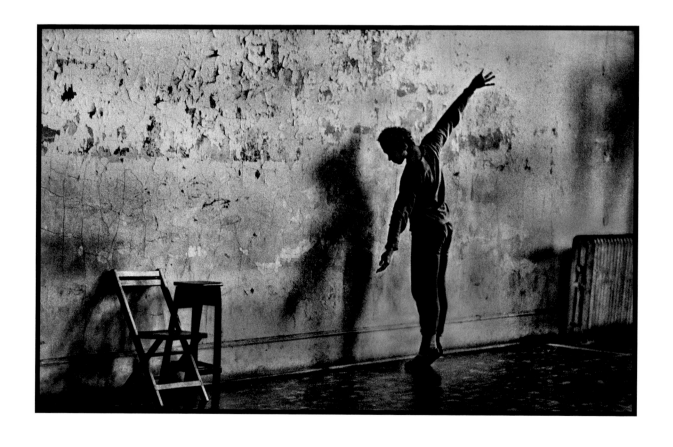

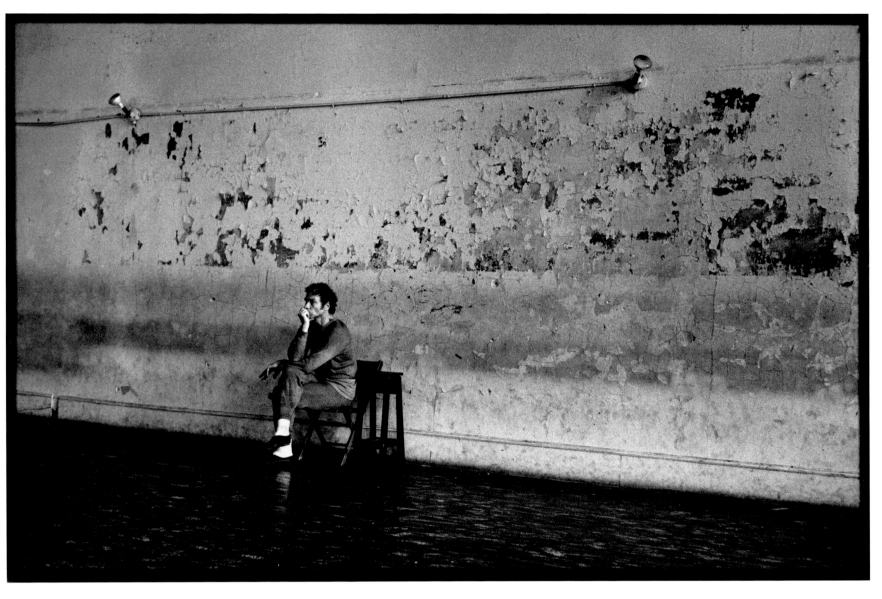

Left and above: Merce Cunningham in rehearsal room

Douglas Dunn and Merce Cunningham

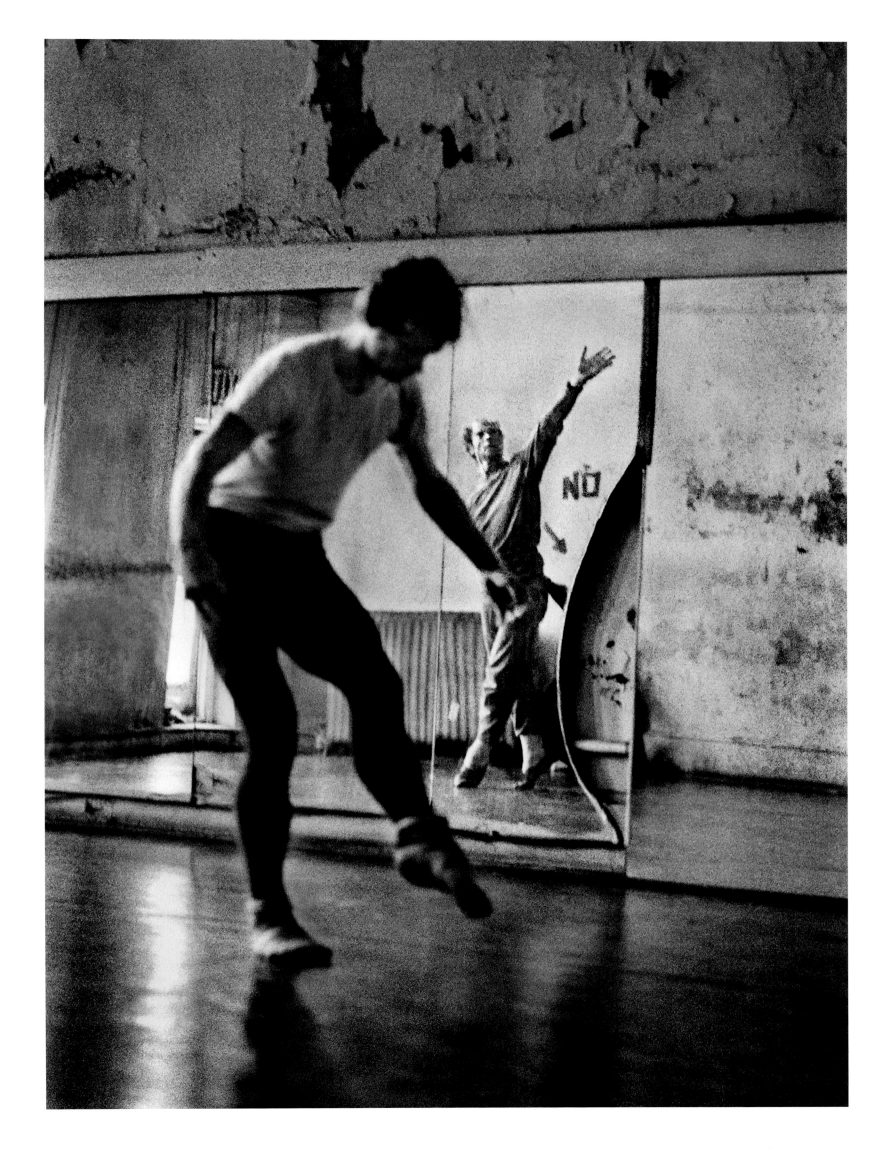

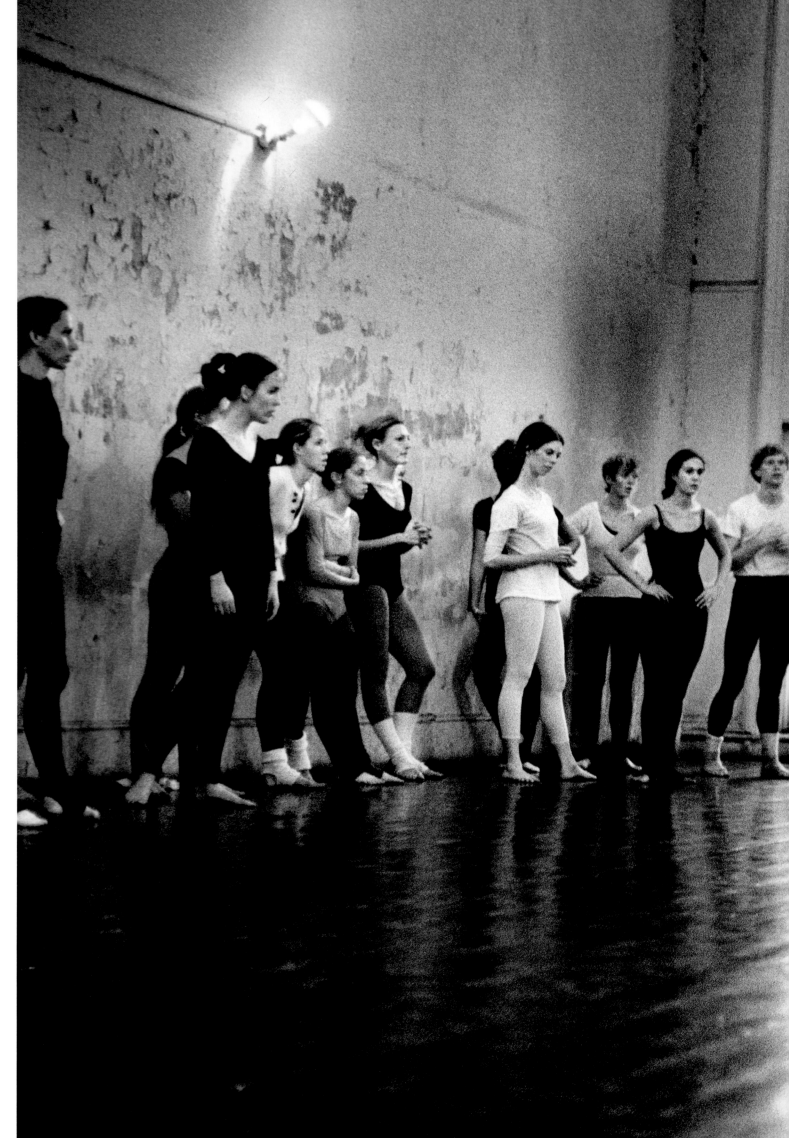

4:30 advanced class

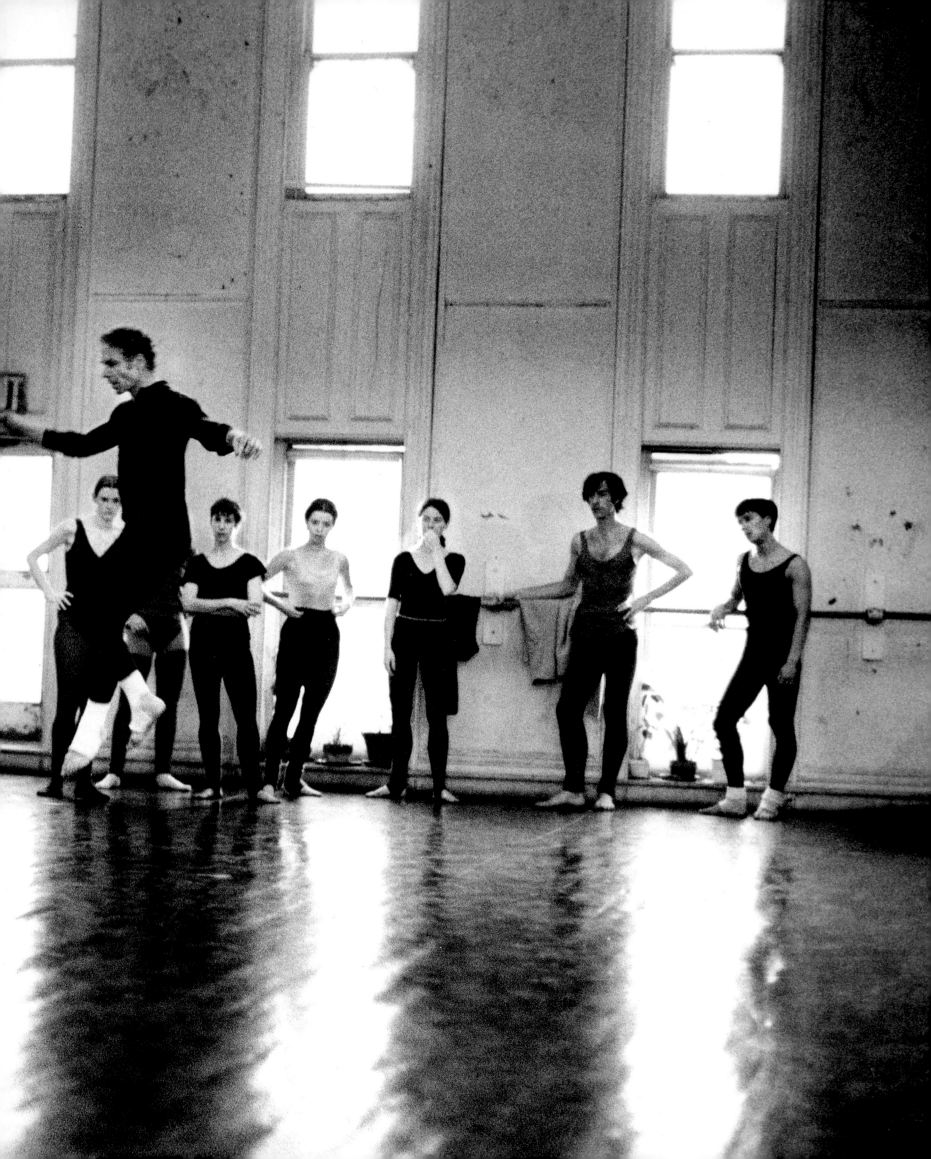

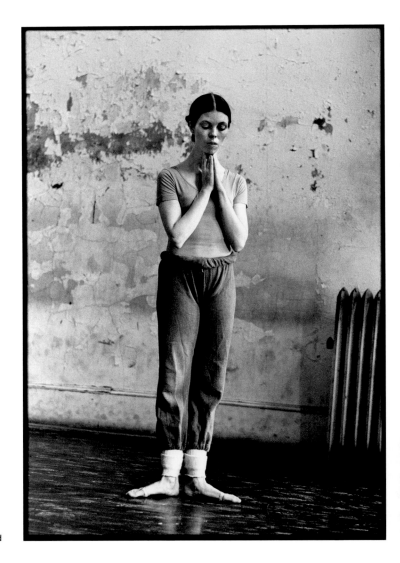

The beat before crossing the floor—Sandra Neels, Douglas Dunn, and Valda Setterfield

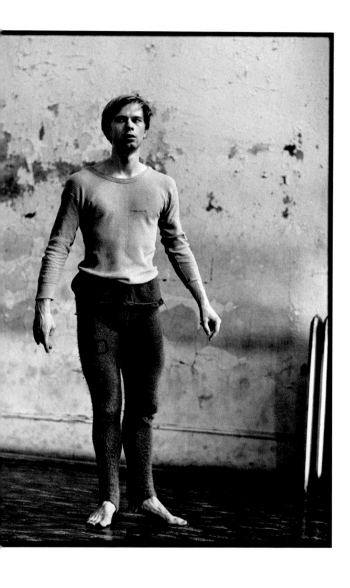
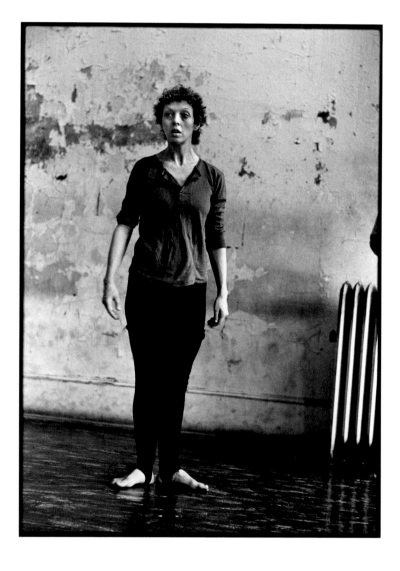

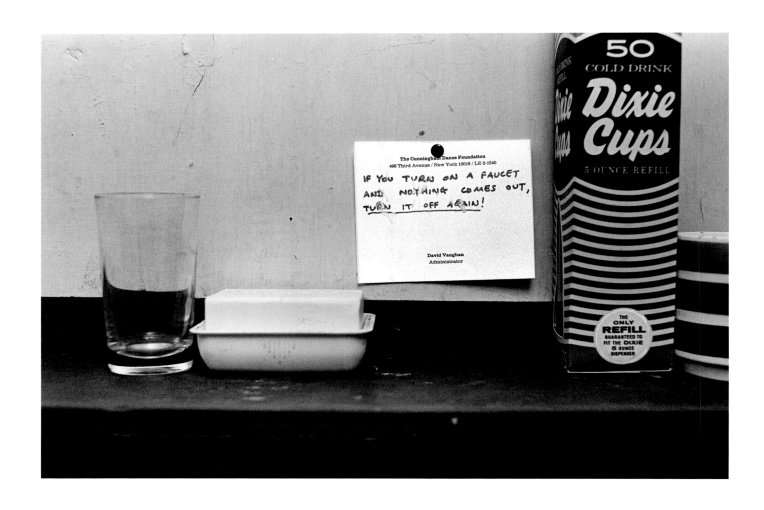

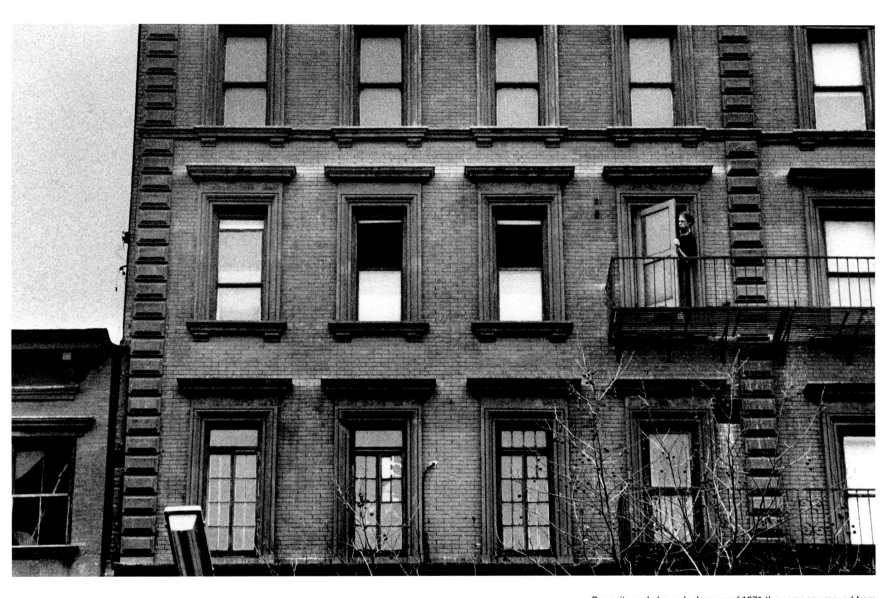

Opposite and above: In January of 1971 the company moved from the homey but dark, dilapidated studio on Third Avenue to the spacious, sun-filled studios on the eleventh floor of Westbeth

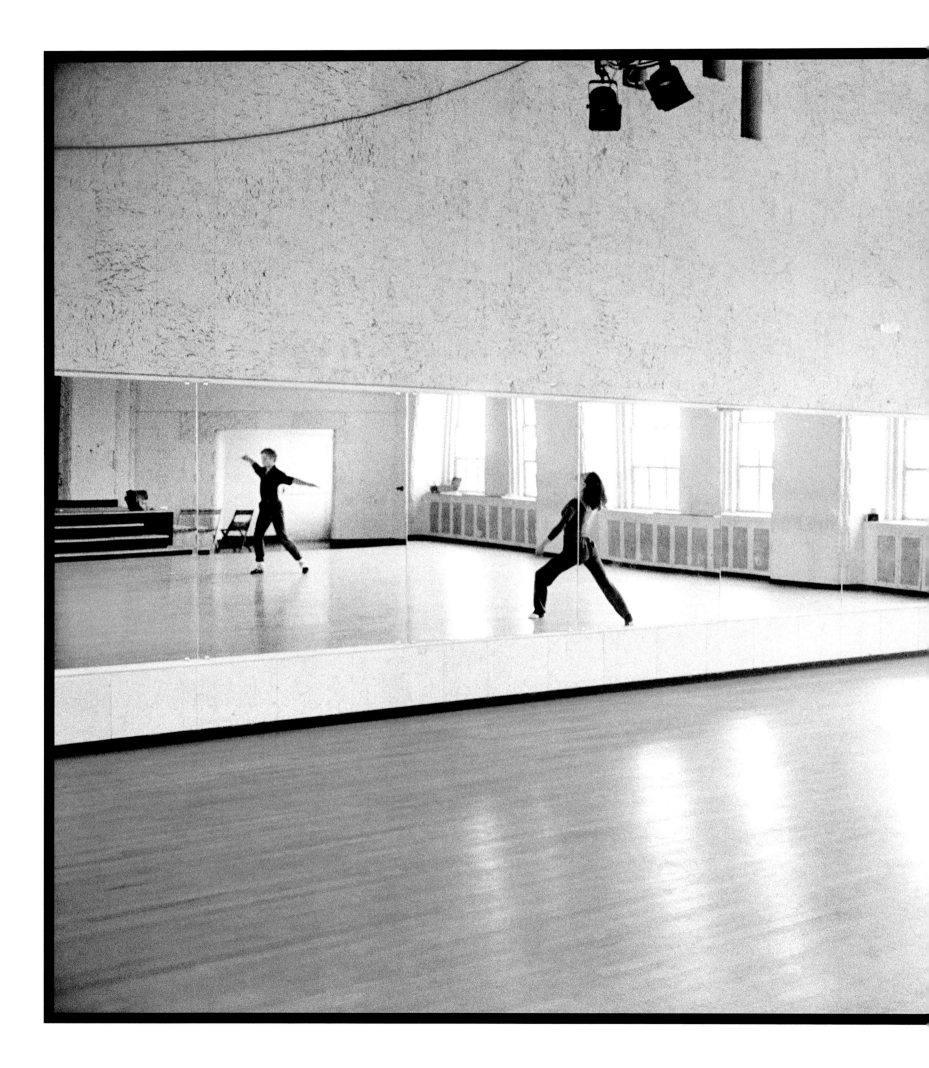

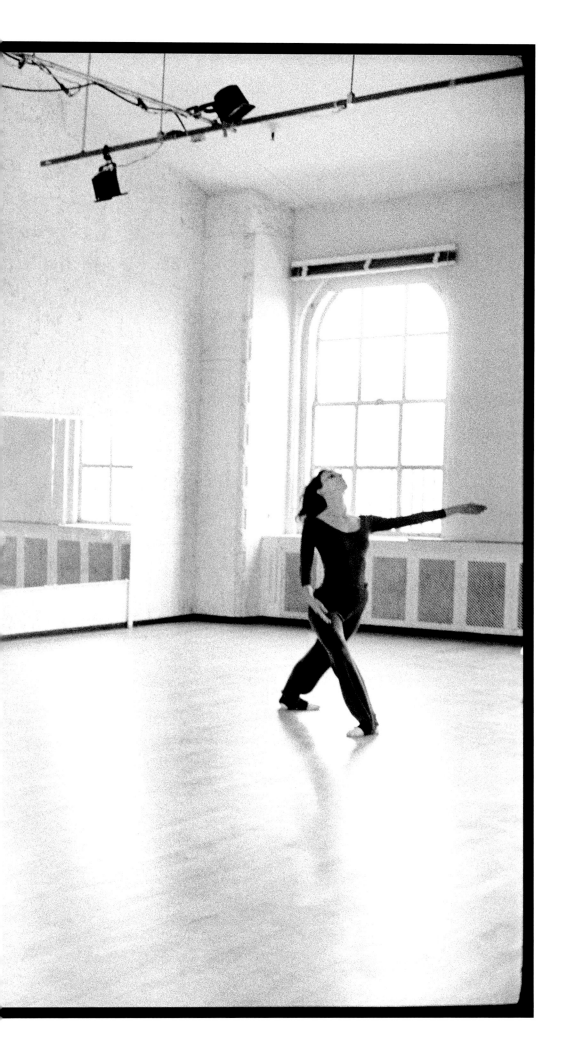

WESTBETH

In this space Merce happily made many, many dances, continuing even after John Cage died in 1992. Some, of course, were forgettable. Others, like *Second Hand* and *Biped*, the two most important to me, were unquestionably masterpieces. *Biped* (1999) was one of the dances made possible by Life Forms, a computer program Merce adopted enthusiastically. It permitted him to continue creating work long after his body ceased to be a useful instrument.

Merce died on July 26, 2009, at ninety years of age. He wished his company to continue on, giving "farewell" performances for two years and to then disband. He could not possibly have foreseen what occurred in 2012. In that year, the Martha Graham Company moved into his Westbeth studio, an irony so dark it can only be called Kafkaesque; I find it difficult to write about this even now.

Merce Cunningham and Carolyn Brown
rehearsing *Night Wandering*, Summer 1972

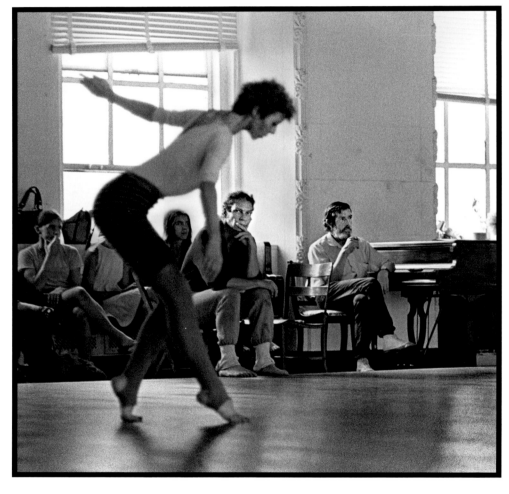

Valda Setterfield, Merce Cunningham, and John Cage at open rehearsal, June 1971

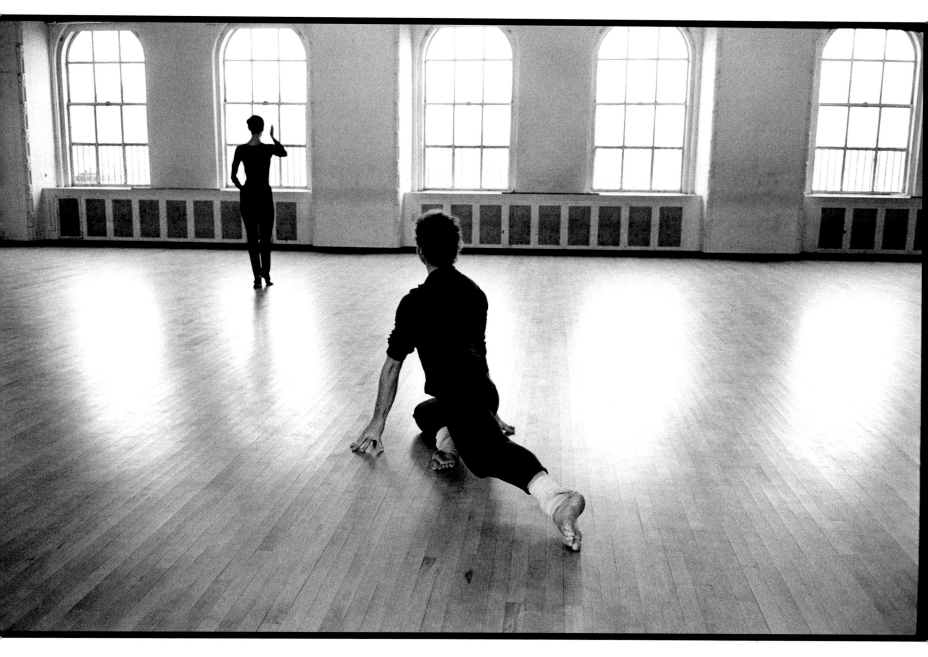

Merce Cunningham and Carolyn Brown, *Suite for Five*
duet rehearsal, January 1972

CAROLYN BROWN

"Who is this Man?" asked the *Saturday Evening Post* on its October 19, 1968 cover, from which a man's face, split vertically by chalk white and flame red makeup, solemnly regards the viewer. It's a good likeness despite the makeup devised by Bob Rauschenberg for a dance called *Nocturnes*, but when Merce Cunningham passed this face staring out at him from a magazine prominently displayed on his neighborhood newsstand, he said he didn't recognize it. In Centralia, Washington, neither did his mother. Jim Klosty's mother, glancing at the magazine on her own coffee table, just assumed the face belonged to Nixon. But scattered around the globe in national capitals and obscure towns and on innumerable college campuses that face is known. It belongs to Merce Cunningham: dancer, choreographer, teacher, and director of his own company. But to answer the question "Who is this Man?" is no easy job. The *Saturday Evening Post* certainly didn't do it. The photographs in this book come closer than all the hundreds of words written about him, though they cannot, any better than can words, reveal Cunningham the dancer. Fortunately, they don't attempt to. Dances and dancing—unique in their utter fragility—will always remain

beyond the camera and the pen. The breath and life of dancing are still immune to permanence; as yet, neither the motion picture camera nor the video machine can capture that aspiration that dance shares with no other activity. But these photographs do reveal a man at work and in love with that work: dancing, making dances, teaching, directing his company in his own singular fashion, and in addition, tending to his administration and to the board of directors of the foundation that bears his name. He does not take these responsibilities lightly. He was born into the Catholic Church, and certainly the manner of its teachings, if not the substance, has influenced Merce's social behavior. He took his turn as altar boy in the Catholic Church, and later, for about five years, in Martha Graham's Dance Company. He says the first prepared him for the second: in both disciplines he spent a great deal of time on his knees, and all those years of being an acolyte wore the knee bones smooth.

As I write I have only a few months' distance from a twenty-year association with this man with whom I have shared the hours and days and months of a consuming and satisfying dance life. In that twenty years few of the people I've known have grown so profoundly as Merce, despite his unchanging need for seclusion and his refusal to reveal any more about himself than that which he willingly offers. One must always meet him on *his* terms; anything else is an encroachment on his territorial rights to privacy. Psychology doesn't interest him. Anthropology and zoology do.

Merce assumes the directorship of his company as though donning an ill-fitting suit that makes him uncomfortable and somehow threatens to engulf him. Direct, immediate communication from director to directed is rare. He finds the role unbecoming. He's actually better with strangers—a group of college dance students, for example, who eagerly absorb his words and gestures. He can seem to give more to them because the involvement is brief. With his own, with those he's chosen and who have chosen him, he is not really at ease. Sometimes he seems even to hate them, so miserable does he find the leader-master role, so greatly does he misunderstand what is needed of him.

But there is no question that Merce is a Master. The distance that he maintains between himself and his company can have an extraordinary effect on the development of the dancers if they are mature enough to realize that his "hands-off" attitude frees them, indeed pushes them, to be self-disclplined, self-critical, and self-moving. Merce's reluctance, for whatever reason, to impose his own values and judgments, his own preferences and aesthetic tastes on those who work with him is on one level baffling and frustrating: one wants to please him! But on another level it can be read as an

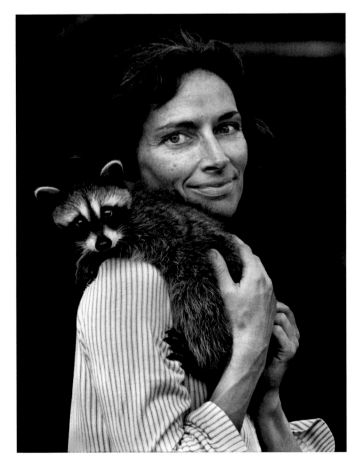

Carolyn Brown and Zoomie the raccoon

affirmation of our differences and an acknowledgment of the worth of those differences beyond his own likes and dislikes. He is unlike many choreographers who attempt to run the lives of their dancers, direct their reading matter, their diet, their choice of wardrobe, and even interfere in their love lives. In fact, he is often reluctant even to express his preferences about the dancers physical appearance on stage in his choreography. No doubt he is concerned, but only three times have I known him to interfere, and that was many years ago: he wanted Remy Charlip to put on a toupée for performances; he wanted Paul Taylor to shave off his Black Mountain–grown beard before the Theatre De Lys season; and he didn't want Shareen Blair to wear false eyelashes. This onand-off attitude toward baldness and beards and eyelashes on stage may not have changed, but he no longer makes his opinions on the matter known. Rarely are his angers or his pleasures revealed spontaneously to those who engender them, and yet he cares about his dancers and worries about their well-being.

The question is: Should the lives of fifteen (or twenty or three) people be crucially dependent upon one individual, upon one man's greatness, genius, madness, self-possessedness, and even cruelty? The answer is yes if a certain kind of work is to be accomplished. John Cage has written (in *Silence*) that the subservience of several to the directives of one is intolerable. He is referring specifically to members of the orchestra under the direction of a conductor, but it is strange that he has not seen it as equally applicable to the life of the dance company with whom he has been associated as musical director and spiritual mentor since its inception. (Actually, Cage abdicated his position of musical director in about 1968. Since then the musicians of the company have worked as a cooperative body, making group decisions.) It is doubtful that he would have written so harshly had he been writing about the Cunningham dance company. He is and has been devoted to it; he has worked for its preservation, its well-being, and its sense of family and community, sometimes as a parent, sometimes as a recreation director, often as selfrighteous preacher-minister, full of zeal and unabating optimism. In his devotion to Merce, he quite easily forgets his written convictions regarding anarchy and revolution. Merce, on the other hand, has heard John's lectures, read his books, and has been profoundly, that is to say, practically, influenced. He carries certain of the ideas into his everyday life (his work), and the results are often curious.

Dance, as Cunningham makes it, is no place for democracy: we are not born equal; we do not have equal gifts; we are not equally driven to success or failure; we are not equally capable or in need to create or perform. Cunningham followed his predecessors in the brief history of modern dance in perhaps its only tradition: he broke away to start anew, to start for himself, his way. At first he created under the aesthetic guidance of Cage. Later, as he grew to accept the worth of his own visions, he became increasingly self-moving. Until 1973, at least, the driving energy to make dances came from an all-encompassing passion to dance. There is no way for anyone to know

if when Merce can no longer dance he will continue to choreograph. The one (choreography) came to exist because of the intense need for the other (to dance). In an interview with Deborah Jowitt printed in the *Village Voice* in March 1973 he said, "People keep asking me when I'm going to stop. And I say, 'Good heavens, I've just got a running start.'" Though this appetite for dancing was the prime mover, Merce did choose to have a company, to choreograph works of a larger scope than the solo dance. (He once remarked to me that he does not consider making solos for himself "choreography.")

Jim Klosty tells a story about asking Merce, as they were driving to Merce's studio for a reception following the wedding of Theresa Dickinson (a Cunningham student and a dancer with Twyla Tharp) and Lew Lloyd (the company manager at the time) if Merce felt like a patriarch. Merce's answer: "I feel more like an innocent bystander who's been trapped." And so he has by a studio jammed with students (many wanting to join his company), a board of directors who until recently didn't understand the necessity of deficits in a performance art, by an administration and office staff sizable enough for a small business, always needing his decision on innumerable questions, by a group of dancers wanting to grow, wanting new material, wanting constant attention, support, and approval. The list goes on to include preposterous details such as a college student wanting him to write her about his technique because she's writing her MA thesis on it, and she knows nothing about it (there's no material in her college library). (His solution to the last problem is typical: "Tell her to come study!") But Merce's own needs haven't changed. Only the pressures and demands upon him have. My guess is he's still happiest alone in his studio and always has been, whichever one it may have been, but especially in the magnificent spacious Westbeth studio with its window-lined walls and eleventh-floor views of the Hudson and Manhattan. His territory is his studio; he stakes it out, paces its boundaries, and is exceptionally possessive about it. There, dressed either in ragged practice clothes or mechanics coveralls, he works: he gives himself a class, waters his plants, choreographs new material, types a letter in an attempt to catch up on a staggering back load of correspondence, watches a ship move up the river, strips and dances for pleasure, eats a lunch of cheese and nuts and fruit and yogurt while he reads a book about apes or bees or the structure of a leaf, plays his radio, plans his technique class, makes a cup of coffee, reviews his notes on a dance to be revived, and for a few hours, if he's lucky enough to go undisturbed by plumbers, painters, building inspectors, the administration requesting program copy for three months ahead, a company dancer calling to say she's ill, or a board member calling to request his presence at a fundraising cocktail party, Merce putters blissfully and enjoys the small clutter of activities that make him whole.

He's terrific in crises, rallying in disasters, and his humor has saved the wretchedness of many nearly hopeless situations (i.e., when a male dancer, in every dance in the repertory including a work-in-progress, quit without warning or understudies a few weeks before a tour preceding the yearly New York season). The demands on him are superhuman, but I don't think it occurs to him that he can refuse them. What has taken place during the twenty years I've known him is a slow realization and eventual acceptance of the millstone he carries, which is that he himself is the weather vane of his company's morale. Nowhere was this more evident than in 1968 on the South American tour where he badly injured himself, and should have stopped dancing, but instead reworked all his dances save one (*Place*), so that he could manage to get through the repertory (on the other foot, so to speak) as programmed, all the while maintaining a gentle cheerfulness despite his extreme pain and the embarrassment and personal anguish of having to perform at about one-fifth of his usual full-out capacity. Added to that was his knowledge of the diplomatic and financial difficulties that plagued the company's management on that tour from beginning to end. But he did not withdraw, as he had done in similar circumstances on the '64 tour. Then, we did not know that he was ill. We knew only that he had withdrawn from us, and each of us wondered what we had done. After six months of performing in France, Italy, Austria, England, Sweden, Finland, Germany, Poland, Belgium, Holland, Czechoslovakia, India, Thailand, and Japan, with Merce for the most part taciturn and in retreat due to illness and injury and stresses few of us knew about, the company was near dissolution. At the final company meeting of that tour, in the lobby of International House in Tokyo, after briefly thanking and commending all of us, Merce requested a decision from each of us whether or not he could count on us for the '65 U.S. season. One dancer had already left the company in London; four more quit then in Tokyo. Of nine dancers, there remained only four and at least two of these had serious doubts about continuing. It was at this time, too, that Rauschenberg left the company. From the 1964 experience Merce learned how perilously affecting his own moods and miseries could be, and it was deeply moving to see the man fight to keep up the spirits of the rest of us that summer in South America. It's no easy thing to dance with others whom you know are in pain. He knows that from a history of experience with his own dancers. I have seen him standing in the wings, tense and immobile, watching an ill or injured dancer on stage, the strain of that worry nearly paralyzing him. It has even made him ill. His concern for his dancers is far more than his concern for his choreography. It is an expression of his caring for the individual person, something he can rarely show in any direct manner. The love he bears us is private, relayed indirectly in curious ways. But I like to think it is there in strong measure nonetheless.

Separate from his relationship to his dancers and artistic associates is his relationship to his studio, to his company administration, and to the board of directors of the Cunningham Dance Foundation. I've heard it said that Merce probably would have made a fine businessman. He's realistic and conservative, and he possesses a pragmatic wisdom and stolidness surprising in someone of his vocation. In the VW days, he was also booking agent, manager, ac-

countant, and even co-bus driver, spelling John at cocktail hour or scrabble time. He kept the books, paid the bills, and taught himself Russian on the side. Since those times, I've seen assistant administrators tremble under his scrutinizing questions regarding schedules, bookings, and accommodations, but they give him highest marks for practicality and foresight.

Merce Cunningham began teaching in order to develop dancers for his own choreography. He had worked in the early years with fellow members of the Martha Graham Company when he first started making his own dances and discovered that he wanted another way of moving without the resonances of the Graham style and vocabulary, and that the best way to achieve this was to start teaching. When I first joined his classes in the early fifties, he taught in a small, drafty studio without central heating. He taught even if there was only one student in class. He usually forgot when it was a holiday, and was there prepared to teach, even if it was Christmas Eve. For most of the years that I worked with him, he taught at least one class, and for many years two classes, daily.

It is impossible to duplicate that charisma that Cunningham possesses as teacher. He sets a pace to his classes that one can emulate but never reproduce. His advanced class is designed to develop flexibility in the mind as well as in the body. Few movement exercises are done by rote. There are no gimmicks, nothing freaky, but his ways of moving are often unfamiliar, difficult, and sometimes odd, demanding both physical and mental strength to cope with the subtleties of shape and the varieties of rhythmic nuance. The concern for rhythm is the first, and this concern manifests itself in phrasing unlike the ballet (even though the actual steps may be reminiscent of ballet) and unlike any I have seen or experienced in modern dance techniques. It comes from the now accepted but at one time truly revolutionary act of acknowledging dance as an entity of its own, separate from music. The rhythms and phrasings come from the movement, not from musical accompaniment. Often he will refuse to sacrifice the rhythm, even for clarity of shape: when a company member asks, "Can we take it slower?" or "Will you count that for us?" he growls softly, "No, the rhythm will be shot." This attitude recalls stories of Charles Ives, who often expressed regret at having to write out a composition at all, because he felt its rhythms would be hopelessly crystallized. Merce's special concern with rhythmic variety and subtlety mixed with his own peculiar passion for movement and his phenomenal gut energy cannot be reproduced by anyone else, no matter how long he or she may have worked with him. Charisma is not transferable.

Merce requires of his dancers that the rhythm come from within: from the nature of the step, from the nature of the phrase, and from the dancer's own musculature; not from without, from a music that

Carolyn Brown, *How to Pass, Kick, Fall and Run*,
UCLA Berkeley, California, January 1971

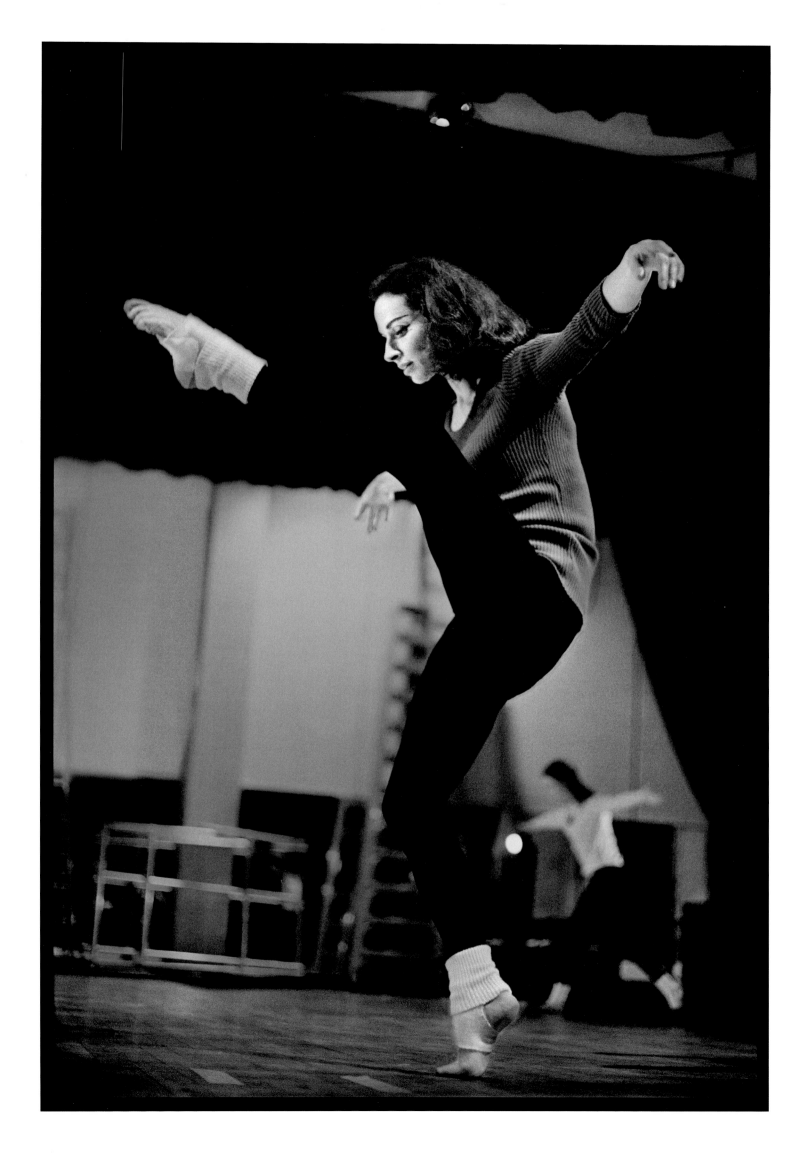

imposes its own particular rhythms and phrases and structure, or from a narrative or "mood." For Merce, I believe, a "musical dancer" phrases from the muscles, the sinews, the gut, and the soul. Each movement is given *its* full value, *its* own unique meaning the movement is expressive of itself. (Margaret Craske, a truly great teacher of ballet, has always maintained this view. Perhaps it is for this reason that so many of Cunningham's dancers have studied with her.) This is what Merce himself does as a dancer, and this is what he wants from his dancers. At the same time he allows for, and in fact expects, each dancer to be uniquely himself.

Merce does not ask for or want imitation of his own personal style and way of moving. What looks on him like sheer brilliance and virtuosity and as natural as walking down the street, on someone else can look dull, or mannered, sometimes even foolish. Few dancers physcally comprehend the deeper muscle knowledge of the body that understands the shadings of attack, what to make big and what to make small without any single action losing *its* complete energy. This knowledge Merce has; it is one of the qualities that make him a great dancer. Again, like Ives, Merce thinks it is desirable that people should not be all alike; both men found it reasonable for a composer (choreographer) to allow for individual variation in performance with respect to tempo and dynamics. Merce seems to feel, as the Zen master described by Eugen Herrigel in *Zen in the Art of Archery*, that the instructor's business is not to show the way itself, but to enable the pupil to get the feel of this way by adapting it to his individual peculiarities. "Shunning longwinded instructions and explanations, the [master] contents himself with perfunctory commands and does not reckon on any questions from the pupil. Impassively he looks on at the blundering efforts, not even hoping for independence or initiative, and waits patiently for growth and ripeness. Both have time: the teacher does not harass, and the pupil does not overtax himself." As a description of Merce it's near perfect.

At a time when some choreographers are looking at the whole idea of technique and virtuosity afresh, and some are giving up specialized techniques of dance altogether, Merce has remained devoted to "dance movement"—training the body to move with speed, flexibility, and control; to move with the sustained control of slow motion; to move free of any particular style. This devotion is perhaps most easily defined as a commitment to energy—not to ideas, to intellection, or even to perception, but to physical energy, expressed through the body moving (or still) in time and space. By example, by the simple fact of his enormous presence, he communicates that energy and passion, and a deadly serious personal discipline that can kindle and fan into fire the inexplicable desire to dance; a kind of spontaneous combustion takes place between master and pupil. But if the student is looking for praise, even for encouragement, he'd better go elsewhere. Merce's expectations are simple but uncompromising: work hard and work consistently. Those who use dancing as an ego trip will get no satisfactions in a Cunningham class—Merce won't be watching.

Company class is over. It's a heavy hot humid day in August 1972, only a few weeks before the company will leave for a two month tour beginning in Iran. Merce has disappeared into his private dressing room at the south end of the Westbeth studio. From there, on a clear day, you can see the Statue of Liberty. No other room in the Cunningham quarters gets that view. That strikes me as symbolic of something. Scattered throughout the studio, members of the company use the half-hour break for their own purposes. There's the stretched out ease of a lazy summer afternoon, but it's deceptive. Soon, Merce appears with notebooks, piles of papers, stop watch, towel, sweater, and pulling the piano chair to face the studio, arranges his paraphernalia. Valda Satterfield, Sandra Neels, and Susana Hayman-Chaffey appear. Douglas Dunn is already moving, working out the phrasing from a particularly complicated combination from class. Meg Harper is practicing her *Borst Park* (1972) solo in a corner. Merce continues along through the office into the company room, nods, smiles again, and the rest of the company assembles itself in the studio. The ritual is not yet complete. Merce pauses to converse with school administrator, David Vaughan, who is closing up after the morning classes; there's some laughter, the key turns in the lock, and Merce enters the studio. He says softly to no one in particular: "We'll take *Walkaround Time*," but only two people hear him, and as they go to their places to begin, the information travels imperceptibly from dancer to dancer. "What did he say?" The rehearsal has begun. Merce is watching this time, not doing his part. He. glances at scribbles on his pad, then at his stopwatch; he jots down some numbers. Except for the slap and thud and caress of feet on the floor and varieties of audible breathing, the room is silent. No music. No director shouting commands or corrections. Those not dancing lean into the walls or mirrors, perch on window ledges, lie on the lecture platform, or stretch and flex some muscle or other; some watch and occasionally they whisper together. Susana's body resounds against Chris Komar's as he catches her spread-eagled against his chest and backs off-stage. The first half is over. Merce checks his notes again, saying nothing. The dancers move onto the floor, talking about steps missed, timings off, spaces in conflict. Merce looks up, saying to no one in particular, "It's one minute and thirty-eight seconds too long." We stop talking. "What happened in the quintet?" Five women try to explain. Merce cuts through the chatter. "Let's take it again. I'll beat, Valda, once you've set the tempo." She starts her run from stage left, breaks into a strongly defined triplet, Merce picks up the tempo clapplng his hands, and the quintet is repeated. The problems are sight cues, space, and rhythm. He irons them out. "The quartet is a little slow. I'd like to see it again, please." He starts snapping his fingers. There's some disagreement about the exact phrasing. "What is it, Sandra?" he asks, not being quite sure of it himself. She shows him, counting out loud. The four do it again, together this time. And so goes the afternoon. No talk about meaning or quality. No images given. No attempts made to nurture expressivity in any particular dancer. The dances are treated more as puzzles than works of art: the pieces are space and time, shape and rhythm. The rest is up to us. We put the puzzle together, making of it what we can, bringing to it what our imaginations allow. What we bring can enrich or detract from his work; Merce accepts that—it's part of the risk, part of the possibility for discovery.

A dancer needs only to have worked with another choreographer to appreciate the working situation in Merce's company. No eight-hour rehearsals for Merce. He works quickly, but patiently. Compared with other companies, Cunningham dancers do very little "hanging around." He values time, his and ours, and uses it economically. When choreographing a new work, Merce usually sketches out a group section first, much as a painter might draw the bold outlines on a canvas before using pigment, teaching all the unison movement; then, later, he adds or deletes, and increases the complexity by varying the material or rhythm or space for individual dancers; the whole process is done with a dazzling speed and skill. Of course I've seen him stuck or bogged down momentarily; but if he is he doesn't waste his or our time with the problem. He moves on to something else. He seldom throws out a whole section or a day's work.

Once a dance is completed, Merce rarely does more than one run-through a day, preceded and/or followed by a cleanup rehearsal of any sections causing difficulties. It was the dancers' responsibility to get it right, to do it as well as we could, and to iron out spacing and/or timing difficulties with other dancers. Merce rarely prodded, criticized, corrected, or encouraged. Only when we couldn't solve a problem ourselves would he step in. Consequently he developed a group of dancers who became individually responsible for his work and themselves. Merce always appeared to be interested only in the correct timing and spacing, seeming to believe that if these elements were right, any other problems would solve themselves. When asked, "How do you do this turn (or fall or jump)?" his answer was inevitably, "You just do it." Viola Farber and I were always amused when after a rehearsal had been a total disaster, Merce's only comment, as he glanced at his stopwatch, would be, "It's two and a half minutes fast."

Merce's way of working with a stopwatch, which so shocked the modern dance world at Connecticut College our first summer there in 1958, led to the company's reputation of being cold, inhuman, impassive, expressionless automatons. But Merce worked with the stopwatch from the belief that rhythm comes out of the nature of the movement itself and the movement nature of the individual dancer. At times he choreographed the movement, then asked, "What time does this particular movement take, what time does this particular phrase take?" We would rehearse it repeatedly until it took its own "inevitable" time in the designed space. It was then fixed and rehearsed in that time. Group works, such as *Rune* and *Aeon*, which had much unison dancing with constantly shifting tempi, took weeks of this kind of careful rehearsal, with sections being counted aloud over and over again while being timed. We worked without a mir-

ror, sensing one another through the pulse of the given movement or phrase. Accuracy of time is necessary to maintain the designed space. Change the space and the time changes, unless the speed of the particular phrase changes in order to keep the time the same. Change the time and the space, and the movement changes. Merce works with all these possibilities. He has often chosen a total time, then structured it into combinations of long and short parts. Sometimes he adheres to a fixed time limit, discovering ways either to speed up or slow down a particular step or phrase to fit it: thus changing the movement and "shaking up" established or familiar ways of moving. In his classes in composition he gives problems relating to time awareness. For example: make three phrases and do them in one minute. Do the same three phrases in two minutes. Do the same three phrases in thirty seconds. Observe the differences in the movement. Of equal importance: be able to do them accurately each time in the prescribed time; that is, be able to repeat precisely. The muscular memory has a built-in time sense. It can go awry, of course. But it can be spectacularly accurate when developed. It is this muscular memory that Merce relied on to make such difficult works as *Rune* and *Aeon* happen consistently.

For years, the most exhilarating times for me came at the end of the making of a new work. The work-in-progress period was a wonderful adventure, both exciting and difficult because we were dealing with unknowns, with strange and sometimes awkward-feeling rhythms and movement. But when it was finished, and we had begun to run through the work in its entirety, there was a time of revelation. At that time, if we had resisted the temptations to make the movement feel and look like something we already knew and had done before (not always an easy task), we could discover something new about ourselves as dancers, as well as fathoming something about the work that Merce had made. Contrary to the often publicized propaganda, most of Merce's dances are much more than "the steps."

Second Hand (1970), perhaps Merce's most programatic work, was originally intended to be performed to John Cage's piano reduction of Erik Satie's three-part symphonic drama, *Socrate*. At the end of our duet, just before I exit prior to Part Three (the death of Socrates in Satie's score), Merce and I run two full circles around the stage, arms around each other's waists. During the run in the final stage rehearsal before the premiere, Merce's expression terrified me. We'd already rehearsed *Rainforest* and *Place* that afternoon, and *Second Hand* is almost thirty minutes long, with Merce dancing the entire time. He'd always smiled at me during this run until that rehearsal, but this time he looked so anguished that my first thought was that he had injured himself or was completely exhausted. Afterward, I expressed my fears to John Cage. "Don't worry," John told me the next day. "Merce said it's at that moment that (Socrates) is preparing to meet death." The point I wish to make here is that, like most of Merce's dances, I believe, *Second Hand* is deeply meaningful to him. Perhaps Merce feels that his dances

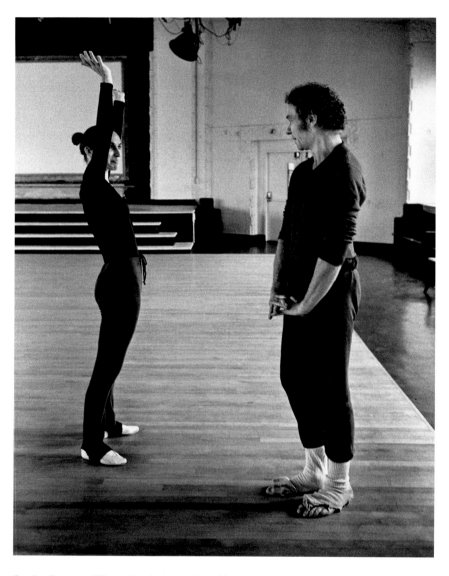
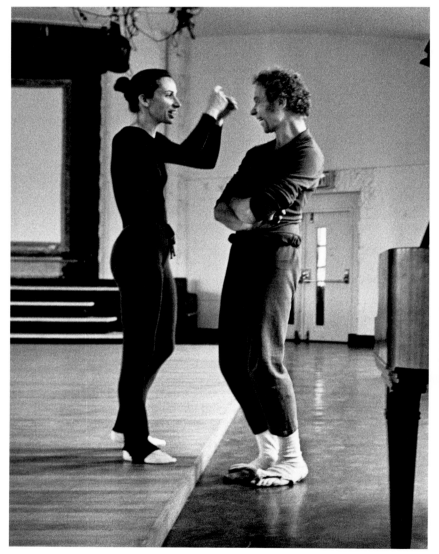

Carolyn Brown and Merce Cunningham, story with gestures, January 1972

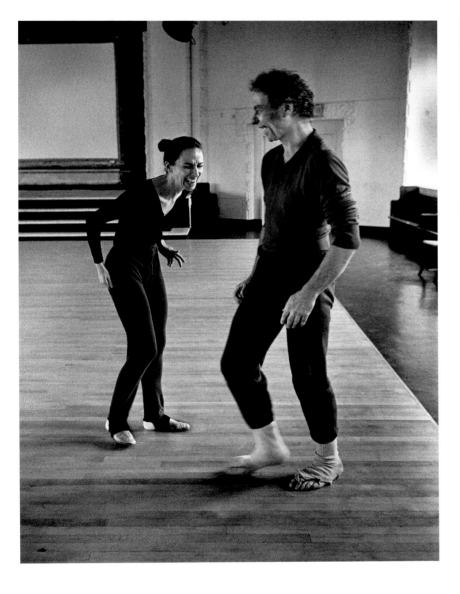
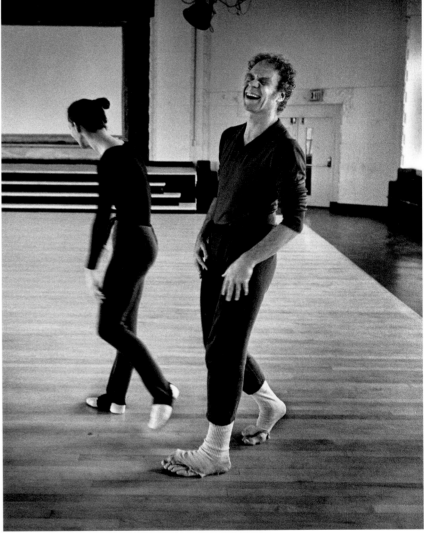

need have no meaning for anyone but himself; certainly he has taken precautions to see that little of it is intelligible to an outsider, or for that matter to an insider. But he does leave clues.

All one need do is look to Merce himself to know that there is much more than steps to contend with. His own dancing is suffused with mystery, poetry, and madness—expressive of root emotions, generous yet often frightening in their nakedness. It's a mistake to forget that at one time Merce intended to become an actor. When he dances, he is a chameleon creature capable of kaleidoscopic shifts of mood and temperament and style. Often the myriad qualities play one upon another within a single dance, within a span of thirty seconds, like a many faceted stone turning quickly in the light. At times the expressions on his face seem fortuitous, contingent upon the moment upon what he may be seeing or hearing or feeling at that precise second. At other times the emotions portrayed are clearly studied and immutable, as in *Second Hand*; at these moments he seems totally aware and in control of the impact he is creating. The virtuousity that Merce reveals as a dancer is little understood. No ballet dancer alive can touch the uniqueness of his physical gifts because his endowments don't relate to any of the conventional balletic skills. His presence alone is so powerful he need only sit on a window ledge in partial darkness, as he did in a studio performance in May 1973, moving almost imperceptibly, and even though ten members of his company are dancing their guts out, it is Merce who commands one's attention. When he stands in parallel position, he is weighted like a tree trunk, roots deep in the ground, all suppleness and ease above. He moves with leopard stealth and speed and awareness and intention. No one else can even approximate the thrusts of energy, the quick changes, the subtle rhythmic variation, the counterpoint of torso and arms and legs and head that occur in his own dancing. It cannot be imitated. It cannot be choreographed. It exists only as a physical fact of his own personal movement, energy, and dynamism.

But Merce has freedoms none of the rest of us has ever had; he made the stuff, after all. The *Village Voice* critic Deborah Jowitt put it this way: "I sometimes think how hard it must be for Cunningham's dancers. He is free—bound only lightly by rules he himself has devised but for the others it's different. I've noticed it takes newcomers a while to find out how to look like themselves and still bring the difficult dancing off."

She's right. It's never been easy. It must be a bewildering and slightly terrifying experience for those dancers who have joined the company in the last ten years or so. For those of us who began with Merce in the early fifties it was quite different. There was no previous history, no world reputation, and most importantly, perhaps, no one's shoes to fill. In over fifty dances, all my parts save four (*Suite by Chance*, *Ragtime*, *Collage*, and *Amores*) were made on me, for me. Merce grew, the repertory grew, and with them, the dancers, each in his own way, were able to grow too.

Although it took me most of my twenty years with him, I eventually learned to trust myself to be myself as fully as I felt his choreography would allow. A clue to performing his dances comes from his own words: "In one of my . . . solo works, called *Untitled Solo*, I choreographed the piece with the use of chance methods. However, the dance as performed seems to have an unmistakable dramatic intensity in its bones, so to speak. It seems to me that it was simply a question of 'allowing' this quality to happen rather than 'forcing' it. It is this 'tranquility' of the actor or dancer which seems to me essential. A tranquility which allows him to detach himself and thereby *to present* freely and liberally . . ."

Merce says he tries to see each dancer individually, not just as dancers but as people, and to draw from this view of them when he makes new works. But since he has always had a repertory company, this often became awkward and sometimes unworkable as dancers left and others came to take their places. New dancers had to take over parts choreographed for the special qualities of someone else. Merce was never happy with anyone else in Viola Farber's parts in *Crises*, *Nocturnes*, and *Summerspace*. Restaging *Paired*, a duet for Viola and himself was never even attempted. I feel that a consequence of the ever changing personnel has been the depersonalization of many of the most recent dances. After a particularly devastating year of losing male dancers, Merce made *TV Rerun* (1972), a dance in which everyone learns the same material but is free to choose spontaneously in performance what parts of it she or he wishes to perform. It is a dance which can be done by any number of dancers, and the whole Is never jeopardized by the departure of any one dancer. It depends for its impact on the counterpoint and almost fugal correspondences of the choreographic material (and Gordon Mumma's score) and on each dancer's execution and presentation of that material. *TV Rerun* presents the curious situation in which each dancer knows that he or she is completely dispensable, and I often wondered when watching it—both in rehearsal and performance—if perhaps it was for this reason some of us often looked it: instead of revealing the uniqueness of each person, we seemed to become anonymous.

Merce's method of teaching movement for a new work varies considerably with each individual. For example, in 1953 during the making of *Septet*, Merce taught us carefully, indicating each movement precisely and filling in the details; generally, he works this way with new dancers, and with some he continues to provide the material in its entirety, demonstrating with exactness both the shape and the rhythm. As the years went by, my own experience with him changed; *Crises* (1960) was a kind of breakthrough for me. When Merce demonstrated my entrance, which followed the brilliant and erotic duet for Viola and himself, he showed it to me so quickly that my impression of it was only of his tremendous vitality, speed, and wildness. I think he purposely blurred the actual steps, forcing me into a way of moving beyond my experience at that time. My usual inclination had always been to want to know precisely what Merce wanted me to do, but on this particular occasion, I didn't want to know the steps—I wanted desperately to be the wildness. Ten years later, after choreographing *Tread* (1970) for two months, he proceeded to teach me a solo in about two minutes. ("I think dance only comes alive when it gets awkward again," Merce has written.) Three days later, Tread was premiered in Brooklyn. I decided it was a dance that Merce didn't want "worked on" and so I rarely practiced it. He never made suggestions about it once he had taught it to me, and even then it was tossed off quickly, a mere indication of shape and rhythm with only the energy of it clearly articulated.

In other solos, i.e., *Suite for Five* and *Variations V* and *Walk-around Time*, each movement, each rhythm, each phrased section was taught with great clarity and attention to detail. He would teach me the dance, and then disappear from the studio to let me work on it alone, reappearing to offer help, explaining a rhythm or illustrating a movement. He would time it with his stopwatch, offer a bit more advice for some part I'd be stumbling over, and disappear again to let me find my way in it. With Valda Setterfield's solo in *Walkaround Time*, he simply sat in a chair and told her what to do, never demonstrating a single movement. Occasionally he would rise and touch some part of her body to indicate from where the movement was to come. He made the dance directly on her body at one sitting.

I believe Merce hopes his dancers will work alone on their material just as he had always done, without guidance or coaching. The first solo Merce made for Sandra Neels was in *Scramble* in 1967, and from that time until she left the company in 1973, Sandra continued to work on it, setting new goals for herself, approaching it in different ways, attempting new solutions to keep herself interested in it. One has to find one's own challenges in Merce's work. (And, I might add, one's own rewards.) There is no "role" or character development to work on, nor any historical precedents with which to measure one's own performance. There isn't the opportunity to reveal one's musicality as related to a musical score. There isn't even a classical technique to aspire to and be judged by. All these challenges exist for the ballerina who attempts the great roles in *Giselle*, *Swan Lake*, *Sleeping Beauty*, *Les Sylphides*, etc. Instead, the Cunningham dancer, like many modern dancers today, is in virgin territory. There is never any critical evaluation or help from an informed body of critics; first, and understandably, because it is Merce's choreography that should command serious consideration (though it rarely gets it); and second, because there are no simple criteria with which the dancing can be appraised.

In the summer of 1971, when the company was in residence at the University of California in Berkeley, an unusual event took place, partly by chance and, as I understand it, partly at Cage's suggestion. For some reason not altogether clear to me, the company was expected to do one more performance than originally scheduled. Instead of repeating any of the other programs, Merce decided to turn the content of the "extra" performance over to the members of

his company. He told us that his contribution would be to design the structure in skeleton. Otherwise, he would participate choreographically as one of the eleven dancers. He organized the stage space in three separate ways, but what went on in the space and how long it went on was indeterminate. There was an understanding that as we exhausted material we had choreographed or chosen from his or other repertories for a particular spacial design we would move on to the next by mutual consent—not a hard-edged ending and beginning, but an easy flow from one concept to the next. As it happened, not all of the dancers were equally enthusiastic about the project; some never joined in the rehearsals. Merce ended up contributing two or three movement ideas, but this was more to encourage activity than to usurp control. Everyone took part in the performance. The event, the first of its kind for our company and probably the last, was received by the Berkeley audience with extreme enthusiasm, perhaps the heartiest reception the company enjoyed all summer. Many of the dancers revealed themselves as individuals quite different from the view of them seen in Merce's choreography. But when a close friend of the company spoke to Merce about the excitement of that event, and especially how strong the dancers appeared in their own choreography, disclosing facets of themselves as dancers and as people never seen in Merce's own work, he acknowledged it, but admitted that his own excitement and pleasure was in the making of dances, and so the experiment has not been repeated as of this writing.

It seems to me, that his experience was quite similar to that of a number of composers in the fifties and early sixties. Earle Brown, whose work is most familiar to me, devised a score titled *December 1952*, which ·is probably the most open score ever written short of handing a performer a sheet of blank paper. It gave the performer close to total freedom. Having gone that far, there were only two choices: quit composing or write more explicitly. Interested in composing, in the making process, Earle's choice was obvious. Merce's choice, like Earle's was to return to making after a single brief taste of group collaboration.

The truth is, Merce is no collaborator. He is a loner. He does not work *with* the lighting designer, set designer, costume designer, or composer. And it is here that Cage's notions of anarchy and of coexistence as practiced by Cunningham work in strange ways. Merce works secretively; the dancers in his company "discover" the set in dress rehearsal, or to be more accurate, in the final rehearsal, since we rarely had true dress rehearsals. Usually we would hear the music and feel the lighting in the first performance. I will not pretend that this is not extremely difficult for the dancers. Loudness, especially unexpected loudness, affects the inner ear, the seat of balance, of equilibrium. Continual loudness can make one irritable, nauseated, even faint. Brilliant lights that come on suddenly can momentarily blind and disorient the dancer and that too affects the balance, and makes quick-moving exits hazardous; darkness cripples one's sense of space and therefore the fullness of the movement itself. Needless to say, lighting rehearsals could alleviate much of the difficulty, but they almost never happen.

What has always baffled Merce's dancers is the extreme attitude of *laissez-faire* regarding most matters of production except the choreography: a strange dichotomy. Cunningham will choreograph a dance for months, rehearse it for months more, working for an exactness of execution and timing that he wants, and yet he then allows a composer to compose what he will, the result often jarring, disruptive, and having the effect of altering what one sees because of what one hears; he allows a lighting designer to plunge the work in murky darkness obscuring spatial relationships, cutting down the visual space, adding "atmosphere," altering what one might have seen by coloring it both literally and figuratively in any number of ways. The inherent problems are maddeningly contradictory. Merce refuses to have proper "tech" and dress rehearsals because he wishes to spare himself and his dancers that tedious, time-consuming, and enervating experience that is so destructive to the dancer's energy. Thus the lighting designer is forced to be a magician of sorts, working miracles from guesswork, with little feedback or even interest shown by Merce, and having to suffer the complaints and wails of the dancers who moan, "It's too dark out there!"; "It's too bright out there!"; "I can't

see *anything!*" Rick Nelson, lighting designer who has been with the company since 1968, is magician, miracle worker, and more important, saint! (He'd have to be to take all the gaff and still love us all as much as he says he does.)

Surely the demands on Merce would flatten a weaker spirit; it is enough to choreograph, perform, and rehearse his dancers, but by ignoring the lighting or by giving near total free play to the lighting designer he constantly risked having the very dance elements he most prized and worked long hours to achieve obliterated. Cage would probably say here that one must give up one's likes and dislikes. But lighting can do much more than coexist with the dance; it can radically alter what it is we see. And then it is the lighting designer's likes and dislikes that prevail. Through the Rauschenberg era, Merce always voiced a preference for "daylight," for the play of light changes to be within the brighter registers, but that was all. In the early years, Merce had to do much of his own lighting. He couldn't afford a designer. The lighting existed to illuminate the dancing, but not to tell us about it, and certainly not to structure it.

Perhaps Merce's work doesn't need a theatrical lighting designer. All he needs is someone to turn on the lights. Merce's choreography can amaze and astonish, bore you or fascinate you, create

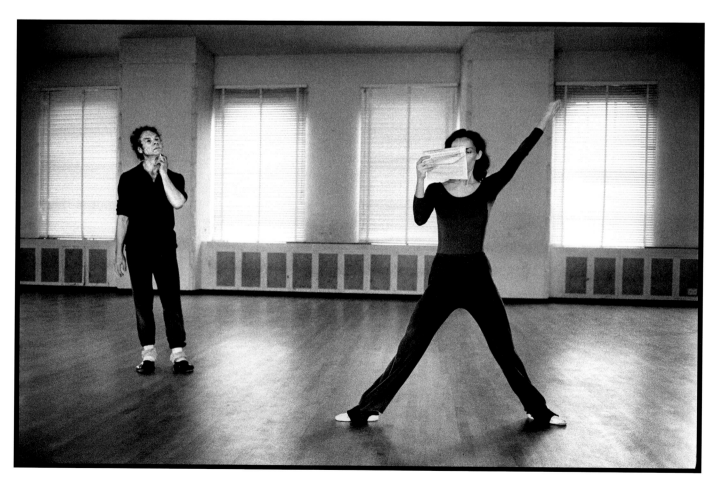

Above and opposite: *Night Wandering* rehearsal, Summer 1972

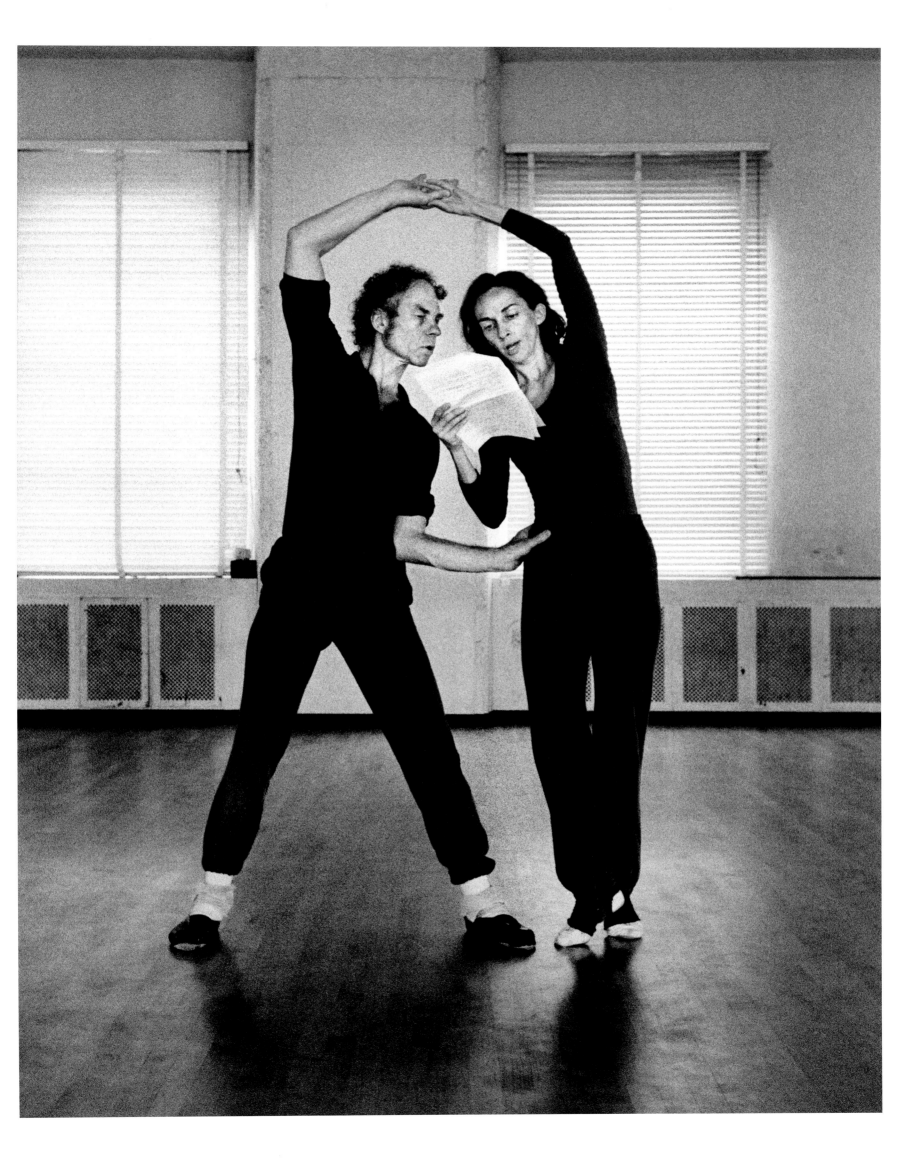

an illusion of romance or the deception of madness merely by the steps he makes and the space and time he uses. The movement says it all if you are willing to look hard. True, one has to love dancing with a special ardor to watch it unadorned and unglamorized by the seductions and glories of the theater, by music, decor, costumes, and lighting. But the official Cage-Cunningham dogma requires the autonomy and freedom of each theatrical element—movement, light, sound, and decor. And so the dancers, the only ones who are neither autonomous nor free, must responsibly do their work, continually at the mercy of those whose flights of fancy with gloom and glare, noise, and obstacle can inhibit their ability to dance well. Of course, it's just possible that these conflicts and tensions, and the dancers' constant attempts to deal with them contribute to making the experience of Merce's theater so extraordinary.

Admittedly, Merce is not so allowing when it comes to costume and set design. At first, practicality was essential. In the fifties and early sixties, everything had to pack easily and fit into the VW microbus. So there wasn't much. And at that time we traveled with a program of six dances to alternate, not a repertory of eighteen or twenty. The priorities were different in those years. Art and life were nearly inseparable. The VW bus symbolized a way of life that included picnics and cookouts, five o'clock cocktail-hour chess and Scrabble

and word games, sharing our books, people piles, storytelling and songsings, kibitzing in the process of Rauschenberg's drawings, and an extraordinary amount of laughter. There was time and space for all these things, and I'm sure that our food boxes must have weighed twice that of any box of costumes or decor or music. The costumes had to pack small to fit into the bus, and since Merce insisted that they should reveal, not obscure, the body, leotards and tights became practically a uniform.

Sets of any kind were rare. Our performing spaces varied enormously, and Merce wanted all the space available for dancing. But Rauschenberg did come up with a number of decors: the *Nocturnes* set a simple scrim and column of white cloth used in the upstage wing, which transformed the stage into a place of elegant, white night mystery; the *Minutiae* set, a brilliant red collage or combine painting on legs, which had a shaving-mirror set spinning before curtain-rise, room to crawl under, and an archway to enter and exit through. Probably his best-known set is the *Summerspace* backdrop cloth—a Monet-Seurat-esque pointillist shimmer of color; since the dancers' costumes were painted in like manner, each different, the result was that of a living canvas. In *Winterbranch*, Bob made a "monster" (as we affectionately called it) out of backstage stuff, different in every performance,

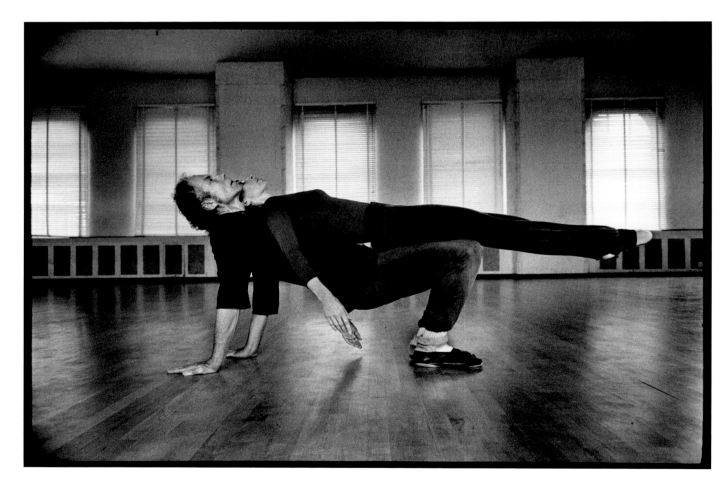

Night Wandering rehearsal, Summer 1972

but always with some kind of light or lights casting eerie shadows as it was pulled across the darkened stage on a long rope. For *Aeon*, Bob made a kind of sculpture we referred to as the Aeon Machine. It didn't get its name until the '64 tour when we were partying in Poszan, Poland. We were sure that there were bugging devices in the hotel rooms, so we carried on cryptically about the maneuvers of our Aeon Machine. It was a peculiar creature like the *Winterbranch* monster; however, it flew slowly across the stage on wire and pulley, trailing smoke from the dry ice held in a battered aluminum pitcher. Also for *Aeon*, Bob devised a series of brilliant flashes that both blinded and illuminated the ten dancers before a step was taken. The *Story* set Bob created anew in each performance from materials which he found in the theater and the streets of the city where we were. Sometimes the set he made was alive; such as at Dartington Hall in England, where he and his assistant, Alex Hay, ironed their shirts upstage. At the Sadler's Wells, Bob dyed clothes many colors and hung them to dry on clothes lines, where they dripped into buckets throughout the performance. We never knew what we would find when we returned to the theater each evening to make up; it was something we looked forward to, a handmade gift. He never seemed to repeat himself, and his enthusiasm never seemed to diminish.

Rauschenberg's greatness in the theater lay in his delight and fascination with on-the-spot problem solving. He had a feel for the outrageous and the commonplace and wedded the two. Compromise was his muse in disguise. The economic necessity of traveling light and small and the limited budget for costumes and decor served as a challenge to his ingenuity. Of course there were times when the budget limitations frustrated him; when he wanted exquisite lace for Viola Farber's "ballet dress" in *Antic Meet*, he priced common lace, bought the expensive lace, and paid the difference out of his own pocket. He toured with the company from 1961 through the world tour in 1964, not only designing sets and costumes but also the lighting, and he once remarked to me that they were the happiest years of his life. During this period he created freshly, intuitively from theater to theater, even from night to night. He learned lighting because he didn't like what other lighting designers had done to his costumes or to Merce's choreographic space. He understood what was needed because more important to him than his own ideas was his absolute devotion to Merce's dances, his respect for the intrinsic worth of the choreography itself. No loss to the company was greater than Rauschenberg's departure from it.

A radical change occurred under the artistic advising of Jasper Johns, who took on the job reluctantly, pressed by Cage's urging. Jasper's devotion to Merce's work was (and is) as fervent as Bob's, but his personality precludes entanglement with a gypsy-dance-troupe lifestyle. Jasper is single-minded in his involvement with his own work, and therefore wisely reticent about taking a participatory role in the crazy chaos of a dance company on the road. He had worked with Rauschenberg on costumes and sets from the beginning of Bob's association with the company through *Crises*, but he does not enjoy working in the theatre; the ambience and the inevitable compromises which were a challenge to Bob serve only as an annoyance to Jasper. Since he did not want to travel with the company nor even to do most of the designing, he chose to invite artists in whom both he and Merce were interested to make sets and also design costumes. This practice was following in the Diaghilev tradition and complimented the variety of contemporary composers asked to write for the company. It also gave opportunity to painters and sculptors to work in the theater, and since it was from painters and sculptors that Merce had received much generous support in the past, it seemed a happy solution to Bob's departure and Jasper's unwillingness to assume a full-time working relationship with the company.

With the single exception of *Second Hand* (one pianist needed), all the dances from 1965 on could be performed in silence, without decor, and without special costumes. Merce's continuing interest was in movement, and those changes in his work were choreographic ones brought about by his special handling of movement in space and time. His innovations usually were unseen and unsung because the physical baggage surrounding his choreography has been louder and flashier. Though some of the sets attempted maneuverability, most were cumbersome and obstructive space-eaters when moved into other less comfortable theater situations. Where do you store thirty helium-filled pillows when a stage has no wing space? The Rauschenberg days of flexibility, happy chance and change, and creative compromise were over. The economy of the company had to change along with the new policy for decor. Fortunately, the change over in artistic advisors coincided with the beginning of the trickle of grant money, commissions for new works, and state and federal aid. The company grew to include as many as four people to handle stage production; it began carrying some of its own lighting equipment. Prior to 1966, the company had two musicians, both pianists. They carried portfolios of sheet music, some prepared piano hardware, a "slinky," and little else. By 1972, there were three musicians plus an electronics engineer, followed by close to 1500 pounds of equipment: electronic stuff, loudspeakers, plus a bandoneon, a French horn, and a musical saw. On the other hand, the costumes remained for the most part the uniform of tights and leotards, with the addition of sweatsuits for events, and the choreography itself required no additional gadgetry. Admittedly, big-name artists attract attention, and a silver helium-filled pillow has very real gravitational advantages over the earthbound flesh-and-bones dances. There are limitations to what the human body can do, and Merce has never tended toward the circus spectacular. Jasper himself, except for his contribution to *Walkaround Time*, chose simply to costume Merce's work because I believe he liked it best unadorned, the space left open. But despite Jasper's personal inclinations, the physical stuff surrounding Merce's work grew one hundred times over, and with it Merce's responsibilities.

After a matinee performance at the Saville Theatre in London in 1966, David Vaughan, company administrator with Lew Lloyd at that time, appeared at my dressing room door to ask if I'd mind talking to a group of students, since the crowds outside Merce's dressing room waiting to talk with him already meant cutting deeply into his precious rest time before the evening performance. Both of us were dancing in six dances that day, with two of the most difficult dances in the repertory that season, *Place* and *Variations V*, still ahead of us. The boys and girls squeezed into the small dressing room, sitting on the floor and leaning against the walls. After the usual questions (How long have you danced?; With whom have you studied?), one of the students asked: "Is he serious? I mean, isn't he just pulling our leg?" I think I was quiet for a rather long time, and finally I said, "Do you really believe that a man would spend his whole life working this hard, even going into debt, merely to pull *your* leg?"

How many people like that student have asked the same question, have even been sure that Merce was a charlatan? I suppose had Merce chosen to remain a Graham performer, he could have basked in the glow of being well loved and risked nothing further. Having chosen to choreograph, not in imitation of his predecessors, but exploring new ideas, he risked everything. The photographer Paul Strand said in an interview that the artist does not grow by pampering himself with his own likes and dislikes. It is in this spirit that both Cunningham and Cage set out to work in the early fifties, influenced by the Zen studies that both men undertook at the time. Because the results of that work were strange and unfamiliar, they were received with suspicion and hostility. The use of "chance" methods in composing dances and music was scorned, the reasons for it misunderstood, and the results written off as "chaotic." "Disorder," says Henri Bergson, "is simply the order we are not looking for," but the difficulty with most people (and most critics) who make up audiences is that they come to a performance armed with preconceptions, looking for confirmation of what they already know. Merce's work satisfied none of their needs, provoked controversy, and made them uncomfortable. As I sat in the half-hostile audience of the Brooklyn Academy of Music in March 1973 during a performance of *Event No. 68*, I thought, how truly remarkable that twenty years later the Cunningham Company is still controversial, still provoking and stimulating.

For Merce, the time between being the "enfant terrible" of the avant-garde and "acknowledged master" of the avant-garde was much like a New York spring—nonexistent. And although it is about twenty years since that summer at Black Mountain College where he began his company, there's never been a period when he was not one thing or the other: "enfant terrible" or "master." No middle period. The reputation grew, almost underground, without much actual exposure in New York City. After the 1953–54 Theatre De Lys season (which neither John Martin of the *New York Times* nor Walter Terry of the *Herald-Tribune* reviewed) the company did not have an extended season in New York until May 1968 (eight performances at the Brooklyn Academy). London and Paris had already seen more than New York. And yet the choreographic output has been extensive, close to one hundred works; the range and variety extraordinary. Cage and Cunnignham and Rauschenberg ideas—which were revolutionary, even scandalous, fifteen years ago—are accpeted by today's younger generation as quite natural and are even mouthed by younger choreographers as though original to them. There were enough ideas to start many separate paths, branches going in different directions, unrelated one to the other. Merce continues to explore whatever interests him at the moment, but more and more, recently, he has been pressed for time. The burdens of maintaining a company, a school, a board of directors, and an office staff weigh heavily, using up precious hours and energy he would more happily expend in making new dances.

Merce is no longer "avant-garde" (he never claimed to be); he's established, if not establishment. Fortunately, I don't think he'll ever be establishment. He's too curious. But he will be liked for the wrong reasons, wronged for the wrong reasons; his early defenders will revert to cries of "He sold out!" when what they really liked then was the revolution, not the work itself. Because finally it is not ideas but dancing that Merce makes, and the meaning is in the activity, which is at once physical, emotional, spiritual.

Thirty years in the life of a long-lived painter or composer is only about half of his years of productivity, e.g., Picasso and Stravinsky. We used to think that a dancer's performing years were numbered, but even they are being extended for longer and longer periods: Galina Ulanova was still dancing at fifty; Merce and Margot Fonteyn are still dancing at fifty-four; Martha Graham didn't stop until she was almost eighty. Though there are physical limitations on the performing life of a dancer, there is nothing to prevent him from continuing to choreograph. Ashton (born 1906), Balanchine (born 1904), Graham (born 1893), and Tudor (born 1909) are all productive to varying degrees today.

Merce traces his beginnings as a choreographer from a concert given at the Studio Theatre, 108 West 16th Street, in New York City on April 5, 1944. At Black Mountain College in North Carolina in the summer of 1953, there was another beginning with a small permanent company of young dancers. In May 1973, Merce came to the end of the second period of his choreographic life; he gave himself a seven-month respite from company obligations in order to make an evening-length work for the Paris Opera Ballet and to experiment with video as an integral part of his work. He made the stunning decision to drop his entire repertory of discrete dances for the theater, which had taken him twenty years to build. It was another beginning. Surely there will be others.

Carolyn Brown and Merce Cunningham
rehearsing the run ending Part II of *Second Hand*

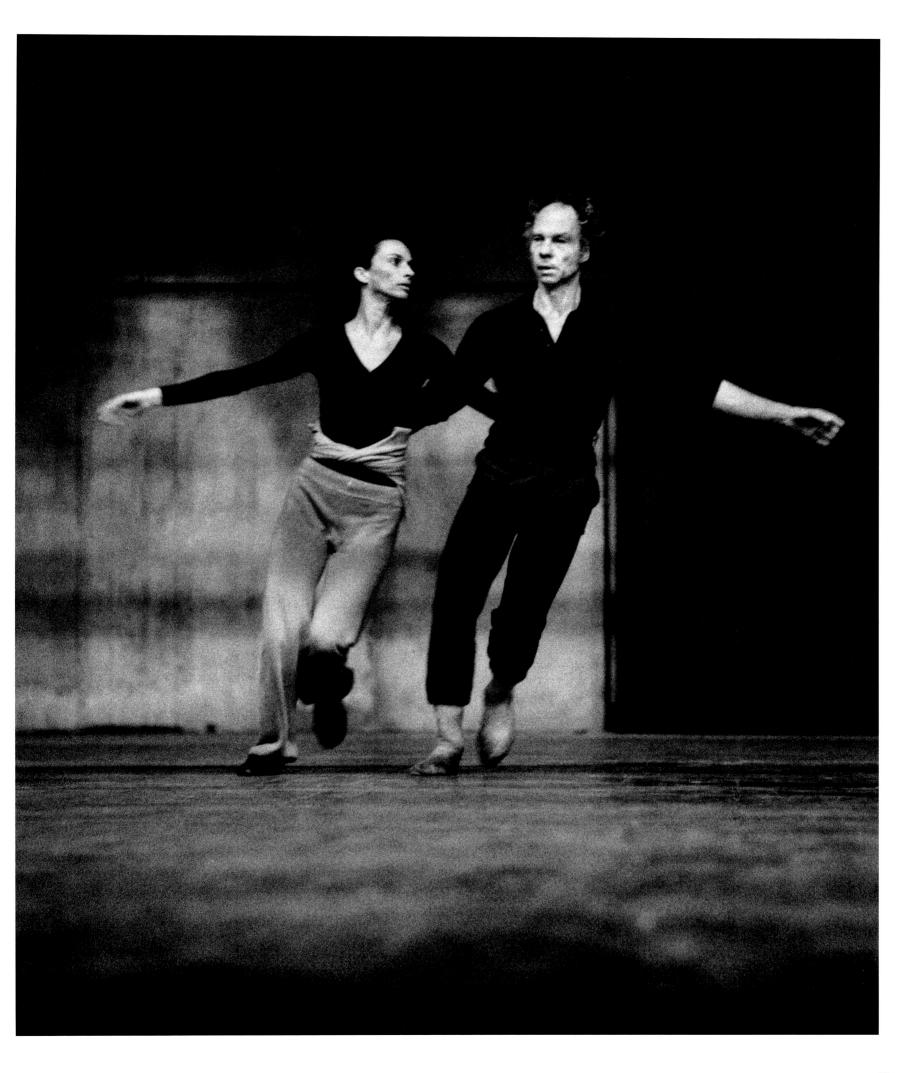

1958 ANTIC MEET

MUSIC
JOHN CAGE
CONCERT FOR PIANO AND ORCHESTRA
USUALLY PERFORMED IN A PIANO
REDUCTION ARRANGED AND PERFORMED
BY DAVID TUDOR

COSTUMES
ROBERT RAUSCHENBERG

DECOR
ROBERT RAUSCHENBERG

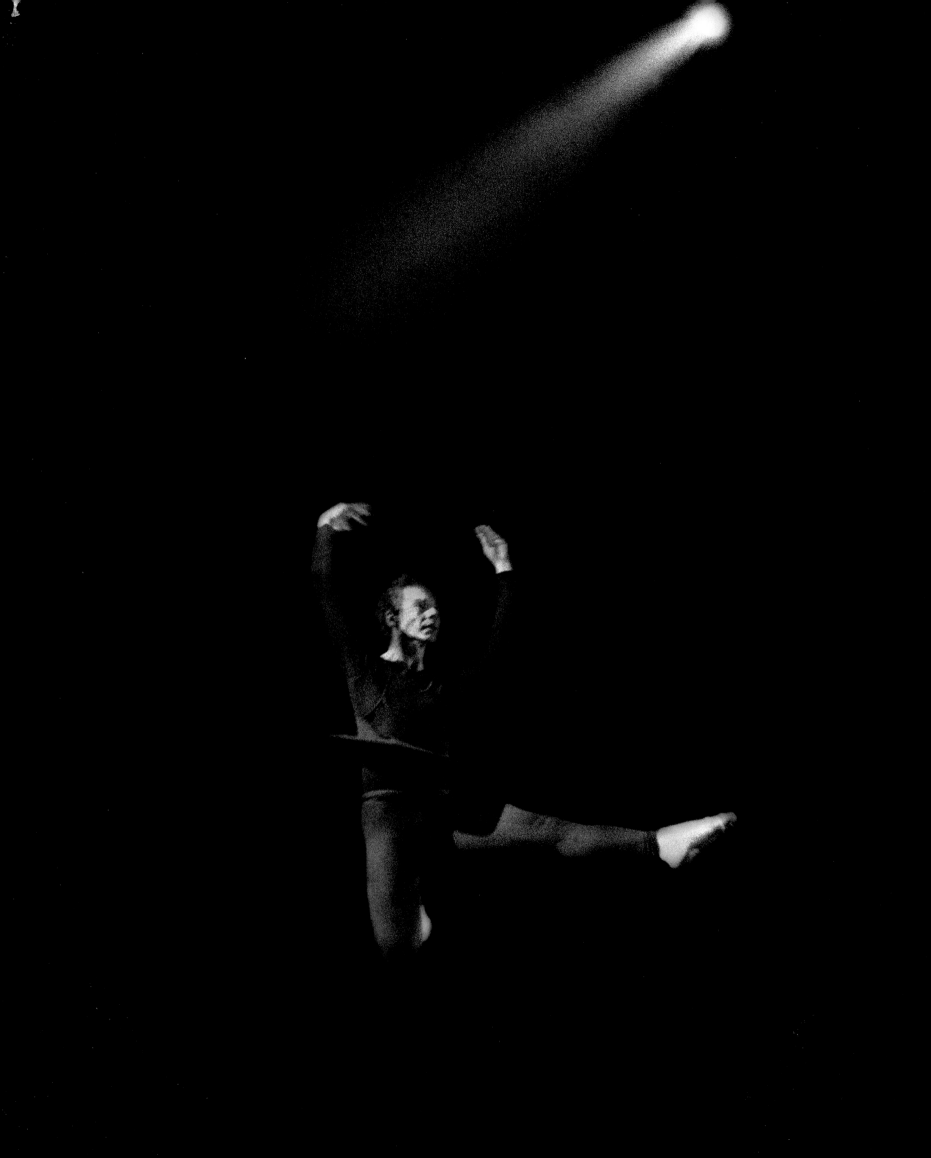

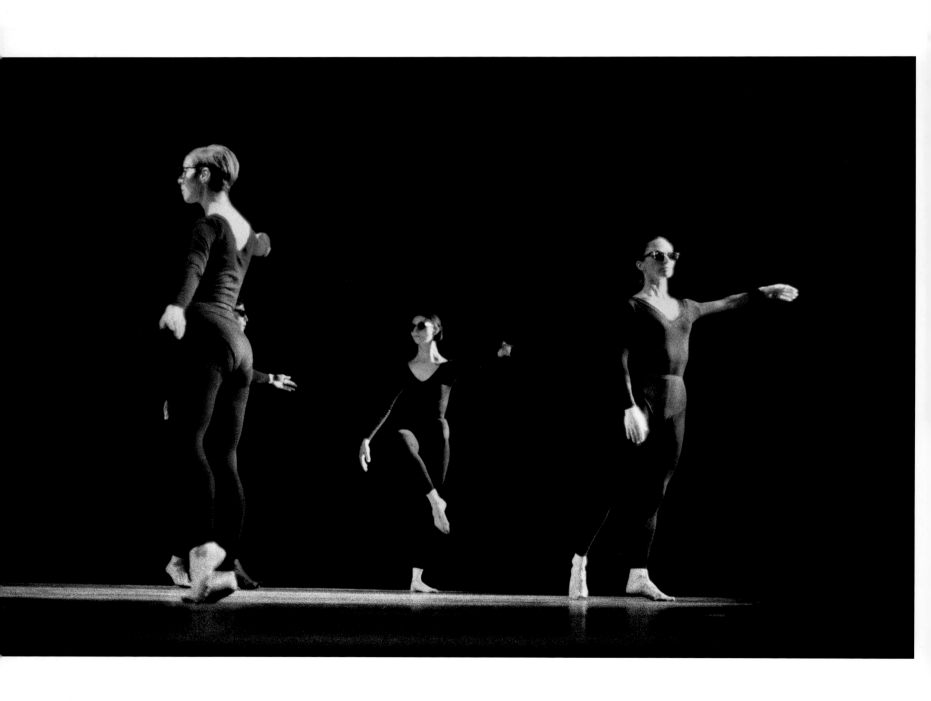

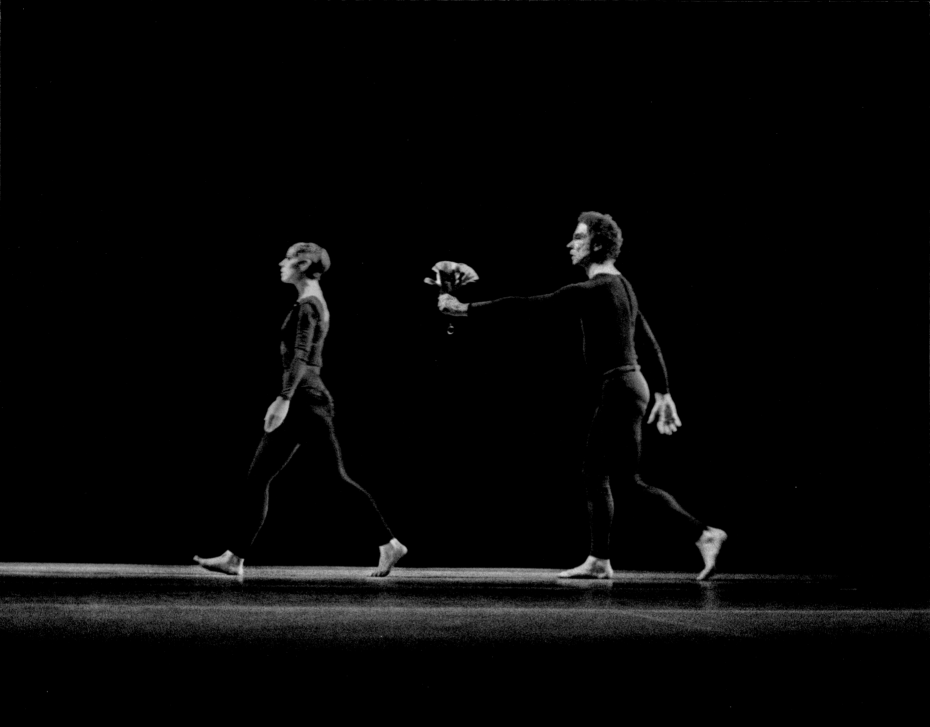

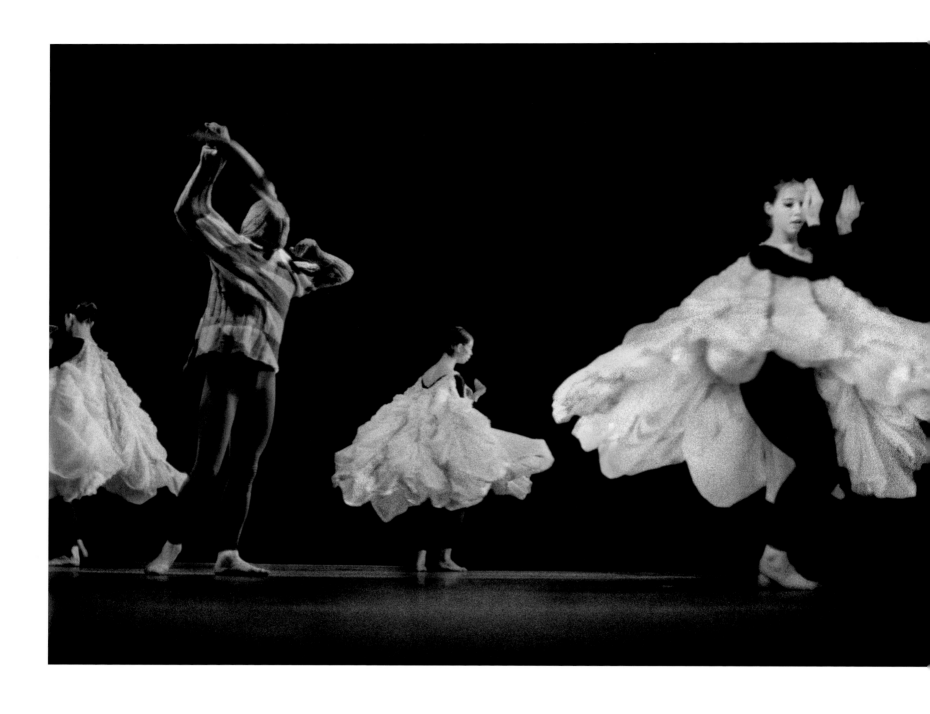

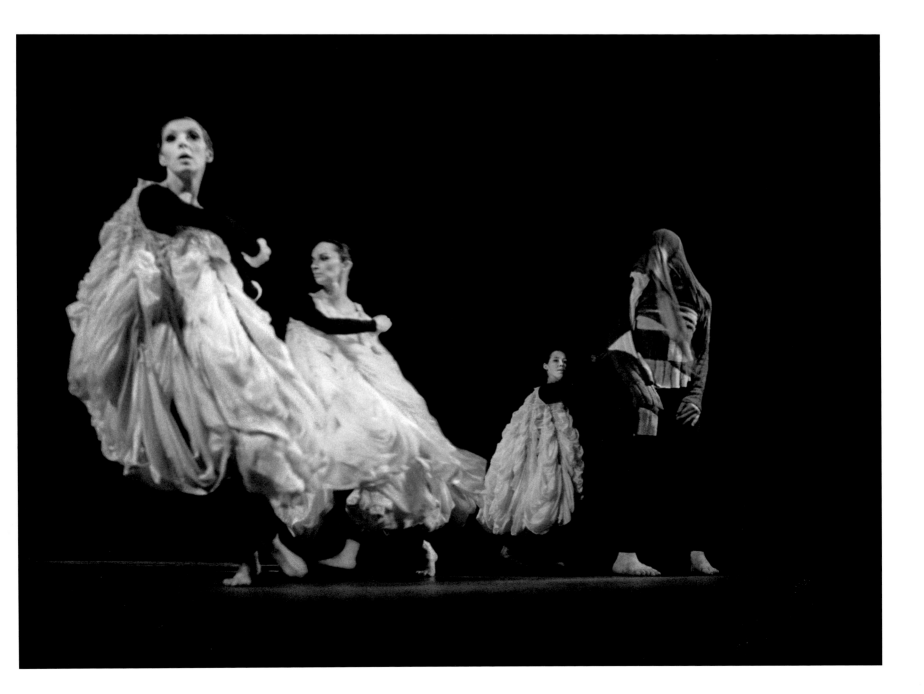

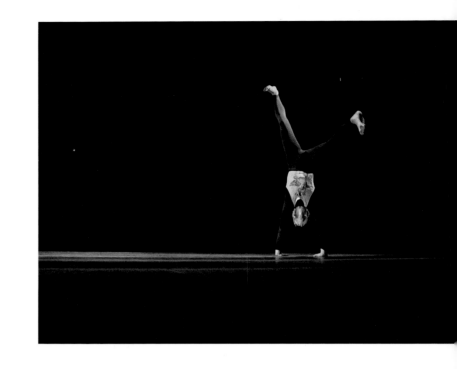

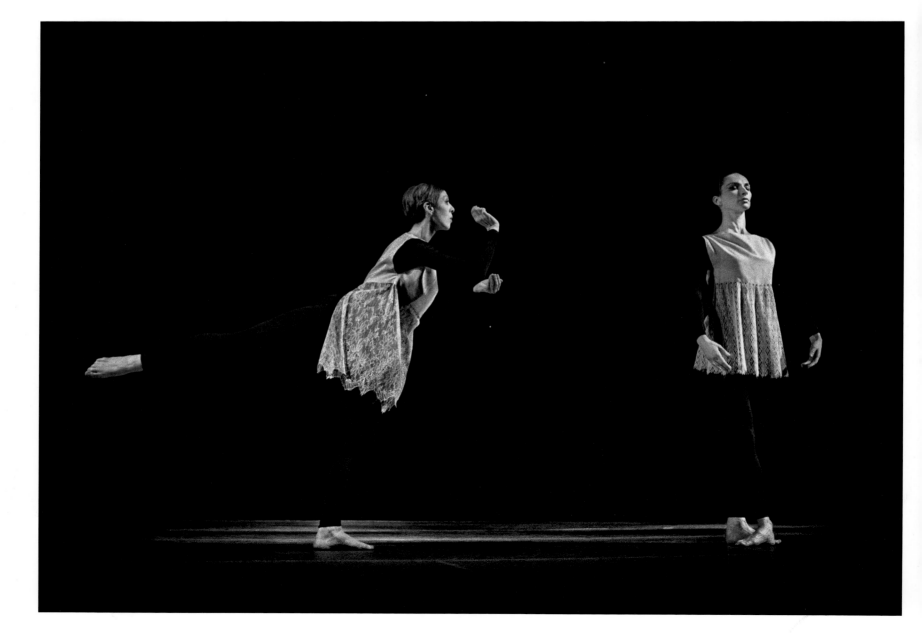

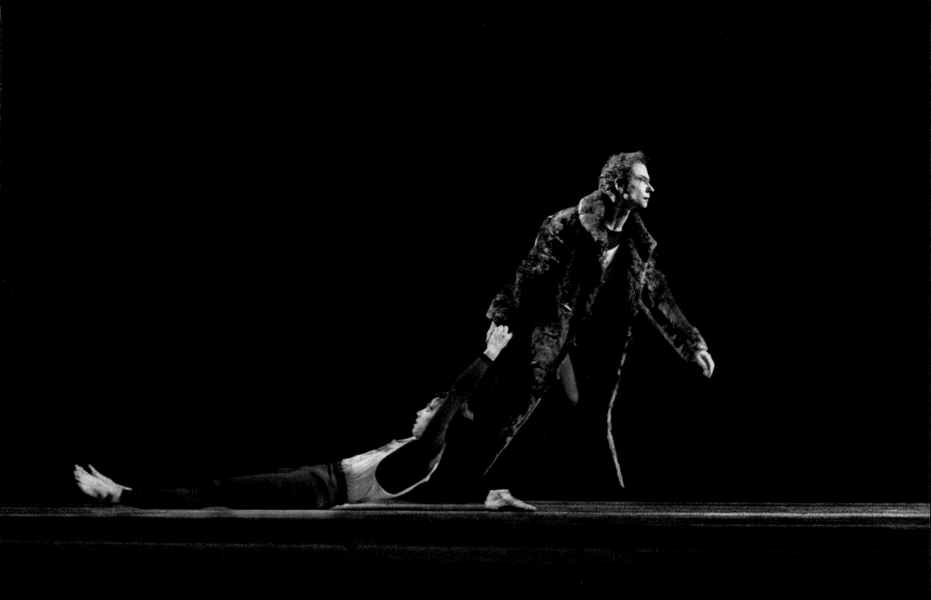

DAVID TUDOR

*An excerpt from David Tudor's realization for solo piano of John Cage's *Concert for Piano and Orchestra* (1958). This was the realization Tudor played in the 1958 Town Hall concert premiere and that he played whenever he accompanied *Antic Meet*. Tudor transcribed his realizations of Cage's long score onto separate small loose-leaf sheets of manuscript paper, which he then compiled in a ring-binder notebook. This allowed Tudor to vary the details of any specific performance, both the internal order and the overall duration, by adding, removing and rearranging the pages in the notebook. The performance time of this excerpt is twenty seconds. The numbers represent amplitudes on a scale of ten.

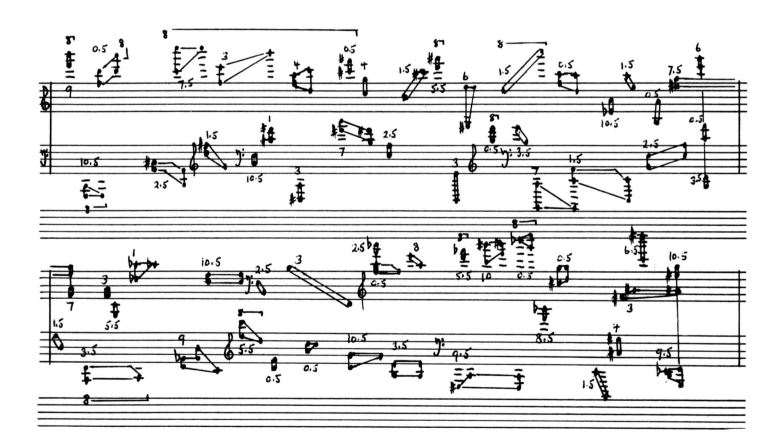

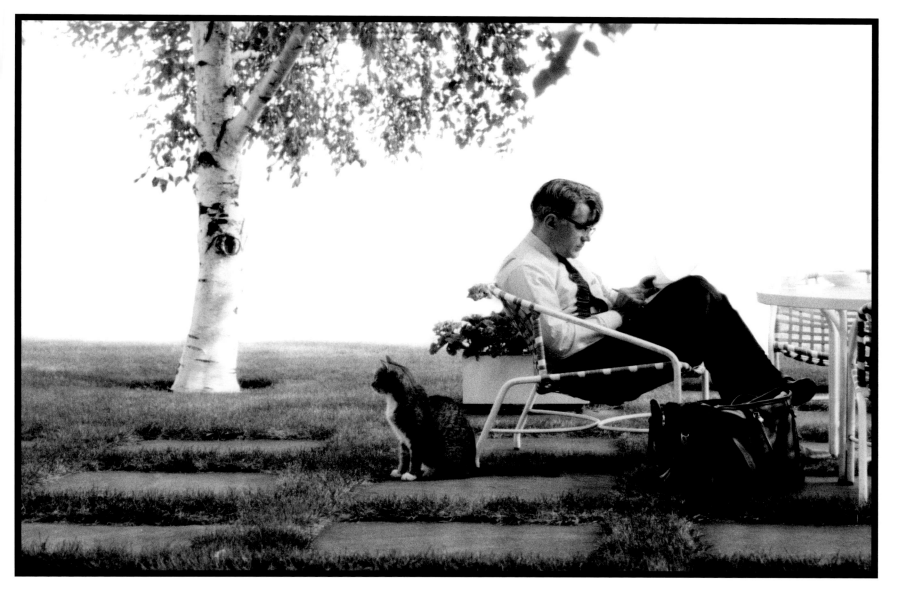

David Tudor and friend, Minnesota, 1969

1958 NIGHT WANDERING

MUSIC
BO NILSSON

COSTUMES
ROBERT RAUSCHENBERG

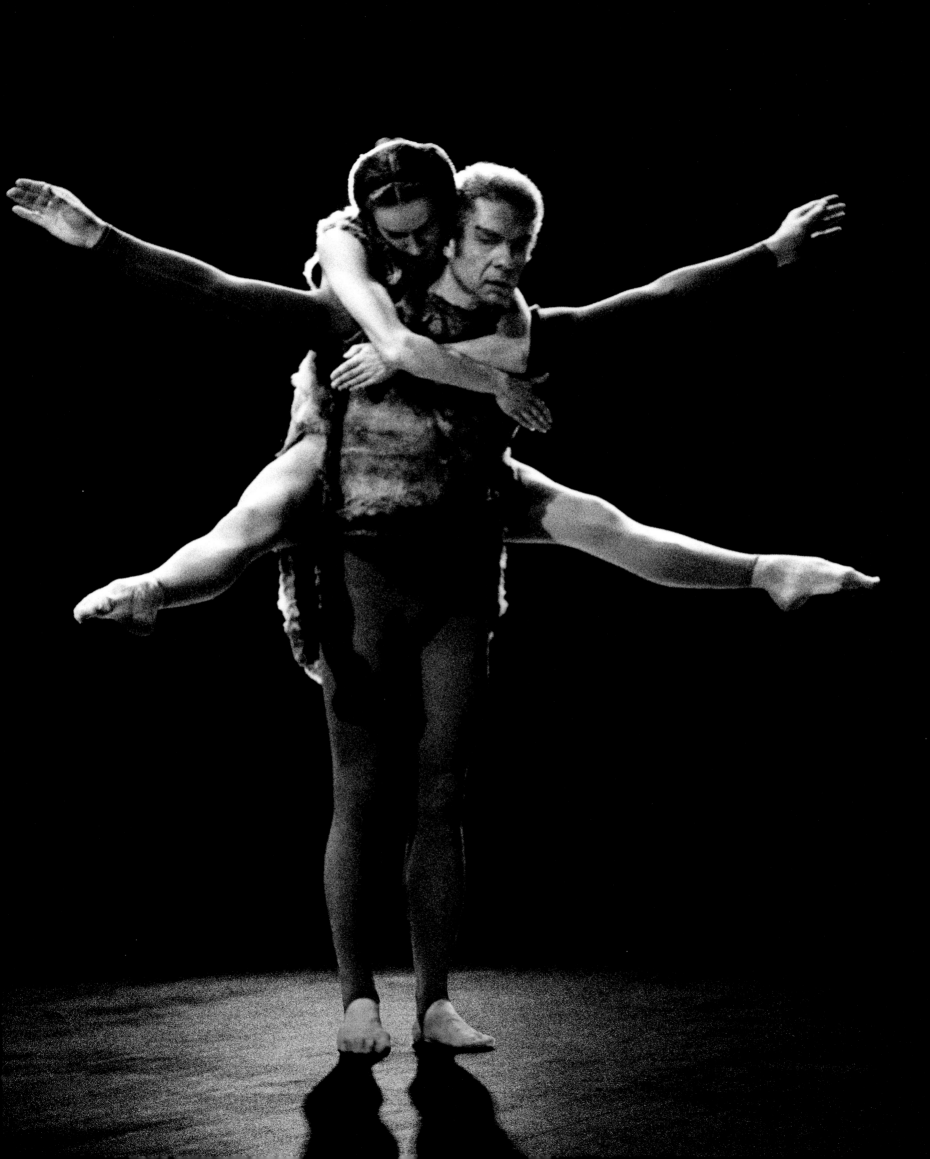

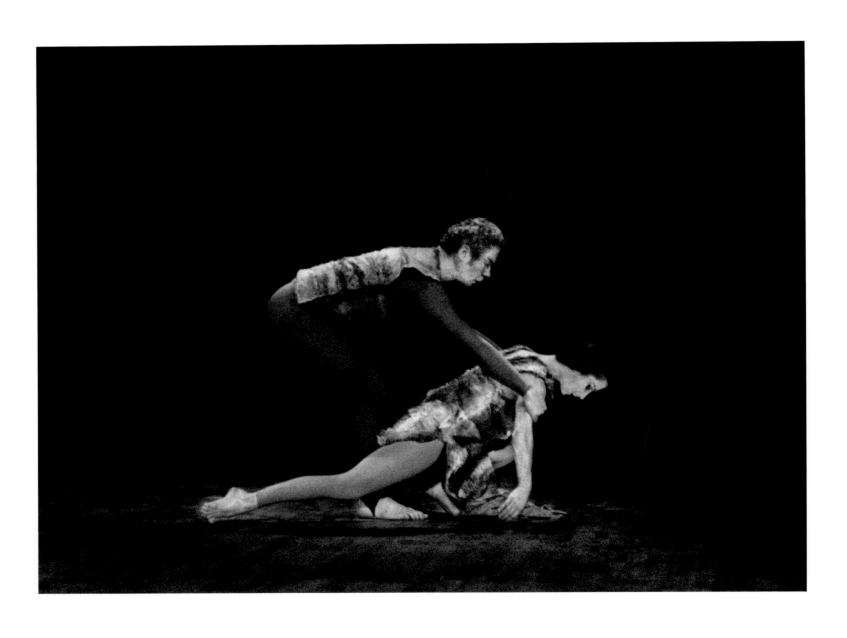

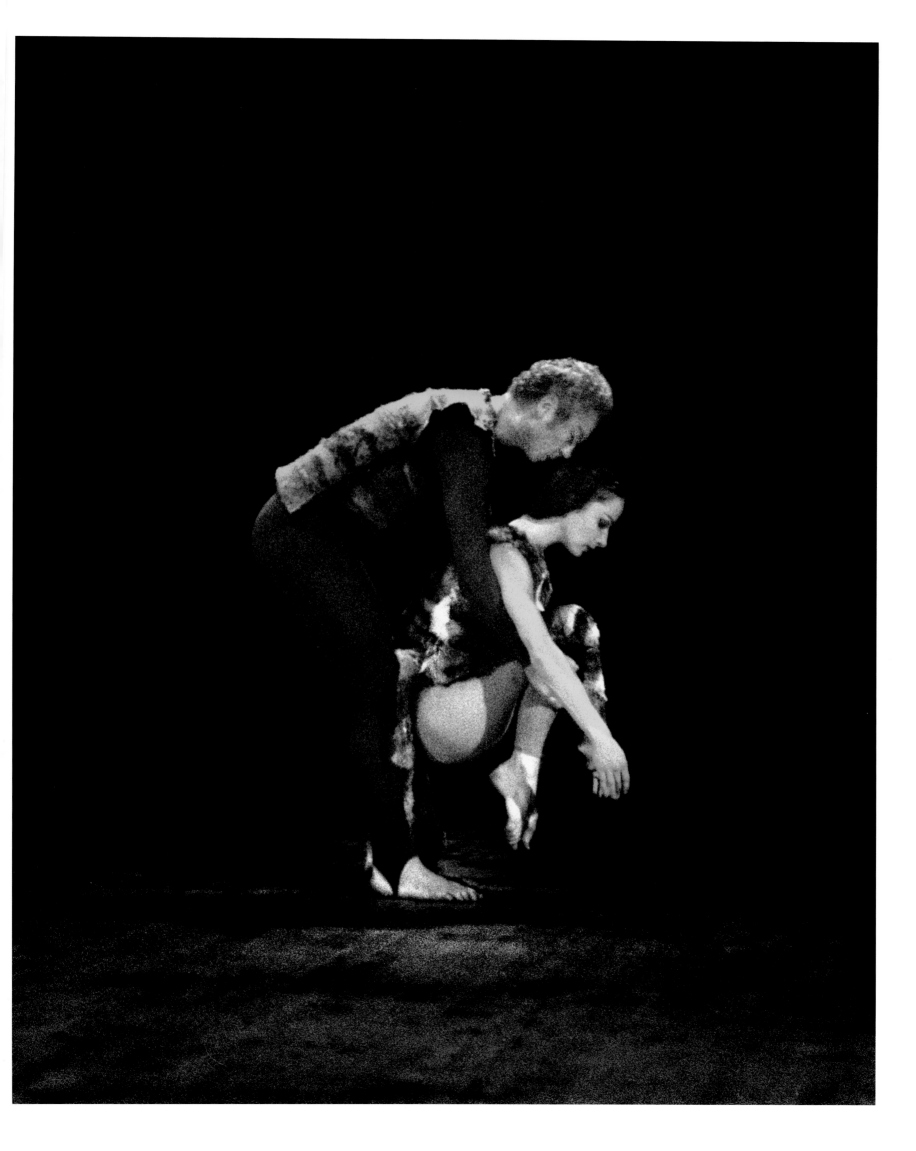

VIOLA FARBER SLAYTON

Merce let Paul Taylor and me watch him
dance a new solo in the
dining hall at Black Mountain College
and took us for a drive afterward.

One afternoon, sometime in the fifties,
I was the only student in class.

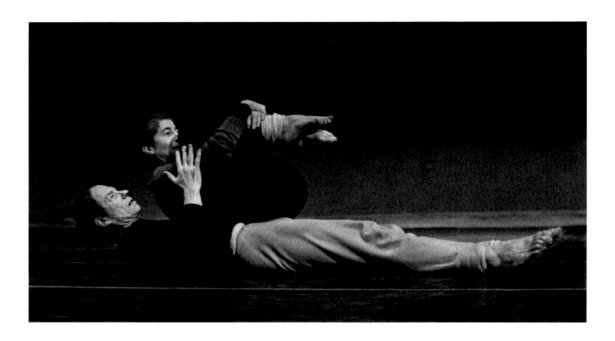

Merce disappeared into his
dressing room while teaching a company class,
and when he came back told us
that we had done very well what we
had done while he didn't see us.

Merce worked with chance,
and our rôles as dancers in the company
became more and more clearly defined.

Variations V was the first
work of the Cunningham Company
that I saw after having left the company.
They had made a world in Philharmonic Hall.

I love seeing Merce dance.

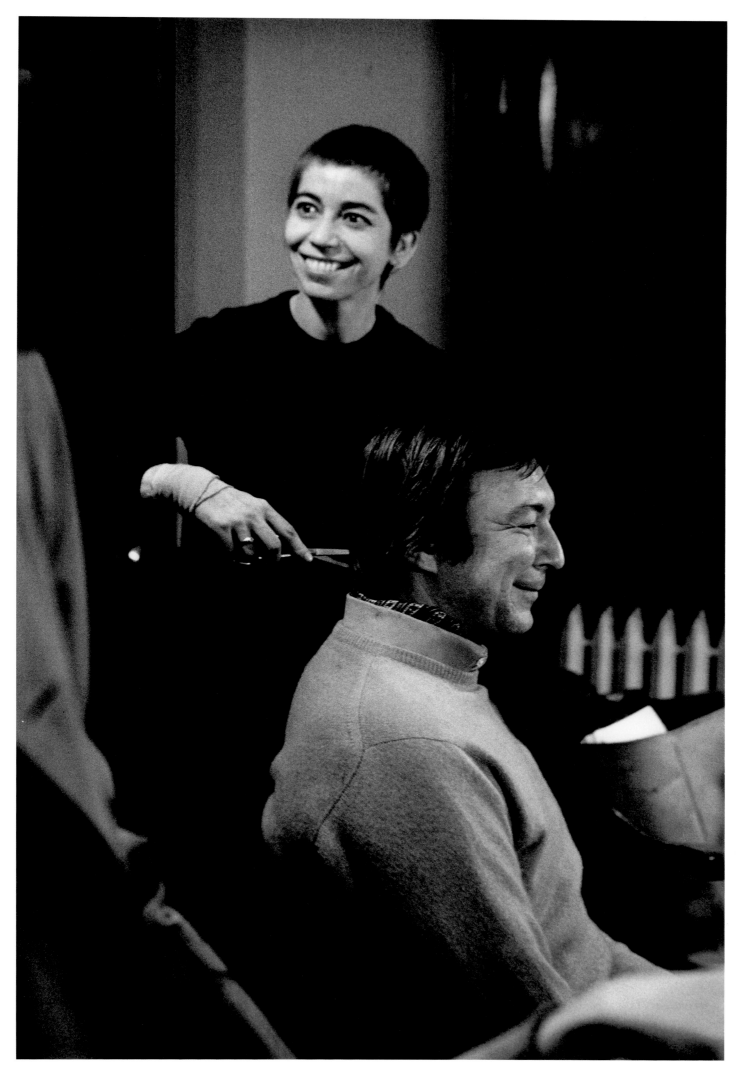

Left: Viola Farber and Merce Cunningham, *Crises* rehearsal at BAM, January 1970; Above: Viola Farber and Jasper Johns, backstage at BAM, January 1970

1960 CRISES

MUSIC
CONLON NANCARROW
RHYTHM STUDIES FOR PLAYER PIANO

COSTUMES
ROBERT RAUSCHENBERG

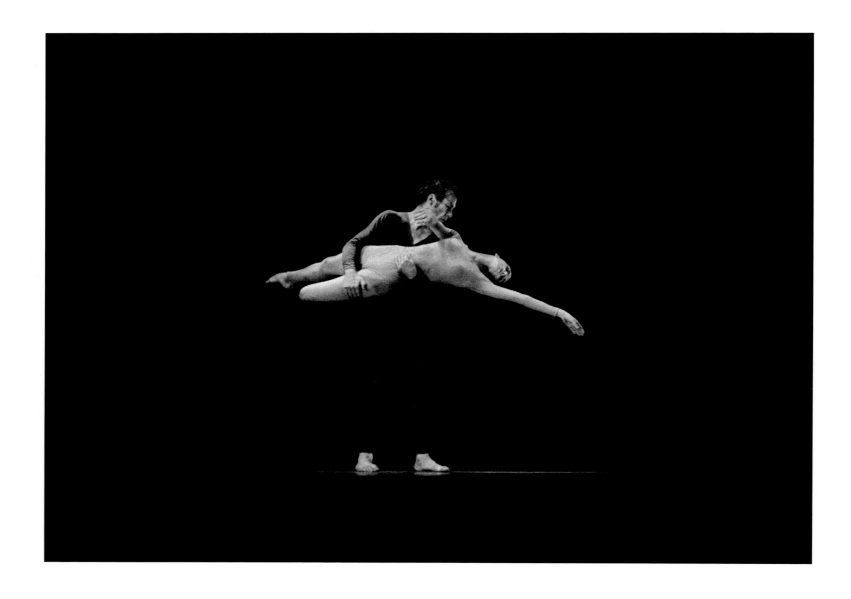

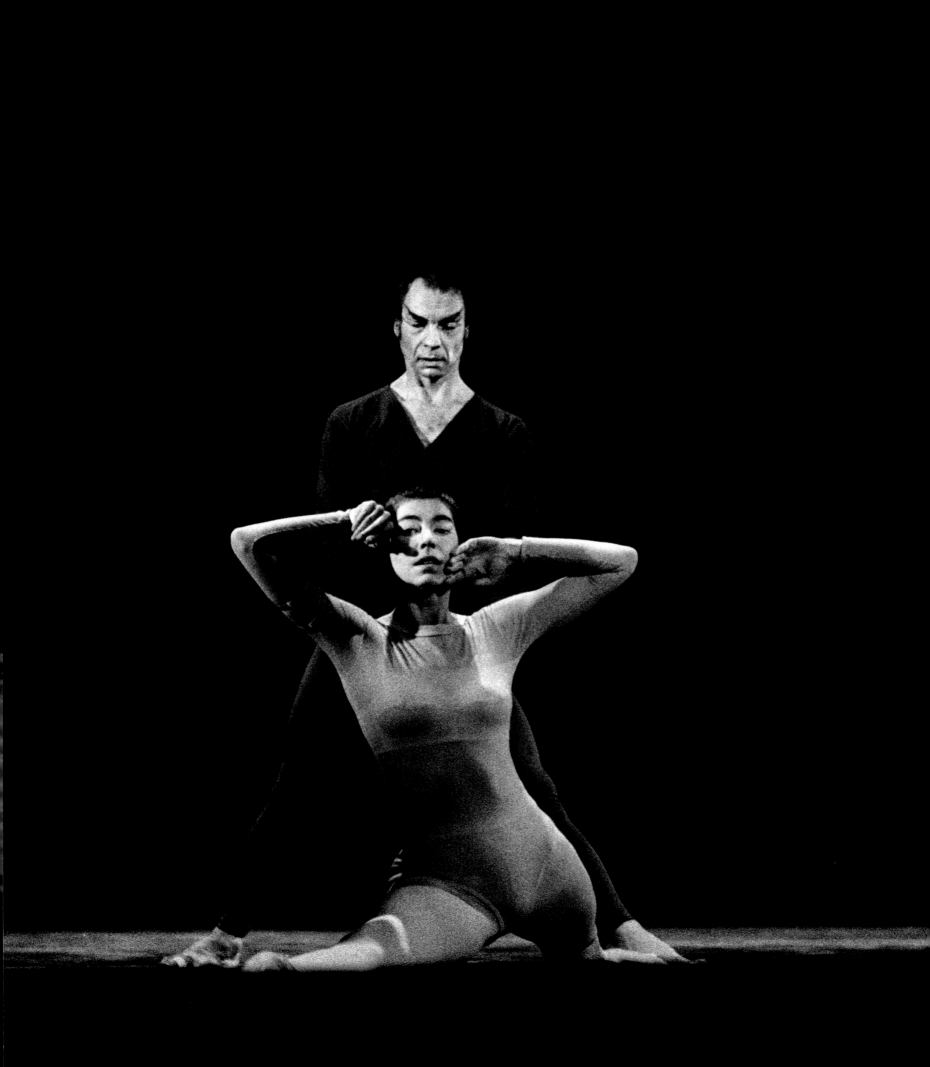

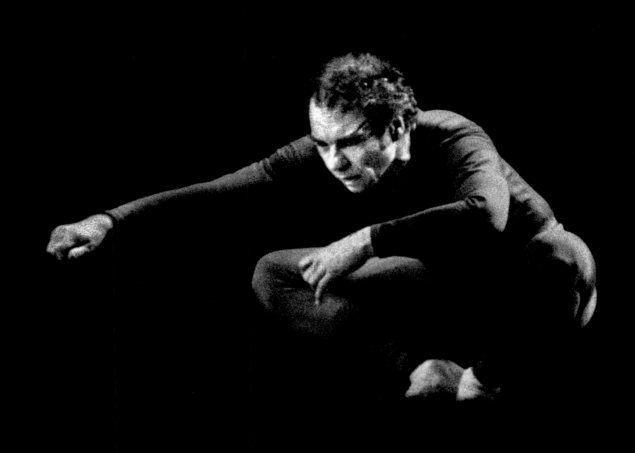

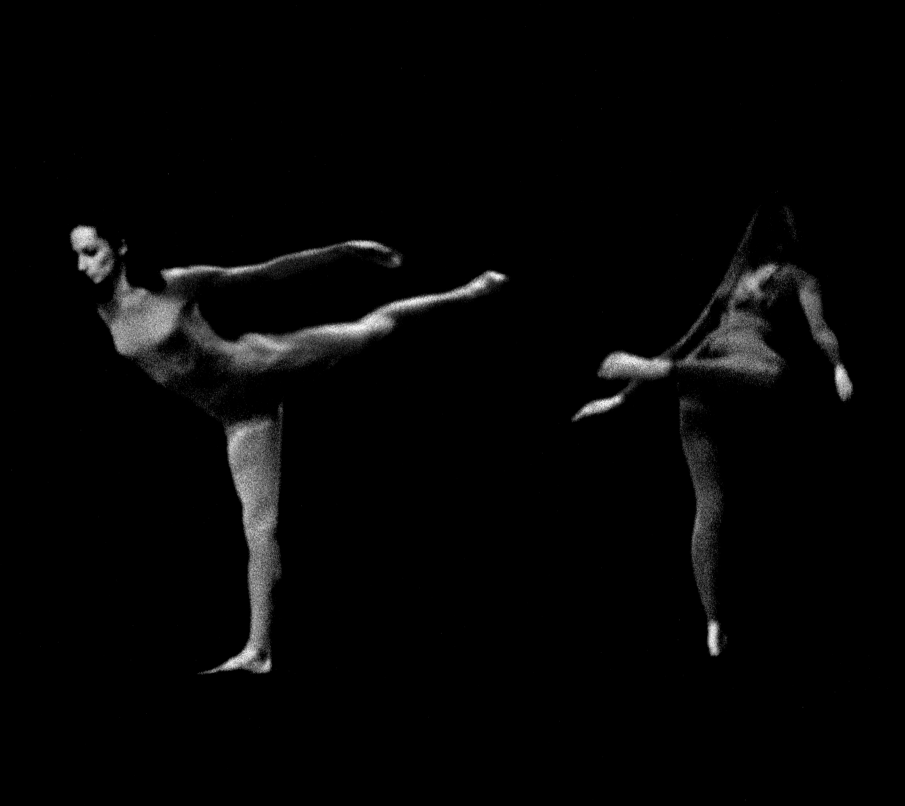

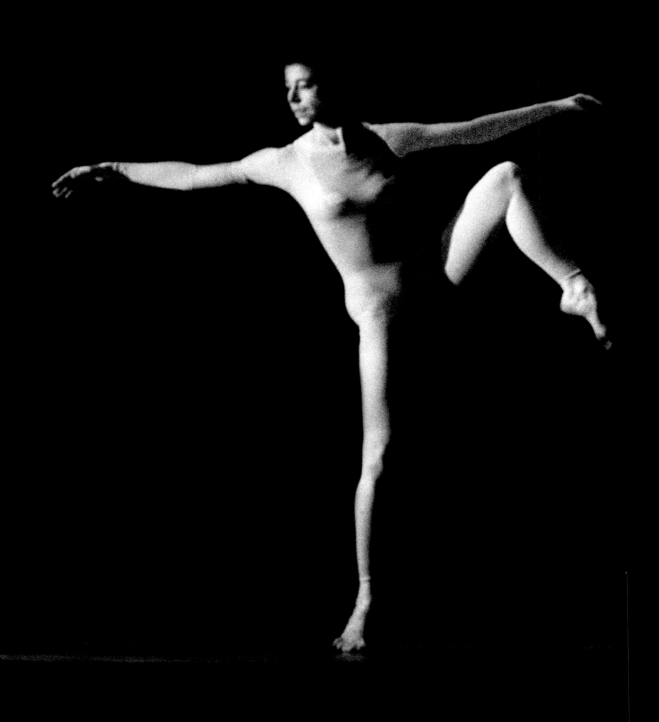

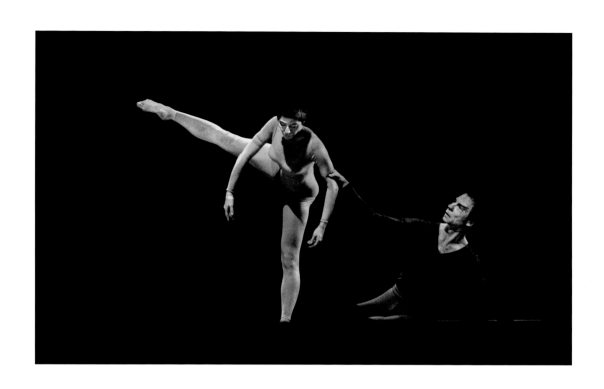

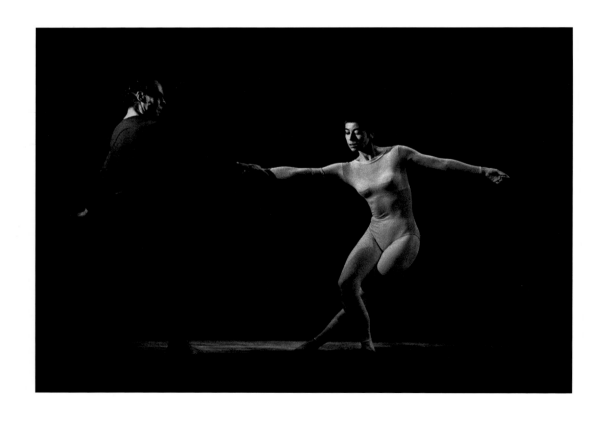

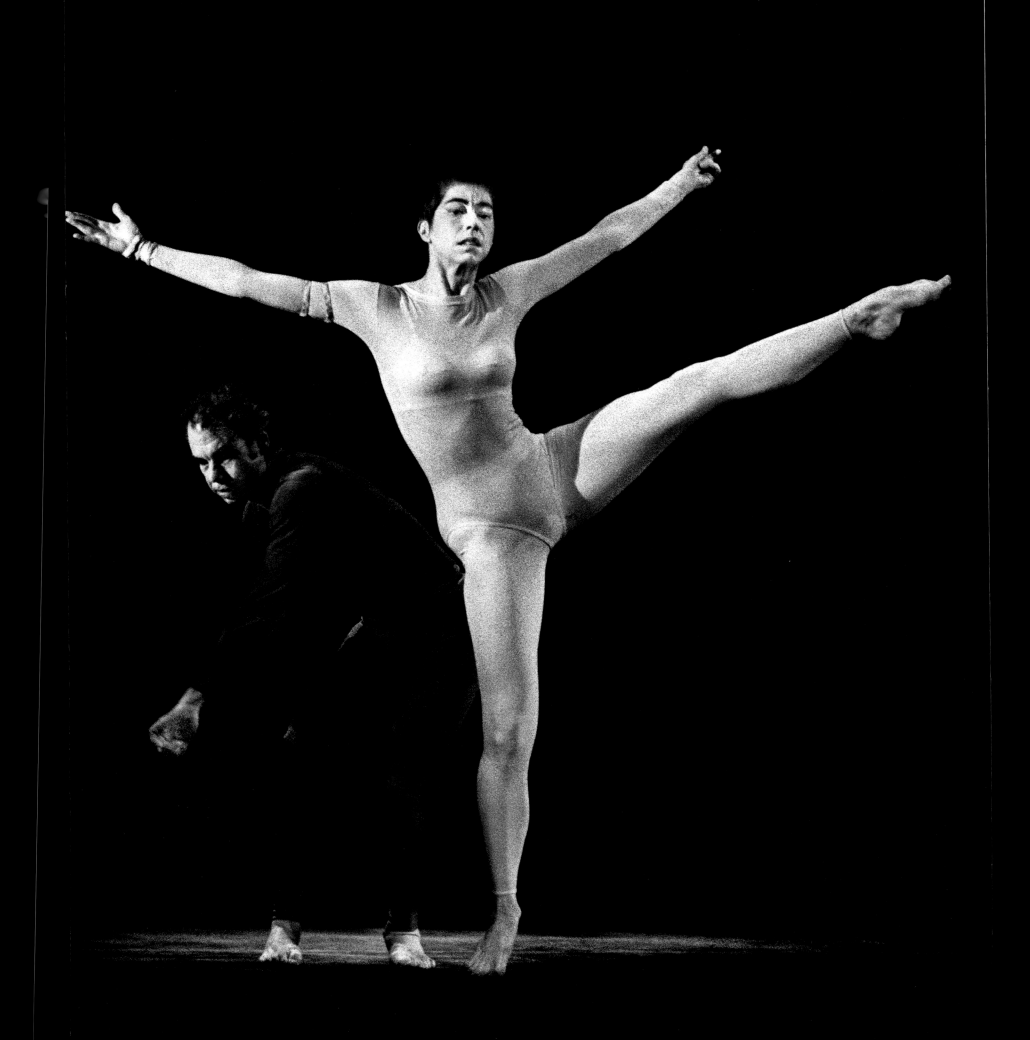

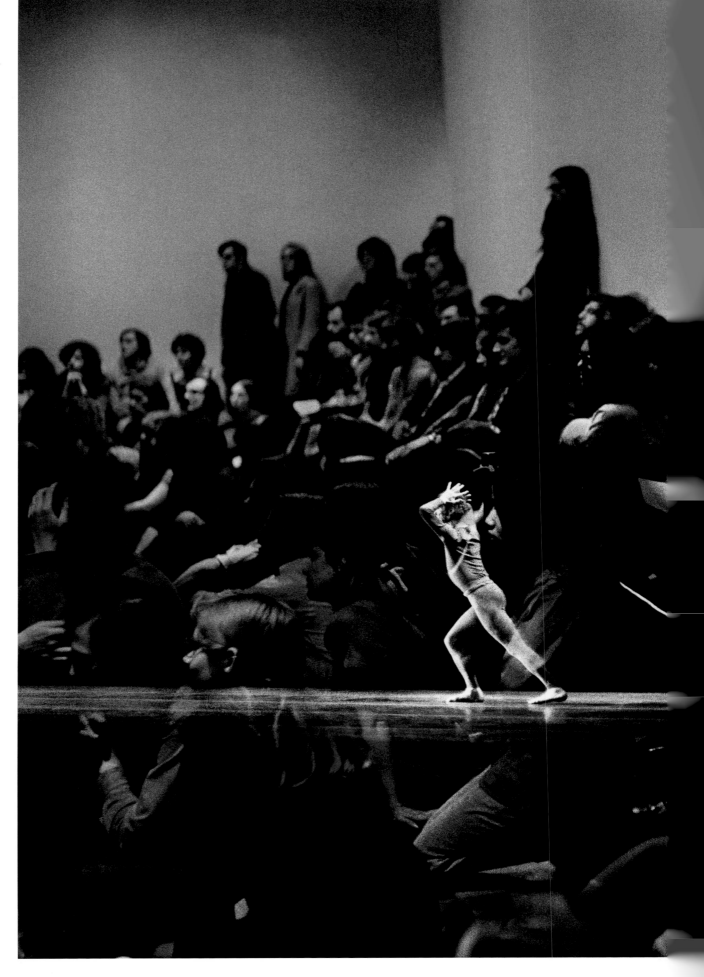

Inadvertently running the same roll of film through the camera at a performance of *Crises* at BAM and subsequently of Yvonne Rainer's *Continuous Project—Altered Daily* at the Whitney Museum permits us to observe Merce Cunningham in the Whitney audience observing his and Viola Farber's BAM *Crises* performance. Similarly on the following pages, from left to right: Yvonne Rainer and David Gordon (with pillows), Carolyn Brown hand in hand with Steve Paxton, and Carolyn Brown and Merce Cunningham with Gordon and Paxton.

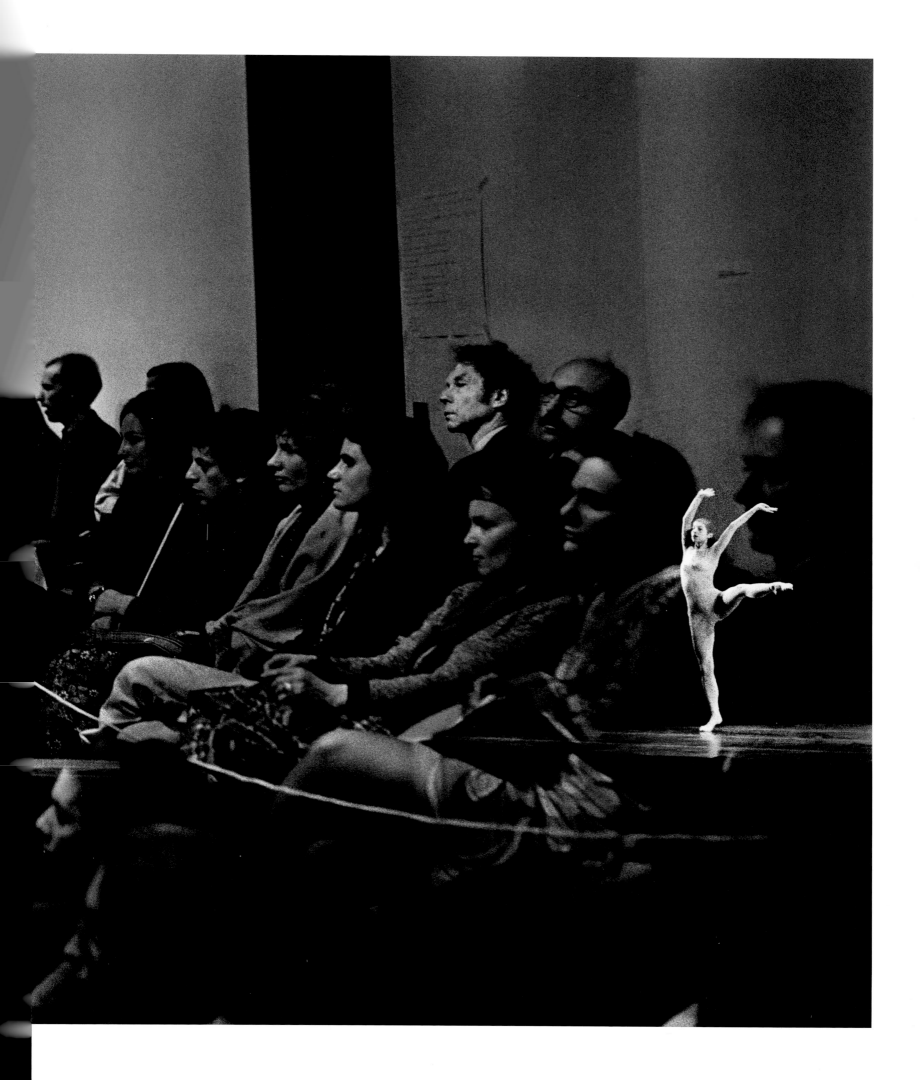

ROBERT RAUSCHENBERG

October 4, 1974

This note is barely meeting the dateline for material to be published in this book for this reason: I don't want to examine and flatten by classification, and description, a continuous moment of collaboration that exists in a group soul. Details are fickle and political and tend to destroy the total events. The rare experience of working with such exceptional people under always unique conditions and in totally unpredictable places (all acceptable because of a mutual compulsive desire to make and share) should not, by me, be shortchanged by memory or two-dimensional facts. All of us worked totally committed, shared every intense emotion and, I think, performed miracles, for love only.

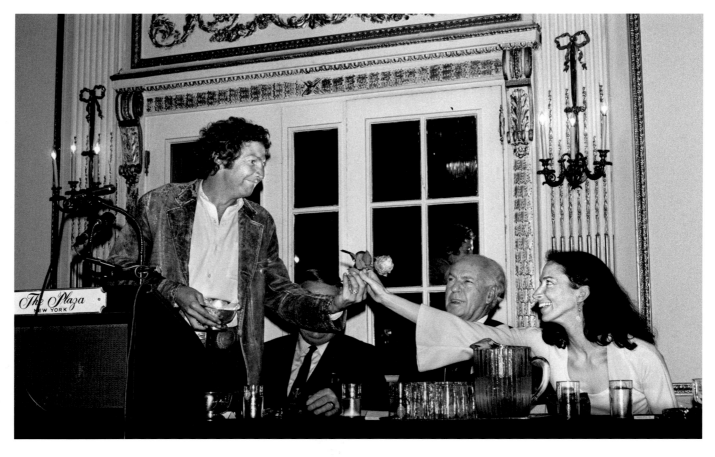

Above: Robert Rauschenberg presenting the 1970 *Dance Magazine* award to Carolyn Brown with Ted Shawn looking on;
Right: Rauschenberg told me he would be using my photos in a Cunningham poster for BAM. Did I want credit?
Assuming he would subsume them under paint I said no. Lesson: When dealing with Rauschenberg, never assume.

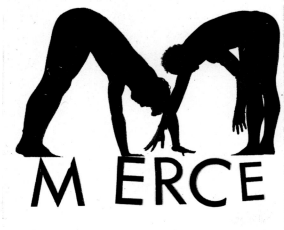

M ERCE CUNNiGHAM in

& dance CompAnY

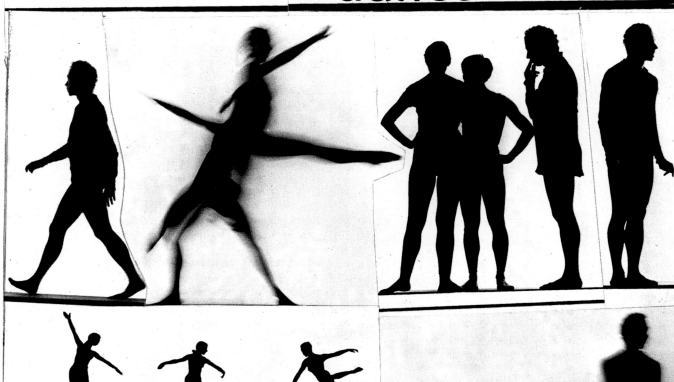

brooklyn academy of music

JANUARY 5 THRU 16

tickets: 5.95, $5, 4, 3, 2 STUDENT PRICES AVAILABLE
FOR IMFO.
783-2434

1964 WINTERBRANCH

MUSIC
LA MONTE YOUNG
TWO SOUNDS

COSTUMES
ROBERT RAUSCHENBERG

LIGHTING (AND OBJECT/MONSTER)
ROBERT RAUSCHENBERG

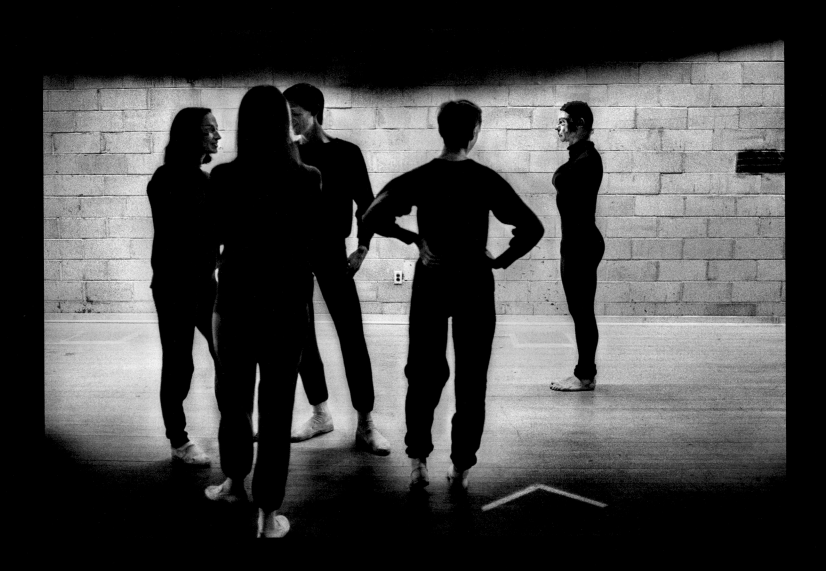

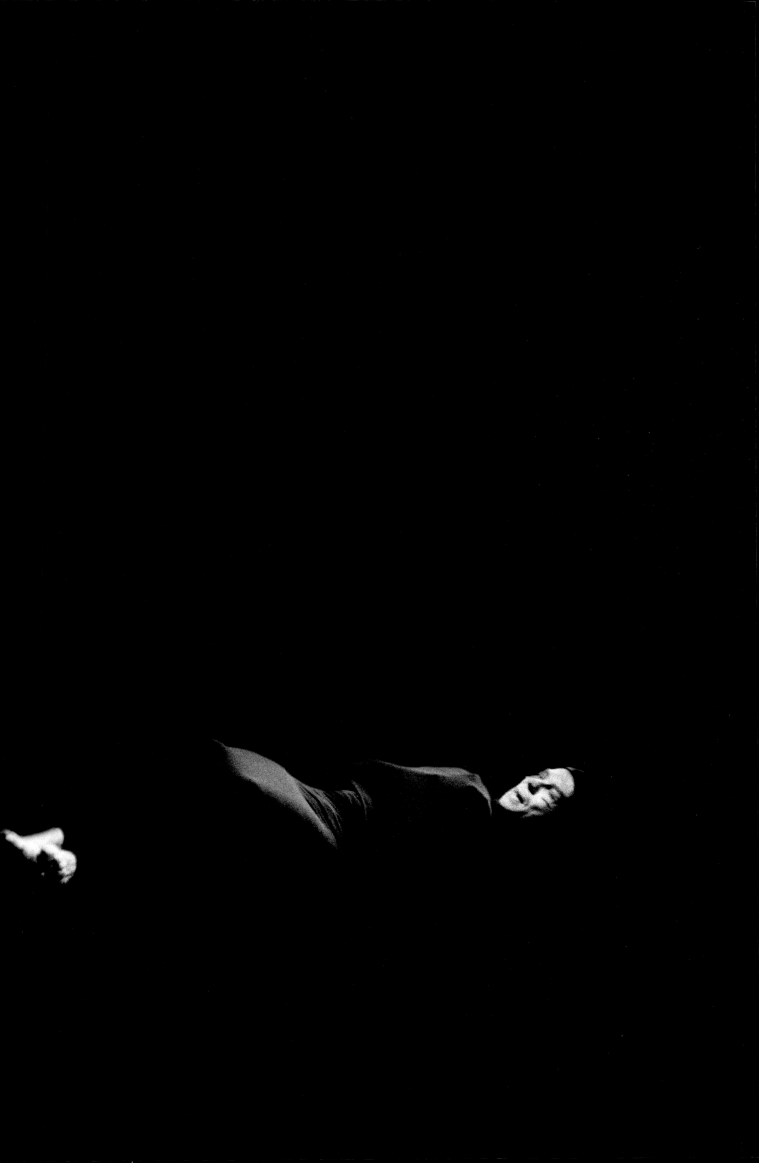

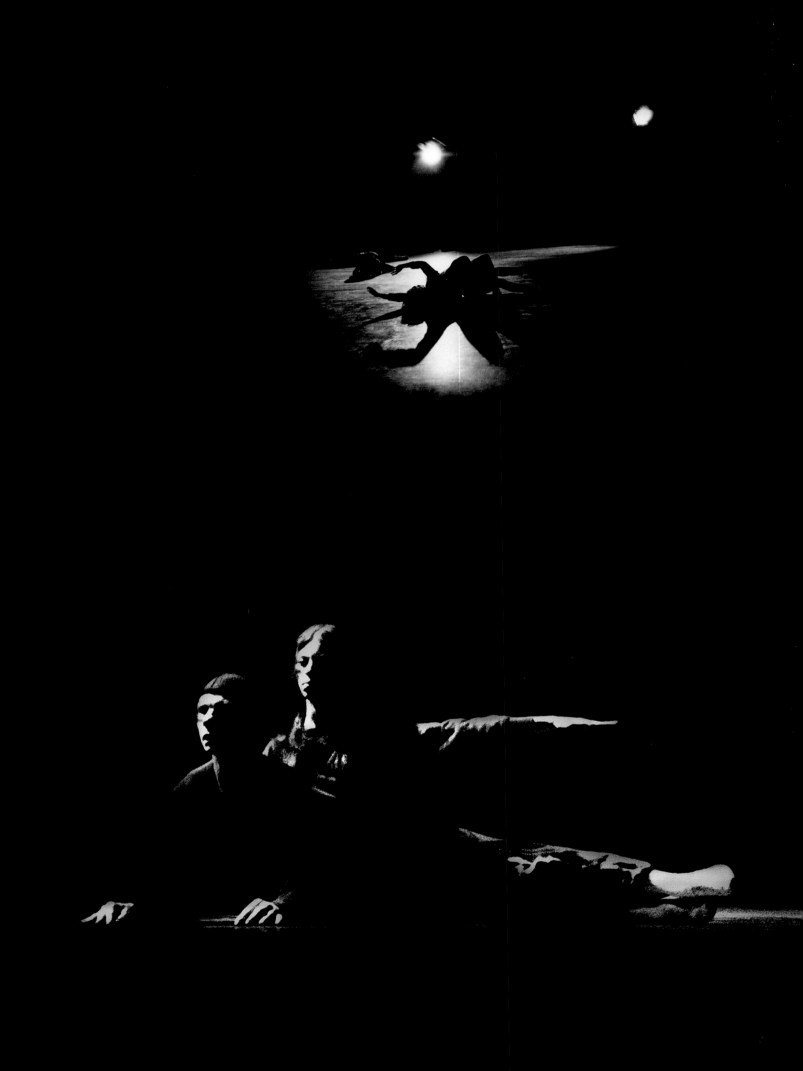

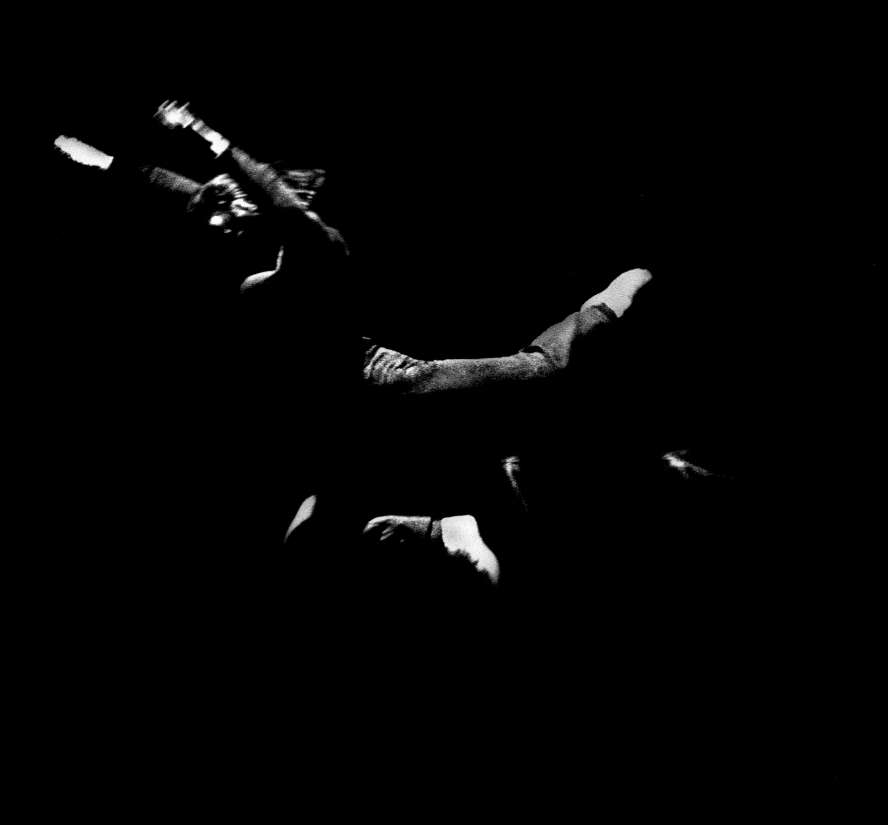

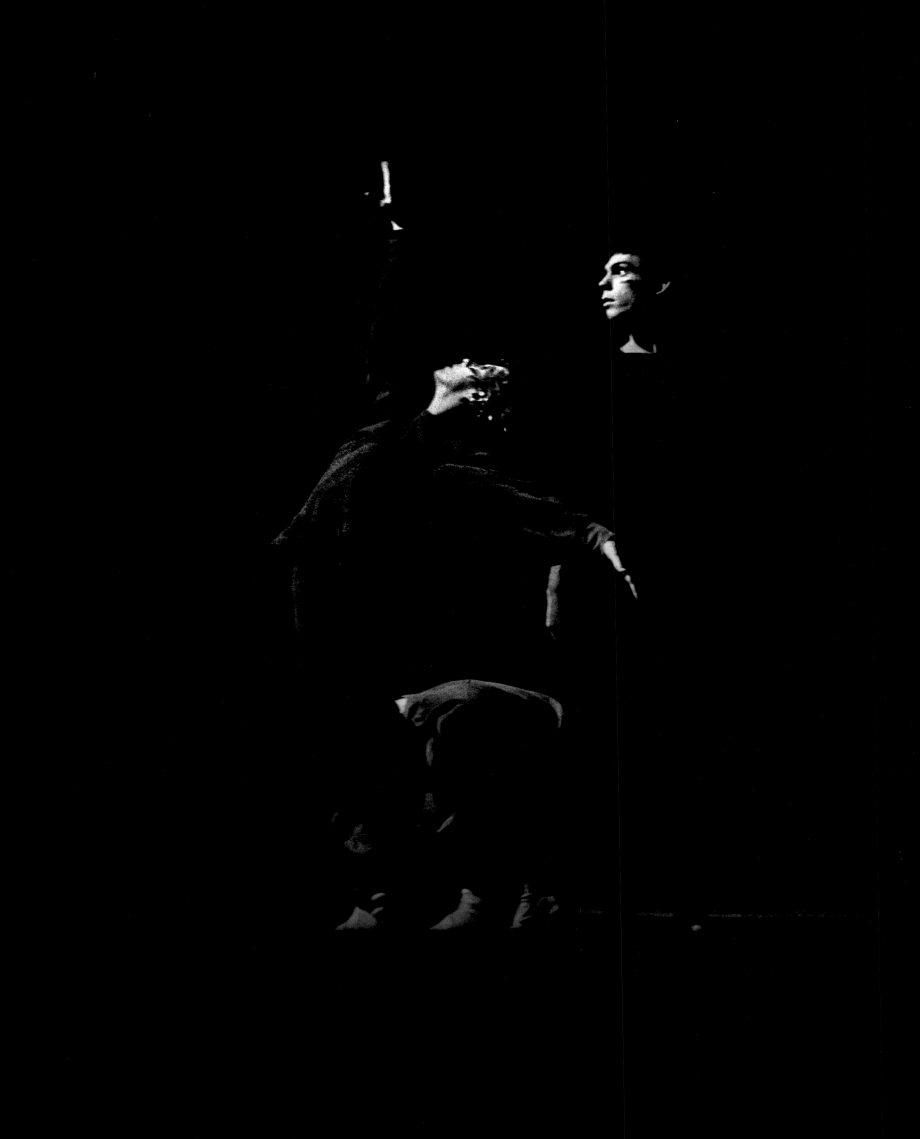

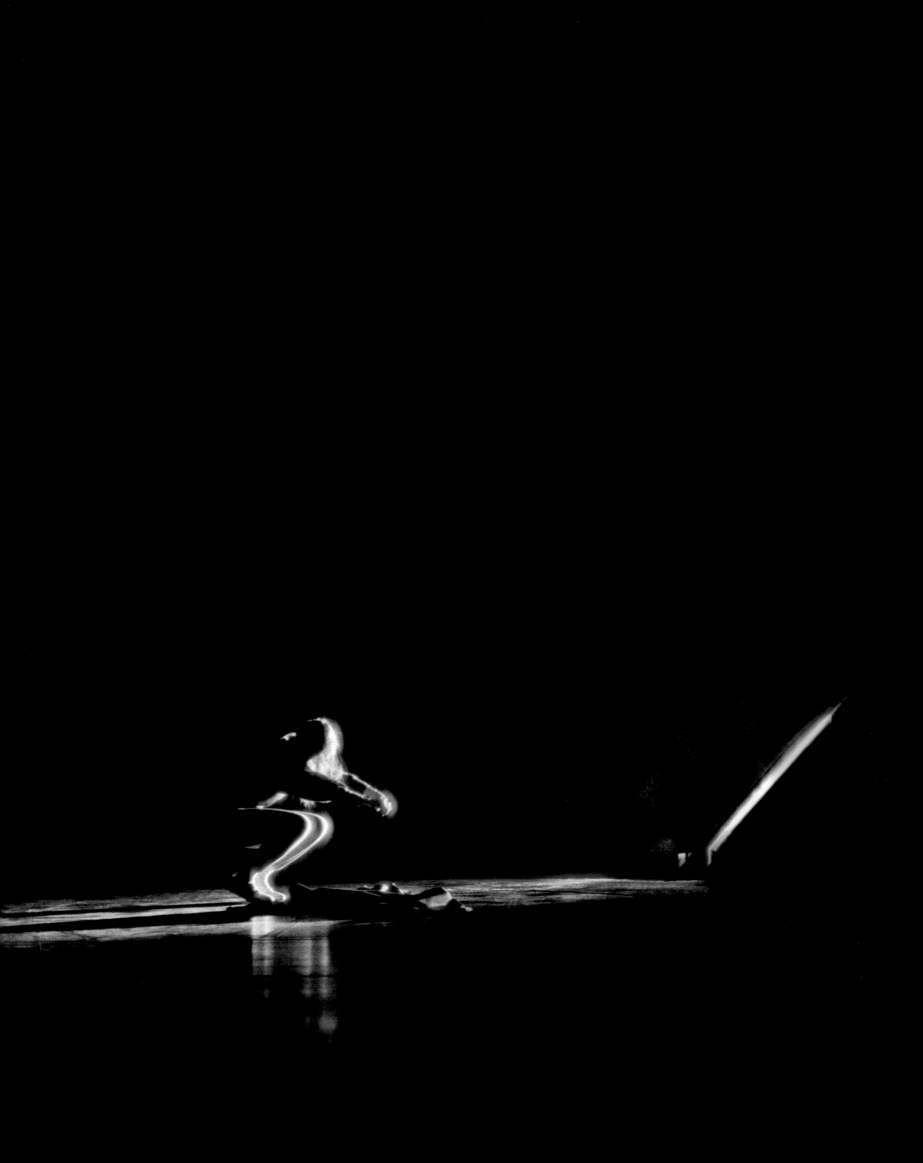

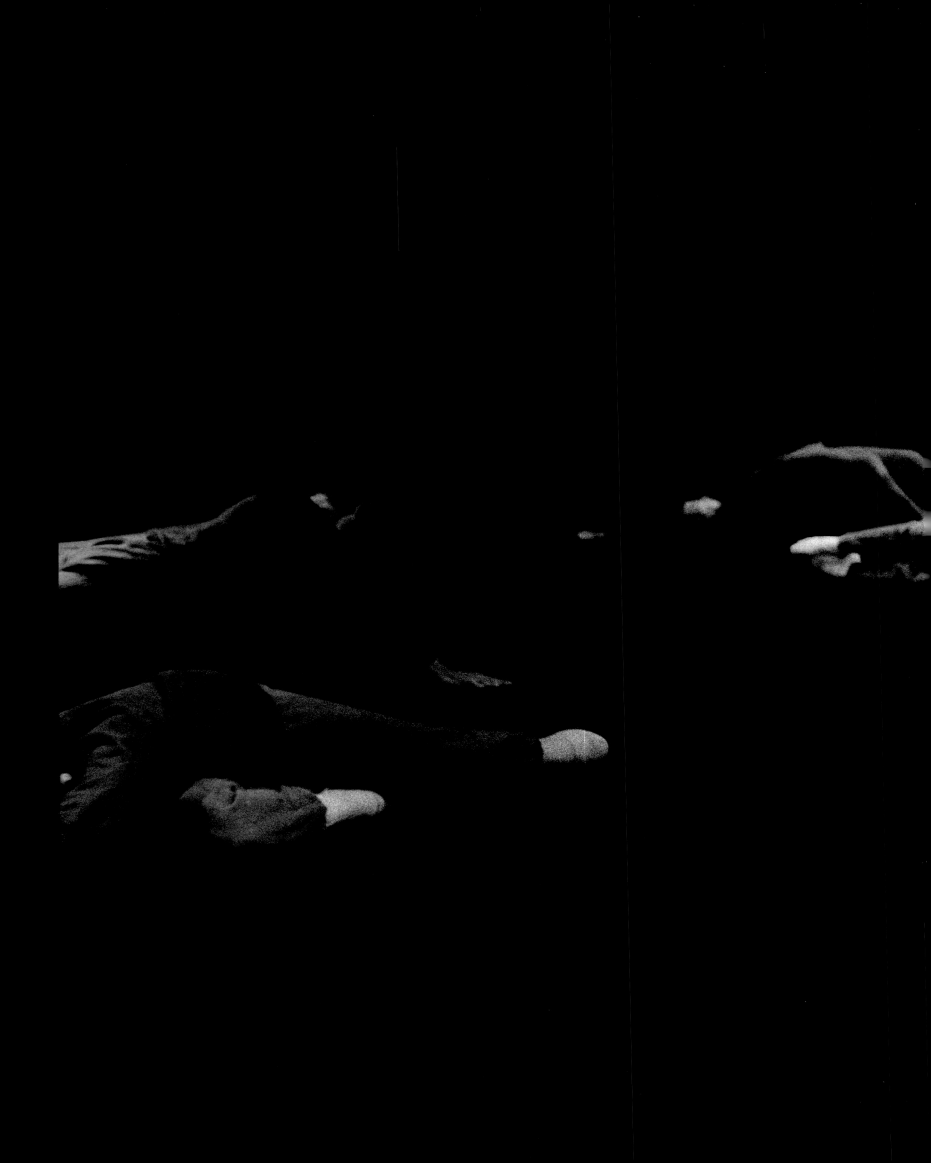

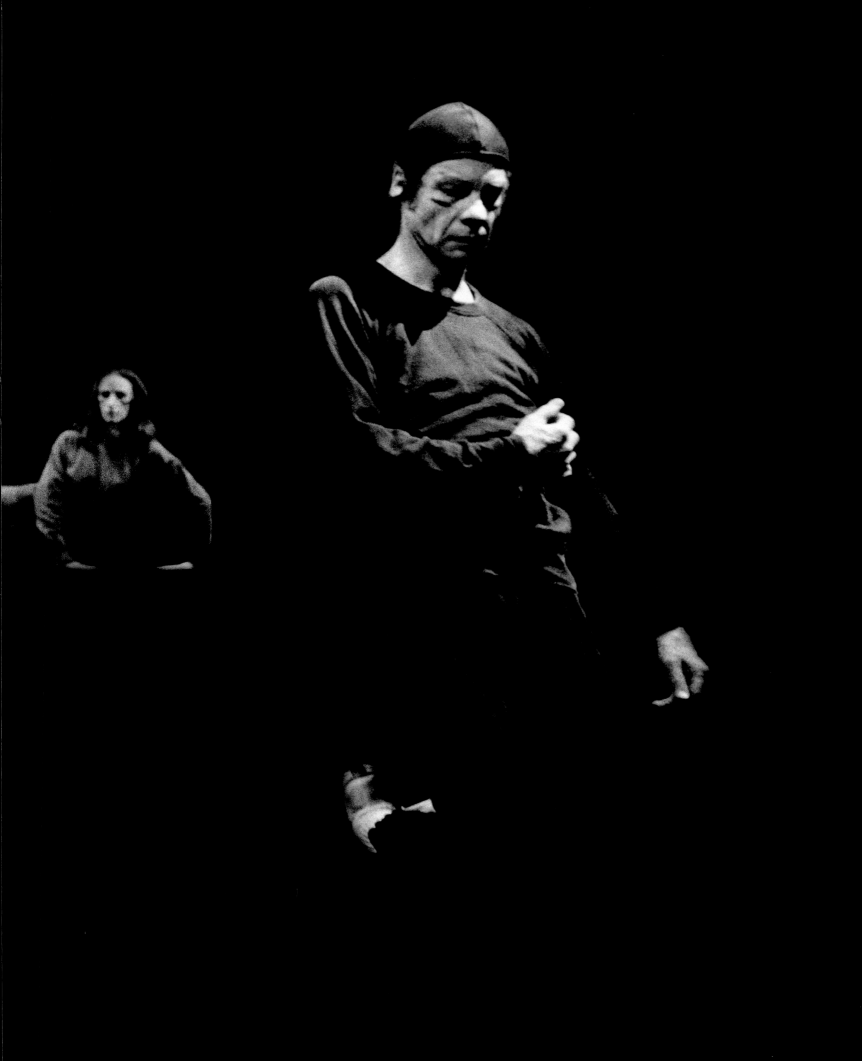

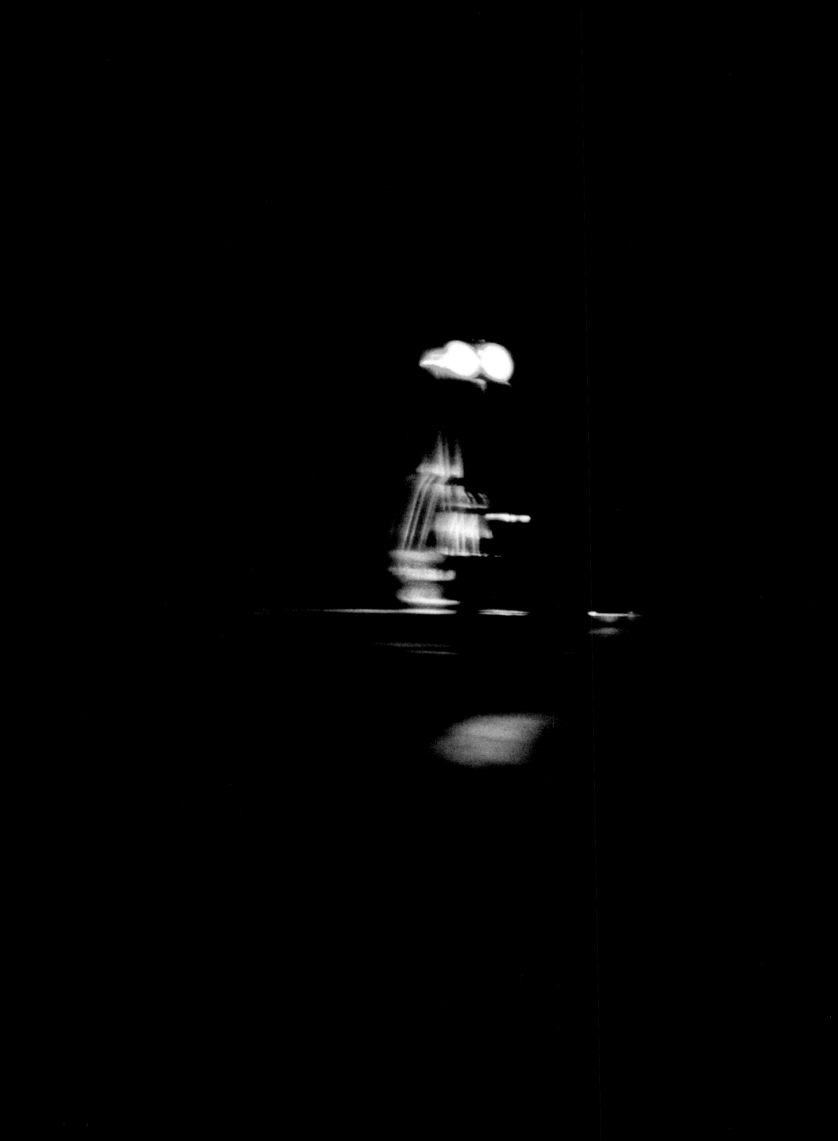

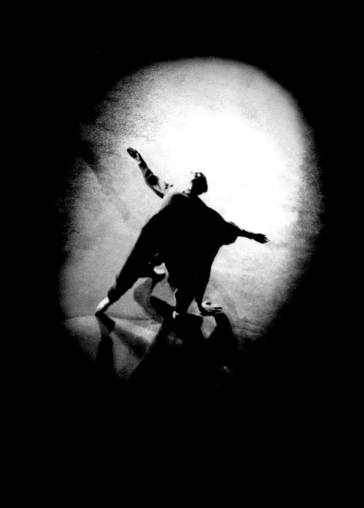
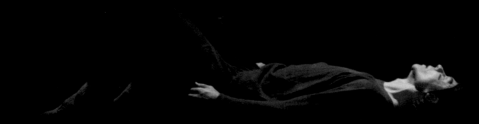

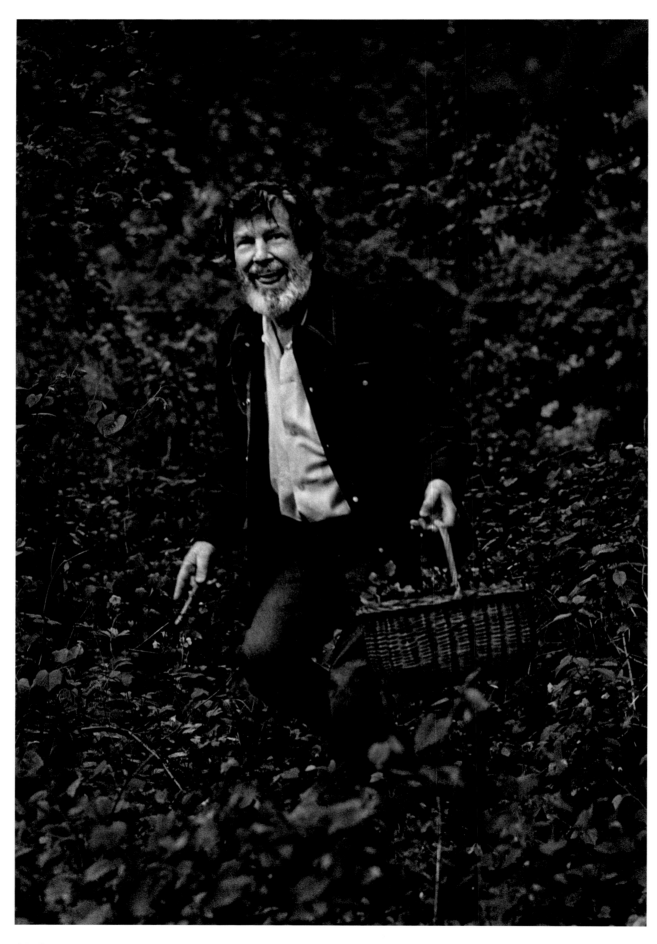

John Cage collecting edible greens, Rockland County, New York, May 1971

JOHN CAGE

—Where Are We Eating? And What Are We Eating?

(Thirty-Eight Variations on a Theme by Alison Knowles)

On the way out of Albany we stopped
at Joe's. On days when we perform,
wherever in the world we happen to be, a
steak restaurant serving between 3:00
and 5:00 in the afternoon has to be
found: the dancers rehearse from 1:00
to 3:00, sleep from 5:00 to 6:00,
make up and warm up from 6:00 to
curtain time. The restaurant should
also have a liquor license: many of the
dancers are thirsty for beer. After
winning the mushroom quiz in Italy,
I bought a Volkswagen microbus for the
company. Joe's was open but said it
wasn't. At Sofu Teshigahara's house,
room where we ate had two parts: one
Japanese; the other Western. Also two
different dinners; we ate them both.

We descended like a plague of locusts
on the Brownsville Eat-All-You-Want
Restaurant ($1.50). Just for dessert
Steve Paxton had five pieces of pie. Merce
asked cashier: How do you manage to keep
this place going? "Most people," she
replied rather sadly, "don't eat as much
as you people." In a pastry shop in Paris
we ran into Tanaquil LeClerq and Betty
Nichols. Both wanted to dance, so
Merce added a trio and duet for Tanny to
his solo program. Afterwards Alice
B. Toklas said, "It was savage."
Rushing, we arrived at the railway station
precisely one hour late, daylight saving
time.

We found a lodge in a meadow surrounded by
a forest near the north rim of the
Grand Canyon. We were so comfortable

there. Fireplaces and good food. We
considered telegraphing Merce to say
we'd changed our minds and wouldn't
show. "What should dancers eat?" Steak,
salad, and Irish whiskey. "I'll leave
off that last when I tell my mother."
Lamb chops. Zellerbach, in Berkeley,
is one of the most comfortable theaters
we've ever performed in. Stage is
wide and deep, has big wings. Floor is
linoleum over wood. Dressing rooms are
like motel rooms. Management,
unfortunately, is aloof, concerned
with ticket sales. Crew's friendly.
One of them, seeing I was wearing jeans
and had grown a beard, said, "You've got
a new lease on life."

We arrived in Delhi. Some of us had lunch
at Mōti Mahal. Tandoori chicken washed
down with dark cider. All of us were there
for dinner. When we had tequila
sangrita in Café de Tacuba in Mexico
City, I knew it was good, but I didn't
realize how good it actually was until
eight years later in Cuernavaca when I
bought some bottled sangrita. I have
vague recollections of a restaurant
in Oregon. Nothing about the food. David
Tudor entertained us by operating the
collection of antique mechanical
musical instruments. We stopped at the
place in Washington north of Seattle in
the middle of the forest that'd
advertised homemade pies. Some of us had
two pieces. Blackberry. While we were
there, some other customers came in and
ordered pie. "I'm sorry: we don't have
any more."

Eat in any municipal, state, or national
park. Build fires: broil steaks or
chickens; roast vegetables in foil with
butter, salt and pepper. Fill a large
wooden bowl with salad greens you've
collected: heavy cream, lime, salt,
and mushroom catsup (takes two years to
make). Buenos Aires: ice cream with
chocolate sauce (after each beefsteak).
Carolyn Brown. Party was given for
us after the show. There was no wine
but lots of tequila, ginger ale, and
beer. Big kettle full of chili. Raw
vegetables with dips. Albany dancers
had made a variety of desserts. Jean
telephoned Joe's to make sure they'd
be open at 10:30 in the morning.
They said they'd be open at 10:00.

London: Sri Lanka. Risotto with
truffles. Heshi Gorewitz: "I enjoyed it
two nights in a row. Standing ovations in
Fredonia! You must be feeling
something." Waiter in the Mediterranée
brought the large pot of *crème fraiche*
so that Merce might put some on his
mousse au chocolat. Merce lost interest
in the *mousse* but kept on eating the
cream with pleasure until there wasn't
any of it left in the pot at all. We
parked and picked bittercress.
Tarpaulin centered on the bus's luggage
rack, luggage fitted on it. Ends'n'sides
were folded over; long ropes used to
wrap the cargo up.

Big Tree Inn in Geneseo. One of
the best restaurants in the United
States. It couldn't make ends meet.
It doesn't exist any more. Merce
rented a large house for the company
on the beach at Malibu. There was a
supermarket out the backdoor.
While the dancers worked at UCLA, I
shopped and cooked. With each
purchase one got a letter of the
alphabet. If you completed the alphabet
you won a lot of money. Have you read
the review? Why should I? Motel
included miserable Chinese
restaurant. Restaurant had a liquor
license. Down the road was The
Villa. Its wine was undrinkable.
Seventeen inches of snow fell. Winds
rose. Traffic outlawed (state of
emergency). Villa closed. Only

restaurant open was Chinese
restaurant. Met in the bar, got
plastered. Went to dining room; food
was delicious.

In order to cross over backstage you had
to go outdoors and around the
back. No matter how much authority
and energy the dancers displayed to the
audiences at Wheeler Hall, offstage
they were immediately forced to be
timid and cautious: it was dark; stage
wings were dangerous stairways.
Dancers' requirement: swimming pool and
color TV. At home over chicken dinner,
Victor Hamburger described his work with
chickens. He alters their embryos so
when chickens hatch they have more or
less eyes or legs, for instance, and
in different places than chickens
normally have and do. I was
hungry. Jean gave me a bag of peanuts
in their shells. Barbara said I
sounded like a squirrel. We stopped and I
had a bowl of chili. Returned to
the bus and began shelling peanuts
again.

When we haven't enough time to go
out, food's brought in. When Joe's saw all
sixteen of us enter at 10:30, they
said, "We're not set up; we're not open."
We said, "We'll be patient." They gave
us the list of sandwiches to study. Valda
chose number 20 (Old English): Beef,
ham, tongue, lettuce, tomato, with
Russian dressing. Dancers never eat
beans before performing. We can look
forward, I believe, to a dance that's
danced by vegetarians. Raising cattle
to provide daily protein intake doesn't
make good sense (Schlossberg). Will new
vegetarian dance be as energetic as
meat-eating dance has been? Probably
it will (Shanta Rao). Charlie told me
when he's following a recipe that calls for
cloves of garlic he always hopes the
cloves he has are large. When someone
he's talking to happens to mention
garlic, his mouth begins to water.

Instant coffee. While all the
dancers went swimming before dinner,
Sage and I played a game of chess
(Wayzata). Merce and Boulez and I were
having luncheon. We'd polished off a

bottle of Pernod. I proudly offered
Pierre peanut butter I'd found near the
Madeleine. Disgusted, he said, "I
don't like peanuts in the first
place." Lenny didn't buy a sandwich. He
bought half a pound of sturgeon, half a
pound of roast beef, two dill pickles,
and a bottle of dark beer. Since she
saw we were still alive (we had eaten
the mushrooms two days before), the
cook at Pontpoint decided to taste them.

Gathered'n'broiled over charcoal
Russulas (virescens), big as pie-plates.
Valda's green sauce (it's made in a
blender): olive oil, lemon juice and
lemon peel, pepper and salt, plenty
of garlic, chives (or shallots), lots
of parsley, fresh herbs (basil or
tarragon). It's good on almost
anything. Food for thought. I was
trying to open the door to my room.
Diarrhea began. I had sent my other
pair of jeans to the laundry. We
were to perform the following evening.
Noit y Dia (Lisbon) never closes,
fits our circumstances perfectly. The
moment you sit down a waiter asks you what
you want.

Brynner got two sandwiches: number 14 and
number 15. He was the only one to whom
potato salad was given. But he doesn't
eat potato salad. He gave it to me. It
was delicious. Was the heaviest
winter I've ever seen. We were drinking
coffee in a truckstop outside Chicago.
Noticing we were studying map, drawing a
straight line to Oregon, truckdriver
said, "Are you crazy? Only way you'll
get there is by going south through
Arizona." Warsaw, 3:00 A.M. Said I
was leaving the hotel. Desk clerk
warned me: "Other hotels are worse than the
one you're already in."
Luncheon on the screened porch (Black
Mountain). Lake and the Smokies beyond.
Student kept plaguing David Tudor with
questions. "If you don't know, why do
you ask?" Day after we got through
Arizona, the road was closed. Food
was brought in by air to keep the
Indians and cattle alive. Pillows and
sheets and blankets. Put them on the
floor. The bed is too soft. We had
one performance: Notre Dame. We drove

all the way from New York and then
back. A prom had been scheduled the
same night. We had an audience of
sixteen: six priests and ten nuns.

Kilina and Charlie helped prepare the
Berkeley dinner. Forty of us.
Spaghettini al pesto (to clean and chop the
basil took five hours), fried chicken,
and salad, and, for dessert, black or red
raspberries (or both) with ice
cream. Suddenly the car went full circle
on the ice: it came to a precariously
tilted stop ten feet down in a ditch.
A truckdriver having all necessary
gear soon stopped and got us back on
the road. We asked how much we owed him.
"Nothing," he said. "It happened to
me once and they charged me an arm and a
leg."

Like Lenny, David Tudor didn't get a
sandwich at Joe's. He didn't buy
anything else there. When we were on
the road to Ithaca, I offered him some
of my sandwich but he didn't want it. I
asked him what he had with him to
eat. "One Jerusalem artichoke; one
red pepper; one flask 'medicine man';
one papaya." I'd played the piano all
evening (no preparations in it).
People came backstage afterward to see
what objects I'd placed between the
strings. Beograd's Festival gave
Canfield first prize. Cologne ridiculed
Canfield. When Clive Barnes writes
about it, he goes berserk.
Englishwoman wrote: "Canfield was
marvelous: I didn't want it to stop
ever."

Sandra: rare roast beef, mustard on
rye. We spent the afternoon on the
lawns of Ricardo Gomis' estate
outside Barcelona. The tortillas were
delicious (omelets with potato and onion).
The weather was perfect. Even though we
were all there (and his five daughters and
many other guests) the space was such
it didn't seem like a large party. We
don't just get gas: we ask the station
attendant where the nearest, best
restaurant is. Susana ate her
smoked salmon and cream cheese. Then
she began thinking about chocolate.
We stopped for the night. Eau Claire,

Wisconsin. Asked the lady who ran the
motel where to eat. "Don't be put off by
the way it looks; go to the restaurant
in the gas station over there." Now,
whenever we're anywhere near, we make a
beeline for the traffic circle on the
west side of town, hoping the restaurant's
still in business.

We were invited to the Ribouds' in
Paris. They had just received a large
box full of fresh mangoes from India. We
kept on eating until they were finished.
In a Buffalo hotel Sandra and Jim stayed on
the eighth floor. They had a large can of
sardines for breakfast. Five they didn't
eat they flushed down the toilet.
After paying the bill at the desk, Sandra
went to the ladies room. There in the
bowl of the toilet were two of her five
sardines. We stopped at a small
crowded restaurant on the road between
Delaware and Baltimore. After our orders
were taken, we waited a long time.
The waitress finally came with some of
our food. Hastily, she said to Carolyn,
"You're the fried chicken," and to
Viola, "And you're the stuffed shrimp."

Picnic preparation in hotel room.
Chicken, marinated in lemon and *sake,*
wrapped'n'foil, left overnight, next day
dipped in sesame oil charcoal-broiled.
Broccoli, sliced, was put with ginger in
twenty-five packages; corn, still in
husks, silk removed,
buttered'n'wrapped. Noticing bathtub was
full of salad, David said, "I don't want any
hairs in my food." In addition to the
roast beef and cheese on rye, Robert had
trisquits, a sour orange from Jaffa, a
banana, and some apple pie. David's sticky
fermented passion-fruit juice geysered on
the way to Grenoble. Bus floor and
handbags were cleaned and the windows
were opened. Then it geysered again.

Three kinds of potatoes (boiled,
French fried, pan fried); *schlagzahne*
(unsweet whipped cream with chocolate
sauce): that was the Holland Festival.
After Merce got the Guggenheim
Fellowship, someone asked him what he was
going to do with all that money.
Answer was monosyllabic: eat! Had picnic
on the lawn in front of Howard Johnsons'.

Went in and used the toilets. Then
drove away. We were in a California
bungalow Japanese restaurant on the
Strip. The food was surprisingly
delicious. The waitress wore a
traditional Japanese costume. After the
meal she asked whether we wanted any
dessert. I said no, but changed my
mind; decided on pineapple ice. She
said, "Oh yes, that'll cut the grease in
your stomach."

There's no indication in any of his
writings that Thoreau ever ate a
mushroom. Asked the waitress in
Sacramento how the roads were to
Oregon. Said she'd had a letter
from her sister two weeks before saying
she was driving south, but she
hadn't seen hide or hair of her. We
parked the car and took the train.
Kamalini didn't eat. She stood
near the kitchen, examined each dish
before permitting a servant to
pass. In four rows, sixty sat on pillows
on the terrace. Woven leaf-cups, each
with oil and wick gave light. Each guest
had a table, raised irregular slab
of grey-green stone, on it a rectangular
tray with bowl for each dish, leaf for
the pickles and chutneys.

Turkey-and-ham sandwich on rye
(tomatoes'n'lettuce); pickle; two
bottles Kirin beer; four candy bars.
Merce ate half of the sandwich on the
bus between Albany and Ithaca, the other
half in the motel before dinner. It's
April 7. Spring's two or three weeks
early. *Helvella* was already seen in
Brockport! I saw hepatica and bloodroot
in Ithaca! We're going to Athens in
southern Ohio. Every mile (we're
going 70!) brings us closer to
morels! During our world tour, dancer
got married, left company; itinerary
changed: Air France confiscated our
tickets, demanded more money. Our new
air-mileage was less than our purchased
air-mileage, we requested refunds.

Kraps told me more'n'more people have
small farms. There's a blurring
of distinction between Amish, Jesus
Freaks, university graduates.
Exchanging food with one another,

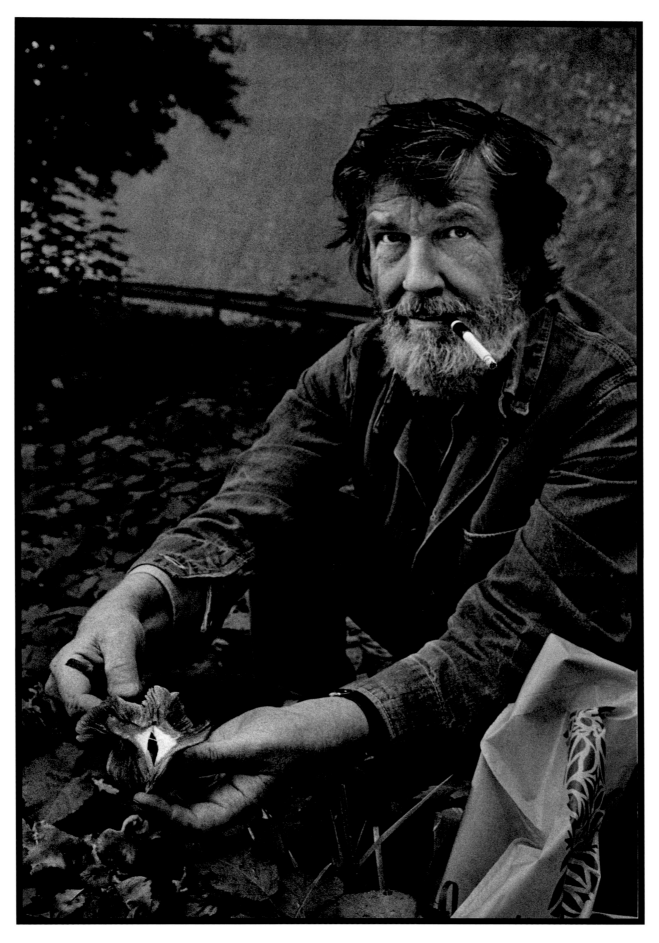

John Cage harvesting *Armillaria mellea* near Grenoble, France, 1972

they make their own economy. "Don't touch money," they say. "That way we'll be free of government." I explained to the cook in the motel how to make the stuffing for the eleven chickens: the giblets, celery, parsley, onion and mushrooms chopped and sautéed in a pound of butter and added with eggs and walnuts to the seasoned crumbs with salt, pepper, and sage. Later he asked whether he should cut the chickens in half before roasting them.

Now that I'm getting older, I think I understand what Wittgenstein had on his mind. He said if he found anything he could eat he would stick to it and not eat anything else. Don't worry about Chicago. Brunch at Carroll Russell's. Omelets and salads after the show at the Sagan's. Skip's home cooking. The French restaurant on the north side that doesn't have a liquor license but's next door to a wine shop. Berghof's in the Loop. One way to tell how hard we're working is whether we have time to eat anything other than hamburgers. Just as

we were on our way down into the desert, I noticed a large stand of *Tricholoma personatum* underneath the pepper trees. We stopped and we picked them. They were in perfect condition.

Birthday cake in Shiraz in Iran had an icing decorated with pomegranate seeds. We'd been on one train from Warsaw to West Germany, our theater luggage on another which hadn't arrived. No way to get information from railway authorities in East Berlin. A day passed. Consulted *I Ching*. Oracle said: Don't worry; relax and feast. While we were stuffing ourselves, news came that our trunks had just arrived. New farms in Appalachia. Farmers take poor land and set to work to improve it. Kraps shares a farm with four friends. This year they're in corn. Next year (they have deep, loose soil) they'll get into potatoes and grains.

We were waiting to be ferried across the Mississippi. We had nothing to eat. We waited two hours. It

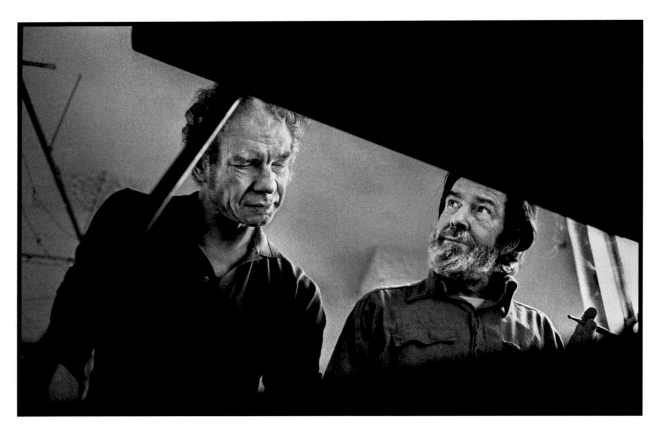

Merce Cunningham and John Cage, Westbeth, 1972

was cold and muddy. When we decided to
leave, Rick and Remy had to push the bus
up the hill. Later we learned that the
ferry service had been discontinued two
years before. Jack Kiefer and Moss
Sweedler introduced me to the Moosewood
Restaurant in Ithaca. Luncheon.
Spinach and mushroom soup. Jack and
Moss had asparagus soufflé. I jumped to
dessert: yoghurt cream cheese pie
(nuts in the crust). Milk that was
actually milk. Backstage: crew's playing
poker. Holiday Inn: Room 135. 4
cups of ground walnuts; 4 cups of
flour; 12 tablespoons of sugar; 2 2/3
cups of butter; 4 teaspoons of
vanilla. Form into circa one hundred
and twenty-five small balls. Bake at 350°
in motel oven. Now back to room 135.
Roll in 1 pound of powdered sugar.
Nut balls.

About 8:00 P.M. we arrived in Durango.
There were two or three
conventions. All the motels and hotels
were filled up. Drove up and down the
main street until we finally landed in
an old whorehouse. Each room had a bed
and that was all. No windows. No water.
Bathroom with toilet was down the
hall. Sign on Tennessee Thruway:
You've just passed the best fried
chicken in the world. We got off at the
next exit and drove back. Except for
Lois Long's fried chicken, it *was*
the best we'd ever had. There were
collard greens, black-eyed peas, okra.
You could eat as much as you wanted.

Asked Moosewood waitress how many
people and how many hours were
necessary to keep Moosewood going.
She said: "There are fifteen of us; we
choose our own hours." What about
shopping? "We do it by telephone."
Health food. Théâtre Experimentale.
Théâtre Gonflable (inflated rubber
theater at St. Paul de Vence). For
rehearsals during the day it was as
hot as an oven. For the evening
performances it was freezing cold.
There was no room for the musicians.
Sound was piped in from a truck
outside. Air France's so large it's
impossible to know what part of it to
talk to (even within *our* company

there's a certain lack of
communication).

Meg Harper had three apples and a
bottle of red wine. She bought a dill
pickle and several slices of roast beef.
When Merce was in residence at Illinois,
he stayed at the Johnstons', took all of
his meals with the family. Betty made
box lunches when he was too busy to return
home. Betty's cooking is delicious,
nutritious. For two years, I got
heavier and heavier. "When it comes
to desserts," Betty advises, "throw
health out the window." (Through
eating nothing but thistles, Mila Repa
took the form of a thistle. He was able
to transport himself wherever he
wished.) High above, thistle floated
past. One farmer to the other: "Pay no
attention: it's just Mila Repa."
Vitasok's thick fruit juices are
great. Had'em first in Zagreb, and
recently in Beograd. In Ljubljana's
supermarket, I bought twenty-four
bottles of raspberry. When we come into a
new town, David Tudor goes over the list
of restaurants in the Yellow Pages. "How
do you read it?" "I read the ones in
large type face first; depressed by
that I start from the top
regardless of type face and read all the
way down to the end." Julie read the
list of sandwiches in the delicatessen but
didn't buy one. She had just had a
cheese omelet for breakfast. After
six weeks in Japan, we went back to Stony
Point. How was Japan? The pickles
were delicious.

We had stopped for gas in Ohio.
While the dancers were going to the
toilets, buying snacks, and doing their
exercises around the pumps, the station
attendant asked me if we were a group of
comedians. I said, "No. We're from New
York." Waiting for air tickets to
Prague. Outside his Albany room, on
the window ledge, Charlie had left some
apricot yoghurt and a package of
Swiss cheese. The sandwich he bought
at Joe's had three kinds of meat: bacon,
turkey, and chopped liver. Friends
in Gaudeamus wanted to take us to a
special restaurant in The Hague.
But we couldn't get in because of the way

I was dressed. The same thing
happened in Bremen. There,
however, Hans Otte persuaded the
manager of the restaurant to let us
sit down. But the people at the next
table immediately got up and left without
finishing their food.

I think it was Remy who got the idea to
advertise the company as America's
Best Fed Dance Company. That was in
pre-AGMA days, when Merce paid for
all the food, gas, and motels, and
then gave each of us twenty-five
dollars for each performance. When
world tour was ancient history, Air France
gave a small refund on our tickets.
Valda was talking with the busdriver.
He seemed to be a family man, often
mentioned his wife and children. After
leaving us, he was going south; it
would be warm and beautiful. "Are you
going to take your wife?" "Would you
take a chicken salad sandwich to a
banquet?"

Jean's sandwich was turkey: white meat on
white bread, Russian dressing. In
retrospect the Ceylonese restaurant
in Boulder reminds me of Sri Lanka
in London. In each case the
cuisine was light and delightful,
and we were given a multiplicity of ways
to vary the taste of a dish.
Albert's luggage included many cartons.
Butane stove, basic utensils, staples
on hand. While we were reading menus,
he was cooking elaborate meals in
his room. Dancer on dressing room
floor, tormented, refusing to perform.
What'd she eaten? Driving along in
the late afternoon, we generally brighten
up: it is time for snacks and a drink.

Drought; found *tabescens* in Oklahoma city
park. They only had two kinds of bread,
white and rye. Chris chose rye (with
Virginia ham, sliced egg, tomato,
chicken salad, and mayonnaise). He drank
grape soda. Cunningham's breakfast: two
parts yeast, one part liver, one
part wheat germ, one part sunflower-
kernel meal, one part powdered milk (cold
pressed), pinch of kelp, one part lecithin,
one-half teaspoon powdered bone meal.
At home, mixed with milk and banana in a

blender. On tour USA, mixed with
milk in portable blender. On tour
elsewhere, mixed with yoghurt or
what-have-you. Sue Weil turns her home
into a hotel at the drop of a hat. I
always stay in the room opposite
Peggy's.

Dinners at Sri Lanka generally begin
with egg hoppers. An egg hopper is an
iddiapam made with rice flour and coconut
milk in the bottom of which fried egg
sunny-side-up is placed. On top of
the egg your choice of condiments from a
tray of many. EAT (Experiments in Art
and Technology): Merce never got involved
in it; David Tudor and I did. The
inefficiency of the engineers nearly
drove me crazy. They had no
realization of the truth of the fact
the show must go on. Began to give
Doolie the nut ball recipe. She said,
"Stop! I can't eat nuts. I have an
allergy."

Pontpoint: the company ate by
candlelight. Everywhere we've gone,
we've gone en masse. A borrowed
private car took two, two such cars took
six to eight, the Volkswagen bus
took nine. Now airplanes and chartered
buses take any number of us. Soon
(gas rationing) we'll travel like Thoreau
by staying where we are, each in his own
Concord: transmission of images, not
of bodies, television. Mila Repa. I did
most of the driving except in
emergencies. Going east from
Buffalo, we couldn't see a foot ahead
because of a blinding snowstorm.
Merce took the wheel. Barbara found the
sandwich she'd chosen very good. Dressed
with lettuce, tomato, mayonnaise and
mustard, and accompanied by half a dill
pickle, it was Swiss cheese and turkey on
rye.

After Jean'n'I'd rolled one hundred
balls, I remembered I'd forgotten
the vanilla. We started over.
Moosewood in Ithaca; Whole Earth
Restaurant in Santa Cruz. It's clear
what's happening: young people all over
America turning the country into a place
to be matriotic about. We reached the
western Pennsylvania park toward

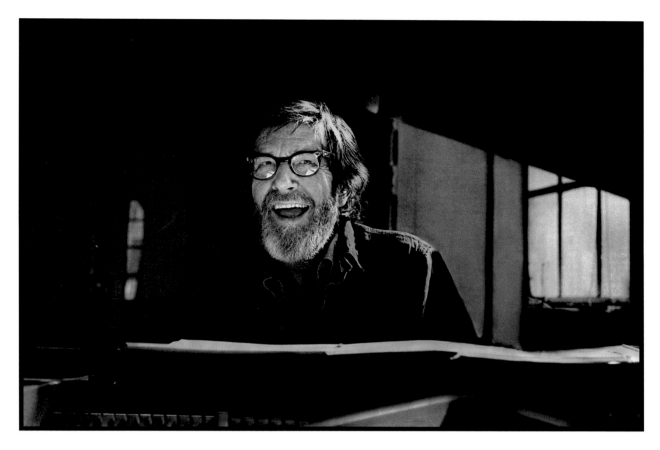

John Cage, Westbeth, 1972

midnight. Using flashlights, we carried
charcoal, food, and drink down the
path on the side of the cliff to the
grounds below where the fireplaces were.
May apples were blooming. Nick took
charge. We had drinks while the yams
were roasting. Mrs. Pylyshenko's stuffed
cabbage with mushroom cream sauce. Then
poker. That's how I met Fred Kraps,
Lighting Designer, Brockport's Dance
Department. Following day, Kraps
mentioned farm and counterculture while
we were eating Sicilian pizza.

Boos and bravos. Doug ate roast beef
on rye and drank Dorfmunder Action
beer. The simplest thing in the
technological world is amplification
by means of contact- and throat-
microphones. We arranged a banquet on
stage at the Y all the noises of which were
to go through a multichannel
sound-system. EAT's engineers managed to
foul it up. Azuma (Japanese
restaurant in Ithaca). Excellent
tempura (not greasy; flaky, delicate
batter). I wrote to Black Mountain in

'39 asking for a job teaching music. No
reply. In '48 they said they'd put
us up if we'd perform there but that
they didn't have any money. We parked
the car and stayed three days.
While backing up to leave, we noticed
the space beneath the car had been filled
with presents.

"You go home now?" No; this ends the
first of five weeks. Toward the
end, Black Mountain didn't have a
cent. The cattle were killed and the
faculty were paid with beefsteaks. Chef
in Kansas motel-restaurant cooked
the mushrooms I'd collected. Enough
for an army. They came to the table
swimming in butter. Carolyn, who isn't
wild about wild mushrooms, had seconds. I
complimented the cook. How'd you know
how to cook'em? "We get them all
the time: I'm from Oklahoma." There's a
rumor Merce'll stop. Ten years ago, London
critic said he was too old. He himself
says he's just getting a running start.
Annalie Newman says he's like wine:
he improves with age.

111

1968–1972 EVENTS

The concept of an "Event" was inevitable considering Cunningham's interest in unconventional, nontheatrical spaces. It was a simple, sometimes not-so-simple, but certainly flexible way to mesh the deep resource of the company's extensive repertoire into segments that could vary, be combined with one another and recombined depending entirely on the space involved. The first Event was in a Vienna museum on the 24th of June 1964 and was titled *Museum Event No. 1*.

Right: "Dialogue" Event, Walker Arts Center, Minneapolis, 1972;
Following spread: *Event No. 45* in the Piazza San Marco, Venice

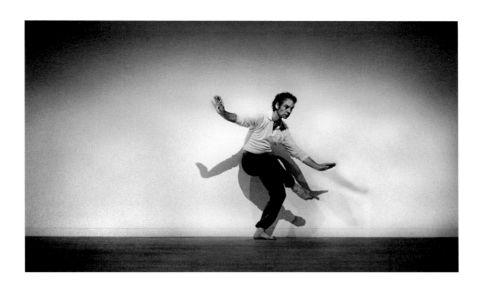

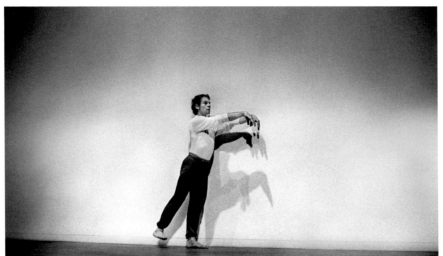

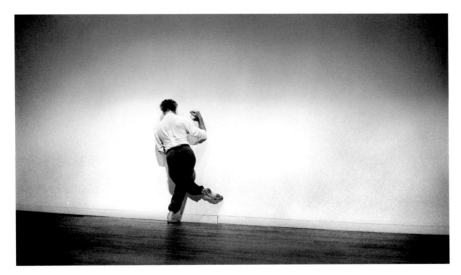

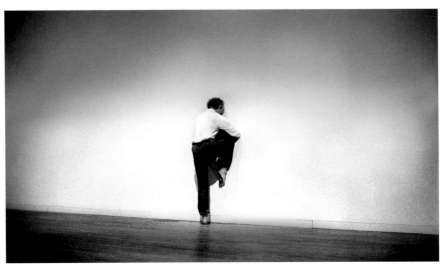

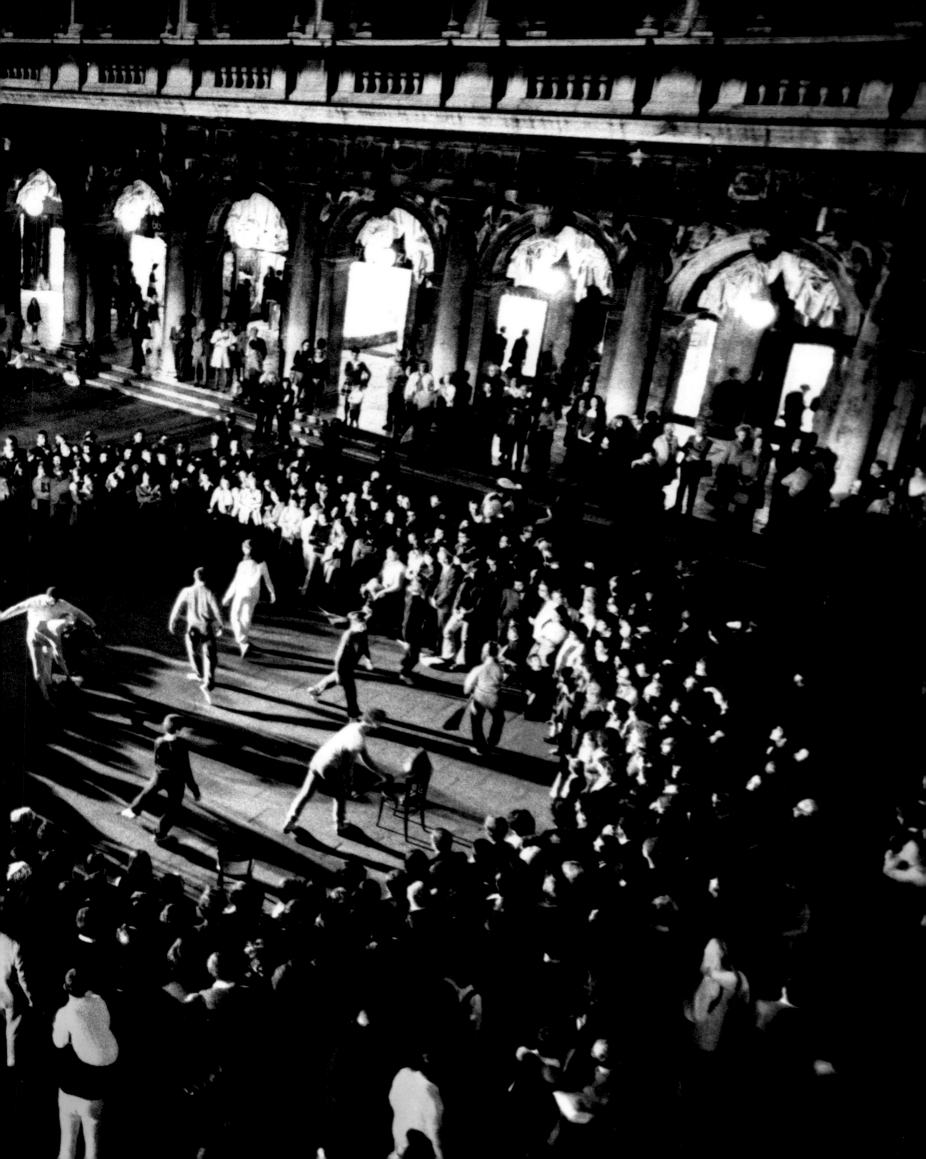

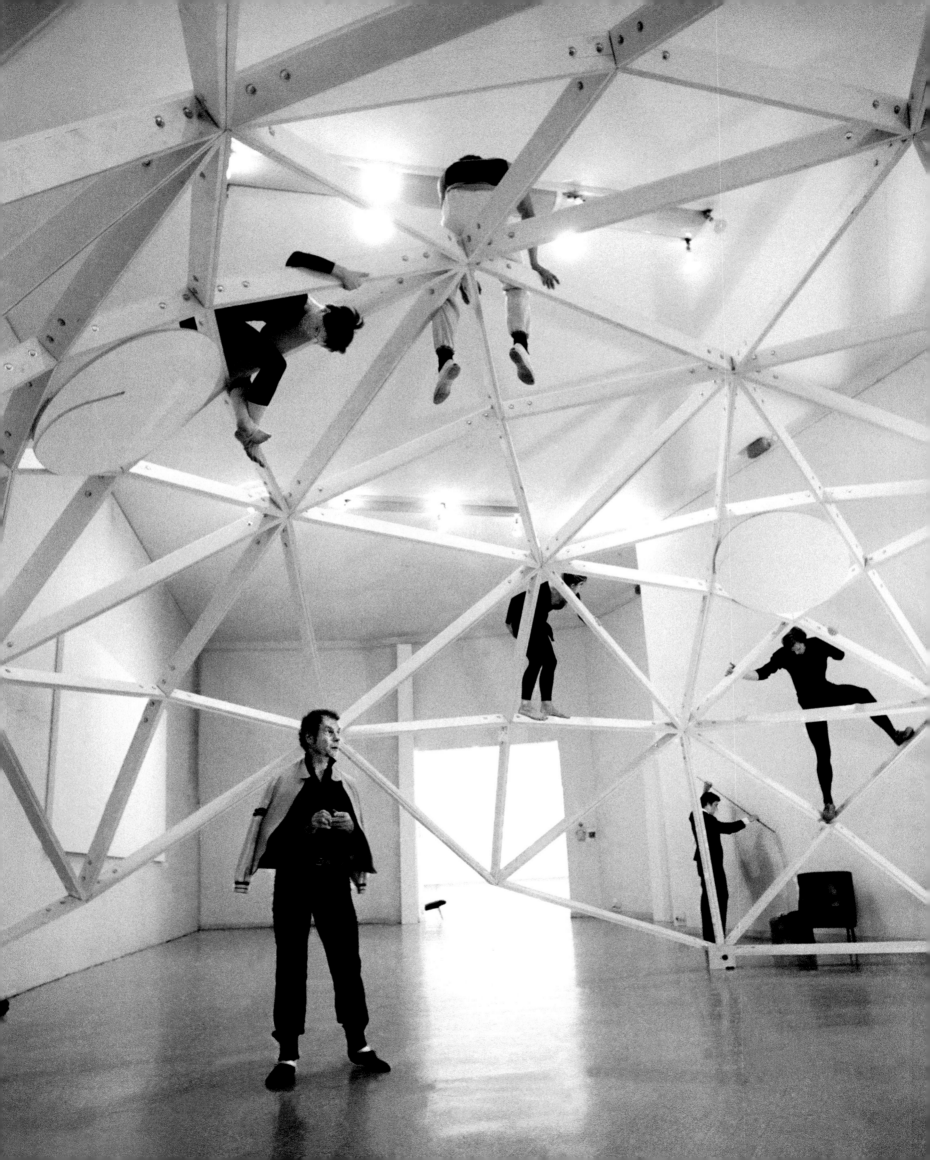

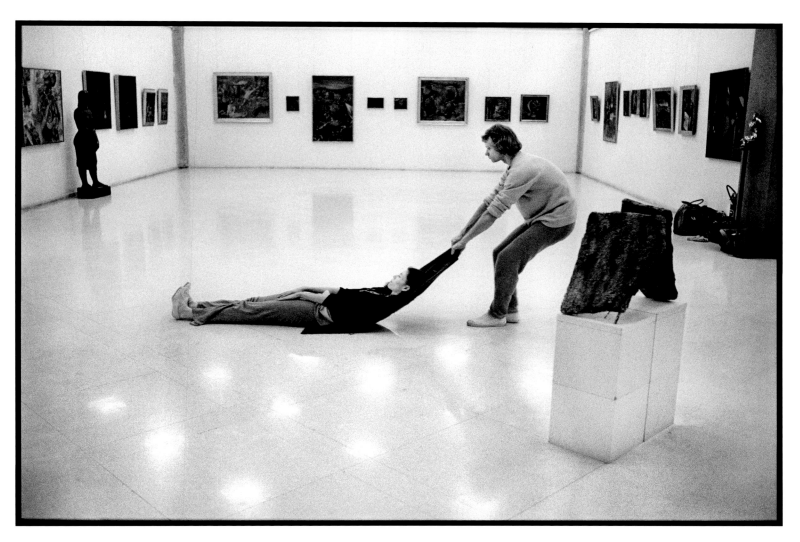

Left: Rehearsal for an Event at the Musée d'Art Moderne, Paris, 1970;
Above: Sandra Neels and Chris Komar at a rehearsal for an Event in the Belgrade Museum, 1972

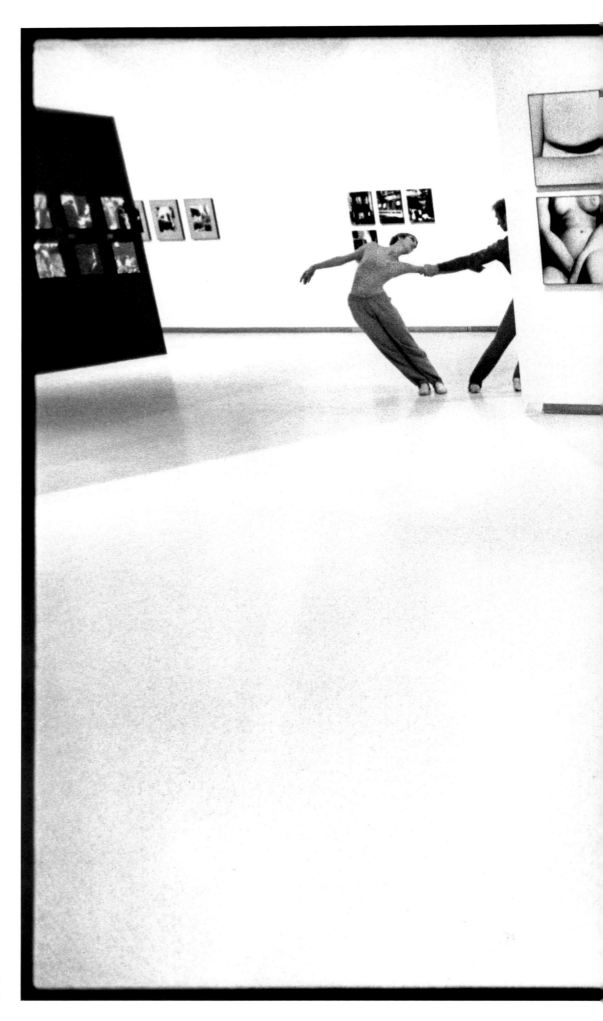

Event No. 32, Valda Setterfield,
Merce Cunningham, Walker Arts
Center Minneapolis, 1972

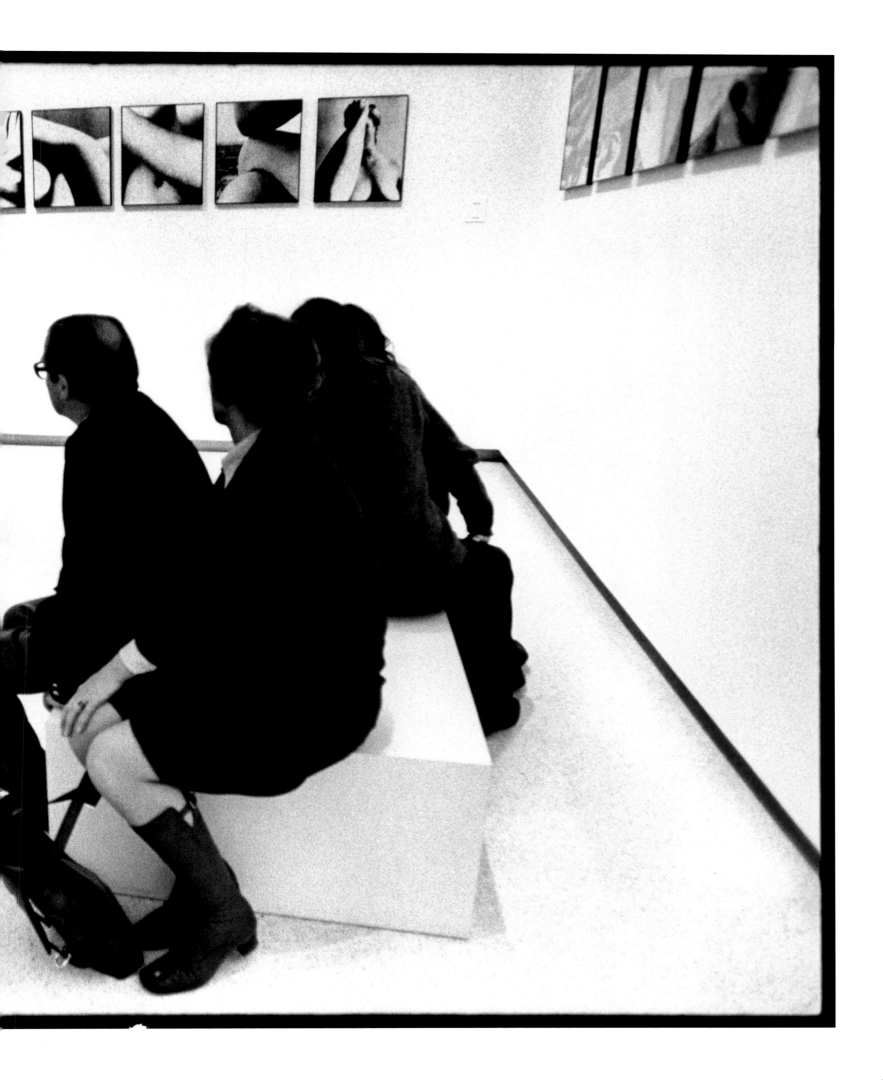

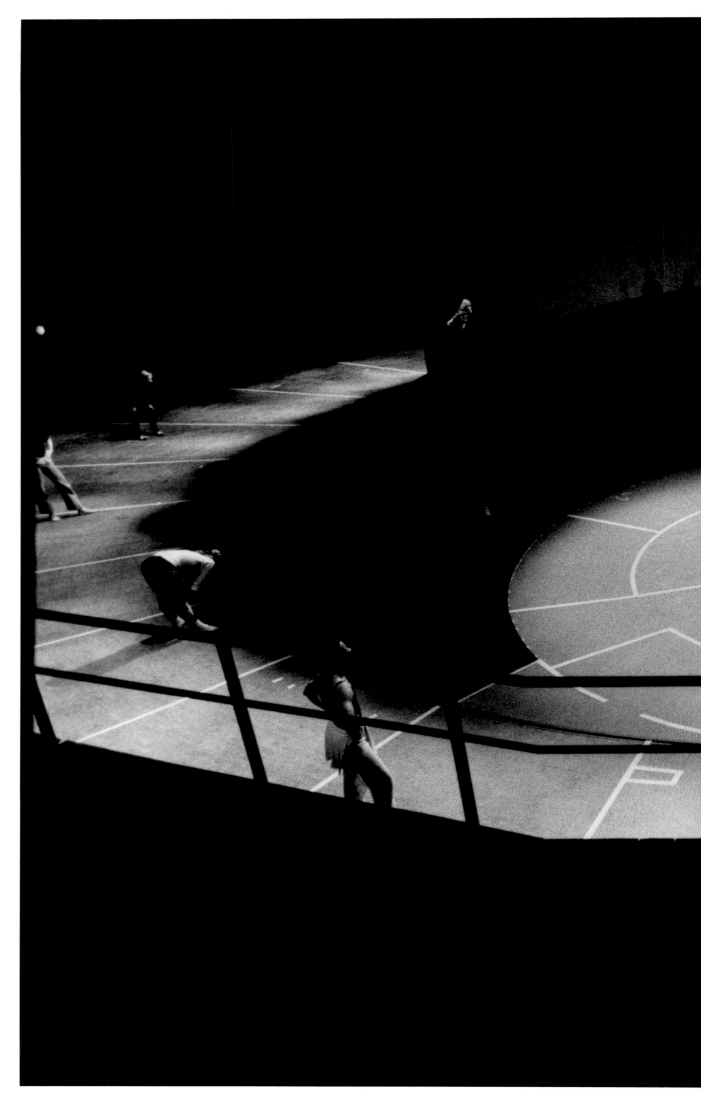

Rehearsal for an Event in the Théâtre
Mobile, Grenoble, France, 1972

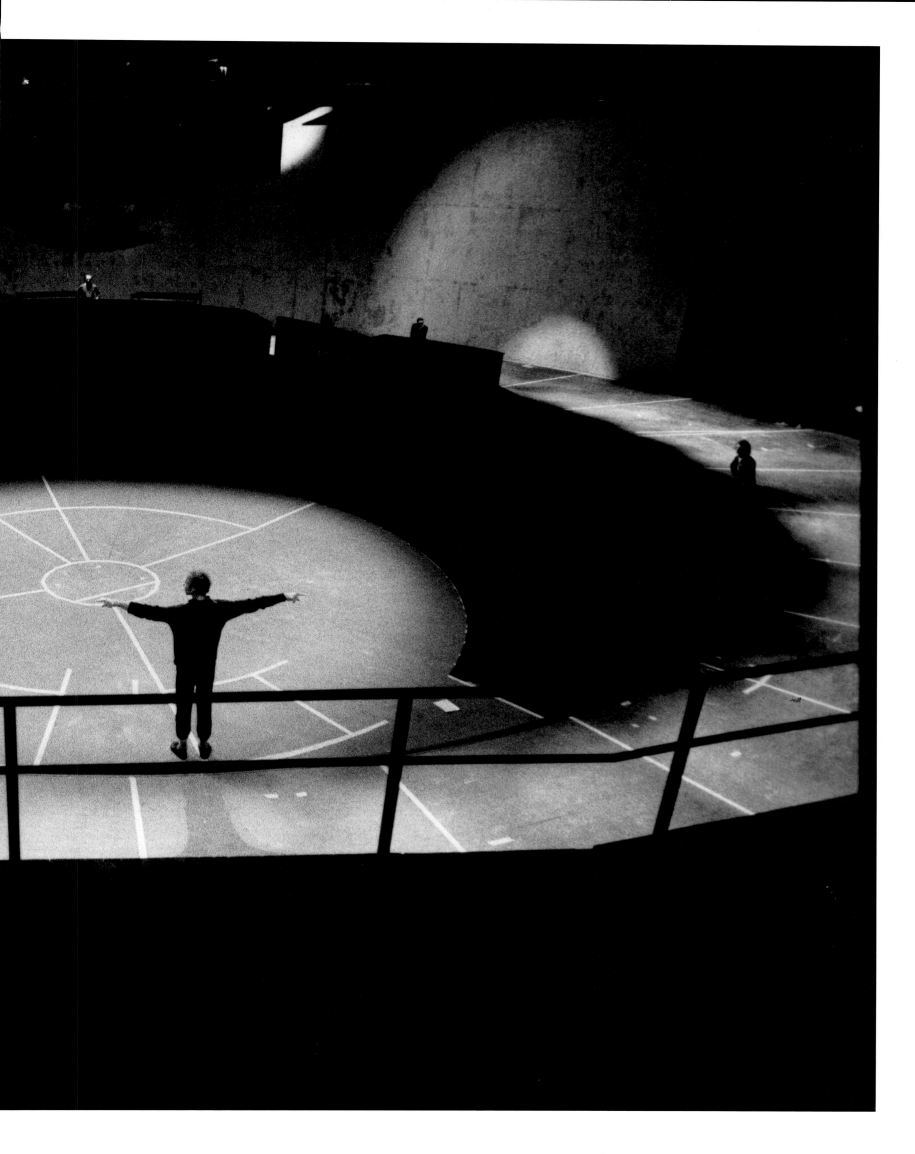

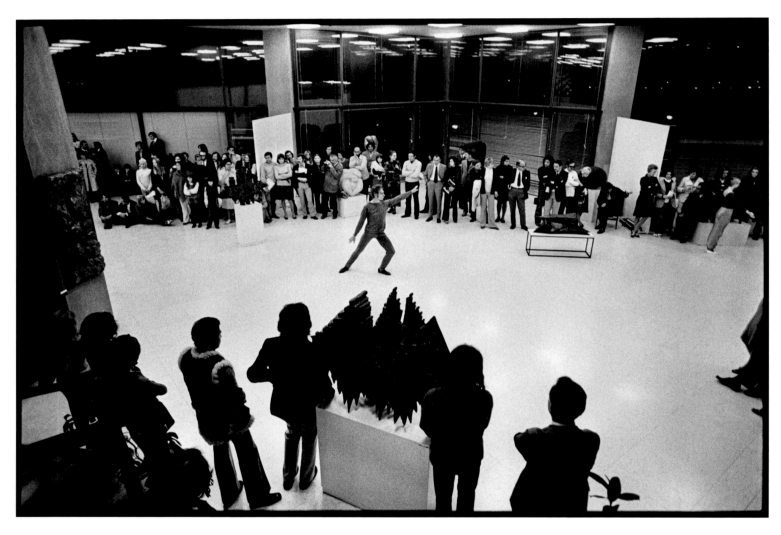

Above and right: Event performance at the Belgrade Museum

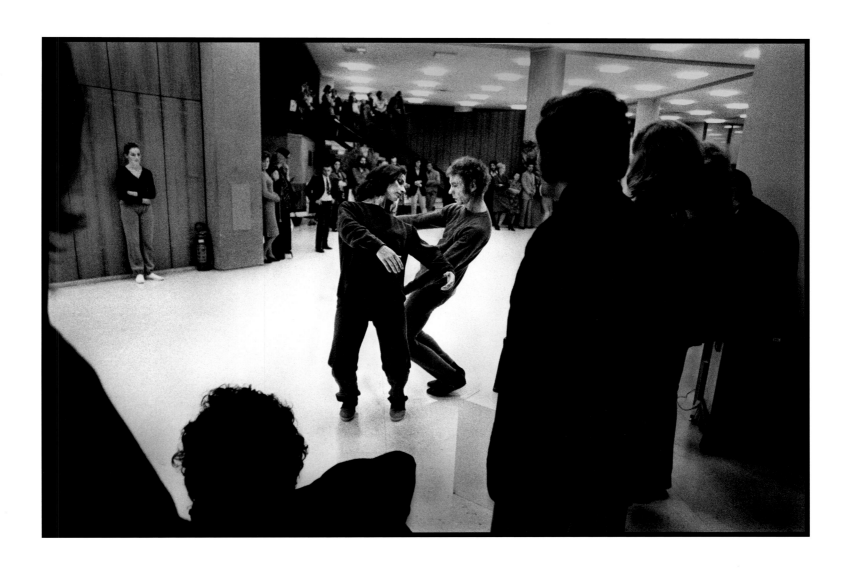

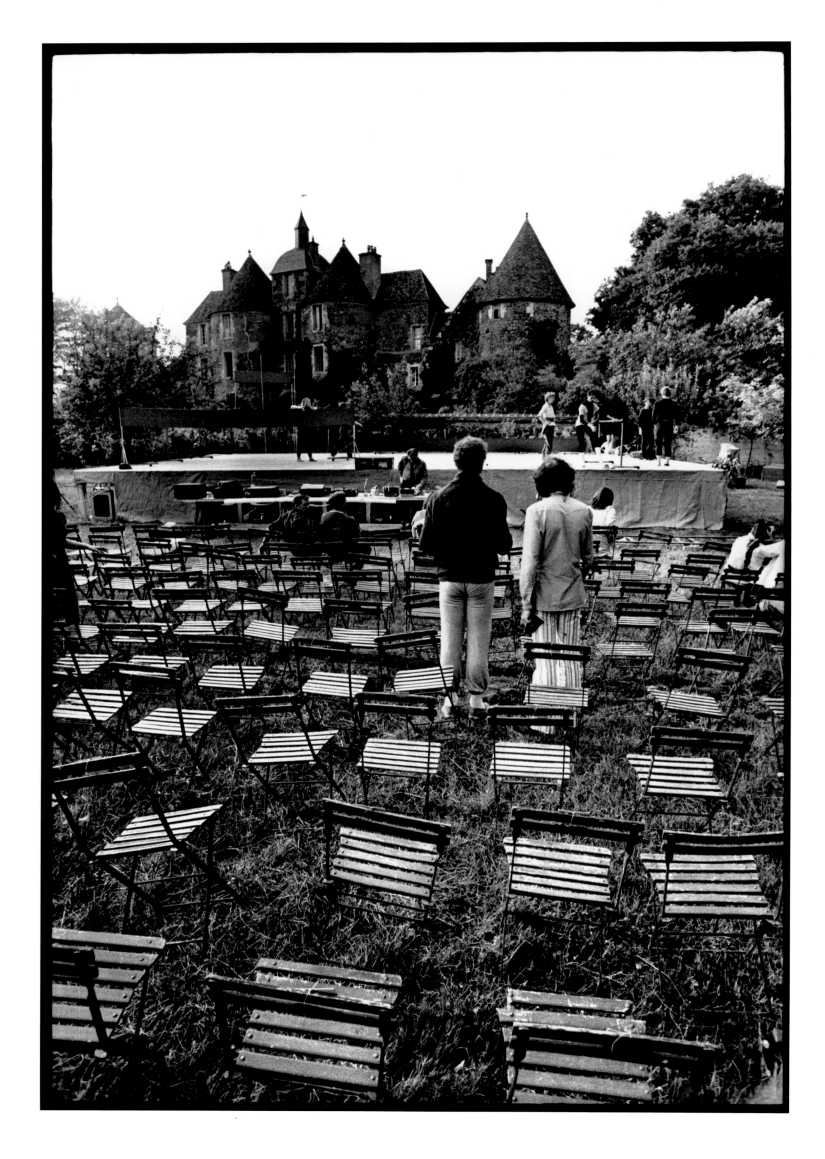

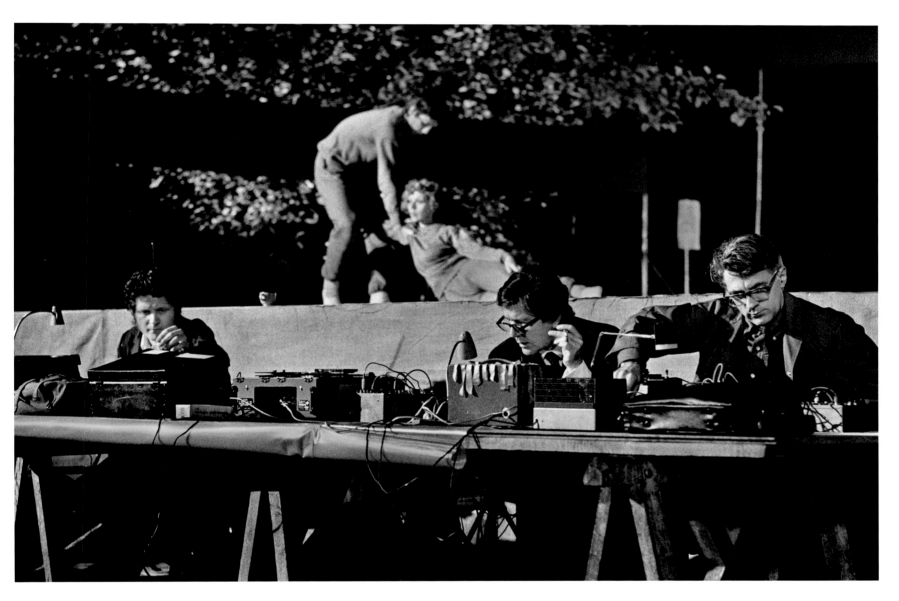

Left: Merce Cunningham and Richard Nelson, rehearsal for an Event at the Château de Ratilly, Treigny, France, 1970;

Above: Ratilly Event performance

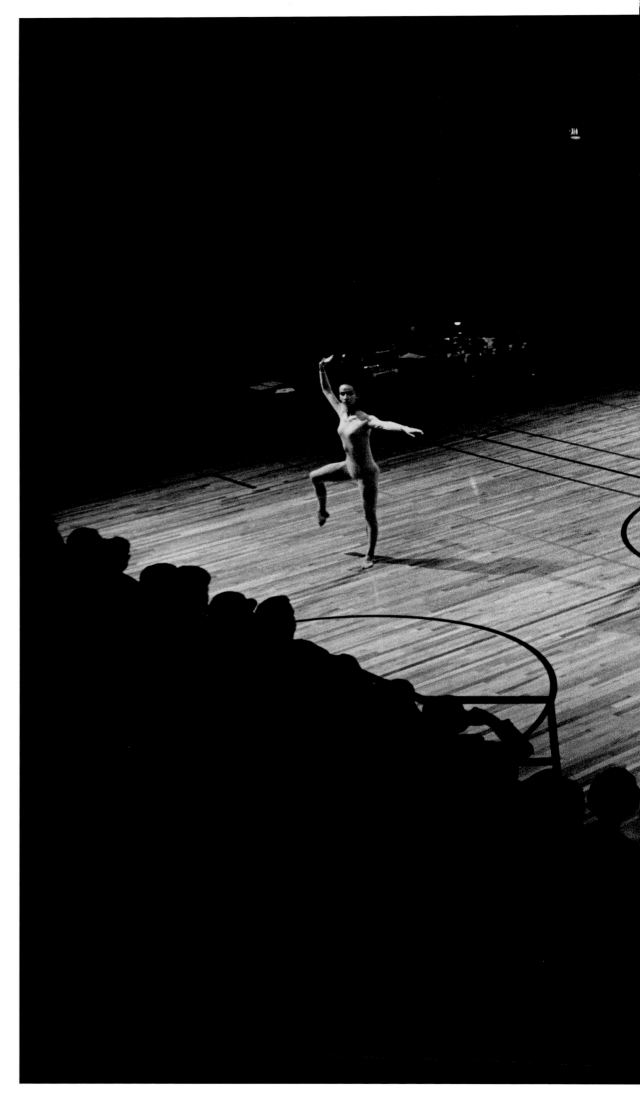

Right: *Event No. 22*,
Mills College in Oakland,
California, 1971;
Following spread:
Ulysses Dove and Merce
Cunningham, Event,
Milan, Italy, 1972

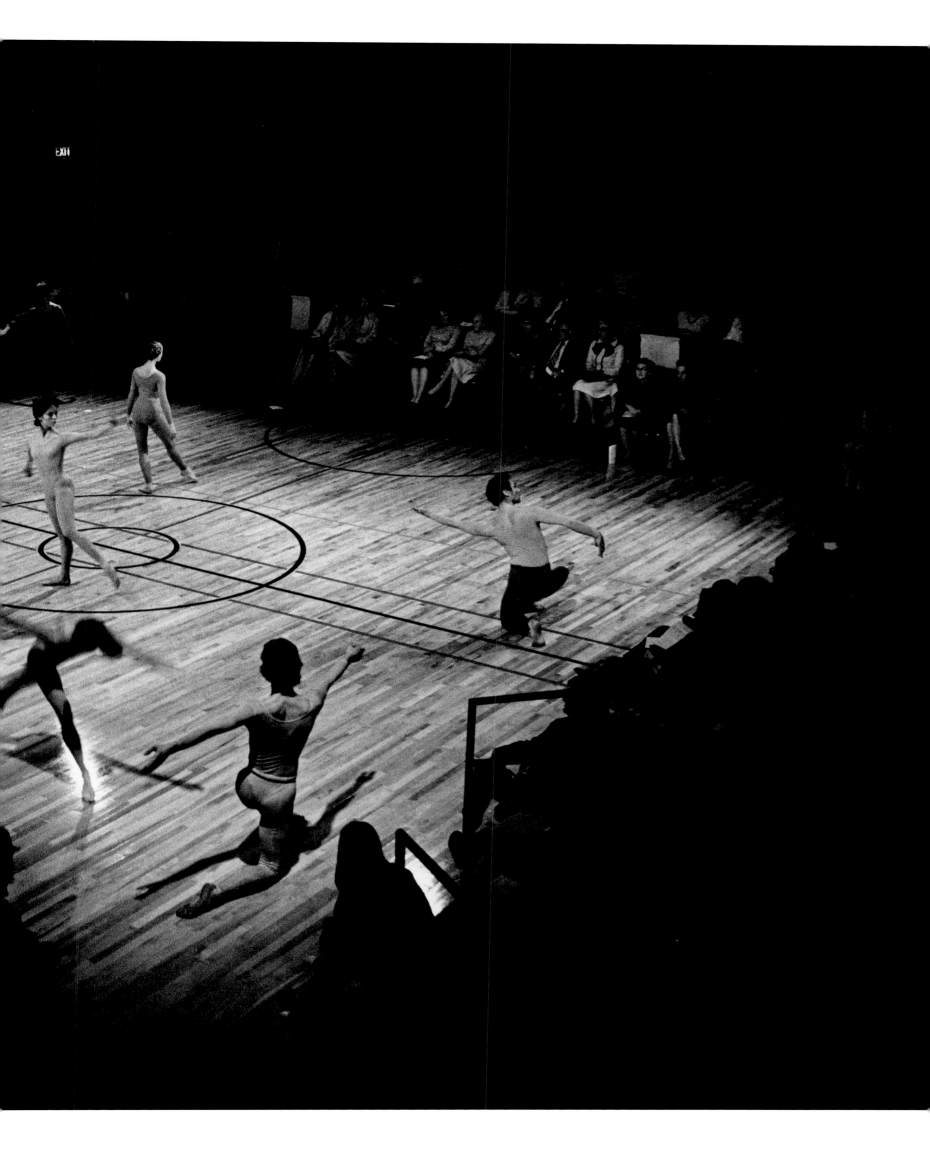

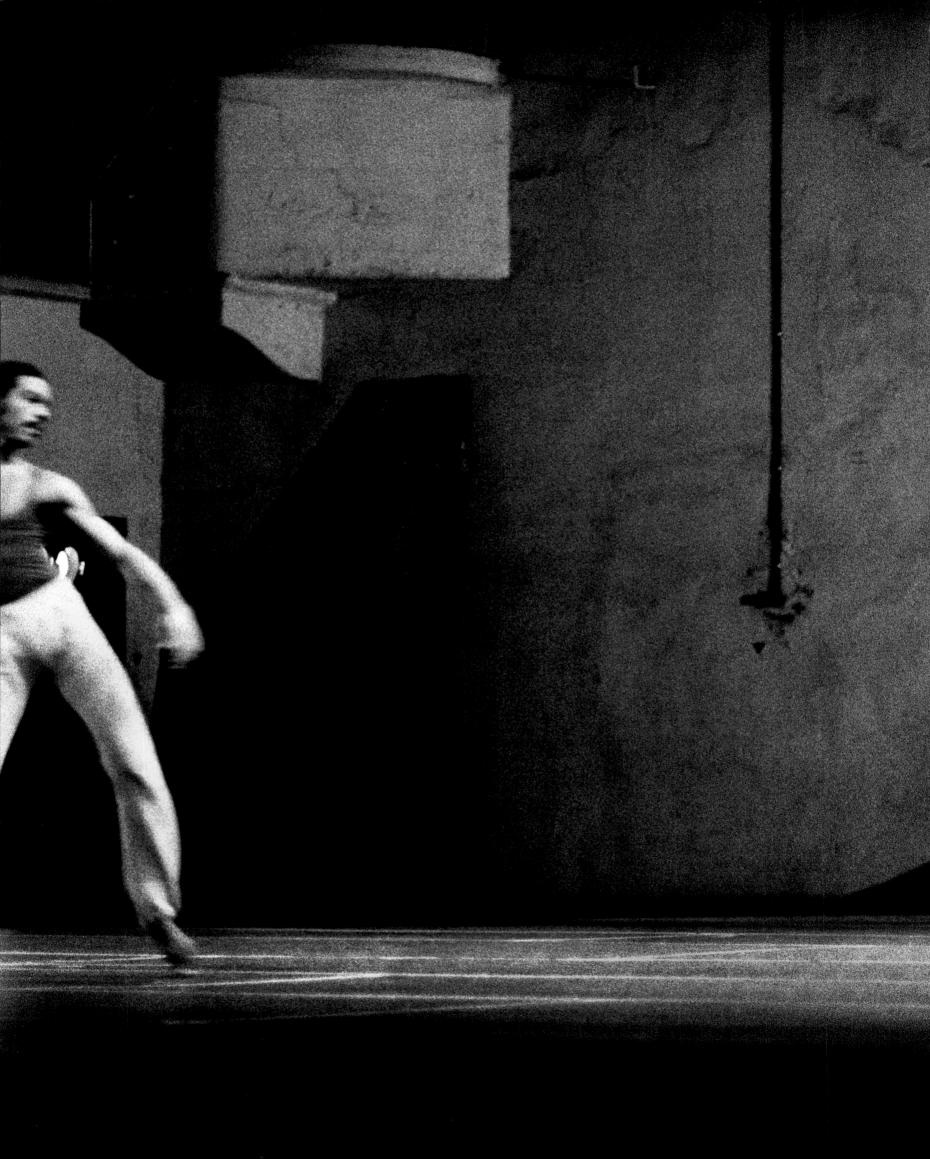

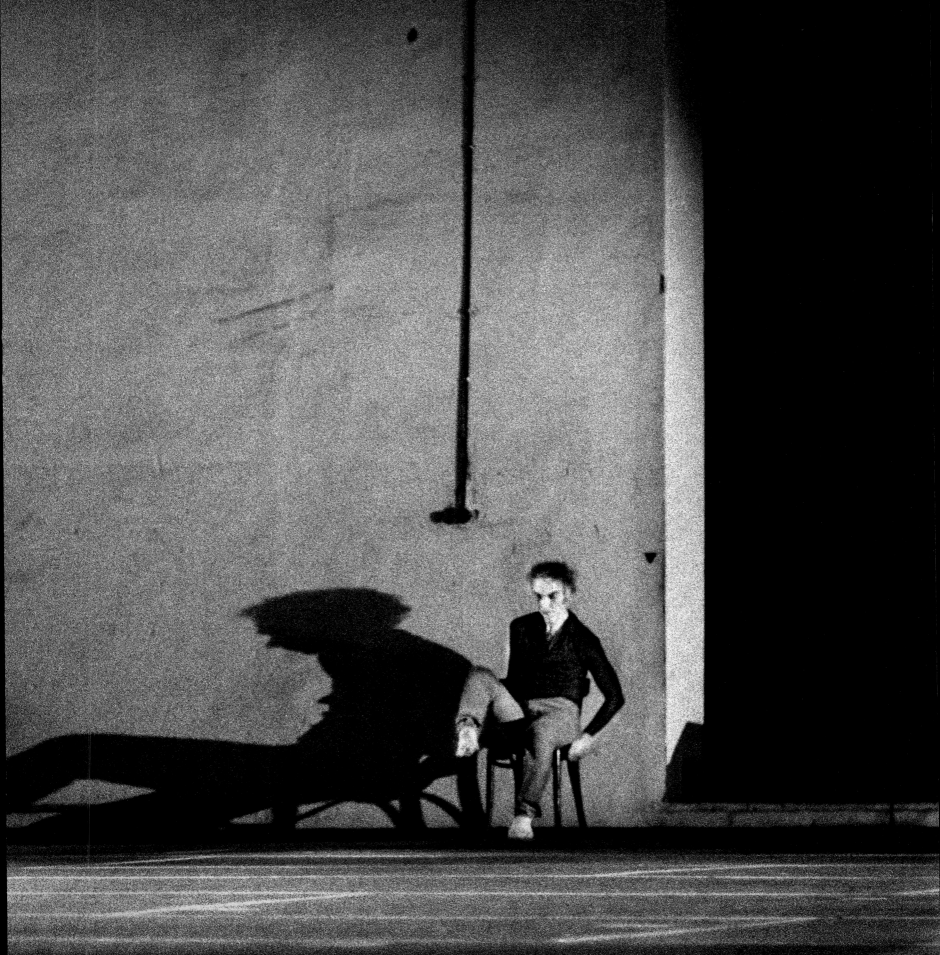

EARLE BROWN

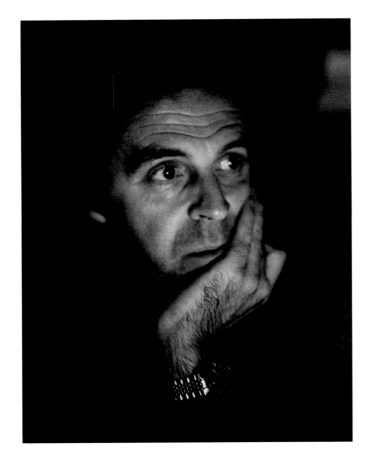

Earle Brown, Saint Paul de Vence, 1970

Merce: My first memory of Merce is seeing his eyes follow Carol in diagonals across the studio floor of Jane McLean's loft in Denver . . . Merce and John were working their way across the country with master classes and the *Sonatas and Interludes*. Personally startled and amazed by the incredible amount of sound and energy Merce generated in the class using only finger snapping, thigh slaps, ªnd hand clapping, embellished by insistent and sonorous vocal counts. We really knew very little about either Merce or John (in 1951 . . . I think) except that Jane McLean's pianist had recently returned from New York saying that he had heard and seen Cage (and/or his music) and that he was completely off his rocker. . . .

The only work that I wrote specifically for Merce was *Indices*, for chamber orchestra, completed in December of 1954. The dance was called *Springweather and People*, first performed in May 1955 with costumes by Remy Charlip with the artistic collaboration of Robert Rauschenberg, Ray Johnson, and Vera Williams.

Somewhere in the spring of 1954 I began sketching some thoughts about a work for chamber orchestra that was to be generated ("constructed") by a book of ten thousand random numbers, called *Random Sampling Tables*. Although I had never been (personally) particularly interested in "chance" as Cage used it, my interest in the random tables was probably influenced by that way of working. But more than anything, the *Indices* idea was very close to the Schillinger concepts of ratios, densities, statistical distribution, rather than to the pure (or impure), "uninfluenced" CHANCE activities of Cage. . . . While sketching, it occurred to John and Merce and me this could be a commission from Merce that would be in payment for all of Carol's lessons with Merce before she became a member of his company. Carol was by this time a member, but we still (technically) owed for the past. Given that Merce had no money to pay for my score and we had no money to pay for the classes, it was "good thinking" all the way around.

It took me two or three months just to set up the "program" (in the computer sense) for *Indices*, and about eight months to carry it out. It is called *Indices* because that is what the two points on the abcissa and ordinate, the intersection of perpendicular horizontal and vertical lines drawn from the two points, are called. The *Indices* "program" was intricate and terribly complex in all dimensions. The piece was not written from left to right (start to finish) but the "program" (of composing) was such that each sound was a completely self-contained "Event," each being able to appear anywhere within the twenty-nine-minute duration of the work as the program produced it . . . subject to the structural "stress" conditions. (There were 175 pages of ruled score paper, which equalled twenty-nine-minutes at mm. 120. According to "program" the first sound composed might have entered on page 107; the second sound might have entered on page 22; the third on page 136, etc.) It was a discontinuous process of composing the material and obviously the piece was not "finished" when I reached the "end" of it but when it became sufficiently "saturated" (event-full).

Merce worked on the choreography and, as he did then and perhaps still does, made a time structure for the dance. Merce and John's idea of music and dance "coexisting in time" rather than being dependent of one another is well known. While I never considered that that was the only interesting relationship for two or more events to be in (or thought of it as a revolutionary cause), it was perfectly compatible with my thoughts about the collaboration. I remember getting a copy of Merce's time structure, but by that time I had already programmed my own structure for the music, and they (quite expectably) did not coincide. Apart from agreeing on the total time duration of our pieces we made no attempt to synchronize the structural sections, because dependent relationships or "Mickey Mousing" between music and movement were equally abhorrent to both of us.

Springweather and People was performed for two years with a piano reduction. The piano reduction was no transcription but a literal reduction of the score. It was extremely difficult for Tudor to play, in that there were long accumulations of notes of long duration all over the keyboard (orchestra) and he had to use all of the pedals and handheld notes at a furious rate. The use of pedals was constant and violent, and in one performance in California that I didn't hear, the entire pedal structure came adrift from the piano and John Cage had to lie on his back under the piano and hold it in place for most of the piece. He said it sounded pretty good from down there but it hurt his arms. An abbreviated version of *Springweather and People* was performed as a duet for Merce and Carolyn Brown in Europe in 1958, with the piano reduction.

I used to feel that Merce had at least three distinct kinds of pieces: the very strange, seemingly psychologically oriented, solo works, usually to music of Christian Wolff, such as *Lavish Escapade*; the rather severe and "abstract" works such as *Solo Suite in Space and Time*; and the "romantic-classic" kind of piece, which always seemed to be about something, but one could never quite grasp what it actually was. *Springweather* was distinctly the latter type. It was very elegant and beautiful and "classic" in feeling. The coexisting of sound and movement left long, still sections of the dance "accompanied" by furious orchestral sound and great complex dance groupings "accompanied" by simple and/or long quiet sound colors. I like the whole thing *very* much.

I remember being at a Merce rehearsal once and he handed me a stopwatch and asked me to time the run-through, saying that it was supposed to finish in fifteen minutes. He counted out loud sometimes, and thigh-thumped and handclapped, but not often. Neither Merce nor the dancers had any reference to a clock or to music; only their own interior time and their remembered relationships to one another and the space. I stopped the watch at the the end of the dance, and it read fourteen minutes and fifty seconds. Perhaps it is a normal thing for dancers to do, but it absolutely astonished me that they could be only ten seconds off over a fifteen minute span of time. It must have been 1953 or 1954 because I was working on *Music for Cello and Piano* and looking for some confirmation that I could do away with clock time and metric notation and still have a flexible but highly controlled "togetherness" between the two instruments. What I expected and hoped for was what I called a "time sense," which would develop in each part and between parts as the musicians rehearsed and became familiar with the music. (There is a clock time reference in the score, but the piece is not to be done "to the clock" in performance.) It was "time sense," "event sense," "muscle memory," or something, but I could see that it *did* develop and work for dancers and, as I felt, gave a much better feeling than counting or reading or clock watching. I wanted, as in the dance, for the impulse to arise from instinct and intuition *in relation* to "composed" events, rather than from an exterior, imposed pulse. The resulting notation I called "time notation," and it is now generally called "proportional notation" and used (in one way or another) by nearly every "new music" composer. I had used it since 1952 in solo works, but Merce's "lesson" confirmed that it could work with larger groups without everything falling apart (or being overly and *mechanically* together).

I think that Merce's *Galaxy*, to my *Four Systems* (1954), was his first truly "open form" dance. (There was something "variable" in his *Dime a Dance* but not really in this way.) It was a very severe and "classic" dance and very difficult to do, and perhaps to watch, Merce made *Galaxy* in 1956, and I always wondered why he had not tried the open form thing before. During and after *Galaxy* he was always a little worried about it. He said (in effect) that while the four systems and their sound-events could be sequenced, juxtaposed, and combined in any way, and sound collisions were what it was all about and not dangerous (except to a sensibility now and then), four dancers careening around a limited space, doing their own things in unknown relation to the other three, created a distinct threat to his nerves and to their lives and limbs. The "kamikaze" image and its dubious esthetic charm was pretty clear. I think that Merce later made other "open form" pieces (*Field Dances*, *Story*, *Canfield*), but not with the classic virtuoso density and pace of *Galaxy*. If you choreograph enough time and space and flexibility to allow looking and avoiding tactics, I guess it can be done, but *Galaxy* wasn't like that, as I remember.

I think that *December 1952*, from *Folio* (the score that was farthest-out graphically of that set) was the only other music of mine that Merce used with his choreography. It was a solo for Carol made in 1960 for a European tour that he, Cage, Tudor, and Carol made that year. I saw it for the first time in Venice, at the Fenice. The title was an entire poem of M. C. Richards; "Hands Birds," and the poem, the dance, and the dancing were extraordinarily beautiful. Sadly, the dance was never performed in the U.S. The score is a single page or "field," with horizontal and vertical lines of various thicknesses, indicating only vague suggestions of relative frequency, duration, and loudness; any sounds may be used by any number of performers. In this case it was performed by Cage and Tudor on (and in) two pianos. It is the most ambiguous, "free," improvisational piece that I have ever written. It always intrigued me that John's "realization" sounded very much like his own music and David's sounded very much like my fully composed music at the time, but beautiful and a pleasure to listen to.

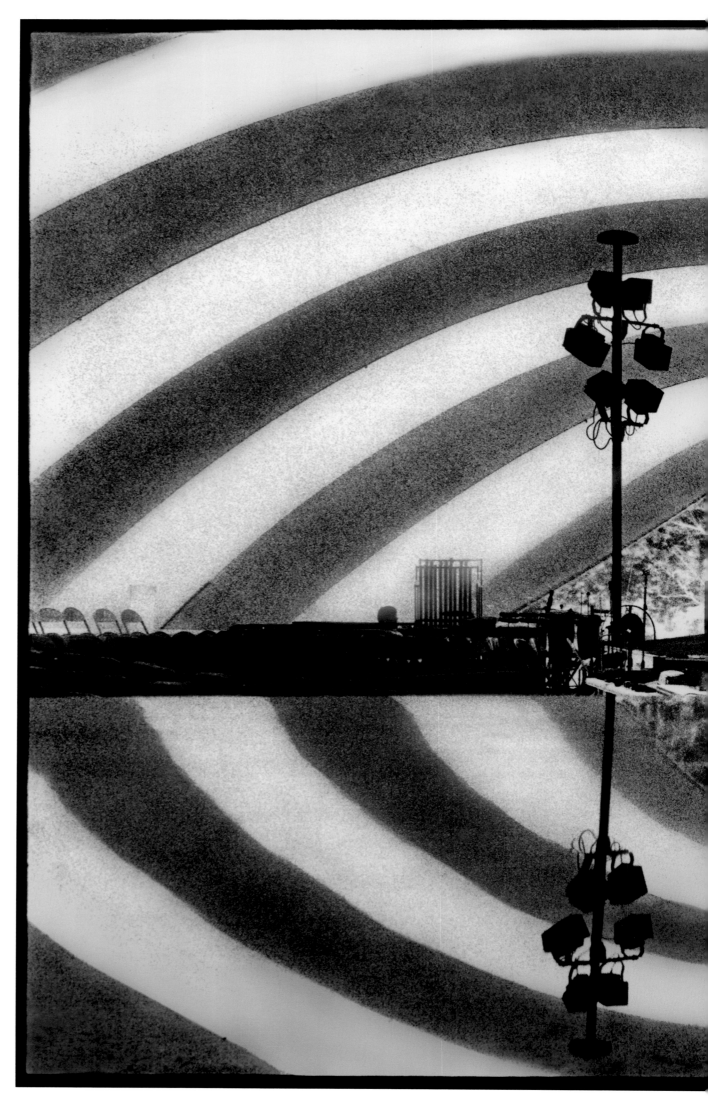

Rehearsal, Théâtre Experimental
(inflated), Fondation Maeght,
Saint-Paul de Vence, France, 1970

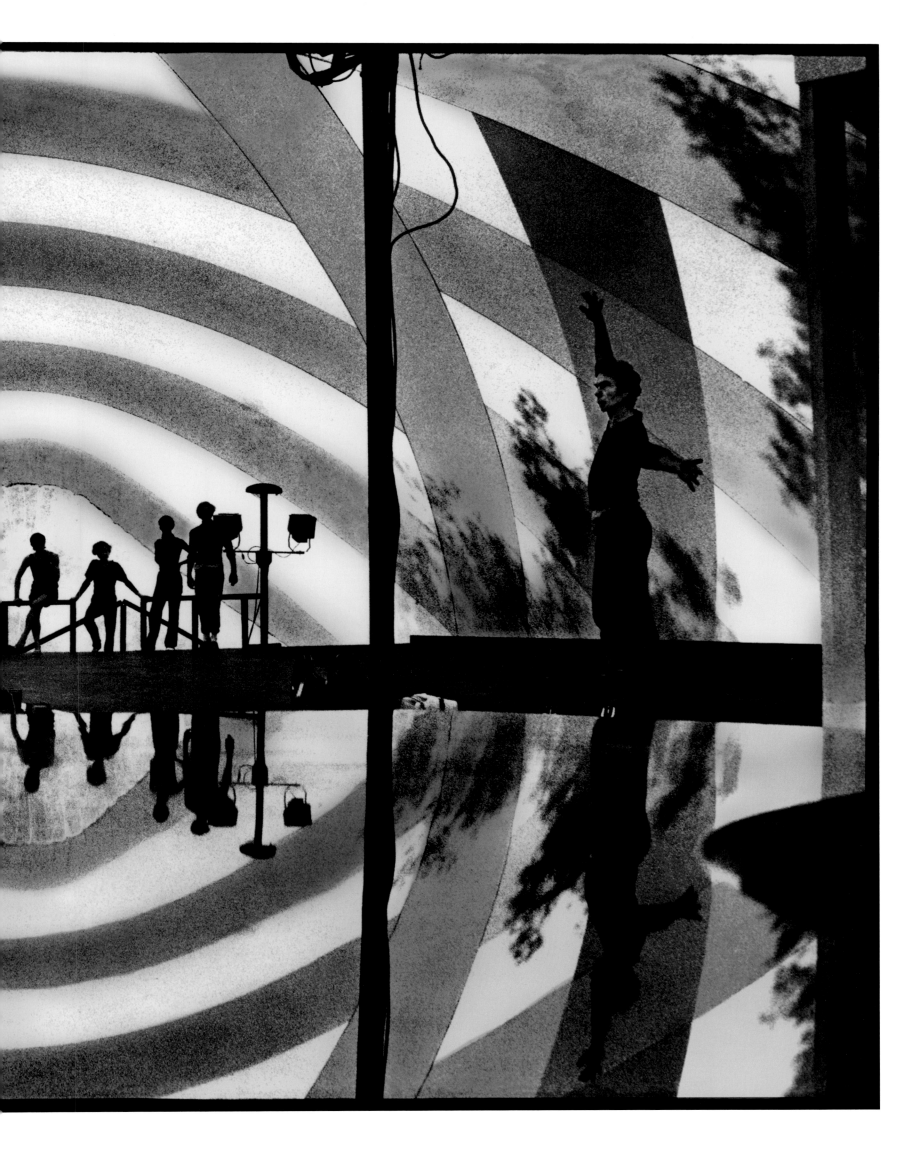

1965 HOW TO PASS, KICK, FALL AND RUN

MUSIC
JOHN CAGE, DRINKING CHAMPAGNE, READING FROM
SILENCE, A YEAR FROM MONDAY, ETC.
JOINED BY DAVID VAUGHAN FOR DUAL READING ON OCCASION.

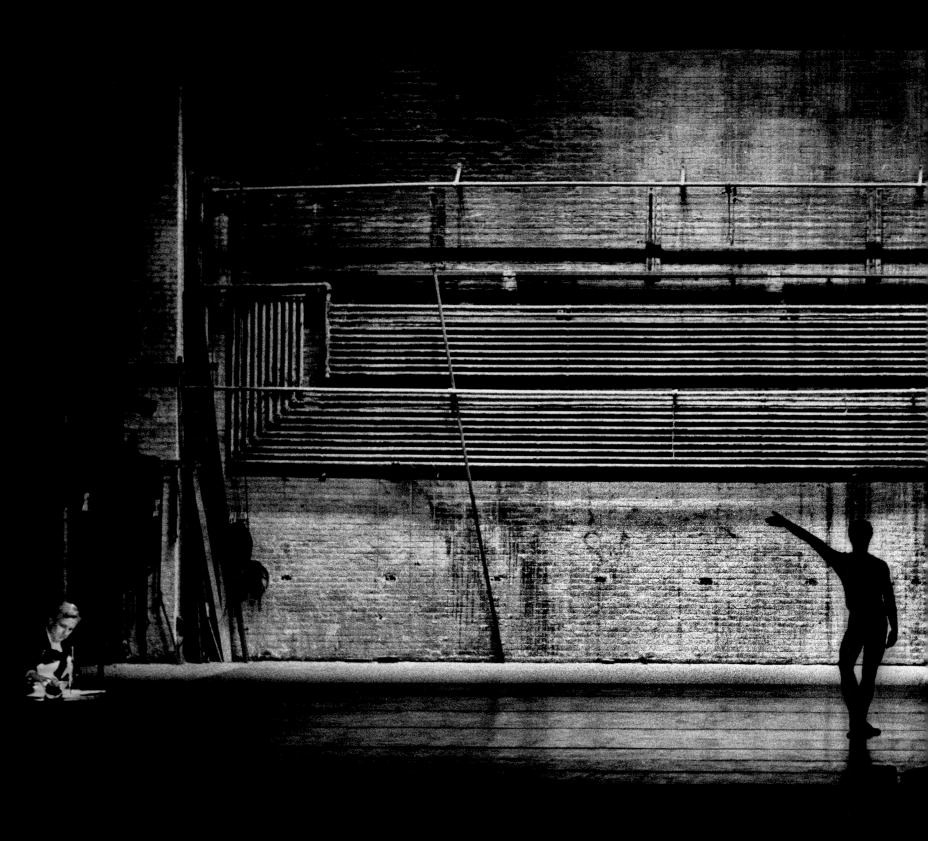

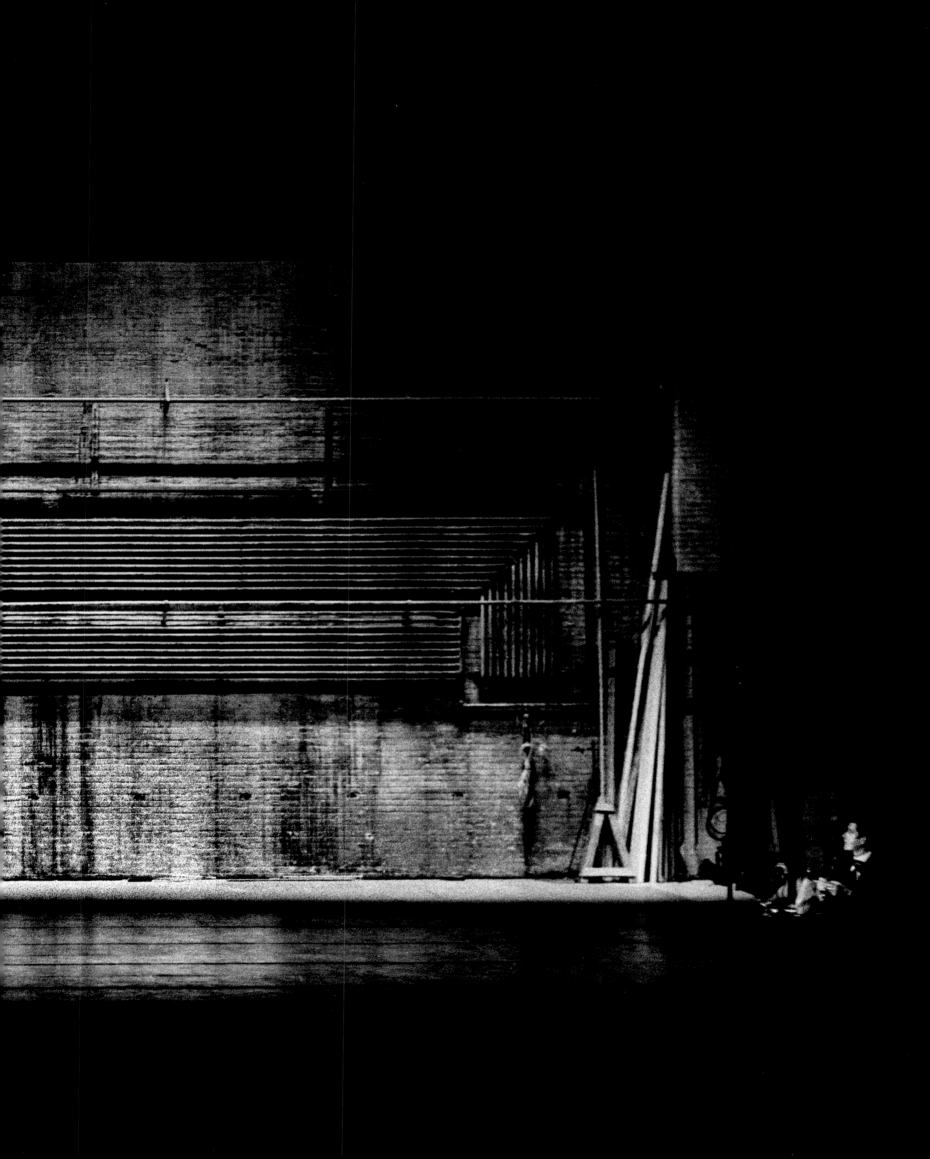

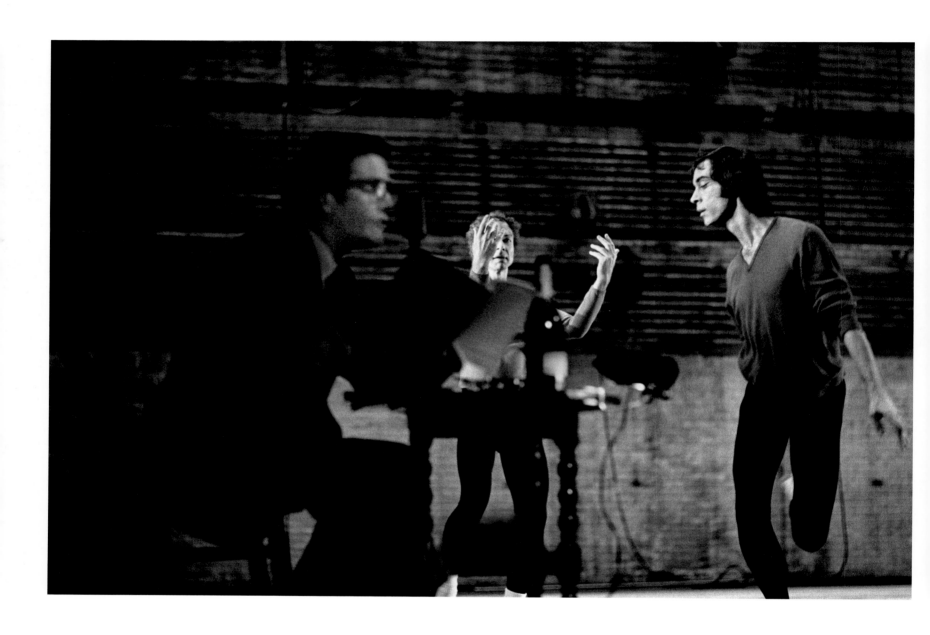

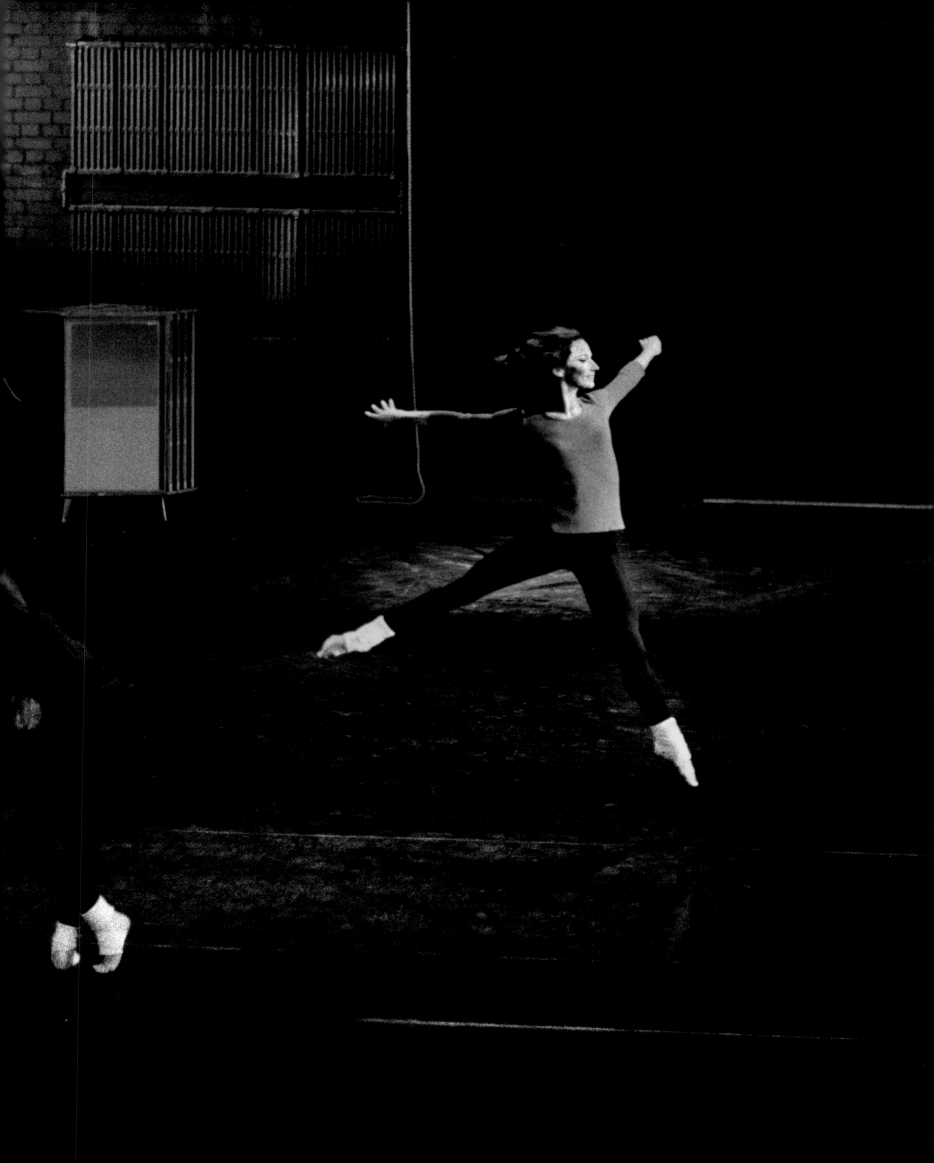

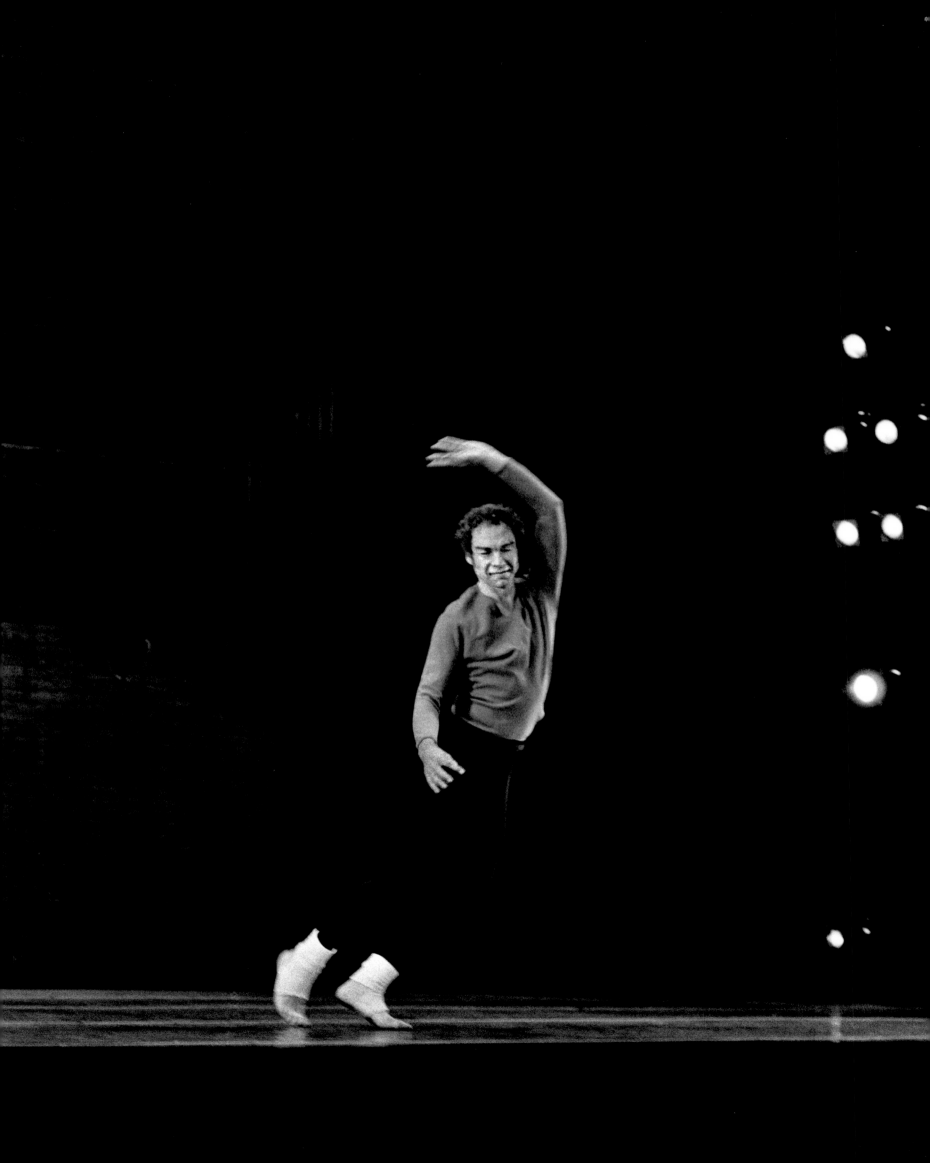

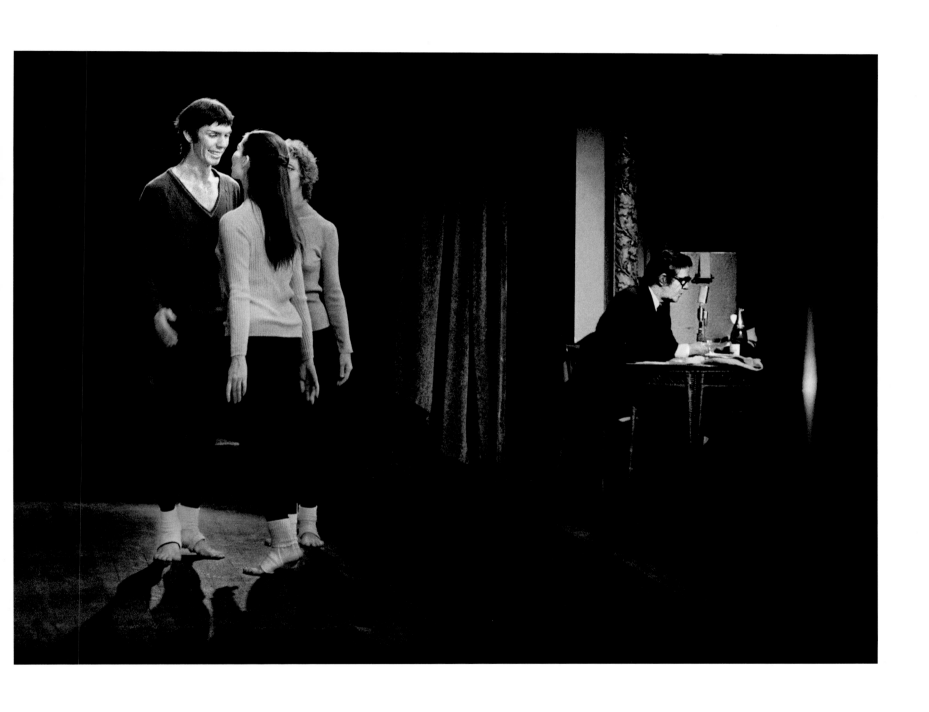

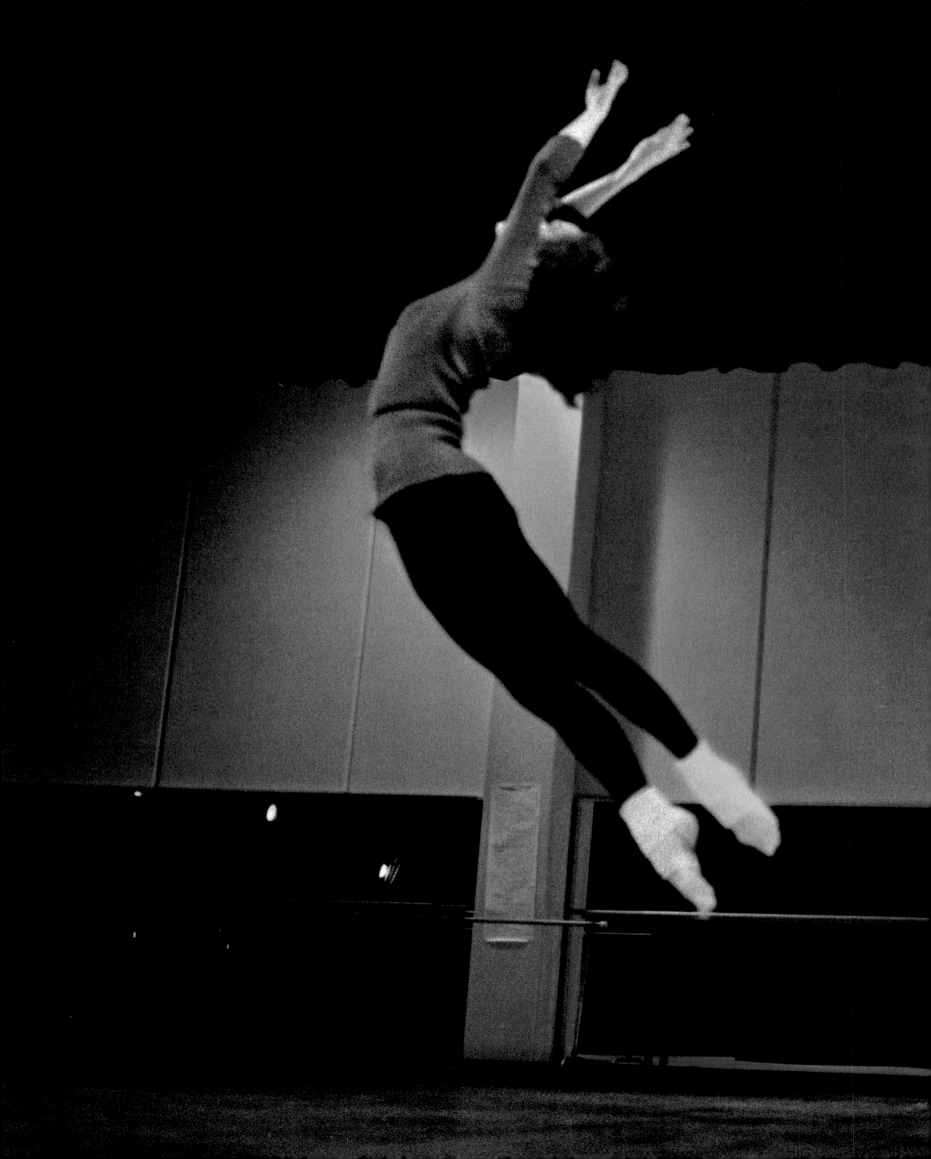

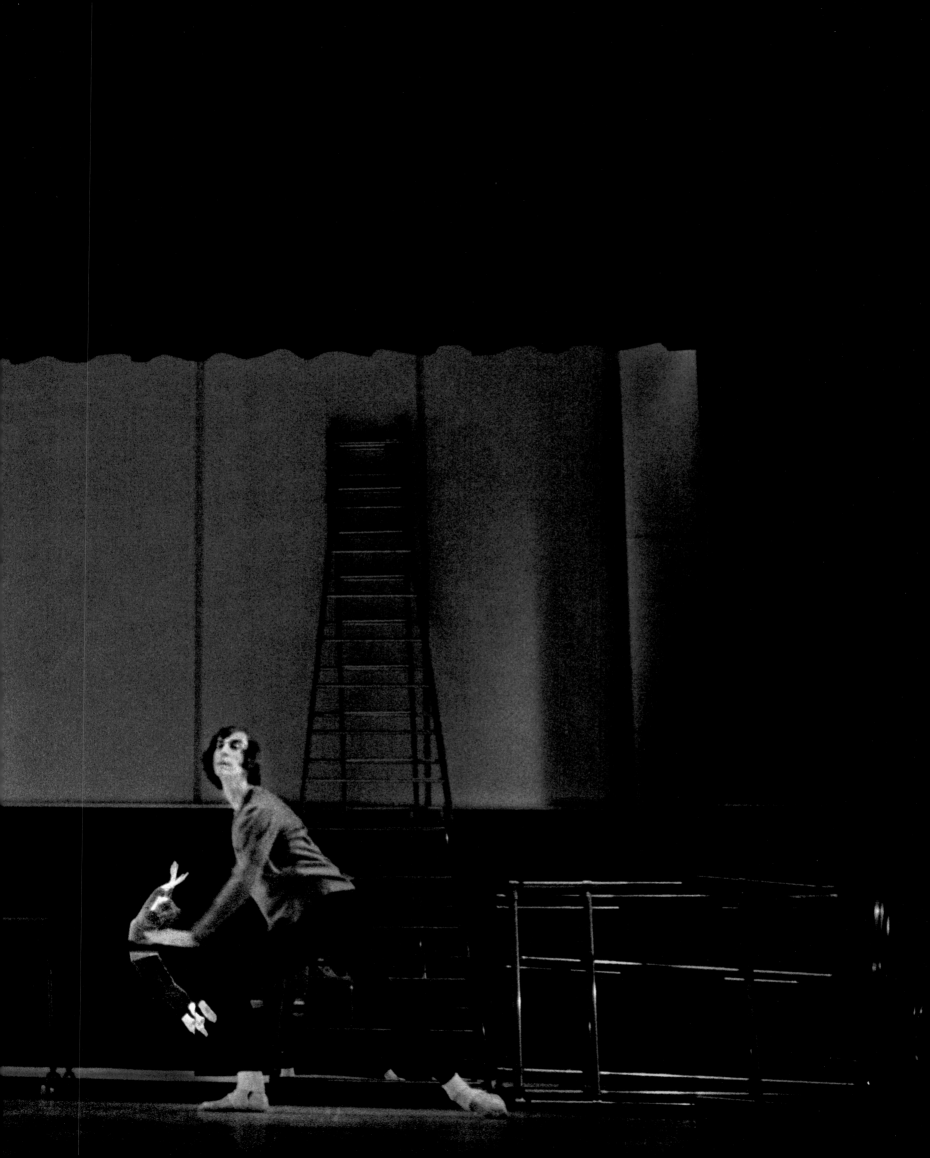

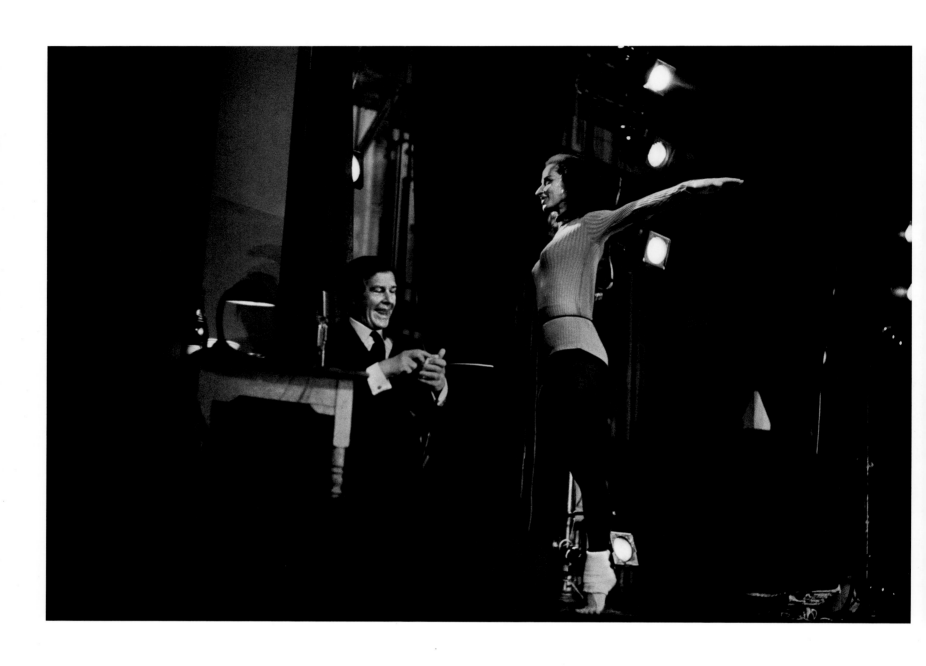

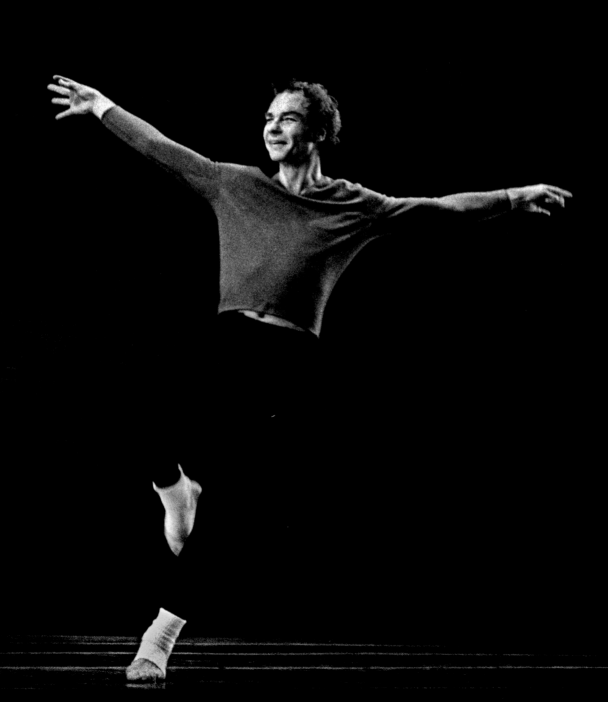

YVONNE RAINER

—This Is The Story of a Man Who . . .

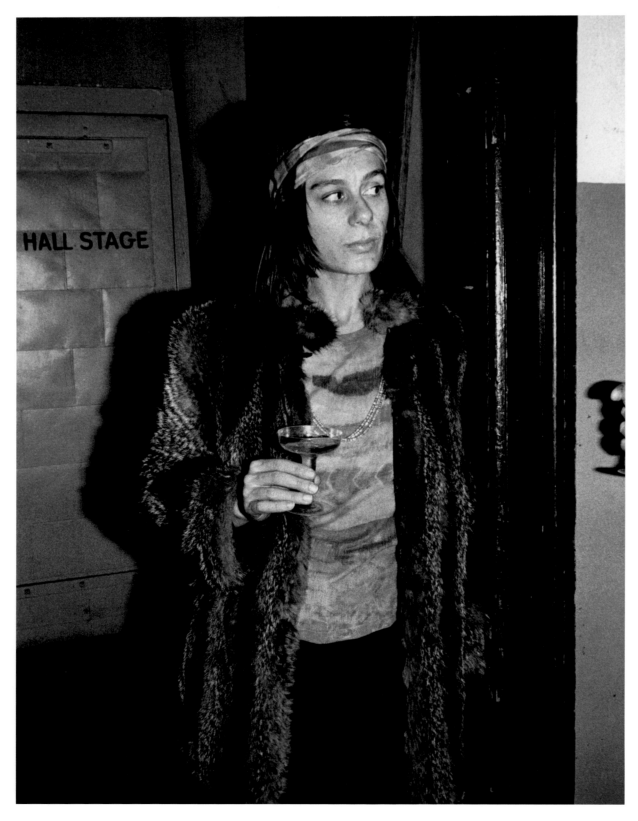

Yvonne Rainer, backstage at BAM, circa 1970

She pondered the problem of writing about him for a long time. She thought about it in several ways. What had she to say? If she were he, what would she like to read? She might find the whole enterprise somewhat unsettling. Milestones are nothing if not loadstones. What would he like to hear about from her? What could be a gift of inspiration equivalent to what he had given her? She had been at the Graham school for a year knowing that she would end up at his place, which had just opened up above the Living Theater on 14th Street and Sixth Avenue. She had heard funny stories about that Cage coterie, but she trusted that she would be no more taken in by all that than she had by all that Graham stuff. She would get what she needed and split. She can't remember her first class with him, but the first impressions he left with her remain:

1. At a big loft party somewhere he was standing with Carolyn Brown. She went over to him and said she couldn't study with him yet because she was still busy with Graham, but it was only a matter of time—or something like that. This sly smile came over his face. If she knew that he had danced with Graham she certainly wasn't thinking about it then; in fact she didn't give that sly smile a second thought. Now, of course, she can attribute all sorts of things to it—like, "The old bag is still raking them in." Or, "racking them up." She now is remembering that her first classes with him were so quiet. *He* was so quiet and unemphatic. He just danced, and when he talked it was with a quiet earnestness that both soothed and exhilarated her. His physical presence—even when involved in the most elusive material—made everything seem possible. "It was truly the beginning of a Zeitgeist," she thinks. "You just *do* it, with the coordination of a pro and the non-definition of an amateur." Of course! It all comes flooding back to her: those early impressions of him dancing with that unassailable ease that made him look as though he was doing something totally ordinary. She knew that she would never dance like that. The ballet part of the shapes he chose she could only parody. But that ordinariness and pleasure were accessible to her. "No," she thinks, "she didn't know that then to articulate it like that, but she knew about 'just doing it' because she remembers saying that to her friend Nancy Meehan, and she knew there were specific things she could copy and other things she would absorb by watching and being around him." So she applied herself to learning the work part of his teaching: careful, sequential placing of different parts of the body on the floor in 4/4 time carrying the body from one side of the room to the other; sudden spurts of furious, swift movement reversing direction on a dime; long, long combinations with different parts—some slow, some fast—like the one from *Aeon* that ends with passé on half-toe and you stay there for a while. And, as Judy Dunn later remarked on that one, "And everybody did it." Stayed there for a while. Then there were the ones where one part of the body did one thing while another part did another, maybe even in a different

rhythm. This, in particular, as a way of multiplying movement detail was later to characterize some of her work. But mostly it was that mysterious ease of his—which he may even have tried to account for when he would say "down down down, get your weight down"—and now she is not really sure if he actually said that or if she *saw* it: him rooted in space, so to speak, even while in motion. She sees him in her mind's eye sailing and wheeling and dipping and realizes that it is always in the studio on 14th Street that she sees him rather than in more recent studios or in performance. That was where she saw him best.

2. The next day she takes another whack at it, and more memories surge in. He had to put up with a lot. They came and went and hung on his every word and paraded their callow opinions and innocence while he already had been doing it so much longer and knew all too clearly that the rewards would only be commensurate with the effort—that is, the reward of more work for work done. "You must love the daily work," he would say. She loved him for saying that, for that was one prospect that thrilled her about dancing—the daily involvement that filled up the body and mind with an exhaustion and completion that left little room for anything else. Beside that exhaustion, opinion paled. And beside that sense of completion, ambition had to be especially tenacious. But while absorbing the spirit of his genius she fought its letter. Her fantasies of her *Show of Shows* incorporated frenzied Bacchanalias of Cunningham Technique performed by the rankest of amateurs. Or ten dwarves and one bearded lady did the exercises-on-six. Or a contortionist performs them backward (bodywise). Etc. Sophomoric fantasies of vindication against the tyranny of his discipline, which—even as she was objecting in terms both moral and aesthetic—was moving her ever nearer to her own body-ease. Now It is almost impossible for her to separate the fused lines of his influence. She has given much thought to teaching, to the two modes of the teaching-learning process—the one that can be codified and articulated, and the one that resists such efforts yet exerts perhaps an even more powerful influence and lies somewhere in a kind of reciprocal empathy, not to be confused with equality. "Oh Christ," she thinks. "Don't get into a discourse on education now. What you were actually talking about was the fusion of your need to make a polemic out of your physical inadequacies with his technique—the fusion of that with his real effect on you." Then she visualizes herself running some years back and remembers the exhilaration and freedom and knows that she came as close as she would ever come to what she imagined he must have felt as he wheeled and dipped and glided in the studio on 14th Street. And she gives him his due for the part he played in that running.

Now she doesn't see very much of him anymore, but when she does she feels very happy.

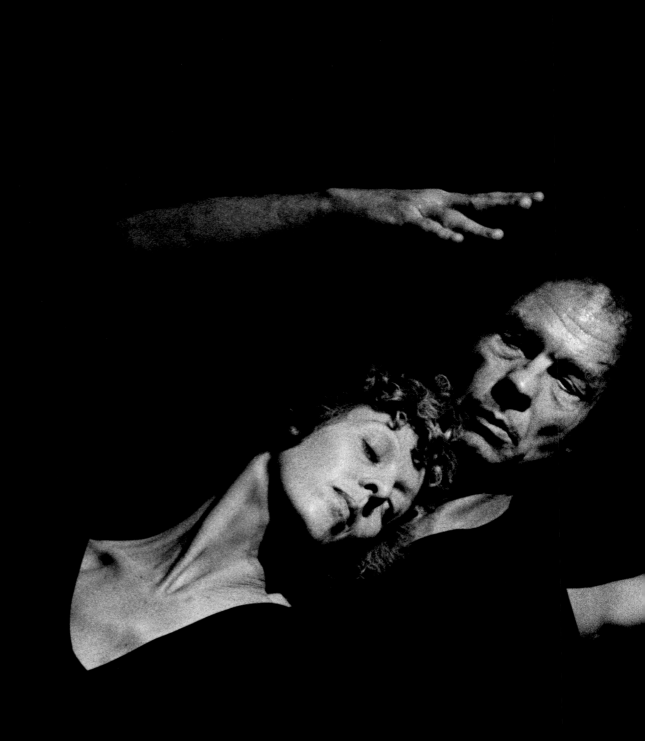

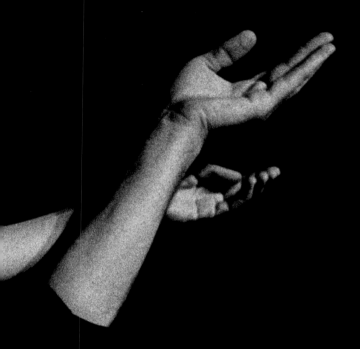

1968–1972 **REHEARSALS**

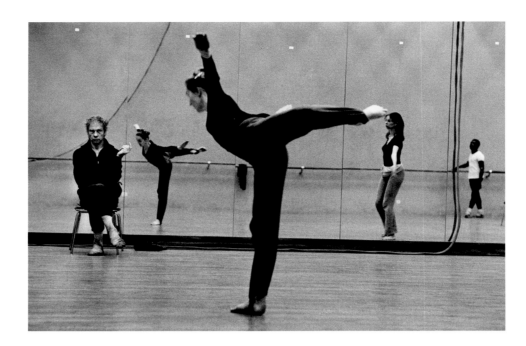

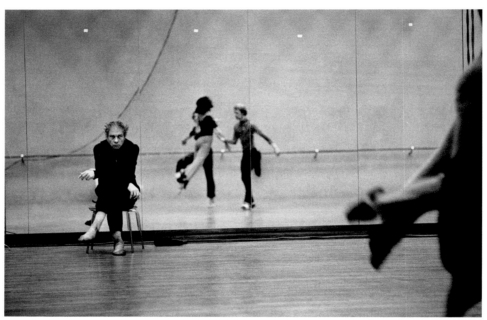

Previous spread: Valda Setterfield
and Merce Cunningham, *Second
Hand* rehearsal, Paris, 1970;
Right: Merce Cunningham,
Sandra Neels, Ulysses Dove,
Carolyn Brown, Douglas Dunn,
Valda Setterfield, and Susana
Hayman-Chaffey, *Landrover*
rehearsal, Grenoble, 1972

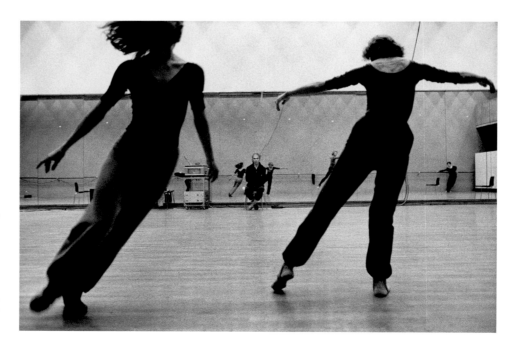

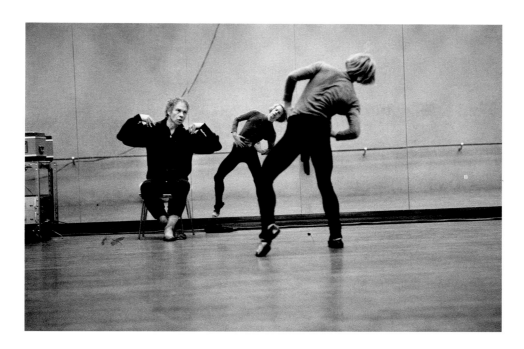

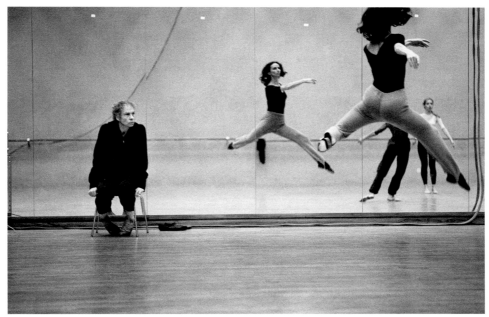

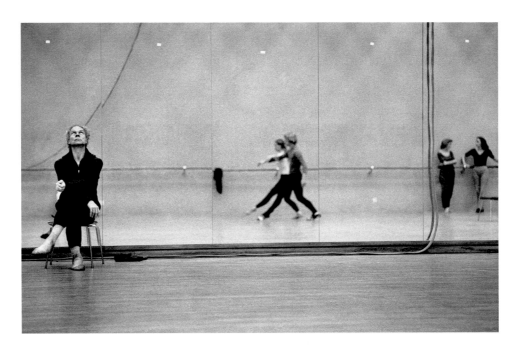

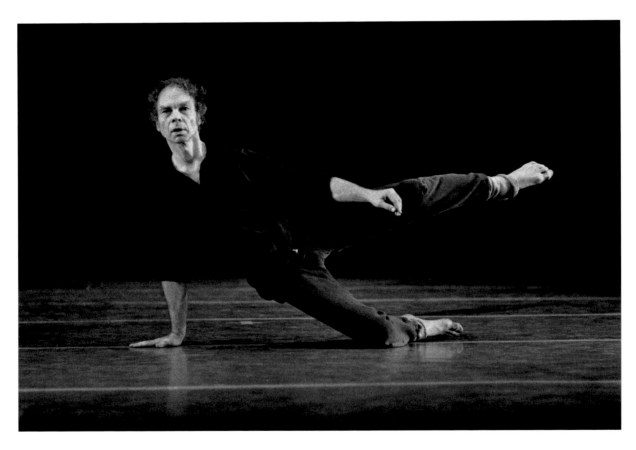

Merce Cunningham rehearsing *Borst Park*, 1972

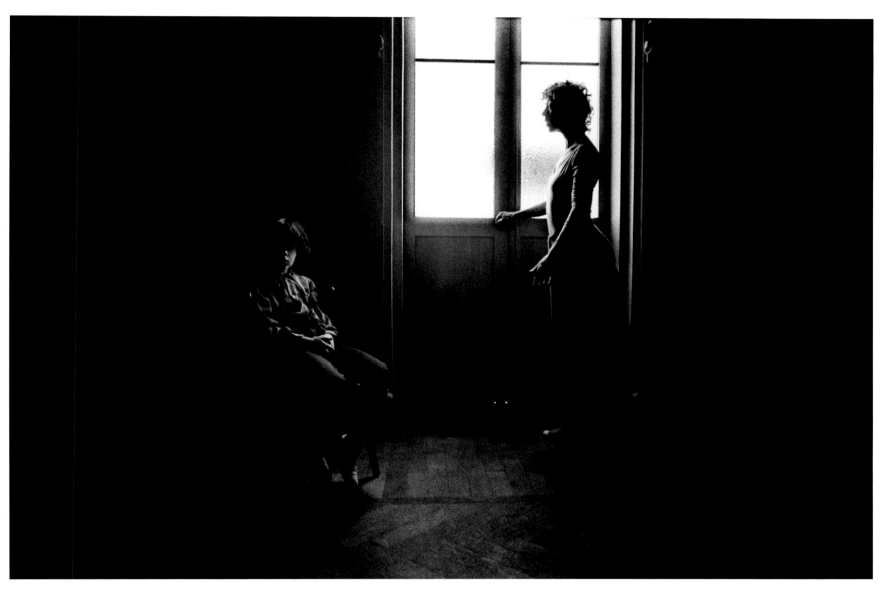

Aine Gordon and Valda Setterfield, Spoleto, Italy, 1970

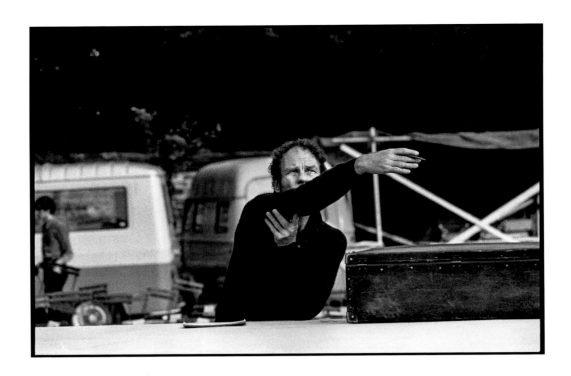

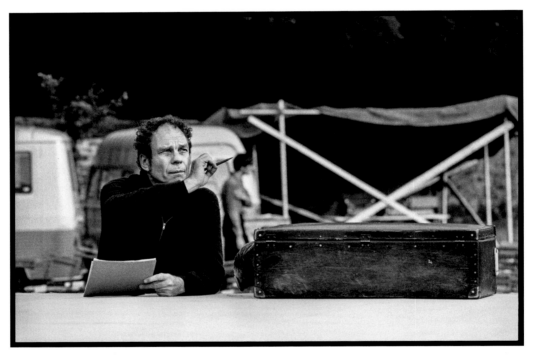

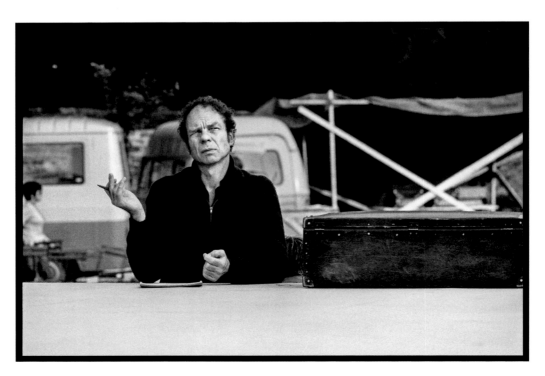

Event rehearsal, Théâtre Experimental,
Fondation Maeght (which had
collapsed due to high winds),
Saint Paul de Vence, 1970

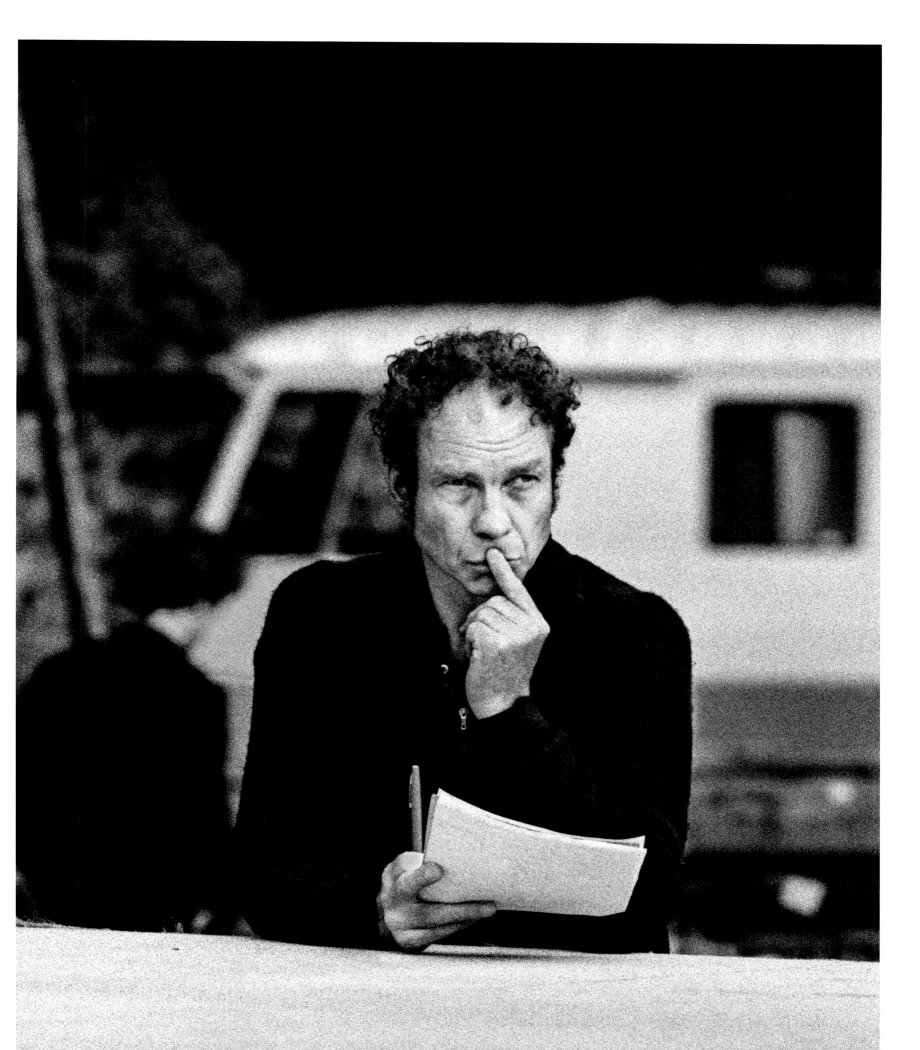

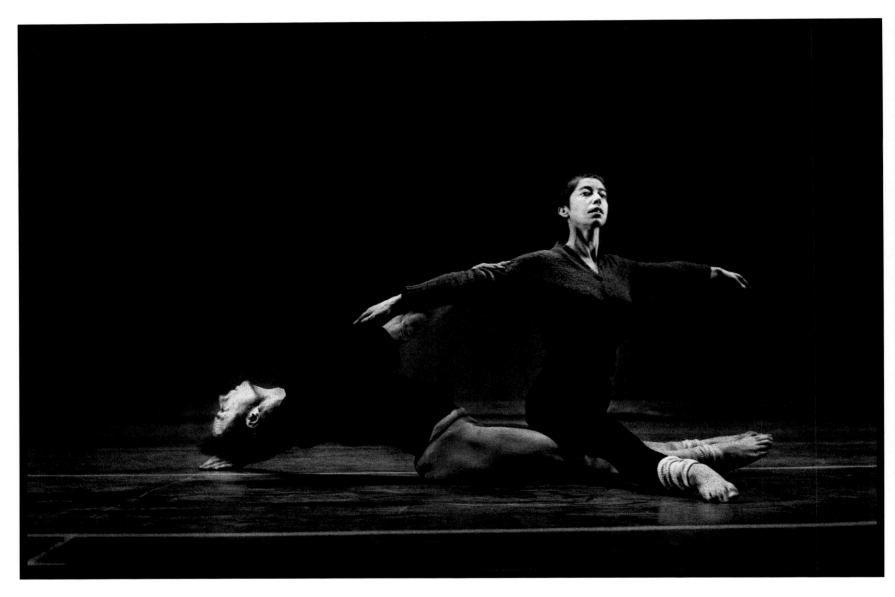

Above: Merce Cunningham and Viola Farber, *Crises* rehearsal, BAM, 1970;

Opposite page: Merce Cunningham and Carolyn Brown, *Crises* rehearsal, BAM, 1970

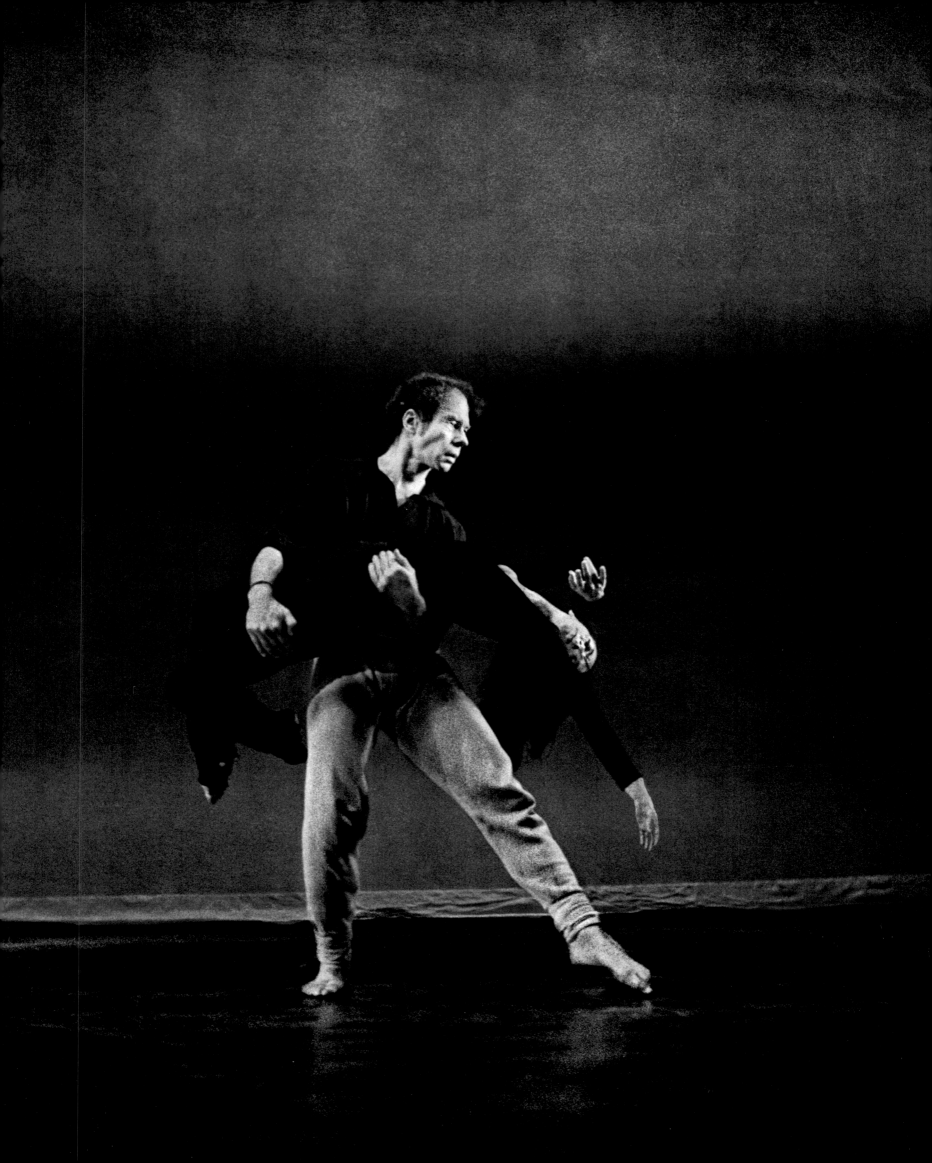

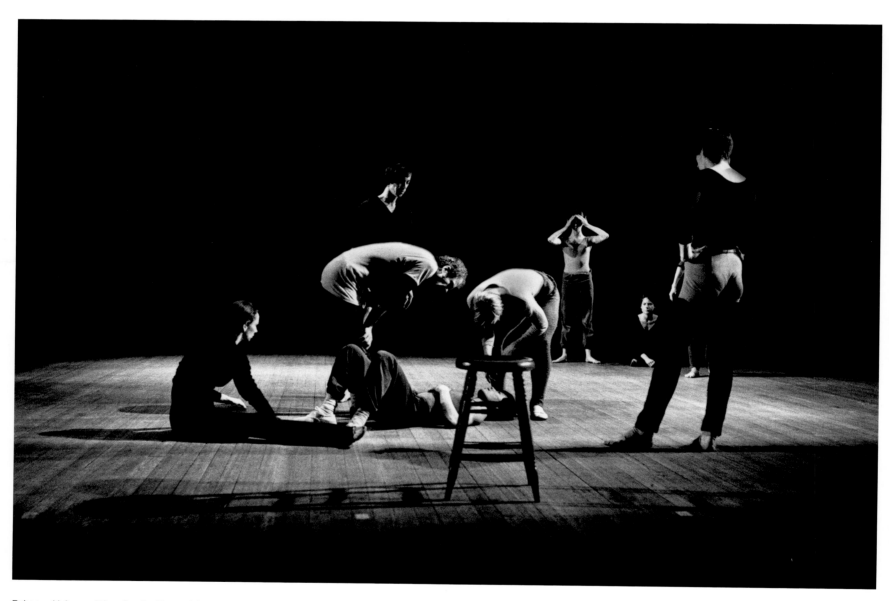

Rehearsal injury—sitting, Carolyn Brown; lying, Mel Wong; bending over him, Merce Cunningham and Douglas Dunn;
looking on, Chase Robinson, Sandra Neels, Meg Harper, and Jeff Slayton

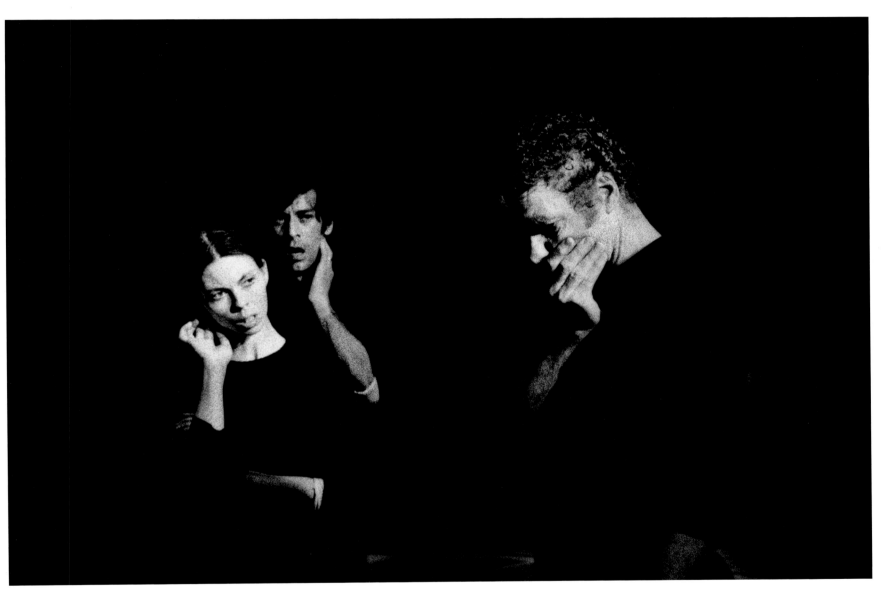

Rehearsal communications—Sandra Neels, Chase Robinson, and Merce Cunningham

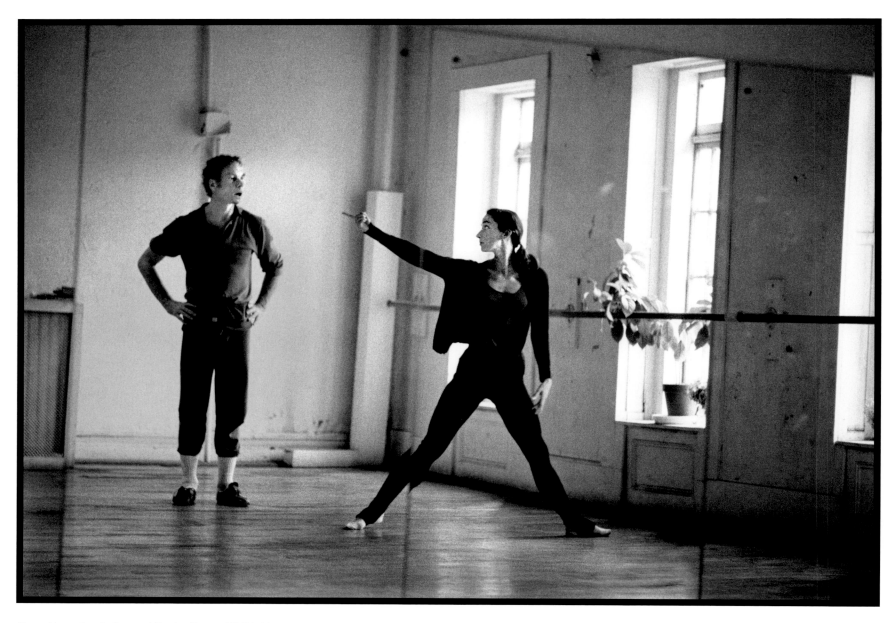

Above: Merce Cunningham and Carolyn Brown, 498 Third Avenue, a disagreement, 1969;
Right: Mel Wong, Susana Hayman-Chaffey, and Merce Cunningham, *Signals* rehearsal

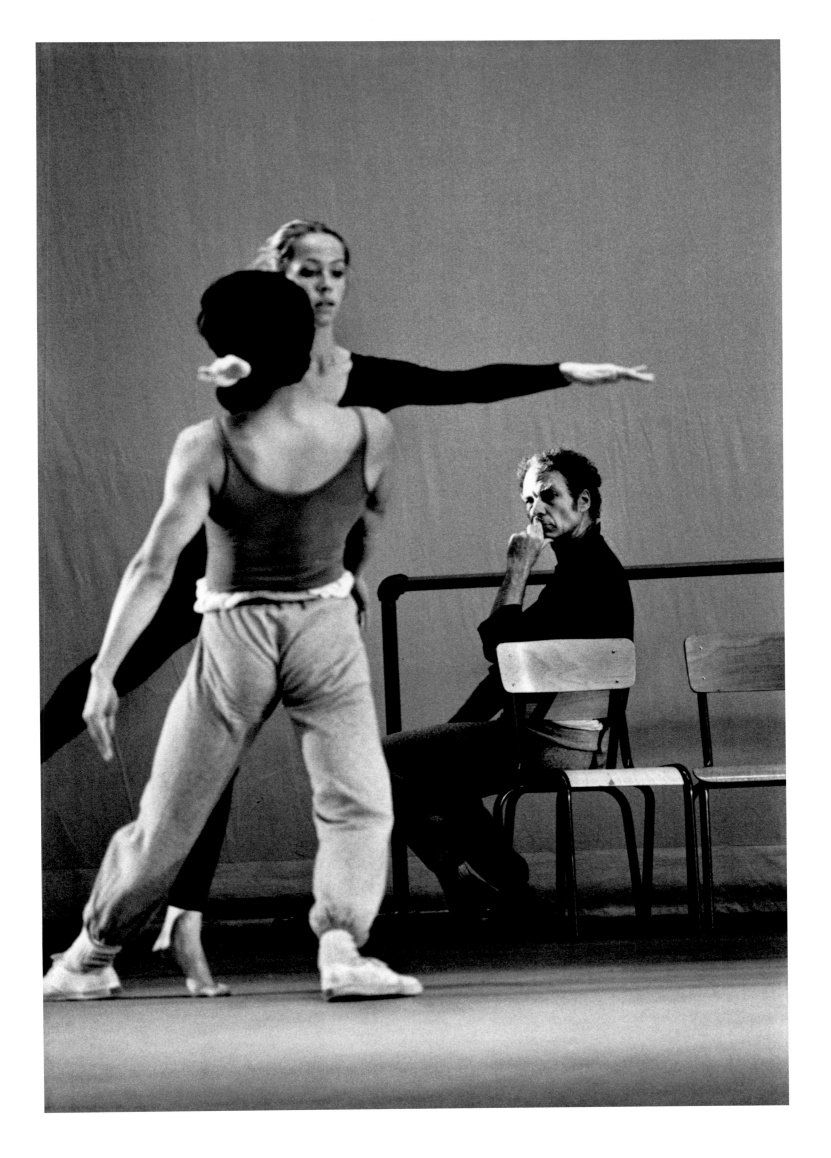

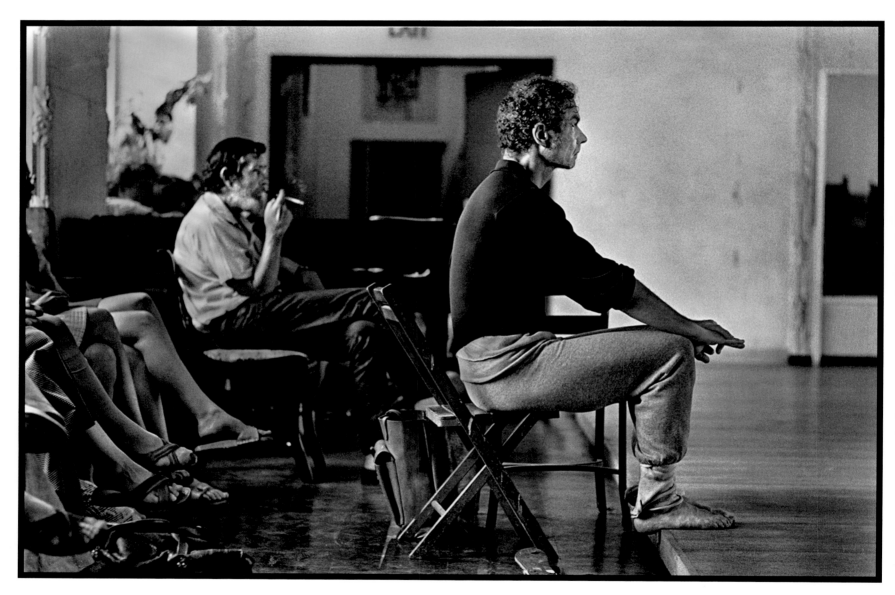

John Cage and Merce Cunningham, open rehearsal, Westbeth, June 1971

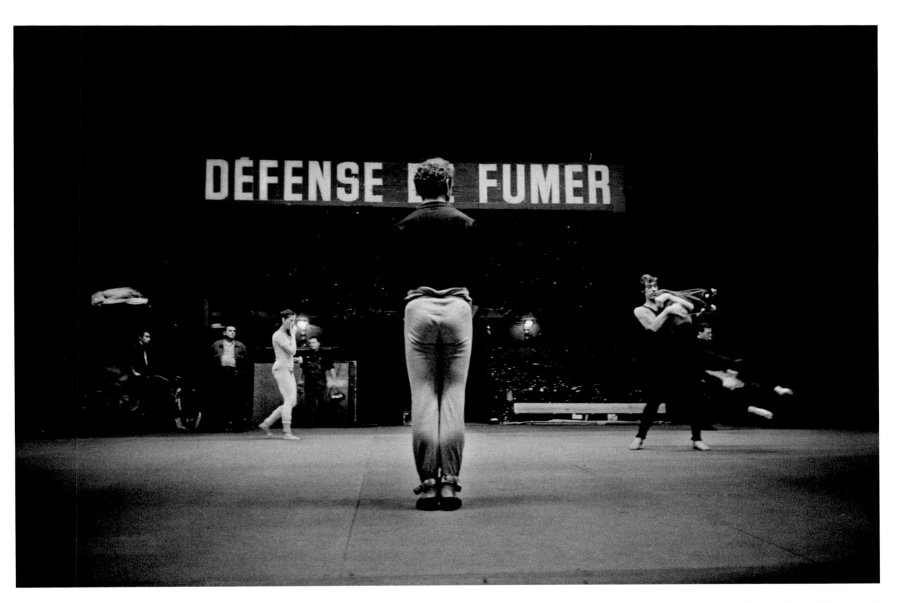

Rainforest rehearsal, Théâtre d'Odeon, 1970

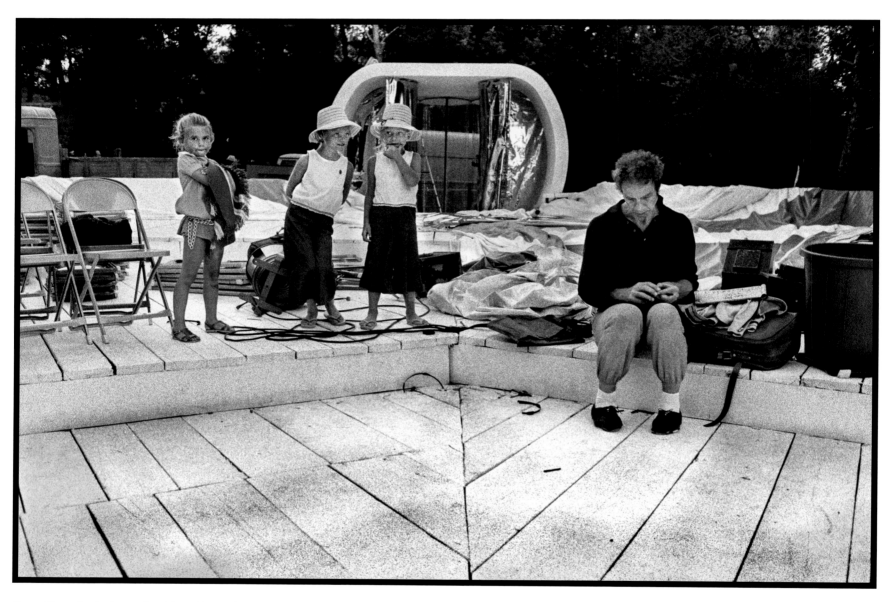

Above: Merce Cunningham and assistants, Event rehearsal in collapsed Théâtre Experimental;

Right: Spoleto, Valda Setterfield, Merce Cunningham, Douglas Dunn, and Susana Hayman-Chaffey, *Signals* rehearsal;

Following spread: Company class, Amherst, Massachusetts, 1970

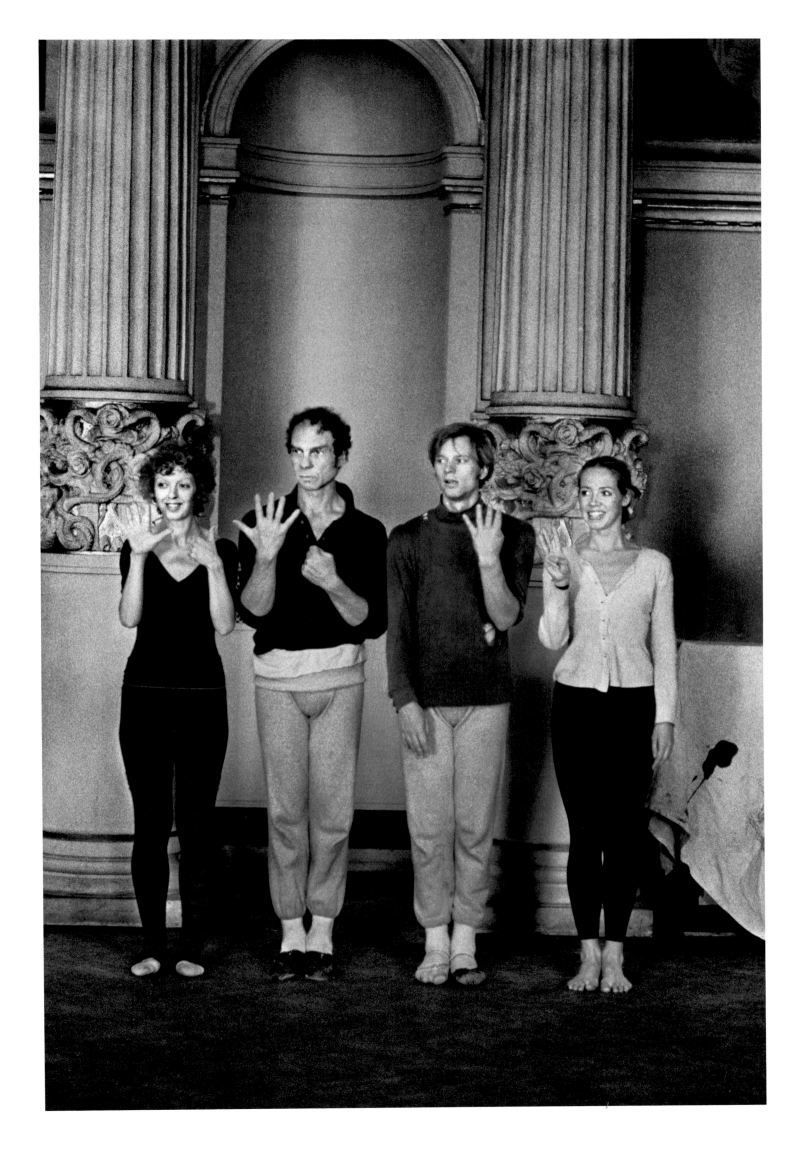

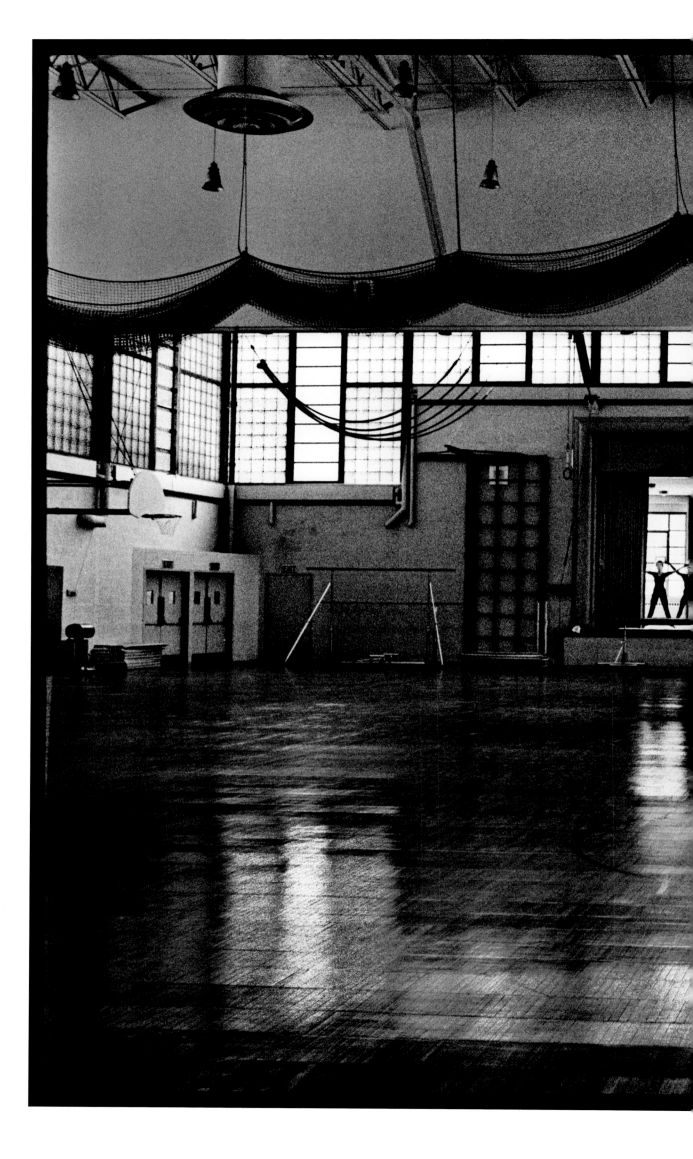

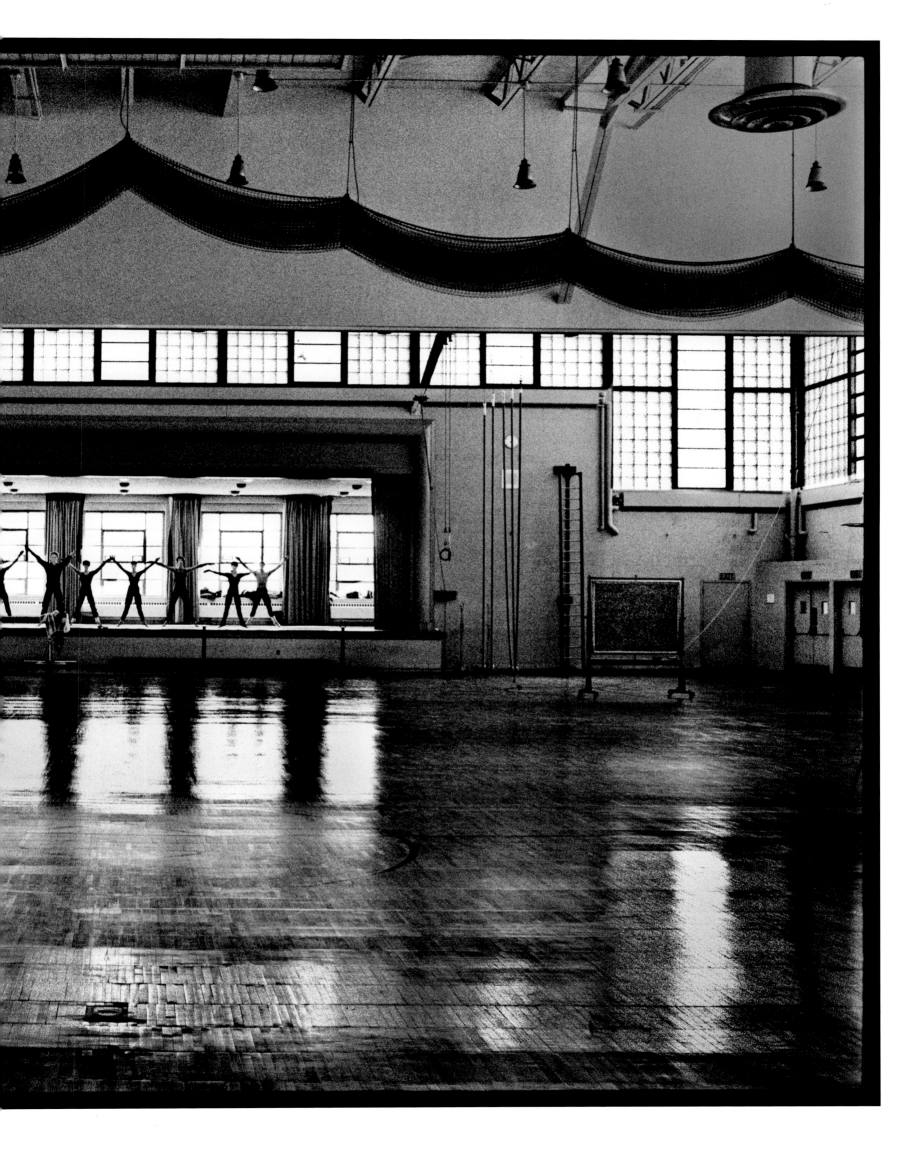

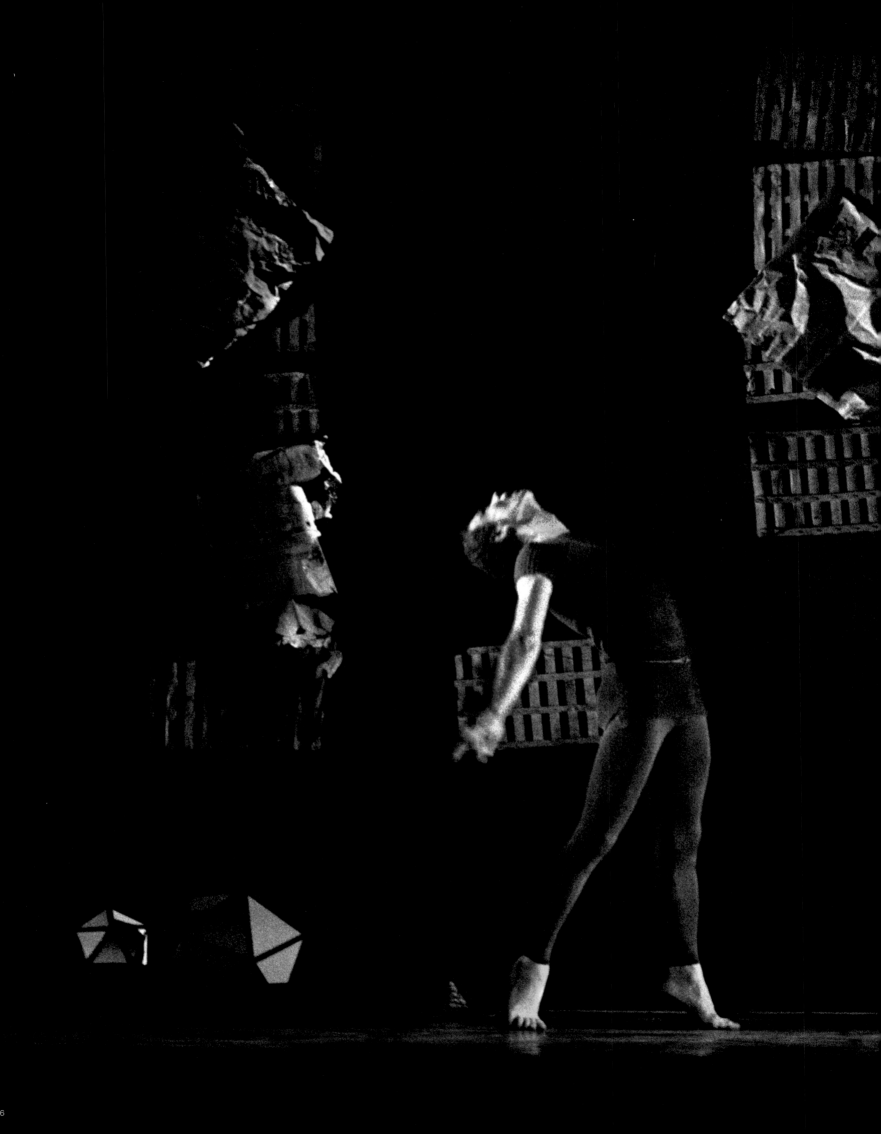

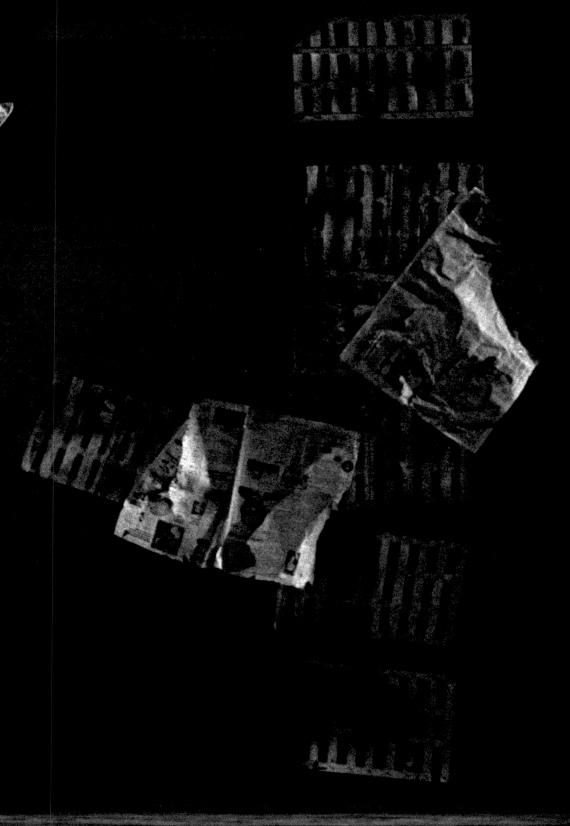

1966 **PLACE**

MUSIC
GORDON MUMMA
MESA

COSTUMES
BEVERLY EMMONS

DECOR
BEVERLY EMMONS

LIGHTING
BEVERLY EMMONS

In *Place*, as in *Second Hand*, Cunningham
inhabits a persona. But unlike *Second
Hand*, here it is one of aggrieved
alienation. *Place* is a very dark dance.
The men's manipulations of the women
are harsh. Cunningham, perpetual
outsider, approaches society warily
and with distrust. His ultimate fate,
desperately thrashing his way upstage
in a large plastic trash bag, is
profoundly chilling. Abstract, it is not.

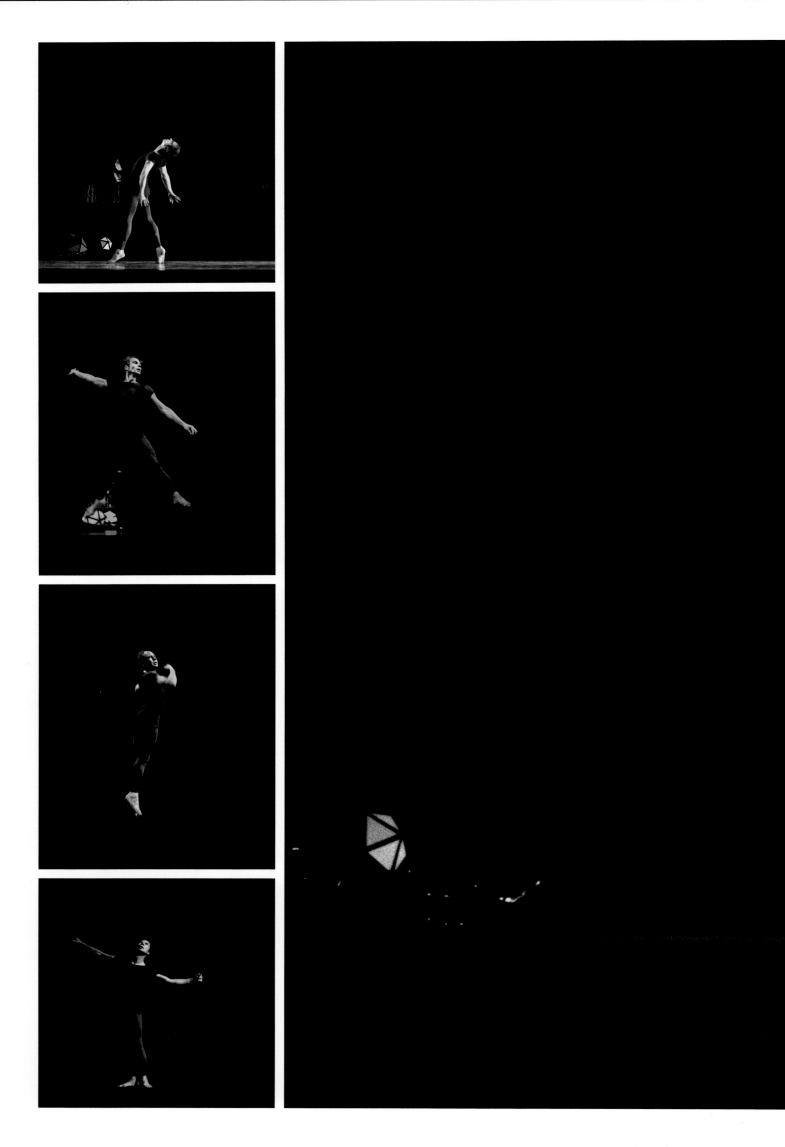

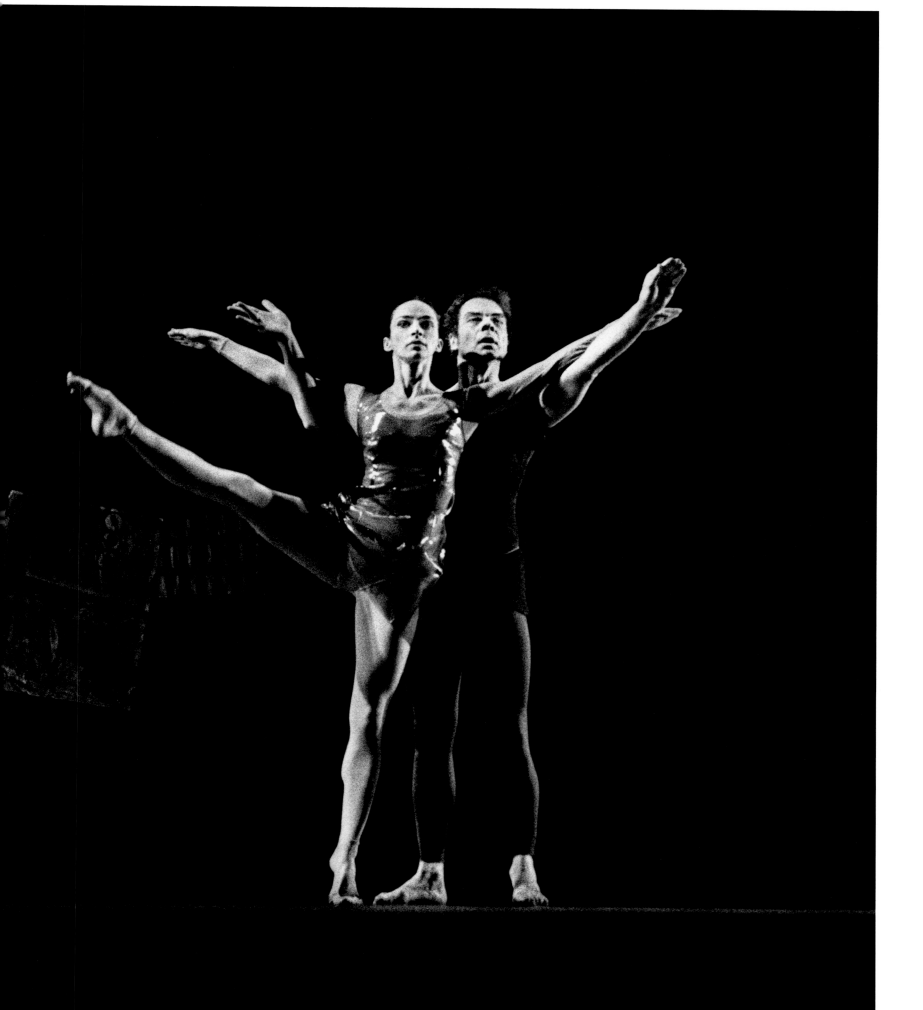

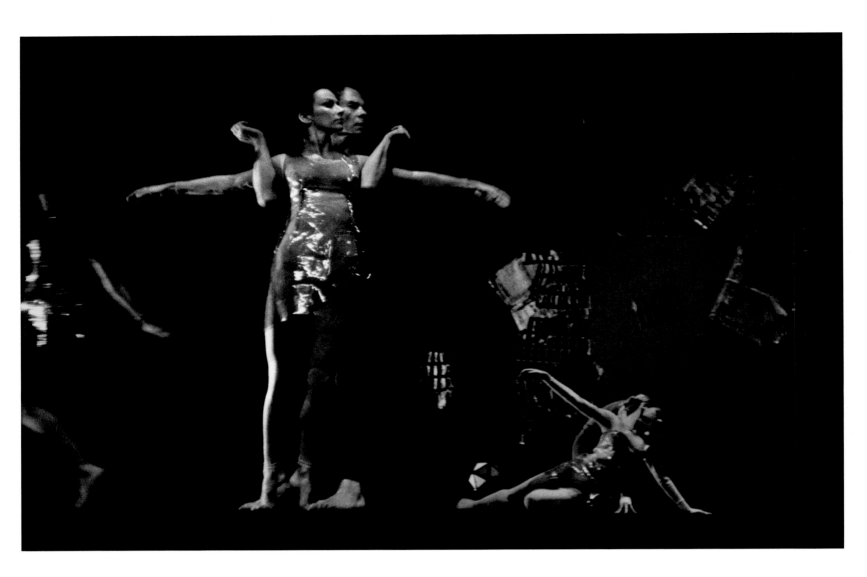

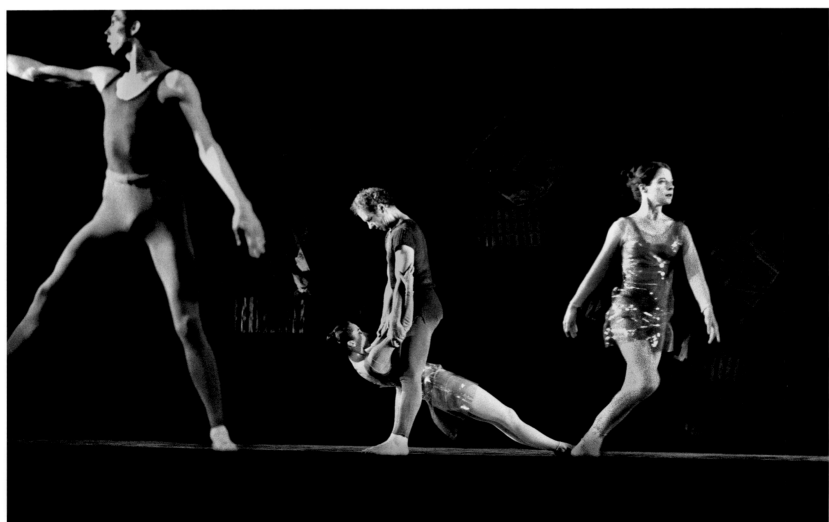

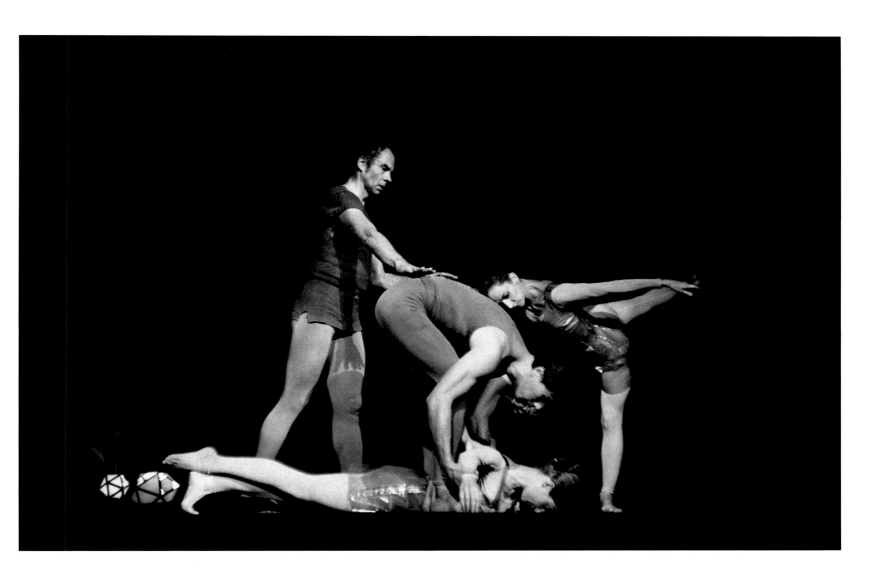

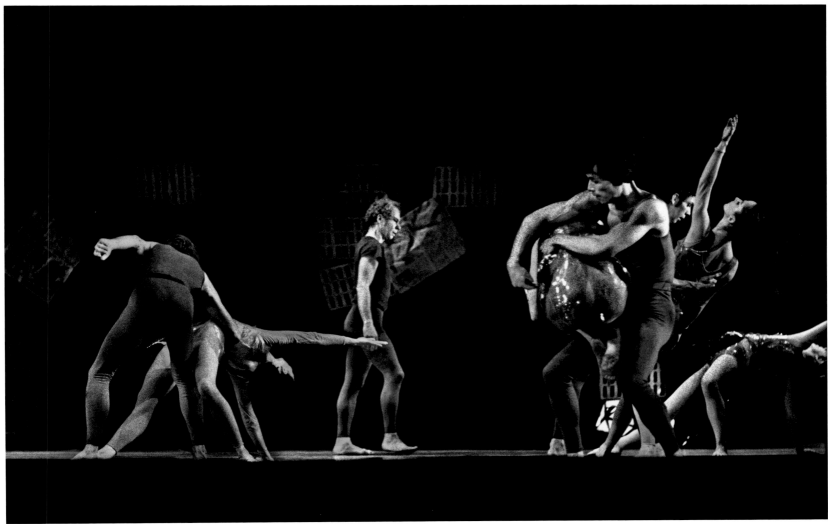

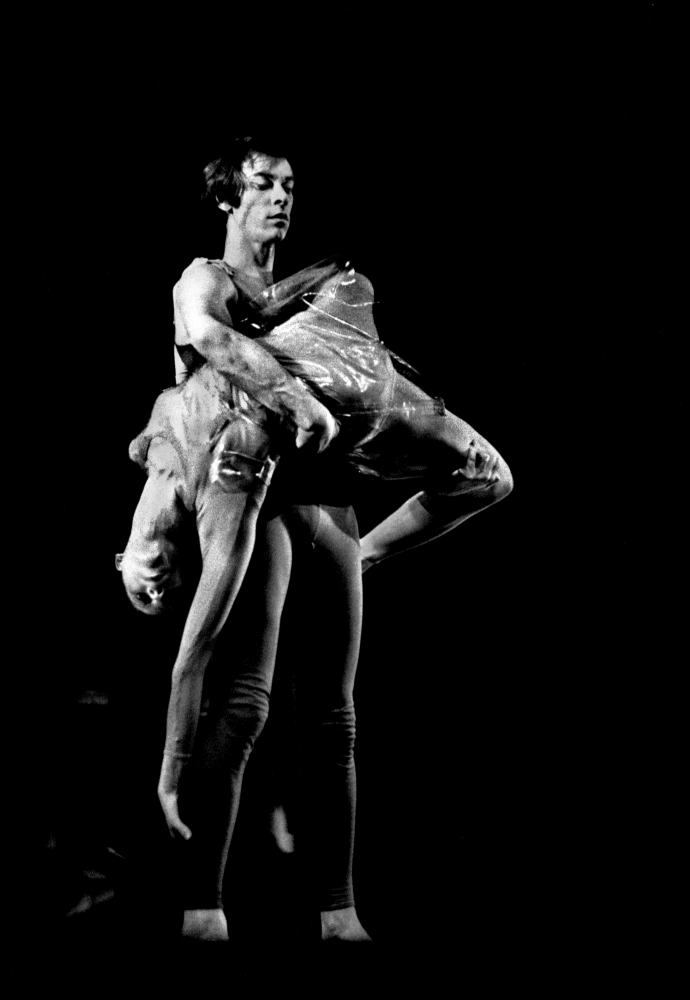

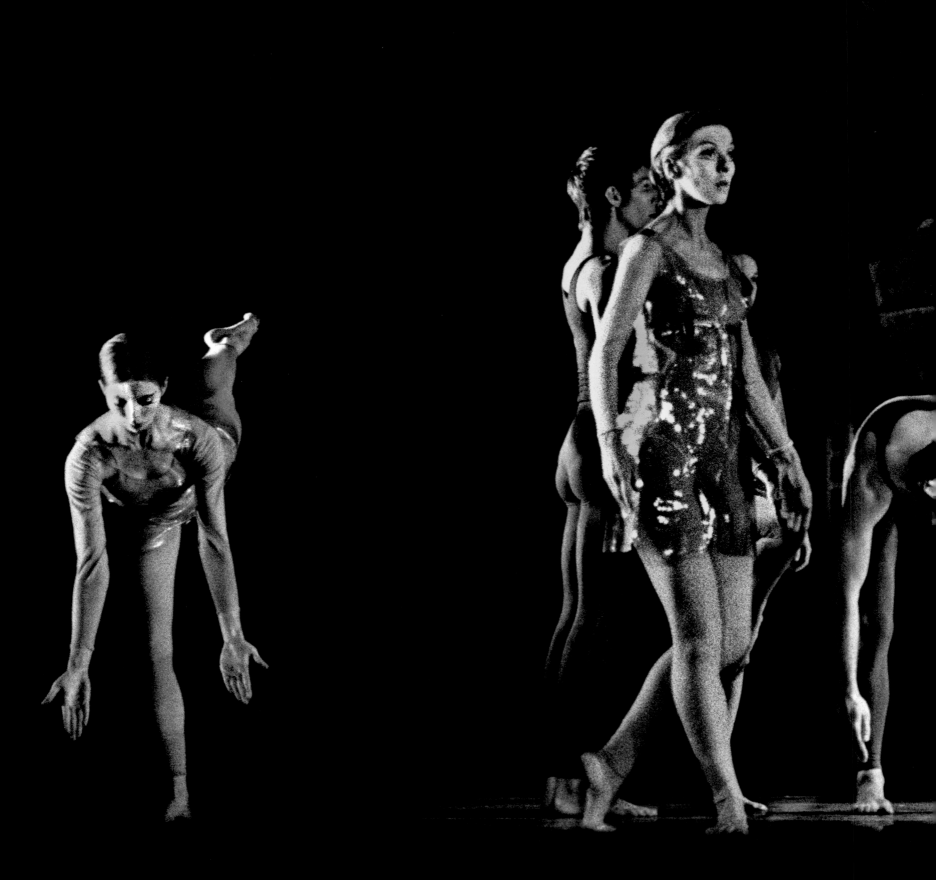

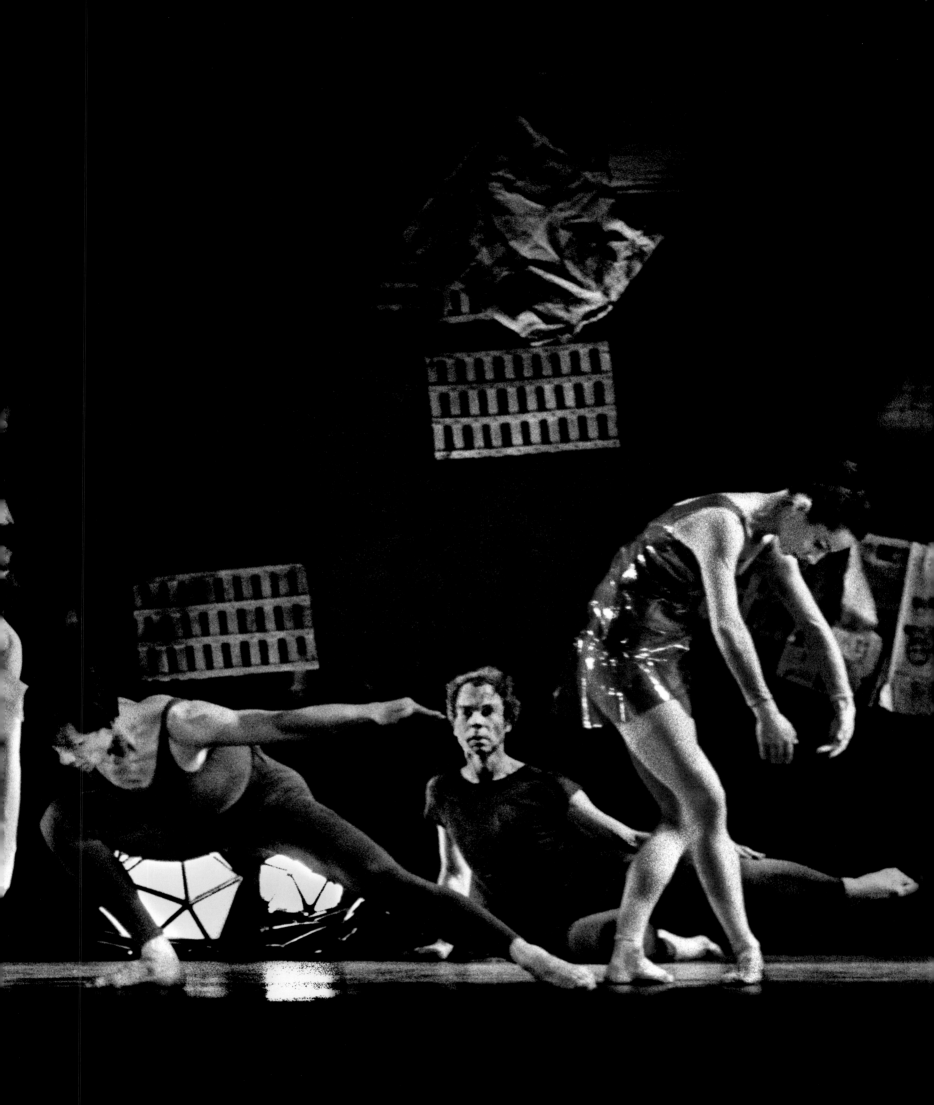

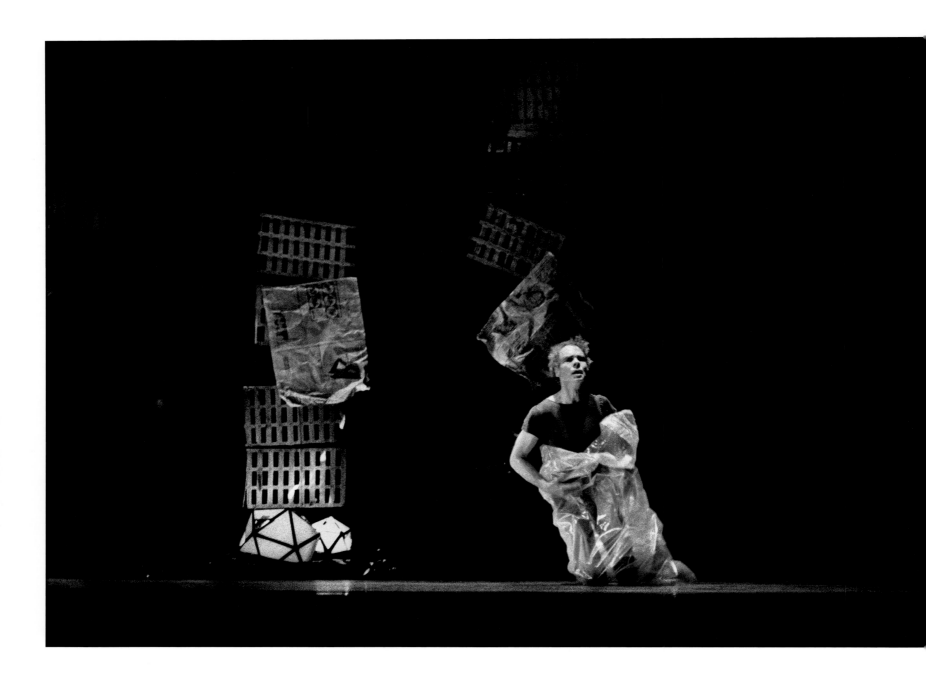

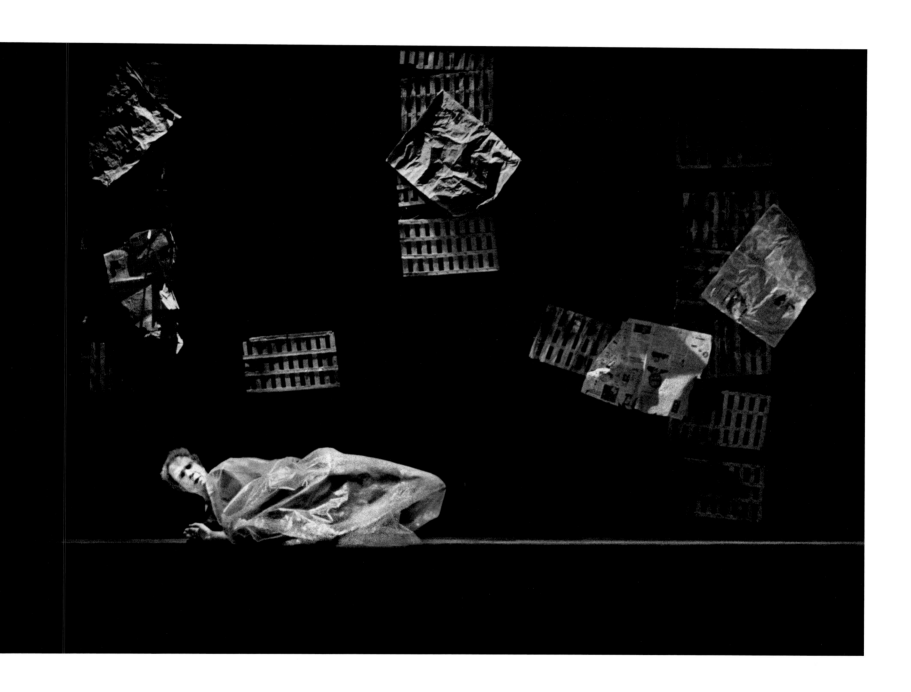

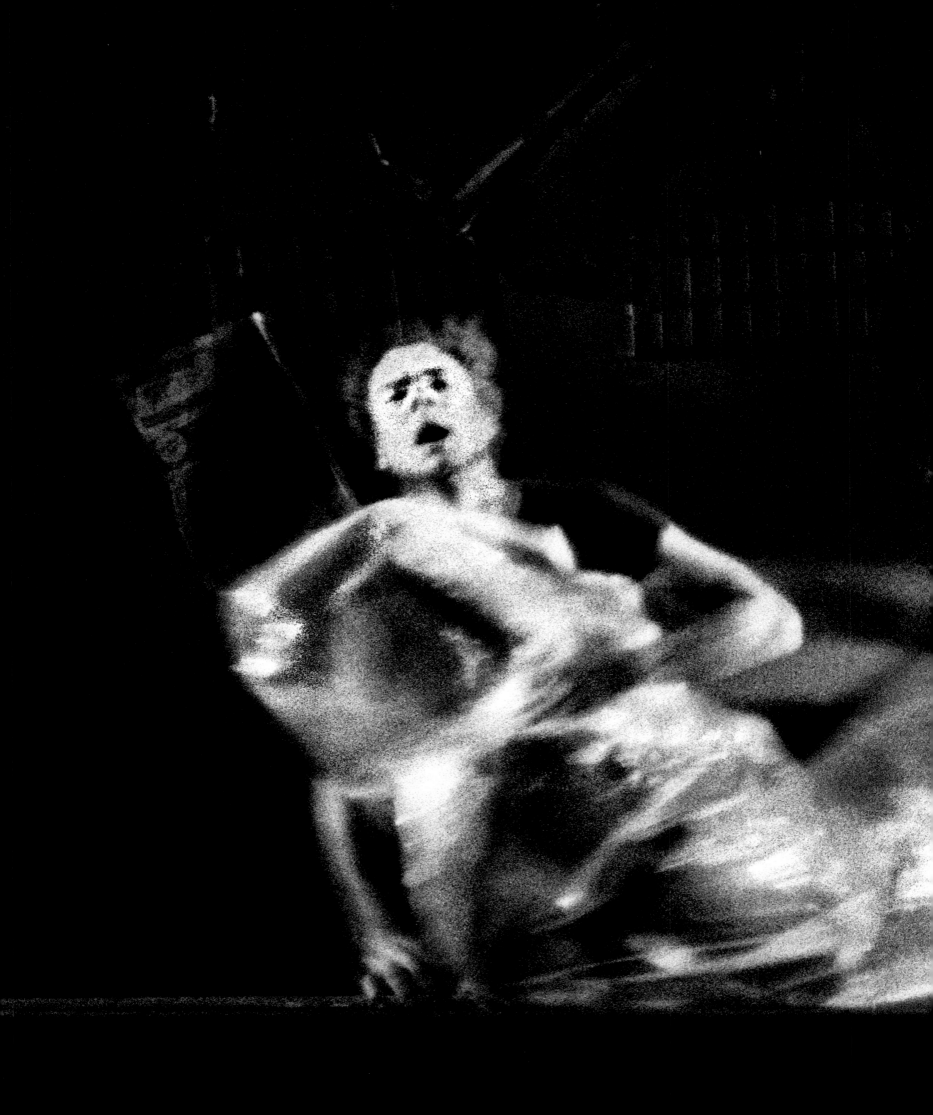

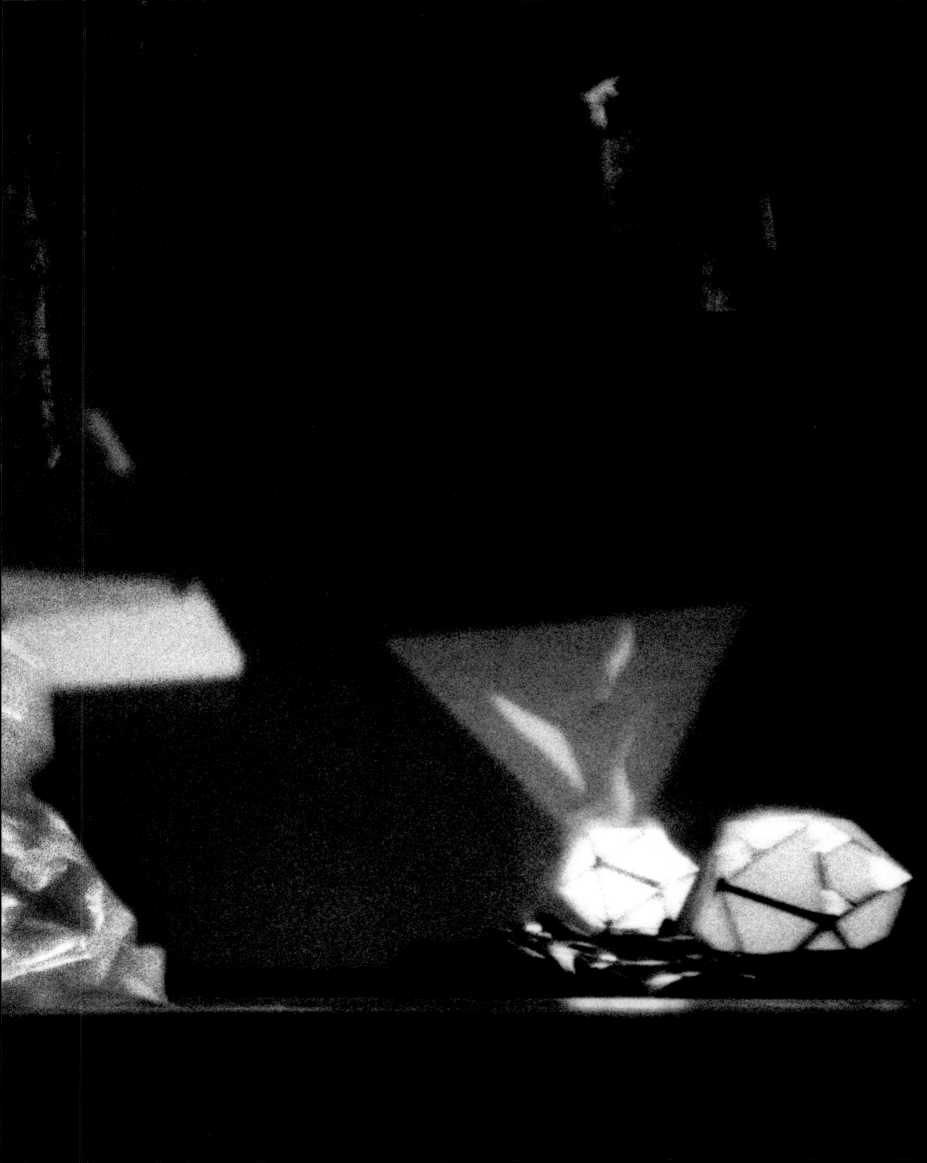

1967 SCRAMBLE

MUSIC
TOSHI ICHIYANAGI
ACTIVITIES FOR ORCHESTRA

COSTUMES
FRANK STELLA

DECOR
FRANK STELLA

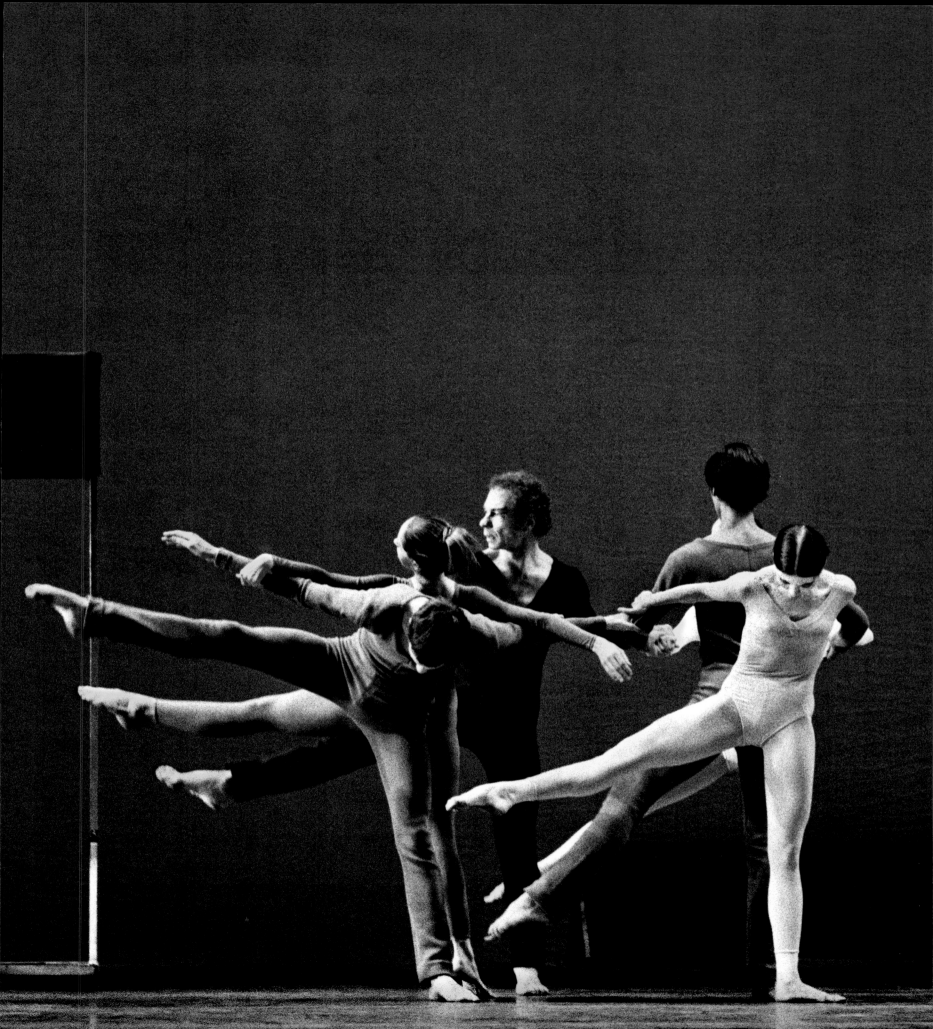

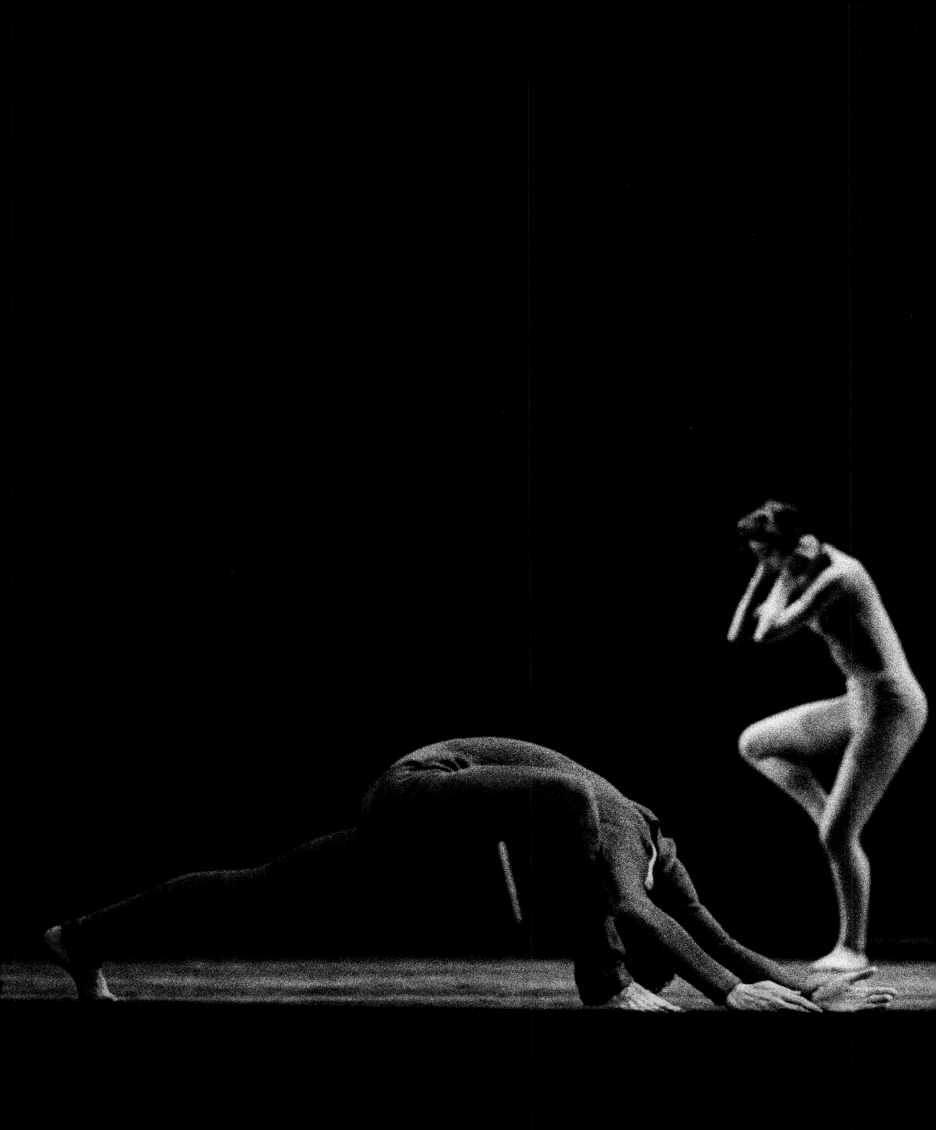

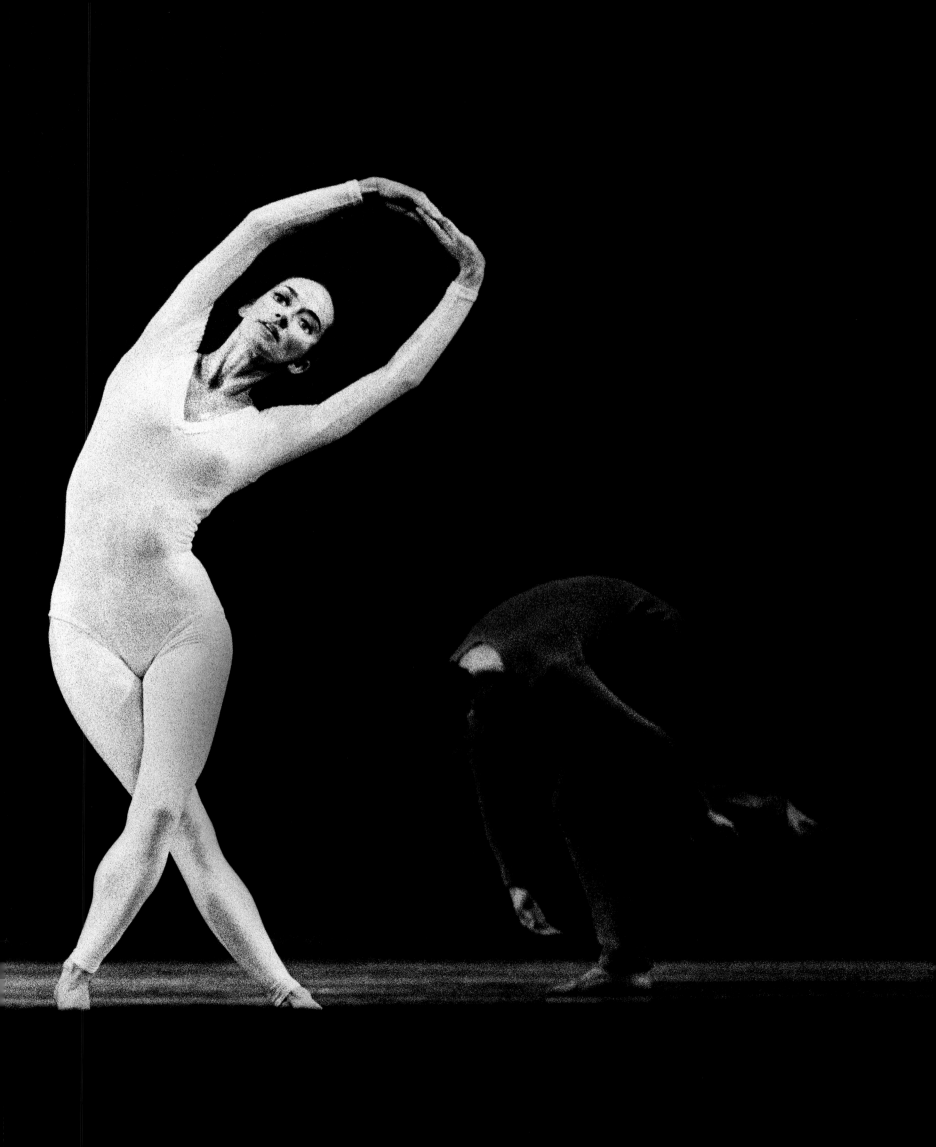

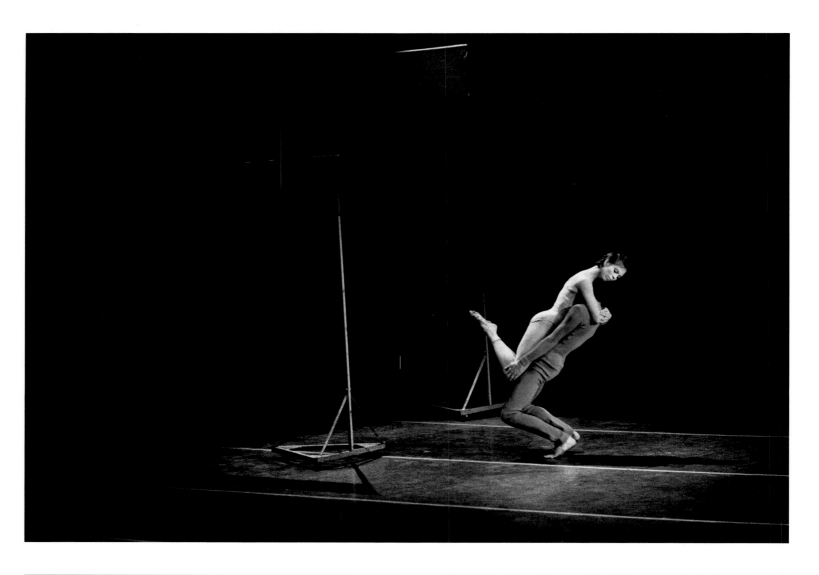

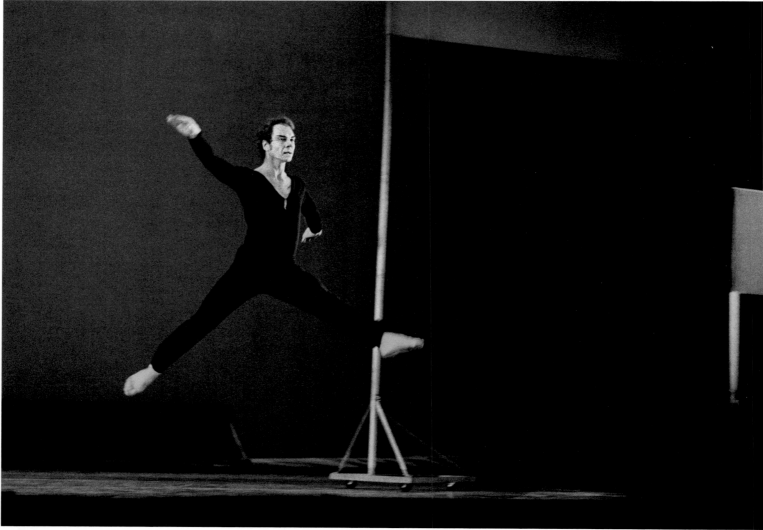

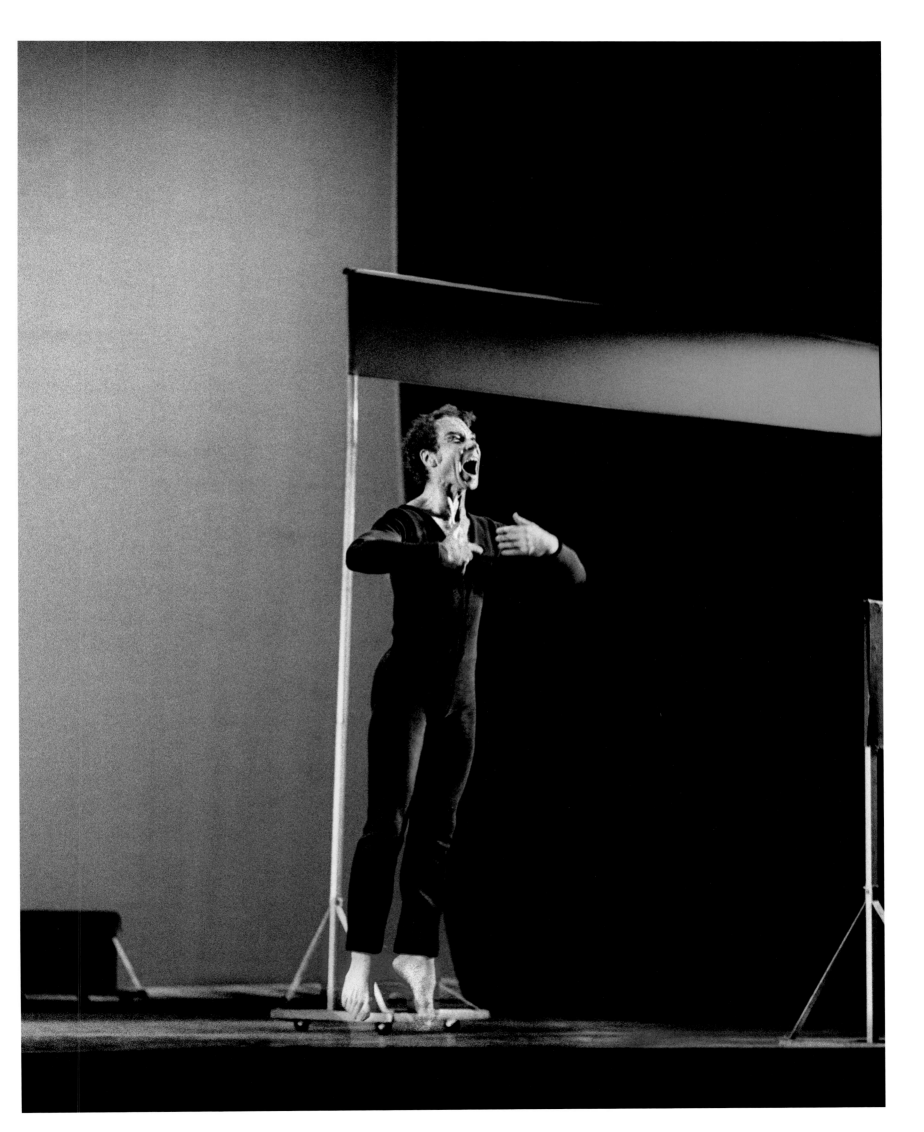

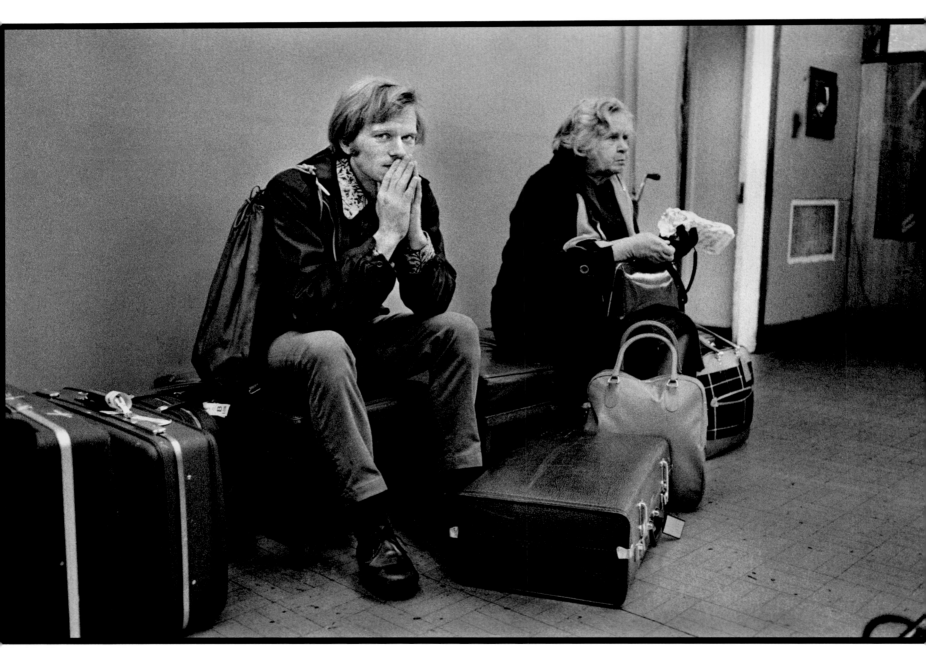

Douglas Dunn, Heathrow Airport,1972

DOUGLAS DUNN

Talking is talking
Dancing is dancing

Not talking is not talking
Not dancing is not dancing

Talking is talking and not talking
Dancing is dancing and not dancing

Not talking is not talking and not not talking
Not dancing is not dancing and not not dancing

Talking is not dancing
Dancing is not talking

Not talking is not not dancing
Not dancing is not not talking

Not talking is not dancing
Not dancing is not talking

Talking is dancing
Dancing is talking

Dancing is talking
Talking is dancing

Not dancing is not talking
Not talking is not dancing

Dancing is talking and not talking
Talking is dancing and not dancing

Not dancing is not talking and not not talking
Not talking is not dancing and not not dancing

Dancing is not dancing
Talking is not talking

Not dancing is not not dancing
Not talking is not not talking

Not dancing is not dancing
Not talking is not talking

Dancing is dancing
Talking is talking

1968 **RAINFOREST**

MUSIC
DAVID TUDOR
RAINFOREST

COSTUMES
JASPER JOHNS

DECOR
ANDY WARHOL

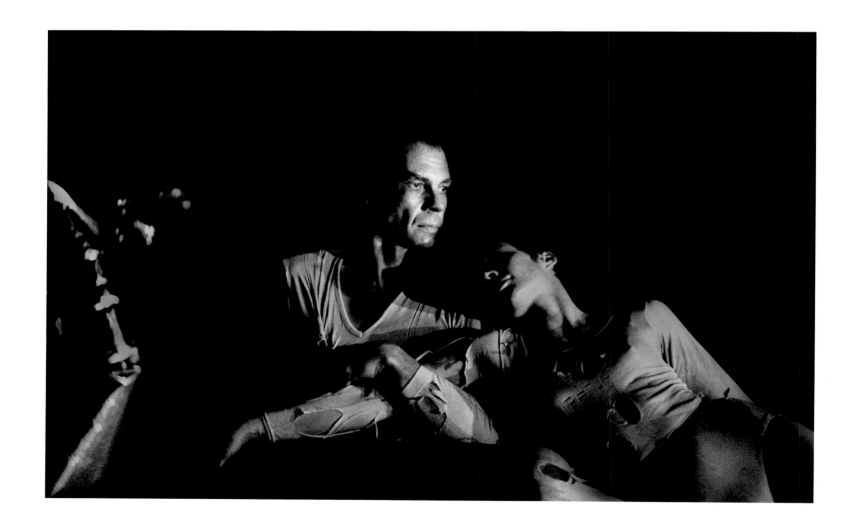

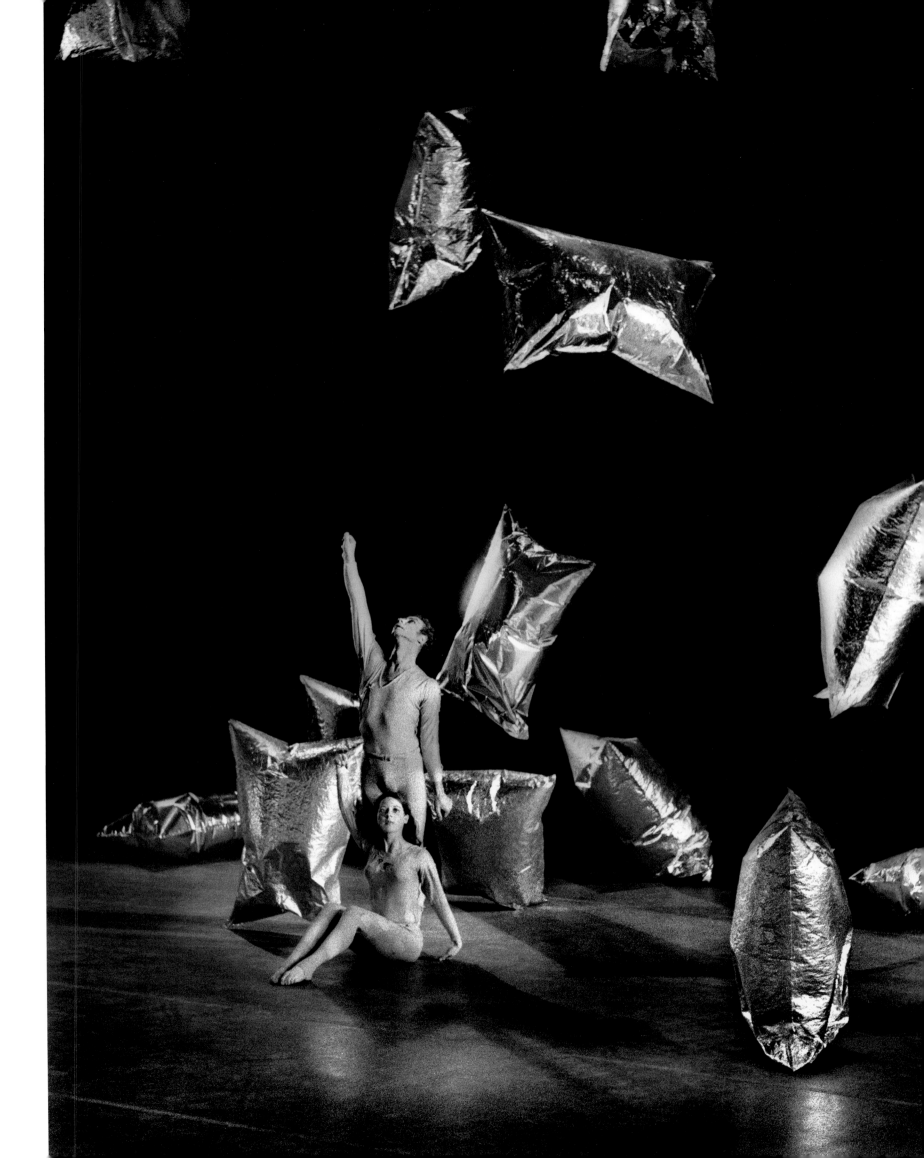

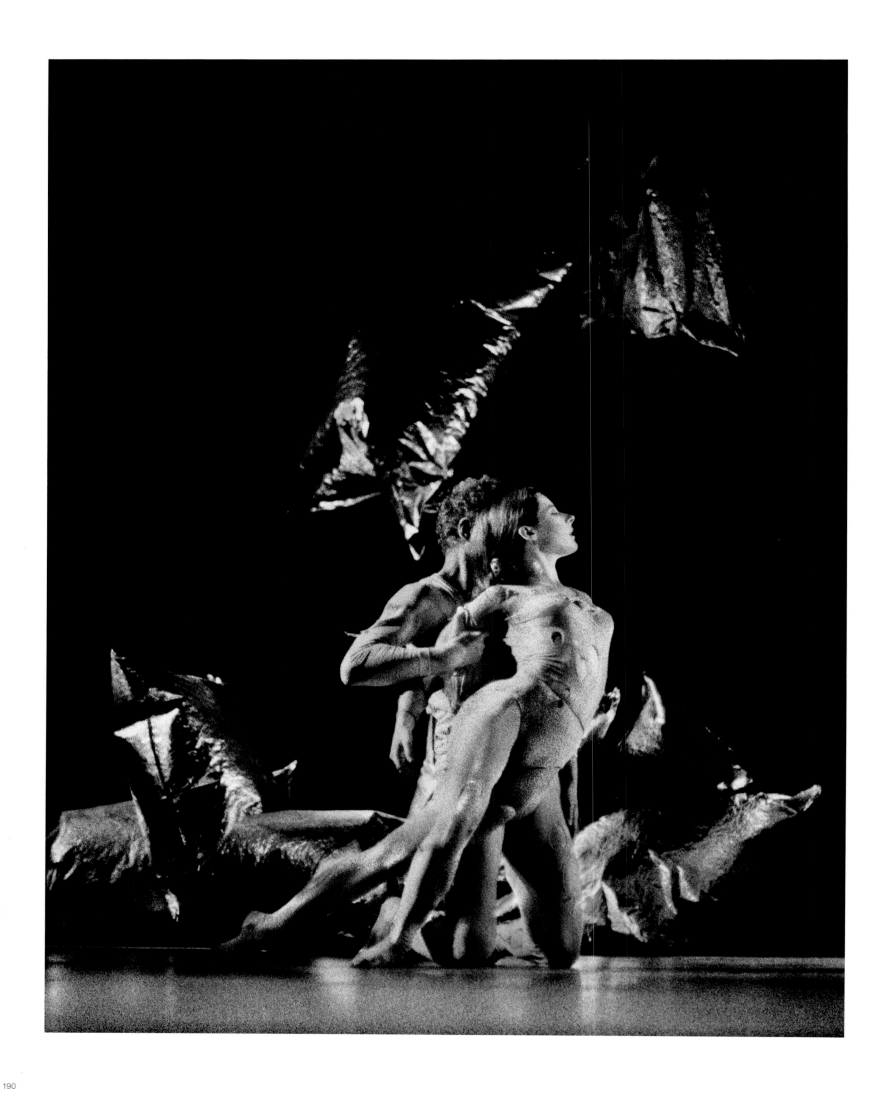

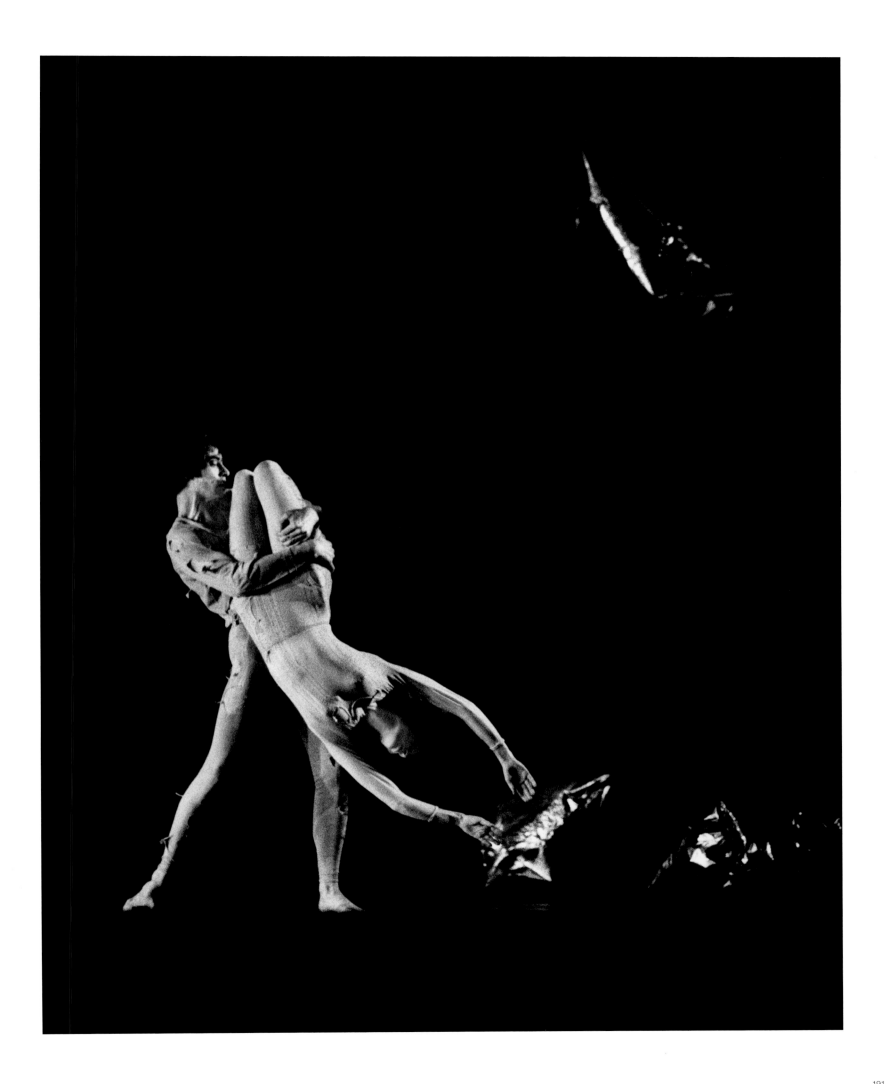

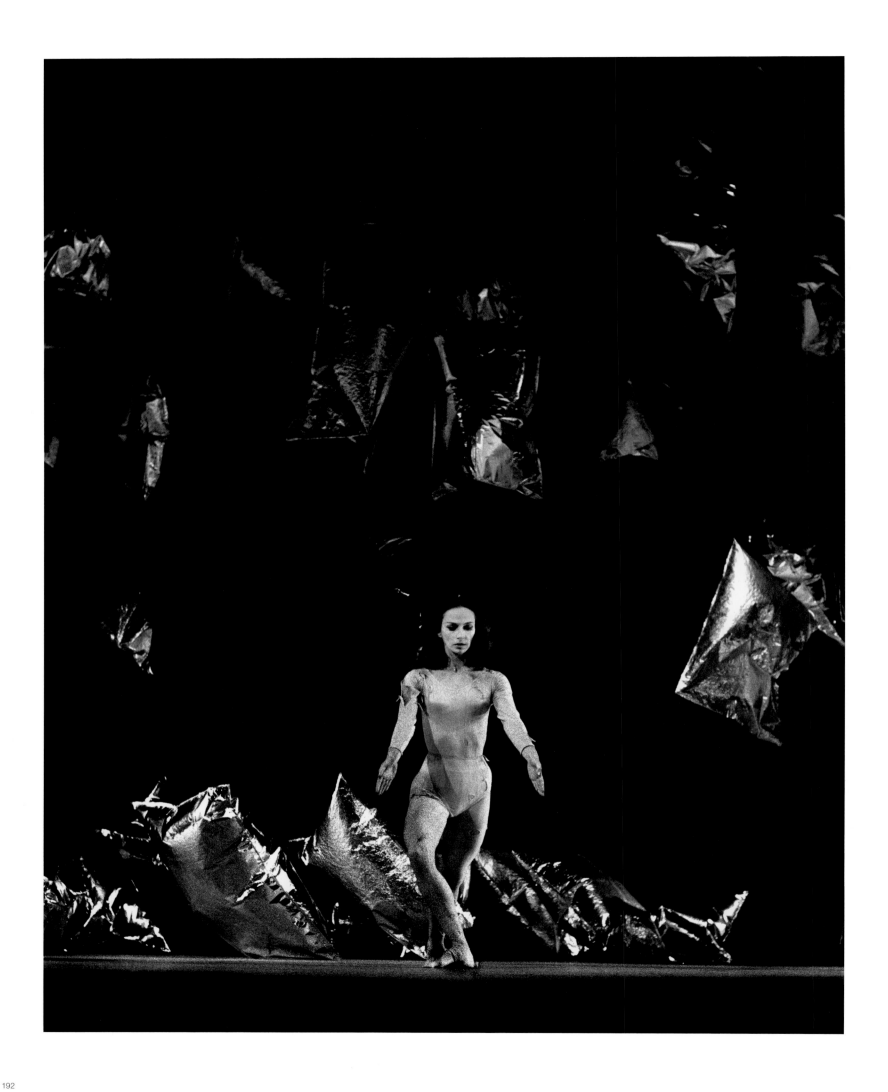

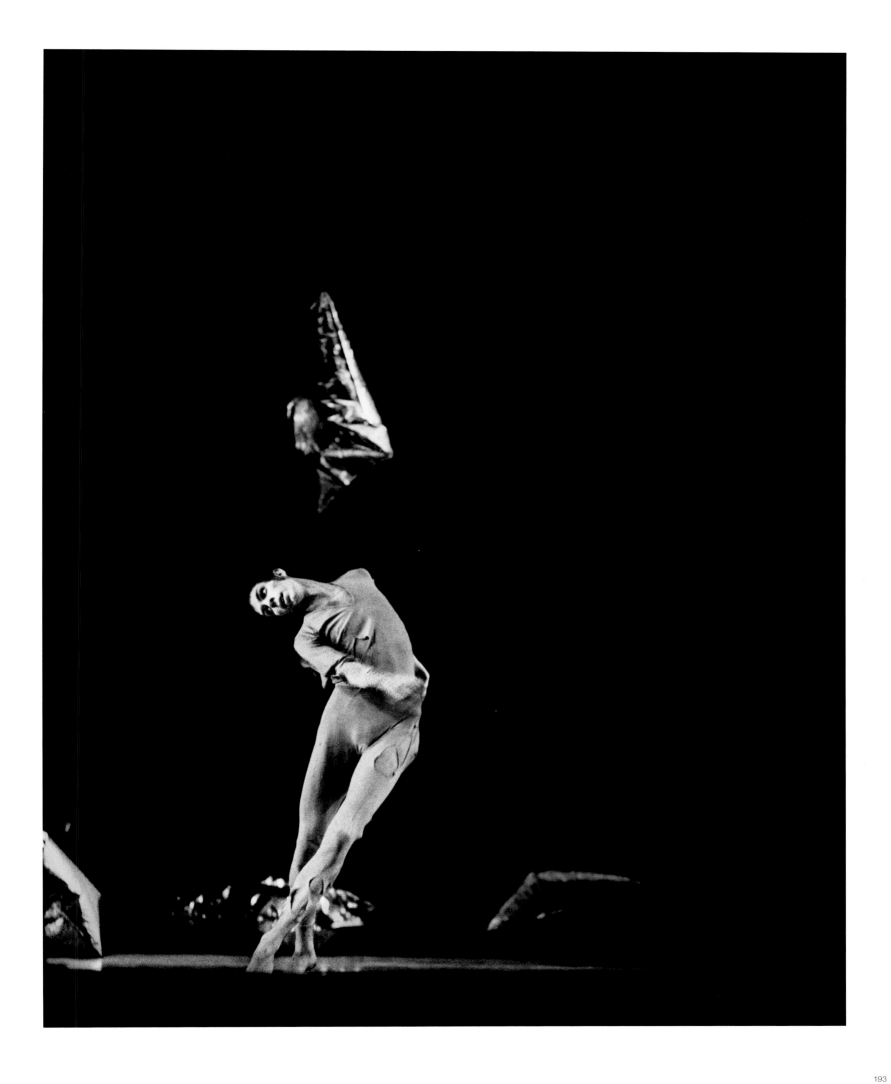

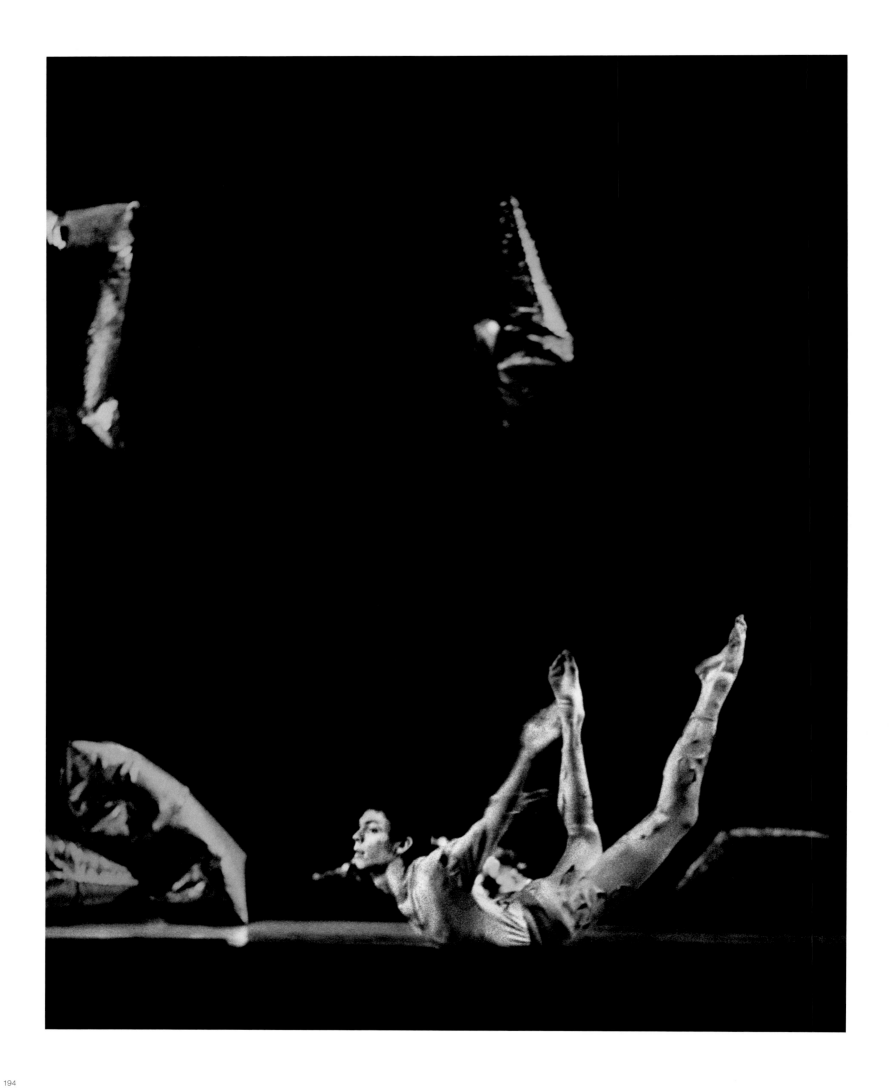

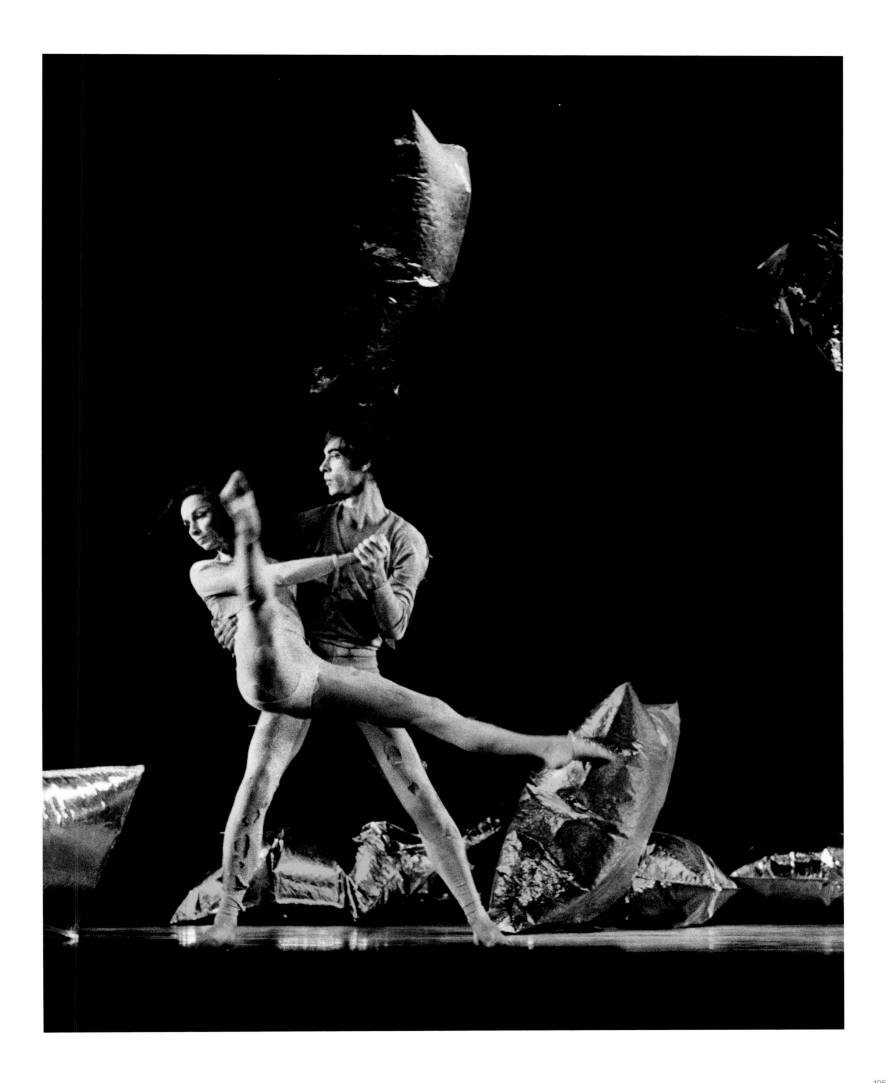

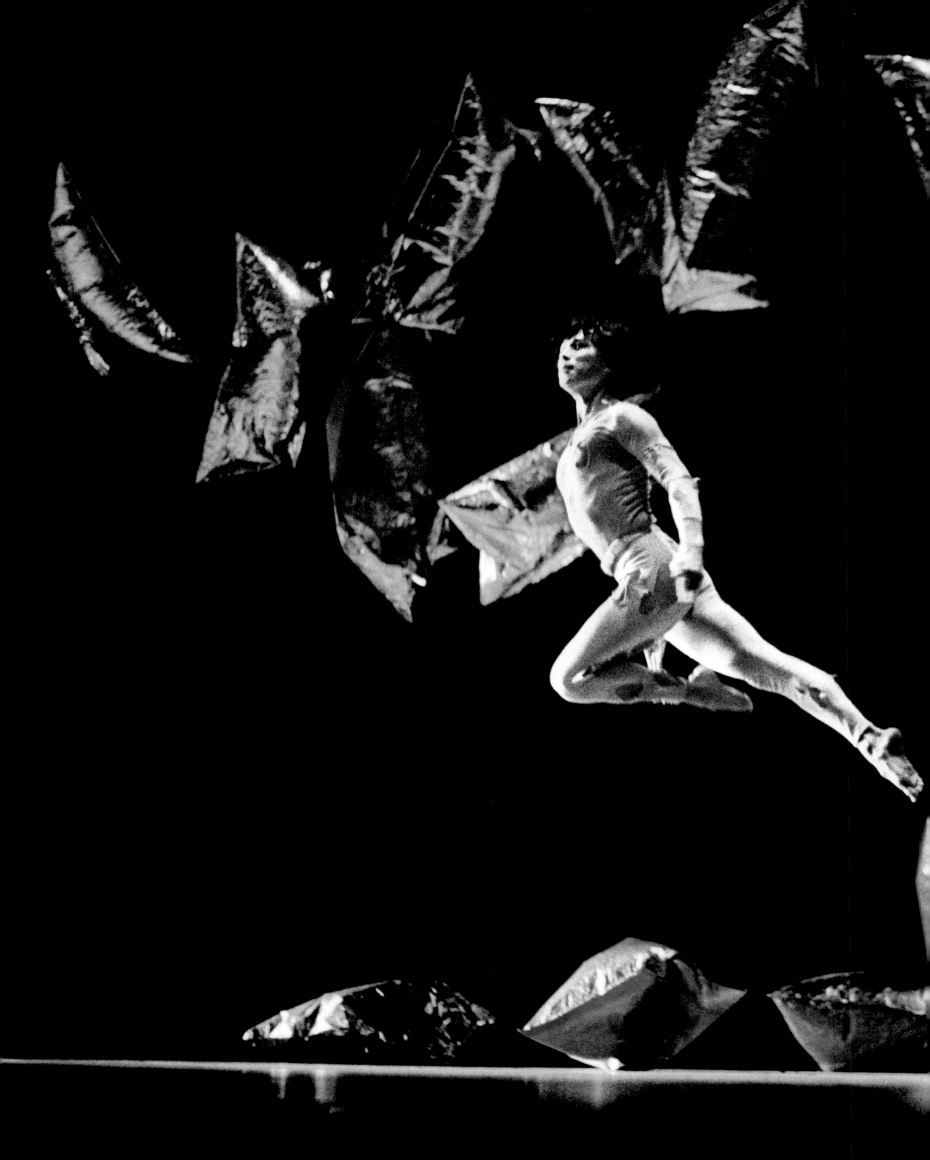

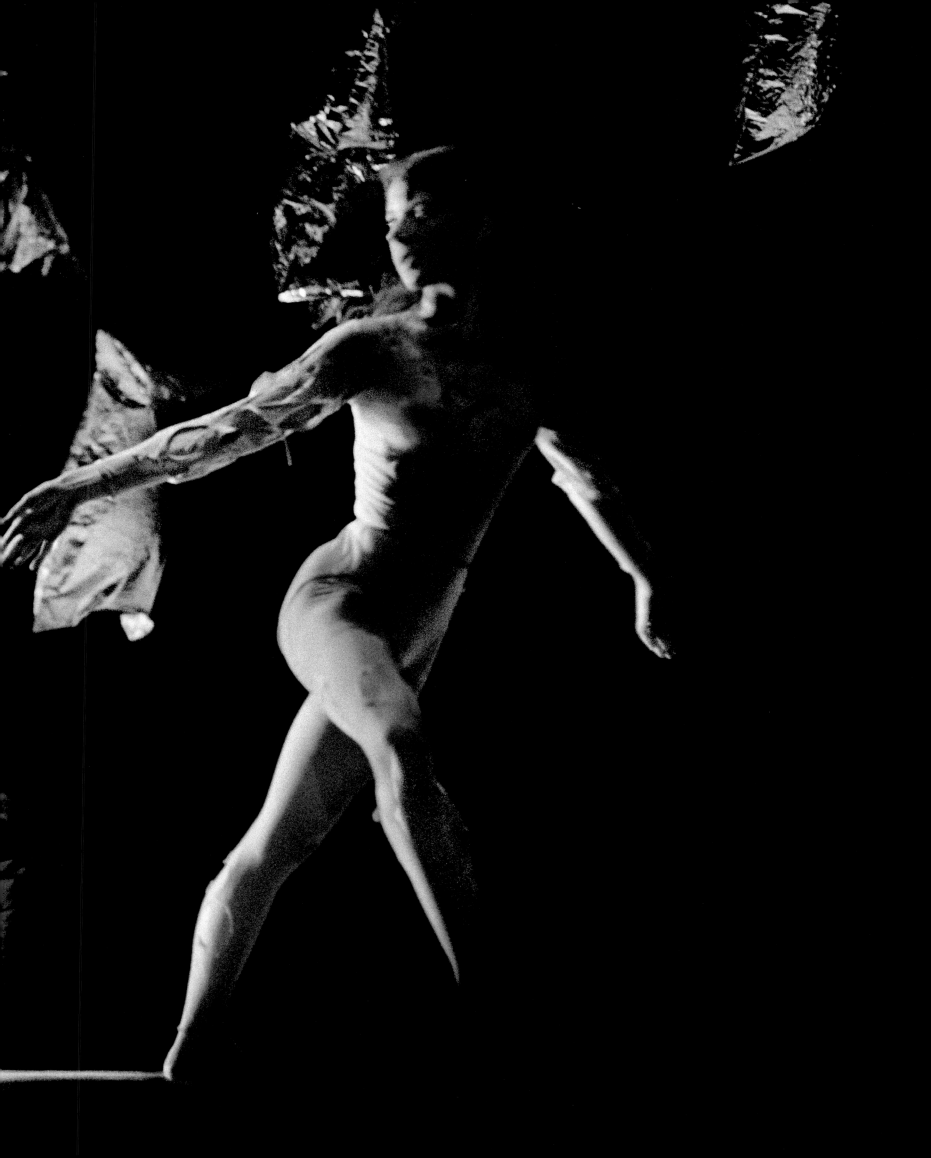

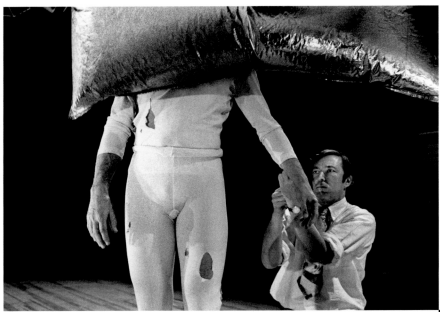

Jasper Johns, finishing touches, Buffalo, New York, March 1968

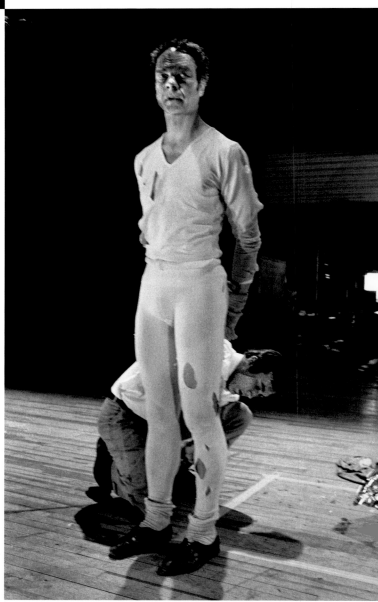

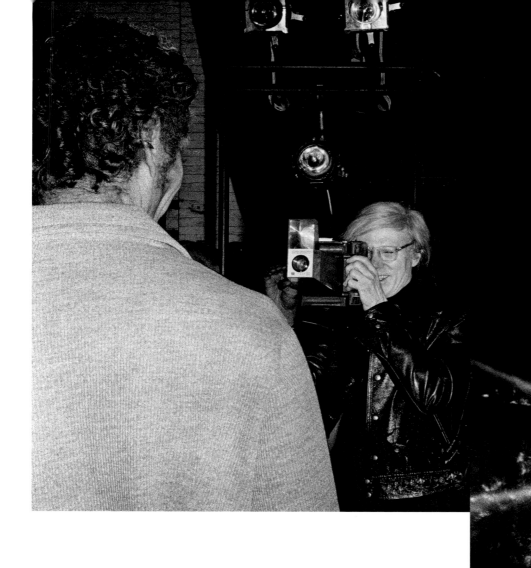

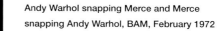
Andy Warhol snapping Merce and Merce snapping Andy Warhol, BAM, February 1972

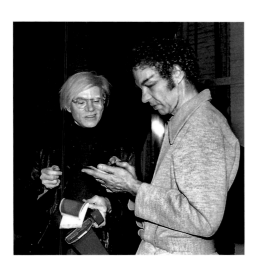

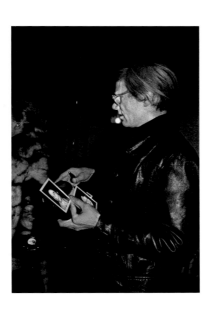

1968 ASSEMBLAGE

FILM DIRECTOR
RICHARD MOORE

MUSIC
JOHN CAGE
DAVID TUDOR
GORDON MUMMA

In 1968 the Cunningham Company was asked
to participate in an experimental film in
Ghirardelli Square, produced by
San Francisco Public Television, WKQED.
A very "effects-dominated" fifty-eight-
minute enterprise, I don't think anyone who
has seen it thinks of it as a dance film.

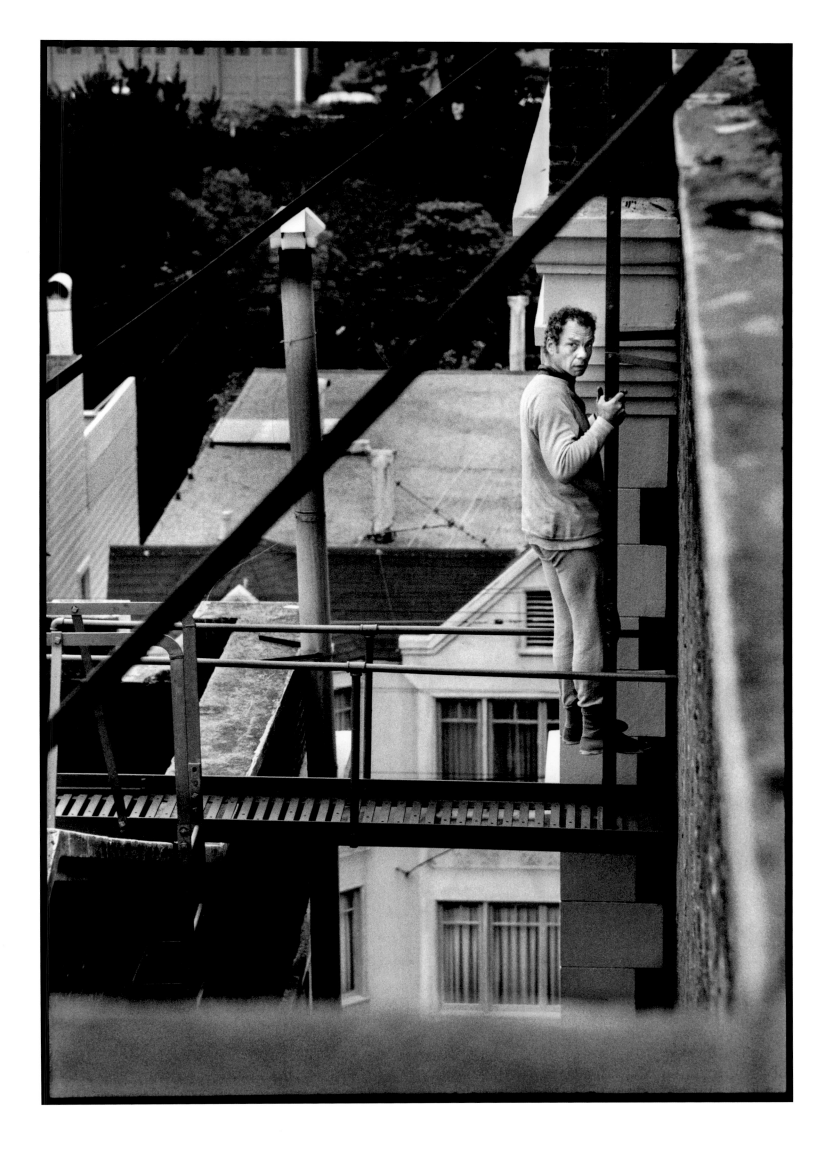

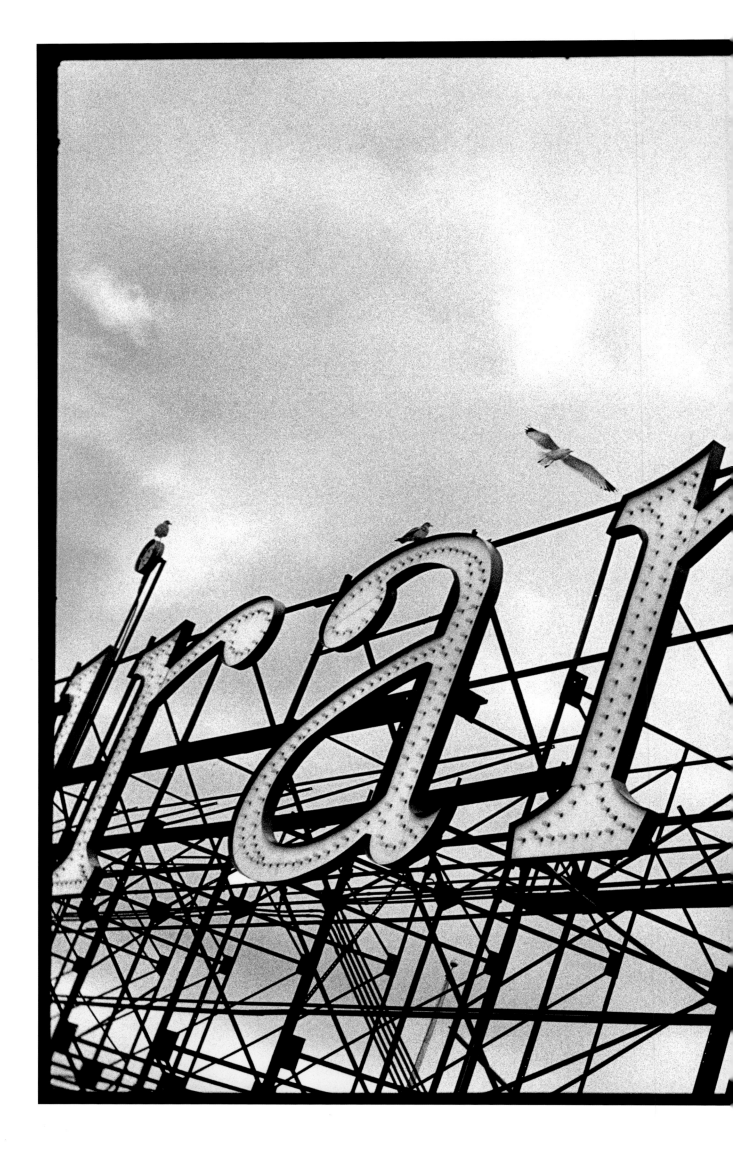

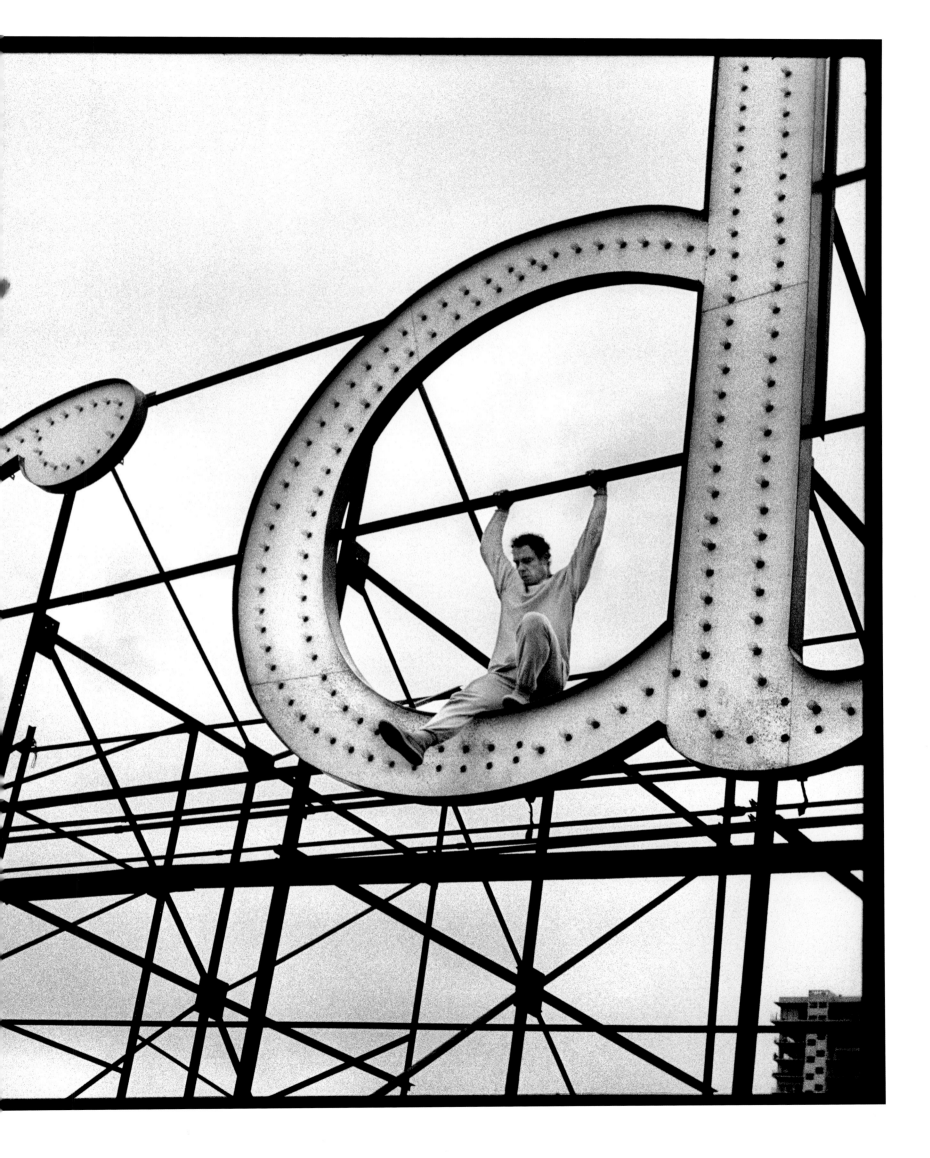

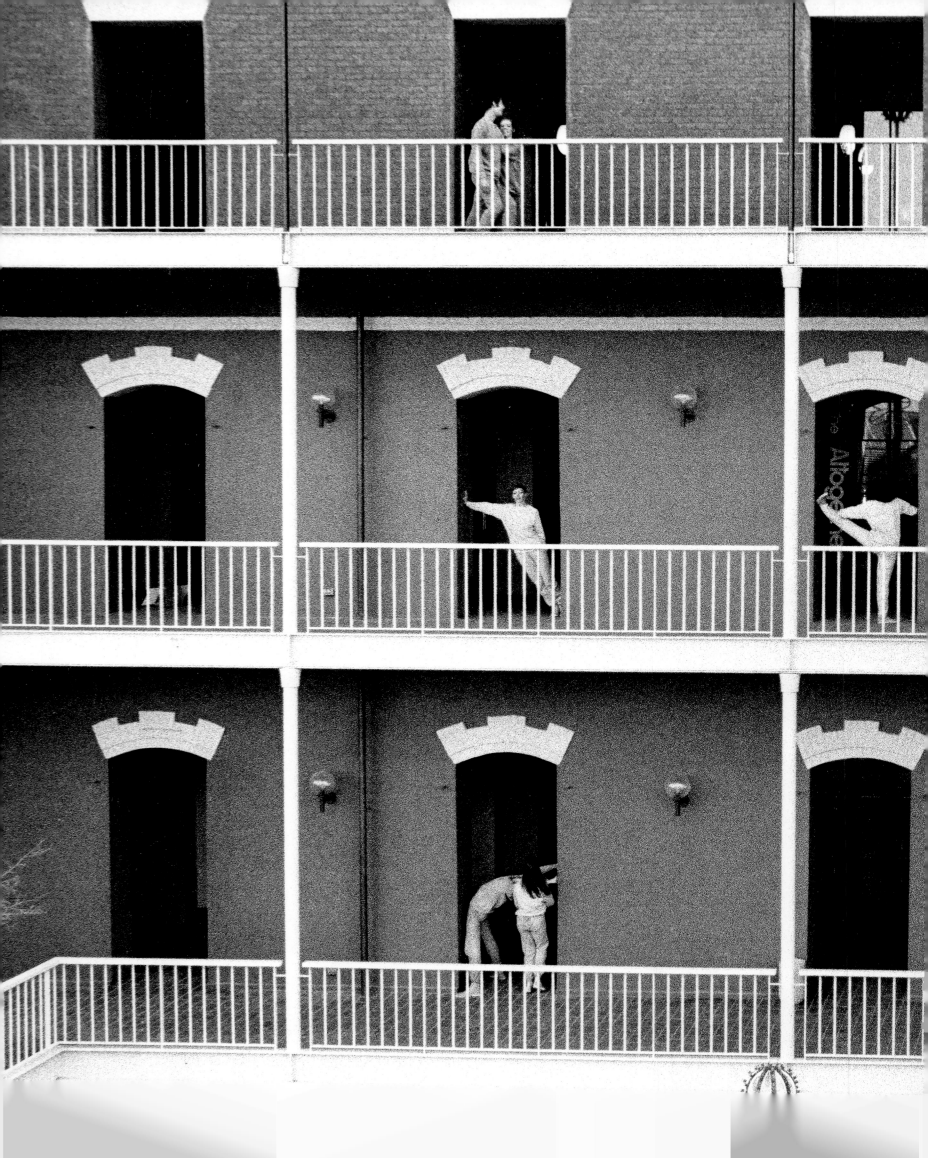

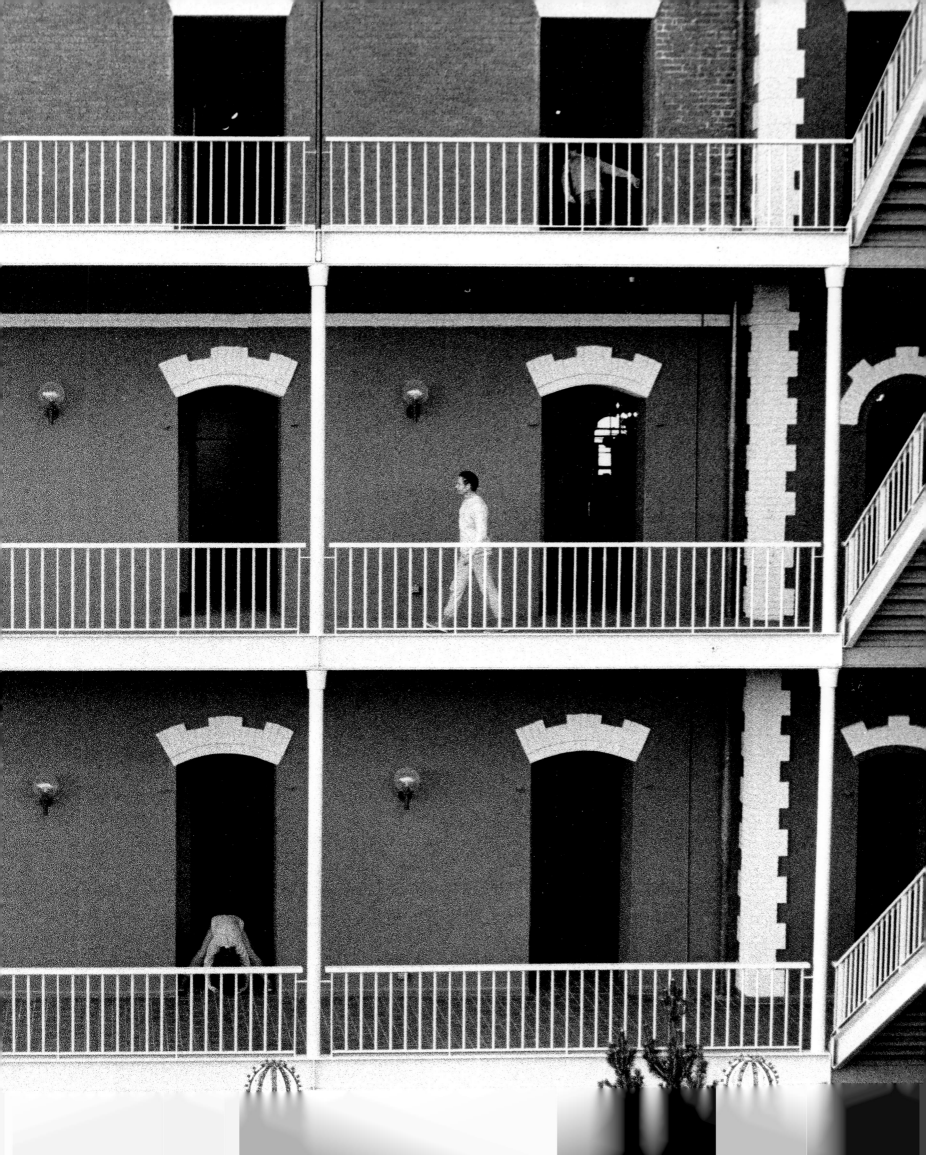

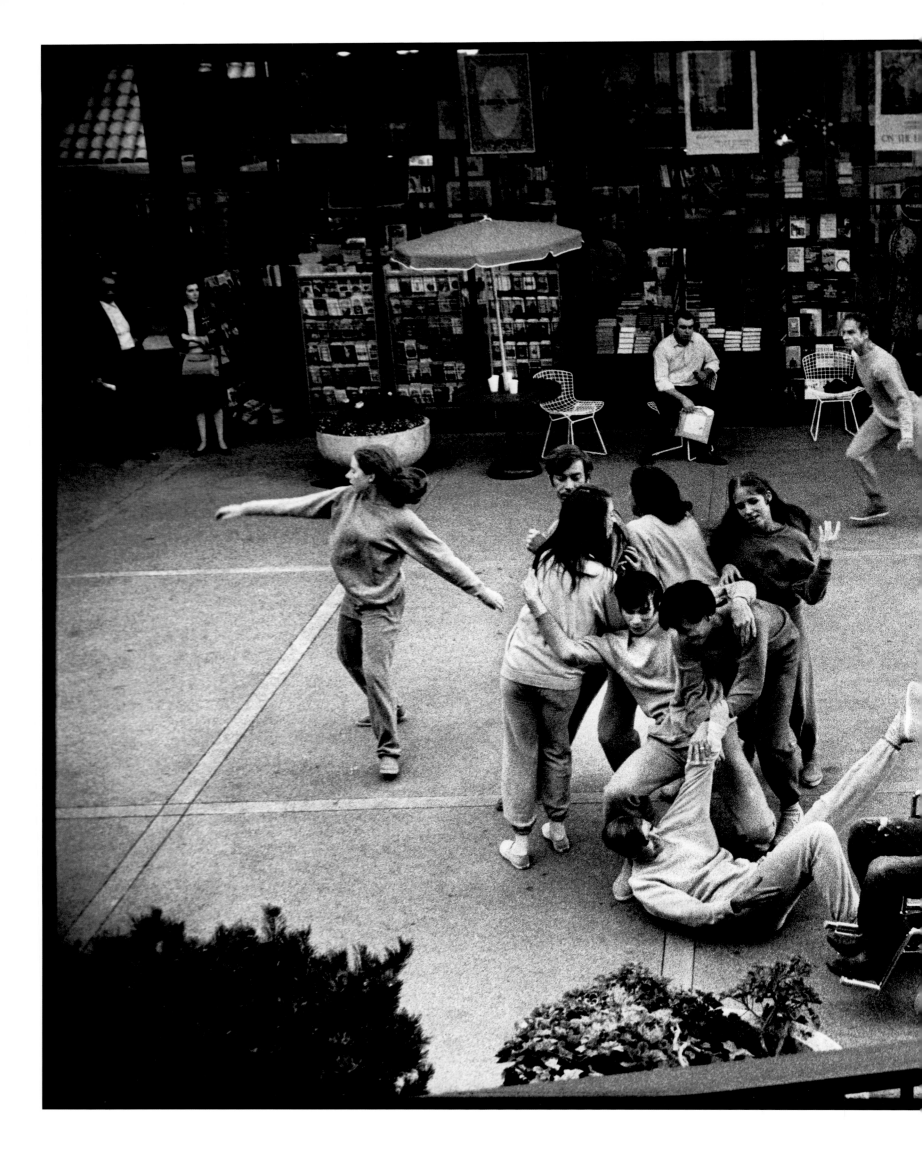

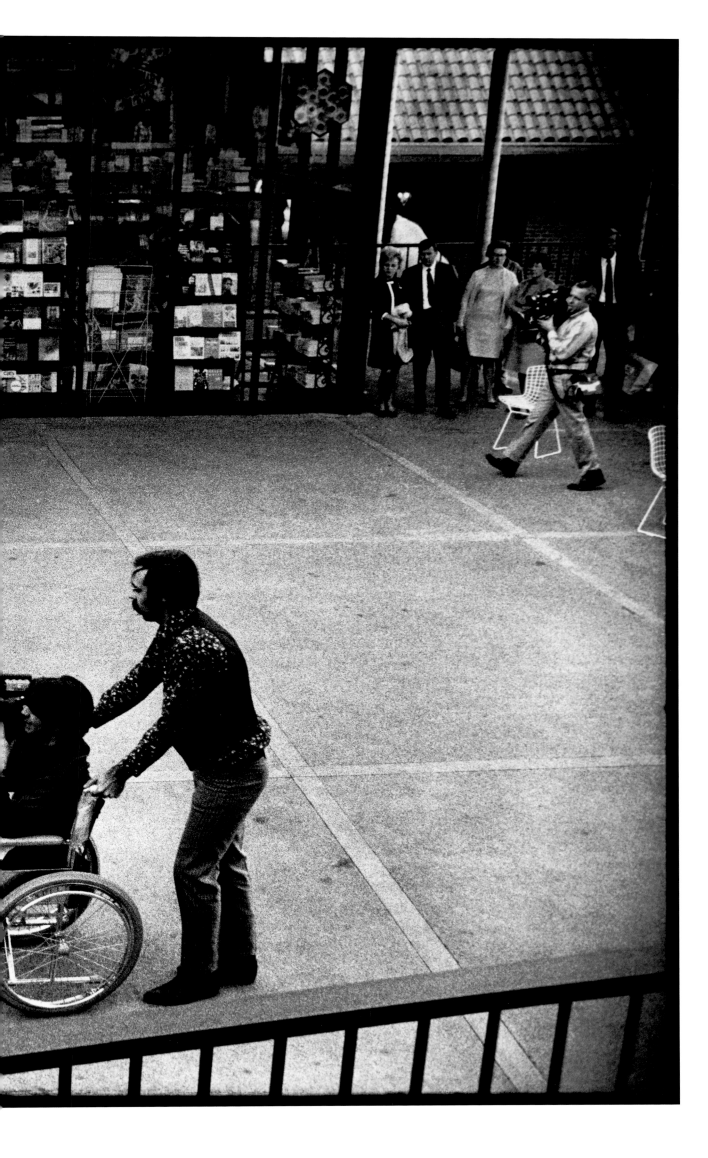

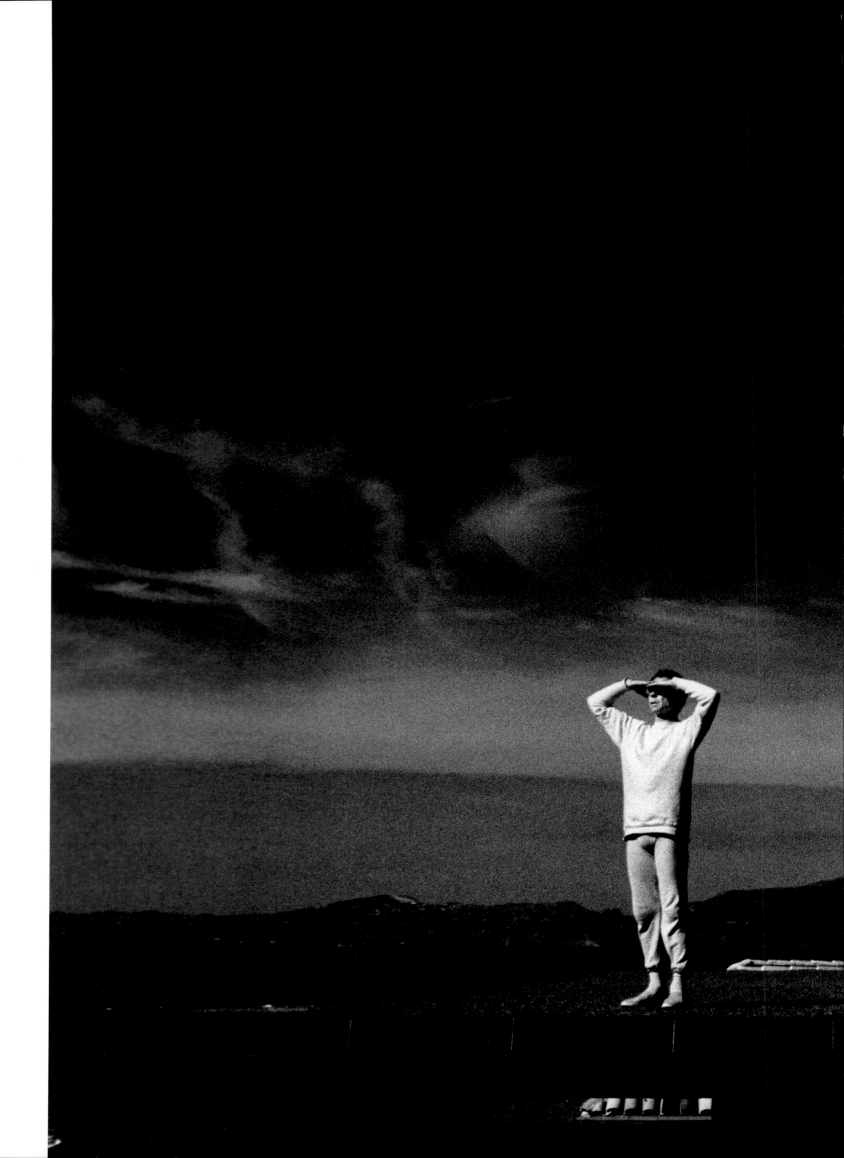

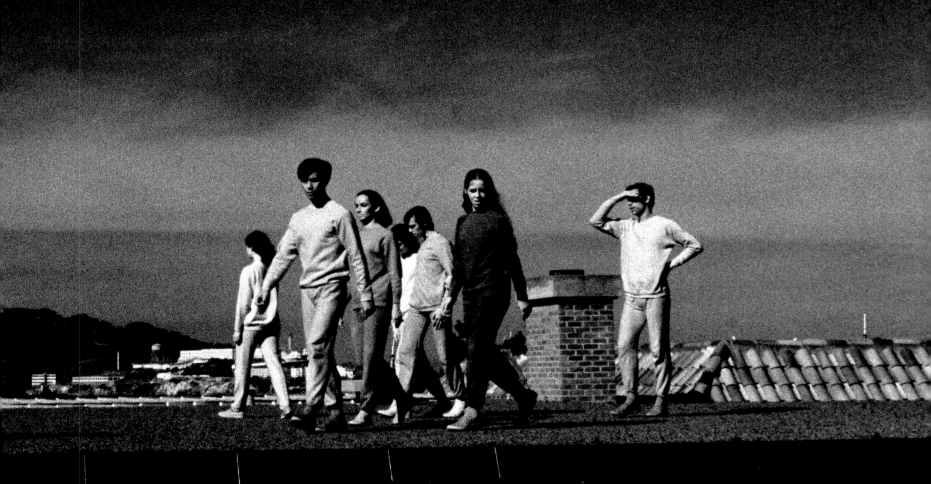

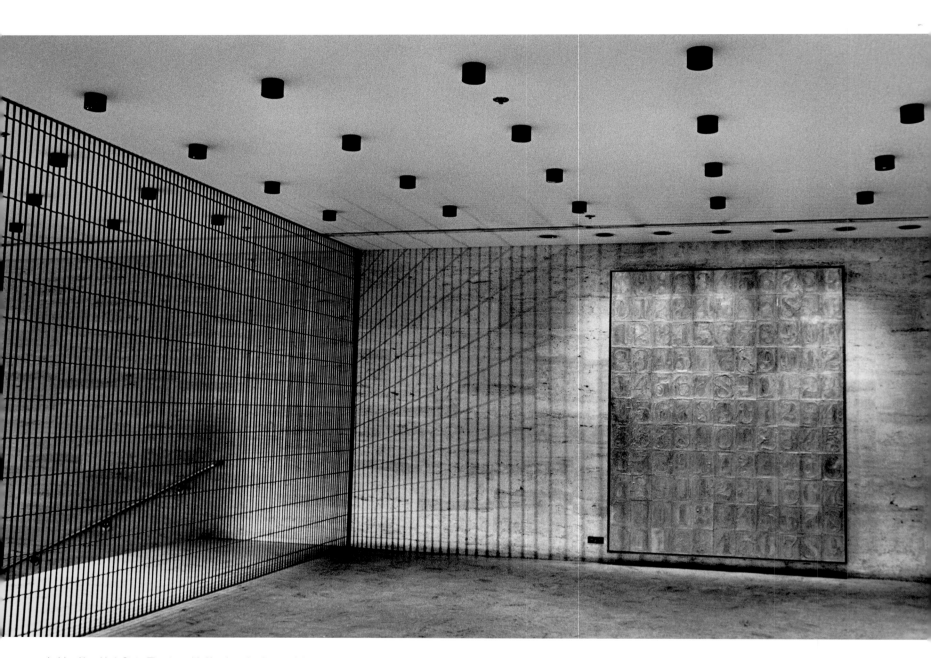

Lobby, New York State Theater, with *Numbers* by Jasper Johns

LINCOLN KIRSTEIN

I met Merce in 1938 in Seattle at the Cornish School and knew him when he was first working with Martha Graham. I admired him as a dancer, and I met and liked John Cage. I asked them to compose *The Seasons* with scenery by Isamu Noguchi for Ballet Society in 1948. This was an orchestral piece, and it sounded rather like Sinding's *Rustles of Spring*. The ballet itself was tender and pretty, but it had little virtuosic interest and was not particularly interesting for ballet-trained dancers to do. I had thought, naively, there was some ground upon which the idiosyncratic "modern" (concert-type) dance might meld with academic ballet; we tried again with Paul Taylor and Martha Graham in *Episodes*, but it was a success due only to the personalities of the two stars, and when they no longer danced it, it had no real value. As for *Summerspace*, the stage we had was too big for it; it worked well with Merce's own dancers, but when he put it on *pointe*, it seemed too bland to hold a public. The music was without any bite; the whole thing seemed to attempt to be some sort of an advance-guard manifestation but it was all rather *deja-vu*. I like Merce and John very much personally, but our philosophies of dance and theater are disparate, to say the least. If you want what I (finally) irreducibly think, and it will not please you, it is this. Without acrobatic virtuosity based on four centuries of logical exercises, a dancer cannot hope to attract the mass public that overlaps onto athletic events, ballgames of whatever category, foot-, base-, or basket-. (The mass public is what pays $125,000 a *week* tor *forty* weeks of the NYC Ballet Company.)

The *soi-disant* "modern" -dance (How modern can you get? Twyla Tharp, Erik Hawkins, Paul T.??) is a self-limited form since it depends on the several Selves of the individual performer, all of whom attach to a heterodox tradition, roughly stemming from Denishawn and a little overflow from Wigman via the early thirties (Kreuzberg, Georgi, etc.). Half the reason for the development of the nonproscenium theater in America was based on the erroneous idea that it would save stagehands. Half the vocabulary of the modern dance derives from the fact that from Ruth St. Denis on down through the Humphrey-Weidman-Graham formulations, they consoled themselves with the Duncanesque doctrine which was freedom; i.e., there were no good opera-house ballet schools around at that time. So they did oriental numbers and Spanish and American Indian, until the Germans developed eukinetics based on a further detheatricalization of Dalcroze's eurythmics. Purity was antitheatrical, and the world was to be saved from the dreadful corruption of the ballet.

Essentially, the modern dance tradition is a meager school and is without audience, repertory, or issue; it never gained a mass public, a central system, nor a common repertory, and the subsequent generation of improvisers depend on multimedia bastardization with not much Intrinsic DANCE interest; *vide* Alwin Nicolais. It is pretty enough as far as it goes, but there ain't much dance if that is what you're looking for; and that is what I, and Balanchine (the Academic Establishment), are always looking for. The Modern Dance, like *M*odern *A*rt and *M*odern *M*usic are all victims of what Baudelaire called one hundred years ago the decrepitude of art: the insistence of personalism, expressionism, idiosyncrasy against the service of the de-selfed Self.

I am personally very fond of Merce and admiring of John, but I think they are self-restricted to an audience which is both blind and deaf to the orthodoxy and apostolic succession of four centuries. They complain of small audiences after a quarter of a century of instant and constant "innovation." And the aesthetic of Jasper Johns and Rauschenberg has had an odd effect. They are so supremely monetarily successful with their particular brands of second-generation pretenderized avant-gardisme that they make the scale of Merce-John more publicity-conscious of a self-considered "failure," in the sense of equating operahouses with one-man shows at big museums, if you see what I dimly mean. I feel they have missed the big boat and console themselves with charming hand-hewn yachts. I grant your amusement about my preference for big boats over hand-hewn yachts, and the question is exactly as you put it: how do you get there or where do you want to go? I want to go into very large theaters with very large and expensive companies with very big possibilities for a very large public. And WHERE I want to go is determined by HOW. In Tantric Buddhism they brandish the *derje*, the thunderbolt bell of method and material; me too, and the method is the classic academic theatrical opera-house ballet. Non-Euclidean geometry has its various developments, but ballet is where solid geometry crosses gross anatomy in a sphere black with crammed movement. Individual geometries, or logics have their reference, and there is nothing in any proposals over the last century that cannot be mastered by an "academic dancer," yet the reverse is patently untrue.

Oddly enough, I could be as wrong as Merce and John. Perhaps we are all, historically, out of luck. But Balanchine has attached himself for fifty years to Stravinsky, and subsequently, Berg, Webern, Ives, Hindemith, and of course Tschaikowsky, Bach, Glinka. I wish John and Merce well, but I am I, and they are they, and never the twain shall meet.

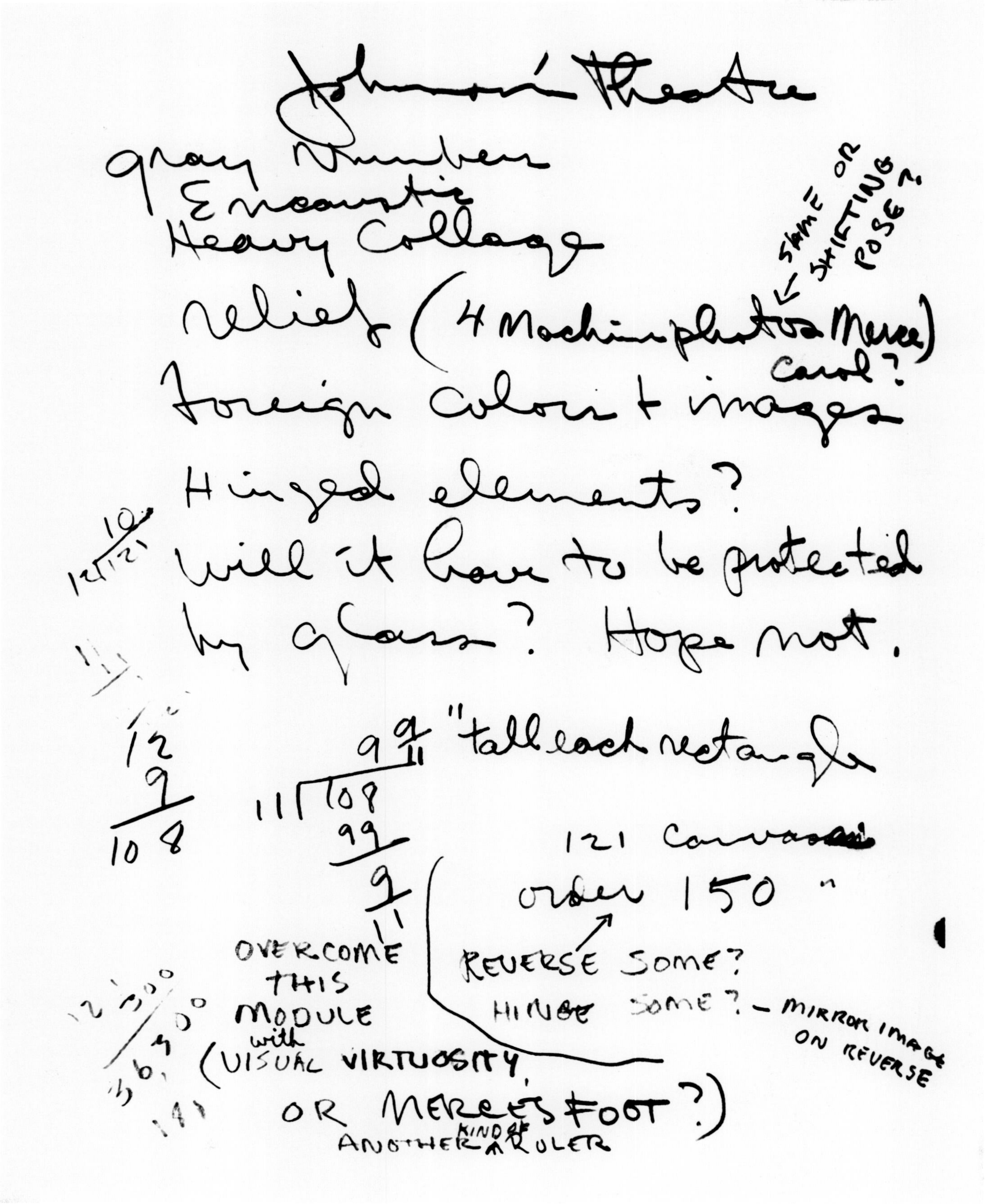

Johnson's Theatre

gray Numbers
Encaustic
Heavy Collage

relief (4 Machine photos Merce) ← Same or Shifting pose?
Carol?

Foreign Colors + images

Hinged elements?

Will it have to be protected
by glass? Hope not.

$$\frac{12}{9} \quad 10\,8$$

$$9\frac{9}{11} \quad 11\overline{)108} \quad \frac{99}{9}$$ "tall each rectangle

121 Canvases

order 150 "

OVERCOME THIS MODULE with
(VISUAL VIRTUOSITY,
OR MERCE'S FOOT?)
ANOTHER KIND OF RULER

REVERSE SOME?
HINGE SOME? — MIRROR IMAGE
ON REVERSE

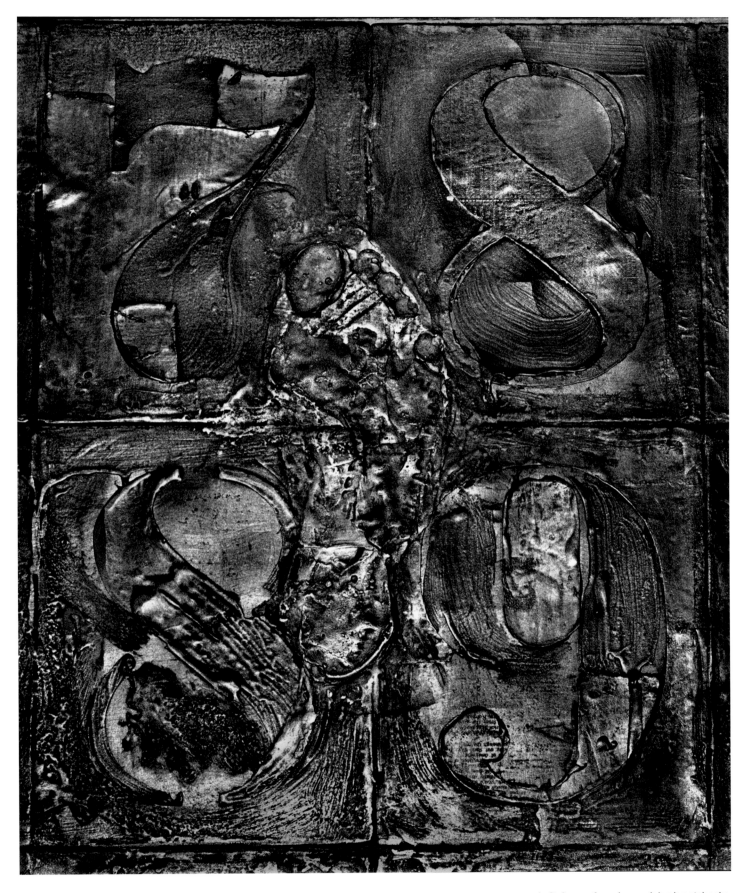

Left: A page from Jasper Johns's notebooks;

Above: Detail, Jasper Johns, *Numbers*, or "Merce's foot? Another kind of ruler."

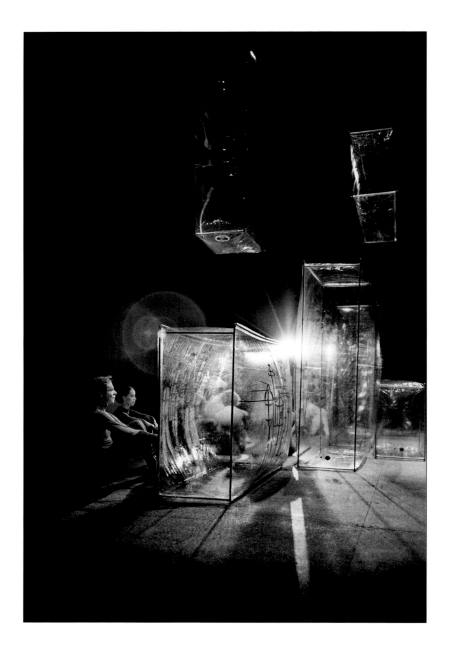

1968 **WALKAROUND TIME**

MUSIC
DAVID BEHRMAN
...FOR NEARLY AN HOUR...

COSTUMES
JASPER JOHNS

DECOR
JASPER JOHNS
(AFTER *THE LARGE GLASS*
BY MARCEL DUCHAMP)
(pictured in inset on following spread)

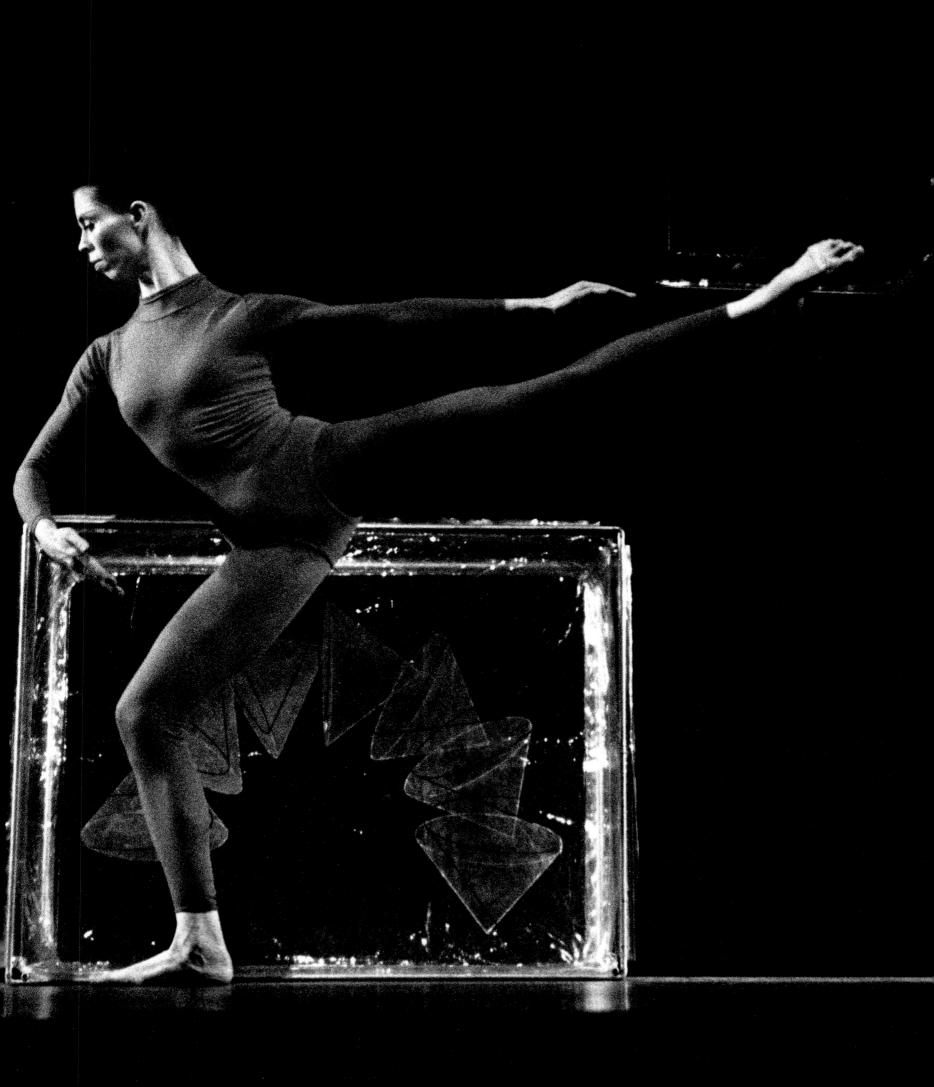

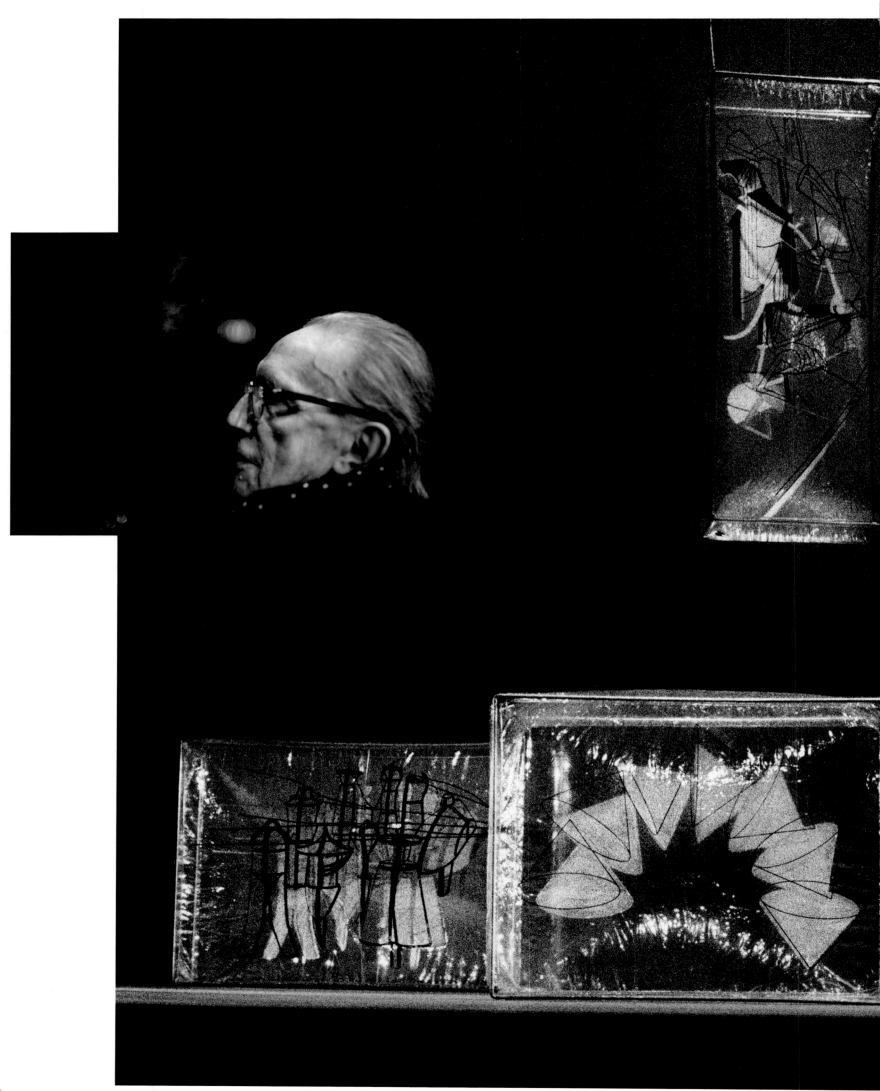

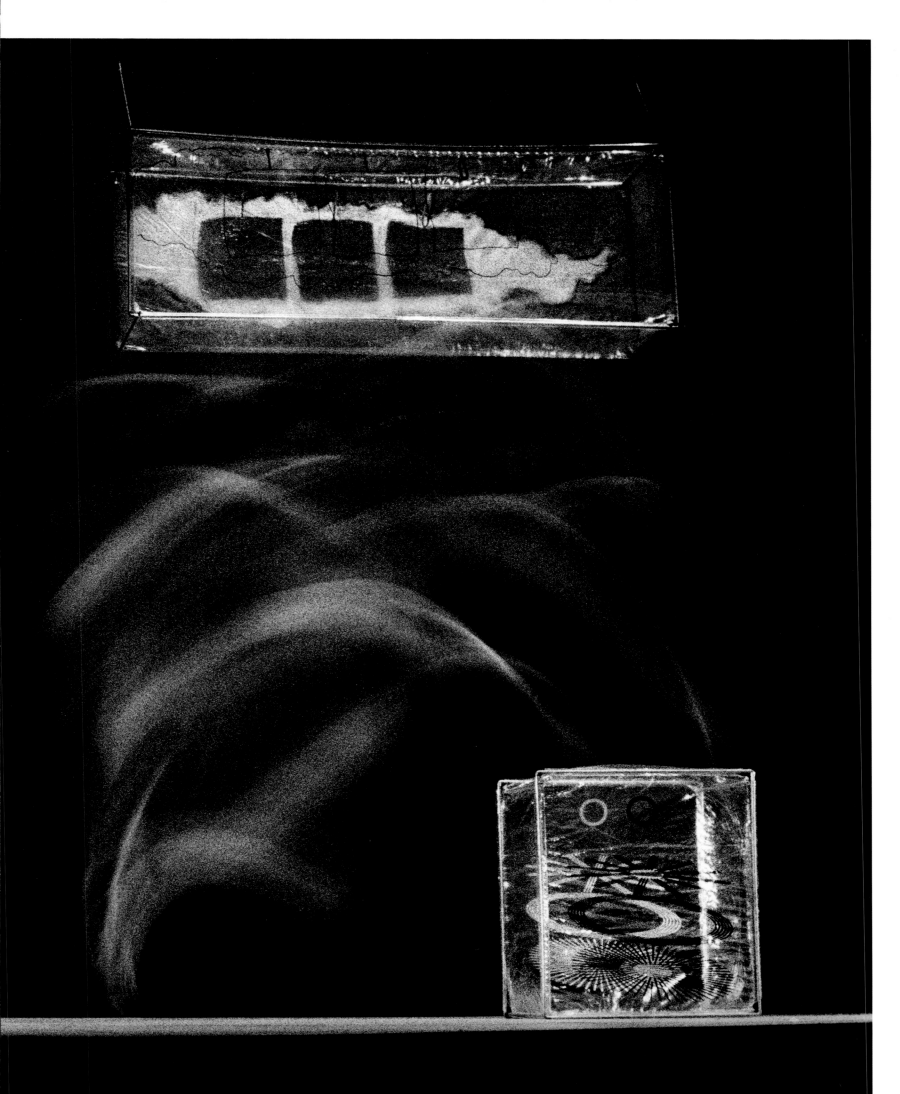

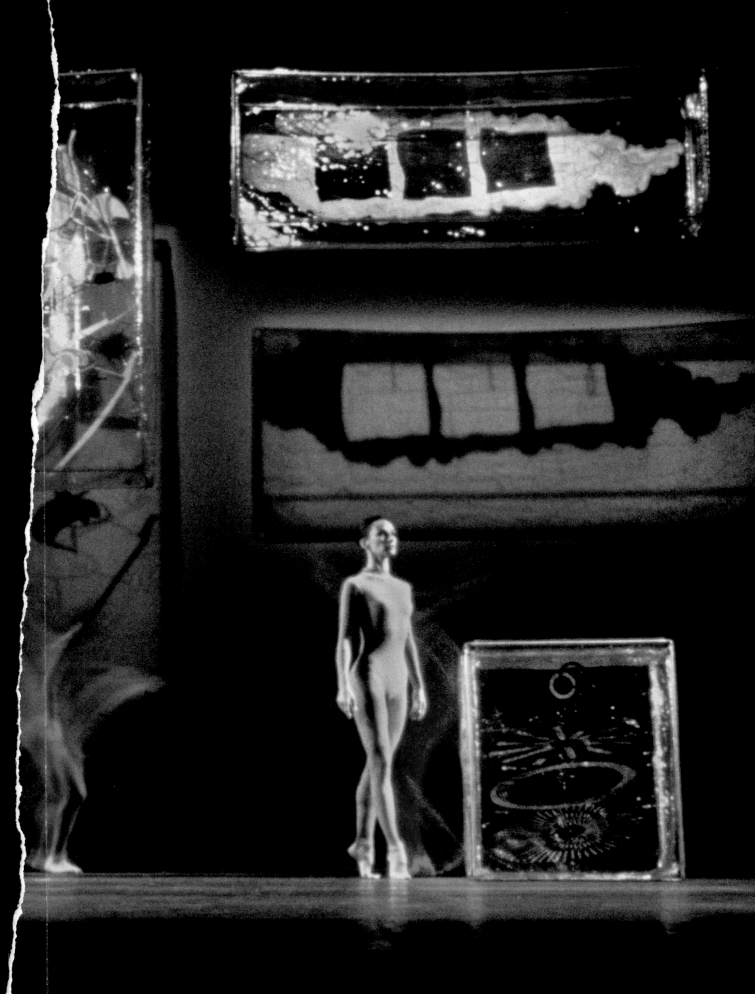

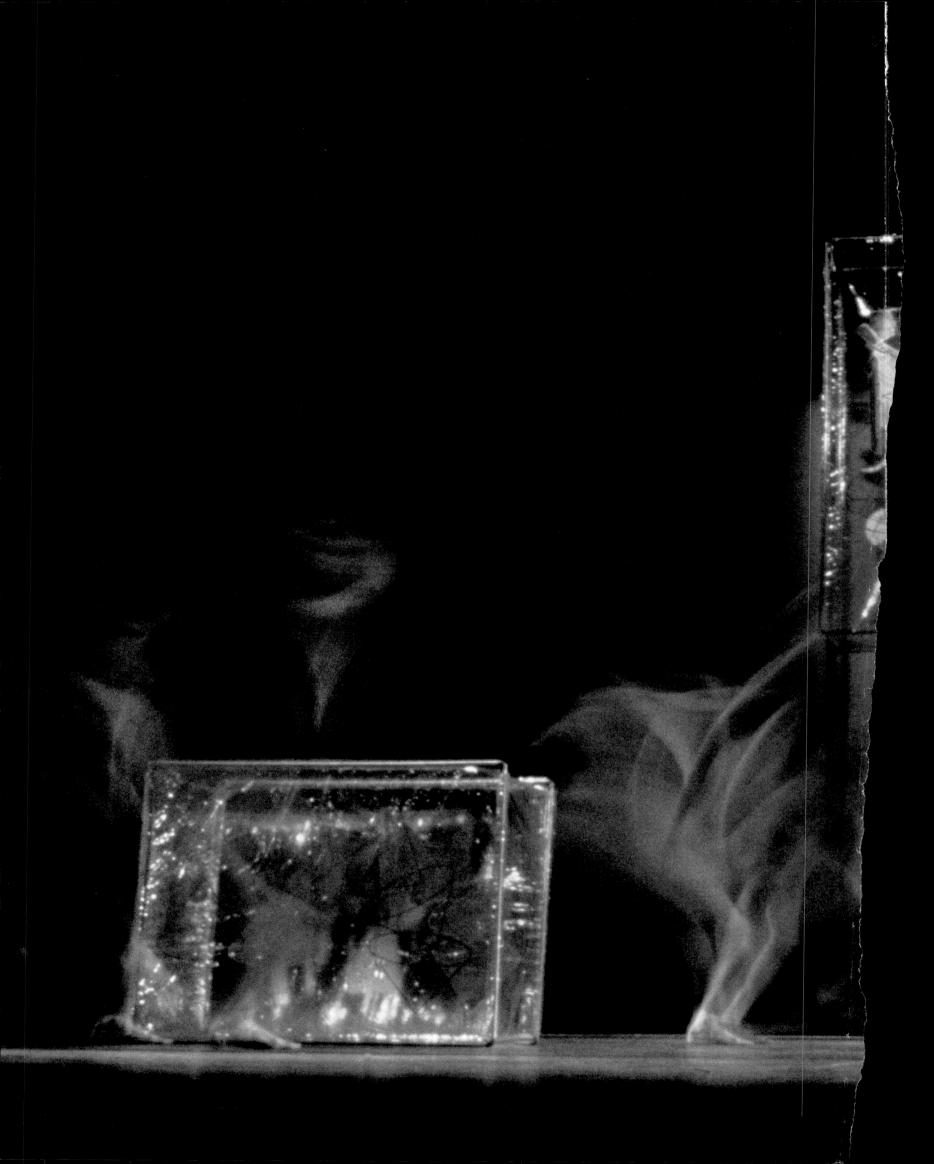

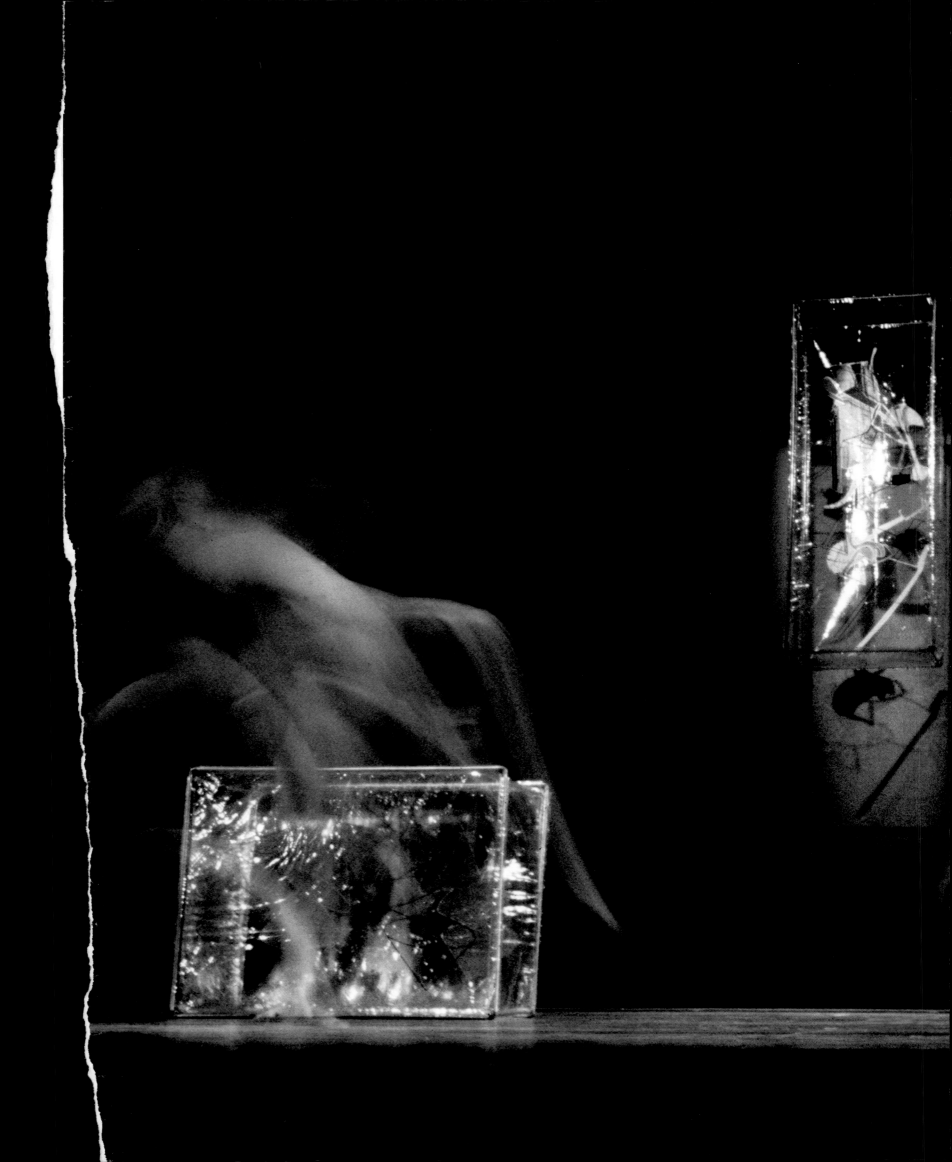

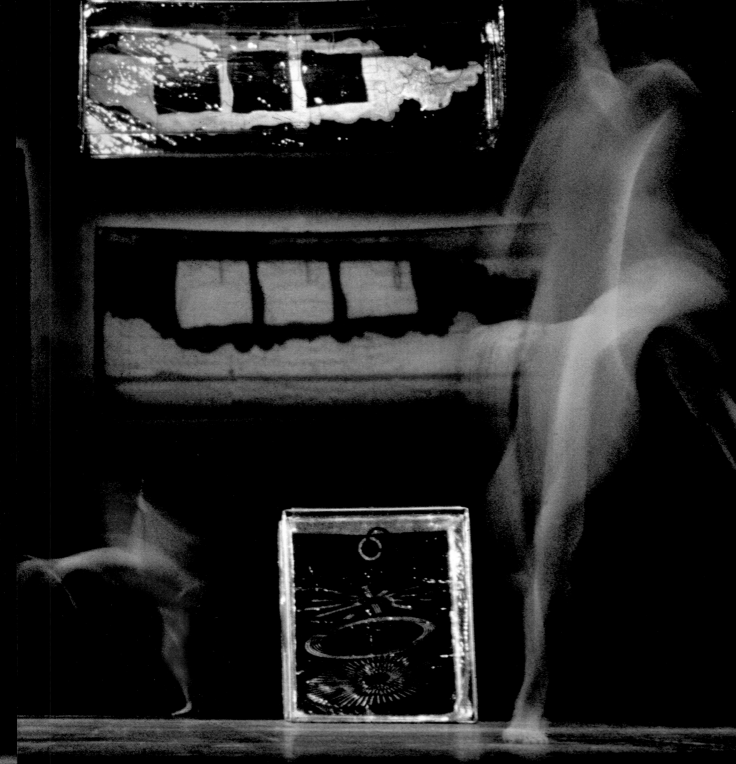

JASPER JOHNS

JAMES KLOSTY: While other artists have chosen to make sets and/or "decors" for the company, with the exception of *Walkaround Time* you have chosen simply to costume the works. Why?

JASPER JOHNS: I don't see the necessity for objects on the stage during a dance. That may be why I rarely have any ideas for sets. Or maybe I have it backward. Perhaps it's because I don't have any ideas that I don't see the necessity.

When Merce suggests that he wants or needs a set, then I try to see to it that he gets one.

I have always felt that each dance should have its own distinctive costumes. A sort of visual novelty is provided that helps make it clear that one dance is not another dance. But I'm beginning to wonder if this is necessary.

JK: Since you have been with the company, the emphasis has been on having different artists contribute designs/decors. What were the chief concerns in selecting artists (if any)?

JJ: I have suggested artists for whose work I have a high regard, who could understand a difference between theater and studio, or gallery scale and space, (sometimes) who could work quickly.

JK: More than once, during rehearsals and elsewhere, I have heard you say—with much enthusiasm—"I *hate* the theater!" For what reasons?

JJ: I think I meant working in the theater.

I don't like the deadlines, the putting up and taking down, the success and failure, the moving about from place to place, the wear and tear and repair, the community of personalities with its and their aches and pains and religions and diets, etc. . . .

JK: How much did you work with Rauschenberg in making costumes and sets in the period before you became artistic advisor?

JJ: I would have to check a catalog of Cunningham dances to be sure. I know I had something to do with helping him to get the set for *Minutiae* to stand up and not fall over and, with the possible exception of *Night Wandering*, I think I assisted him with his work for every dance through *Crises*.

JK: In your notes for the New York State Theater painting, you say that Merce's foot could be used as "another kind of ruler." Were there any other considerations in your mind tor having Merce's foot in a work for this particular building?

JJ: I didn't feel that my work belonged in the theater and I felt that his did, I thought his foot should get through the door.

JK: The book contains photographs of you spraying the dancers in their *Canfield* costumes. Did Robert Morris provide specific sketches, instructions, and details for this dance or simply a generalized idea? It the latter, what was it? Visually, did the dance work as was intended?

JJ: Bob Morris gave me either written or oral instructions. I think that he and Yvonne Rainer had recently performed a dance in which they wore only "coats" of oil. His first idea for *Canfield* was that the dancers should be naked but coated with a substance that changes colors in response to changes in temperature.

Jasper Johns, Gemini G.E.L., Los Angeles, 1971

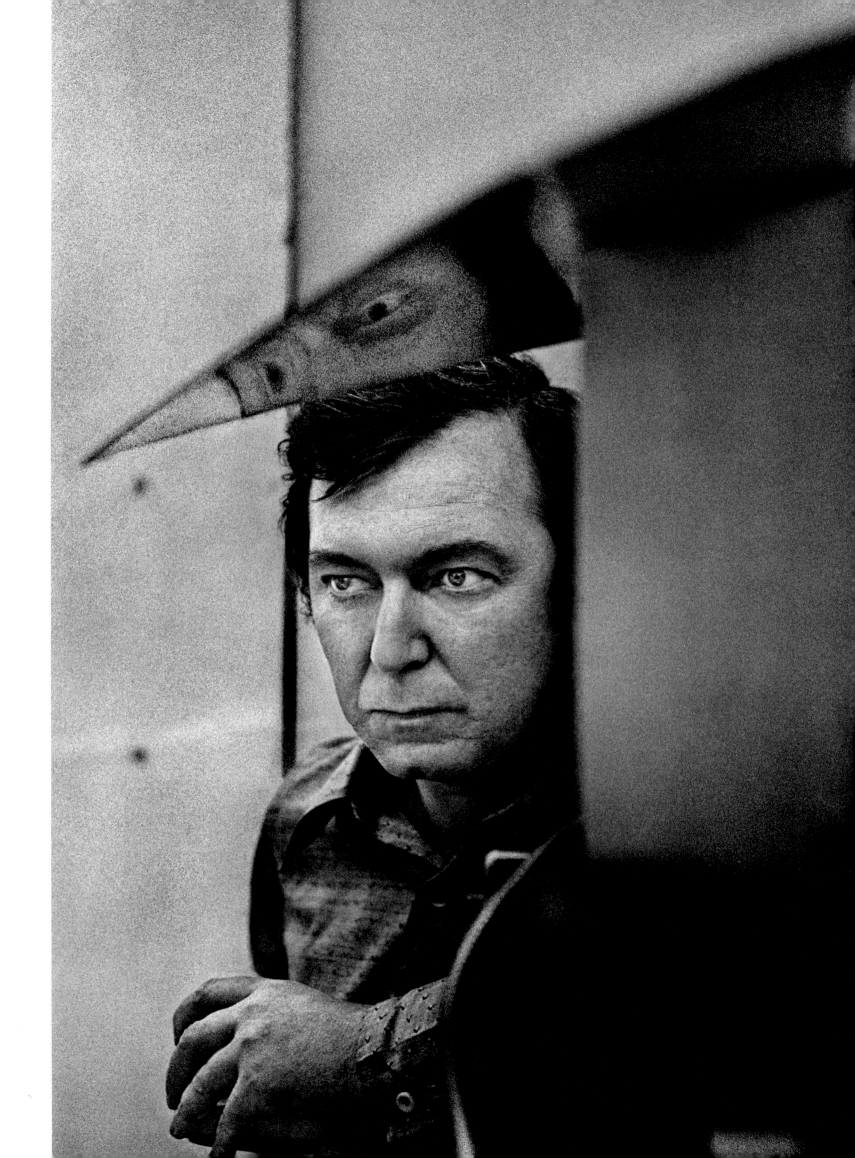

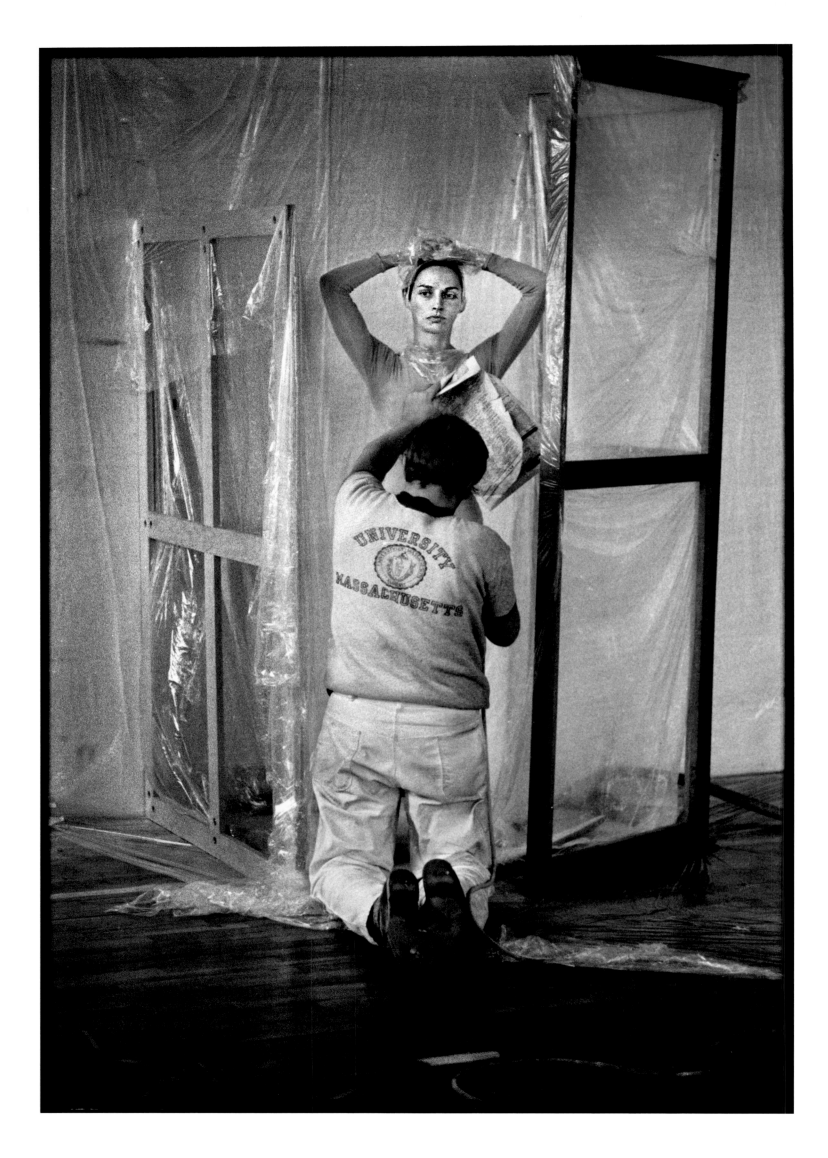

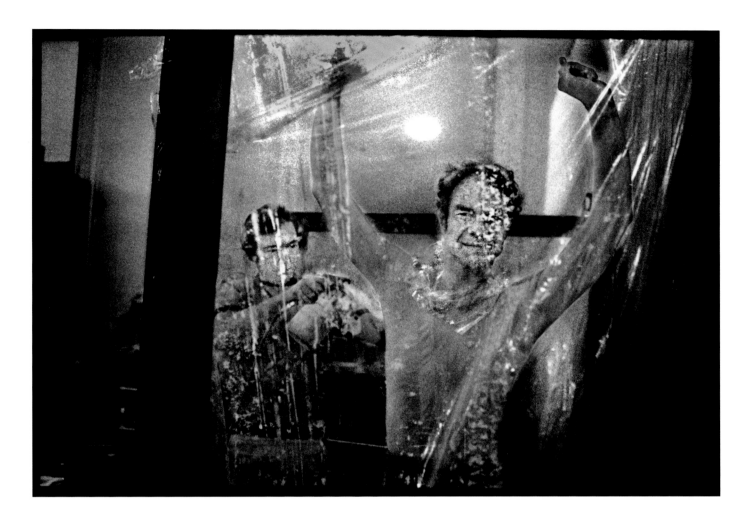

Cunningham didn't care for the nudity or the body makeup idea, and Morris then decided that there should be a backdrop coated with a highly reflective substance, made of minute glass beads, which is often used on traffic signs on highways. At night these signs appear to tight up as one approaches them in a car.

The dancers were to be dressed in the same material. Moving at a constant speed back and forth across the proscenium, there was to be a vertical panel of lights directed upstage.

Kenneth Noland loaned us a large studio that he had just acquired but was not yet using, and I painted the backdrop there. The dancers came to my studio to put on their tights and leotards for me to spray them. Jim Baird got the panel of lights made.

Everything was finished just in time for the *Canfield* premiere, and nothing worked as intended.

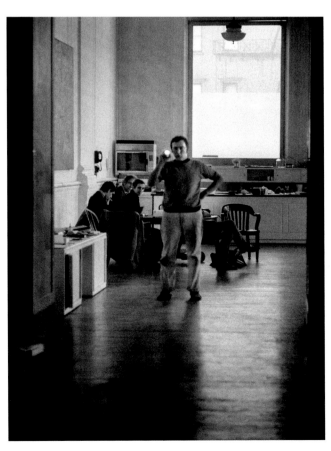

Left: Jasper Johns spray-painting Carolyn Brown's
Canfield costume, Houston Street studio, April 1969;
Above: Jasper Johns spray-painting
Merce Cunninghams's *Canfield* costume, April 1969;
Right: Checking costume reflectivity

The light source must be fairly near the eye of the observer for the "lighting-up" effect to occur. One can sit in the theater and direct a flashlight at the stage and get something of the intended effect, but the audience have never been given flashlights.

JK: How did the idea for the *Walkaround Time* set come about? Were any fundamental aesthetic or conceptual ties between Merce's work and Duchamp's work involved in the choice of *The Large Glass* beyond the belief that visually it would make an excellent decor?

JJ: I said to Merce Cunningham that I thought there should be a Duchamp set. He said that would be nice and that he was working on a new dance. I had just come upon a little booklet with line drawings of details of *The Large Glass* and I thought the set could be based on these. We visited Duchamp, and I mentioned the idea to him. He asked in a shocked tone of voice, "But who would do the work?" I said that I would do it, and he said, "Certainly." I gave Cunningham the approximate number and sizes of boxes so that in making the dance he could work with cardboard substitutes, and said that any of them could be anywhere on the stage.

I painted the images on plastic in David Whitney's Canal Street loft. He and David White helped me with the large silkscreens and with filling in the colors. Jim Baird (I think) found someone to fabricate the boxes.

When they had been completed I took Duchamp to the Canal Street studio to look at them. He seemed pleased and said that at some point in the dance he would like to see the pieces put together so that the different elements would relate to one another as they do in *The Large Glass*.

Cunningham saw the set and I the dance for the first time, I think, on the day before the premiere in Buffalo, and the final decisions about placement were made then.

At the end of the first performance, I told Duchamp that he should go on stage for a bow. He asked wasn't I going too. I said no. He said, as he went, "I'm just as frightened as you are."

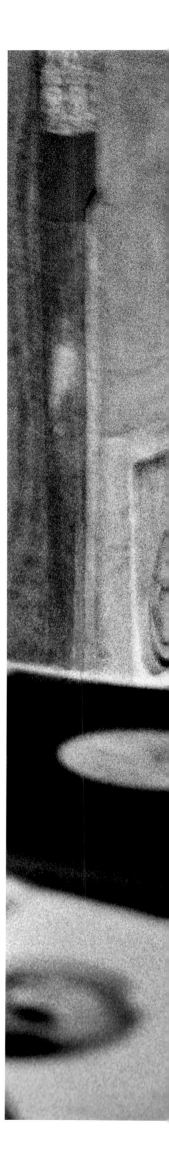

Jasper Johns, Houston Street studio, March 1972

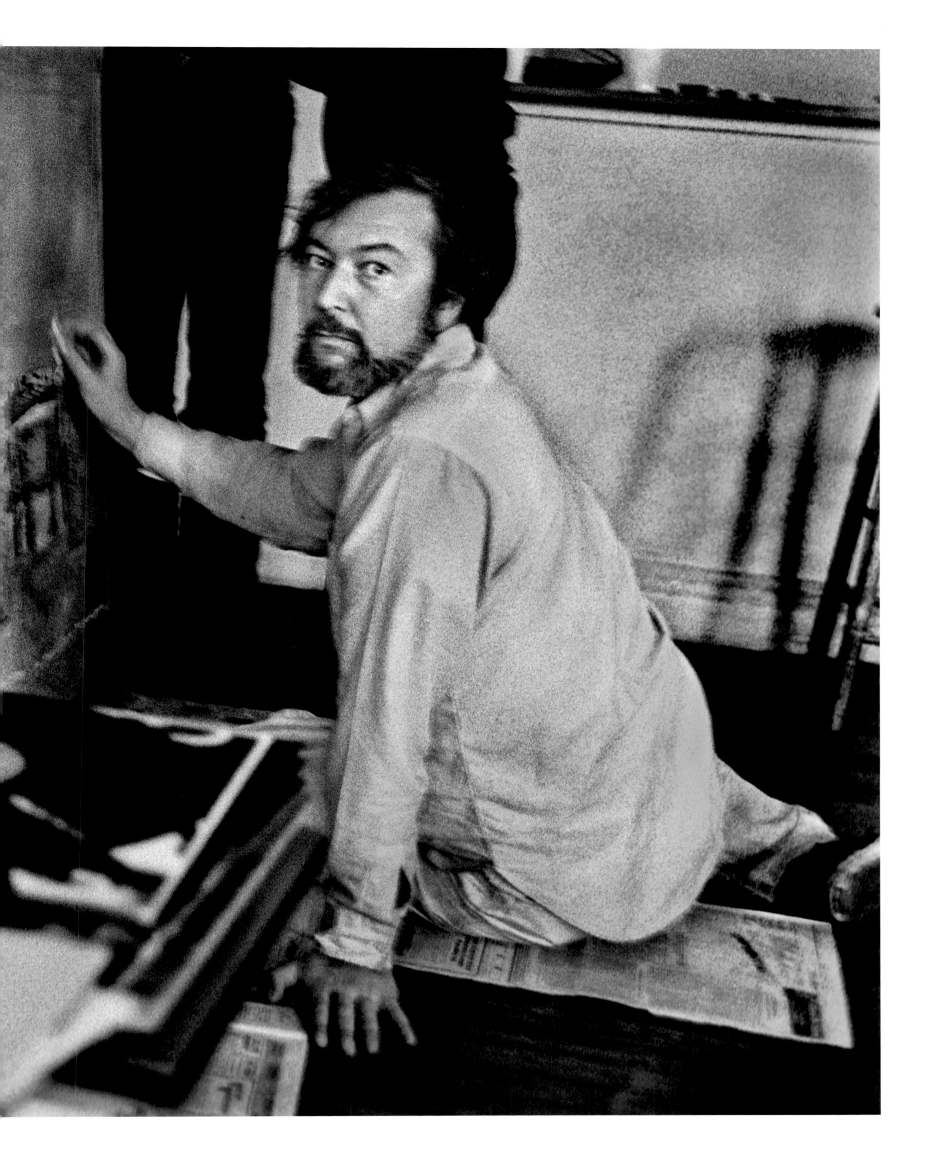

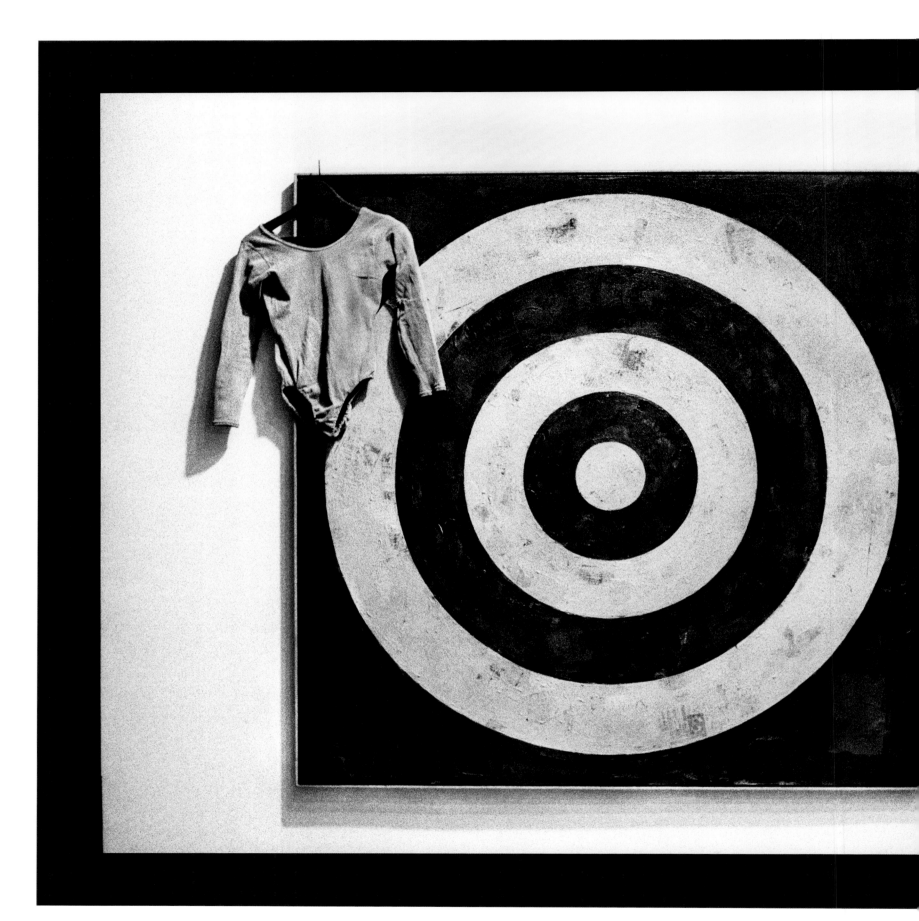

One way to dry a leotard, April 1969

Emotion
is rarely
the subject
of his work,
but it
does seem
to be a
source
of the work.
It prompts
the movement,
qualifies the time,
colors
the kinds
of space
the dances
offer.
I always
felt this,
but maybe the
feeling
is intensified
by the
memory
of old
experiences
from the time
when I felt
there was
only
the present
tense.

—Jasper Johns

1969 CANFIELD

MUSIC
PAULINE OLIVEROS
IN MEMORIAM: NIKOLA TESLA, COSMIC ENGINEER

COSTUMES
JASPER JOHNS

DECOR
ROBERT MORRIS

LIGHTING
UNAVOIDABLY BY THE MORRIS DECOR,
WHEN AVAILABLE, TRAVERSING THE STAGE

ADDITIONAL LIGHTING
RICHARD NELSON

*When performed complete this is a full evening work, premiering as
such at the Brooklyn Academy of Music in silence due to a dispute
between musicians and electricians unions. Often performed excerpted
as one-third of a program and in events.

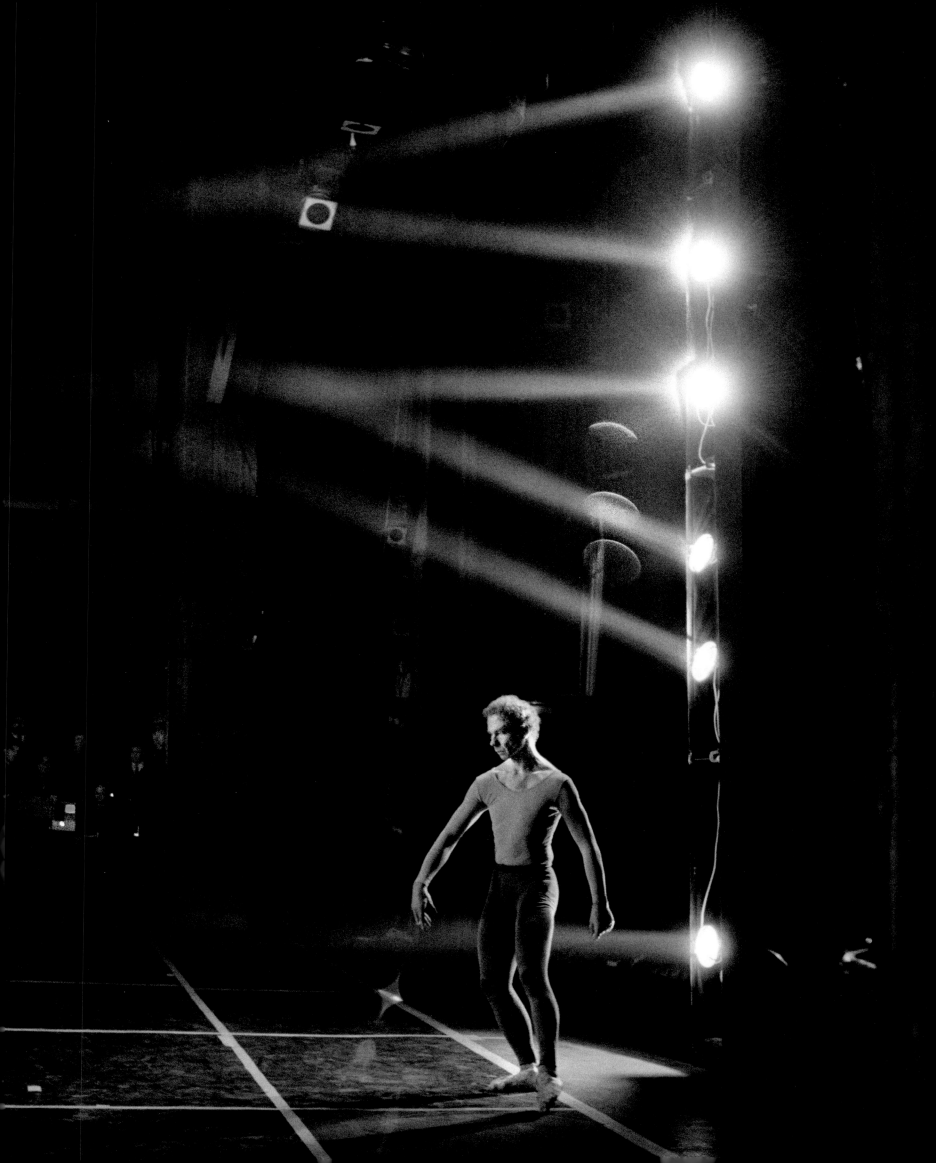

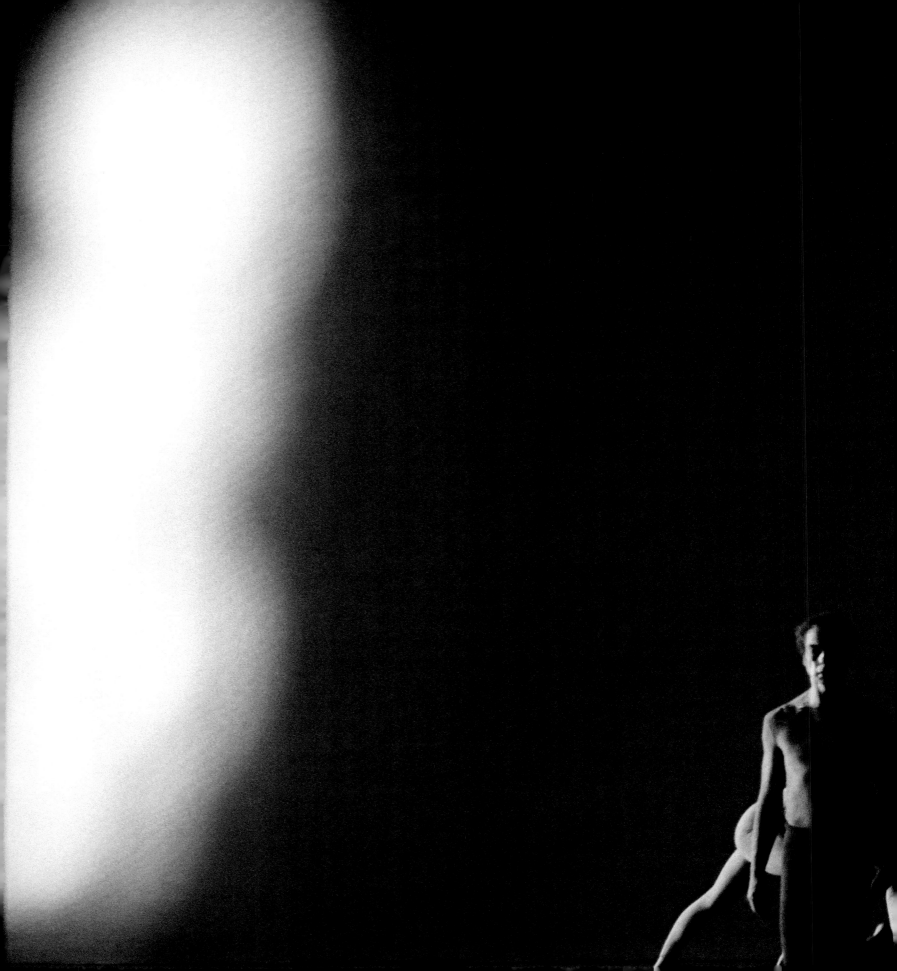

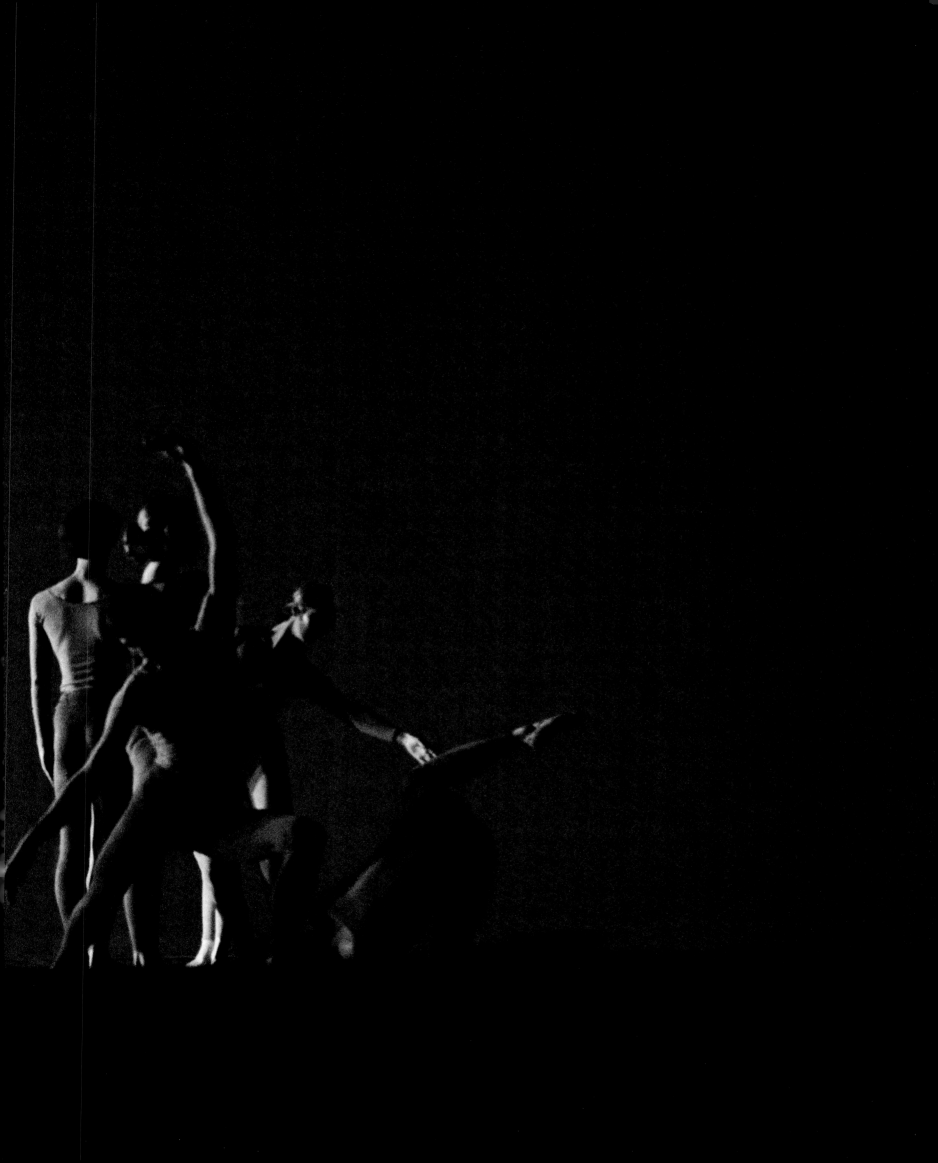

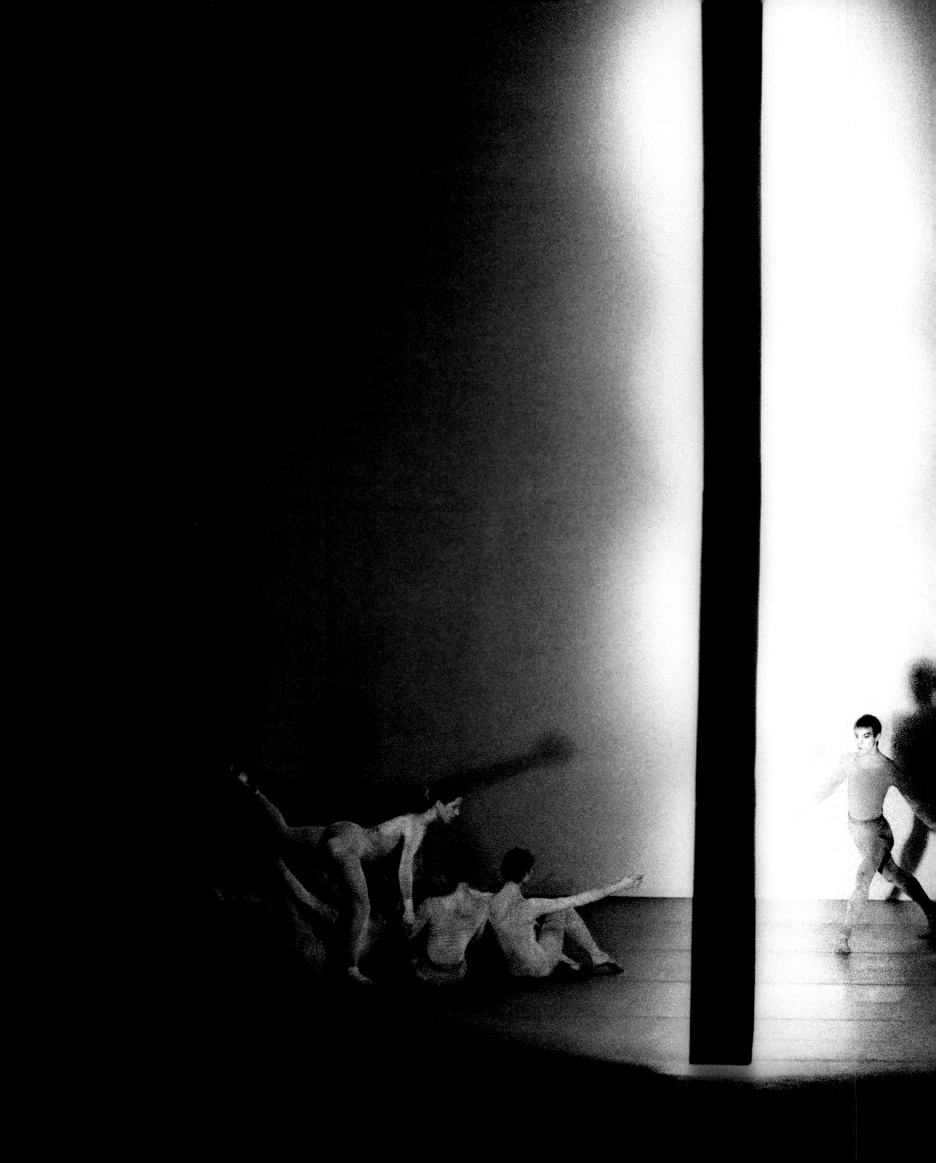

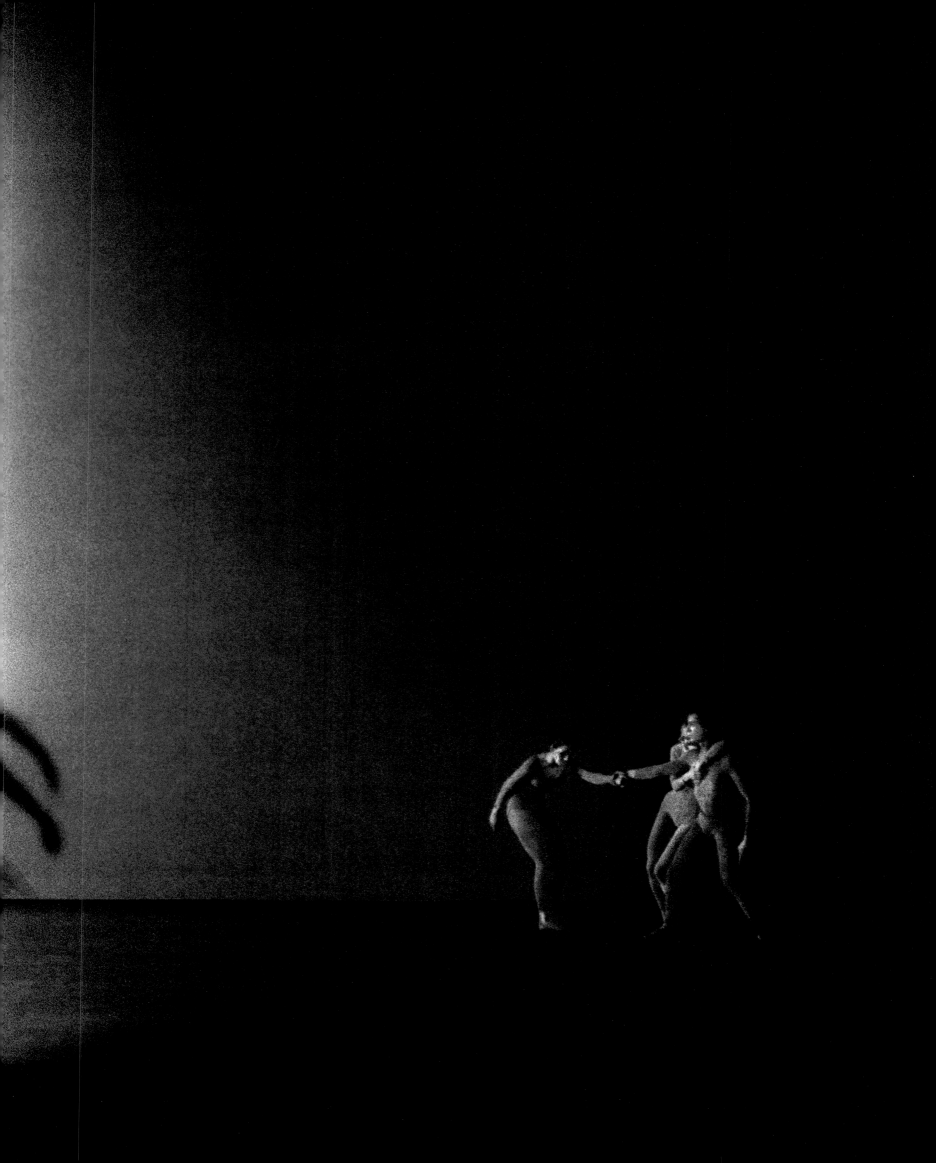

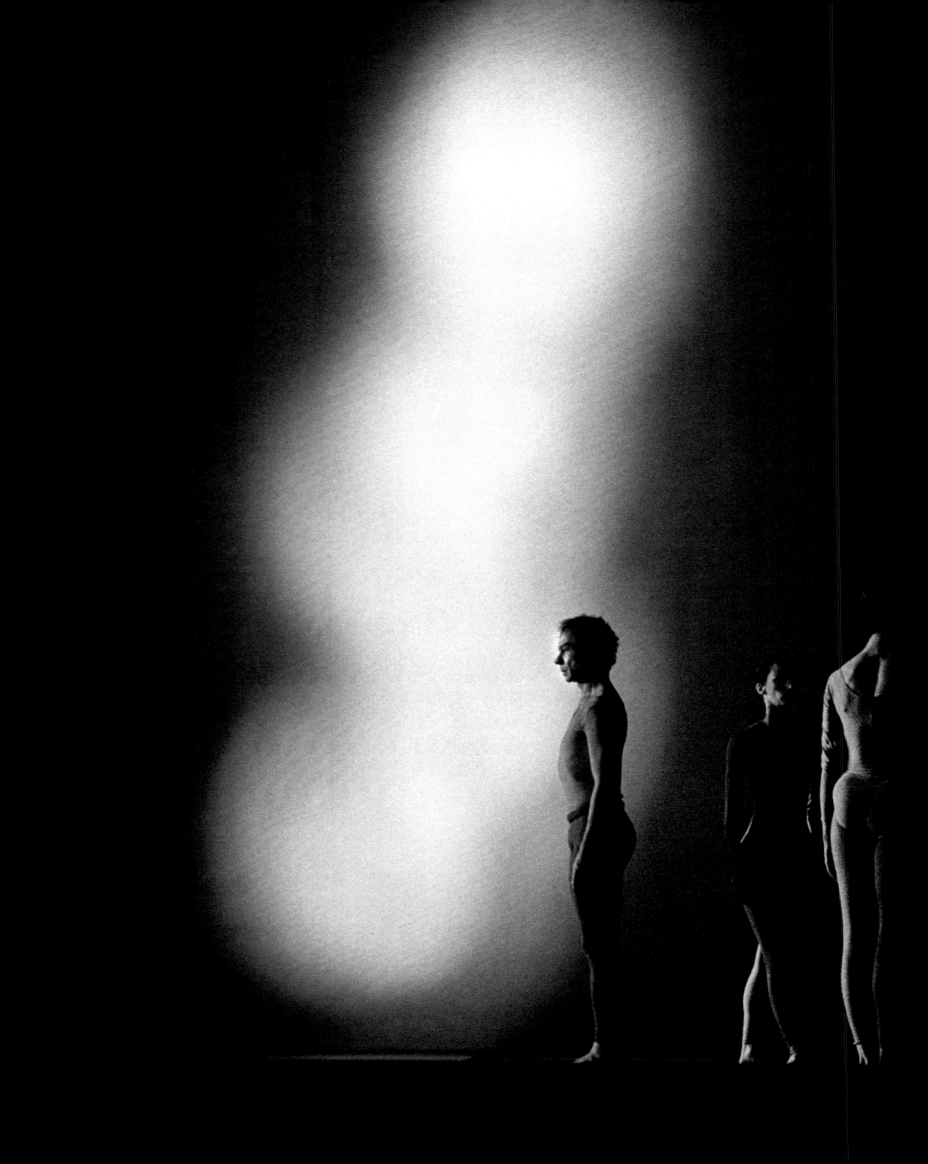

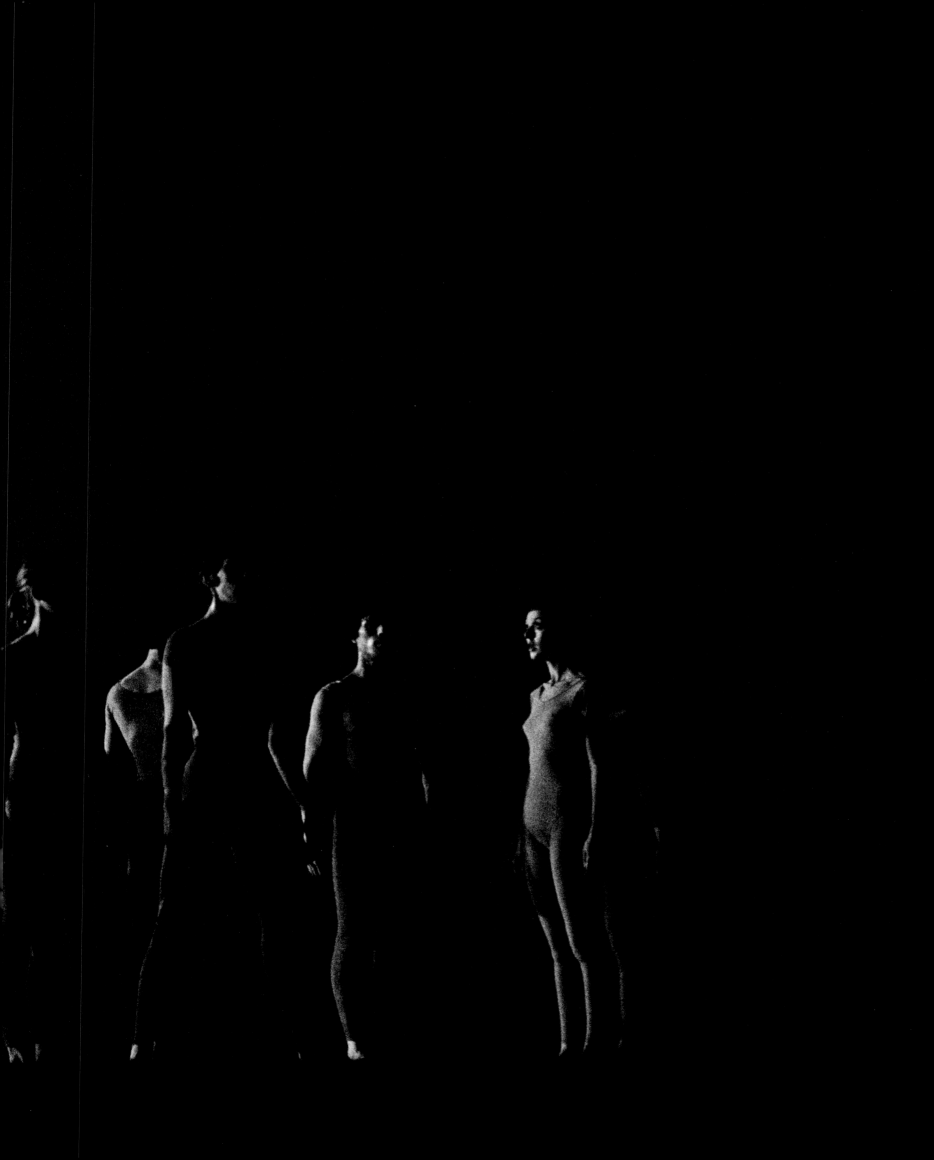

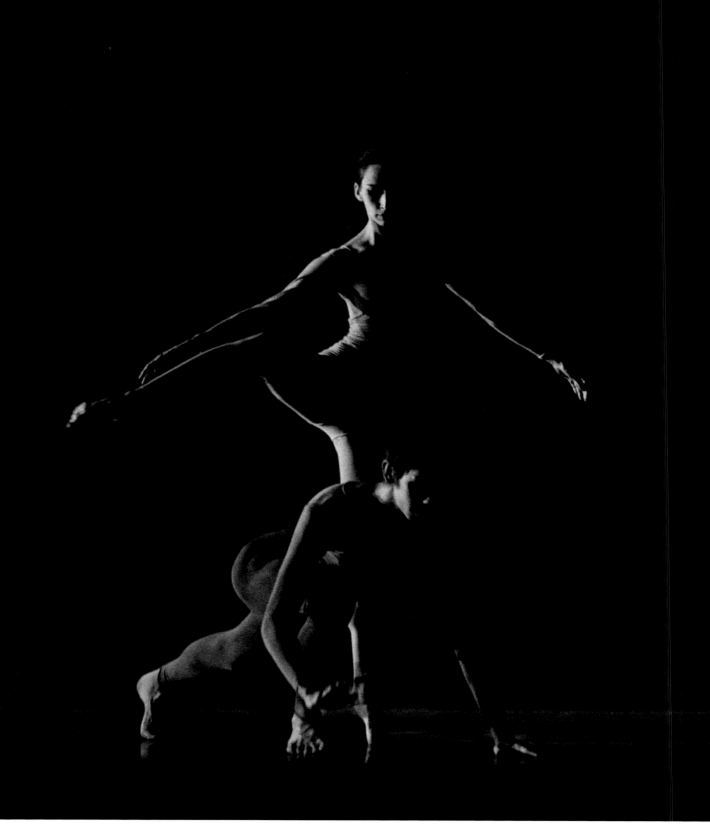

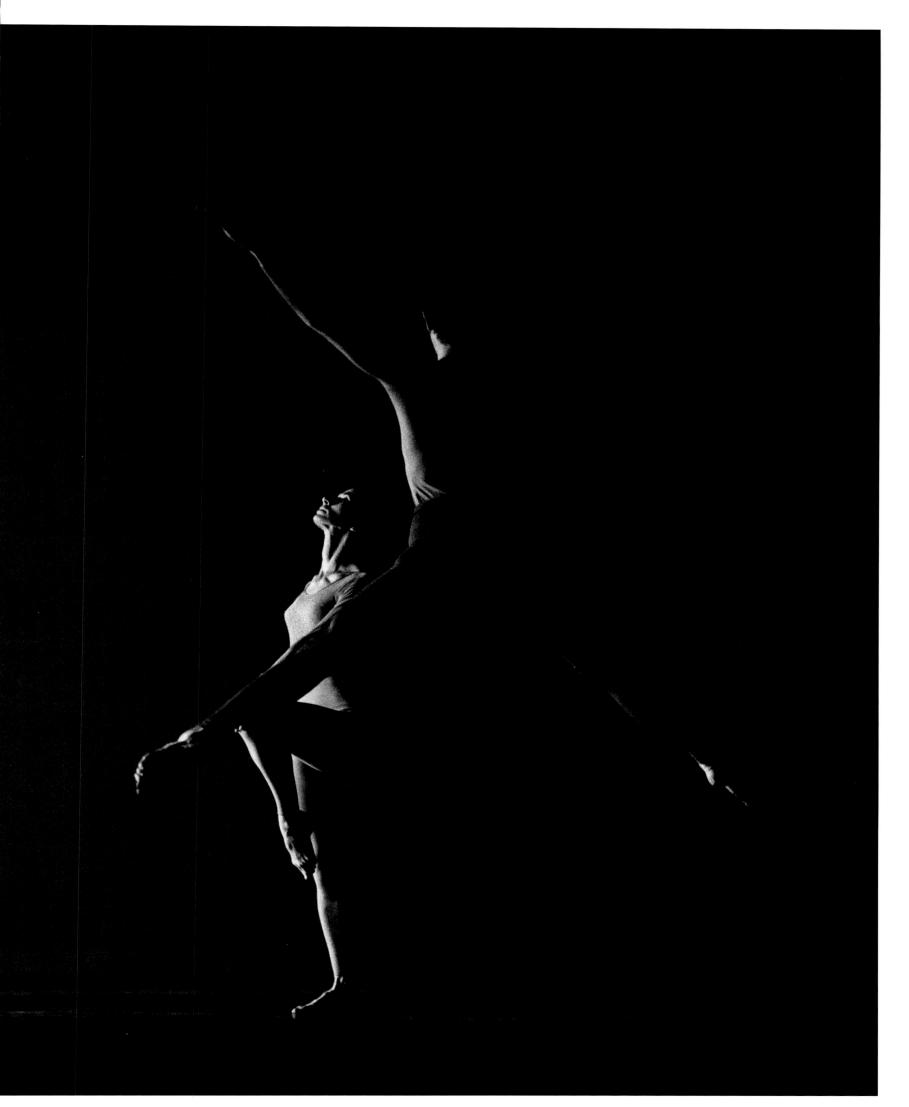

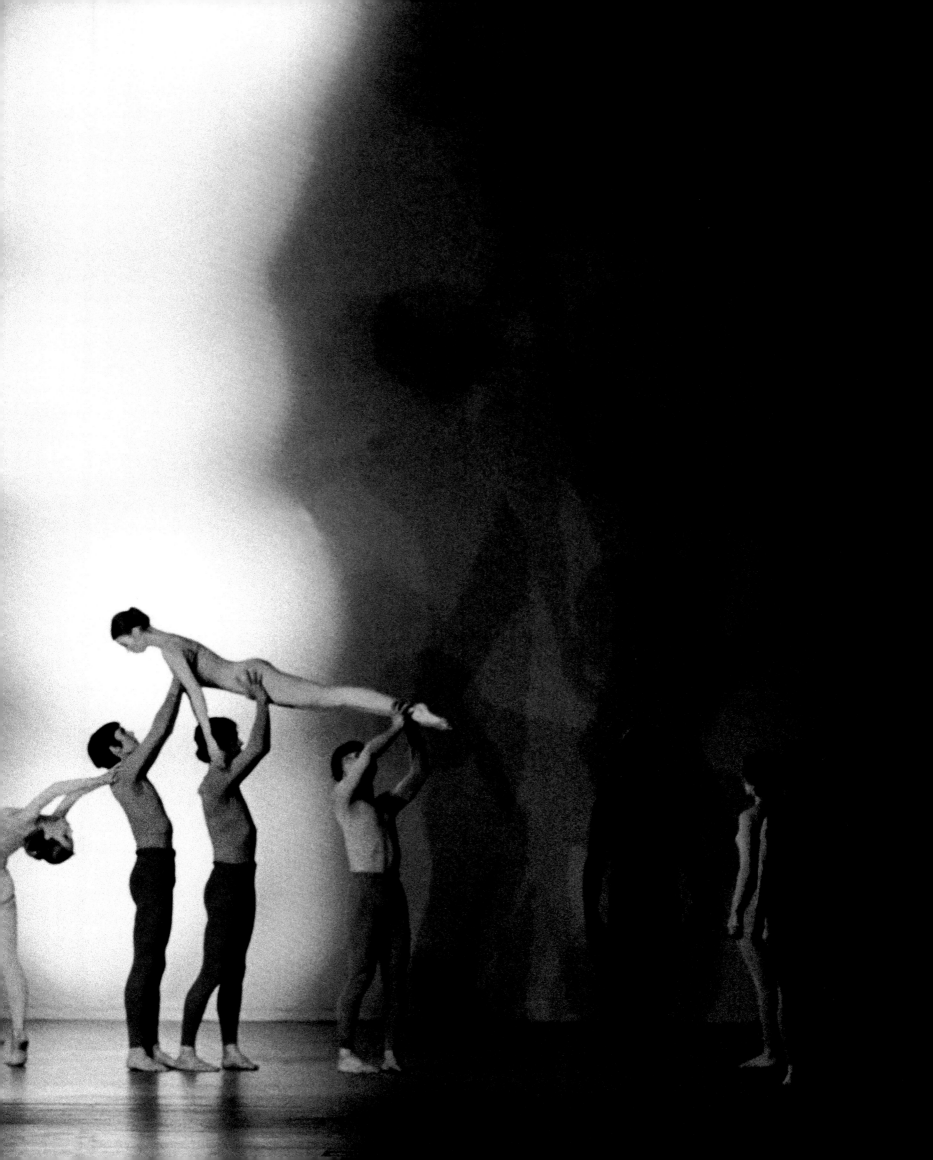

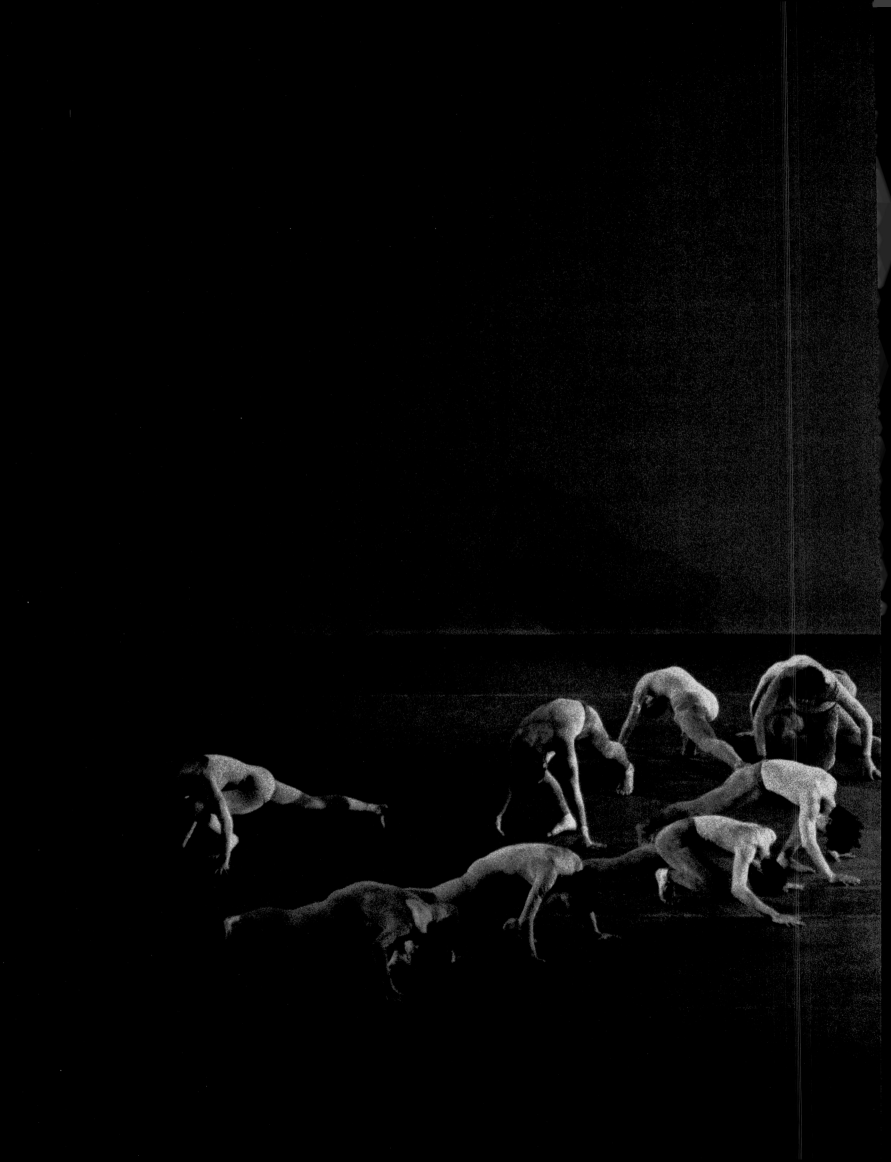

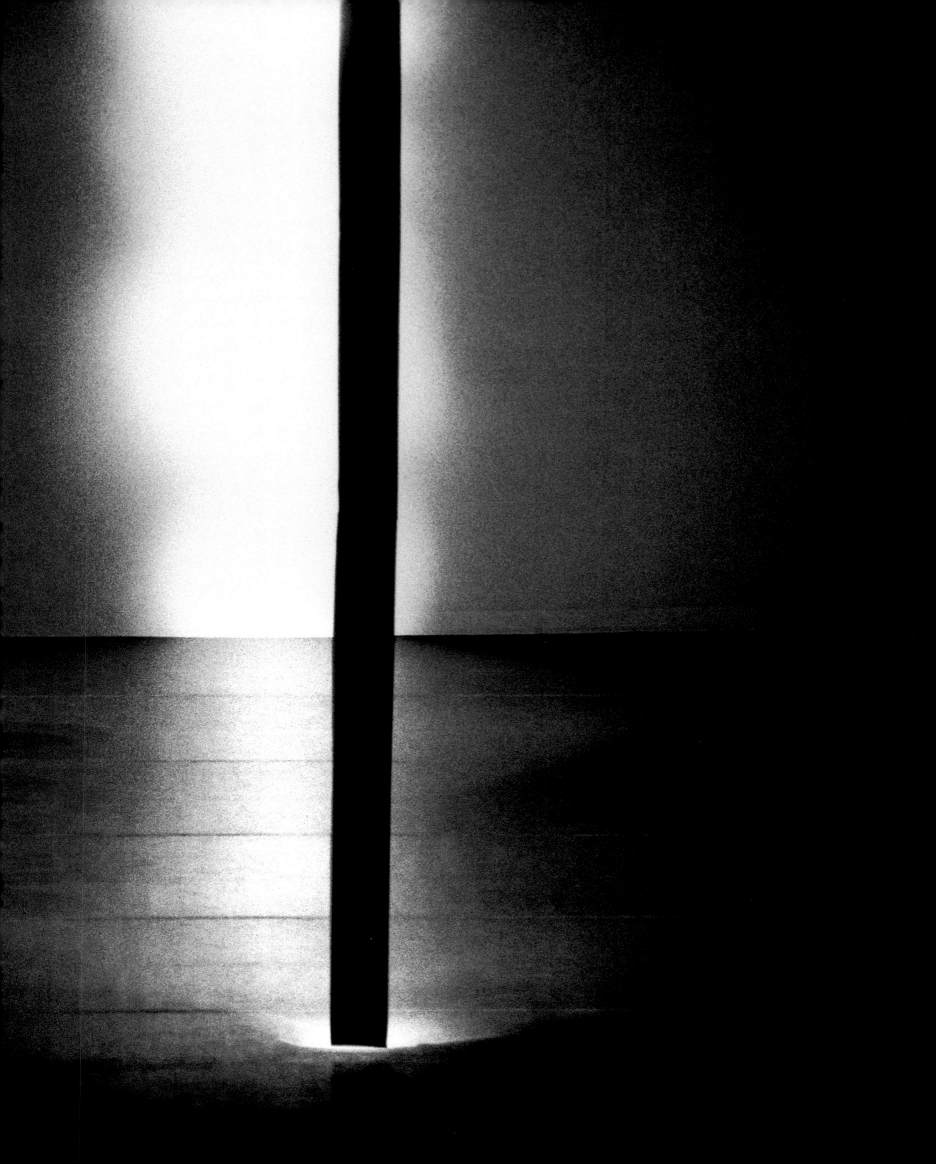

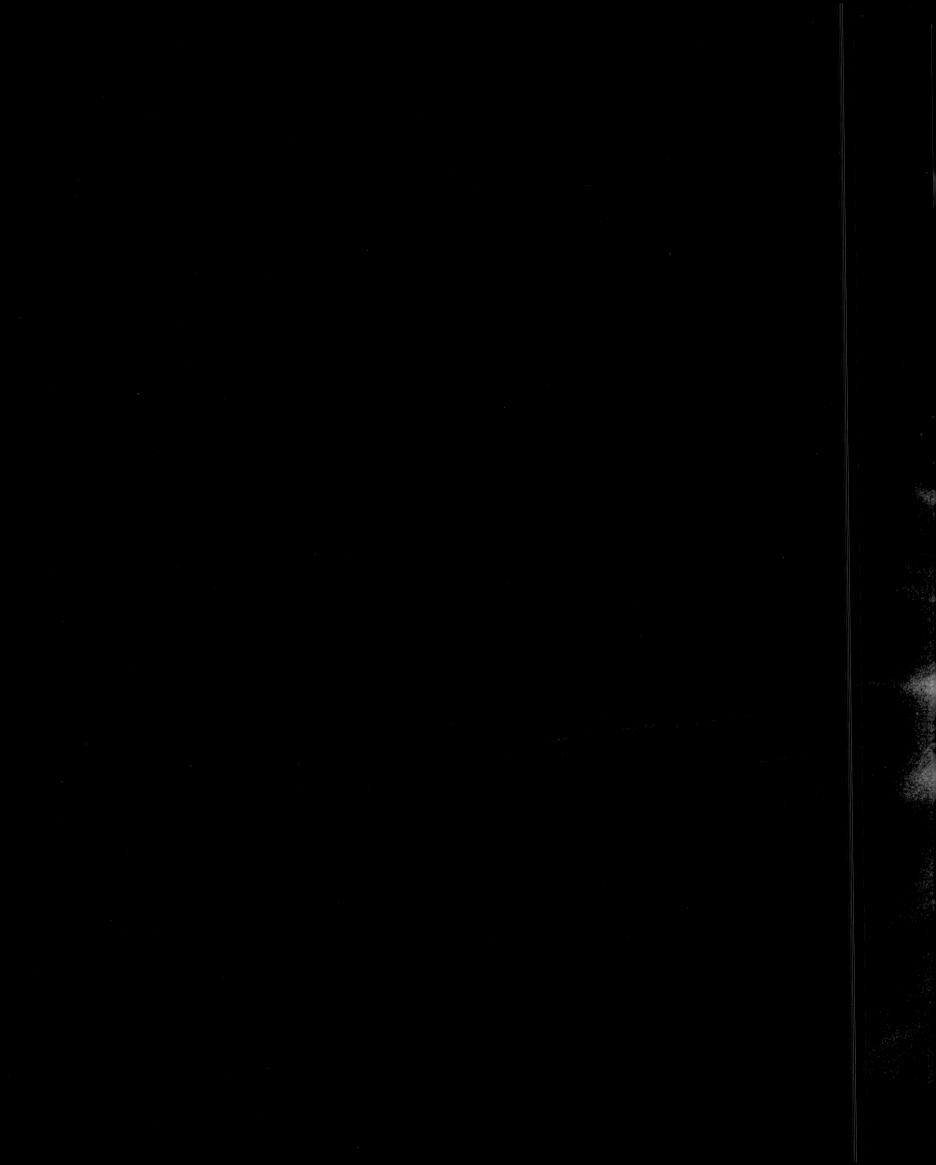

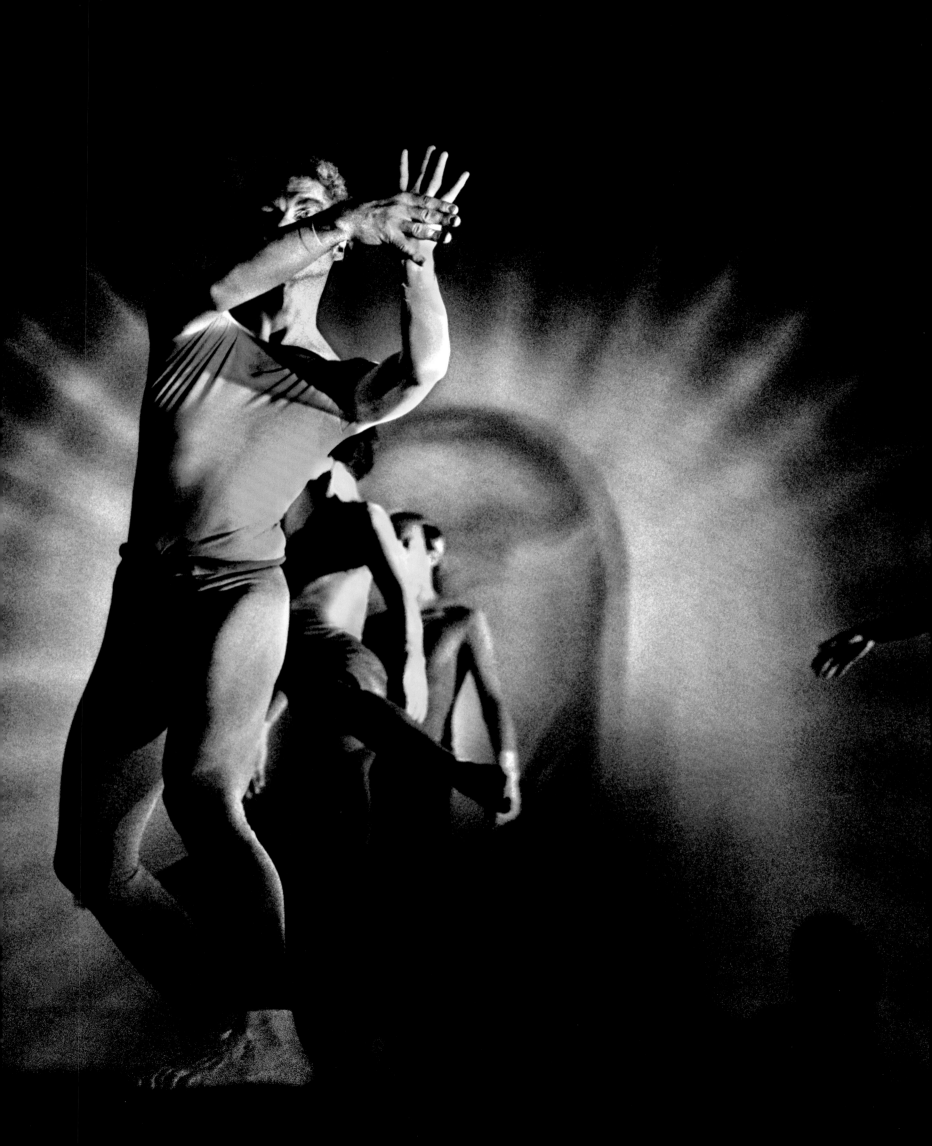

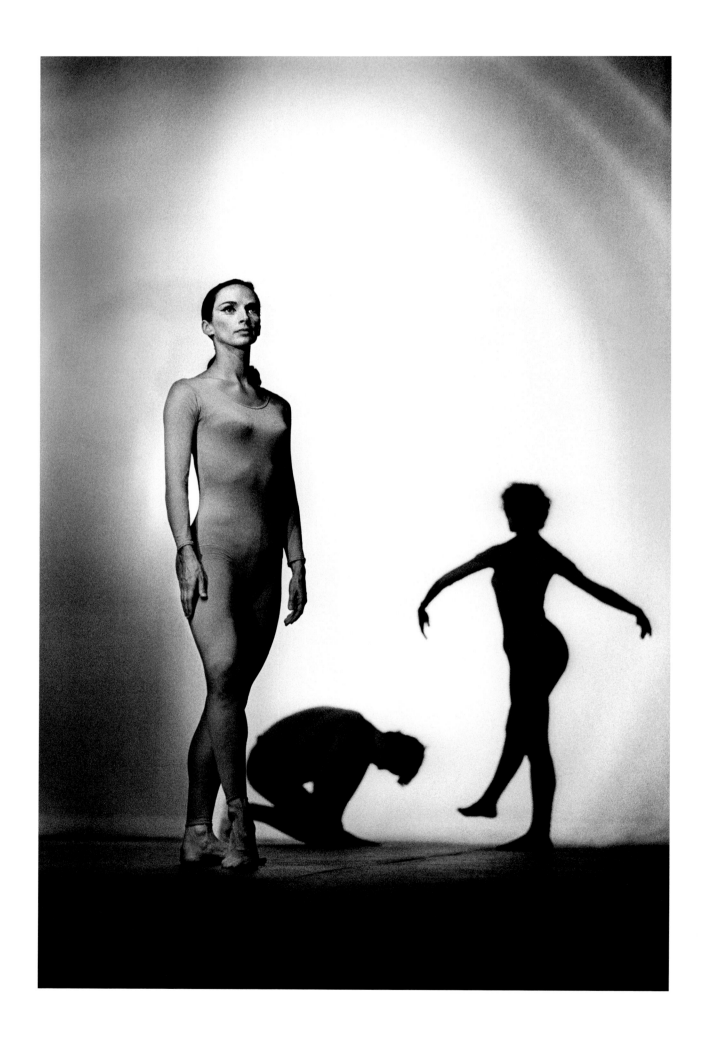

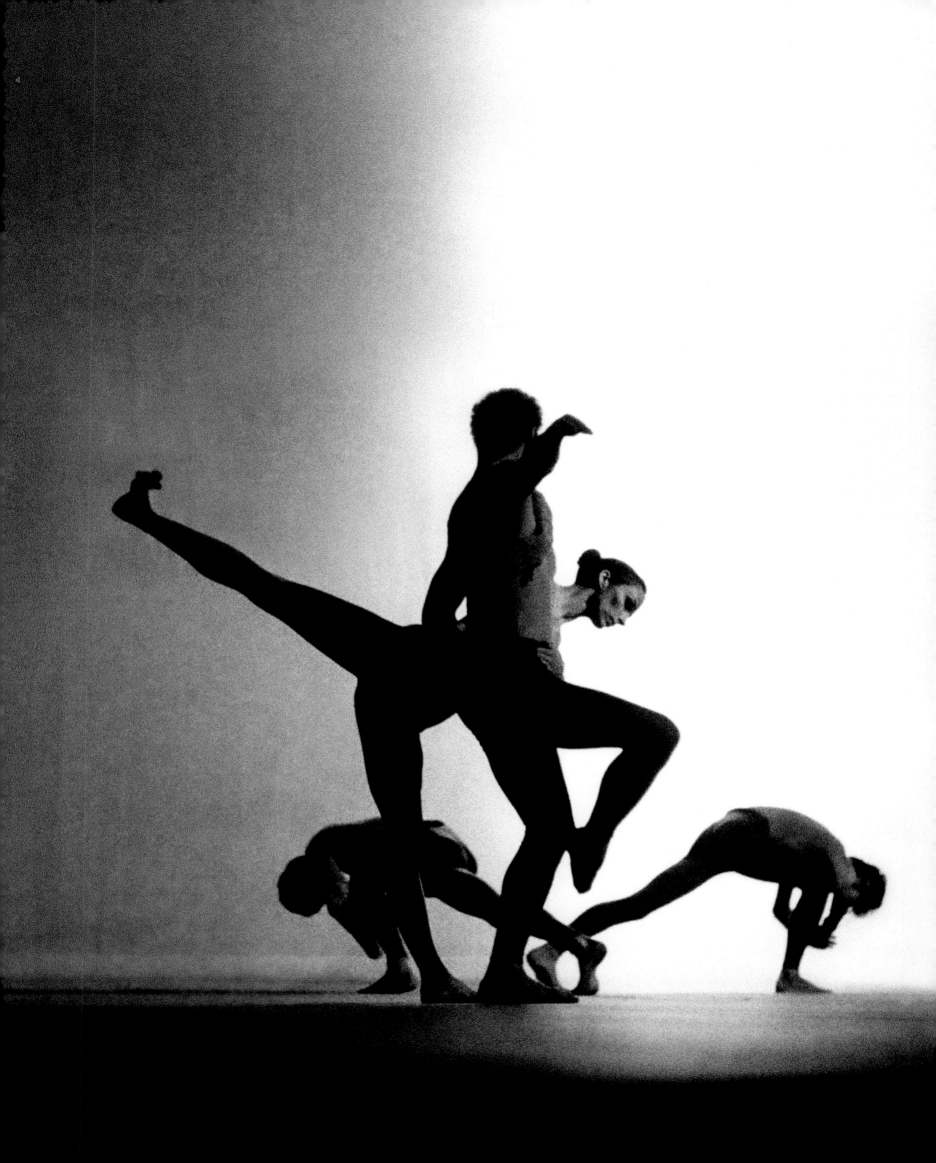

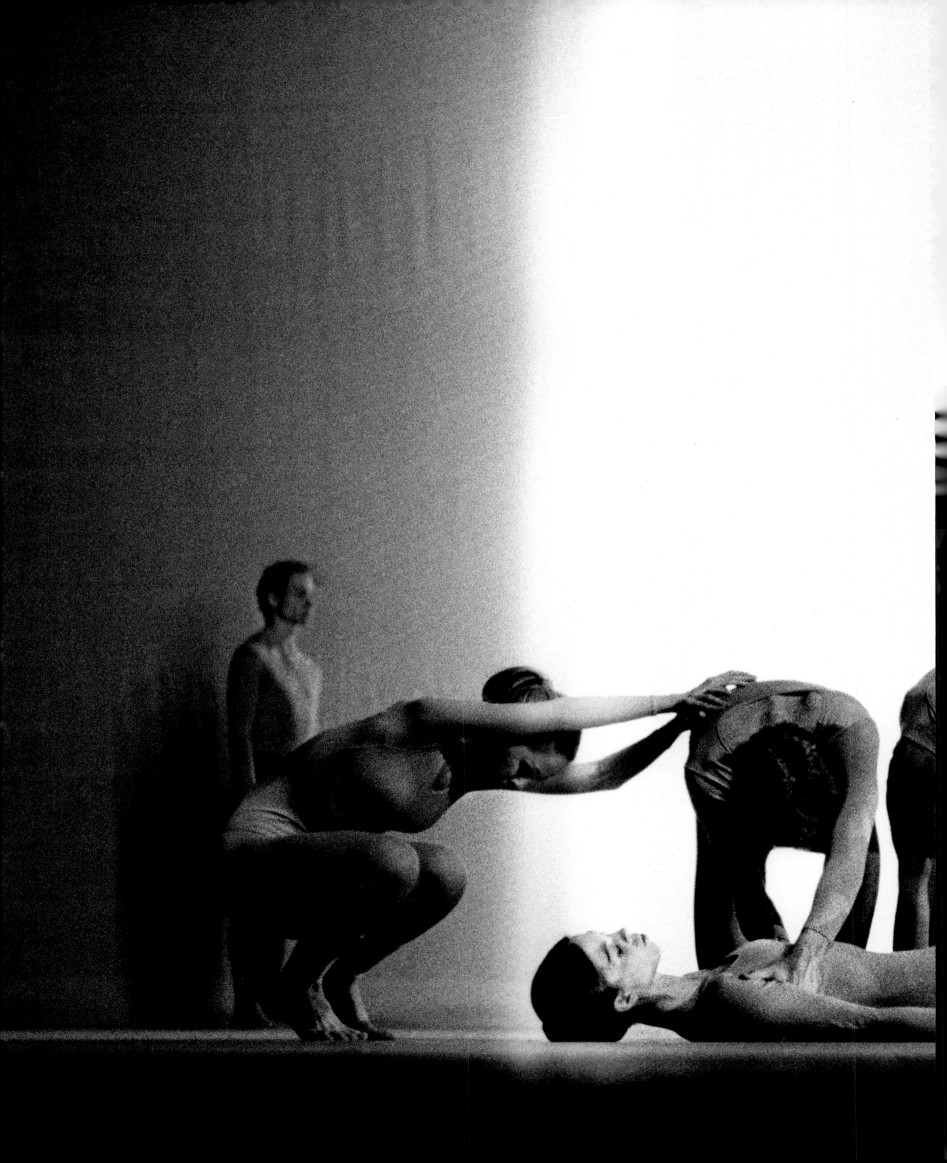

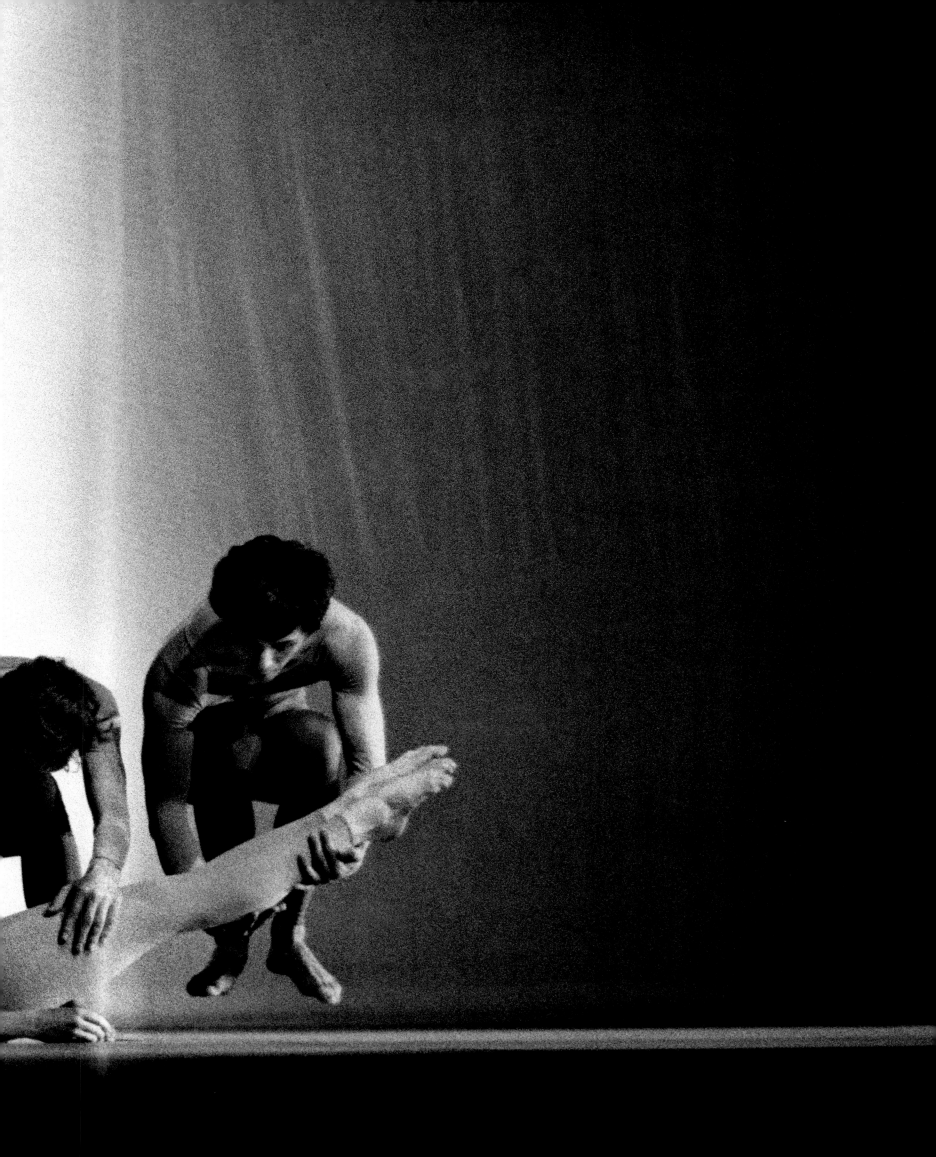

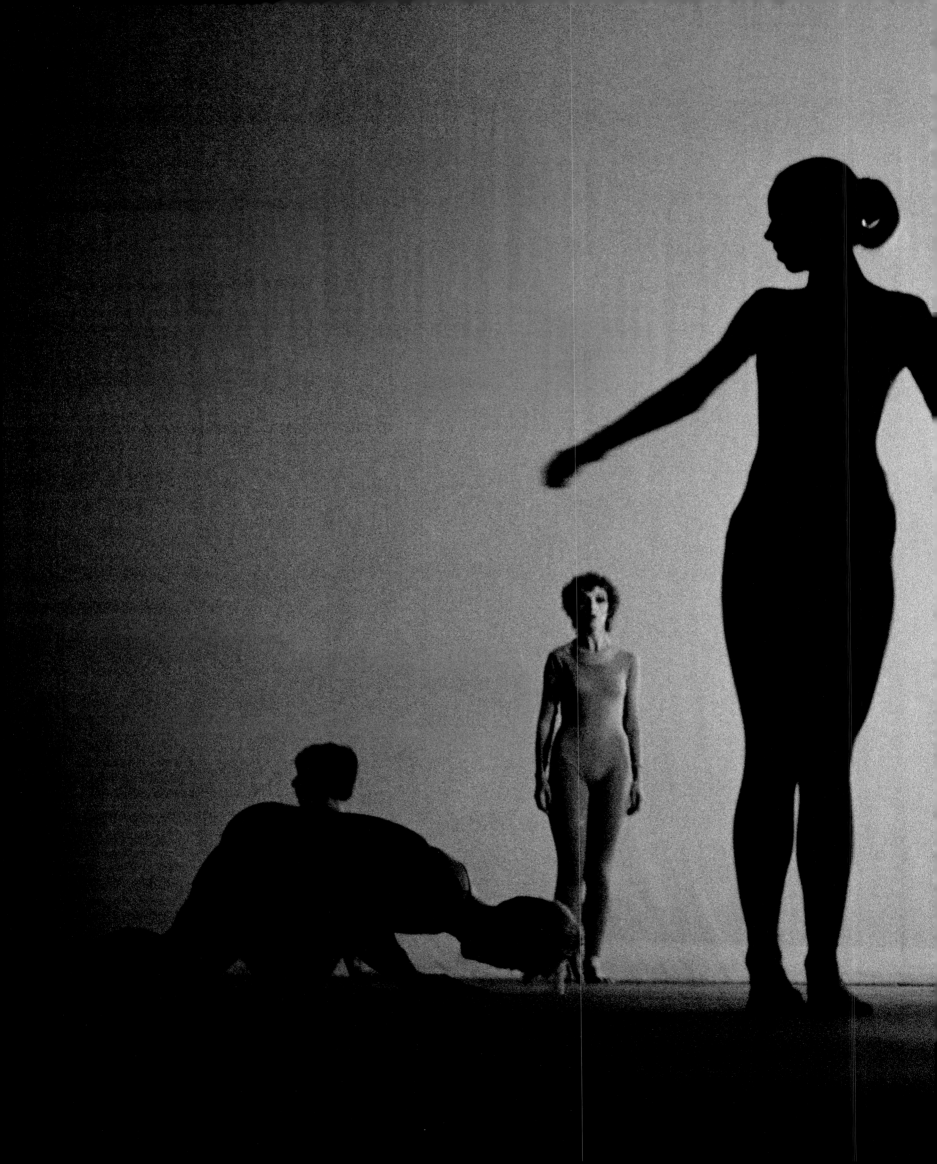

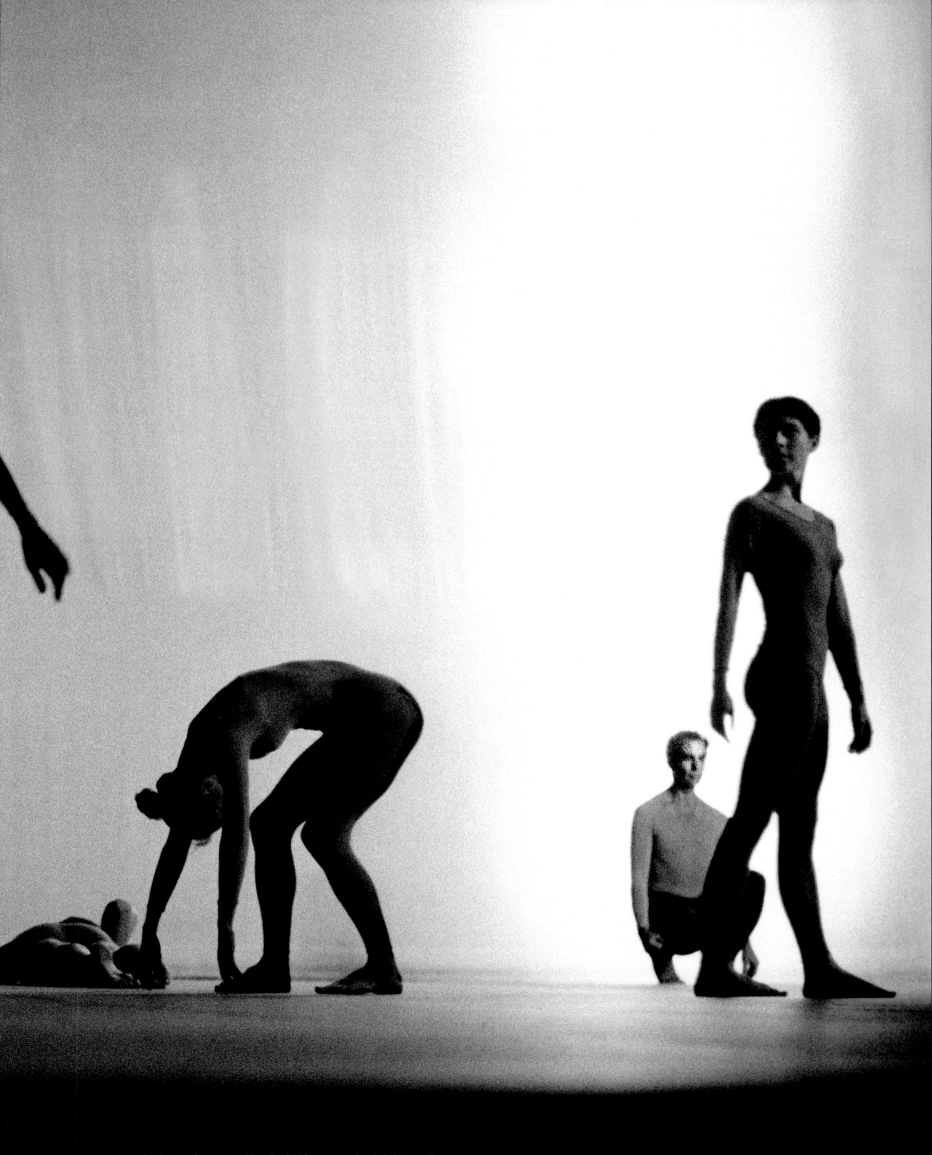

PAULINE OLIVEROS

Since Merce Cunningham has long insisted that "the music goes its way and the dance goes its way," I was very interested in an exploration of that philosophy. When I composed *In Memoriam: Nikola Tesla, Cosmic Engineer* for *Canfield*, which was commissioned by the Cunningham Foundation in 1969, I had no idea what the choreography would be like. Instead, I became interested in the concept of the Cunningham Company as a whole, its impact, and my memory of previous performances in relation to theaters or performing spaces and the adjoining environments, seen or unseen, heard or unheard, and the nature of the virtuoso musicians David Tudor and Gordon Mumma.

The compositional problem was to include, extend, expand, explore, compare, store, and manipulate the auditory space within Cunningham's philosophy, which allows a natural rather than an imposed relationship to arise between the music and the dance. This philosophical relationship is embodied in the following description of a Tesla experiment and the response of the environment and its inhabitants from which the central tasks of the score are derived: Tesla's experiment with mechanical resonance in his New York City laboratory (near the present location of the Cunningham studio) nearly ended in disaster. He adjusted an oscillator to the resonance of the building and then began to give the machine more power. This caused a minor earthquake, which terrorized the neighborhood and brought the police out in full force just as Tesla perceived the magnitude of his procedure and smashed his oscillator before the building began to fall apart.

The musicians are asked to begin the piece by discussing the acoustical environment of the theater with, possibly, comparisons to other performance spaces both real and imaginary. The essential aspect of this discussion is that the musicians actually describe their own real personal responses to the environment. The conversation must be real in order to be dramatically viable. This discussion occurs with the aid of a PA system.

During the second section of the piece the performers are asked to test the environment in order to find the resonant frequency of the space, to report any interesting facts via walkie talkie, and occasionally to broadcast particularly interesting features through the PA system. The differences in quality between the sound of moving walkie talkies and the stationary PA system are essential in the increasing collection and comparison of auditory phenomena.

Simultaneous with Sections One and Two, recordings of the discussions and the adjoining environments such as the stage, the basement, the dressing rooms, and the lobby or other connected spaces are being made. During Section Two these amplified environments may be introduced continuously or intermittently as they are being recorded.

At the beginning of Section Three, all discussion, activities, and recording stop. Two or more audio generators never to exceed 100 cps begin an extensive, slow crescendo from inaudibility to extremely loud. During the course of this crescendo, the stored environmental material from Sections One and Two is played back selectively mixed with the generated electronic sound. The playback is of course modulated by the crescendoing generators, transforming the memory of that material.

If the search for the resonant frequency has been successful, then the frequency of the generators selected by the musicians can cause the performance space to add its squeaks, groans, and other resonance phenomena to the general sound. Thus the space performs in sympathy with the musicians.

The audience, of course, imposes its own drama in this theatrical situation very much like the police in relation to Tesla. The musicians so far have always managed to stop before the theater comes crashing down, which is no small indication of their virtuosity.

While Tesla's experiment went its way very much like the Cunningham Company goes its way, the energy of his activity included and activated the whole neighborhood, causing a central dramatic episode.

The first performance of *Canfield* that I was able to witness was done in silence. Cunningham's philosophy was exquisitely demonstrated that evening. The dance indeed went its way and existed powerfully as a total organism without any necessity for accompaniment. It was an extraordinary experience for everyone, and the subsequent drama was apparent in such ways as a critic's proclamation: "Merce Cunningham goes on in silence. Thank God!"

Since that performance there has been a subtle tuning of the dance and the music to the point of philosophical resonance. The musicians have mastered the materials of a very difficult situation and very much go their own ways. Their performance could exist independently of the dancers'; but the dance and music together resonate powerfully.

Notes for a *Canfield* Event

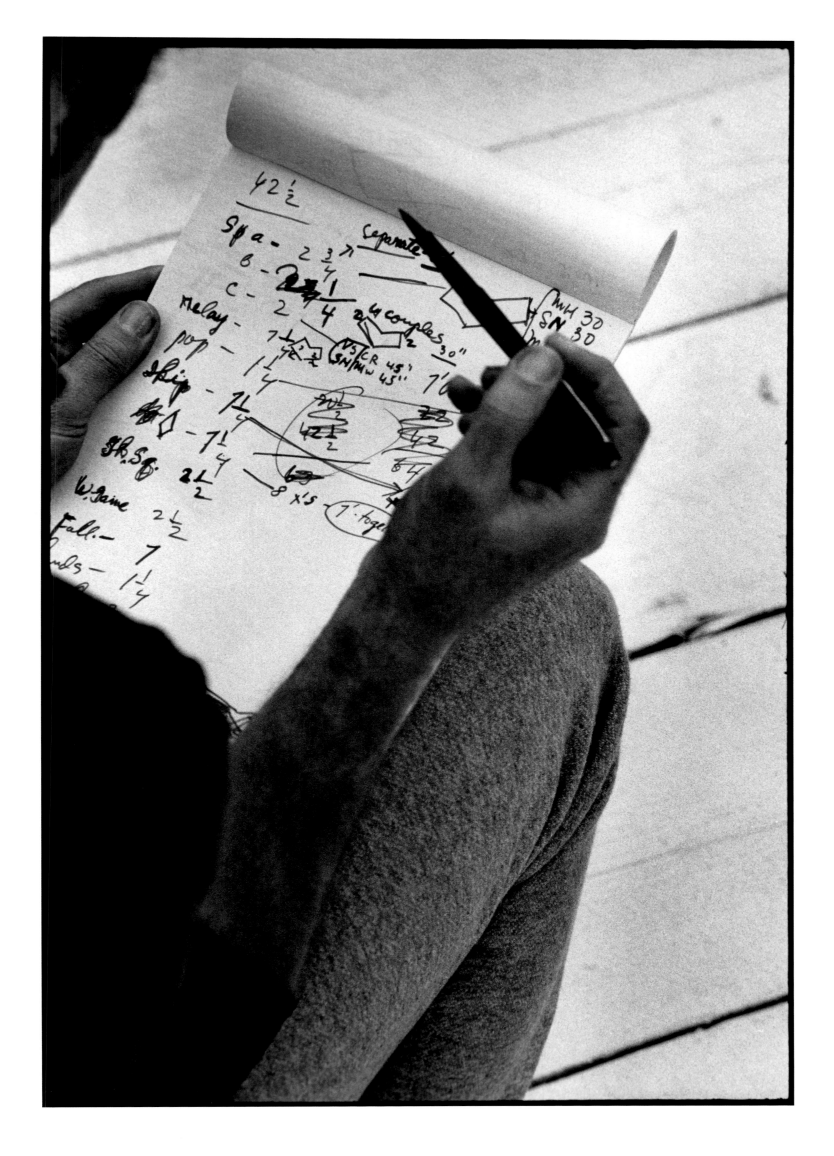

1970 **TREAD**

MUSIC
CHRISTIAN WOLFF
FOR 1, 2 OR 3 PEOPLE

COSTUMES
MERCE CUNNINGHAM

DECOR
BRUCE NAUMAN

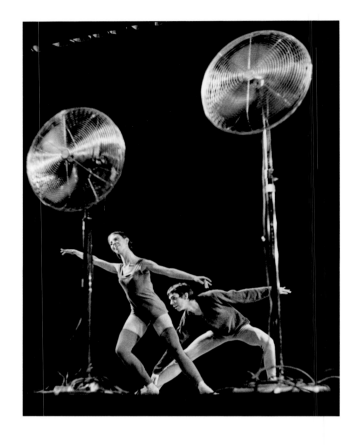

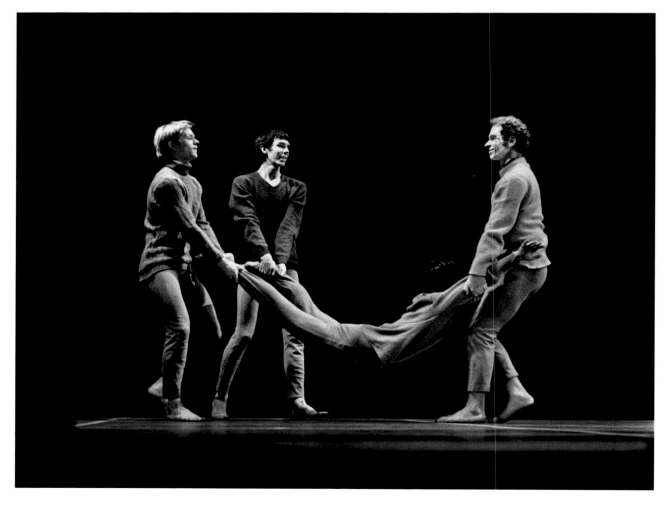

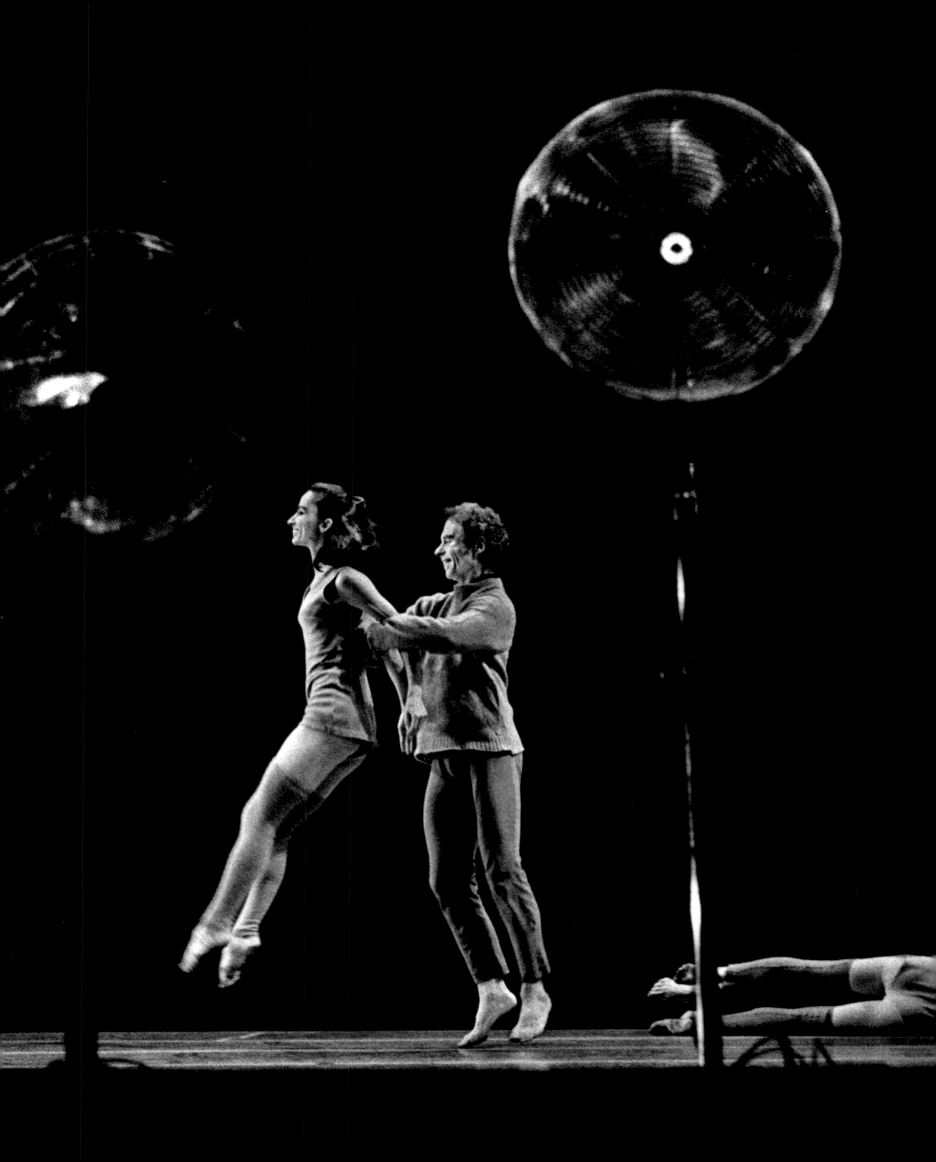

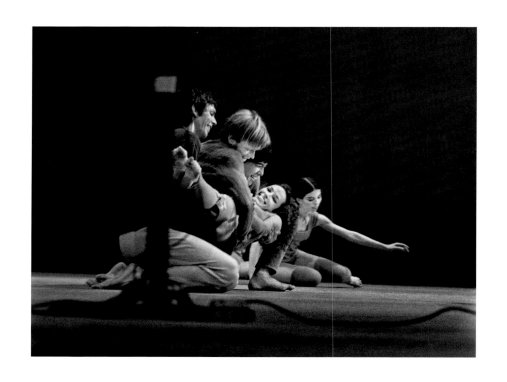

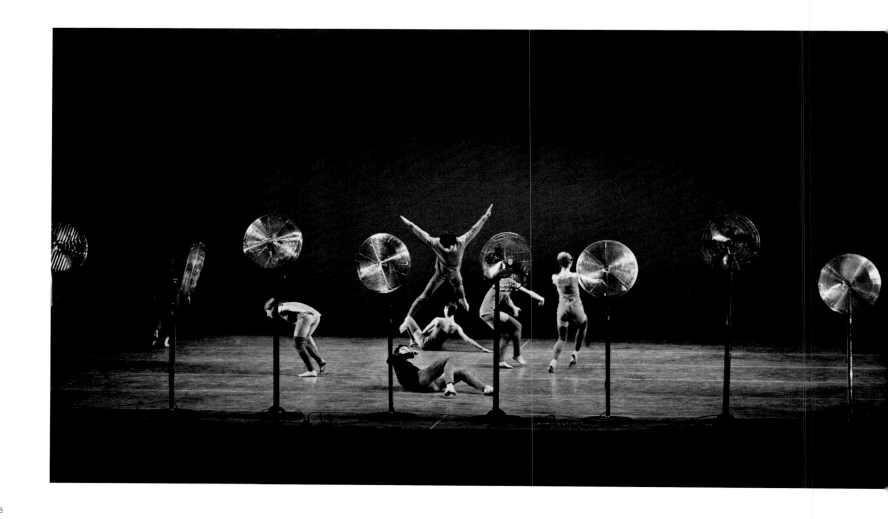

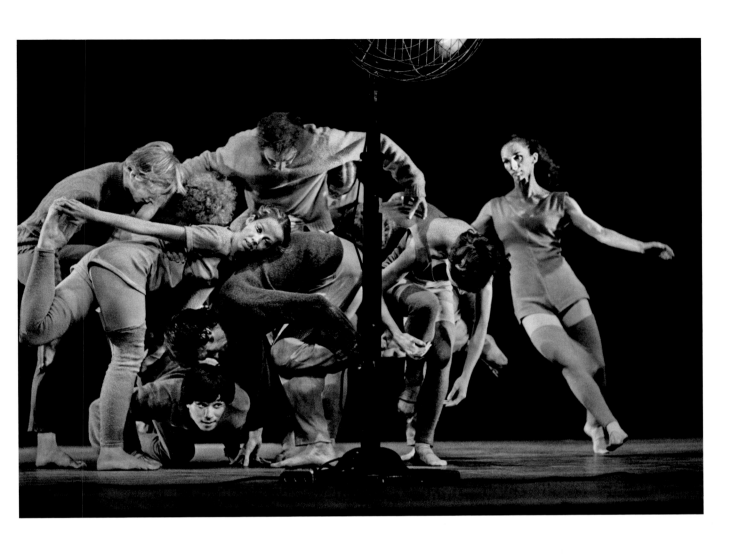

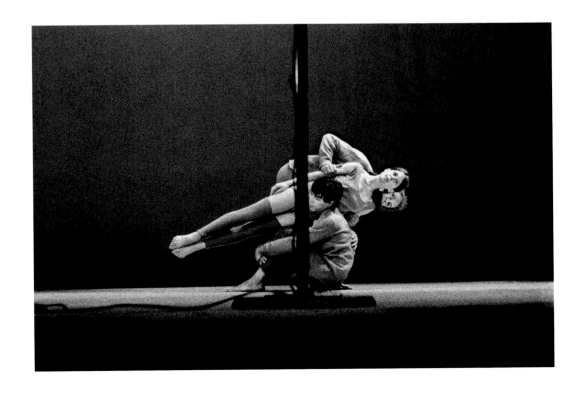

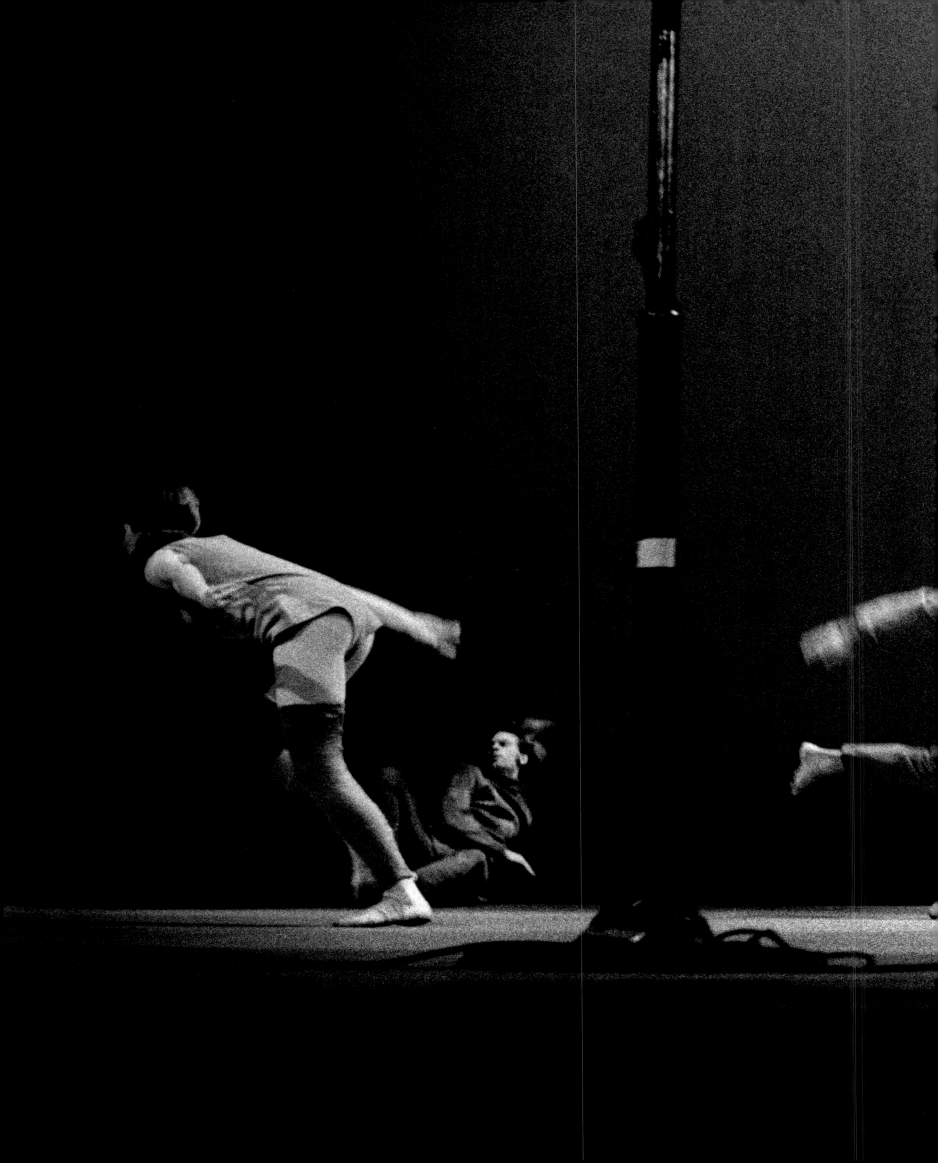

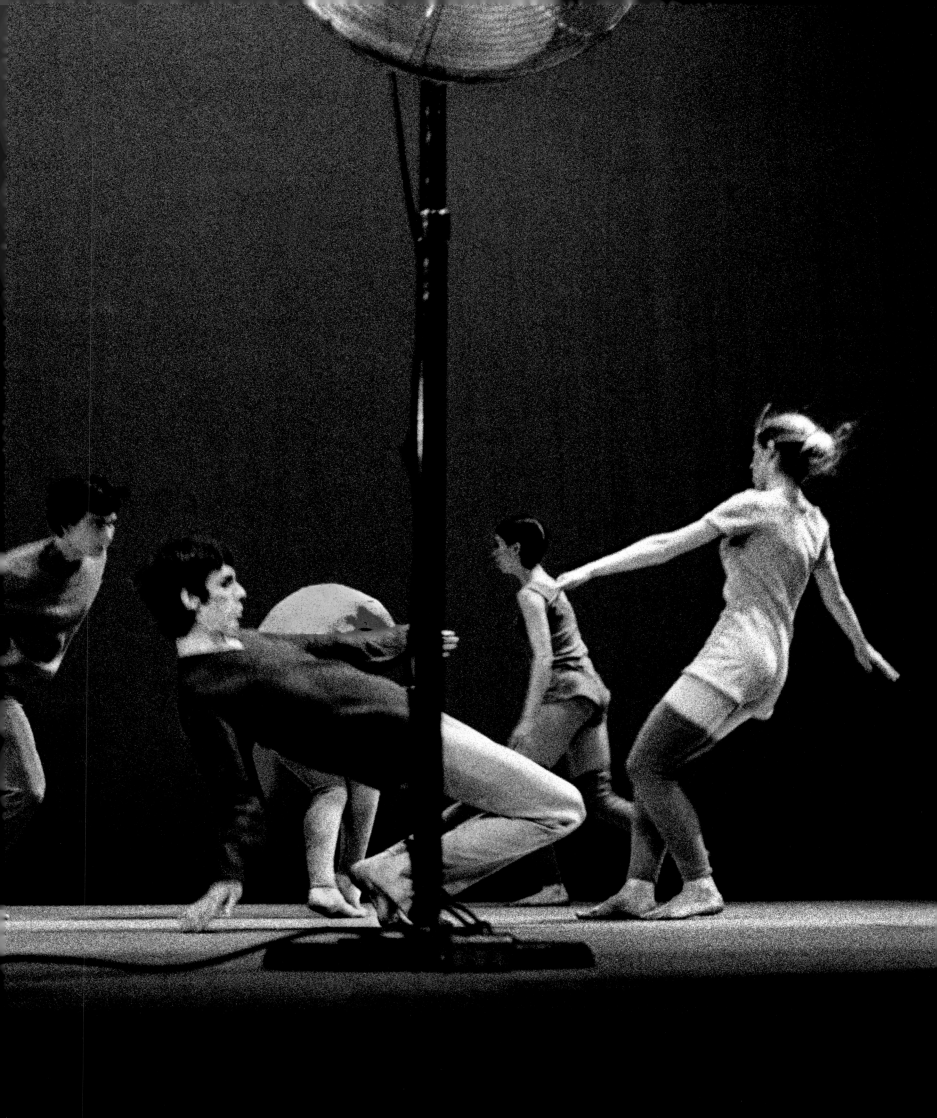

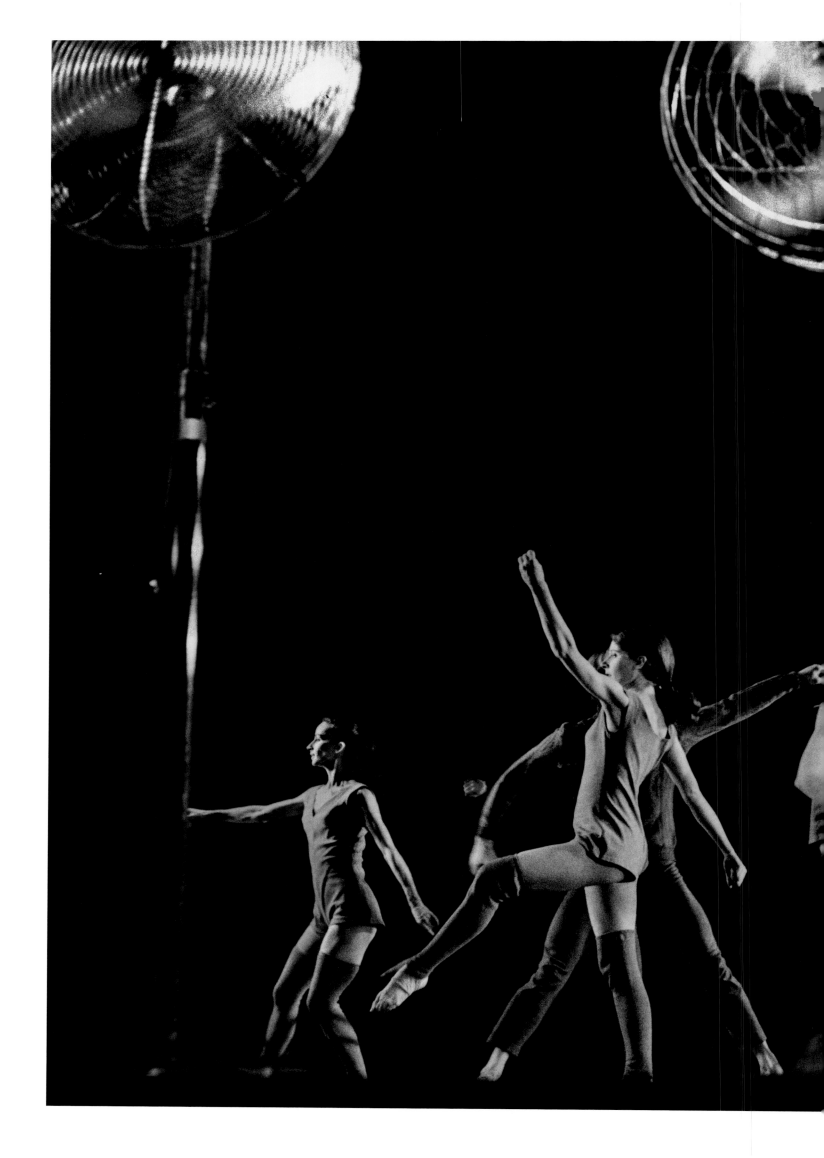

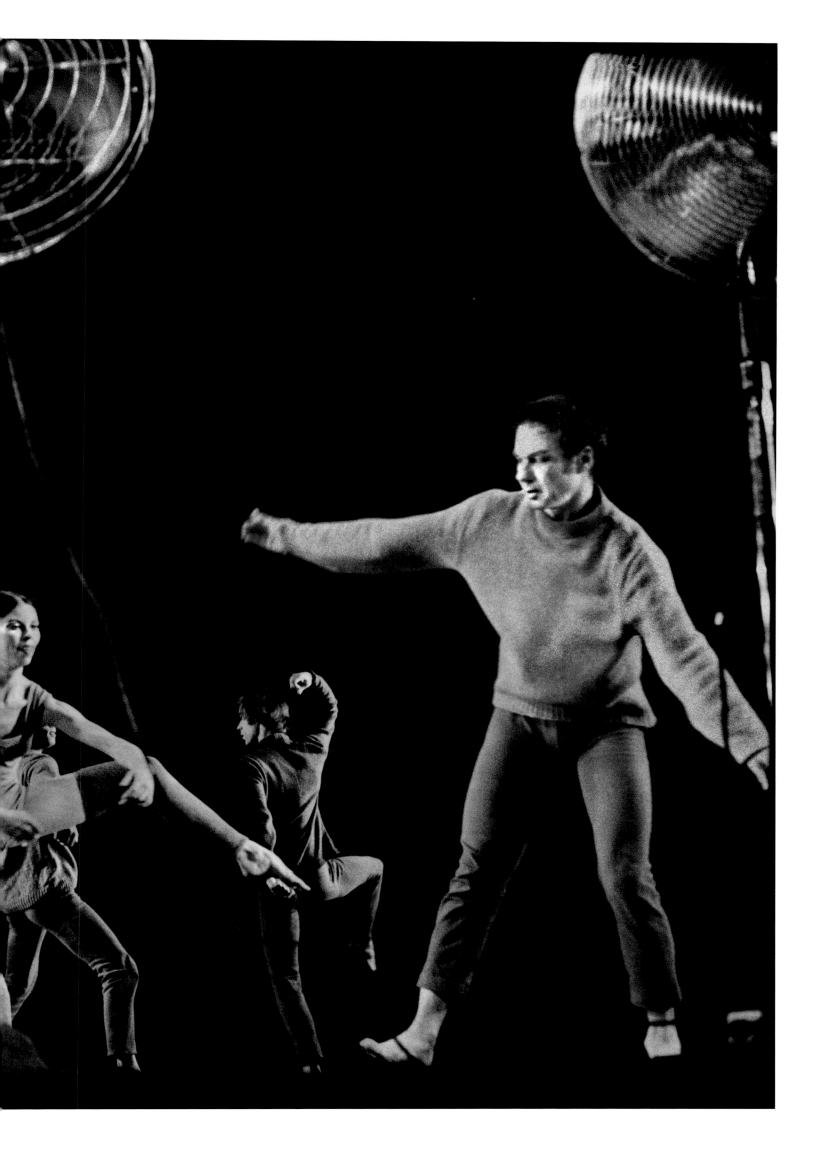

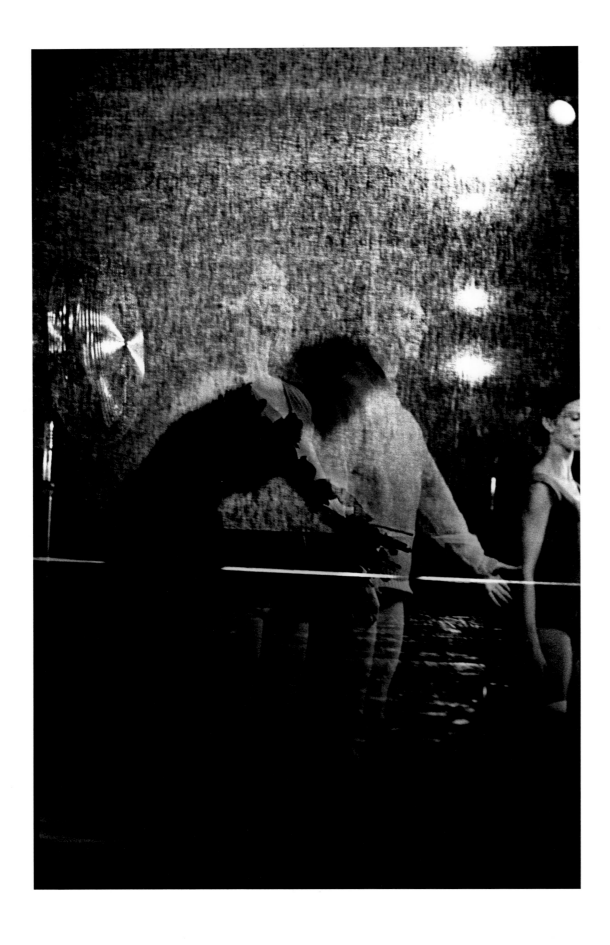

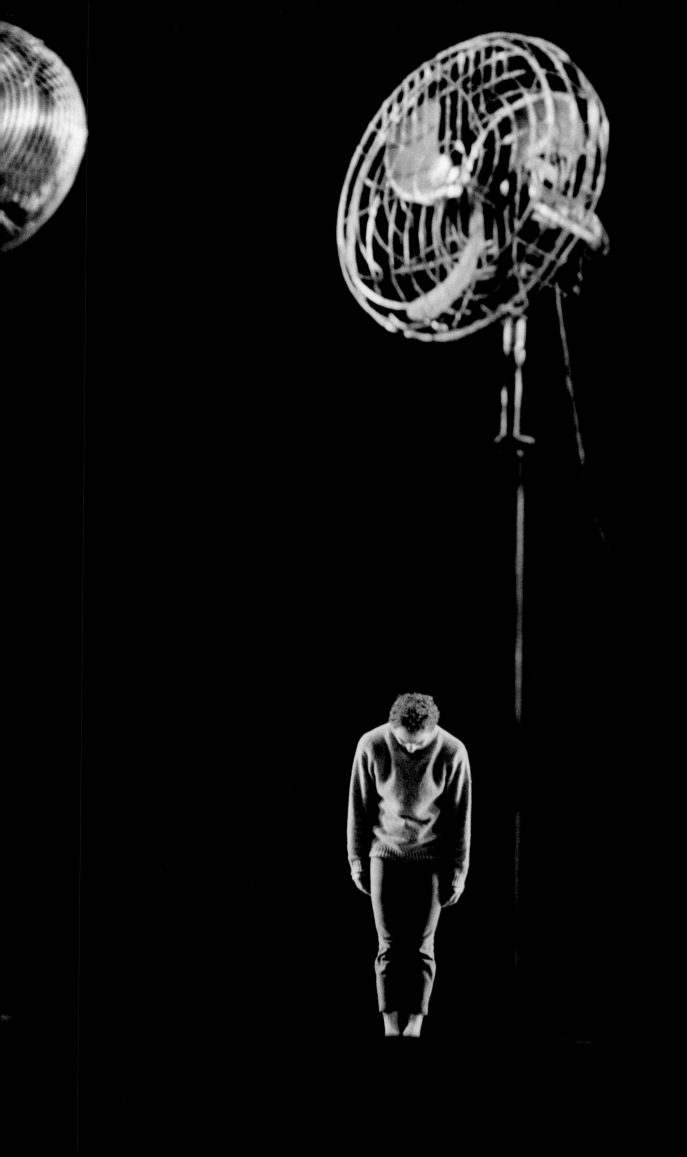

MICHAEL SNELL ON SECOND HAND

—From "Cunningham and the Critics"

Second Hand is a translation of a masterpiece from the language of its original medium into the language of a entirely different medium. It is an homage, but to neither Graham nor ballet. It is an alchemy, a triumphant transformation of "story" into "pure" dance. It is abstract, yet narrative; humble, yet unique. And it is, if you will excuse the expression, a masterpiece.

Its intended title was *Socrate*. *Socrate* was one of Satie's later works (1918) and with the exception of his ballet scores it was by far his most ambitious and extended undertaking. There is nothing like it in the history of music. He chose excerpts from Victor Cousin's translation of the Platonic Dialogues and set them to music in a three-movement score for reduced orchestra and four sopranos. To those familiar with his life and music, Satie's decision to undertake this work is strangely moving.

It is hard to resist the idea that Satie was aware of a sadly ironic correspondence between his own life and Socrates's. Yet no trace of pathos or of pride enters into *Socrate*. The orchestral partition is transparent; the very definition of simplicity. As it ripples past it projects the text, rather than itself, into one's consciousness and rejects all dramatic inflection. As the piece proceeds an accumulation of emotion grows as if from nowhere.

The text of *Socrate* can be summarized as follows:

PART I—From *Symposium*: an excerpt from a speech about Socrates in which Alcibiades praises his spirit and the effect his words have upon men.

PART II—From *Pheadrus*: a dialogue between Socrates and Pheadrus as they walk along the banks of the Ilyssus. Pheadrus is leading him to a place to rest. Their talk is casual; they delight in the clear water, the shade trees, and the grass.

PART III—From *Phaedo*: by far the longest section, it is an account of the death of Socrates.

While it would be a mistake to search for one-to-one relationships between the text and the dance, it is undeniable that *Second Hand* is a mirror held up to Satie's score. We should not forget that Satie is one of the very few composers with whom Cunningham has "collaborated" in the traditional sense of the term. Both *Septet* (1953—to *Three Pieces in the Form of a Pear*,) and *Nocturnes* (1956—to Satie's music of the same name) are dances built upon the musical phrase rather than upon a self-reliant structure independent of the music. Other works, unfamiliar to most of us, the *Monkey Dances* (1948), *Two Step* (1949), *Waltz* (1950), *Rag Time Parade* (1950), used Satie's music. So it is safe to say that Cunningham clearly cares about Satie, and I would go so far as to suggest that the correspondence between himself and Satie in terms of their own careers and their somewhat "Socratic" natures is something that probably has entered his head at one time or another. In any case there exists a remarkably detailed parallel between Cunningham's creative position relative to his time as a choreographer and Satie's position relative to his time as a composer. If one considers their immediate predecessors, contemporaries and successors, one finds some fascinating substitutions are possible. For Wagner one could substitute Martha Graham—the parallel is perfectly delicious. For Ravel and Debussy one might try Paul Taylor and George Balanchine—the parallels are imperfect but useful. For Darius Milhaud, Francis Poulenc, Arthur Honegger et al. one could substitute Yvonne Rainer, Twyla Tharp, Rudy Perez et al. Or for Les Six as a whole one could substitute Judson. If Satie had any reason to consider himself a Socratic figure (which he most certainly was to Les Six), Cunningham has even more. Not because he played the mentor to a gathering of disciples but because of the very fact of the modern dance as it has evolved in the last two generations as a result of his existence.

Within *Second Hand* the connection between the persona of Socrates and the person of Cunningham is explicit. A glance at the structure of the dance makes this obvious, and one can find in each section's choreography distinct echoes of the text of *Socrate*. These echoes move in a steady trajectory from abstract to concrete as the text emerges from an intellectualized description of Socrates' qualities in Part I (a hieratic solo for Cunningham) to a more direct personal interchange between friends in Part II (the duet for Cunningham and Brown) to a deeply personal, involved and detailed narrative in Part III.

What occurs in the third part of *Second Hand* is not only astonishingly beautiful, it is also simply astonishing. Satie had succeeded in distilling all the emotion of the Phaedo's death scene into a melodic line and transparent accompaniment devoid of any traditional emotional gesture; yet the reconciliation of music and text was virtually perfect. Cunningham, God knows how, has discovered a choreographic equivalent for Satie's accomplishment and his translation of sense and sensibility from vocal

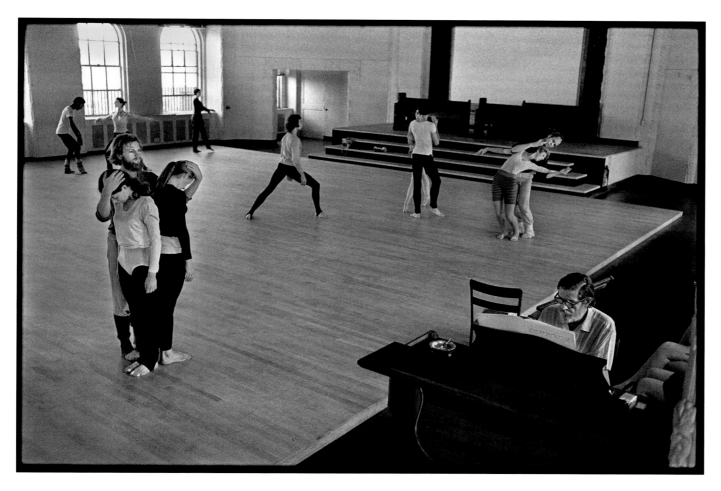

Rehearsal of *Second Hand*, Westbeth, 1971

music to a purely choreographic expression is uncanny in its faithfulness to the spirit of *Socrate*. *Second Hand*'s third movement is a threnody of leave-taking that is unmistakably and— considering the choreographer—amazingly programmatic. Yet somehow it manages not to violate the anti-narrative values Cunningham's work has always maintained. It transforms stage space into juggled multiple points of focus that, while emotionally weighted into a matrix of evolving relationships, remain bound by spacial tensions more complicated and more extended than even the complex tableaux in *Canfield*.

I do not intend to point out every correspondence between the text of *Socrate* and the third section of *Second Hand*, for there are a great many and it would take too long. But here is an example: the first to occur and the clearest. The third part begins with Cunningham standing alone, isolated against the cyclorama. Slowly, legs bent as in some solemn, dreamed procession, the company enters one by one. At this point in the score of *Socrate* Phaedo is recounting what occurred on the day of Socrates's death:

> Since Socrates had been condemned, not a day passed that we did not go to visit him. As the public square where the judgment had been handed down was not far from the prison, we assembled there in the mornings and waited, talking together, for the opening of the prison doors, which never occurred very early (my translation).

Of course nothing happens on stage that exactly mimics the text. All is metamorphosed, yet emotional landmarks remain, such as the poignant series of farewells taken with hands raised in the gesture of parting. The one that moves me most deeply is between Cunningham and (originally) Jeff Slayton, who are separated by the full space of the stage while the rest of the company moves between them. Another is between Cunningham and Sandra Neels as she is carried bodily away from him (page 279). In this fashion the dance unfolds in continual invention for almost fifteen minutes. The death of Socrates ends the dance, as it ends the score:

> Shortly thereafter he made a convulsive movement. The attendant uncovered him; his eyes were fixed. Crito, seeing this, closed his mouth and his eyes. In this way, Echecrate, did our friend die . . . the wisest and most just of all men.

Second Hand, like all Cunningham dances, reveals itself to you in terms of what you bring to it, and can be spellbindingly beautiful even if you are unaware of the narrative hidden within. Risking a simile, *Second Hand* is like an expanse of mirror made of one-way glass. Looking at it unsuspectingly you see your own face, but walking round to look from the other side you discover others are gazing through.

Whether performed to Cage's *Cheap Imitation*—which Cage conjured up when the Satie estate refused permission for Cunningham to use Cage's original reduction of the orchestral score of *Socrate* to two pianos—*Second Hand*'s narrative origins would remain unperceivable because the music of *Socrate* is so undramatic, the melodic soprano line so unassertive that a faithful piano reduction would not have given the dance a more dramatic foundation than it has now with Cage's curious, peaceful, meandering accompaniment. Whether Cunningham would like the metamorphosis he has wrought to be fully visible, whether he would like *Second Hand* to be accompanied by performances of the full *Socrate* is a question I cannot answer. I think the effect of the choreography under such circumstances would be absolutely extraordinary. But as it stands now the dance, accompanied by *Cheap Imitation*, definitely obscures its origins. It unfolds without references, complete in itself. The empty stage becomes a quiet, spiritual arena where dance, music, and literary humanism confront one another, blend, and re-emerge as a new and single thing. I think that was Cunningham's intention: to unify text, music, and choreography into a completely round, spherical expression with no visible seams. Satie managed more or less the same thing.

But much of my enthusiasm for *Second Hand* comes from the knowledge that those seams are there, and from an awareness of the exquisite manner in which they have been hidden. Cunningham had not expected the audience to know *Socrate* and he was careful to cover all tracks leading back to it. That the end product nonetheless works at face value was proven to me by a review that appeared in *Ballet Review* 3, no. 3. Although Jack Anderson apparently did not know the nature of Satie's *Socrate* he recognized its qualities in Cunningham's choreography:

> How paradoxical . . . that a work whose title is a pleasantly trivial "in" joke should be heroic in scale, gesture and implication . . . The confidence and modesty of the choreography lead me to relate the Cunningham figure to those courageous people who seek to bring truth, beauty and goodness into the world. This sort of heroism is romantic in the grandness of its aspiration, classical in its lack of self-dramatization.

> —From "Cunningham and the Critics"
> Ballet Review 3, no. 6 (1971)

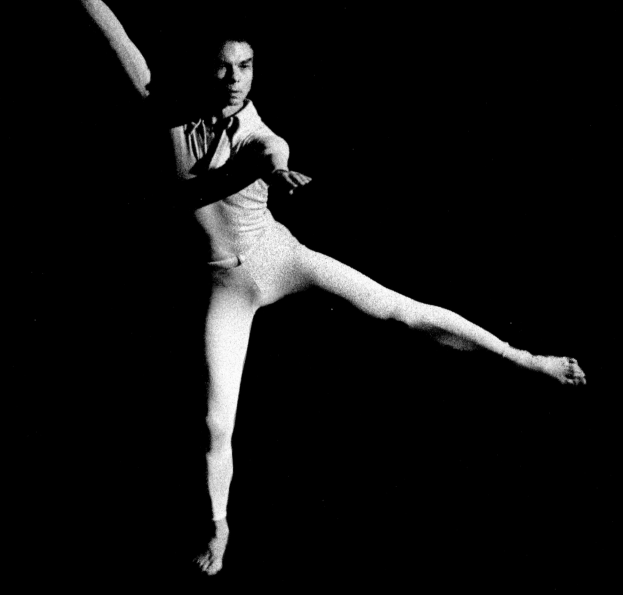

MUSIC
JOHN CAGE
CHEAP IMITATION

COSTUMES
JASPER JOHNS

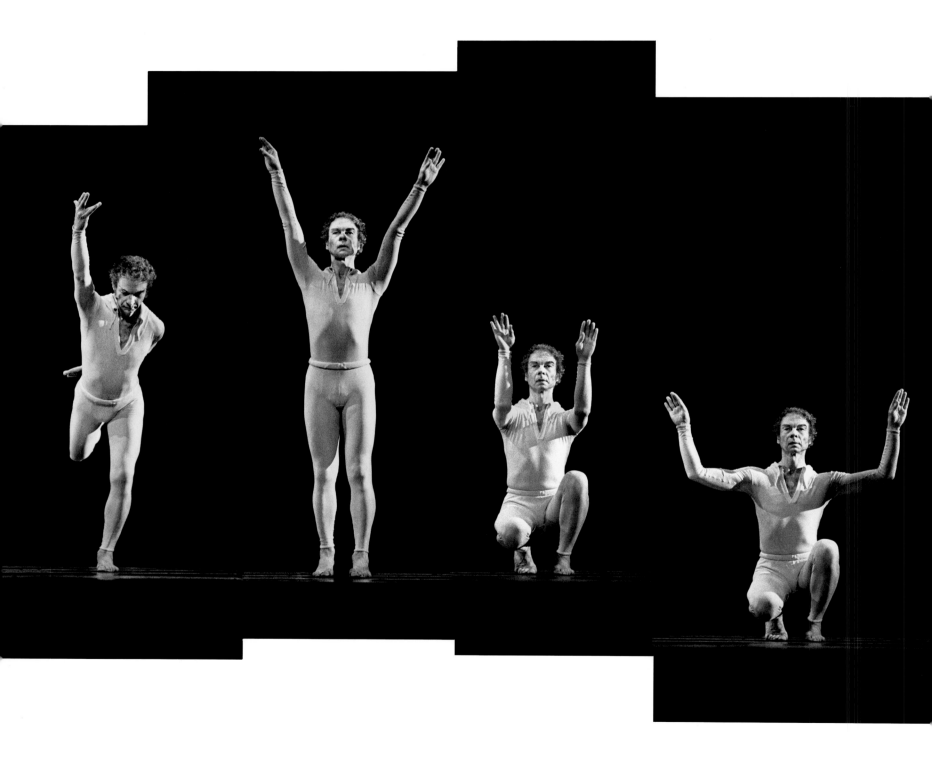

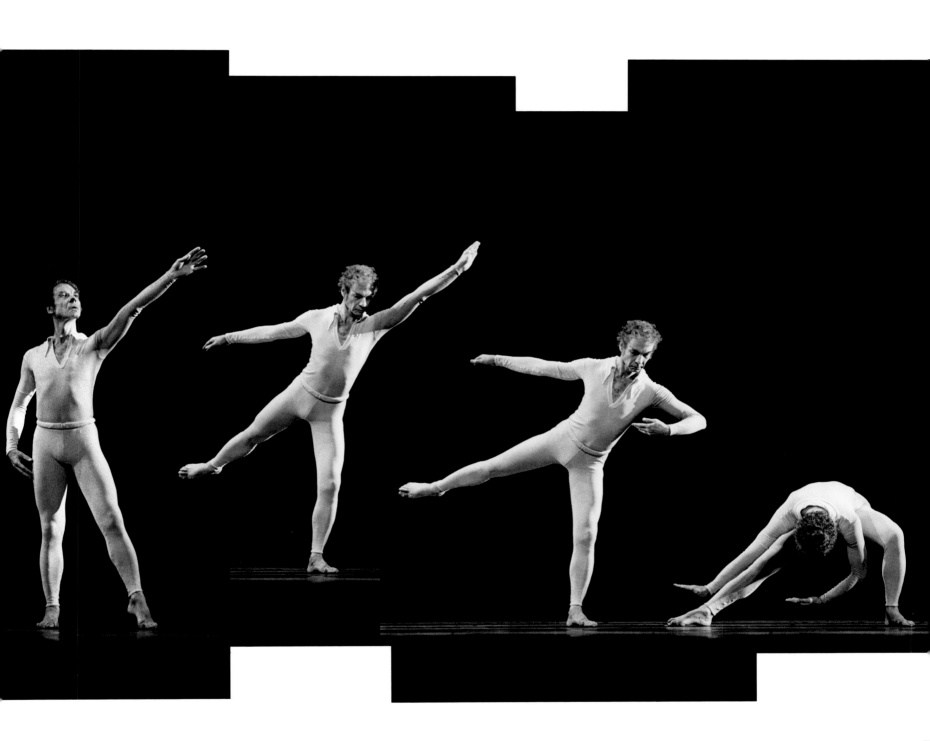

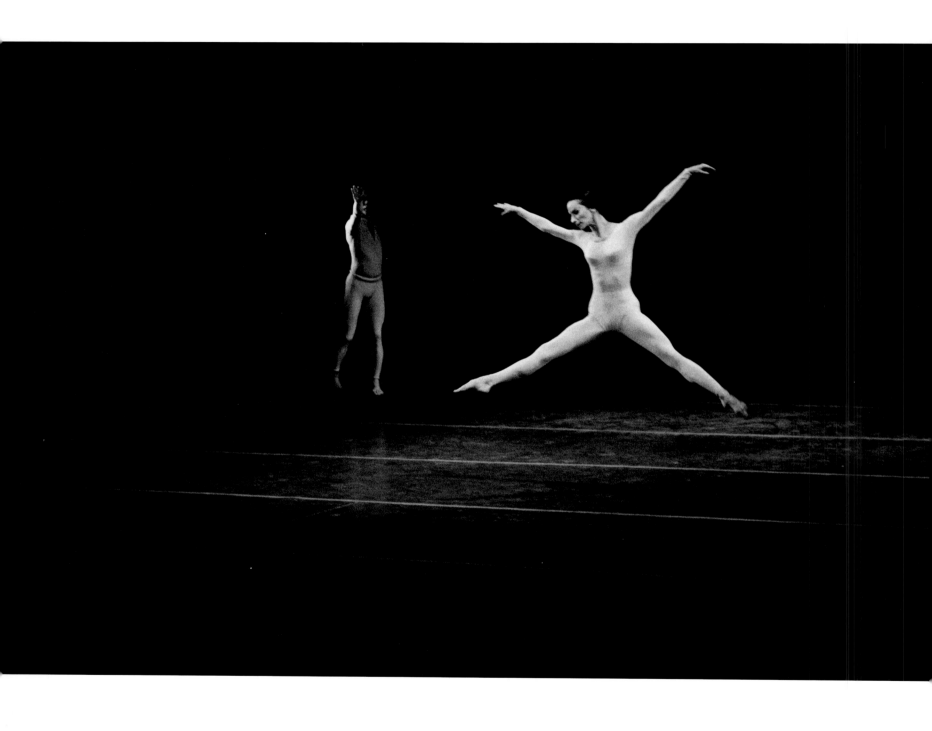

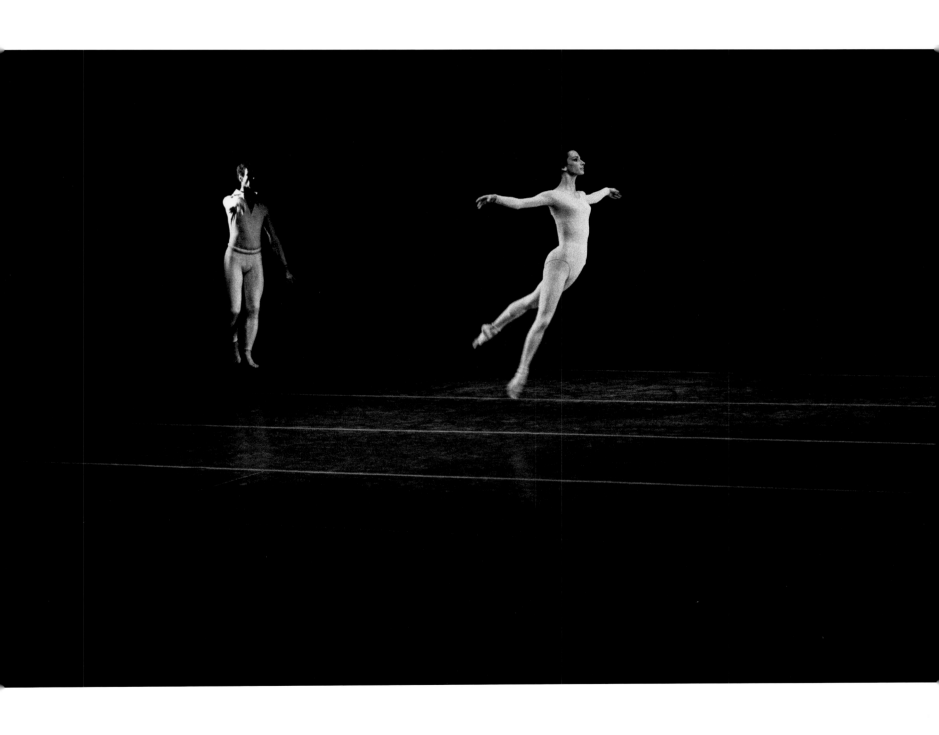

SOCRATE PART II—LES BORDS DE L'ILLISSUS (The Banks of Illissus)

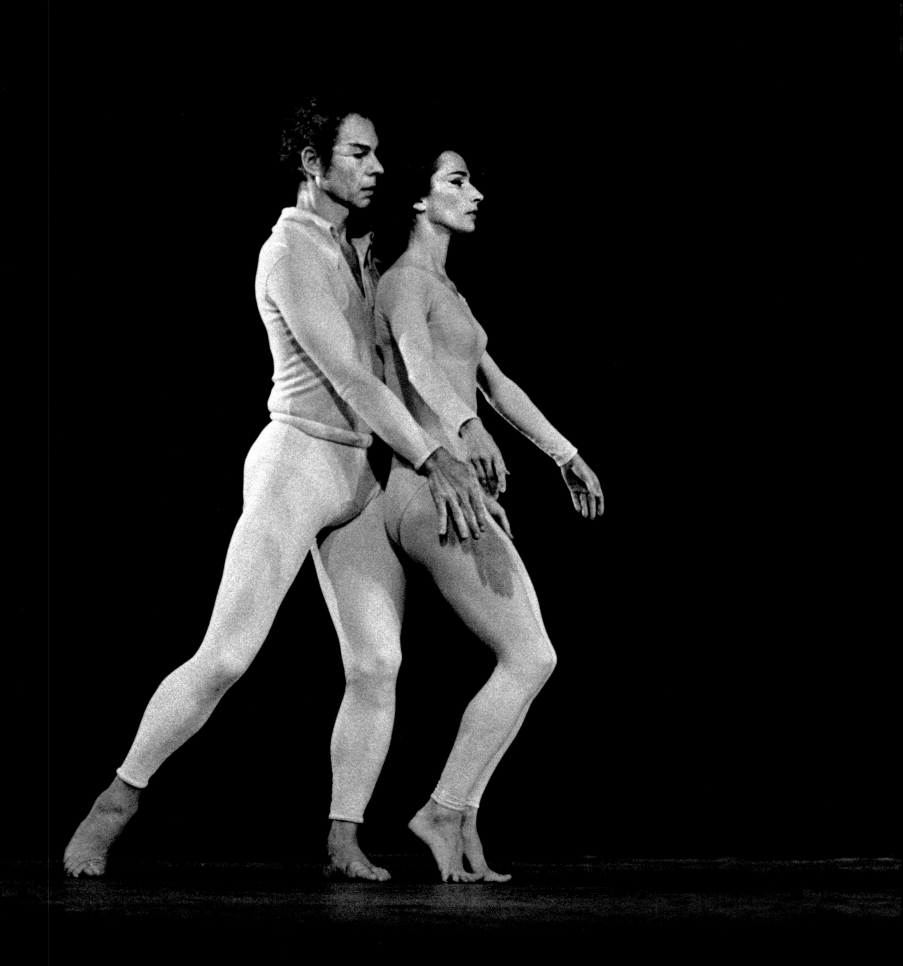

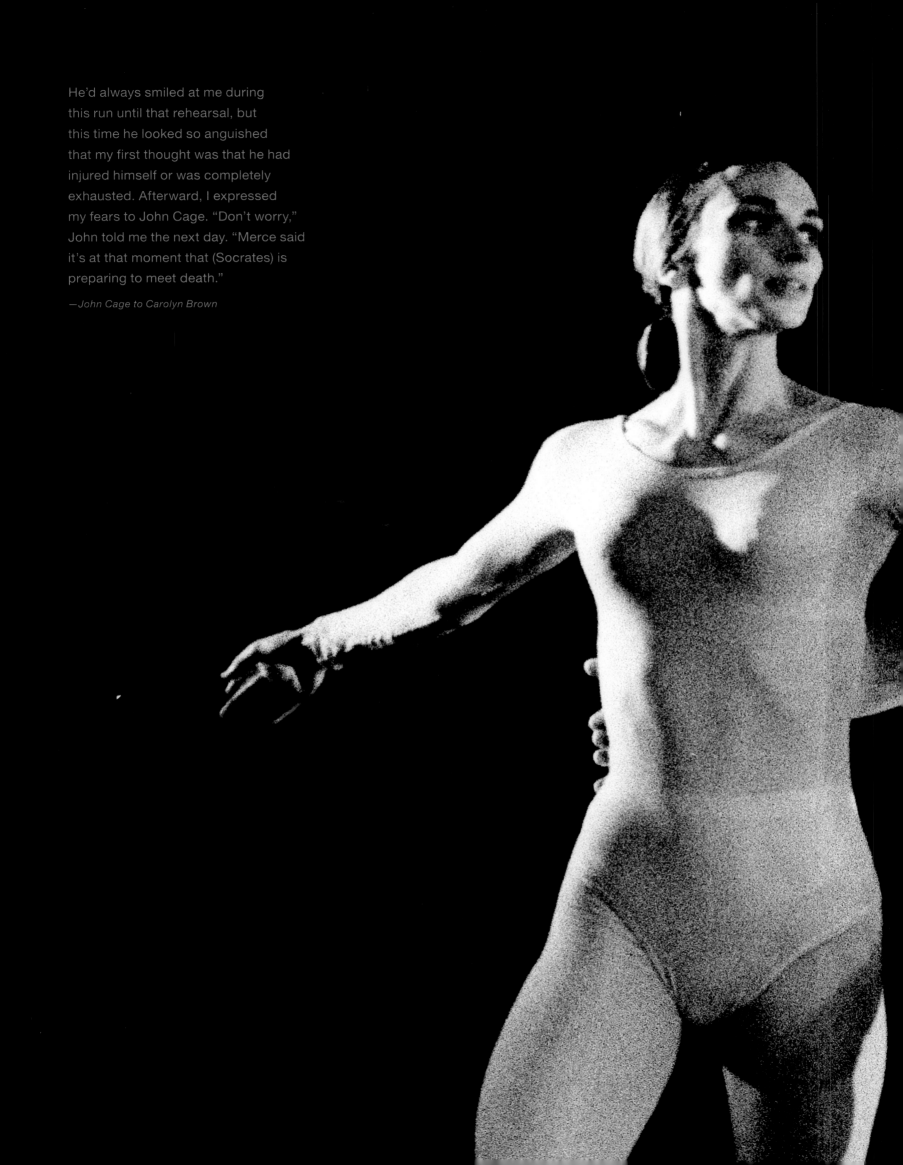

He'd always smiled at me during
this run until that rehearsal, but
this time he looked so anguished
that my first thought was that he had
injured himself or was completely
exhausted. Afterward, I expressed
my fears to John Cage. "Don't worry,"
John told me the next day. "Merce said
it's at that moment that (Socrates) is
preparing to meet death."

—John Cage to Carolyn Brown

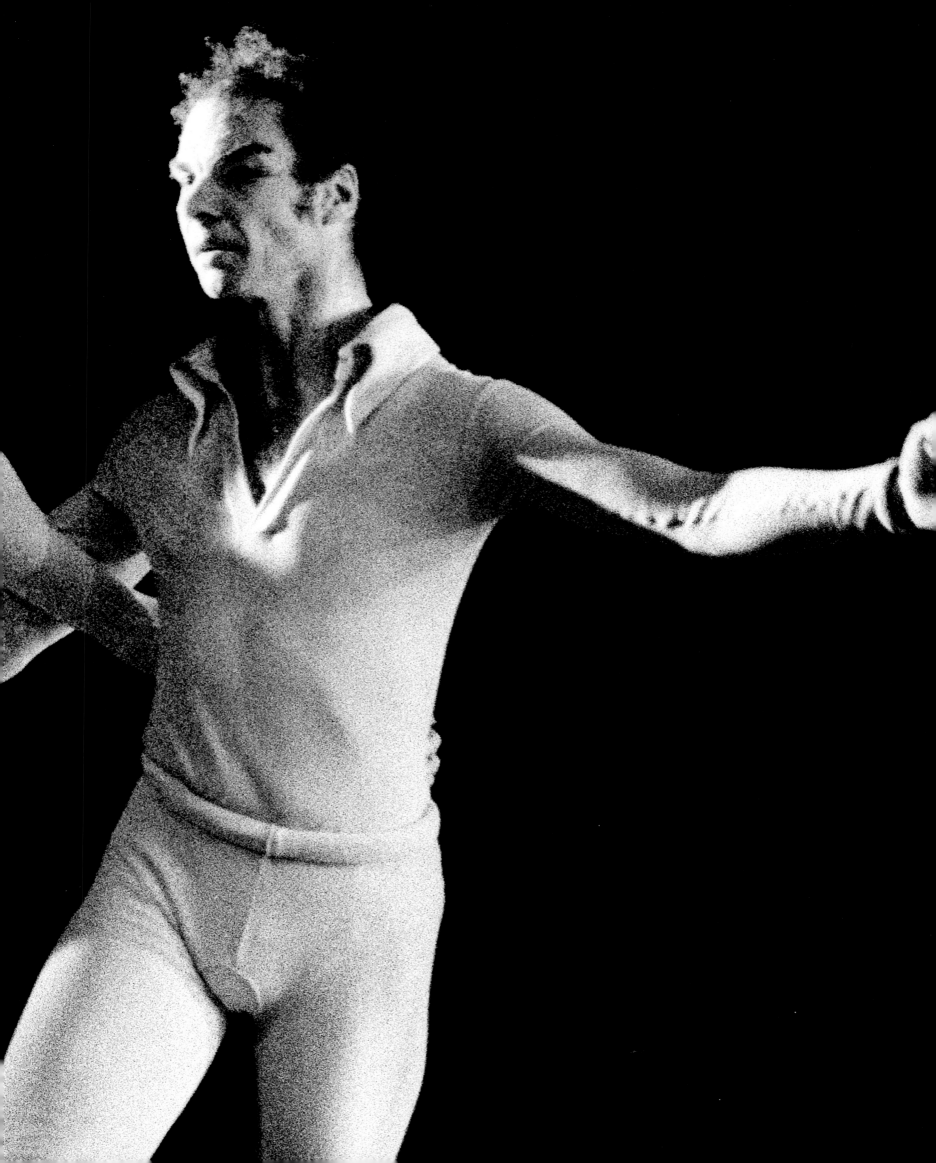

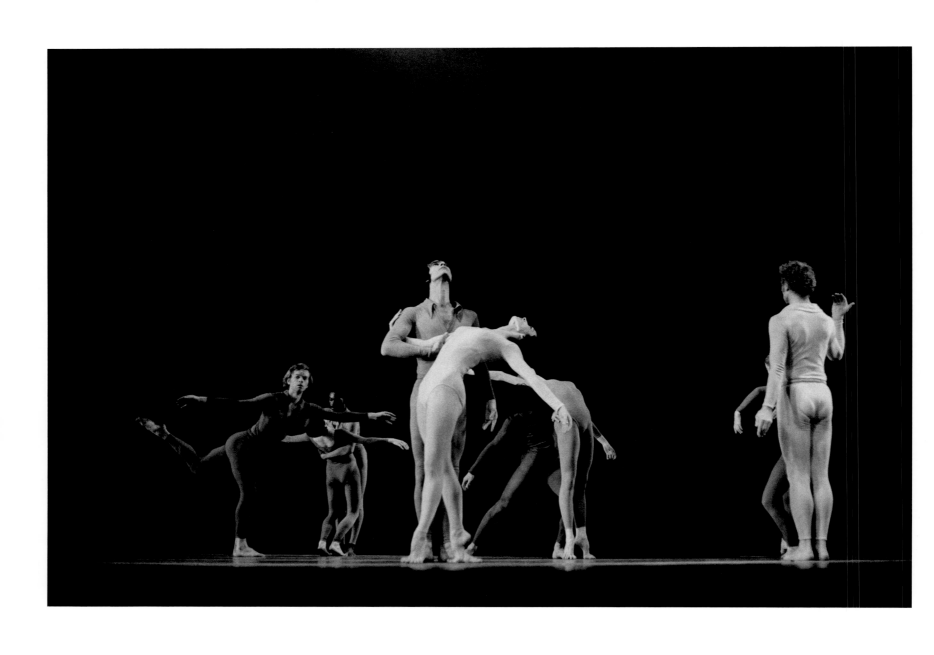

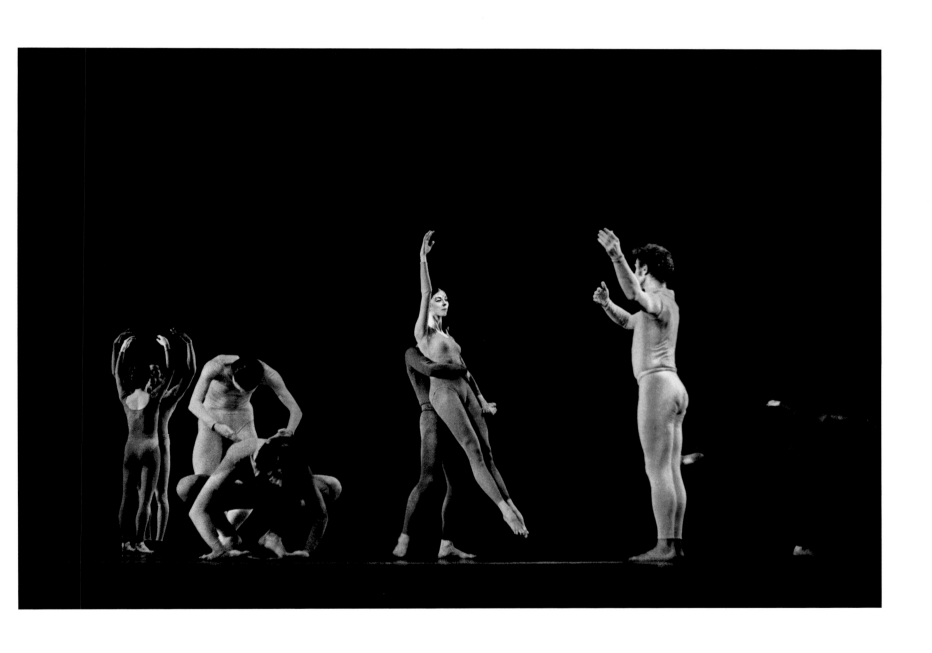

SOCRATE PART III—PHAEDO (The Death of Socrates)

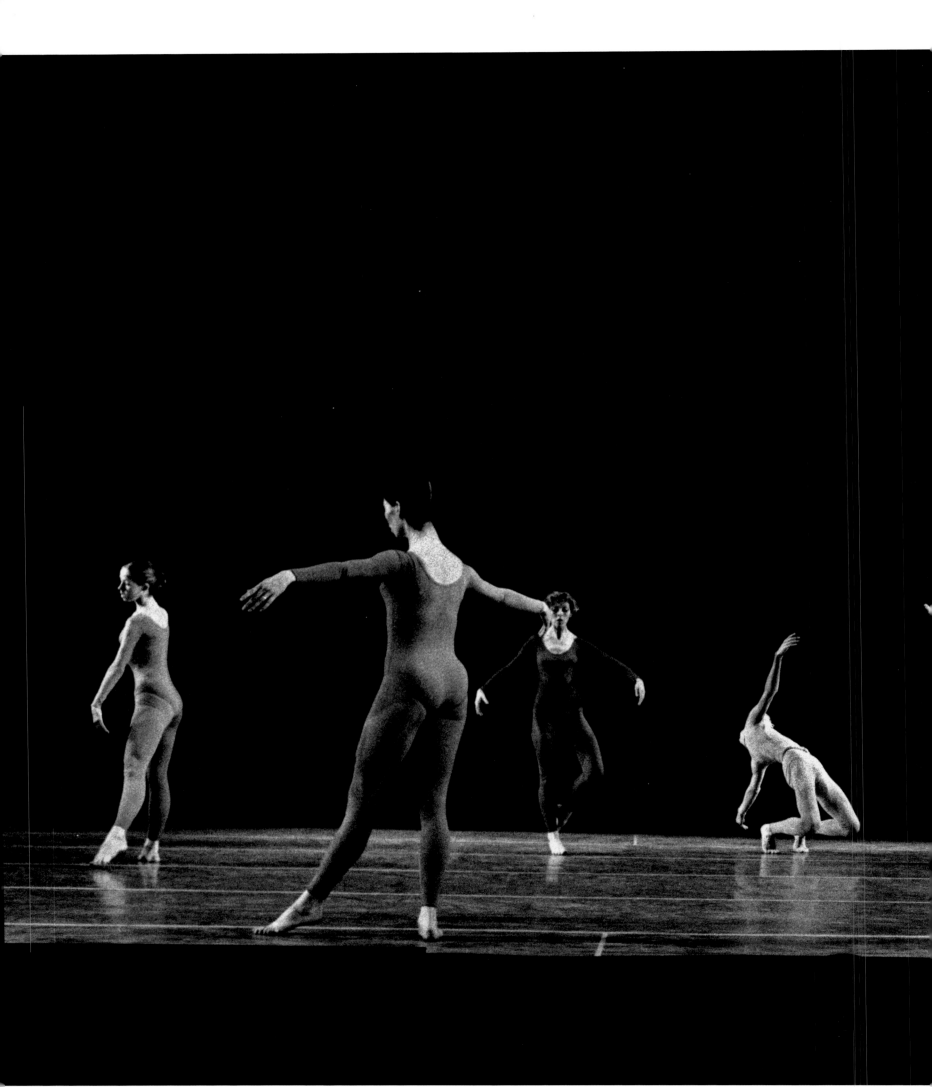

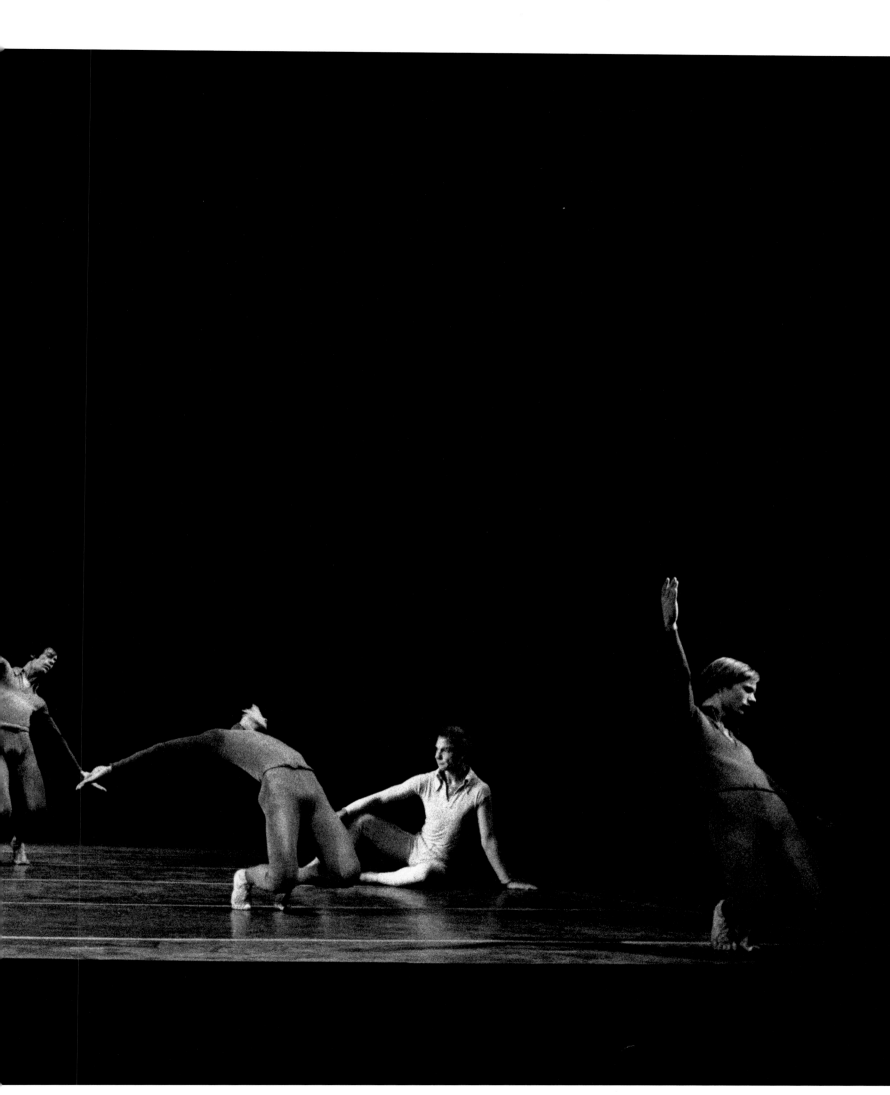

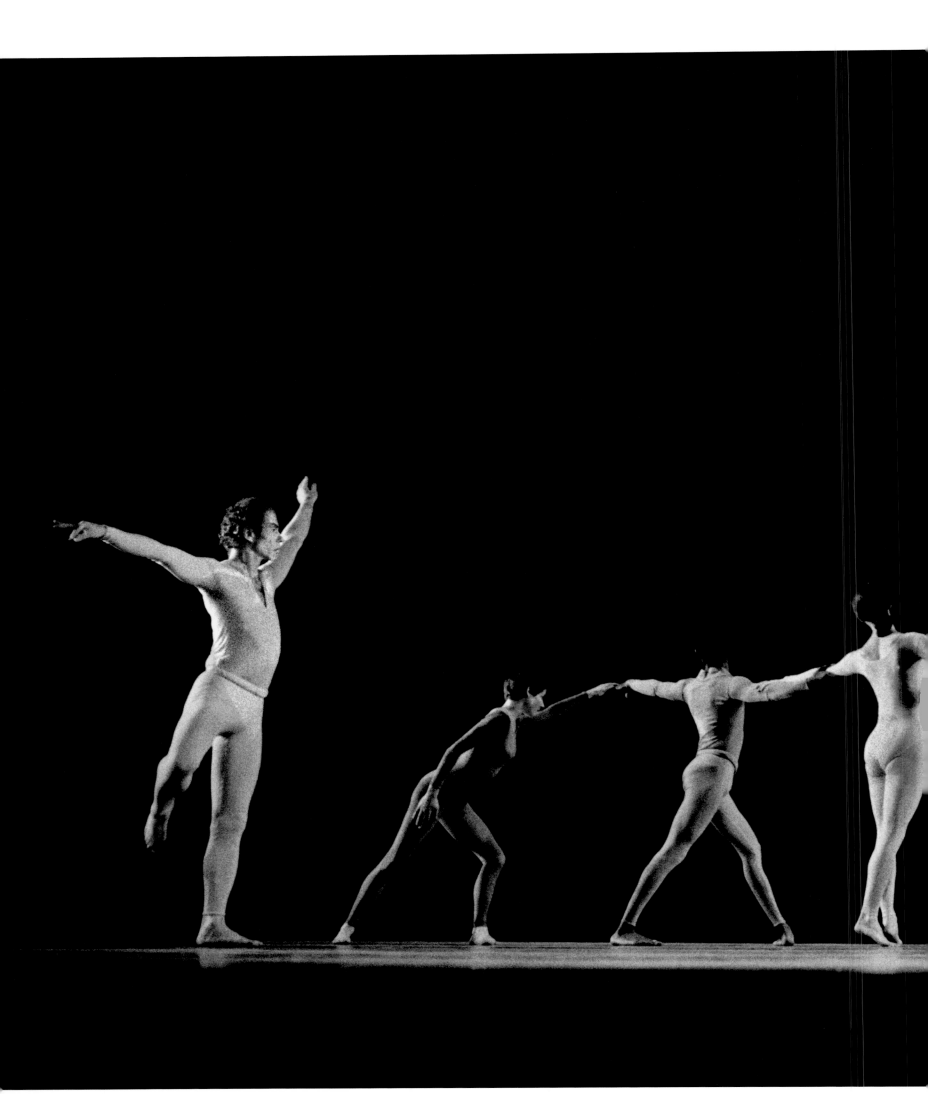

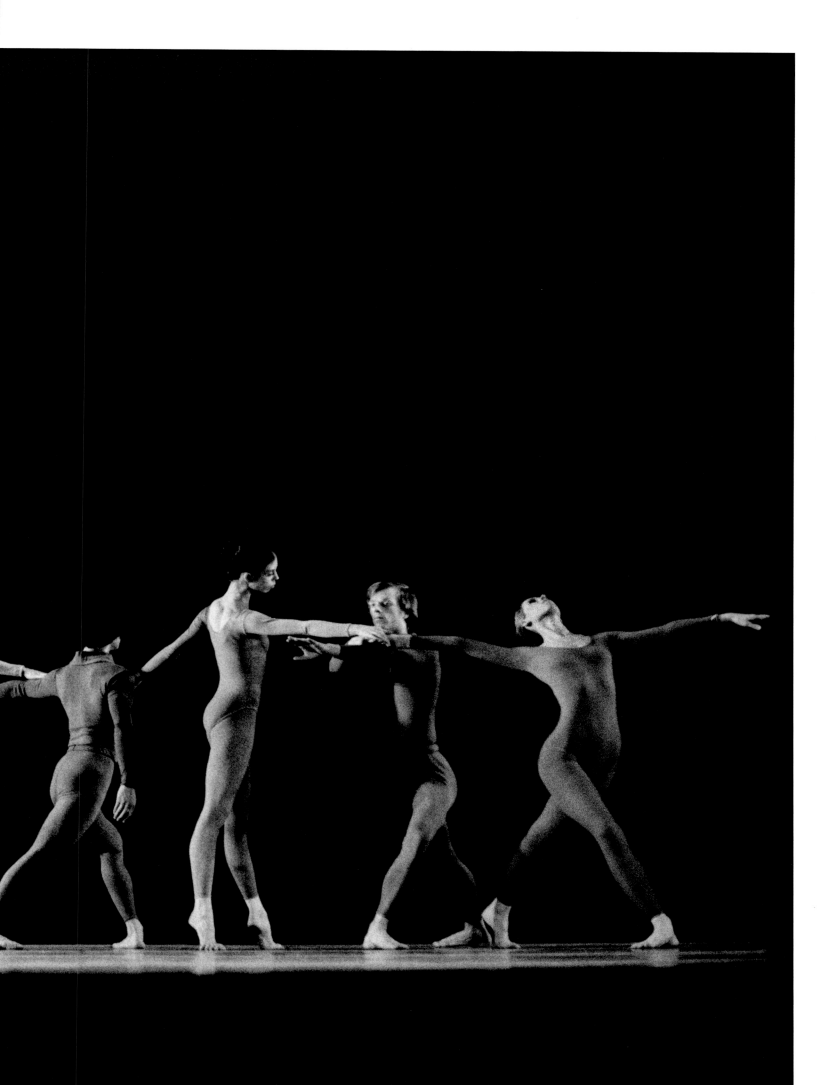

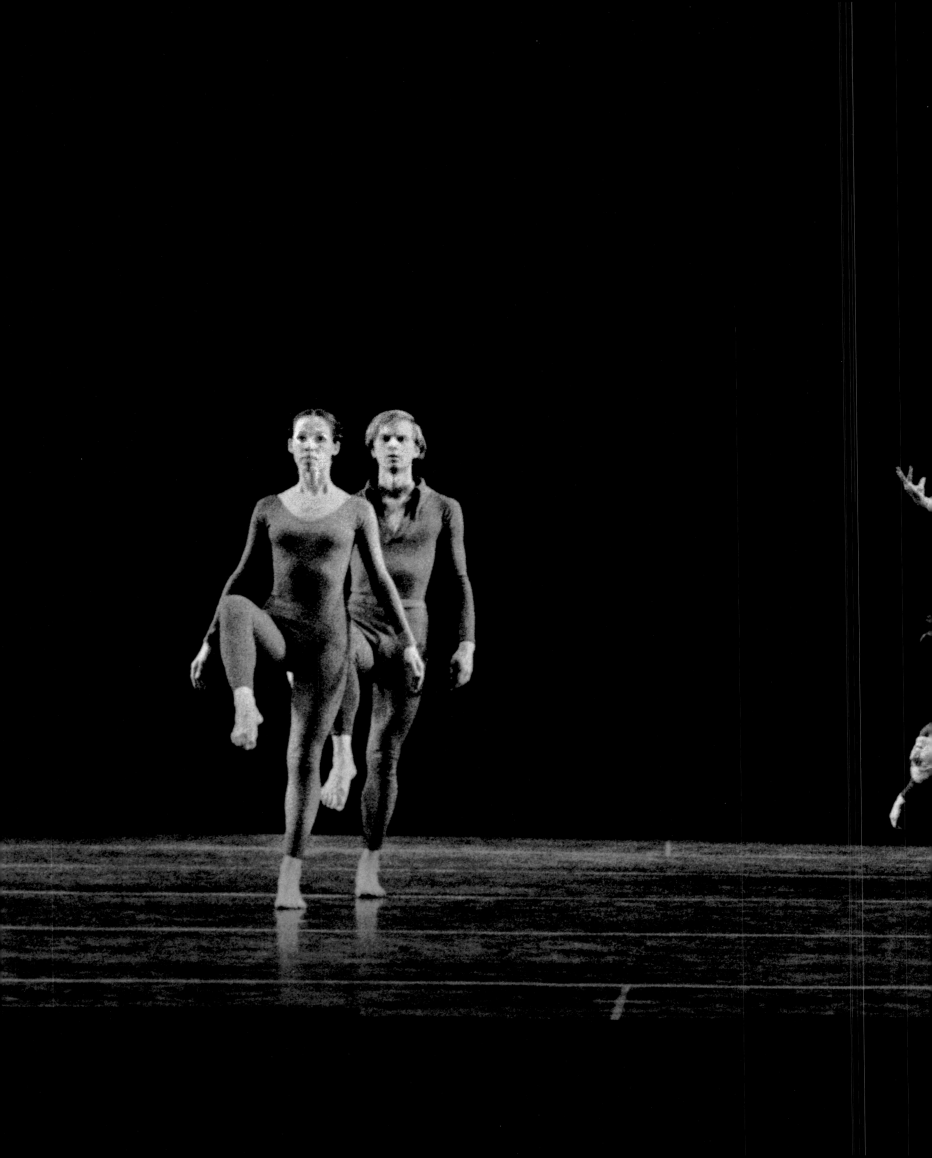

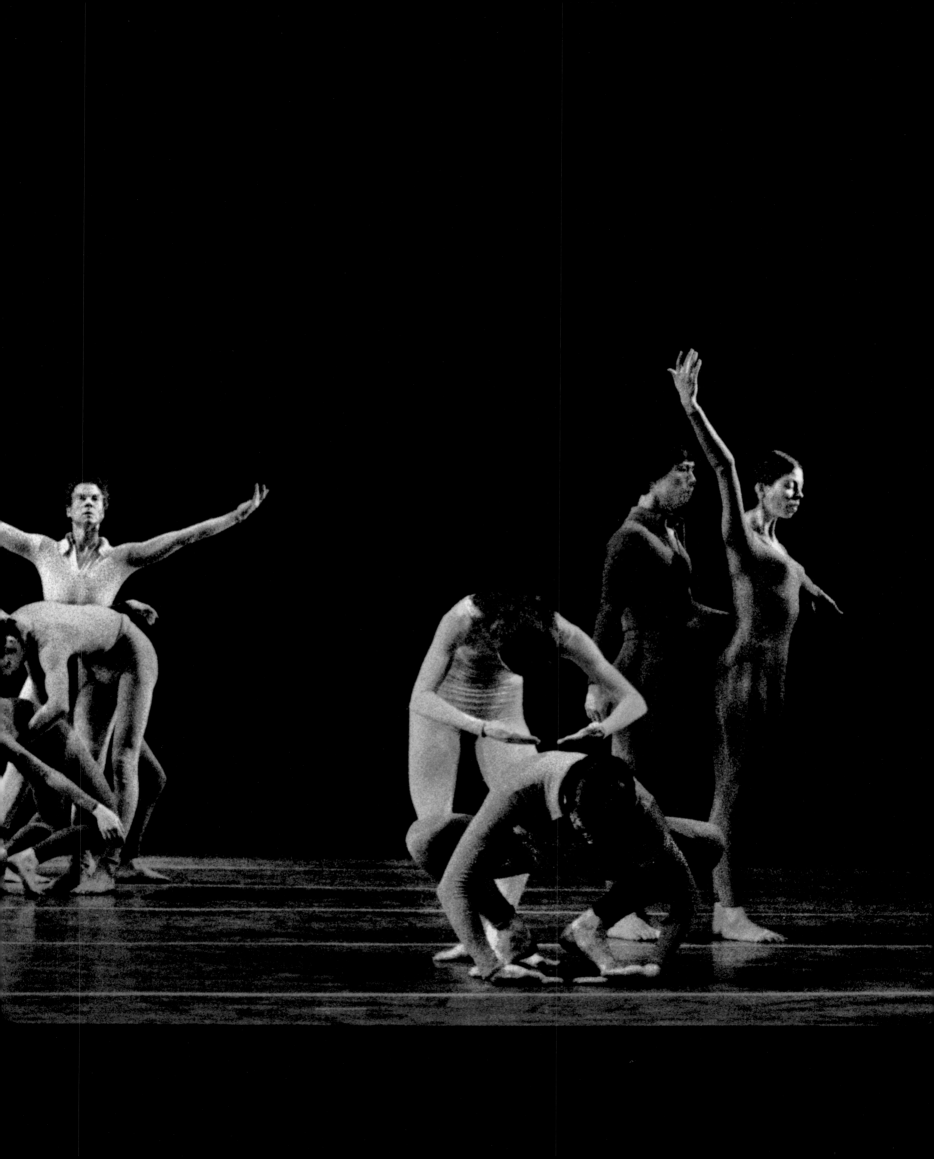

RICHARD NELSON

Morning, too early. Must; do. Open curtain: Cue One. Yellow sunlight, fast. Maximum. Move to bathroom, switch on: Cue Two. Buzz and flickerrrrON, blueish. Don't like the look. Well, someone will. (A few minutes.)

Three; switch off. Cue Four. Door open, admit light. Five (this happened some time ago but I've only just noticed it), yellow to gray, sunlight gone. Very slow. Six, back on again, brighter than maximum.

Etcetera to theater. Eight A.M. Crew of six. Event tonight. Gymnasium, old, small, several lights up. Windowed room, wood. Low ceiling, poor hanging positions. Beam angles not wide enough to cover space; inadequate electrical power; low-intensity gray general illumination. Open windows. See trees. Hang lights in. Power from transformers outside. Controls at one side of the space. Wait for darkness to permit focus through closed windows. Darkness will come too late, focus in daylight. Flood the lights and aim in general direction. Check all

working. See some rehearsal? Can't, ended, dancers resting. Rest and wait.

Six P.M., dancers to warm up. Learn program material, what and when. Where? Well, in the space, of course, no need to ask that. Make list. Will I use it? Don't know, but it is nice to have if I want it . . .

A dancer has a question. "Rick, what will the lights be like tonight?" Perhaps I've waited a long time to say this, but I'm *serious!* "Depends on the weather." "No, now come on, you know what I mean, I mean makeup and all, and, you know, we're VERY tired, and . . ." Valda says it nicest. She really doesn't WANT to be blinded by the sudden bursts of low sidelight, or find her shadow darting about while she's balanced in one of those amazing conditions. (They are more these than positions.) Nobody wants it to be difficult, and they have reason to be concerned. "Actually, Valda, the lights are in the trees. (Don't tell.) I haven't been able to see them, but it will probably

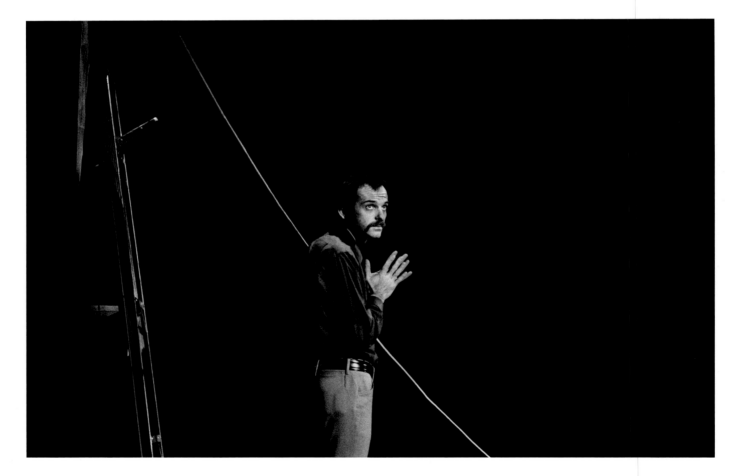

Richard Nelson, Minneapolis, 1969

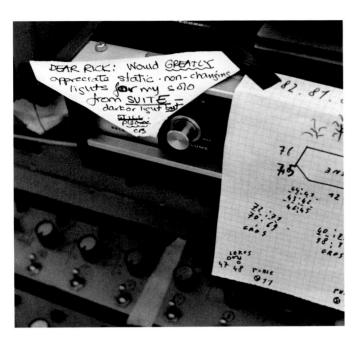

Note for Richard Nelson from Carolyn Brown left
on his lighting board, Fondation Maeght, 1970

be a rather *still* evening. Lots of people, close." Then Sandy: "I just wanted you to know . . . last time we did the (name of thing from name of dance here), we really couldn't see each other. Poor (name of another dancer here) couldn't see at all, I was OK, but . . ." Others are more optimistic; "Got something neat up your sleeve, huh?" Perhaps he's seen my smile. Or the trees. Carolyn smiles Her smile, The Smile of I Know We Can't Talk About This (Again), and What Is There To Say Anyway But Well You Know, and it (this smile) is happy and sad . . . a certain kind of sad . . . and we do our Hug, which is warm and quiet. We too are silent collaborators.

Maybe Merce says something before we start. It is probably "Have fun." Perhaps "Bon chance." It's rarely possible for me to know what's behind his expression. Like the dances, his face doesn't connect with recognizable emotions. I wonder if he's seen the lights in the trees. I think not. He occasionally glances up at the spotlightless area, but goes about his business without comment. That's nice. In any case, what could he say at seven-thirty? "Hang some lights"?

I've decided to let the program start ahead of me. If you prefer, you could consider that I started at the same time and that my first cue was "stillness." Usually the musicians begin when the houselights, or their representatives, dim or go out. Sometimes they begin earlier, but we usually know how we will begin. This is some condition we somehow never thought about eliminating. Or just never got around to eliminating. Tonight I've forgotten and said nothing. Since, the room lights remain on, the musicians make no sounds. However, the danc-

ers have been told they should "begin when ready" and have done so.

Sometimes I can dissociate myself from the sounds, whatever they are. However loud or soft, I do not receive. I think some of the dancers can make this happen. When I turn off my ears my responses are generally with respect to an already existing condition of light, not with respect to the dance. Sometimes feelings of light and movement intermingle. Sometimes I open my ears for awhile to see what I'll feel; sometimes respond "to" the feel, sometimes "against" it. I don't know that those terms mean anything; I would prefer to leave the space blank and have you know what I mean. In person, you and I could be silent collaborators.

Tonight I have prepared some "cues" on paper. They are activities or actions that I have thought would be nice to loak at during the performance. I'm more interested in them than I would be if I had had the opportunity to "set" them during a rehearsal. I enjoy seeing the performance as the audience sees it.

Here is a space. The dancers will perform in it tonight. What will they dance? Well, parts of the repertory. Oh. Which parts? We'll figure that out later, during rehearsal. When is the rehearsal? We'll begin at about two, and finish at four. The performance is at eight? Yes, we'll be back to warm up at six. Ah, I see; we have from four to six to set up the lights.

What's happening could be, and often is, considered an outrageous departure from traditional and "sane" or structured work methods. A degree of disorganization is implied in a description of the work; whereas, in fact, our technology demands more organization, more careful planning than most. In addition, since we cannot depend on feeling a certain way at a certain time, we must be ready and alert always for any possibility. For the technicians, musicians, stage manager, electricians, an unusual awareness backstage and in the pit makes the air crackle.

Everyone else would be aghast at our technique. Some who think they understand it, and refer to all our activity as "chance" operations, might call our work "unstructured." I have not yet heard the word that really suits the work. It is not "un" anything. It consists of positive action. "Free" does not describe it; the limitations on everyone are strict. "Improvisational" is grasping at straws. Perhaps "open"? Well, why bother? You could miss what you're seeing for all the thinking . . .

We don't speak much about it. I used to try, before I knew better (or learned to forget). Speaking is for speakers; dancing for dancers; lighting for lighters. Merce and John are presenting (or are presented in) a "dialogue." John speaks; Merce moves. That about sums it up.

1970 SIGNALS

MUSIC
ORIGINAL PERFORMANCES BY
JOHN CAGE, DAVID TUDOR,
AND GORDON MUMMA.
SUBSEQUENT COMPOSERS
VARIED DEPENDING ON WHO
WAS IN THE PIT.

COSTUMES
MERCE CUNNINGHAM

LIGHTING
RICHARD NELSON

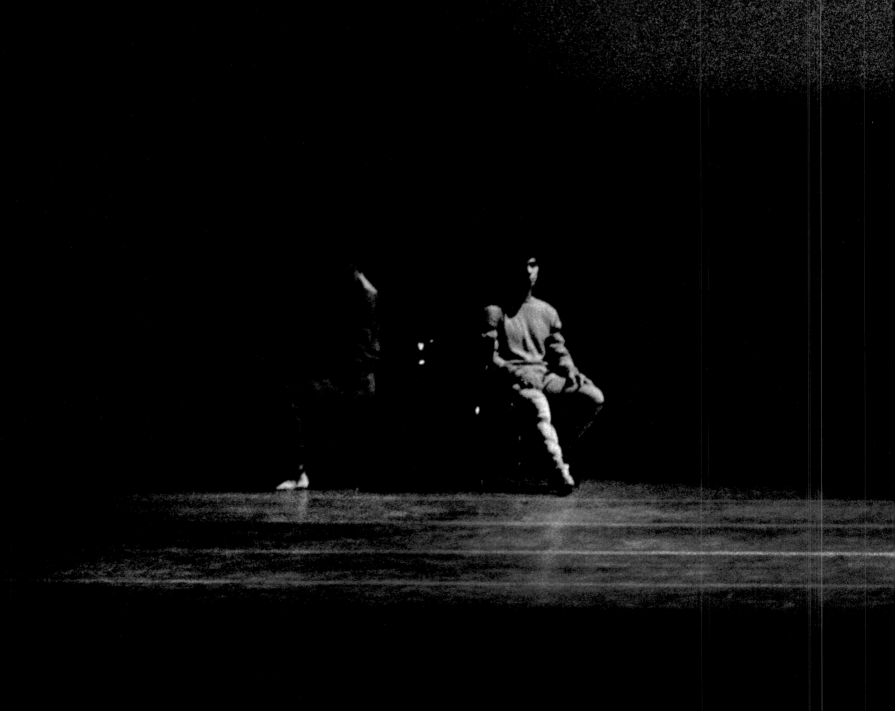

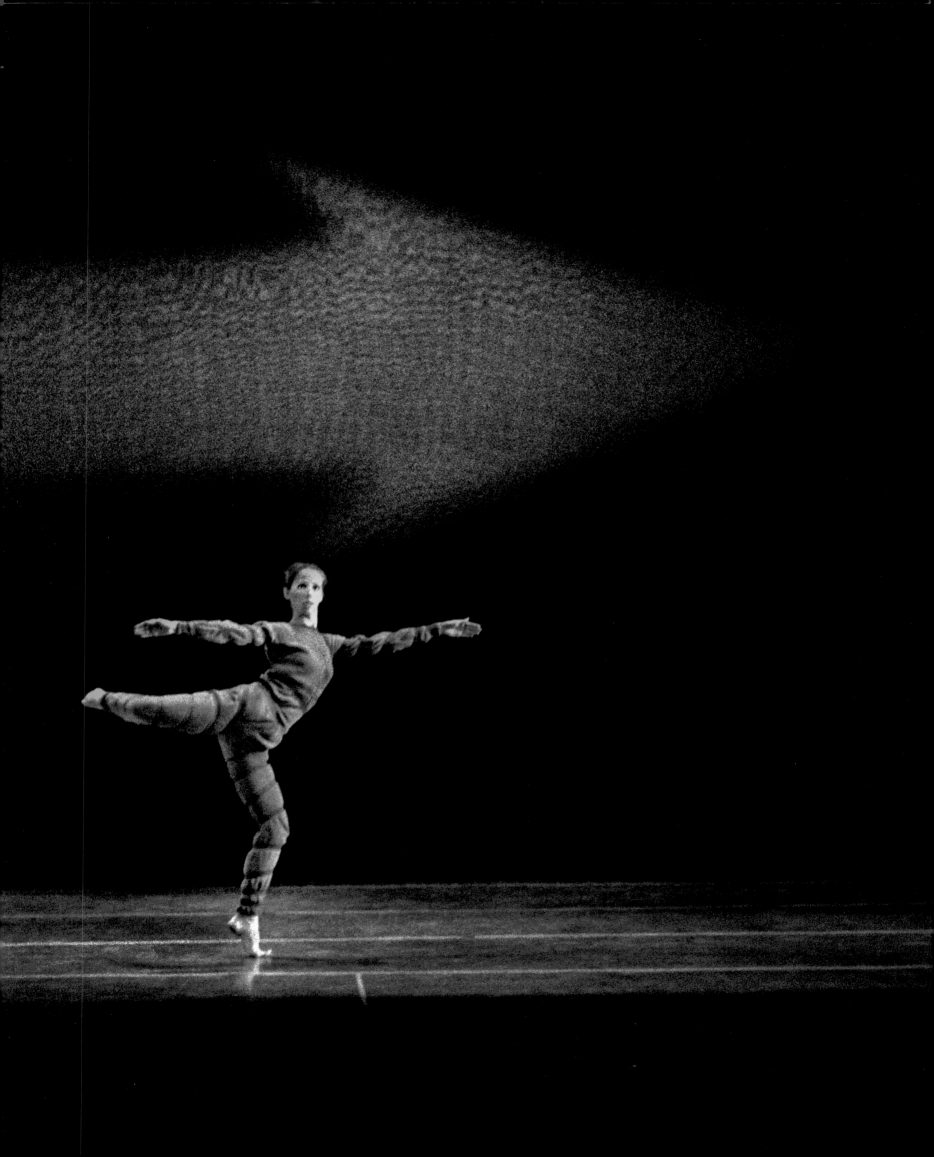

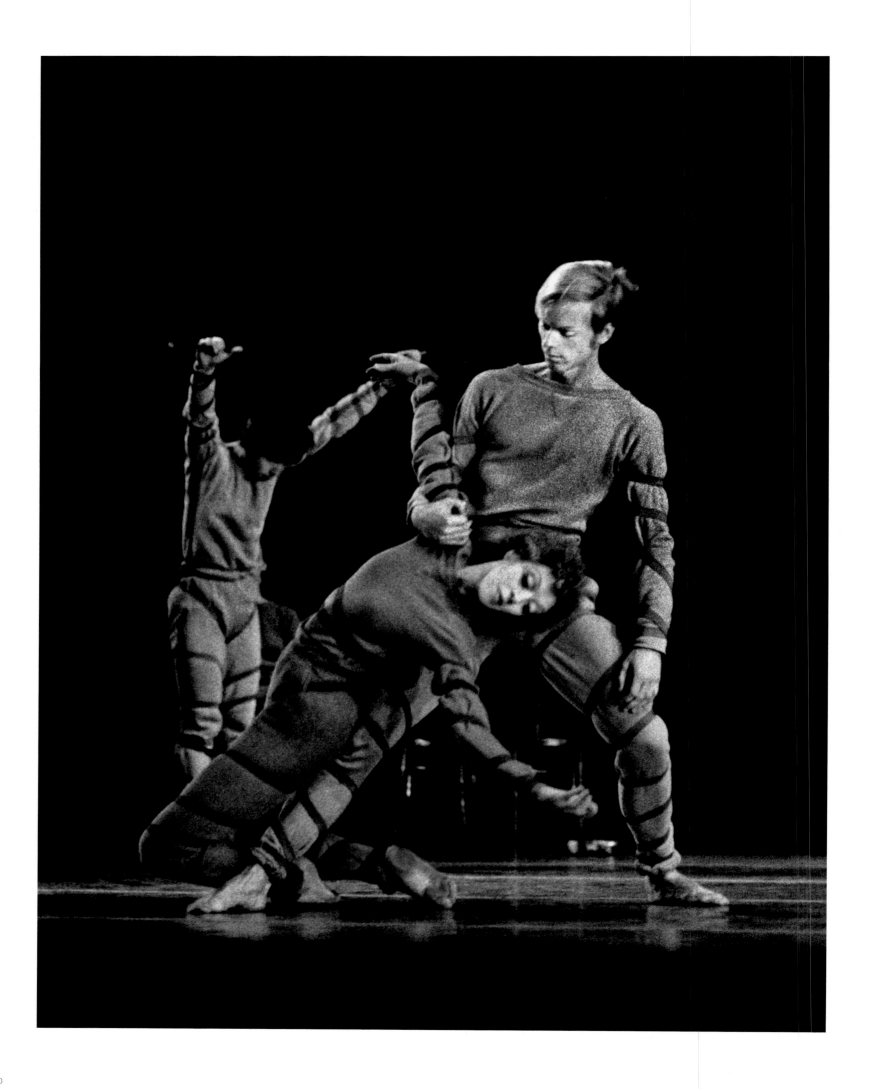

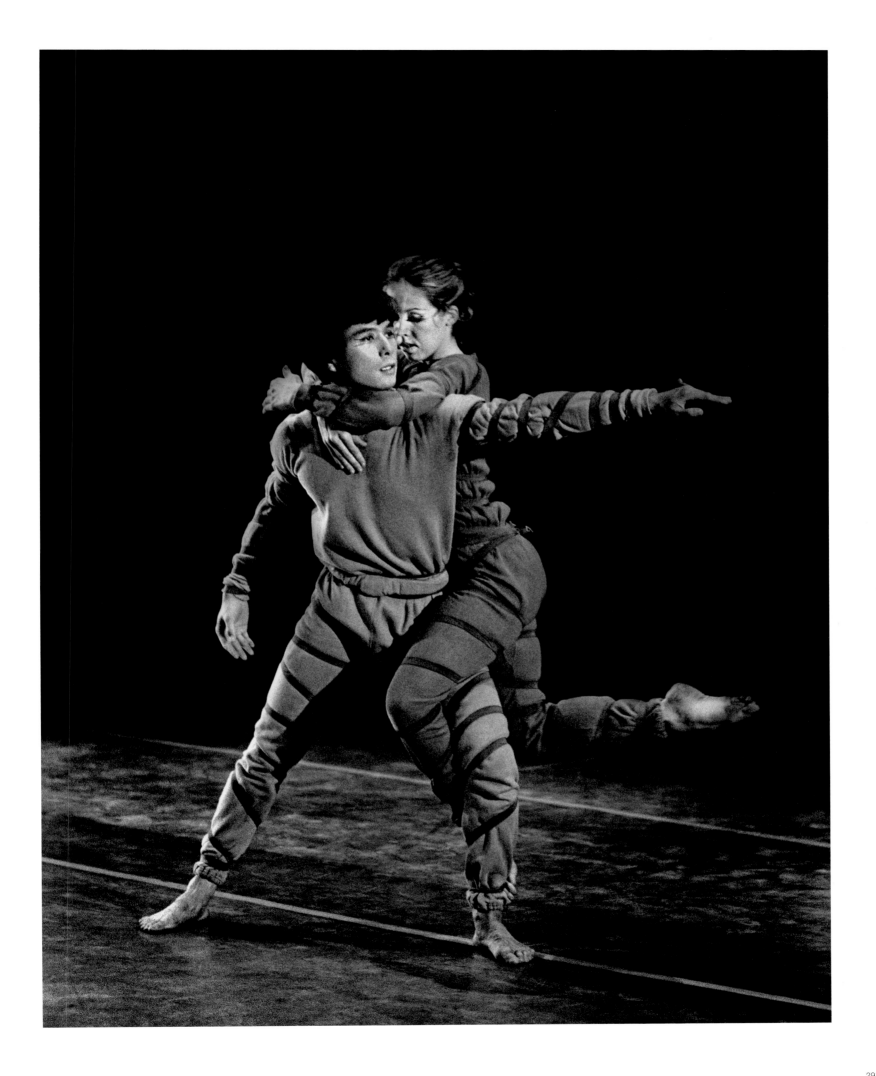

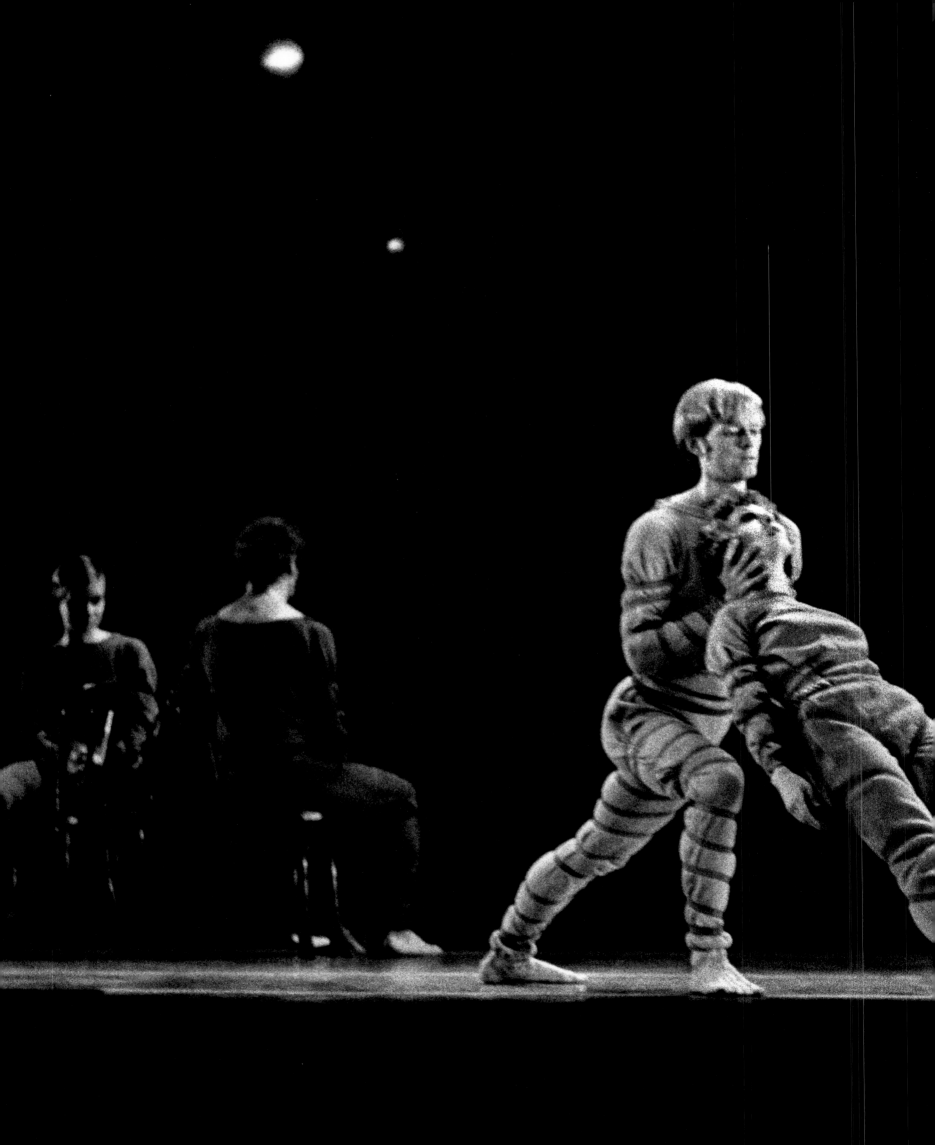

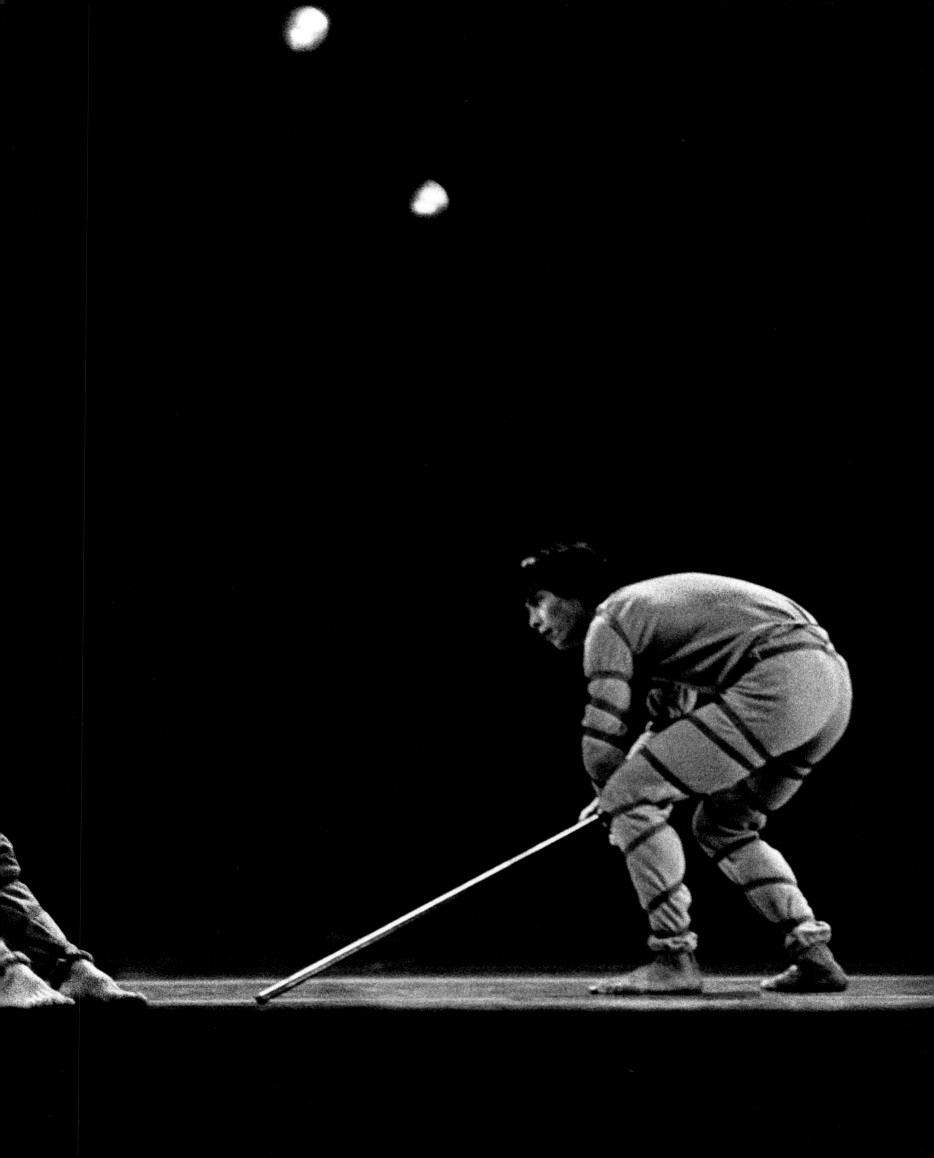

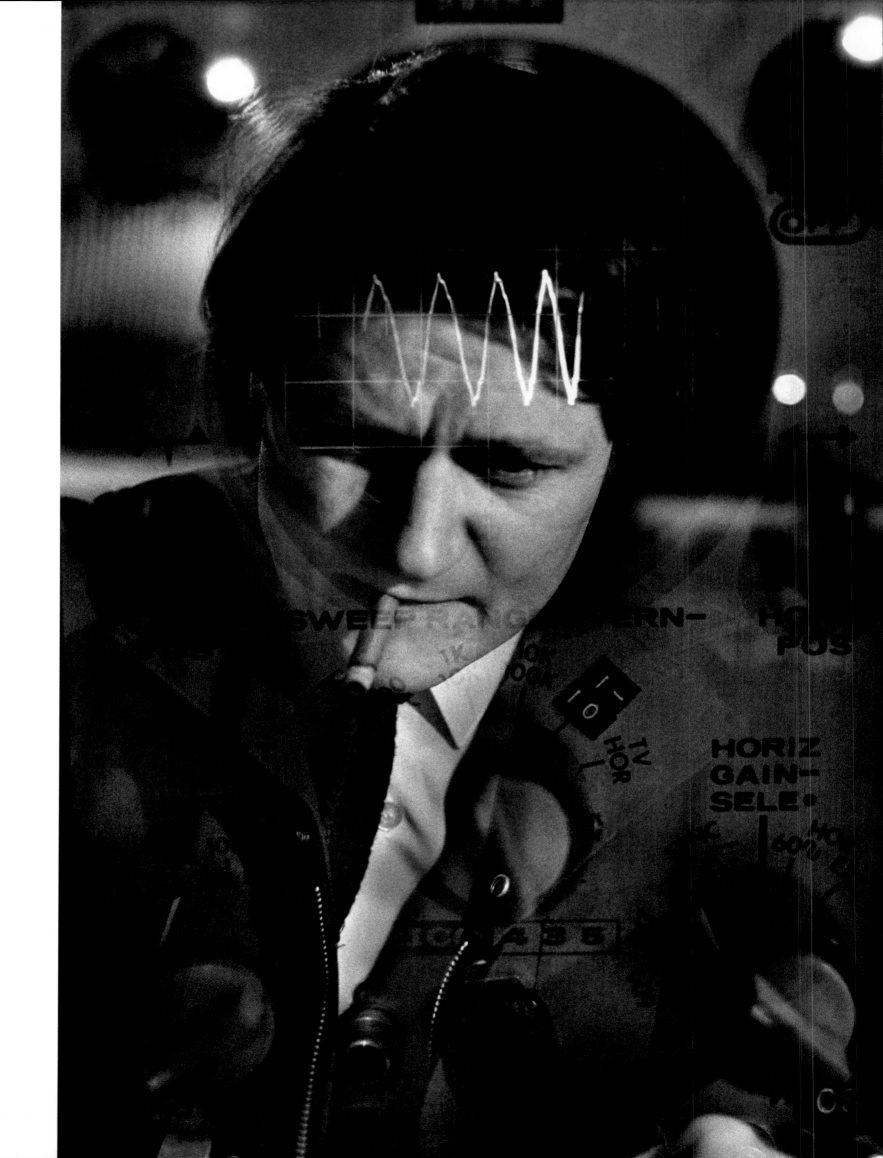

GORDON MUMMA

—From "Where the Circus Went"

How I joined the Cunningham Dance Company was never very clear, and of the nature of the proverbial "grapevine." My previous relationship to John Cage and David Tudor had been as a musical collaborator and technical assistant in several concerts. I had built special electronic music equipment for them, and at Tudor's request I was beginning work on a composition for his Bandoneon, a none-too-common Argentine instrument. On several occasions Tudor had mentioned that they were considering someone to assist them with the increasingly complex sound equipment of the dance company repertory.

It became official in June 1966, when I received a direct invitation from Cage by long distance telephone. I accepted. A week later Cage called again to ask if I would compose the music for a new dance that was to be premiered on a European tour in August. A bit stunned, I again agreed.

Merce Cunningham phoned a few days later to discuss details of the new work.

"I'd like it if you could do something for David Tudor to play."

I agreed, and asked about the title of the new dance.

"I haven't decided yet."

"How long will it be?"

"Between twenty and thirty minutes."

"I wonder what else I should know, maybe how many dancers?"

"Eight dancers, and we perform it at St. Paul de Vence, in France, on the sixth of August. It's beautiful there."

That was all. I had seen the Cunningham dancers perform in 1961, and again in 1963. Each time had been an awesome experience. I was now attempting to accumulate enough information over the telephone to compose a work for them in less than three months. To meet the deadline I decided to recast the elaborate composition I was already preparing for David Tudor and his Bandoneon.

Gordon Mumma, Buffalo, New York, 1968

Though the information Cunningham had given me was minimal (I didn't have the presence of mind to probe further), his comfortably matter-of-fact tone of voice was reassuring. I doubted that he knew any of my music, but I had the feeling that he trusted me. At least he seemed comfortable taking the risk.

In the ensuing years it became clear that this initial encounter was representative of much of the Cunningham Dance Company collaboration. The best and worst aspects of "grapevine" communications and telephone arrangements, the minimal specifications between choreographer and composer, the blended sense of freedom and responsibility, and a pervading ambiguity about details and commitments were nourished by Cunningham's immediate trust of his collaborators and his invitation to artistic risk.

People familiar with the tradition of dancing to music sometimes find it difficult to comprehend the possibility of dance that is simultaneous with but independent of the music. Actually, the procedure has become a tradition and is now practiced by many other dancers. The surprise is often greatest for those of the audience who inquire about the coordinations and correspondences that they have noticed between the music and the dance, and learn that these happen by chance at each performance. Not everyone agrees about these correspondences, of course. Though they attend the same performance, it is often a very different experience for each.

Further, this independence of music and dance is true only for a part of the Cunningham Company repertory, and as an artistic procedure it has evolved over many years. In the 1940s Cunningham and Cage collaborated in a relatively traditional way. Cage composed fixed, notated music, often to a previously fixed Cunningham choreography. Given this procedure, there was still innovation aplenty. Cage was preparing the piano with miscellaneous hardware, Cunningham was creating movement independent of literary references, and the critics were already unsettled.

Following the Second World War, Cage returned from a trip to Europe with "musique-concrete" by Pierre Schaeffer, to which Cunningham established a precedent by making the first major choreography to original music on magnetic tape. Cunningham had also used music by Eric Satie, Ben Weber, Alan Hovaness, Alexi Haieff, and the jazz musician Baby Dodds. David Tudor's introduction to Cunningham had been as a pianist for Ben We-

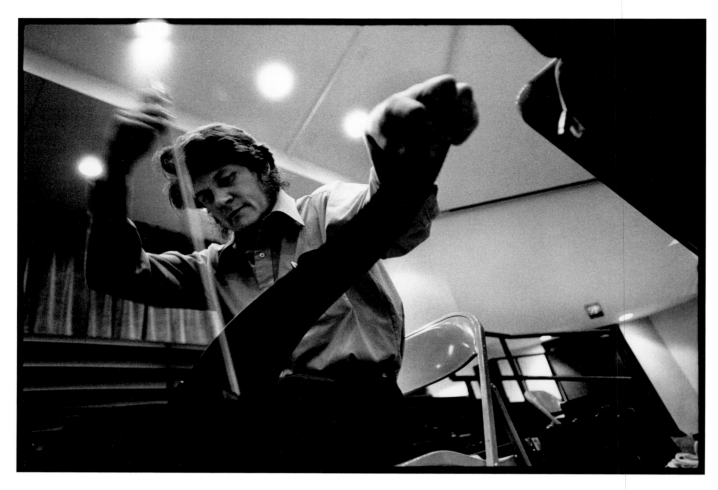

Gordon Mumma, the Yo-Yo Ma of the musical saw

ber's music. In the 1950s the collaborations were extended to less wellknown, more experimental, and considerably riskier composers: Earle Brown, Morton Feldman, and Christian Wolff.

Listed on the programs as "pianist," Tudor's relationship to Cage's (and others') music became an increasingly interdependent collaboration. Tudor often supplied fundamental ideas as well as innovative performance procedures. By 1958 they were at work on the bizarre, virtuoso collaboration called *Antic Meet*, and shortly after its introduction in 1961 were beginning to amplify the pianos that accompanied the dance *Aeon* with Cage's *Winter Music*. The diverse repertory now included dance coordinated with traditional music (the conventional piano of Satie's *Nocturnes*), connected with mechanically innovative music (the prepared duo pianos of *Suite for Five*, and the player piano of *Crises*), and coexisting with all manner of sounds (the electronically modified pianos and nonistrumental resources of *Aeon* and *Antic Meet*). That repertory also included traditional and innovative instrumental ensembles, and electronic music, by other composers.

Along with the development of chance procedures in the 1950s, there were the beginnings of shared creative respon-

sibilities: the functional distinction between composer and performer was becoming blurred. For Cunningham musicians this distinction became more obscure with the increasing use of electronic technology in the 1960s, and it had become irrelevent by the 1970s.

The increasingly heavy touring schedule that culminated in the 1964 world tour left little time for creative innovation. I once asked the prolific Cage, who had always made several new works each year, why he had no compositions dated 1964. Surprised with the recognition, he replied,

"I spent that year writing letters to raise money for the touring."

1964 was a difficult year in many ways. The Cunningham Dance Company became world famous, Rauschenberg won the Venice Biennale, and the human and financial costs were staggering. Heavy touring usually decimates performance ensembles, and the Cunningham Company was no exception. The "classic" Cunningham ensemble developed through the 1950s was at an end. Rauschenberg and over half the dancers departed from the collaboration at the end of the world tour. Undaunted, the company determined to further its explorations with chance procedures, theatrical innovations, and particularly electronic technology. The largest step was *Variations V*, which was premiered in 1965 at Lincoln Center. With virtually no precedent, this work established at once a coexistence of technological interdependence and artistic nondependence. Every complicated production of *Variations V* was logistically precarious, and no two people could agree about its artistic merits. The implications of *Variations V* have changed my life in many ways. It was my first experience with this recurring dilemma: I loved the work and absolutely dreaded the exhausting preparation of every performance.

For the audience *Variations V* was like a multiringed circus. For the performers it was participation in a man-machine environment, chock full of images and gadgets: movies, TV images, slides, a bicycle and gym mat, plastic plants, furniture (all of them rigged with electronics), and a garden of vertical antennas projecting upwards from the floor.

These vertical antennas were capacitive sensors that responded to the locations of the dancers on the stage by sending electronic signals to the musicians. It was one of two systems of sensors. The other system was a network of photoelectric cells that responded to changes in light intensity as the dancers moved past them. Electronic signals from these photoelectric cells were also sent to the musicians.

The musicians operated an orchestra of electronic sound-producers: tape recorders, radios, phonographs, and the like. The signals from the two sensor systems directly articulated these sound-makers. That is, by their movements the dancers articulated both the performance space and the sounds of the music. The interaction of the systems with the performers was complex, and contained a measure of technological unpredictability. The audience rarely perceived a one-to-one or "mickey-mouse" correspondence between the dancer's movements and the sound. Further, differences of performance space, lighting, and musical materials

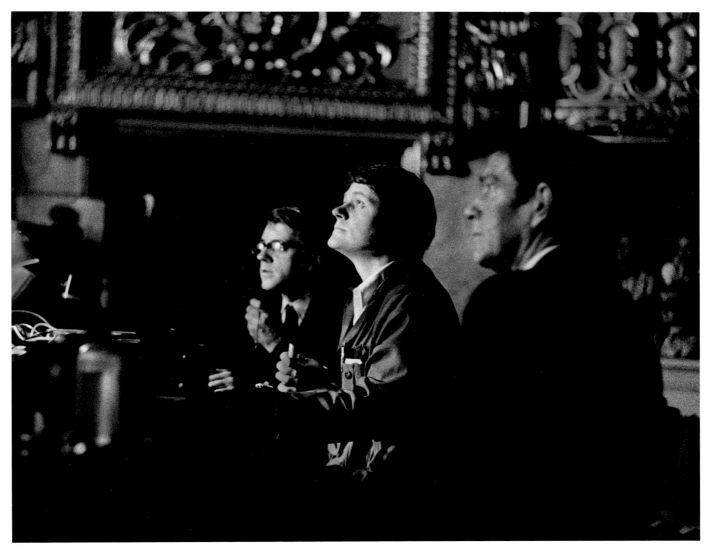

David Tudor, Gordon Mumma, and John Cage in the pit at the Théâtre de l'Odéon, 1970

from one performance to another contributed to a nonrepeatability of the result. Because of these multi-leveled complexities, *Variations V* had the unsettling effect of being the same and different at each performance.

Besides *Variations V*, several other repertory works from the 1960s indicate workings of technological, artistic, and social collaboration in the Cunningham Dance Company. Three of these, *Story* (1963), the notorious *Winterbranch* (1964), and the smaller-scale *Field Dances* (1963), were made previous to the world tour. The fourth, the extremely popular *How to Pass, Kick, Fall, and Run* (1965), was made right after *Variations V*.

The music for *Winterbranch*, *Variations V*, and *How to . . .* was the result of electronic technology. But where *Variations V* was a complicated spectacle, *Winterbranch* and *How to . . .* were elemental simplicity. *Winterbranch* used "canned" music: two tape recorded sounds of La Monte Young were played at a sustained, near-deafening level over loudspeakers. For *How to . . .* the "music" was the product of that most common live electronic instrument: the public-address system.

The sensation of *Winterbranch* was in its theatrical impact, and due largely to its lighting. Rauschenberg lit *Winterbranch* with strongly focused, noncolored lights in such a way that the light rarely hit the performing dancers directly except by chance. He distributed this light activity over the duration of the piece differently at each performance. Cumulatively, more than half of *Winterbranch* was often in total darkness. The choreography was derived from the physical gestures of falling. The performance began in silence. After a few minutes, just as the audience invariably grew restless with this theatrical ambiguity, they were pinned to their seats by the massive shock front of La Monte Young's excruciating *Two Sounds*, which continued to the end.

How to . . . was also a relatively simple production. The choreography was inspired by the movements of sports and games and (as with *Winterbranch*) was specific and fixed. The "music" consisted of John Cage, as raconteur, reading from his one-minute-long stories.

During the first year of *How to . . .* David Tudor performed with Cage, using Cage's voice as a sound source for his complicated electronic modification procedures. The result was a montage of sonic fragmentation that increased in verbal unintelligibility with each performance.

Complaints came not only from the audience but from the dancers. Because of that mysterious "grapevine" procedure of quasi-consensus, which is a typical feature of the Cunningham Company, the electronic modification of Cage's reading was eventually abandoned. On occasion, though, the performance was elaborated when David Vaughan joined Cage in the simultaneous, but independent, reading of those stories.

The artistic and social collaboration of *Story* was more daring. The music for *Story* was Toshi Ichiyanagi's *Sapporo*, a notated but open-ended ensemble work that allowed for considerable interpretation on the part of the performers. More telling is the procedure of the choreographic and scenic resources of *Story*. Rauschenberg (collaborating on the world tour with the artist Alex Hay) made the decor anew during each performance, using materials found on the spot. Thus they were themselves performers. Also, during the performances the dancers chose what they would wear and what they would do with it from a great pile of clothing and other paraphernalia on the stage.

In *Story* Cunningham had given the dancers some creative freedom that they had not previously enjoyed in earlier repertory works. It was a social and artistic direction being actively explored by the pioneers of "happenings" at that time, and seemed particularly fertile in the context of the Cunningham Company because its performers were a highly trained ensemble.

The collaborative restraints of *Field Dances* were more specific. The duration of *Field Dances* was indeterminate, and the "choreography" that Cunningham presented his dancers was essentially a vocabulary of physical gestures. The dancers were free during performance to develop their own syntax for that vocabulary. Further, the dancers Individually chose whether they would perform in it at all, and on occasion noncompany dancers were included in performance.

In the signal year of 1964 the first three of a long series of Event performances took place, one in Vienna, the other two in Stockholm. These *Events* were made specially for each occasion. They were generally complete, uninterrupted performances in nonproscenium spaces, and they held implications of greater collaborative endeavor than most of the repertory works.

The departure of Rauschenberg and the arrival of Jasper Johns as "artistic advisor" shortly afterward brought about a significant change in the nature of the decor. In one sense there was an expansion of collaborative activity: many other artists were invited to participate. The decor for *Place* (1966) was by Beverly Emmons, for *Scramble* (1967) by Frank Stella, for *Rainforest* (1968) by Andy Warhol, for *Walkaround Time* (1968) by Johns and Marcel Duchamp, for *Canfield* (1969) by Robert Morris, for *Tread* (1970) by Bruce Nauman, and for *Objects* (1971) by Niel Jenny. The decor for *Second Hand* (1970), *TV Rerun* (1972), and *Landrover* (1972) was by Jasper Johns. An impressive list, comparable in many ways to the era of the Diaghilev Ballet.

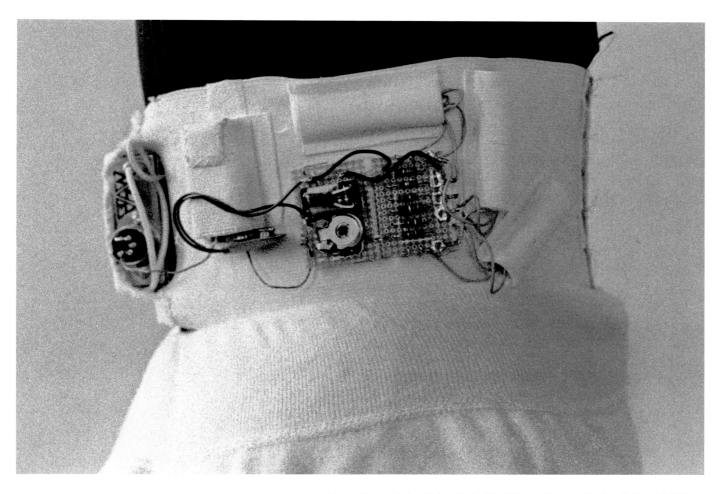

Mumma's sound-signal telemetry belt for *Telepos*, his score for Cunningham's *TV Rerun*

On a very elementary level the decor for *Scramble*, *Rainforest*, *Walkaround Time*, and *Objects* involved a collaboration with the dancers. They moved the scenery around the space during performance, and the helium-filled silver mylar pillows of *Rainforest* were often moved by chance encounters with the dancers. But elegant as some of it was, this decor was still basically a collection of decorative props. The audience might gasp with appreciation when the curtain opened, but except for the mysterious, animallike character of Warhol's pillows in *Rainforest*, the dancers didn't sense any particular collaborative affinity with either the decor or its production.

The lighting designer Richard Nelson found himself in a more interesting position. In 1968 he made a special score, *Lightgames 1^R*, for *Rainforest* that changed from performance to performance, thus extending an aspect of the *Winterbranch* tradition. For *Signals* (1970) Nelson employed several unusual procedures, including laser projection. He treated each performance as a new challenge to his ingenuity and produced a tour-de-force series of scenic wonders.

Robert Morris's decor for *Canfield* included the conception for the lighting design. The dancers, wearing irridescent gray leotards and tights, were lit by a vertical beam that extended from the downstage floor to a place above the proscenium arch, and it moved slowly back and forth across the proscenium opening. The light itself came from a series of aircraft landing lights, mounted within the beam and focused on a gray drop at the back of the stage. The effect was a vertical plane of brilliant light which, slowly sweeping through the space, was interrupted by encounters with the dancers, who seemed like the intermittantly fluorescing population of some lunar landscape.

As impressive as these various decors were, if any collaboration existed between Cunningham and the designers it was a private affair, and not shared by the dancers. Many people had the sense that the potentials suggested by works like *Story* and *Variations V* were being held in suspension.

Repertory collaboration between the dancers and musicians was also suspended following *Variations V*, and occurred only once, again in an elementary way, in my own music for *TV Rerun*. For this composition, entitled *Telepos*, I designed lightweight elastic belts for the dancers. The belts contained acceleration sensors and radio transmitters. The dancers'

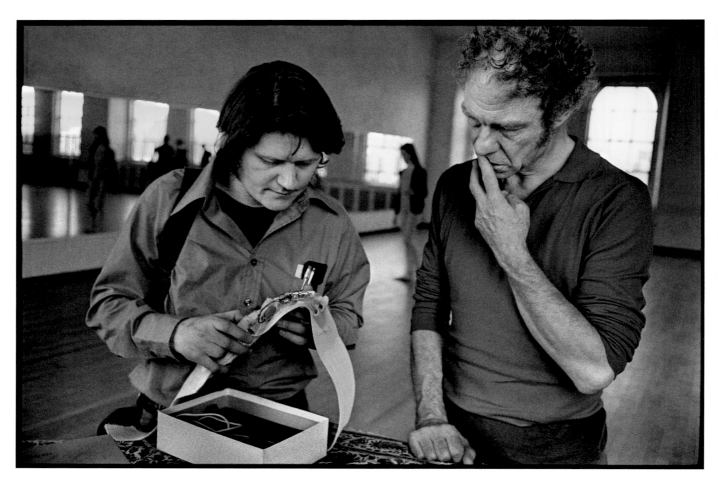

Merce Cunningham's first look at Gordon Mumma's telemetry belt for *TV Rerun*

movements were translated into audible pitches, transmitted to special electronic equipment in the orchestra pit, and heard from loudspeakers around the audience. This process of telemetry was like that used in space travel. Thus the dancers were collaboratively responsible for the nature and continuity of the sound, though the implications of this technological extension of human activity suggested more collaborative potential than we (the dancers and I) actually felt in the making of this piece.

However, the collaborative activities among the musicians themselves were becoming increasingly complex and fruitful. The performance of my composition *Mesa*, the music for Cunningham's *Place*, with Tudor's performance of his *Bandoneon* and my performance of the electronic equipment, was a closely interdependent collaboration. Ichiyanagi's music for *Scramble*, called *Activities for Orchestra*, like his earlier music for *Story*, was a notated but open-ended composition. It allowed for ensembles of various sizes and required difficult new ways of performing acoustical and electronic instruments simultaneously.

The two new works of the following year (1968) were *Rainforest* and *Walkaround Time*, with music by Tudor and David Behrman,

respectively. Tudor's music for *Rainforest* was a collaborative duo between him and myself, performing with a forest of electro-acoustic transducers of his own uncanny design.

The next repertory work, *Canfield* (1969), was notable in many ways. The choreographic structure was thirteen sections with interludes between each, analogous to the form of solitaire invented by Richard Canfield, a gambler at the casinos of Saratoga Springs, New York. The sections and interludes were arranged in a different order for each performance, usually on that day, and not all were necessary to constitute a performance. Thus the continuity was different each time and the dance varied in length from 20 to 105 minutes. The character of the choreography was one of extreme contrasts, with elements of the lyrical, preposterous, baroque, serene, and surreal juxtaposed with one another in often jolting succession, and displayed in all manner of solo and ensemble activities.

The music, by Pauline Oliveros, is entitled *In Memoriam: Nikola Tesla, Cosmic Engineer*, and is as much a theatrical as a musical composition. In performance it occurred simultaneously with, but independently of, the dance and lighting/decor.

Independently, both Morris and Oliveros had fulfilled their commissions by supplying the Cunningham Company only with ideas about what should be done, leaving the implementation and execution of those ideas to the lighting designer, stage-production manager, and musicians. For example, the score of Oliveros's piece was three pages of typewritten instructions that specified, often in general terms, the nature of the equipment that the musicians had to obtain or develop, as well as the characteristics and continuity of the performance with that equipment. In the sleep-depriving tradition of Cunningham Company new-work production, the music, lighting, and decor specifications arrived within only weeks of the scheduled first performance.

The stage-production manager, James Baird, was responsible for the design and construction of the mobile, vertical light-beam. The *Canfield* light-beam project was more intimidating than most because Baird was responsible for implementation of an idea that required a series of interdependent innovations: the aircraft landinglight configuration within the vertical beam; a light-weight multi-sectioned, horizontal aluminum I-beam from which the vertical beam was suspended; and a unique electric motor and reduction-gear mechanism that travelled back and forth along the I-beam and pulled the vertical light-beam hanging below it. All of this mechanism had to be adaptable to the various sizes of proscenium stages that we would encounter for the next several years; operate with wide variations in mains, voltage, and frequency; and be efficiently installed and dismantled on one-night stands by a different (often foreign-language) stage crew at each theater.

For Baird the successful confrontation of a challenge and a modest salary was ordinarily more than sufficient reward for his efforts. But consider: if the light-beam succeeded, Morris got the credit; if it failed Baird got the blame.

The musicians were in more generous circumstances in *Canfield*. The Oliveros score was more open-ended in its possibilities of implementation. The musicians were committed to specific kinds of sounds and theatrical effects, but not to specific hardware. And though we used lots of equipment for Oliveros's piece—by the end of a performance the orchestra pit was an awful mess—the physical scale was comfortably small. The *Canfield* sound equipment was packed into a few suitcases. The light-beam apparatus was shipped in large crates.

More than any work in the repertory at that time, *Canfield* was a continual production-in-progress. The impact of performances of the complete *Canfield*, which filled an entire evening, had become very great. By the early 1970s we were rarely presenting the abbreviated versions, as we once had, in performance with other repertory works. *Canfield* seemed to be metamorphosizing into the genre of the Event performances, which had come to occupy more of our creative time. In several nonproscenium Event performances the entire choreography of *Canfield* was danced, but with different, specially made lighting, decor, and music.

Increasingly preoccupied with the idea of a collaborative creative process, and encouraged particularly by the results of our Event collaborations, the musicians decided to share in the creative responsibilities for the next repertory work. We decided in advance that each performance would have different music; each musician would make an independent contribution of sound materials; and each contribution would be sparing in its resources and might have a specific character, idea, or image. Furthermore, we would title this collaborative music by the week and month of each specific performance, e.g., "the second week of November." Finally, the names of all participating musicians would appear on the program, allowing for the possibility that more than the three regular Cunningham Company musicians would collaborate, and their names would be listed in rotating order.

This new work was called *Signals*, and I have mentioned Richard Nelson's contribution to the lighting and decor. Sensing the various implications of the title, *Signals*, Cage generally played sparse "abbreviations" of early music on the piano, which he derived during performance by chance operations with the *I Ching*. I chose the idea of a sound ambience, often of signal-type sounds like bells, which occurred quietly at a great distance, often in the outdoors. Tudor commonly selected a continuous sound from a single source, such as insect activities, electroencephalic signals, or a sentimental example of parlor music.

The musicians collaborated in a later repertory work, *Landrover* (1972) in a different way. Like *Canfield* and *Scramble*, which preceded it, the choreography of *Landrover* existed in sections, the order of which could be arranged differently for each performance. Taking our lead from this procedure, Cage, Tudor, and I decided to do the same with the music. The choreographic sections of *Landrover* were of unequal length and four in number, but did not all have to be performed. We established the musical sections to be equal in length and three in number, with the total length equal to that of the choreography. Each of us was completely responsible for a single section, and immediately preceding the performance straws were drawn to determine the order of the three musical sections.

For his contribution Cage chose to read a short fragment from his *Mureau*, which he would place somewhere in the large, remaining silence of his section. For the entire length of his section Tudor presented seismological signals, which he speeded up to an audible range and modified gently with electronic equalization. I made a set of verbal instructions, in the event someone else wanted to perform my section, though I invariably performed it myself. These instructions specified "a phenomenon unarticulated insofar as possible and sustained at the threshold of perception." Though that phenomenon doesn't necessarily have to be sound, for my section of *Landrover* I created a kind of supersonic blanket with special electronic equipment. In accordance with the instructions I adjusted this phenomenon at the threshold of perception—my perception. Of course, since everyone's perception thresholds are different, it was above some and below others. I could barely hear it, Cage said he never heard it, and Tudor found it obnoxiously audible. Critics described it variously as "absolute silence," "intolerable roaring," and "something like crickets."

The putting-together of *Landrover* seemed almost too simple to deserve being called a collaboration. (I don't mean to imply that a lot of energy wasn't spent, particularly by Cunningham and the dancers!) Yet the combination of elements that were chosen by the participants, in that inexplicably independent yet parallel way, would have been inconceivable to me In any other circumstances.

The work called *Objects* (1971) turned out to be an interim production, and for various reasons it didn't last long in the repertory. The music for *Objects* was Alvin Lucier's *Vespers*, a live-electronic piece in which the musicians moved blind through the performance space, finding their way by echolocation with the use of clicking, sonar-type instruments.

When a composer outside the Cunningham Company was commissioned to do music for a new production, the choice was usually made as a consensus between Cunningham and the regular musicians. If Cunningham had a specific person in mind at the outset, everyone else was likely to concur. It was likely to have been a parallel idea in the other minds as well. Alvin Lucier had been in our minds for several years. However, the Cunningham Company procrastinated in making a commitment to him.

One way out of the dilemma was to ask Lucier for an already completed work. For several days I carried with me everywhere a portable tape recorder and a tape of Lucier's *Vespers* performed by the Sonic Arts Union. Eventually my path crossed that of Cunningham, in a dressing room between rehearsals. He listened to *Vespers*, and replied:

"I like it, don't you? Will you play this tape in performance?"

"No, we'll do it live, with the original instruments. Besides meeting the requirements of Lucier's score, it will allow us to adapt to various performance circumstances of the new dance. It can be any length, and the texture can be more transparent."

Merce asked, "What are the instruments called that make that clicking sound?"

"Sondols."

"Well, if we all like it, let's give it a try. Thank you for letting me hear it."

Only seven days remained until the premiere.

In the productive year that Cunningham introduced *Landrover* and *TV Rerun*, he was also preparing a third work, *Borst Park*. Here, a very quick musical decision was made.

Christian Wolff, Frederic Rzewski, Jon Appleton, and I were performing a small-ensemble version of Wolff's recent *Burdocks* at New York University a few months before the Cunningham Company premiere of *Borst Park*. *Burdocks* was an expandable, transcendental music of one to ten sections and for one to ten orchestras (an orchestra consisted of a minimum of five musicians). Cunningham was in the audience and immediately wanted *Burdocks* as the music for *Borst Park*. Thus we enjoyed nearly two months of preparation time before the premiere of *Borst Park*.

The production of Events increased considerably in 1972, and the musical collaboration became more diverse. Since Cage, Tudor, David Behman, and I were performing independently at a new-music festival in Bremen, Germany, in May 1972, Christian Wolff and fourteen student musicians from Dartmouth College collaborated with the Cunningham Company for *Event No. 36* at the University of New Hampshire. With the exception of a single performance of Canfield at the Brooklyn Academy of Music, all the performances of 1973 were Events or lecture-demonstrations, for which our musical endeavors were expanded by the full-time collaboration of David Behrman.

Besides repertory performances and the growing production of Events, in the late 1960s the Cunningham Company became more involved with university residencies. A residency lasted as little as three days or as long as four weeks, and made use of all the resources of the ensemble. Besides lecture-demonstrations, repertory, and Event performances, the dancers taught classes in technique, repertory, and composition. The musicians presented seminars, workshops, and concerts, and the lighting designer taught stage design courses. The residency schedules sometimes allowed for the making of new works as well.

One aspect of our work is uncomfortably clear. As much as we may aspire to it, we do not have a sense of collaborative equality. There is hierarchy in the social dynamics of the Cunningham Dance Company, and this narrative may seem to indicate that the musicians are in a privileged position. But if hierarchy is the proper word to describe the company, it is an extremely complex hierarchy that is constantly changing.

There are inequalities inherent in the situation because so many skills and specializations are necessary for the elaborate production the Cunningham Dance Company requires; and the practical risks taken by the various categories of people are quite different. The dancers risk physical confrontations that are of a magnitude greater than those of the musicians. The dancers have to avoid knocking each other over, while if one musician overwhelms the sound of another, the result rarely involves physical injury. Thus the dancers plan their actions with a greater vigilance than required by the musicians. For the dancers it is perhaps a situation of having inherently less freedom.

In contrast, the social dynamics of the musical production have had a relatively simple and inspiring course. The history began in the 1940s with Cage as "pianist and composer." In the 1950s Cage was "musical director" and Tudor was "pianist." In the 1960s these categories became irrelevant, the functions were increasingly shared and complicated, and I joined the ensemble. When Cage became uncomfortable with the idea of being "musical director" all categories disappeared. By the 1970s, with the addition of Behrman (and others on occasion) we had evolved into a remarkable collaboration. We were not equal: each had specializations and some of these were not interchangeable. No one could imagine me reading Cage's stories for *How to Pass, Kick, Fall and Run*, Cage (instead of Tudor) performing Bo Nilsson's music for *Night Wandering*, or Tudor (or anyone except Cage) performing Statie's music for *Nocturnes*. Everyone worried if I wasn't around when some complicated electronic problem had to be quickly solved, and I lost sleep over the prospect of Tudor's not setting up his own electronic menagerie for *Rainforest*. But with the Events of the 1970s the musicians had reached a remarkable coexistence of specialization and comprehensivity.

There are very few persistently innovative groups of performing artists that, like the Cunningham Dance Company, manage to survive their preposterous economic circumstances and thrive for a quarter of a century. If, on the one hand, their economic situation improves as they become famous, on the other, they must learn to survive the erosion of their private lives. The constantly widening gap in generation between the oldest and youngest member of the ensemble has its own consequences.

The question of age disparity has consequences in other contexts, too. When the practice of art and technology advance rapidly, innovation is largely the province of the young. The older practitioners are nervous and tend to react through their institutions, including their unions, which may take an unattractively repressive position. For example, the union may hold that a dancer whose actions produce sound threatens the security

of the musicians. Likewise, electronic musical instruments performed by musicians "threaten" the security of electricians. Choreography that affects the decor "threatens" the security of the scenic artist.

Changes in artistic traditions sometimes conflict with politics in ways beyond our knowledge and control. We performed *Event No. 23* in a large ballroom in Southern California. The format of the evening and physical arrangements of the hall allowed the audience freedom to move, leave and re-enter the performing space at will. A corps of nervous ushers, nurtured in an era of constant civil unrest, actively discouraged the audience from moving at all or else intimidated the people who left the performance area.

In other situations we must be conscious of our influence. Jean Tinguely once suggested to me that it was immoral to condone a repressive and elitist regime in the Middle East by accepting an invitation to perform in that country. This is a delicate argument, but what is viewed as a condoning action from outside the country can be in reality a subversive action, seen from inside it. And in countries with heavily controlled communications, declining an invitation, particularly for political reasons, usually has no effect. It is unreported and virtually nothing is accomplished. An opportunity for cultural confrontation and the exchange of nourishing ideas is missed.

The decision to decline an invitation, or refuse to perform, requires astute consideration and an honest search for perspective. When Cage was challenged about why the Cunningham Company would perform in one politically appalling country he replied, "You must remember what country we come from."

For me the South American tour of 1968 and the ten-week European tour of 1972 were our most important overseas accomplishments. With the exception of a few places, these were not comfortable or glamorous occasions. We were pioneering: producing cultural confrontations in circumstances where the risks were not always easy to accommodate. In South America we confronted hyperconservative ballet lovers with our relatively extreme manifestations of modern dance. Many political and ideological reactionaries of those audiences had trouble with the very *ideas* of freedom embodied in our work.

It continues a precious opportunity: to collaborate in a process with an ensemble with exceptionally high performance standards. An ensemble of different people meeting perhaps at only a single point: the congruence of disparate ideas, based on the premise of rigorous discipline and risky experimentation.

"A continual preparation for the shock of freedom," as Peter Brook called Cunningham's work.

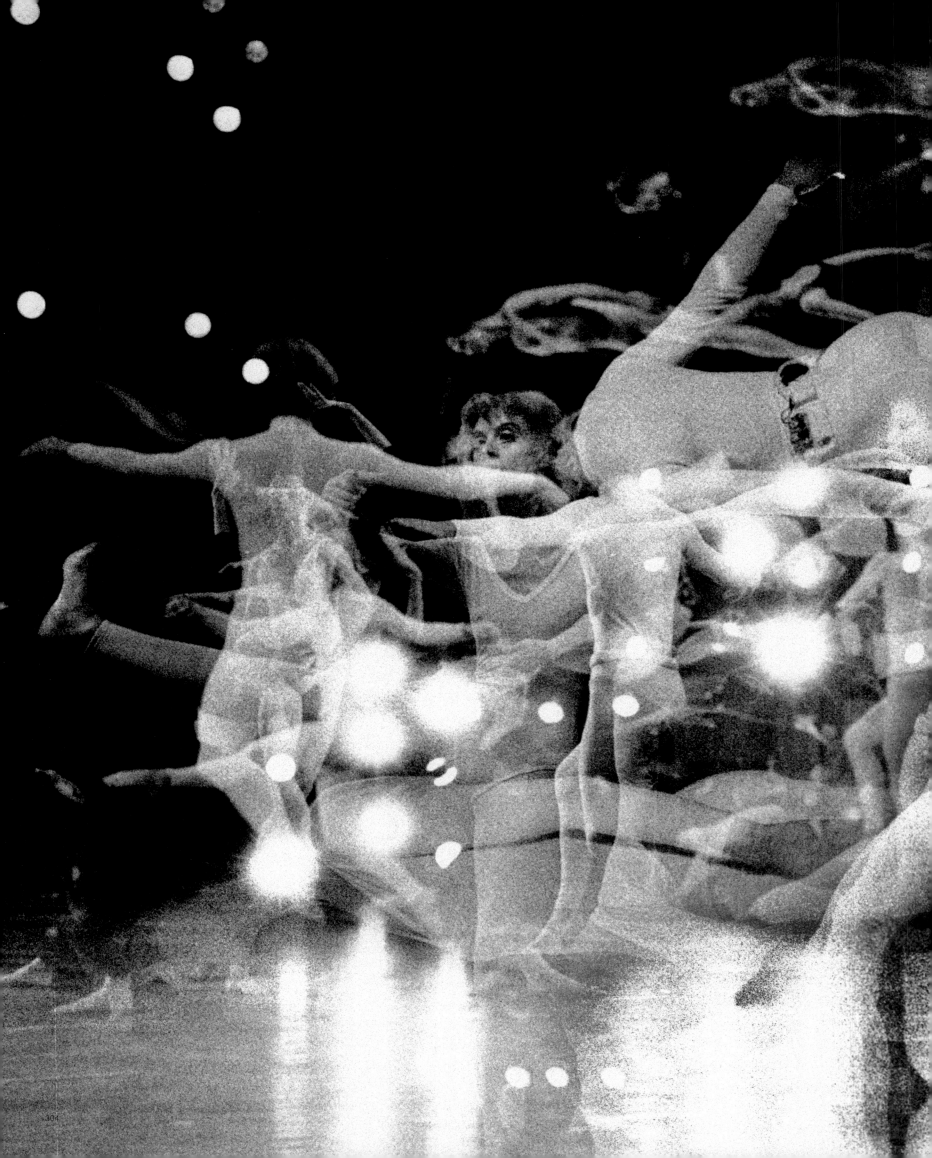

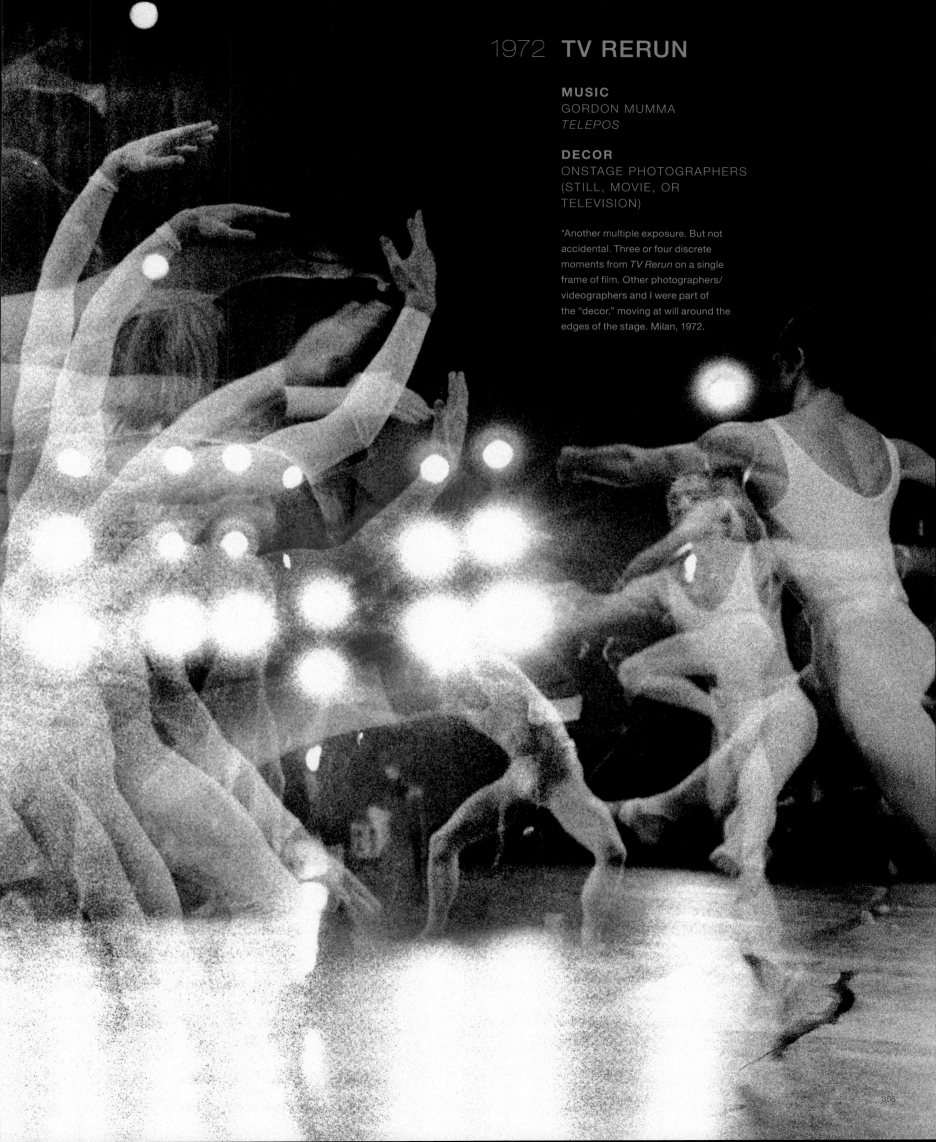

TV RERUN

MUSIC
GORDON MUMMA
TELEPOS

DECOR
ONSTAGE PHOTOGRAPHERS
(STILL, MOVIE, OR
TELEVISION)

*Another multiple exposure. But not
accidental. Three or four discrete
moments from *TV Rerun* on a single
frame of film. Other photographers/
videographers and I were part of
the "decor," moving at will around the
edges of the stage. Milan, 1972.

1972 BORST PARK

MUSIC
CHRISTIAN WOLFF
BURDOCKS

COSTUMES
THE COMPANY

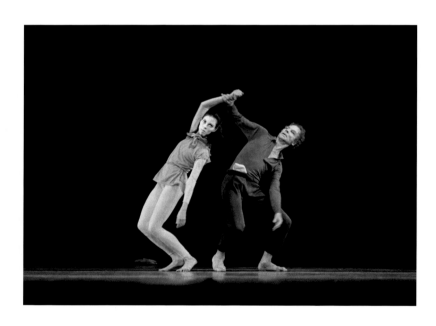

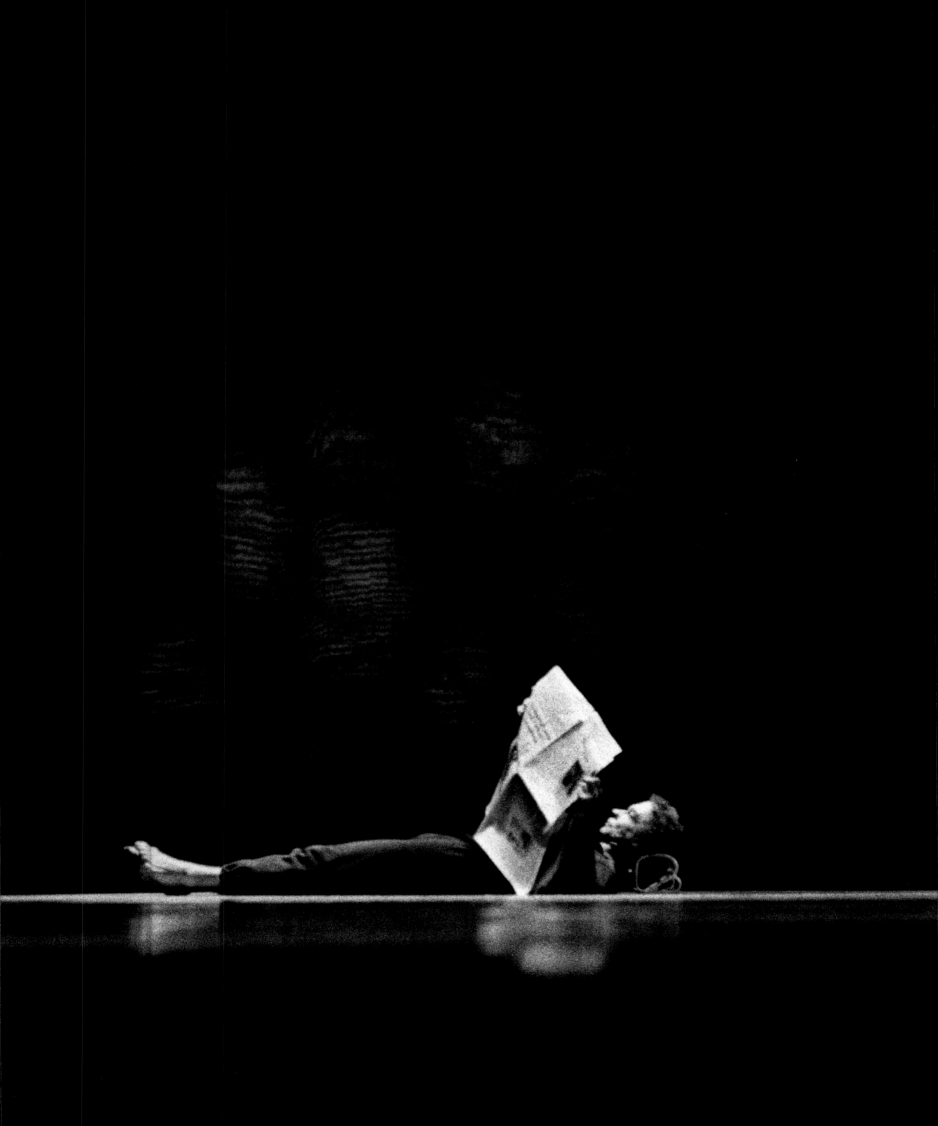

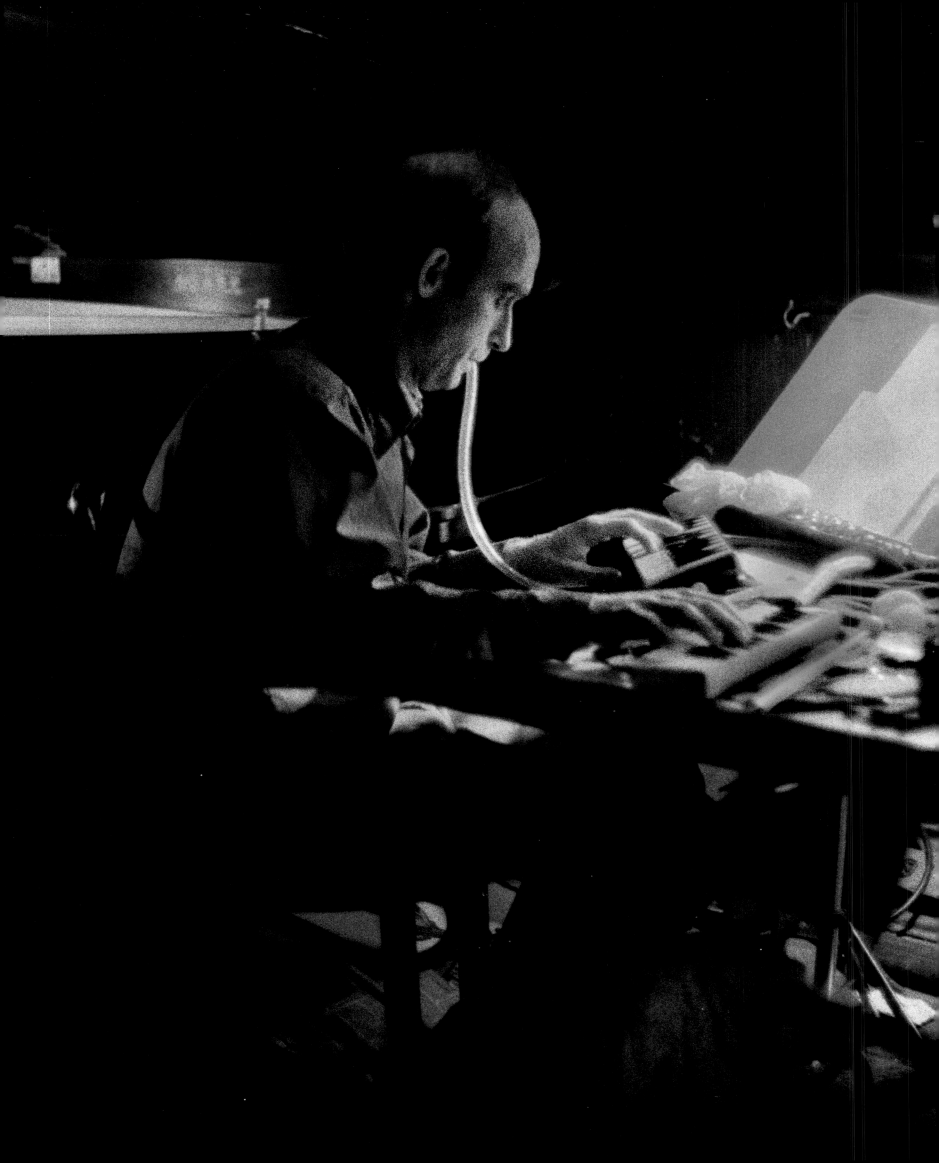

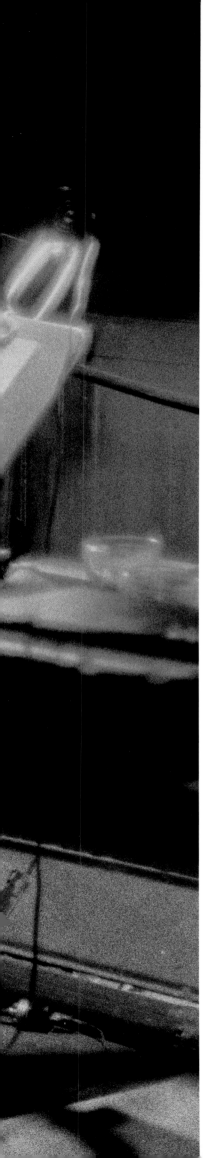

CHRISTIAN WOLFF

Written, tried, *Burdocks*, before I knew of *Borst Park*, was then dedicated to Merce. This, partly, is why. I took encouragement from the many things I had seen him do. Particularly, the mix of things and the spirit which kept them both apart and together; the changes one after another; the complicatedness of things together. Many various processes, activities, states felt as if they were coming—spinning, breaking off, drifting, walking, just moving—from a source which was magnetically there, and kept eluding you; and each element of that variety could still be itself. There were also unisons (we can all play the melody together). Then again different bodies making the same movements (i.e., bass or treble clef). The groups coordinated within one another but separately active. The cheerfulness. The gravity. The endurance (511 times). The abstraction, and the chance, each one's own, of something's becoming evocative. Other qualities generated by the dancing I could at best hope for, though they are the very means of that encouragement: pleasure, generosity, and a sense of danger made sometimes light, sometimes piercing and harsh by concentration and discipline. *Burdocks*, sounds, can be unruly and messy; they cannot do each other bodily damage, unlike the dancing, and I think they feel the lack of that possibility.

Christian Wolff performing his *Burdocks*, the score for *Borst Park*, BAM, 1972

1968–1972 **BACKSTAGE**

Jasper Johns onstage at BAM inspecting the decor by Neil Jenney
during a rehearsal of *Objects*, 1972

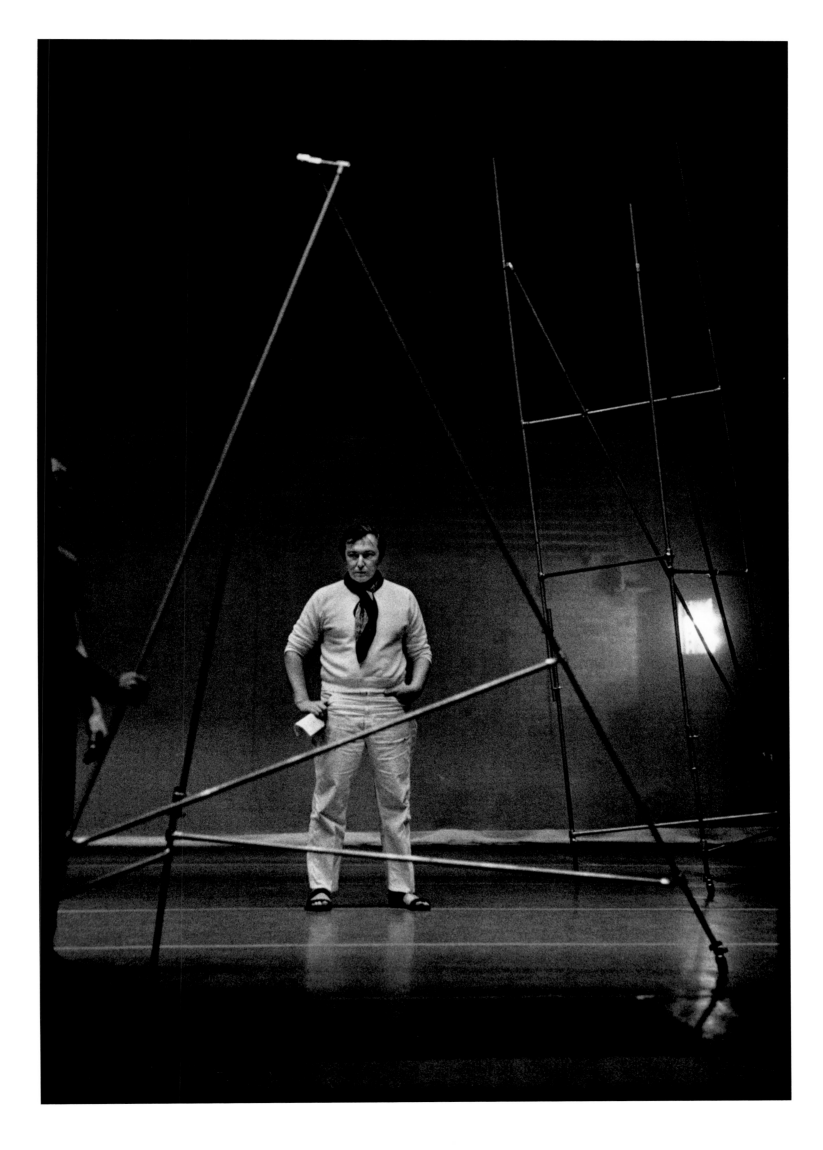

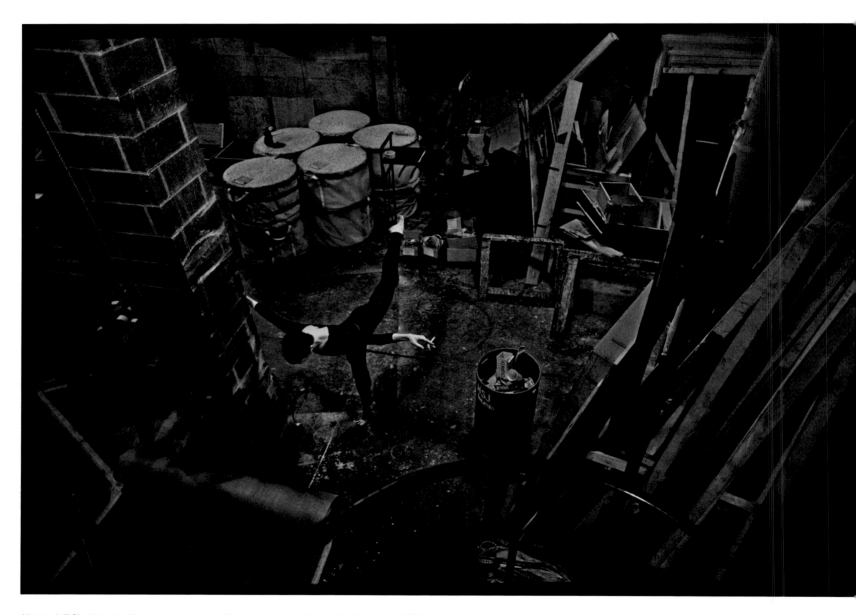

Above: Jeff Slayton warming up somewhere in Massachusetts or Connecticut, February 1970;
Right: Merce Cunningham backstage reviewing notes

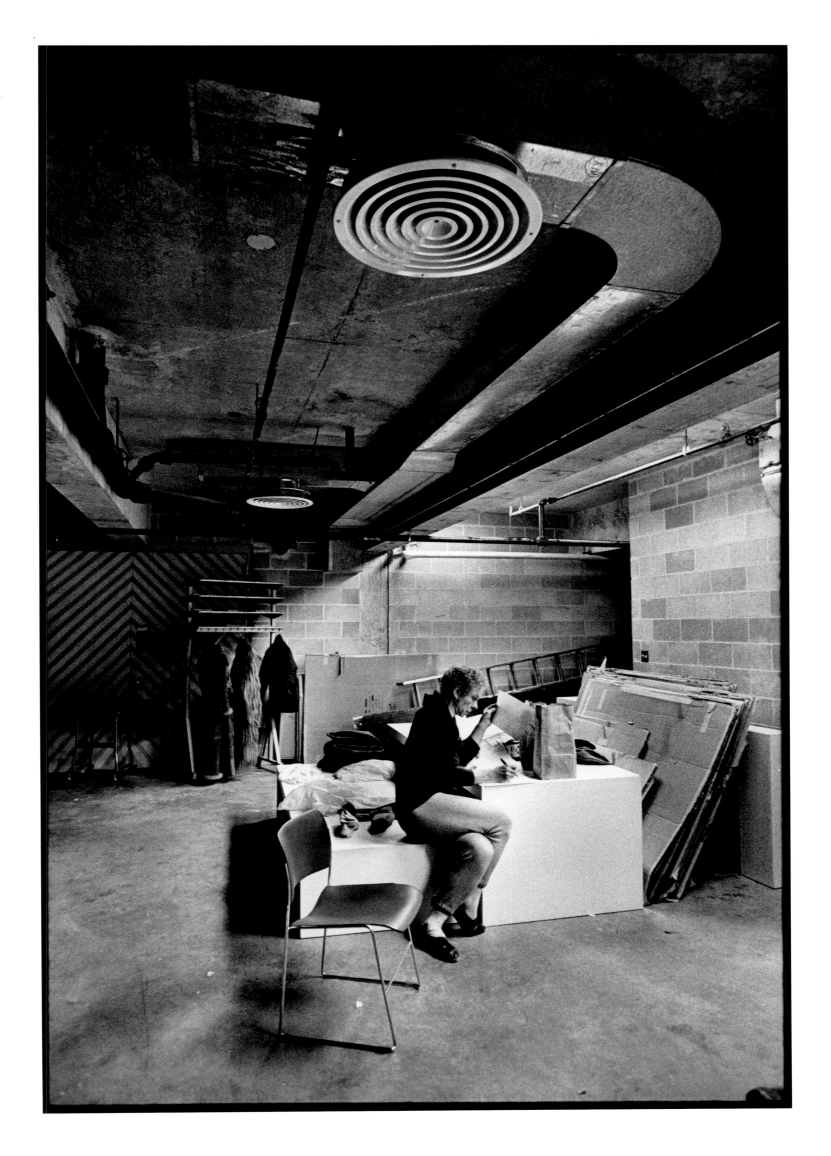

Right: Merce Cunningham and students, Stony Brook, New York;
Following spread: Merce Cunningham, Westbeth, 1972

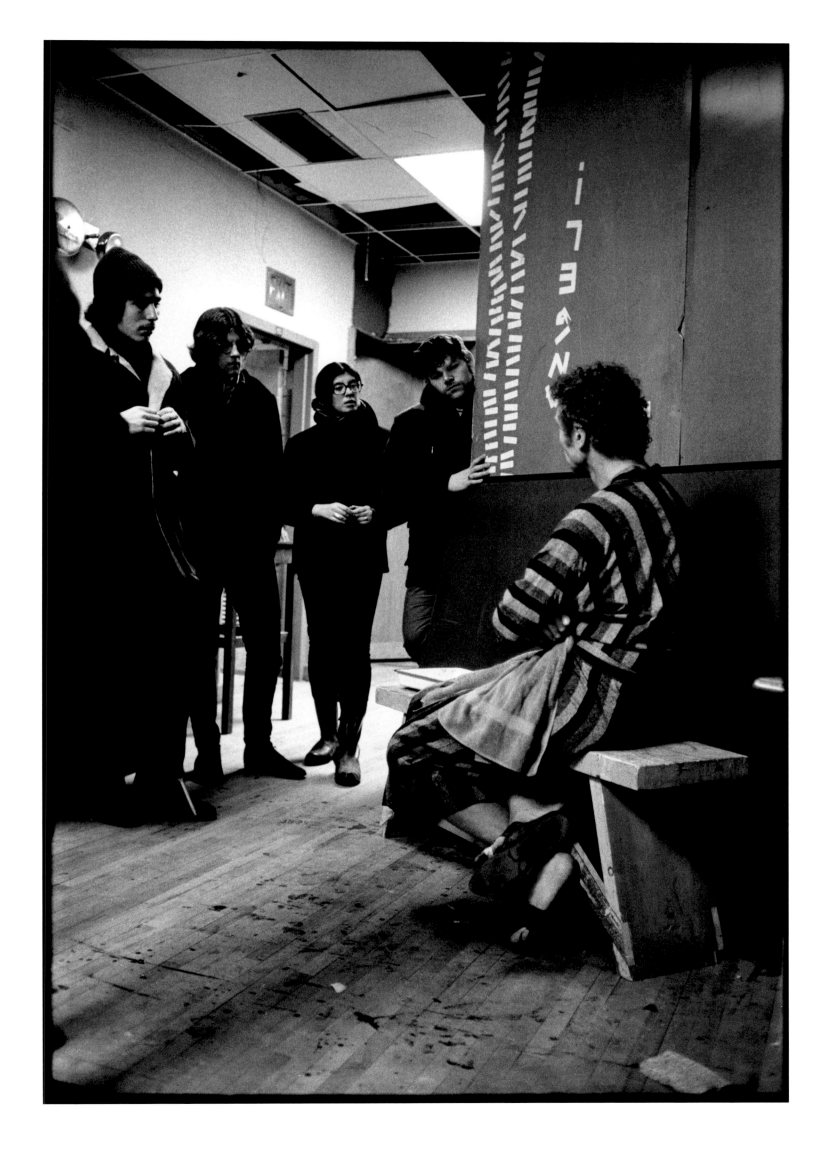

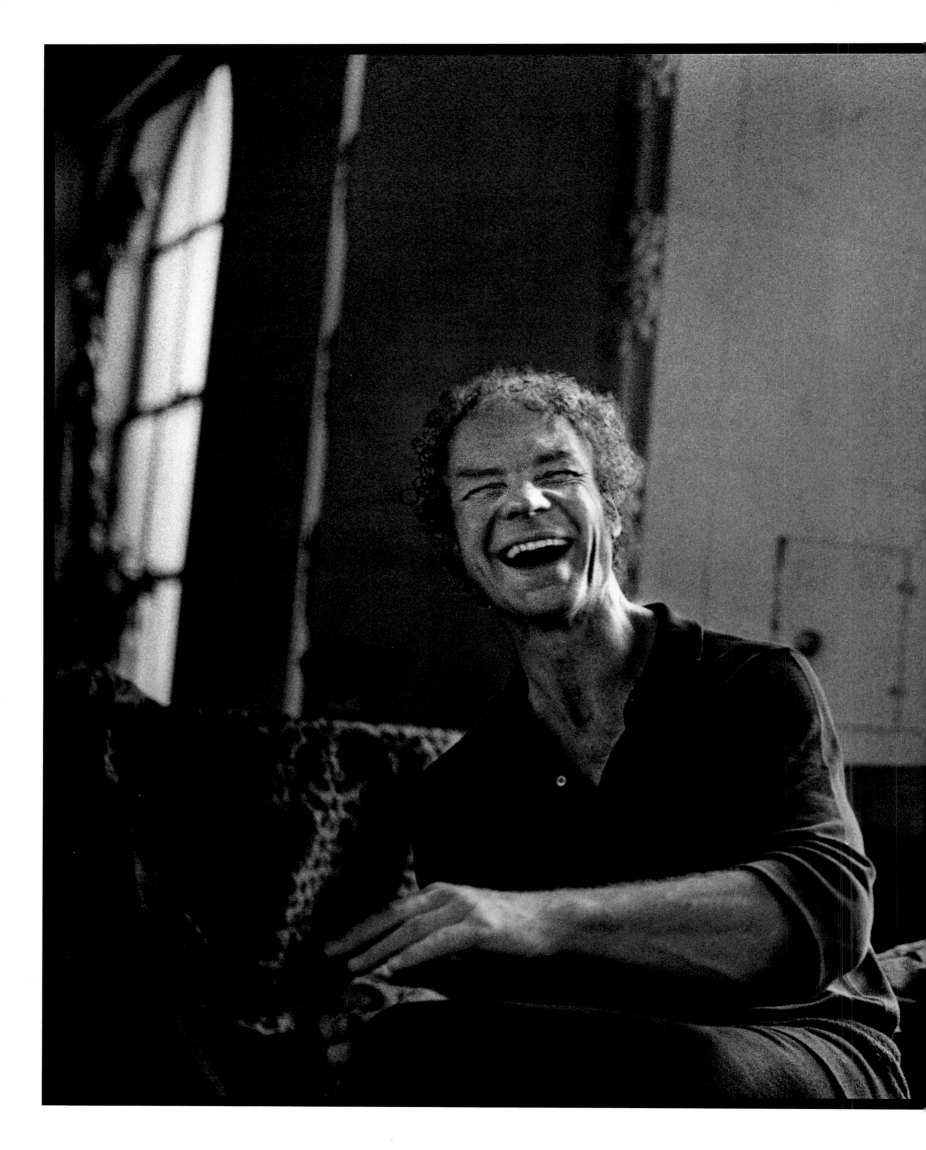

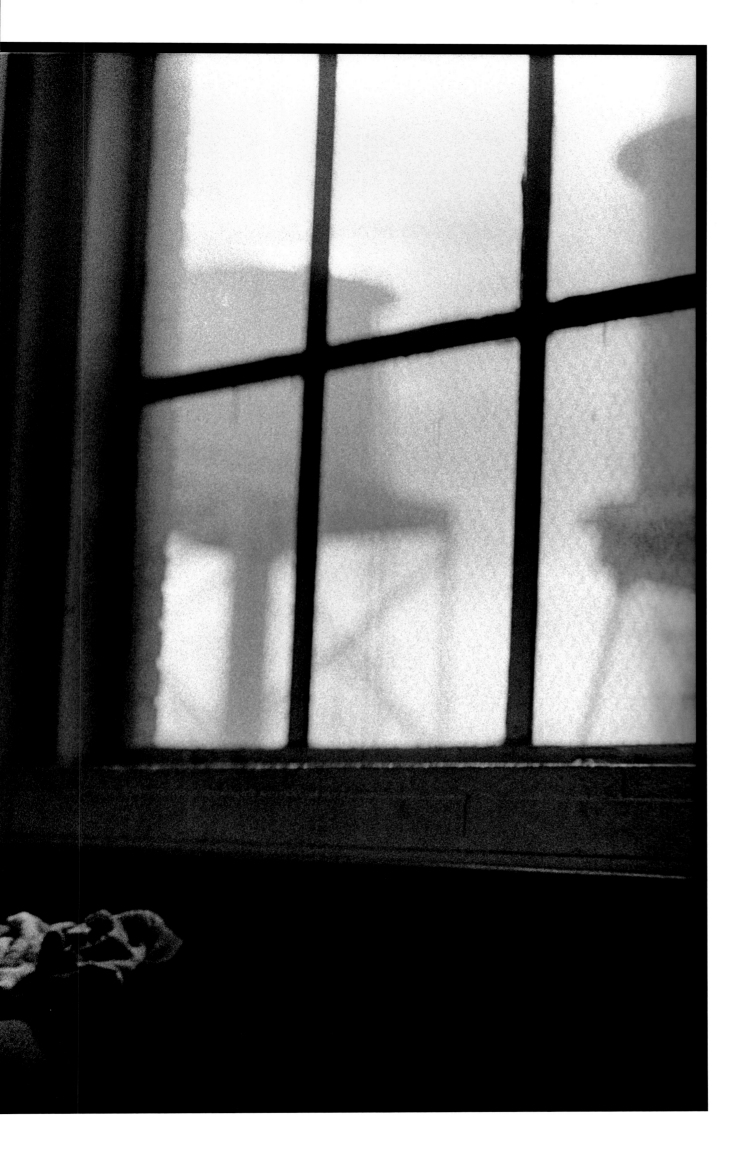

"Merce is my favorite artist in any field. Sometimes I'm pleased by the complexity of a work that I paint. By the fourth day I realize it's simple. Nothing Merce does is simple. Everything has a fascinating richness and multiplicity of direction."
—*Jasper Johns*
Herbert Saal, "Merce," Newsweek, May 27, 1968

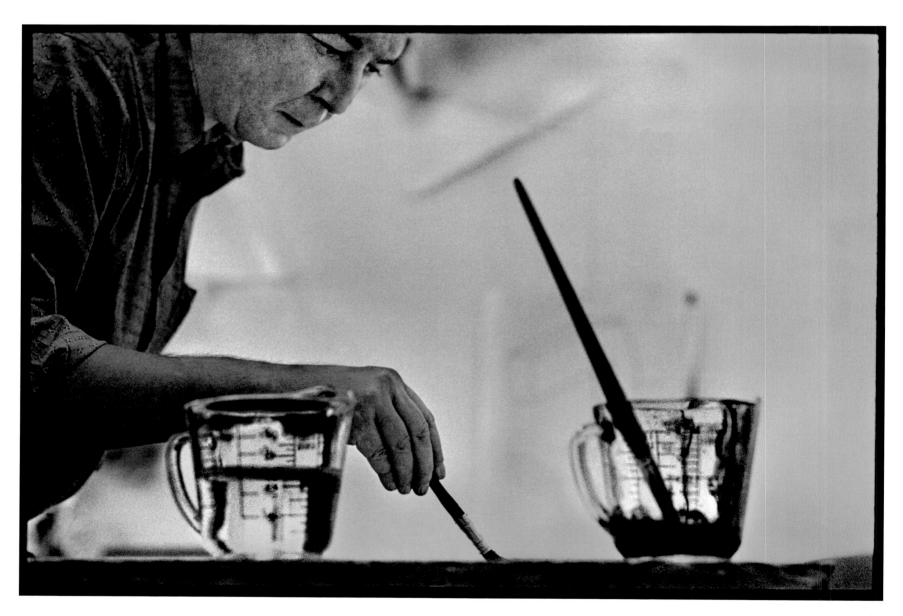

Above: Jasper Johns at Gemini G.E.L., Los Angeles, January 1971;
Right: Merce Cunningham, *Suite for Five* rehearsal, Grenoble, France, 1972

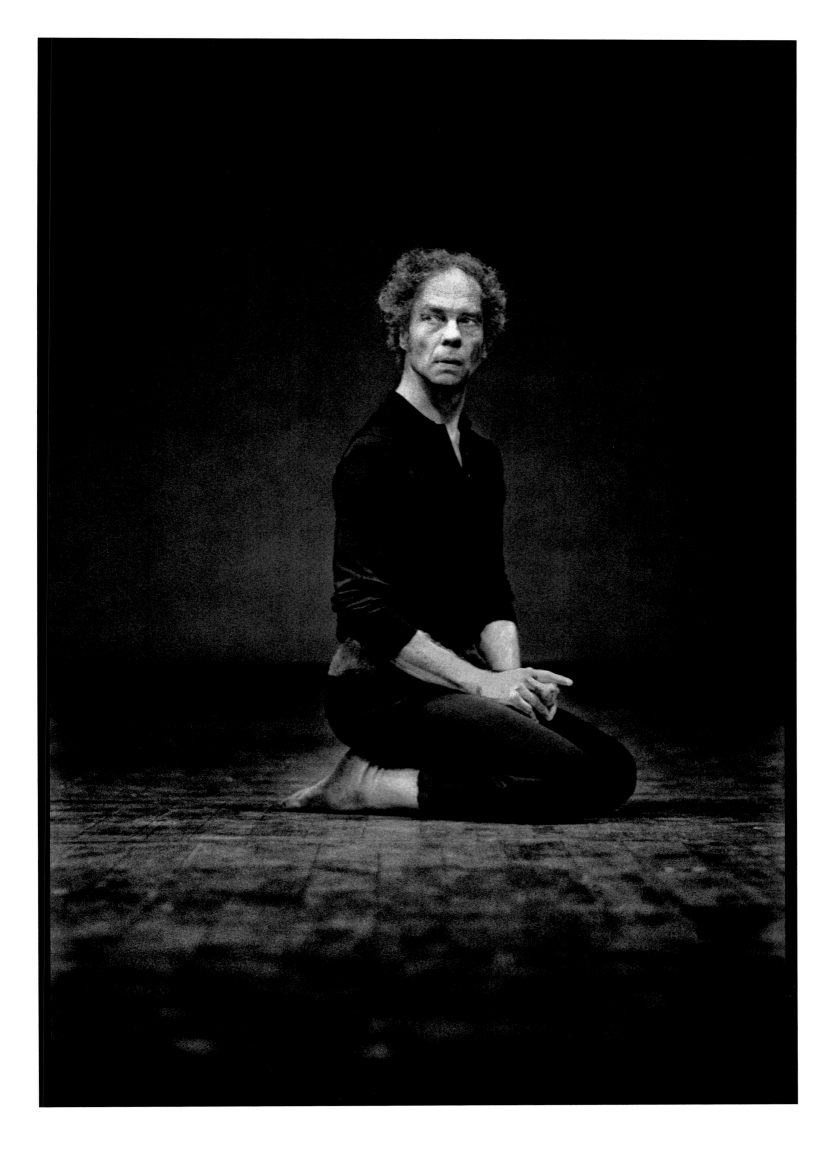

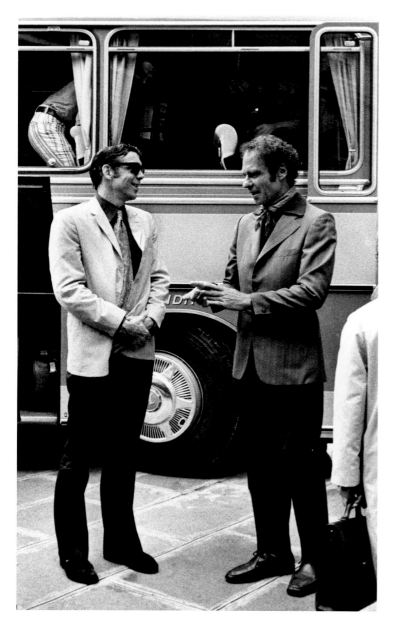

Paul Taylor and Merce Cunningham, Paris, 1970.
Changing of the American guard at the Théâtre d'Odeon
(see bottom photo on page 337).

PAUL TAYLOR

It is strange that of the various things worth remembering of the time I worked with Merce Cunningham, the experience that comes to mind is a secondhand one. Perhaps it is because it was one of my first impressions about him and, in my mind at least, likens the man to his work.

In 1952 Merce did a commissioned *Les Noces* at Brandeis University. Since I was interested to work with Merce, I asked a dancer who danced in the piece what it had been like to work with him. He told me this: after the performance, he stopped by Merce's dressing room to say goodnight. Upon seeing Merce alone, sitting perfectly still in the middle of the room, he withdrew, not wanting to intrude.

That is the whole story. That such a trivial incident would be remembered by the dancer and selected to answer my question seemed unaccountable. Until later when I thought it perhaps said a great deal.

That picture of Merce could be an image of a solitary and private world. It could also picture Merce's stoic reaction to the fact that there then seemed to be no throngs of backstage admirers; his fierce determination in presenting a work he believed was right, in spite of, or even because of, the public's unwillingness to accept it.

Or the image could have been one of quiet dissatisfaction and unfulfilled feelings that some dancers experience after the rigors of a performance. Or could it have meant that Merce was waiting for the chiropractor to come unlock him from some kind of allover muscle spasm? Or maybe he could have been just plain resting.

In any case, one can only guess. The story is like the images in the man's works—open, as he says, to individual interpretation. It is a random and seemingly unconnected incident, and one that lingers after many others have faded.

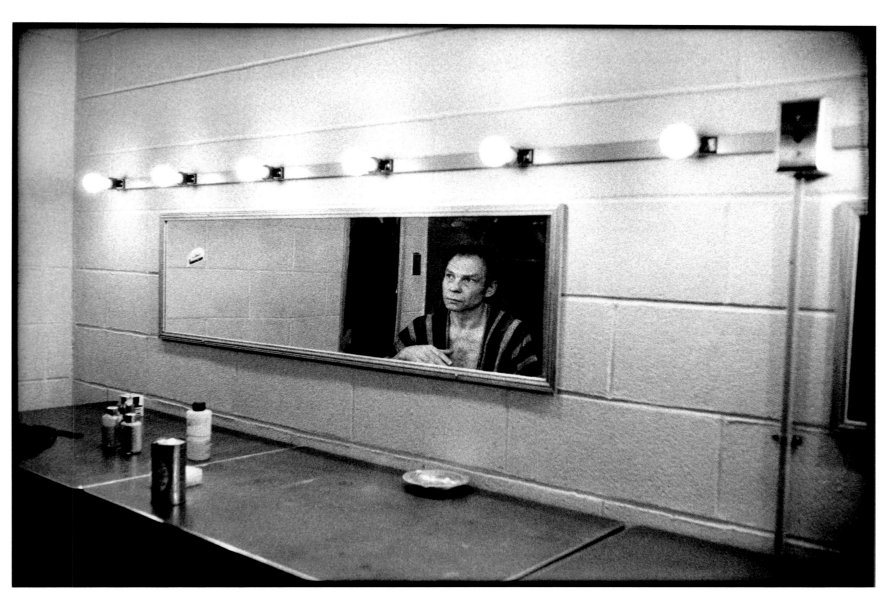

Merce Cunningham in his dressing room

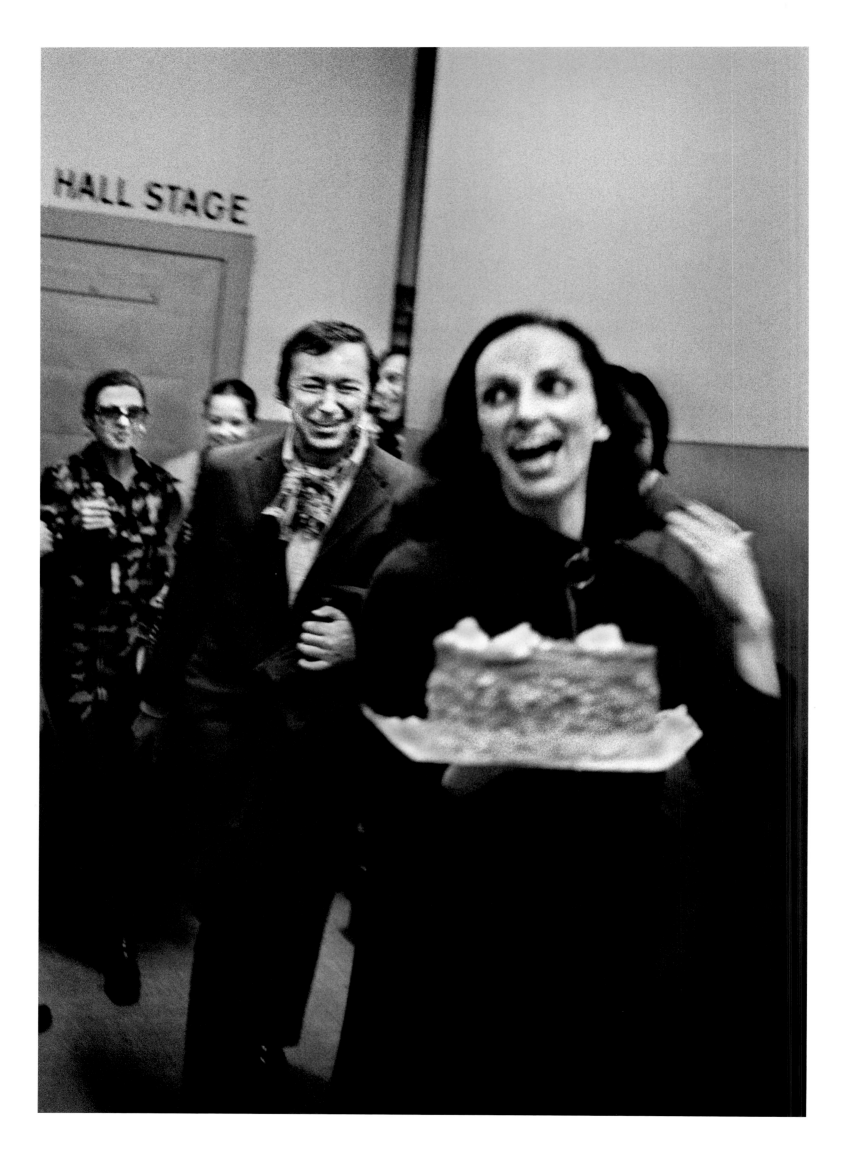

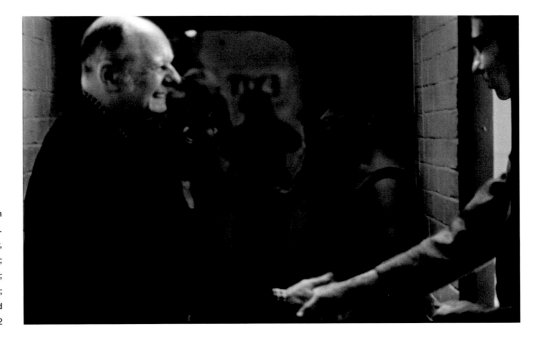

Opposite: Post-performance birthday procession to Cunningham's dressing room at BAM, April 16, 1969. Left to right: Valda Setterfield, Susanna Hayman-Chaffey, Jasper Johns, Chase Robinson, and Carolyn Brown; Right: The classicist, John Geilgud, London, 1972; Below: The visionary, Peter Brook, Paris, 1972; Following spread: Douglas Dunn and Merce Cunningham, onstage warmup, Milan, Italy, 1972

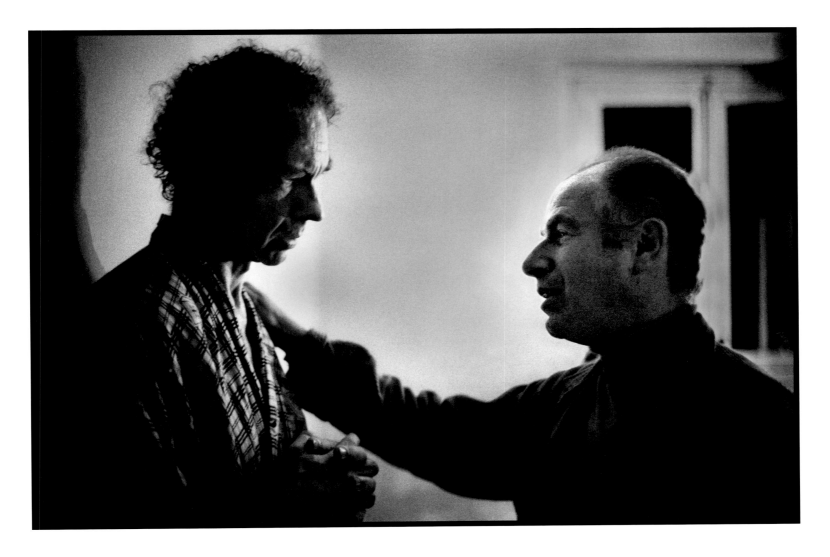

"Merce Cunningham has evolved a company whose daily exercises are a continual preparation for the shock of freedom."

—Peter Brook, 1968

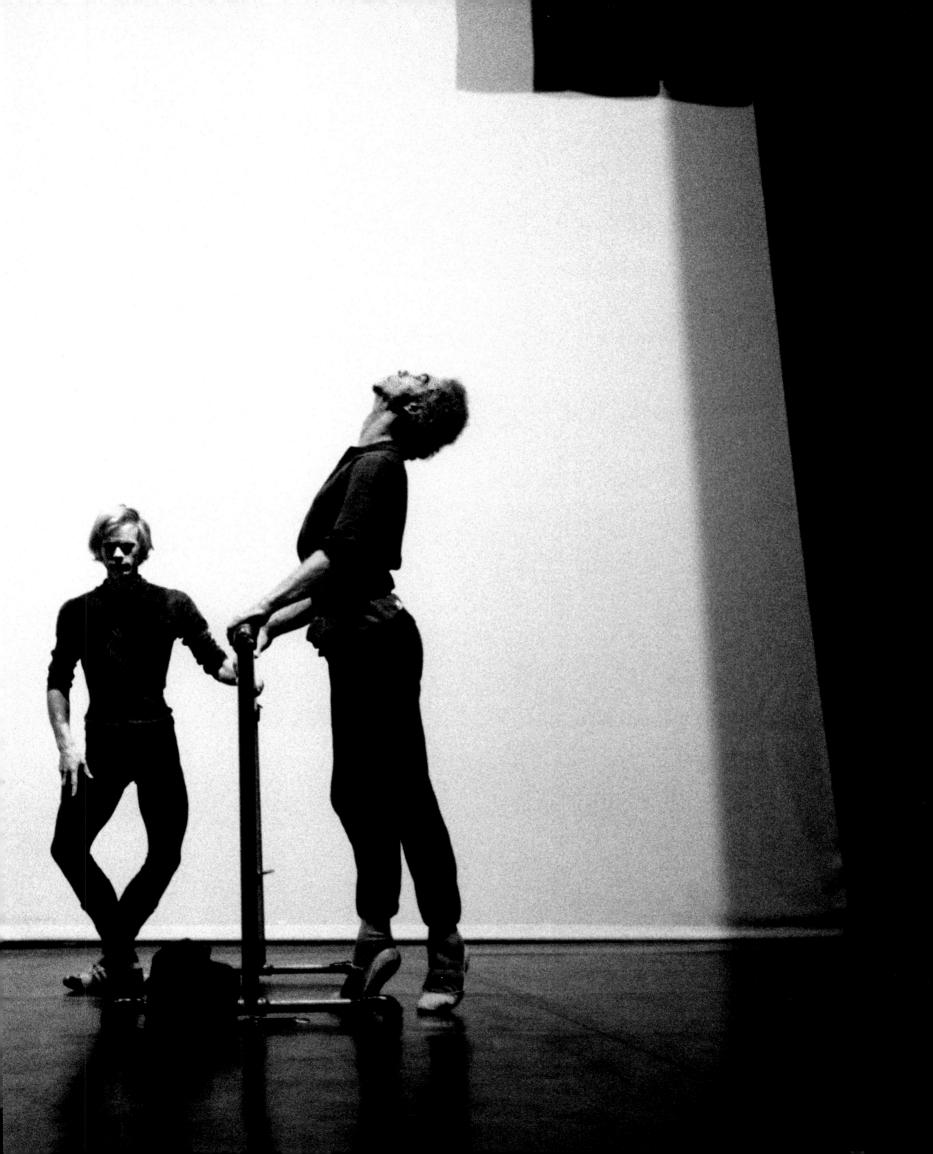

LEWIS L. LLOYD

I

Merce Cunningham's dance company came together as a formal entity at the 1953 summer arts session at Black Mountain College. The six dancers were Carolyn Brown, Remy Charlip, Jo Anne Melsher, Viola Farber, Marianne Preger, Paul Taylor, and Anita Dencks; the musicians were John Cage and David Tudor. Cunningham had agreed to waive a salary in return for which the college agreed to house and feed the company for the summer. Cunningham also paid for their travel expenses down to and back from the college. During the summer, the company prepared works it was to present in its first New York season the following winter, at the Theatre De Lys in Greenwich Village.

A friend with some means, Paul Williams, had lent Cunningham and John Cage the money necessary to secure the theater and promote the season. According to Cunningham's recollection, Robert Rauschenberg made up the posters for that week, which were then put up around New York by all the members of the company. This serious and important Event drew "not bad houses," Cunningham recalls, and the company members were actually paid for the performances, which was an important event in itself.

Not one review, not one critical evaluation of the work of Cunningham, Cage, and their collaborators appeared in print in connection with that week of performances.

Following the disastrous silence that greeted that first New York season, Cunningham and Cage set about trying to get work to support the company and Cunningham's studio on Sheridan Square, as well as themselves.

They soon evolved a pattern of existence thath was to sustain them for many years. A fortuitous Guggenheim Fellowship ("that Guggenheim saved my life," Cunningham has said) helped pay the rent at Sheridan Square, and kept the wolf from the door. The pattern that evolved at the studio was one that depended on Cunningham working by himself on his choreography in the mornings, then teaching two classes in the afternoon. He also wrote letters with John Cage "to friends and enemies like mad," hoping for performance dates.

When the dates materialized, the company—the six dancers and two musicians, along with a stage manager/lighting designer—would pack off to do the performance, with Cunningham and Cage guaranteeing the travel, meals, and lodging expenses of the company, and, if the fee was high enough, ten dollars, then later, twenty-five dollars apiece on their return to New York.

In 1955 the company purchased the vehicle that defined both the company size and the company's personal character for the next nine years the famous Volkswagen bus that held the nine company members, and could carry as well whatever personal possessions, scenery, and costumes that could be jammed in. Between the tours in the Volkswagen bus, and the teaching, rehearsing, and "creating" schedule in a succession of studios in New York City, Cunningham eked out a meager existence. In the late fifties two important events helped stabilize the company for the next five or so years: in 1958 the company was invited for the first of several summers to the dance festival at New London, Connecticut, and in 1959 Cunningham leased space for a fine new studio in a building that also housed the Living Theater, at 14th Street and Sixth Avenue in New York.

The festival work in the summers in Connecticut provided a coherent work period for Cunningham, during which his company was economically secure and at his disposal. Carolyn Brown has said that much of Cunningham's finest work was produced during those summers. Unfortunately, however, the directors of the festival were not well disposed toward the Cunningham/Cage aesthetic, which ran against the grain of the prevailing spirit of Doris Humphrey and her disciple and resident practitioner, José Limón. The decisions that determined placement on the programs and, much more importantly, the amount of money available for the company's orchestra and scenery requirements were inevitably in favor of the Limón group. It was with some bitterness that the Cunningham Company severed its relationship with the Connecticut festival in the early sixties.

The 14th Street studio, aside from a leaking roof and a bleak climb up four long flights of steps, was a warm and congenial place for Cunningham's work. Cunningham himself regularly and sometimes cheerfully repaired the roof, tar bucket and brush in hand. The studio itself was somewhat cramped, especially in the dressing rooms and so-called "office" areas. But it did provide a setting for the work Cunningham needed to do,

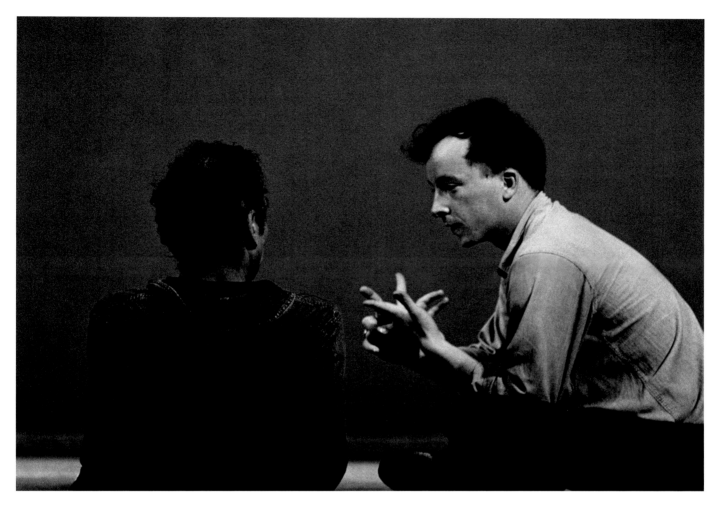

Lewis Lloyd and Merce Cunningham, 1968

and it became, without proclamation or self-consciousness, the gathering place for some of the most talented of a generation of younger choreographers, surely the highest testimony to the genius that Cunningham himself so very quietly presented.

II

I first saw a performance by Merce Cunningham and the dance company on August 17, 1961, at New London. At the time, I was producing a musical off Broadway, and I was married to Barbara Lloyd, a dancer who was studying with Cunningham. John Cage decided that a formal Broadway season of Merce's works was necessary if Cunningham's career was to prosper further. My work in the Off-Broadway theater had been brought to Cage's attention by Barbara. In the summer of 1962 Cage came to see me. He said that he wanted to see the Cunningham Dance Company's works presented on Broadway the following season and he wondered if

I was interested in becoming their producer. He said, too, that the reason he had come to talk to me was because I was almost, "a part of the family," and in any case, he said, Carmen Capalbo had already turned down the job.

Cage later explained that the season on Broadway would be subsidized through the sale of art works, donated by painter and sculptor friends of Cunningham's. It was decided that a nonprofit corporation would be created to be financed with the proceeds of the sale scheduled for that fall. In all, eighty artists participated, including Willem de Kooning, Marcel Duchamp, Philip Guston, Mark Rothko, Barnett Newman, Jack Tworkov, Richard Lippold, Larry Rivers, James Rosenquist, David Cornell, Saul Steinberg, Robert Motherwell, Robert Indiana, Frank Stella, Andy Warhol, Jasper Johns, and Robert Rauschenberg. The nonprofit corporation, the Foundation for the Contemporary Performance Arts, Inc., was created, the sale was held, and enough money, some $45,000, was raised.

Although the subsidy necessary to guarantee two weeks of performances on Broadway was in hand, the season had to be postponed beyond the winter of 1962–63. New York suffered its first major newspaper strike in many years in the middle of the winter, and the strike proved to be a long one. Shows that had been scheduled to open on Broadway remained out of town. As time passed, it became apparent that the waiting Broadway productions would create a booking jam in the theaters late in the spring, as the shows sought to open before the traditional summer business slump, and in fact the interim booking we were counting on never materialized. The Cunningham Company then packed itself into its Volkswagen bus and headed west—for teaching and performing commitments at universities in California. So the New York season was put over to the fall of 1963. But during the summer, two of the six dancers in the company decided to retire. I was still trying to line up a theater for the fall when Cunningham and Cage called me from California to say that they had decided to cancel the New York season altogether.

On their return Cage and Cunningham said that instead of performances in New York, they had decided to organize a tour abroad, responding to the many inquiries they had received over the years. The administrator of the Cunningham Studio, David Vaughan, had been working on this correspondence with potential sponsors for some time. Cage asked me to work with him. Cage said that he would approach the Foundation for Contemporary Performance Arts, Inc., the group organized to support the Broadway venture, and ask that the funds raised for the New York season be set aside to assist the Cunningham Company in its new project. The directors of the foundation were Cage, myself, Elaine deKooning, David Hayes, Jasper Johns, and the attorney for the foundation, and it was not difficult to arrange for the necessary approval of funds for the Cunningham tour abroad. The money was to be used to cover the cost of air travel.

But to make this transfer, a nonprofit corporation, the Cunningham Dance Foundation, Inc., had to be organized in the spring of 1964, and the dance company's formal relationship with the Foundation for Contemporary Performance Arts, Inc., ended with the funding of the pending tour. In line with Cage's thinking that only artists understood the needs of the artists, the new corporation's board of directors was made up of people directly connected with the Cunningham dance company: John Cage, the company's accountant Ruben Gorewitz, myself, Lois Long, Robert Rauschenberg, David Tudor, David Vaughan, and Christian Wolff.

As things turned out, the tour abroad in 1964 was much more important in establishing Cunningham's artistic position in America than the New York season could ever have been. Almost certainly the Broadway engagement would have been an expensive, sparsely attended, poorly reviewed affair. On the other hand, the company's appearance at the Sadler's Wells Theatre at the end of July 1964 created the kind of European critical acclaim that turns American heads.

The problem of financing the 1964 tour around the world, for that is what it turned out to be, did not end with the commitment of the Broadway money. As the planning for the tour progressed it became clear that we had overestimated the company's willingness to live like paupers abroad. Also, never having collected the scenery and costumes in one place for the eighteen dances being taken along on tour, I was not prepared for the sheer mass of bits and pieces, including the "found objects" Robert Rauschenberg had collected over the years. In fact, on the day we left, Rauschenberg was still buying footlockers and stuffing them with things in his loft on lower Broadway.

Prior to departure day, two more major benefactors appeared on the scene to contribute an additional $40,000 to the company's coffers. John Cage offered to sell for the company's benefit a wire sculpture made for him by his friend Richard Lippold. When a willing purchaser paid $20,000 for it, the company got the money. And the John D. Rockefeller III Fund came across with another $20,000 through the interest of the fund's director, Porter MacCray. This money was to be used to make up the difference between weekly expenses and the fees available from sponsors in India, Thailand, and Japan. The other major supporter of the world tour was Robert Rauschenberg himself, who sold a painting at the last moment before the company left, in order to donate the proceeds of the sale to the company. Later he advanced cash to the company on the road, as they regularly faced severe cash deficits.

However, the company left without any support from the U.S. government. Although appeals had been made to the State Department Cultural Exchange Program, through the panel on dance, no response was forthcoming. Actually, this was not surprising, since this same panel had supported the previous year's tour of the Far East by José Limón's dance company, and, in any case, Cunningham and Cage had been refused support for a planned trip to the Orient some years earlier.

Still the lack of support annoyed us all, and Cage particularly went out of his way to be critical of the government cultural exchange program during press conferences early in the tour. As the tour progressed and the publicity surrounding Robert Rauschenberg's painting prize at the Venice Biennale built up, we received overtures from additional sponsors, which we eagerly followed up, since our calender of working weeks had several lengthy gaps in it. I think that it is precisely because of the fact that we did not receive government aid and were highly vocal about it that the Czech government permitted performances by the company there in September, during the fourth month of the tour. Prior to these performances in Prague and Ostrava, though, a more important series of performances had occurred in London. Several people active in the theater in London had come to see the company during the first performance abroad, in France, in June. One of these was the English producer Michael White, who had been encouraged by the cultural attache at the American Embassy in London, Francis Mason, to take on the task of producing the London performances, scheduled for late July. Mason was one of the very, very few men in the State Department with a serious interest in American dance, and it was through his interest and good will that White agreed to produce the company, and that the Sadler's Wells Theatre was booked. With a very few exceptions the performances in London were greeted with extremely enthusiastic critical notices. We had to extend the week at the Sadler's Wells Theatre into an additional two and a half weeks at the Phoenix Theatre in the West End. The London run succeeded in establishing an attitude about Cunningham and Cage's work that had been lacking before, and even their severest critics at home in New York had, now, to evince respect.

IV

As the company finished the tour in December 1964, they realized they had outgrown touring in the Volkswagen bus. An attempt had to be made then to improve the conditions under which the company worked in the U.S.A. On the long tour, for the first time, unemployment insurance coverage had been provided for everyone. Back in New York, an agreement was made with a concert booking office, and the management of the company, such as it was, undertook the development of a more or less continuous supervision of the studio, the company, and the supporting nonprofit corporation, Cunningham Dance Foundation, Inc., or C.D. Finc, as the dancers came to call it.

At this time, there were only six or eight active major American modern dance companies. Only one of these companies, Martha Graham's, had any regular, dependable sources of private subsidy. Two of the other companies, those directed by José Limón and Alwin Nikolais, benefited from their director's affiliation with a larger institution; in Nikolais's case this was the theater of the Henry Street Settlement House, and Limón was attached to the Julliard School. Both facilities had tangible advantages to these two choreographers; at least they had a roof over their heads which didn't leak. The other active companies, those headed by Cunningham, Erick Hawkins, Alvin Alley, and

Paul Taylor, somehow existed from tour to tour, usually in the studio in New York where the man whose name was on the door held forth as local choreographic abecedarian. This combination of teaching and touring made it possible for these few creative artists to get their work done, though under difficult conditions, since their income from their work simply could not support all the people necessary to perform it.

How then to achieve a measure of artistic and economic prosperity? Artistic prosperity had been Cage's goal for years, of course, and the world tour in 1964 had helped the Cunningham Dance Foundation, Inc., gain a *small* measure of it. In Cage's mind the foundation, no matter how necessary or well constructed, was to be *only* a device to serve the needs of the artists associated with the dance company. It had then, and has now, no meaning or life of its own.

When I was asked, in 1962, to join the Cunningham dance company as an "administrator," I was regarded with suspicion by the dancers in particular. They had endured bad times with profit-oriented managements, and all administrators or managers tended to get stained by these experiences. Some managements, even those dressed in the nonprofit suit of clothes, still did (and do) act as if the theater business is just a "business" in the sense which private enterprise in America has defined it where only a *profit* justifies its existence.

It is possible, however, for a small nonprofit corporation to function responsibly as a producer in the arts *if* the management of that corporation can abandon about a hundred years of business gospel about profit. Administrators of many of the nonprofit corporations working in the performing arts in recent years have become aware of the basic conflict between the old-line commercial impresario's attitude of "the guiding principal is that the theater is a business," versus the acknowledgment that "profit" and "business," in the sense which private enterprise uses those terms, have no place in the arts.

The commercial attitude, of which performers should be suspicious, can only lead to a continuation of the practices that have degraded the arts over the years: elitism, by restricting access to the art works through high ticket prices; commercialism; by restricting the kind of work offered to only that which "sells"; and exploitation of the performers and creative artists by the managers, by perpetuating the miserably low wage scales that have traditionally been the lot, with few exceptions, of the performing artist.

Yet, over the years, Cunningham and Cage recognized that their course of action would not take them along the way of box office success. Cunningham has often said that the size of the audience doesn't matter to him if size represents "success." What he cares about is whether or not the people in the audience care, one way or another, about what they are seeing. In that sense, based on first hand experience both with audiences that threw vegetables at the dancers (Paris, 1964) and audiences that roared their approval (Cologne, 1964, one month after Paris), he is, and has been, a success. The fact is, though, that virtually no one working in modern dance in 1965 had the means to support the numbers of people necessary to produce this form of theater or could figure out how to get those means. Box office was not the solution for Merce Cunningham and Dance Company, but an acceptance of a deficit operation was, along with a commitment to active fund-raising.

In part because of its growing reputation, the company was able to command larger fees for its performances. Also, the foundation, as an employer of dancers, was able to wrestle successfully with the vexing problem of union affiliation for its "employees." During the tour around the world, the foundation discovered that it had been put on the dancers' union's "unfair" list, because it could not pay the premium due the dancers under the terms of a union "overseas contract." This premium had been devised by the union to take advantage of State Department funds which ordinarily supported dance companies working abroad. Of course the Cunningham Dance Company did not have any such support, and the tour had to be a low budget affair. This problem was untangled on the company's return in December 1964, and discussions then began with the dancers toward developing a "basic agreement" between the foundation, on the one hand, and the dancers, on the other, covering working conditions, salaries, etc.

Beginning in the spring of 1965, there began a three-way negotiation between myself, the dancer's union, and the dancers (who saw themselves as quite distinct from the union). I believed that a basic contract with the dancers was necessary for several reasons, including the aim to formalize and at the same time stabilize the dancers' positions in the company; I wanted the dancers to demand more of their employer, C.D. Finc, and by those pressures force the newly reorganized board of directors of the corporation to accept a funding obligation they might otherwise let slip. I also wanted the Cunningham contract to be a model of its kind, one not based, as all others had been, on either the "Large Ballet Contract" or the "Small Ballet Contract" of the dancer's union. Our new contract, eventually concluded in 1968, recognized what I thought was a key fact—the dancers worked as hard in rehearsal as they did in performance, and therefore the pay for both kinds of work should be basically the same. A system of "units" was devised that allowed the employer to build the required minimum number of employed weeks from rehearsals, performances, college residency work, and the like, as long as the basic minimum weekly salary was paid.

Cunningham himself didn't care for this sort of institutionalization for what had been a very informal structure. But I thought that, for the foreseeable future, anyway, Cunningham could count on having a management that could deal with these developments.

From 1965 to 1968 the company made many appearances in the United States and two more tours abroad, both to Europe. The first of these, in the summer of 1966, was once again financed through the generosity of other artists—the painters Joan Miro and Jean-Paul Riopelle. Miro had wanted to see the company perform in Spain, and, with his help also, performances were arranged at the Maeght Museum in the south of France. A videotaping contract in Hamburg completed the work for that tour, which was short, well funded, and relatively trouble free. I say "relatively" only because of a mishap at the border between Spain and France, where I lost all the company baggage—scenery, costumes, the lot—for a tense twenty-four hours.

The third tour abroad, in the fall of 1966, was not well financed at all. There had been no painter-patrons for this trip, and, although the Gulbenkian Foundation had funded the performances in Portugal, the tour ran up a deficit almost every week.

Almost as aggravating as this financial difficulty was a problem that developed, once again, with the State Department. Cunningham had been awarded a prize as the result of the company's performances at an international festival in Paris. The prize itself was awarded at a ceremony after the tour had ended, and Cunningham was no longer in Europe—David Vaughan stayed, though, to receive the prize on Cunningham's behalf. He was dumbfounded to discover a representative of the State Department on hand at the ceremony. The State Department man felt that, in spite of the company's total lack of support from the U.S. government, the U.S. government should get the credit for the prize. And he proceeded to take the prize from David Vaughan and send it on to Washington! Many weeks later, much to Cunningham's disgust, the prize, a small gold star, arrived in a little package from Washington, with postage due, which Cunningham had to pay at the post office.

During the following winter the Board of Directors decided to produce a major benefit event in June 1967, with the hope of eradicating debts. John DeMenil and Philip Johnson collaborated with the board to plan the evening at Johnson's house in Connecticut. A stage was constructed in the meadow beside the house, and the company gave a brief performance for the benefit guests at twilight. It was all immensely successful, and the $30,000 or so netted on the evening provided a brief moment of financial security for the corporation. Another important development of 1967 was the agreement entered into between the two people (the director of development and myself) responsible for running the affairs of the dance company: we pledged always to plan our international tours at least one year in advance, so as to give the director of development the maximum amount of time to raise the necessary funds I would need for the tour. Immediately upon making this understanding between us, we signed a contract with an impresario in Santiago, Chile, for engagements in South America in the summer of 1968.

We proceeded with our efforts at internal organization as well, and, by the middle of 1968, clear contract agreements were being sketched out with the performing musicians, composers, the lighting designer, and the scenic artists. A structure of fees, salaries, and royalties was worked out with each group of these artists. One of the most difficult distinctions

to work out was what constituted the composer's own tools, with which he created his electronic music score, and what constituted the materials to be left behind to perform the work in the repertory. There were heady discussions abou the definition of "art works," "realizing musical compositions," and the ownership of the apparatus needed to produce the electronic music. Agreement was not always unanimous though, on how best to deal with these questions, as this excerpt from a letter I wrote will show: "John Cage, however is irritated at the letter to the composers that went out from me; he says that once the equiptment is purchased from the composer to realize the piece, the composer has no right to it and must rent it from us at a modest rate. This has to do with property, he says, which once bought remains the property of the buyer. Art, though, is something else. The rights to the art work must not be limited, thus presenting the composer with a flexible situation regarding his art. He wants a qualifying letter sent to the composers saying this. Clear it with him first." But probably the most important development of 1967–68 was the creation of the first, modest, annual salary for Merce Cunningham. In spite of having worked harder than any human being should ever have to for over twenty years, Cunningham had never been assured of a living wage from his own work. Of all the

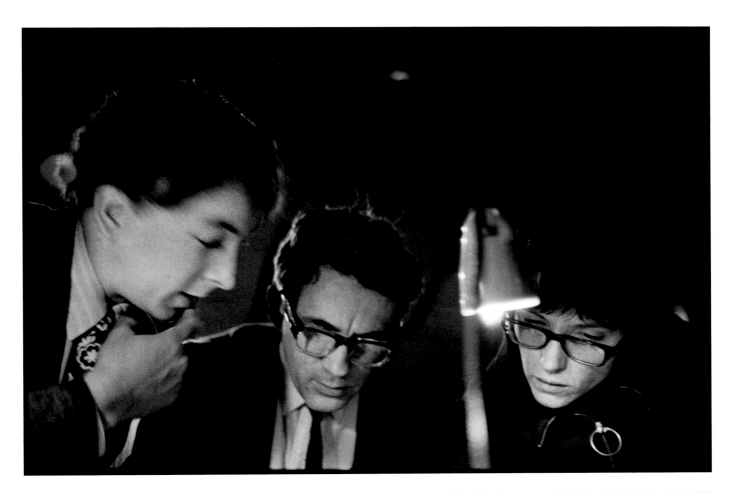

Lewis Lloyd, David Tudor, and Jean Rigg (company administrator), Buffalo, New York, 1968

things accomplished by the foundation, this accomplishment seems to me the most worthy.

As the spring wore on, it became clear that the necessary funding for the South American tour was not going to materialize, in spite of a year's lead time for the project. At the end of May we notified the producer that we were breaking our agreement with him due to his inability to provide us with advance information, and I then left for South America myself, to try and pull together some dates that we could count on. A tour of five weeks was possible, it turned out, and we decided to proceed with appearances in Mexico City, Rio de Janiero, Buenos Aires, and Caracas.

This was an epic tour in many respects; certainly managerial and contractual problems were monumental. The cash deficit became weekly more pressing, while the accumulated deficit in New York, represented mainly by unpaid bills to suppliers and back taxes on payroll, grew as well. No special funding, save $5,000, which was our first and only support from the State Department, had been arranged. The estimated loss for the tour had been planned at about $20,000; it ended up larger than that.

And so we completed the tour only to face the most critical financial situation in the foundation's short life—just one year after the successful benefit we all thought would solve our problems. Our internal agreement to plan one year in advance had been carried out, yet it too had failed due to the director of development's inability to raise sufficient funds. I wanted to take over fund-raising responsibilities myself, since I was planning the budgets for the foundation and actually spending the money. But Cage, particularly, was uneasy about this, because he feared the consolidation of power in any person save Cunningham and himself.

Almost as important as the lack of outside funding for the South American tour was the fact that Cage and I had never really agreed on what was the proper balance between work time and creative time, so to speak. Here, Cage was concerned with the damaging physical effect too much touring would have on Cunningham as well as the less tangible damage that might occur to Cunningham's work.

On one hand, it was necessary to work constantly, to perform, to generate touring income from performances, all of this supporting our effort to obtain a decent livelihood for all those associated with the company. Too many performances, on the other hand, would interfere with the periods of creativity necesary for choreographing new works, bringing old works back into the repertory, and teaching dances to new dancers joining the company. In one of his letters to me Cage said: "I suggest . . . that in your objective of thirty weeks of work at performance level there is good business thinking, good employment thinking, etc., but very poor artistic and human thinking. You will answer that the dancers have to eat, live decently, etc. But there won't be good dancing if that economic objective alone is met. Try to find a way to get the company subsidized, not worked to death, but subsidized . . . so that the pace of performance is in relation to the life of creative people in the company, not workhorses." By the fall of 1968, then, after six years of work with the company, it was apparent to me that an impasse had been reached. Cage and I could not agree on two crucial points of operating the company: how much paid work was proper for the company, and who was to raise the money necessary to sustain the company at its modest level of economic security. It was clear to me, anyway, that I was the expendable part of the situation.

On reflection, I was sure that the foundation would be able to develop in the long run quite satisfactorily, whether or not I was around. So thinking, I chose to leave. Mechanically, the leave taking was as simple as crossing the room, since the company had moved its offices to the Brooklyn Academy of Music, where I became the assistant director in charge of the dance program: my office and the Cunningham office were in the same room during that fall. Practically, though, the effect was a real one; the new administrator took over the management of the company and studio and the multitude of financial problems that came with those responsibilities. My own work then took me into the development of a new ballet company, directed by Eliot Feld, and from about that time my substantive relationship with Merce and John ended. Since that time, I'm pleased to say, the company has achieved many goals. It moved to excellent new quarters in Westbeth, the artists' housing facility in New York City. It has appeared regularly in New York City, it has toured Europe twice more, and has continued to appear all over the United States to great acclaim. The Board of Directors became the most active and responsible body of its kind in American modern dance, and the company has even survived the renegotiation and renewal of its contract with the dancers' union.

Right, top: Notes for a *Canfield*-based Event
Right, bottom: Dressing room door, France, 1970

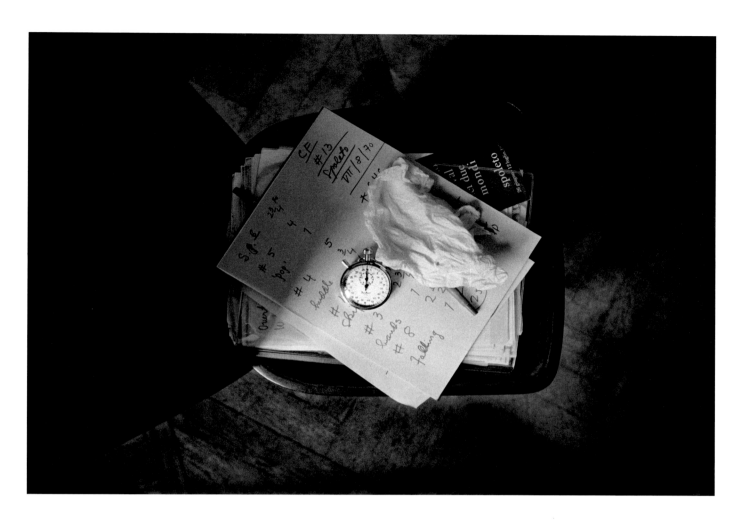

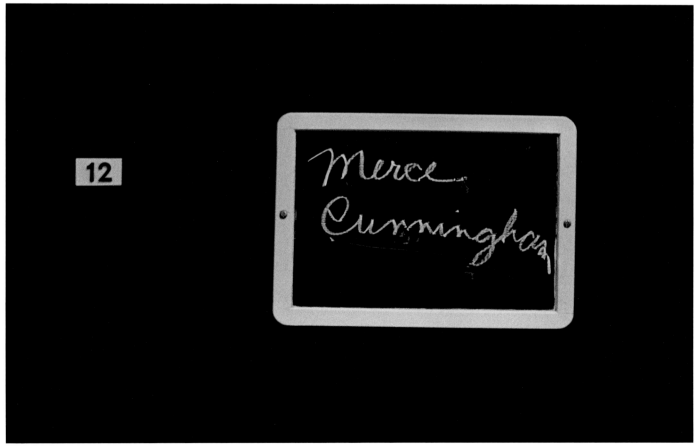

12

1968–1972 **TOURING**

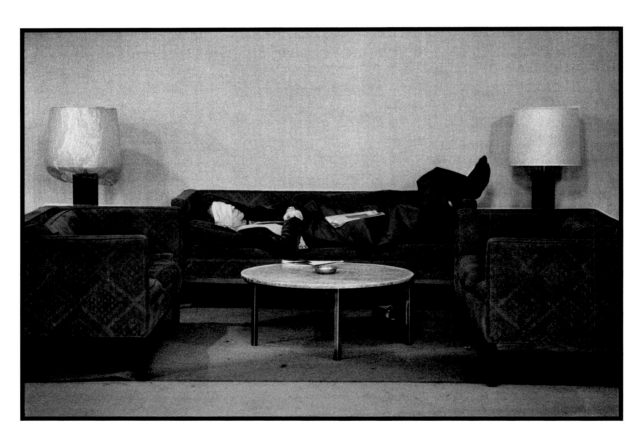

Above: Staten Island, 1969;
Opposite: Merce Cunningham, Fondation
Maeght, Saint Paul de Vence, 1970

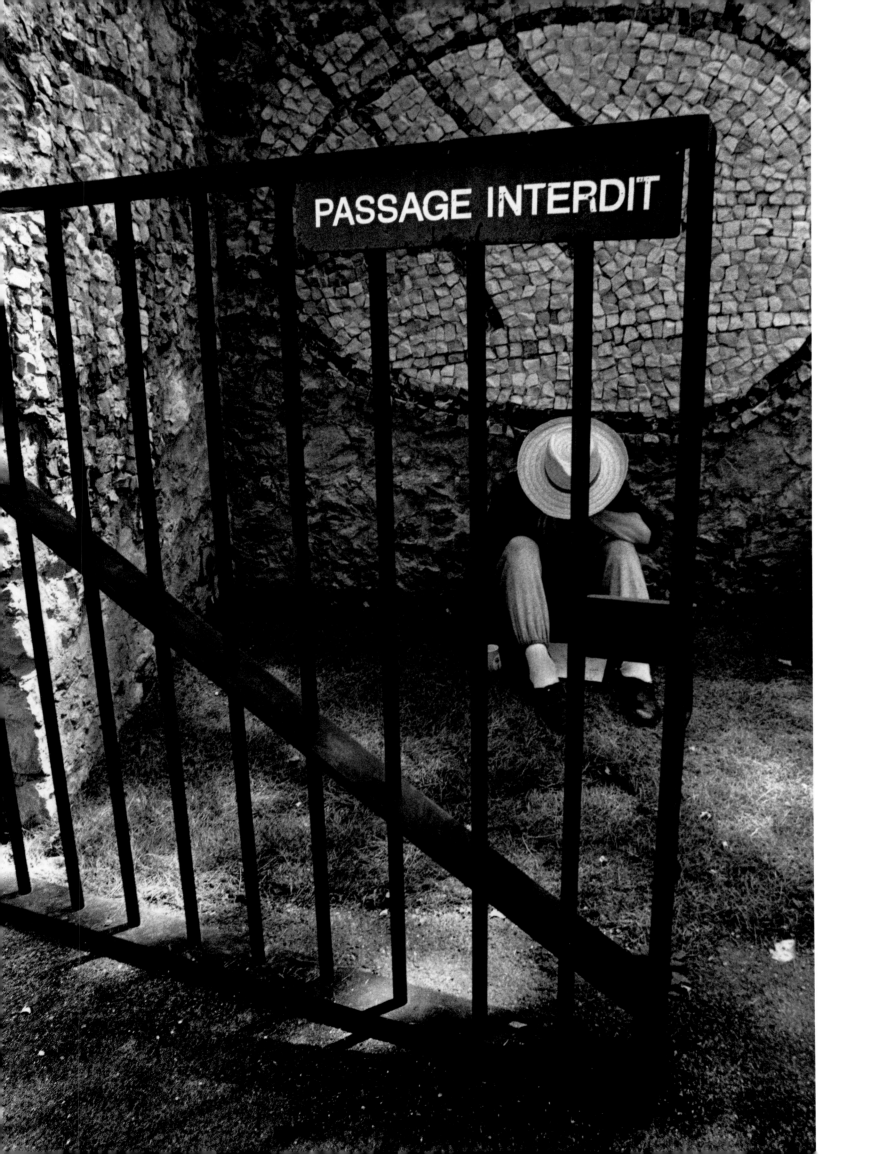

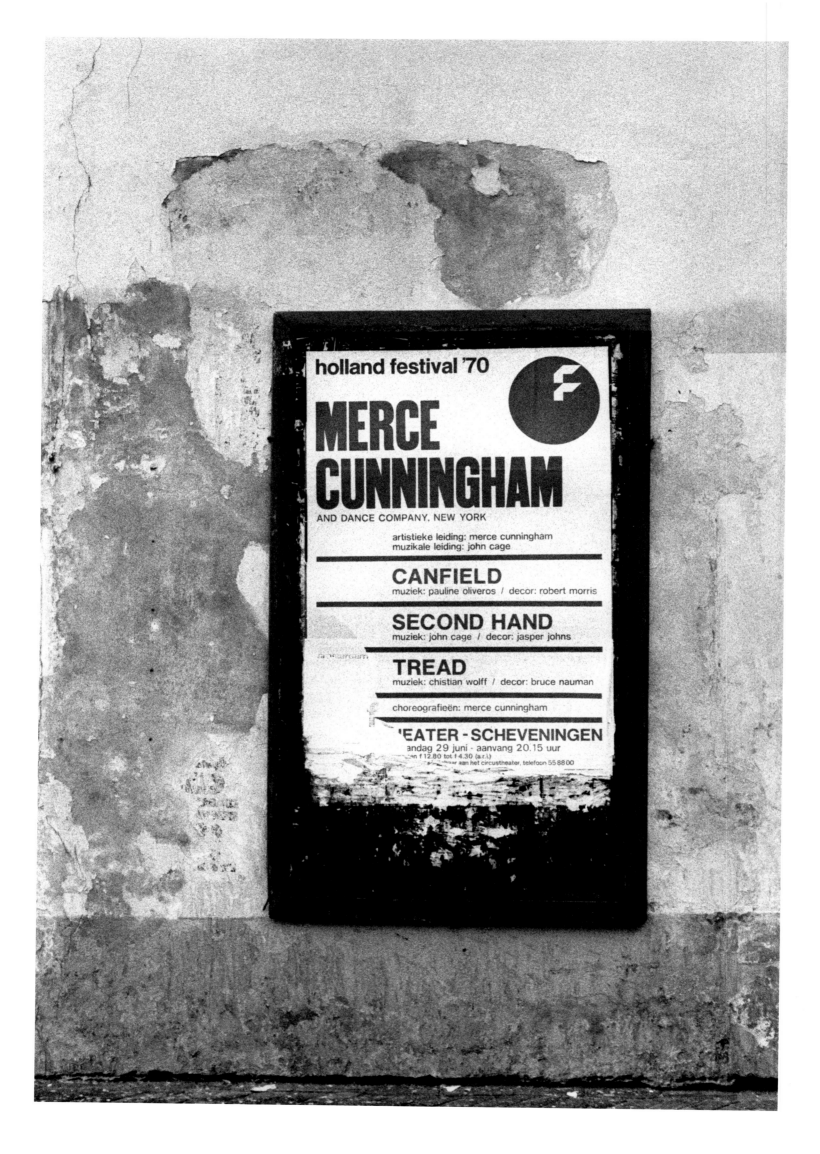

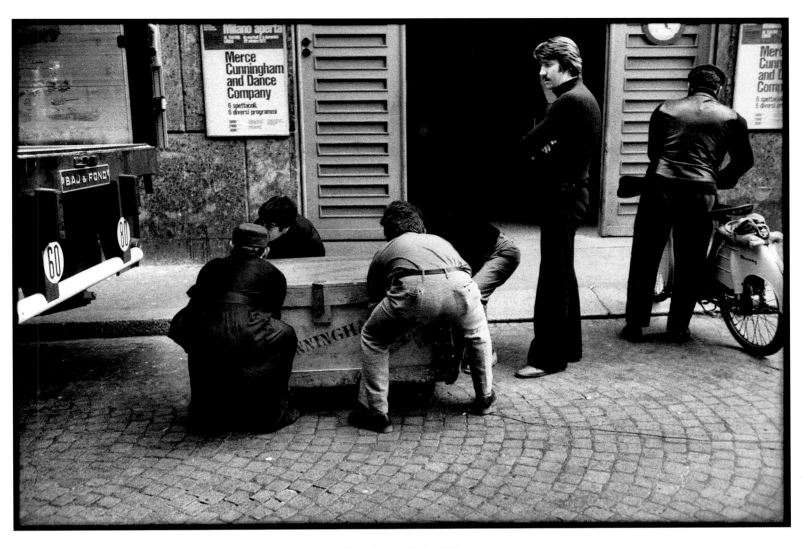

Left: Scheveningen, Holland, 1970; Top: Milan, Italy, 1972; Bottom: Lobby, Théâtre d'Odeon, Paris, 1970

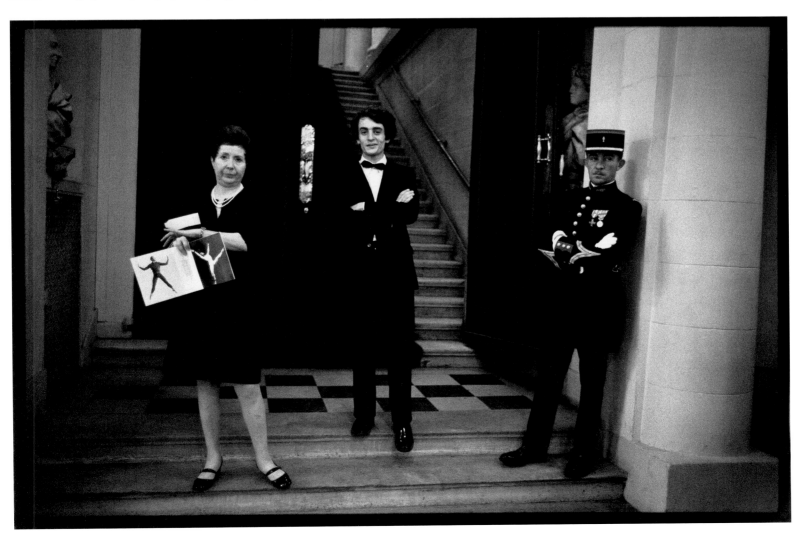

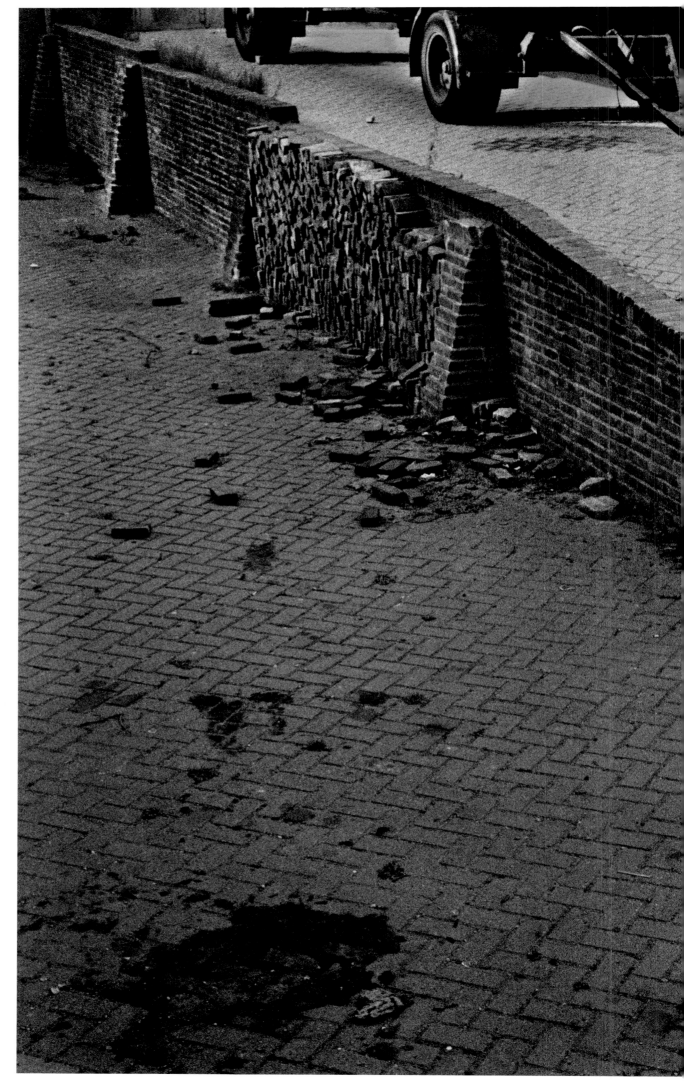

Top to bottom:
Charles Atlas, Gordon
Mumma, Mimi Johnson,
and Carolyn Brown,
Scheveningen, Holland, 1970

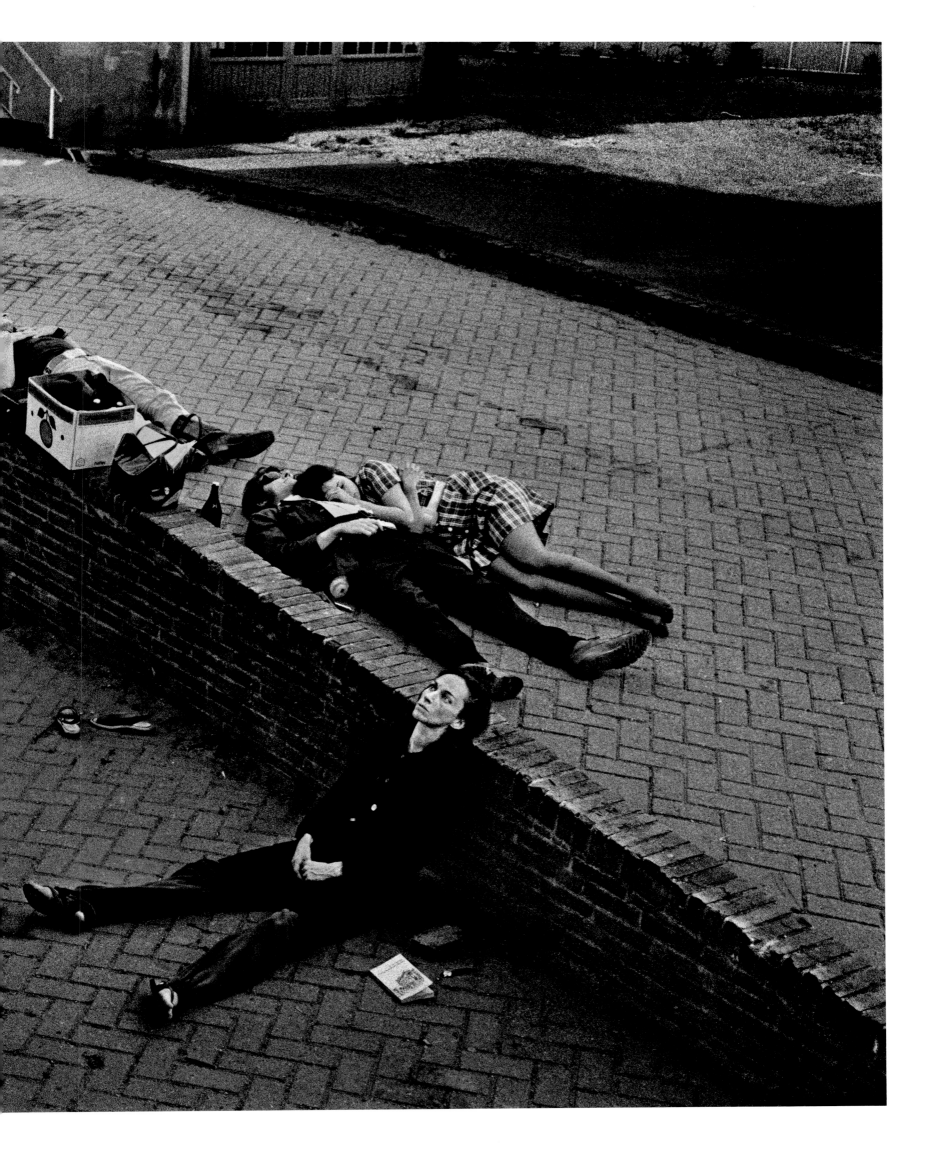

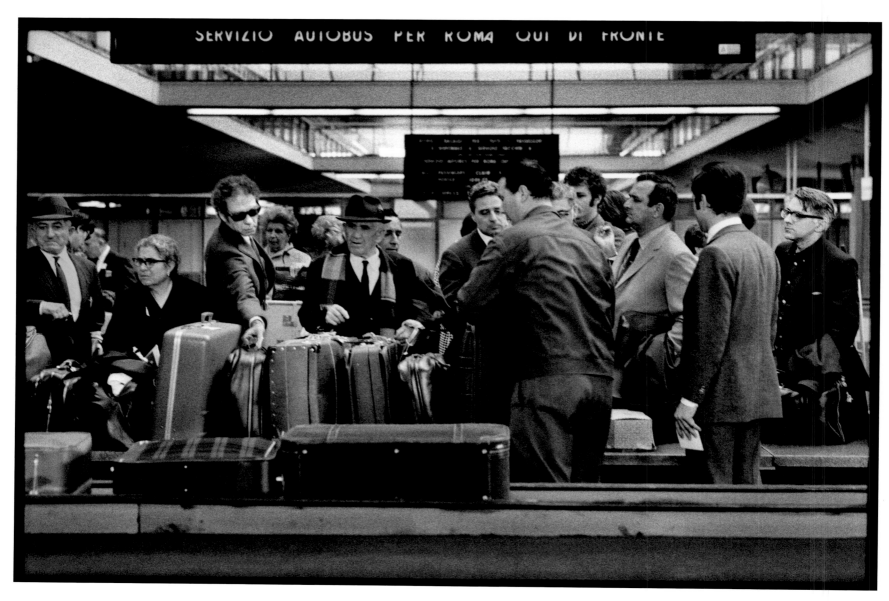

Merce Cunningham and David Tudor (extreme right), Rome airport, 1969

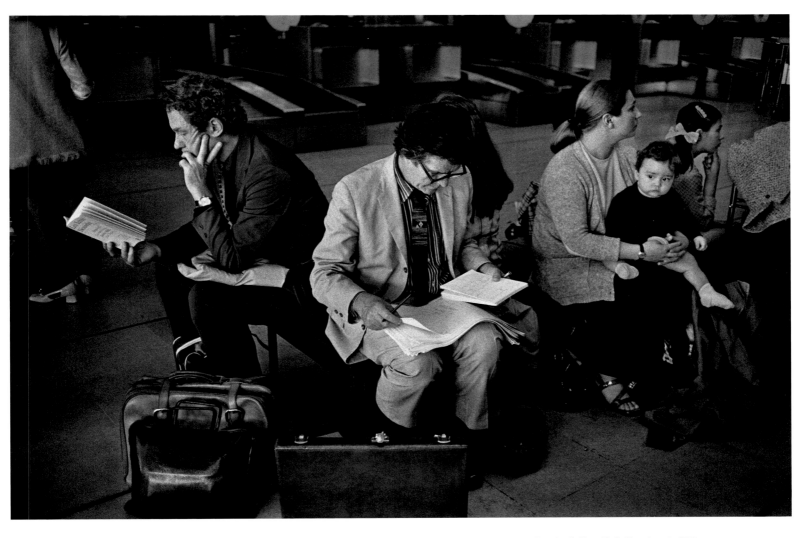

Top: Merce Cunningham and John Cage (working as always), Paris airport, 1970; Bottom: Carolyn Brown and Meg Harper (masked), New York City airport, 1972

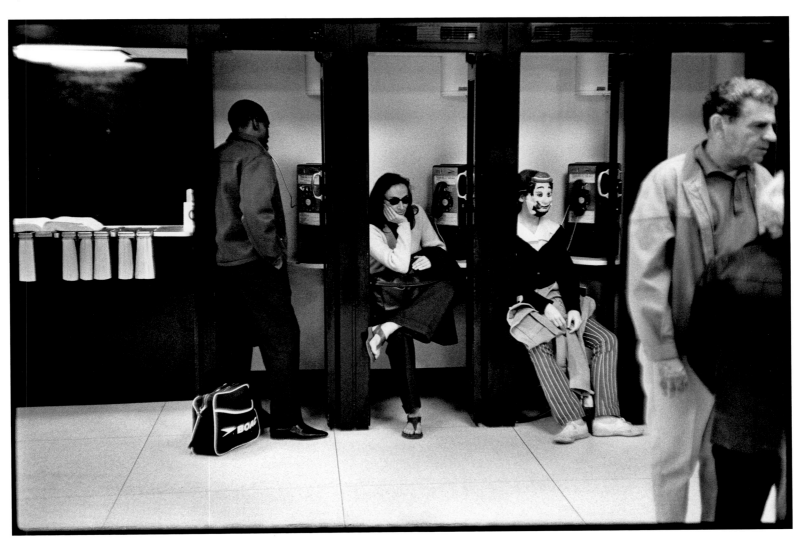

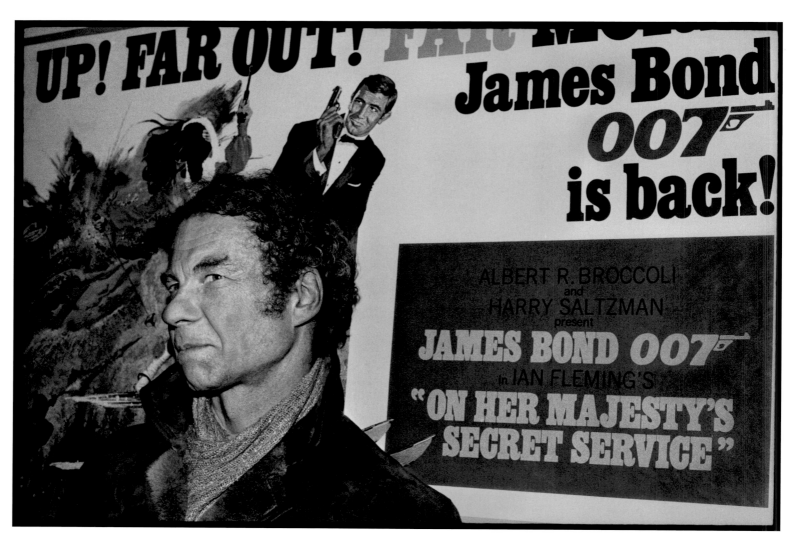

New Year's Eve on the IRT, December 1969

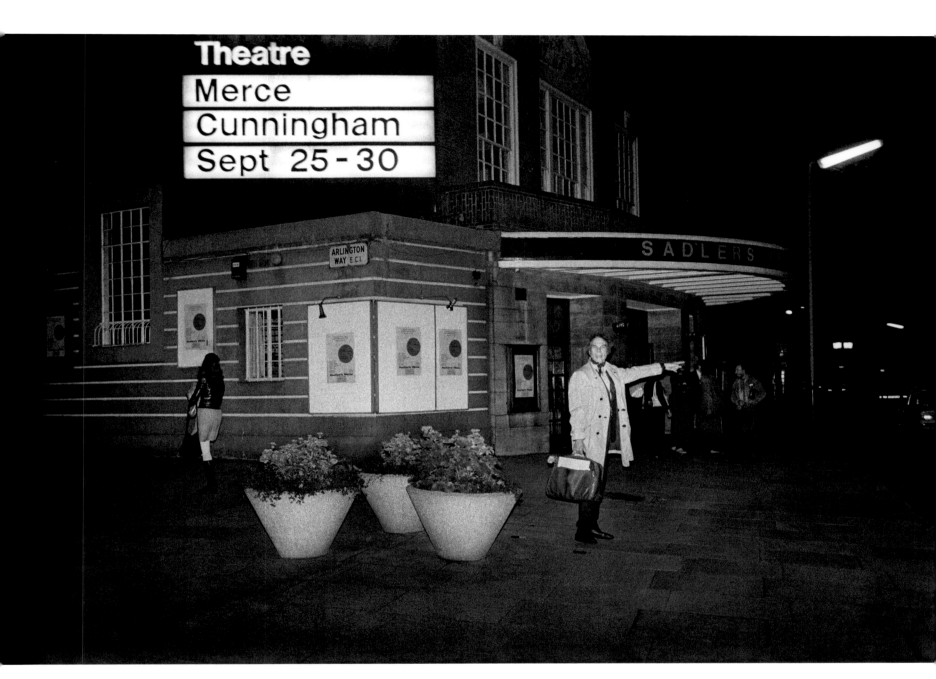

Merce Cunningham, Sadler's Wells Theater, September 1972

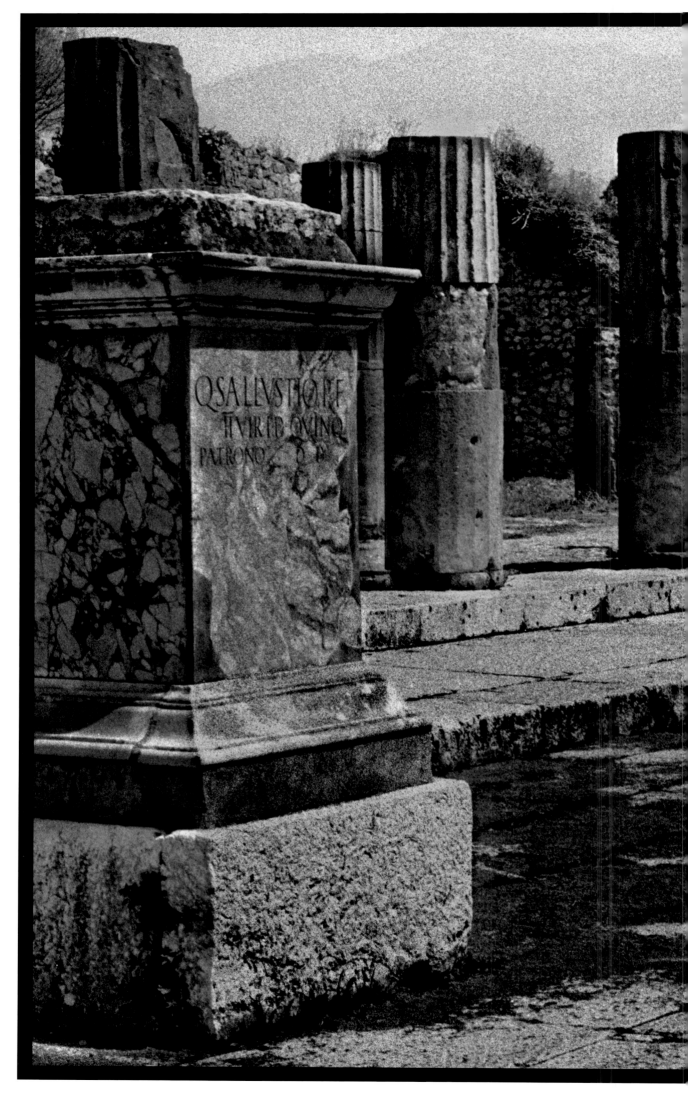

Merce Cunningham,
Pompeii, 1969

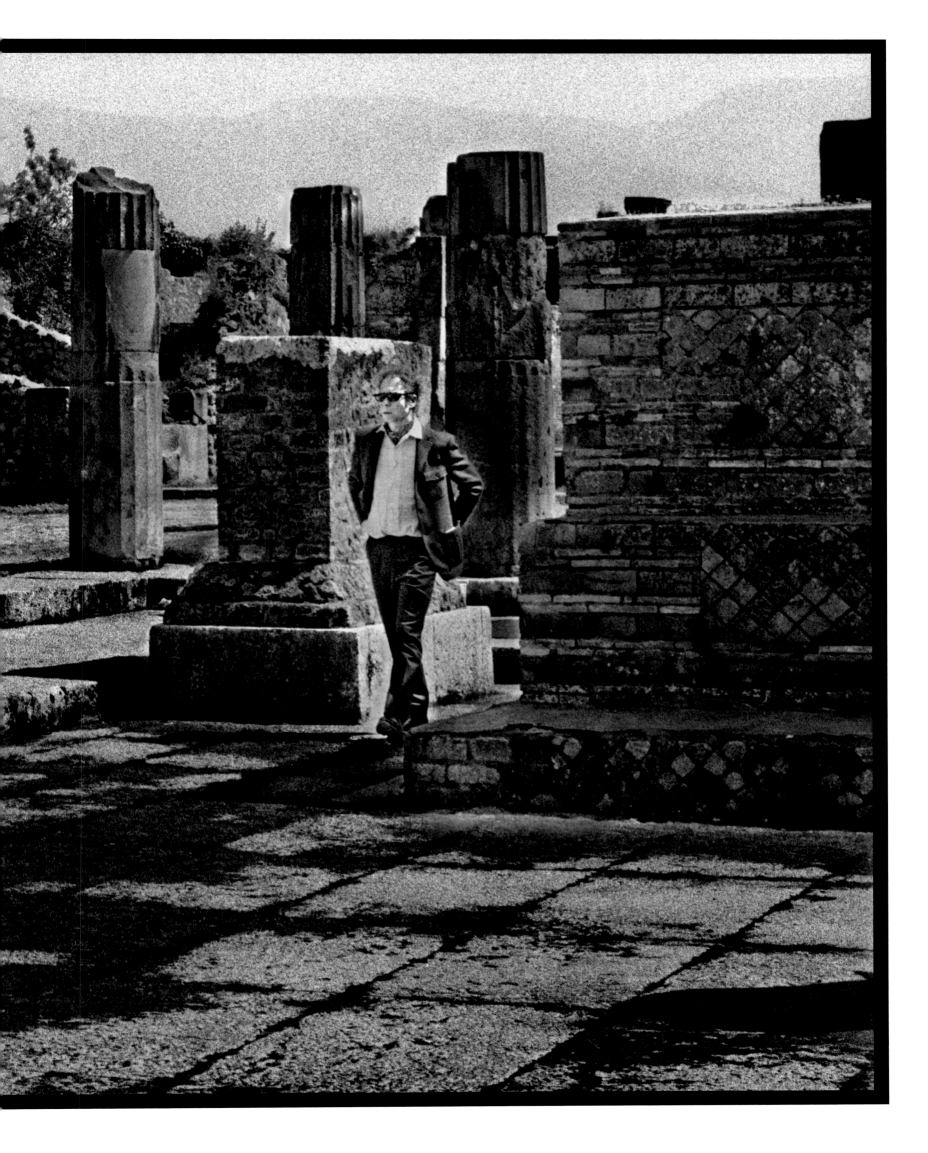

Merce Cunningham,
Cologne, Germany, 1972

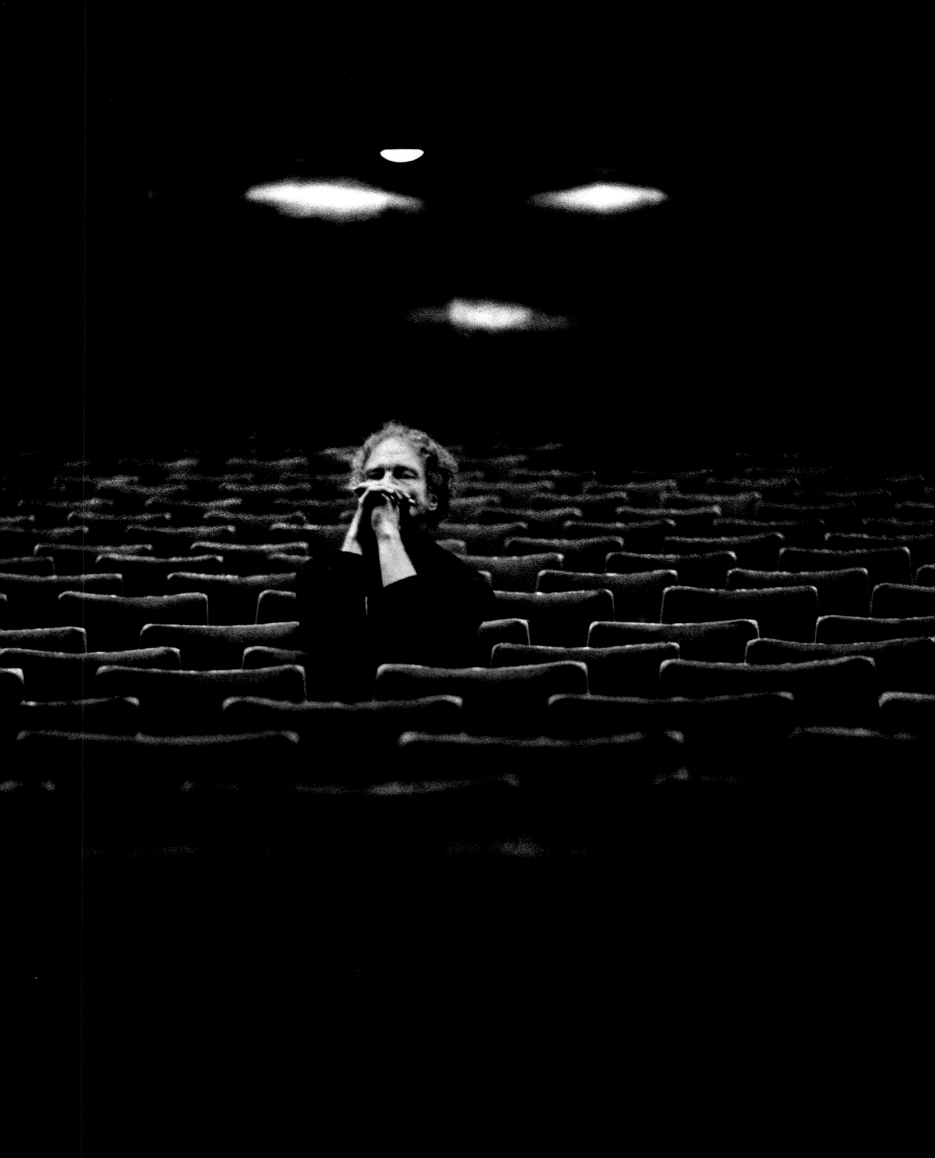

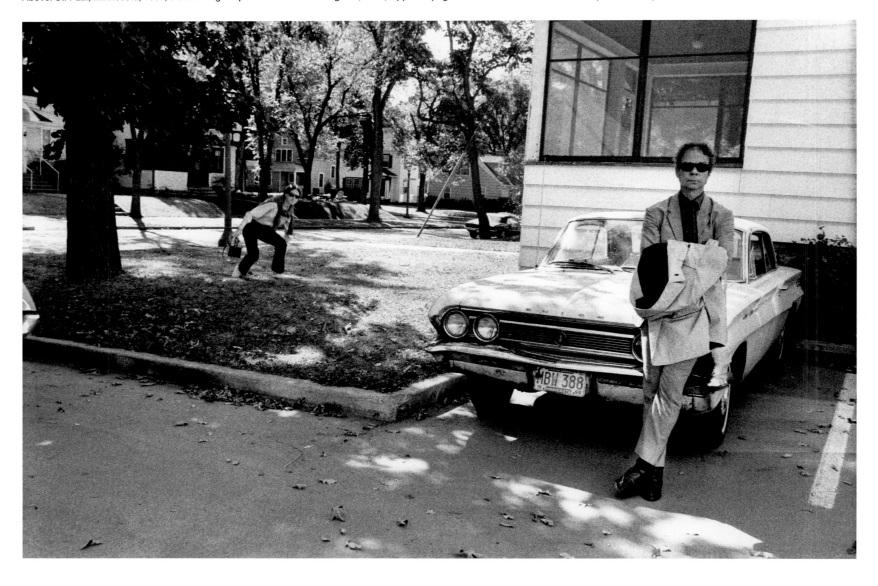

Above: St. Paul, Minnesota, 1969; Below: Meg Harper and Merce Cunningham, 1969; Opposite page: Gordon Mumma and Susana Hayman-Chaffey, Holland, 1970

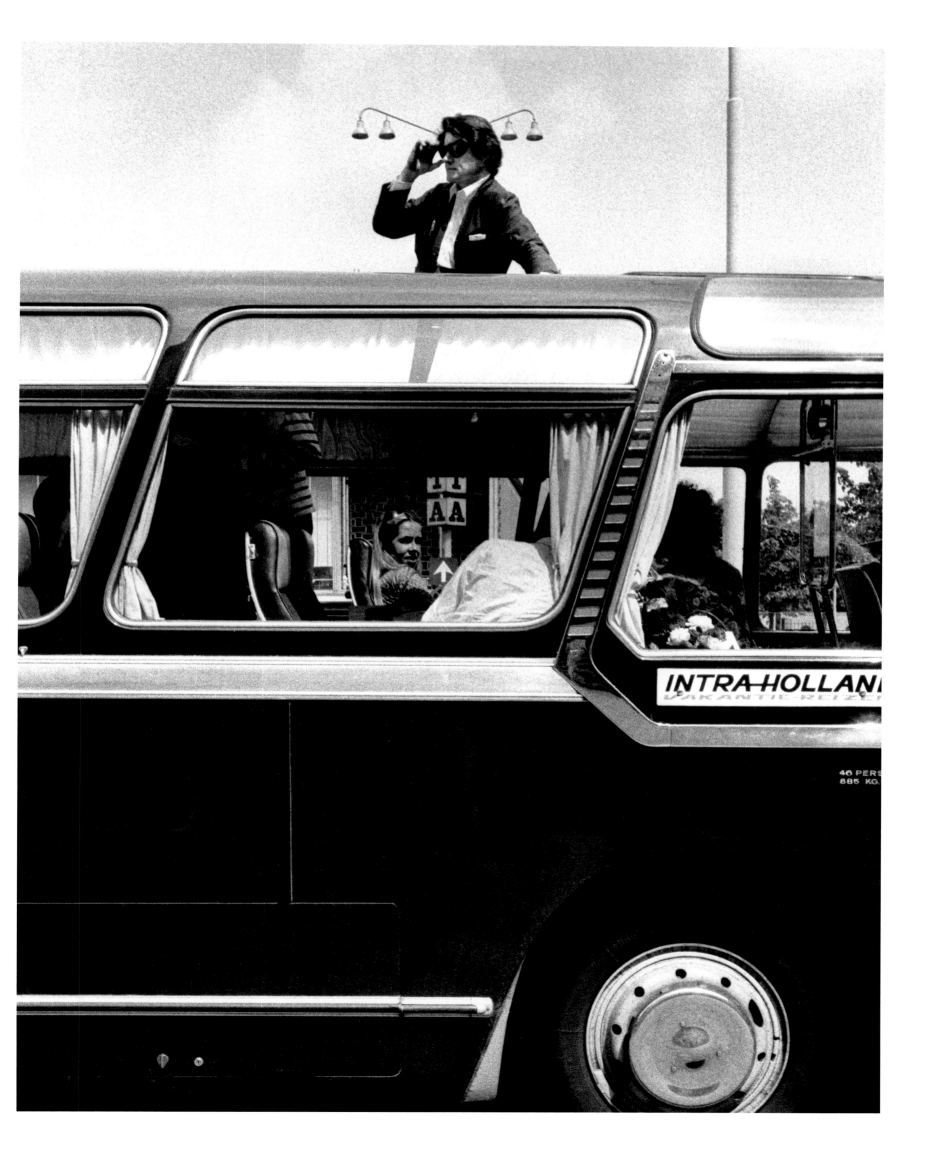

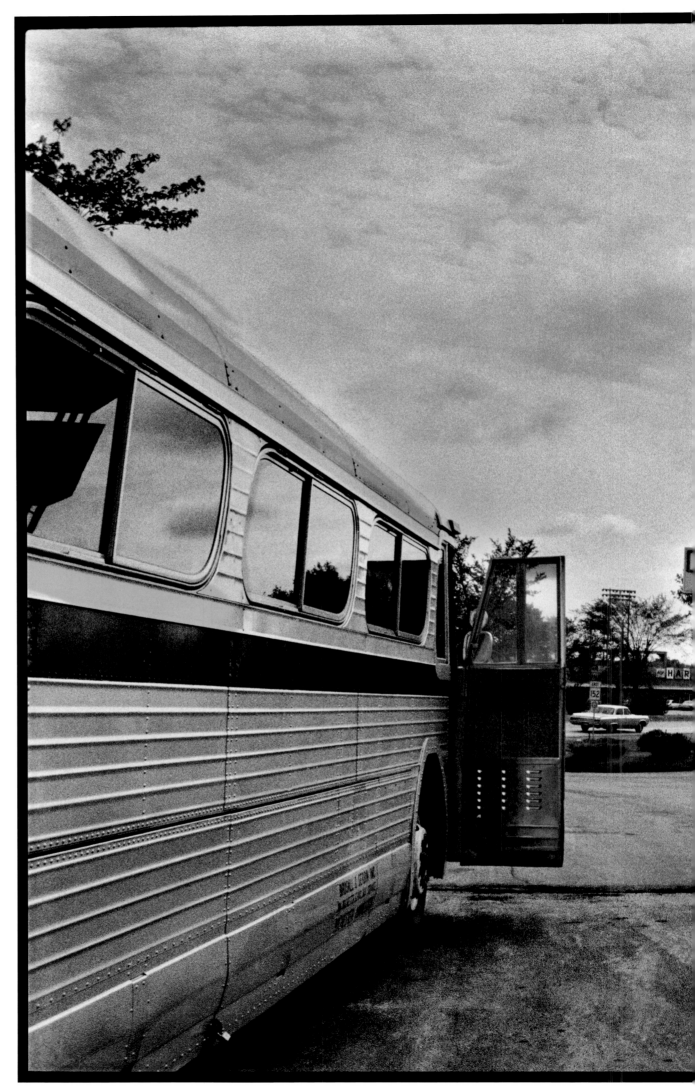

Swiggums Motel,
St. Cloud, Minnesota, 1969

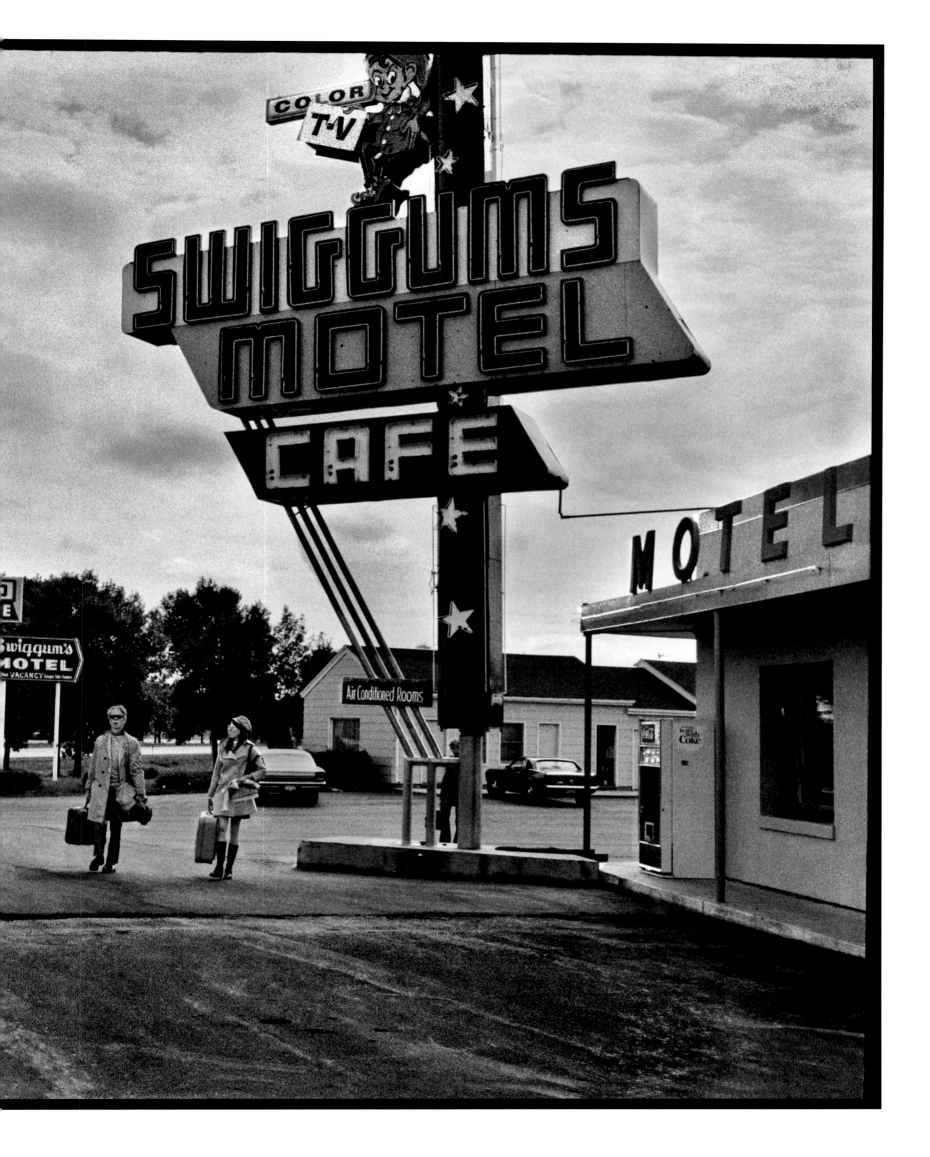

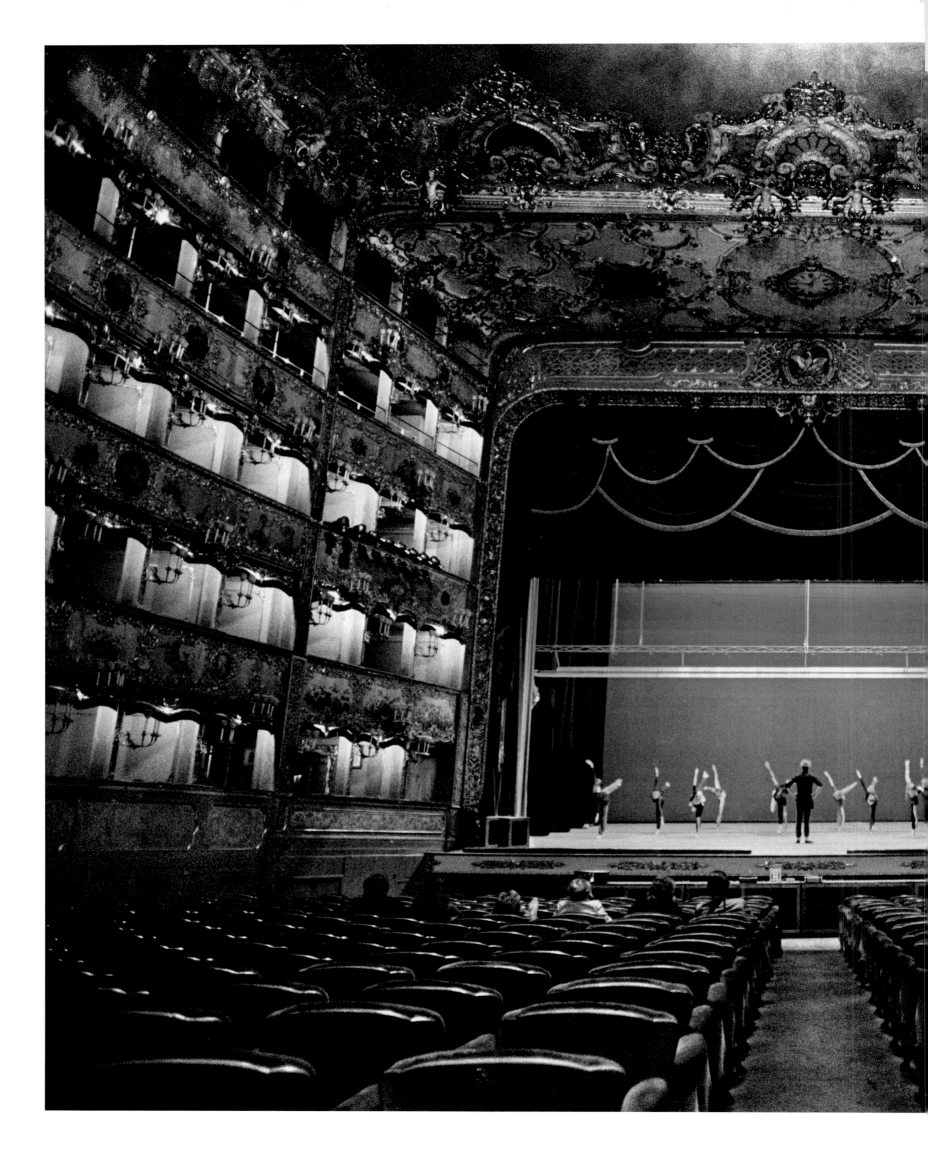

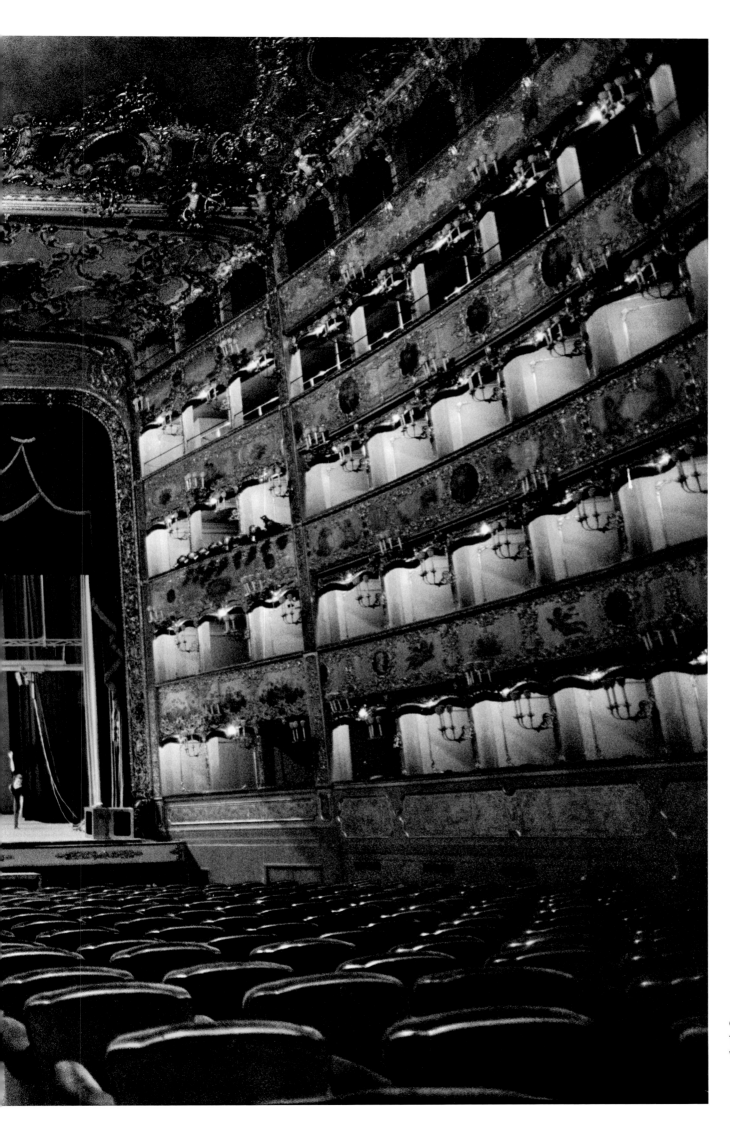

Company class,
Teatro La Fenice,
Venice, 1972

353

FOREWORD BY JAMES KLOSTY

—From the 1986 Limelight edition

Although this book was originally published in 1975, the photographs were made over a period of roughly five years, from 1968 through 1972. If 1970 is taken as their temporal center (the texts were written mostly from 1972 to 1974), this is a reissue of a book now sixteen years old. The obvious question arises: Is this book relevant to the Cunningham Dance Company of today? The obvious answer is yes and no. Yes, because the primary force, the inventiveness, the disregard of what is easy (i.e., popular), the uncompromising adherence to an idiosyncratic aesthetic, to a profound and profoundly influential conception of what dance can be, remains as vital as ever. No, because with the exception of Chris Komar and David Tudor no one pictured herein is officially associated with today's company. Cunningham himself, stubborn veteran of injury, arthritis, and the inevitable restrictions of age, is a very different performer than he was then, though no less remarkable. His interests have broadened to include a serious involvement in film and video dance, his works have entered the repertory of major ballet companies here and abroad, and his long-time associate John Cage has retired from the company to devote himself to his own work.

Some years back, the original publisher offered to reprint this book if I would bring it up to date, photographically. I refused. One does not keep "up to date" with an artist like Merce Cunningham, and it was never my intention to "illustrate" Cunningham's work. The feelings I expressed in my introduction regarding dance photography have not changed. The fact that there is an entirely new repertory of very different dances performed by a very different company is not only beside the point but inevitable. To put the matter as succinctly as possible, the work has changed visually, but not in its primary vision. Clearly the reason to republish this book in 1986 is to help today's public understand something about the central period of an artist whose company has for over thirty years been a critical point of reference for anyone seriously interested in the contemporary arts. Succeeding in that is enough for me.

I think it worth noting that although my admiration for Lincoln Kirstein is as sincere as when I first assembled this book, the opinions he expresses in these pages have not been entirely borne out by time. There is a rapprochement between classical ballet and modern dance that was not, I think, predictable in 1971. True, Kirstein's "mass public" remains largely innocent of knowledge of Cunningham's work. But what are we to make of the 1985 Kennedy Center Awards? On TV screens all across America, Merce Cunningham was honored side by side with Bob Hope (recalling the pre-surrealist evocation of "the chance meeting upon a dissecting table of a sewing machine and an umbrella"). The event certainly must have given Kirstein, as it did me, cause for mild astonishment. On the other hand, also worth noting is Cunningham's recently sharpened interest in at least some aspects of Kirstein's oft expressed espousal of "acrobatic virtuosity based on four centuries of logical exercises."

In December of 1985 I talked with Cunningham in his Westbeth studio about these and other matters.

JAMES KLOSTY: Merce, is the company very different today from the one represented in the book?

MERCE CUNNINGHAM: It's basically the same. We're bigger. There are more dancers, more musicians, more technical people, a larger administrative staff, and something we never had earlier: a wardrobe mistress. We play more, of course, and generally in better theaters. But the *traveling* is so exhausting. Getting on and off airplanes, getting your luggage. That's different And we carry very little scenery.

JK: Your involvement with decor seems less intense than it used to be.

MC: Oh, it is. Partly for economic reasons, because it costs so much. But basically it's so difficult to get it anyplace. You get there and it doesn't. And it's not just the fact that you don't have it, it's the psychological problem that you're standing around wondering what happened to it. It's a terrible problem. We have an enormous amount of freight because of the electronics. If we had *more* scenery, they simply couldn't carry it. So we don't do it.

JK: Do you feel the lack of it in the work?

MC: No, because I never worked from the point of view that I had to have it. It's like a landscape when you look at it and there's not a tree there anymore. It changes the landscape, but you can exist with it. Should the opportunity come once again to work more fully with the visual arts I would do it.

JK: What do you do about food for yourself, now that John [Cage] isn't with the company?

Merce Cunningham rehearsing *Untitled Solo*

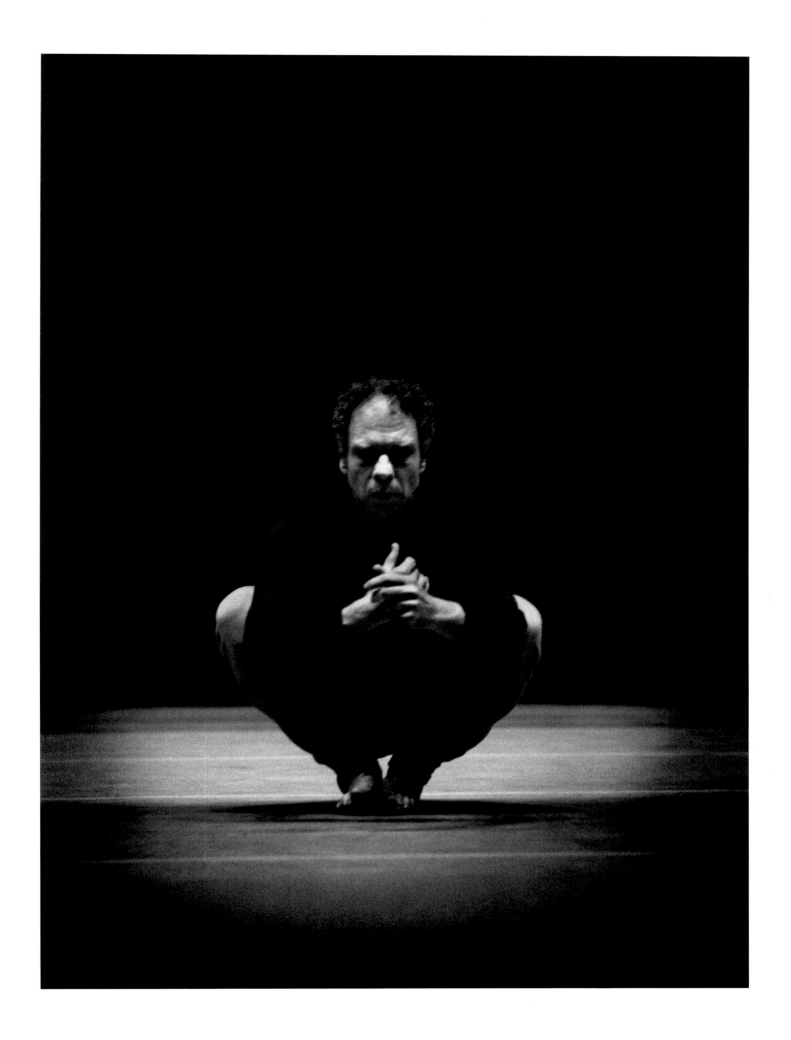

MC: I carry a rice cooker and a wok, and when it's essential I cook in the hotel room. But more and more there are restaurants I can eat in. Macrobiotic restaurants. Around the corner from the hotel in Barcelona; in Madrid there was one three blocks from the theater; in Paris now there are two.

JK: I take it your macrobiotic diet hasn't changed your interest in eating well.

MC: Oh no, no! It's one of the few pleasures about touring.

JK: One change in the new edition will be a photograph of Edwin Denby. There was none in the first edition.

MC: I saw Edwin in June about two weeks before he died. He asked me what I was doing. I told him the company was off and I had been making things in a workshop with students and we'd had a showing. He said, "Oh, I would have liked to have seen that." I said, "Oh, it was just students." He said, "Well, your company and the New York City Ballet have the highest performance level, and I would like to have seen it at the point when it wasn't there so I could see how it got to that." No one but Edwin would have thought that way. So I told him I was doing another one in August, and would he like to come. [*pauses*] But he wasn't around for that.

JK: Is there a difference in the work today, or how the audience sees it, compared to, say, 1970?

MC: I think that lots of the things we do that were strange and new then are not now simply because things have happened in society, so that there are things now they can unconsciously accept that then they couldn't. There's such a splitting up of image today in most anything anybody sees that the idea of splitting images now is not so strange. The music is still a great disturbance for them, but not anywhere like it used to be. Sometimes they don't even bring up the idea of the dance being separate from the music. The question comes up less and less. I'm not even sure they think it is separate. And I think then it was hard for people to see how brilliant, for example, Carolyn [Brown] was. *What* she was doing was strange, so it didn't occur to them that maybe it was difficult. Now I think they can see that what the dancers do is quite difficult.

JK: Your interest in virtuosity itself has increased.

MC: Yes. So that has pushed the dancers in the company, of course.

JK: Does that interest result from your feeling that the company requires a higher degree of virtuosity to compensate for your less frequent appearances on stage?

MC: No. Well, if I feel that way it's unconscious. I simply began to feel there was this area about virtuosity that I ought to investi-gate. I did it a little bit with myself originally, and then began to try to find a way to translate it to the company.

JK: But the idea of virtuosity was not something that concerned you in the period of the 1950s and 1960s?

MC: Not as strongly, no. I tried to do certain things, but because we were dealing with the whole question of chance, and the separation of the music and the dance, there were different things to be concerned about. Virtuosity always necessitates . . . well, there are fewer ways to get in and out of things in virtuosity. There are very few ways to get into and out of certain kinds of jumps clearly. You can always fall down, but that's something else. If a movement is not virtuosic there are many more ways to use it, what it comes from and what it goes into. And diversity of movement was one thing I was interested in. But even then we did things in class that were difficult.

JK: I don't think anyone ever had the impression that what you were doing was easy.

MC: Well, no. But you see people so often still think, "Oh, yes, of course, it's improvised." How can people possibly have that kind of witless thinking seeing these incredibly complicated things going on, dancers leaping and jumping and falling into each others arms and so on; how could that possibly, on that scale, be improvised?

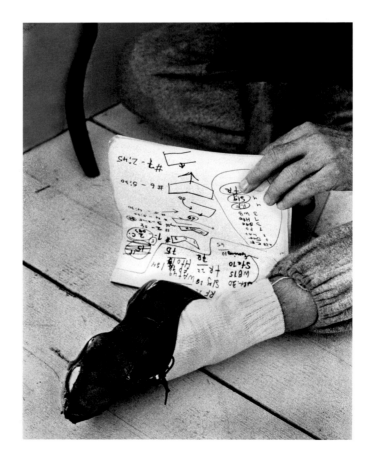

Event notes, Fondation Maeght, 1970

It would be catastrophic! But virtuosity was something I hadn't that much investigated. I'm not sure I have now.

JK: It's fascinating to hear you say that because I always thought of you as a virtuoso dancer.

MC: Yes, but there are many more things about virtuosity: the speed with which you can do things, the variety within speed, for example, which you simply have to figure out. Personally, I always had speed, but the idea of making that more varied one has to look at, to try out. And as I increasingly obviously can't do those things for myself, I try to find ways to show the dancers how to do it. In *Torse*, for example, I figured out things about how the torso is used, then ways for the legs to move, and tried to put them together. That involved going up in the air in ways—change of speeds, change of direction—I had never quite gotten to before.

JK: But you had certainly approached the subject.

MC: Oh yes, I kept *trying* to do that. I was sure there was a way. But *Torse* was the first time, and it took six months of work, that I really thought I had solved some kind of problem. A solution had been found. It might not be the only solution. The same thing happened working with video: other problems came up, other kinds of possibilities.

JK: I'm particularly curious about your recent interest in the film and television camera, because when shooting the book I was positive you were not simply resistant to, but really disliked, being photographed.

MC: Well, I don't like having pictures taken. I never liked having my picture taken in any circumstances.

JK: But I also had the impression you didn't want your dances filmed.

MC: Well, I suppose. But then I thought, there's going to be a lot more dancing on television. . . . This was in the '70s, just before the Dance in America thing. I hadn't seen very much, but what I had seen was so uninteresting. It didn't work. And I thought about Astaire and how it worked in his films, for heaven's sake, and worked marvelously. That's the only way we all saw him. We didn't see him on the stage. I thought, well, he did it, so something must be possible. So Charles Atlas and I simply started. And then I got interested in what it *was:* another way to present dancing visually; to deal with dancing. That I found fascinating. It's terribly difficult to put something on television or film; to get it *on.*

JK: Get it on in the way you envision it . . .

MC: Yes. To make it work. So that it is what it is and not something you think would be better on the stage. I've never seen something that was done on the stage and simply transferred to television that functions.

JK: Do you understand why now, or is it still a mystery?

MC: Oh yes, I understand exactly: because the camera works totally opposite from the stage. The stage, looked at from the audience, is wide to narrow. The camera works just the opposite. That's the first thing I saw when I looked through it. In front the view is narrow, and in back, wide. Right away that changes everything. It changes any kind of stage proportions that you have, and I think it changes the time, how movement operates and how dynamics are perceived. And then there are so many things you can do with a camera. If you cut from one camera to another, for instance, you have the possibility of changing the dancer's size. And that's totally different for the energy.

JK: A whole new world to work into your charts.

MC: Well, on the stage you can do other things. With a camera you do whatever *it* can do. If [*laughs*] you can manage to keep the dancers on the screen. That's the hardest thing.

JK: Has working in video and film changed your work for the stage?

MC: Yes, I think so. It certainly has affected it. It has added certain ideas about movement. Not necessarily new movements, although there may have been some, but what you can do with what you have. The angles you can use, for instance. I was so used to thinking, on the stage, that if the body is facing front and then turns, that makes a visible change. But in the camera if you just turn six inches, it's huge! Visible. OK, if you see that as a possibility in the camera, maybe its possible on the stage.

JK: Do you regret the lack of a filmed record of your early works?

MC: I suppose if I thought about it I could dig up some regrets, but I don't, really.

JK: What about the lack of a record of you as a younger performer?

MC: I somehow don't mind. [*laughs*] I suppose maybe I should, but I don't. [*laughs again*]

JK: What are your feelings about reviving old dances?

MC: First of all, they're pieces I used to be in, so that becomes a different experience. They are different because the other dancers were different as well, and some of the steps aren't exactly what they were because we don't always have records from that time. So they are *remembered*.

JK: And sometimes remembered second or third hand.

MC: Oh yes. Now, of course, we tape them. But in doing a dance again I don't try to change it with some aesthetic idea about now I can make this dance better.

JK: Yet you admit that with different dancers they can't be the same dances anyway.

MC: Oh yes, but that's all right. I understand if someone can only do a certain step a certain way rather than exactly as it was originally. I accept that out of necessity. But I don't change it with some aesthetic idea of improving it. What's interesting to me is what it *was*, what made that particular piece interesting at that time.

JK: In the past you made new work by choreographing on yourself.

MC: I still do.

JK: Yet there are many things you could do once that you can't do now.

MC: Some, yes.

JK: How do you deal with that?

MC: Well, I try to figure out the movements. And then I do what I have always done: I try things out in class. Just to see if it's feasible or *how* it might work.

JK: So class is still a period of experimentation?

MC: Yes. Probably not as much as it used to be.

JK: Why not?

MC: Because it used to be a smaller, more flexible group. Now the classes are enormous. And I don't teach that much. I don't teach consistently. I do when I'm here, but I don't have the consistent relationship with students that I used to, so I don't feel quite so free about trying things out. With the company it's different.

JK: You never really felt positively about teaching . . .

MC: Oh no, I hate it.

JK: That has never changed?

MC: It's mostly because, out of necessity, you have to repeat. It's necessary so that they will get stronger over a period of time, be able to be clearer, I hope, and more flexible. And you don't do that, as far as I can make out in dancing, by haphazard training.

JK: But some people do enjoy teaching.

MC: Oh I know, I know. I think its marvelous when people do.

JK: Why didn't you?

MC: Because there's so much time spent doing rote, repeated things. Like the whole beginning of class. That's absolutely essential, but not interesting. From that point of view, I'm not a good teacher at all because I'm not basically interested in that although I know it's necessary.

JK: Is there anything you want said in the new edition about your work or its presentation in the book?

MC: No. What I liked so much about your book is they're not like regular dance photographs. We're caught also as people, not just as dancers in some kind of flattering pose, or from that point of view only.

JK: One critic took me to task, feeling the book was not serious for that reason.

MC: Wasn't about dancing, you mean?

JK: Not sufficiently.

MC: That's the part I thought was wonderful.

JK: I can't resist asking what was going through your mind sitting in that box at the Kennedy Center, sharing awards with Lerner and Lowe, Irene Dunne, Beverly Sills, and Bob Hope?

MC: I'm trying to remember how I felt, because the next day I had to fly to Paris to restage *Un Jour ou Deux* at the Opera Ballet and it all went out of my head. We were an odd group. The whole experience was really so bizarre; a one-night stand. It was like playing a part, and I was wearing a costume. I thought that in that situation I was like a dark horse: What is this? Who would know? My work was so basically unknown. The dancers did part of *Native Green* and did it beautifully, although that audience must have been stunned by the music. It sounded marvelous, but they were so unaccustomed, most of them. Actually, though, people one knows from television like Maureen Stapleton and Sylvia Fine came up to me and said nice things. I was amazed. So maybe we're not as unknown as I thought. I always have the feeling that even though I know who they are, they wouldn't know much about what we do. But I suppose we've been around long enough! [*laughs*] I was just *relieved* when it was over, and I was very pleased with the dancers. I have no idea what the American public thought. I was just so glad it was over.

JK: One final thing then, Merce. A choreographer of note who knew I was going to be talking with you wanted me to ask you this. And I quote: "When did you think you knew what you were doing?"

MC: Is that the way it was phrased?

JK: Word for word.

MC: I never know what I'm doing. [*laughs*]

JK: Never?

MC: No! I just go ahead and attempt to do it.

—*James Klosty, January 1986*

Merce Cunningham between Rome and Pompeii, 1969

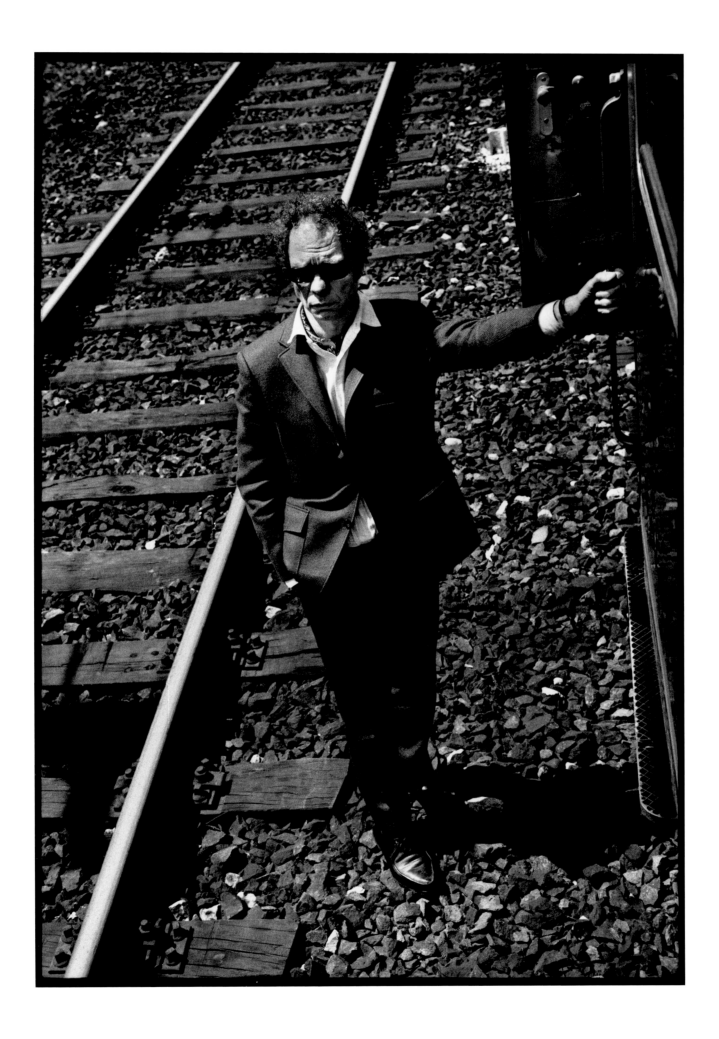

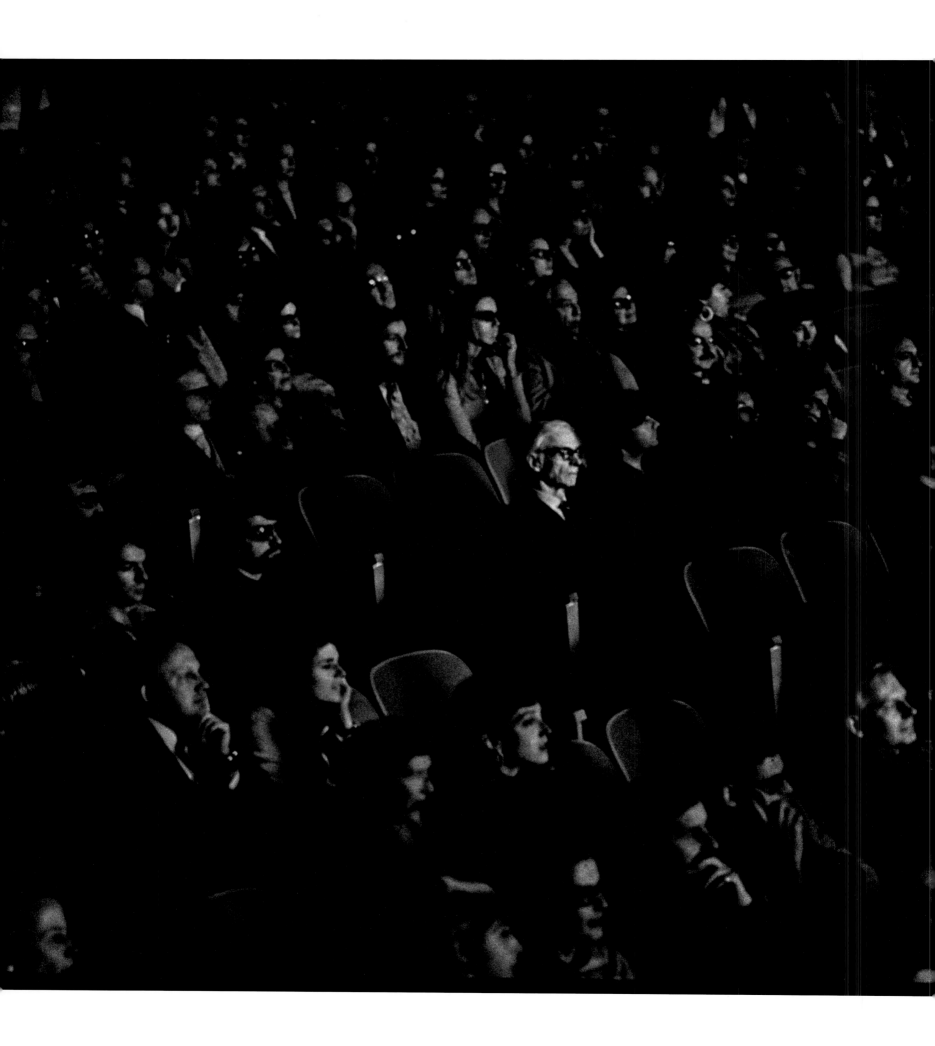

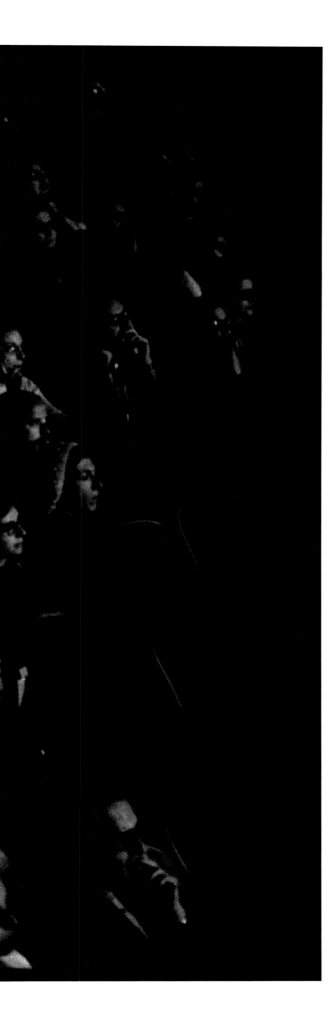

EDWIN DENBY

April 6, 1944

At the small Humphrey Weidman Studio in the darkness of Sixteenth Street, Merce Cunningham and John Cage presented a program of solo dances and of percussionist music last night which was of the greatest esthetic elegance. The audience, an intelligent one, enjoyed and applauded.

It was Mr. Cunningham's first solo recital, though he is well known to dance audiences as soloist in Martha Graham's company. His gifts as a lyric dancer are most remarkable. His build resembles that of the juvenile *saltimbanques* of the early Picasso canvases. As a dancer his instep and his knees are extraordinarily elastic and quick; his steps, runs, knee bends, and leaps are brilliant in lightness and speed. His torso can turn on its verticle axis with great sensitivity, his shoulders are held lightly free, and his head poises intelligently. The arms are light and long, they float, but do not often have an active look. These are all merits particularly suited to lyric expression.

As a dancer and as a choreographer of his own solos, Mr. Cunningham's sense of physical rhythm is subtle and clear. His dances are built on the rhythm of a body in movement, and on its irregular phrase lengths. And the perfection with which he can indicate the rise and fall of an impulse gives one an esthetic pleasure of exceptional delicacy. His compositions, too, were in no way derivative in their formal aspect, or in their gesture; they looked free and definite at the same time.

The effect of them is one of an excessively elegant sensuality. On the other hand—partly because they are solo dances, partly because they lack the vigorous presence of the body's deportment characteristic of academic ballet style—their effect is one of remoteness and isolation. This tone may well be due to the fact that Mr. Cunningham is still a young dancer, who is only beginning to discover his own dramatic resources. But I have never seen a first recital that combined such taste, such technical finish, such originality of dance material, and so sure a manner of presentation.

January 29, 1945

Mr. Cunningham reminds you that there are pure dance values in pure modern technique. He is a virtuoso, relaxed, lyrical, elastic like a playing animal. . . . He has a variety of drive and speed which phrases his dances; and better still, an improvisatory naturalness of emphasis which keeps his gesture from looking stylized or formalized.

The kind of elastic physical rhythm he has strikes me as something peculiarly American, and it is delicately supported by the elastic phrases of John Cage's music. But Cunningham's stage character is still too cautious to carry a solo program. He appears either as a lonesome youth or as a happy hooligan; you would like him to show a franker character, too, or see him in contact with different people. So strong a body should also harden and strike, force one phrase and throw away another; it could risk a firm beat, or an attack open and generous. A serious solo program calls for more risks in expression. Amiable popularizers . . . don't lead you to expect much of a risk. Cunningham does, by his poetic style, by his brilliant gifts. There is no reason why he shouldn't develop into a great dancer.

Edwin Denby, BAM, November 1970

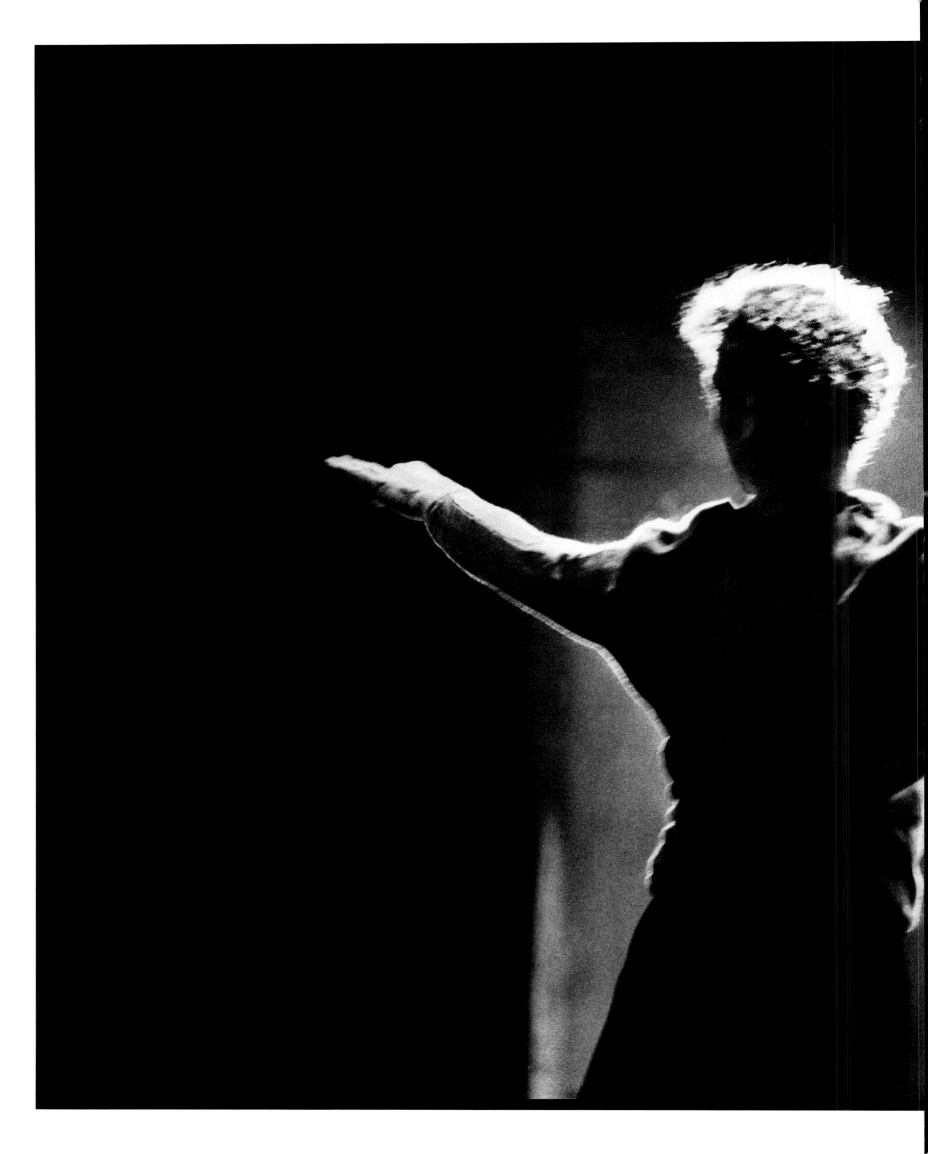

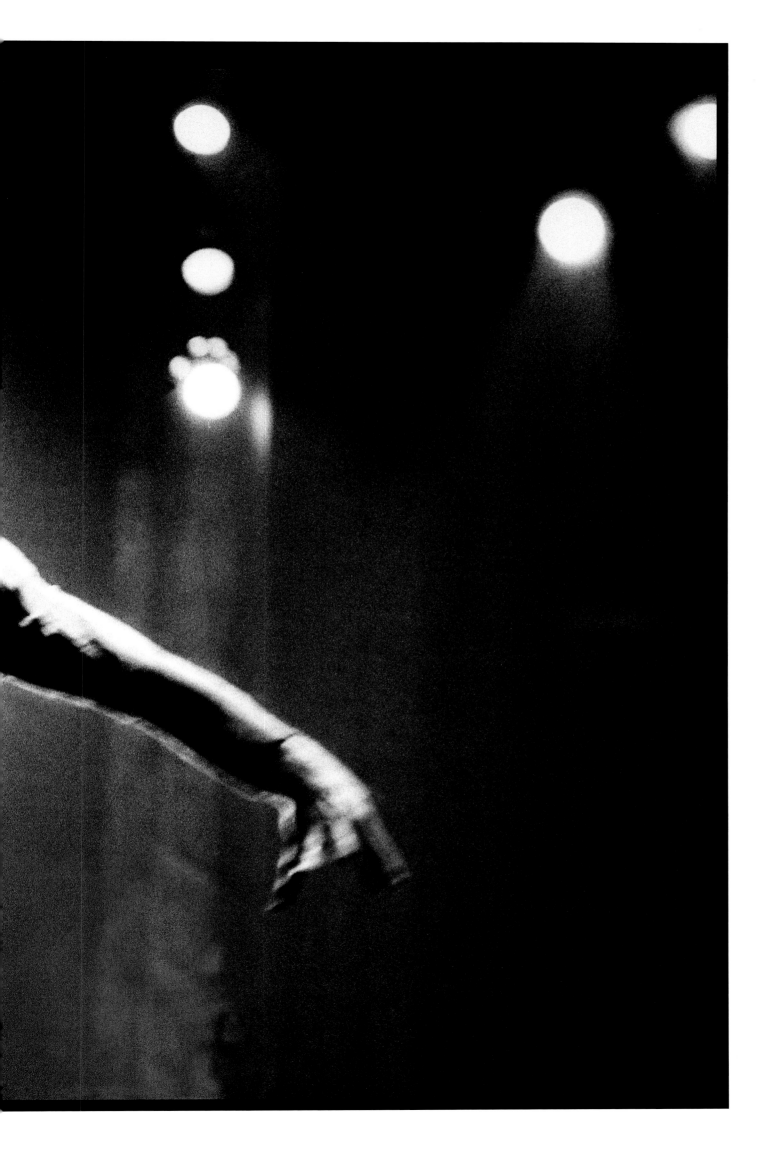

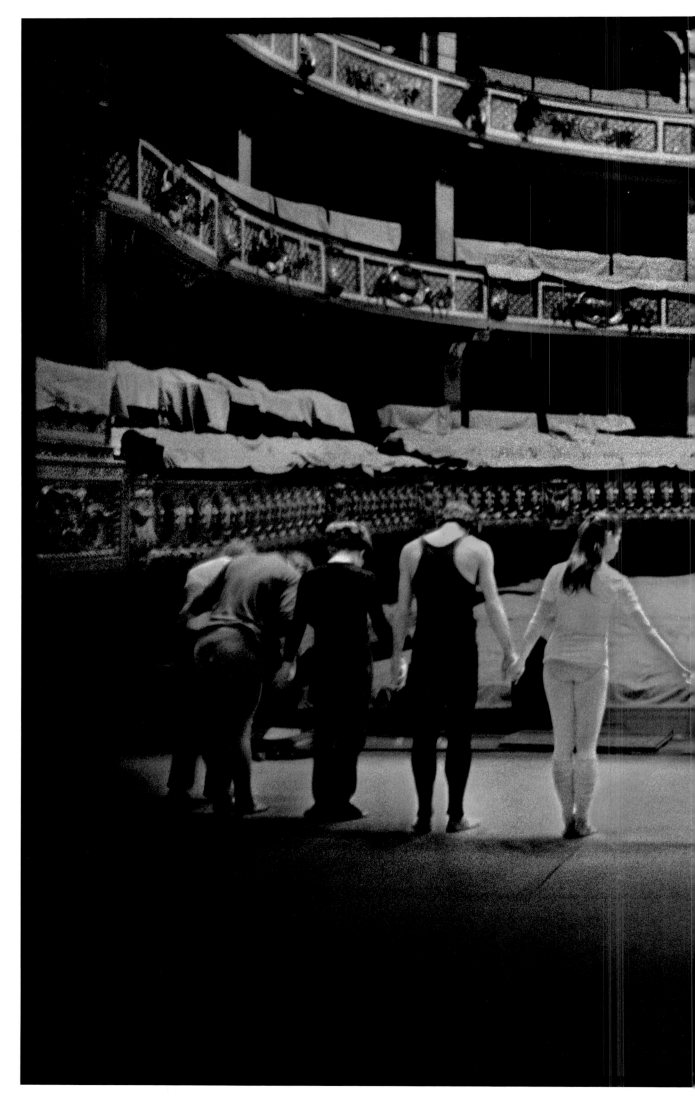

A Concise History of
the Avant-Garde
(as Lincoln Kirstein
would have it)

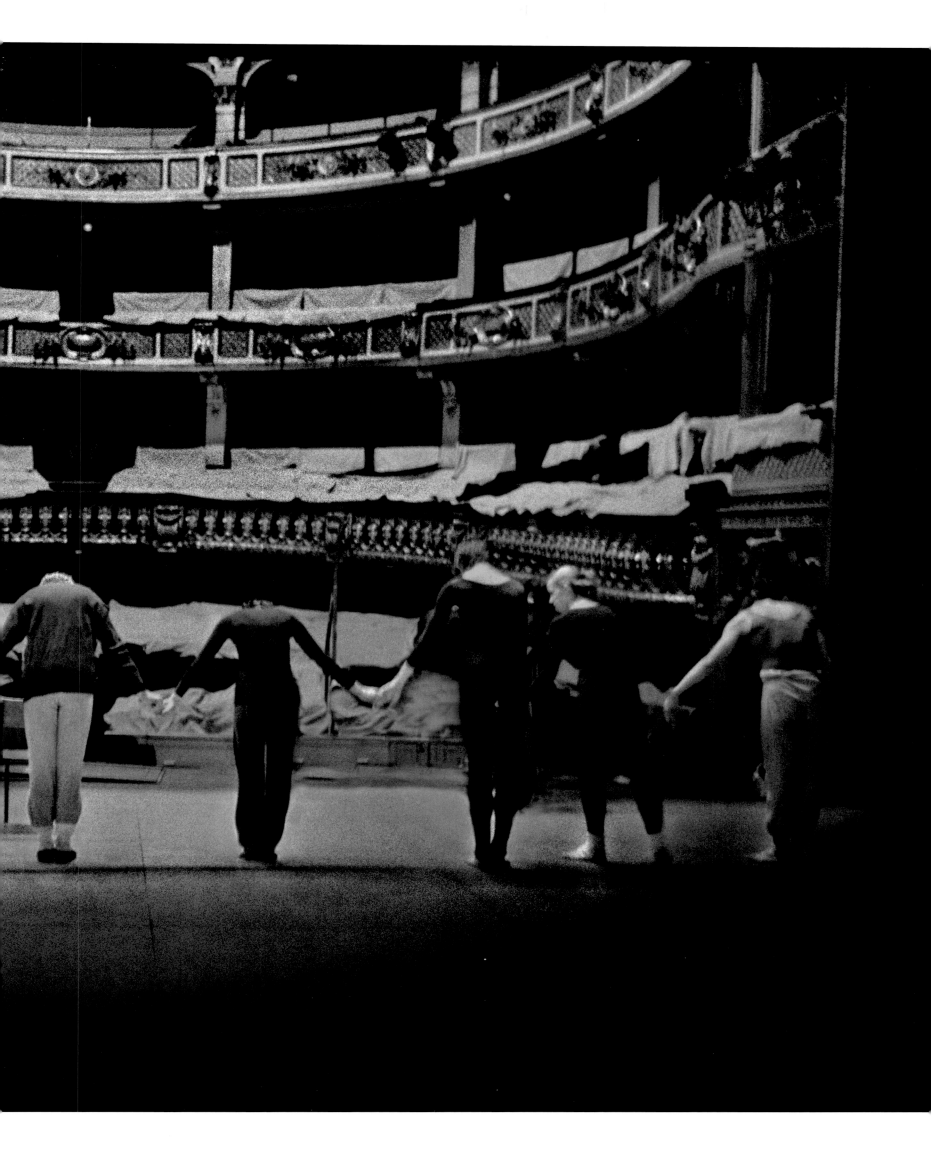

Merce Cunningham solarized print

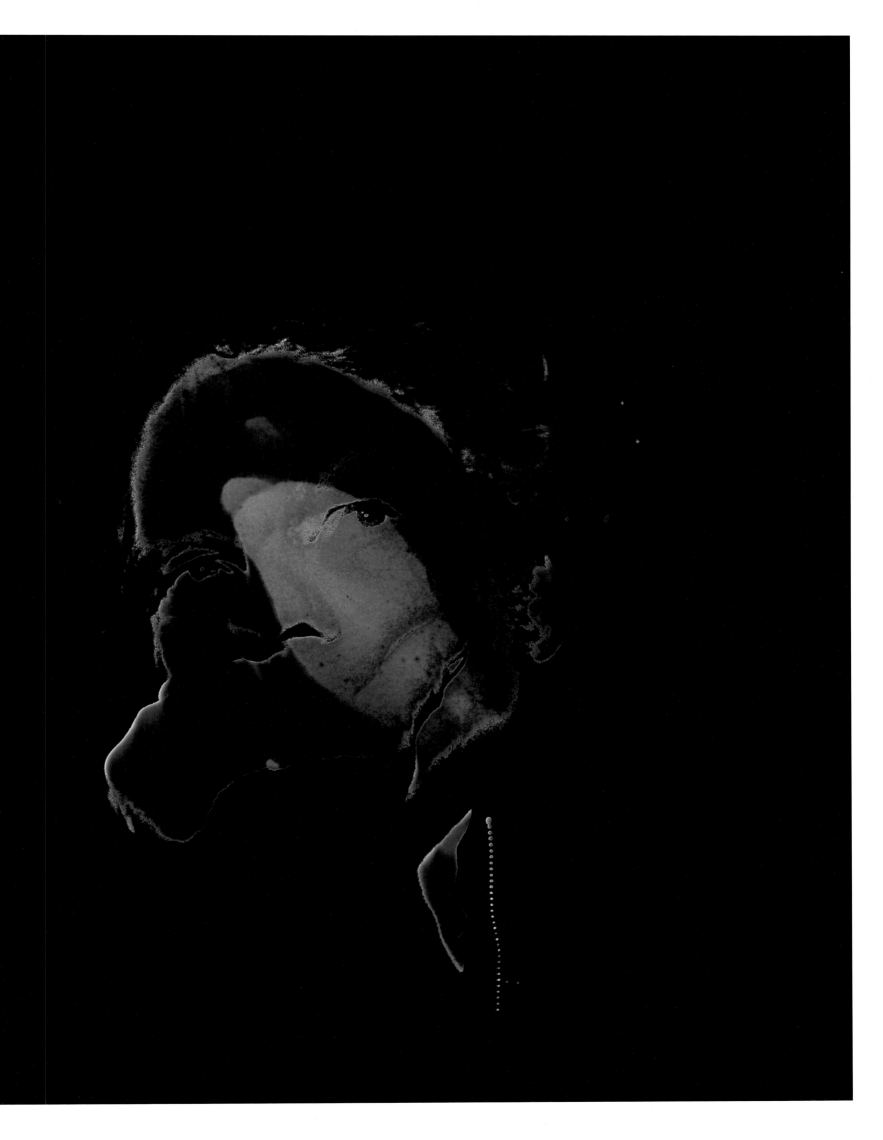

CONTRIBUTORS

CAROLYN BROWN

Carolyn Brown was one of the founding members of the Merce Cunningham Dance Company, a principle dancer and Merce Cunningham's partner for twenty years, performing in forty-three of Merce Cunningham's dances and traveling with the company throughout the United States, Europe, Canada, Mexico, South America, Iran, India, Thailand, and Japan. In addition to performing with MCDC Ms. Brown created her part in John Cage's *Theatre Piece* and danced on *point* in Robert Rauschenberg's *Pelican*. After leaving the company she worked as a freelance choreographer, filmmaker, writer, lecturer, and teacher. In 2007 Knopf published her book *Chance and Circumstance: Twenty Years with Cage and Cunningham* (a 2007 National Award for Arts Writing Finalist). In 2009 the book was published in paperback by Northwestern University Press, and as an e-book in 2010.

EARLE BROWN (1926–2002)

The composer Earle Brown was a member of a group of experimental composers known as the New York School, which included John Cage, Morton Feldman, and Christian Wolff. His early work in graphic and proportional notation, open form, and improvisational techniques was a major influence in the development of contemporary music both here and abroad. His own music was mainly influenced by the work of artists, not composers, especially Alexander Calder and his mobiles, and led to Brown's "open form" and Jackson Pollack's action paintings, which contributed to Brown's concern with "spontaneity." His *Indices* was especially written for Cunningham's *Springweather and People*; his *Four Systems* was the music of Cunningham's *Galaxy* and *December 52* was the music for Cunningham's *Hands Birds*, his solo for Carolyn Brown.

JOHN CAGE (1912–1992)

John Cage, closely associated with Merce Cunningham since Mr. Cunningham's earliest days as a choreographer, was probably America's most influential contemporary composer. His first book, *Silence*, has long since become a classic. After *Silence* he published *A Year From Monday*, *M*, *Empty Words*, *Composition In Retrospect*, *Diary: How to Improve the World (You Will Only Make Matters Worse)*, *X: Writings '79–'82*, and several others. He has edited a collection of music manuscripts published under the title *Notations*. Inventor of the prepared piano, student of Arnold Schoenberg, friend of Marcel Duchamp and Buckminster Fuller, Mr. Cage harnessed the ancient wisdom of the *I Ching* to the uses of art, systematized chance as a method of composition, and generally confounded all those who pretend to know what art is and is not.

EDWIN DENBY (1903–1983)

When he was actively reviewing, Edwin Denby was this country's most respected critic of the dance. His writings have appeared in many publications, and from 1942 to 1945 he was dance critic for the *New York Herald Tribune*. His prophetic review of Merce Cunningham's first solo recital was reprinted in these pages with the kind permission of the author. His books include *Looking at the Dance* and *Dancers, Buildings and People in the Streets*.

DOUGLAS DUNN

Douglas Dunn danced with Merce Cunningham from 1969 to 1973. He first presented his own work in 1971, and his company, Douglas Dunn + Dancers, continues. He has set pieces for many companies besides his own, including the Paris Opera Ballet (Stravinsky's *Pulcinella*, 1980), and has composed numerous outdoor and site-specific events. Renowned as a teacher of

Technique and of Open Structures, Dunn is a frequent guest artist at major institutions across the United States and abroad, and has a thirty-year tenure at New York University's Steinhardt School of Culture, Education, and Human Development. His awards include a Guggenheim, a Bessie, and a Chevalier in the Ordres des Arts et des Lettres. Dunn produces Salons at his studio in Soho, showing dance, music, film, poetry, and painting. He is board member emeritus of Danspace Project, New York City, since 2005. His collected writing, *Dancer Out of Sight*, is available at Amazon.com and DouglasDunnDance.com.

JASPER JOHNS

A friend of Cunningham and Cage since the 1950s, Jasper Johns became artistic advisor of the Cunningham Company in 1967. He has designed and executed the costumes for Cunningham's *Suite de Danses* (1961), *Rainforest* (1968), *Walkaround Time* (1968), *Canfield* (1969), *Second Hand* (1970), *Landrover* (1972), *TV Rerun* (1972), and *Un Jour ou Deux* (1973). He conceived and executed the transcription of Marcel Duchamp's *The Large Glass* as the decor for *Walkaround Time*, and designed and executed the decor for *Un Jour ou Deux*. Needless to say, Mr. Johns is one of America's foremost artists.

LINCOLN KIRSTEIN (1907–1996)

Lincoln Kirstein brought George Balanchine to America in 1933. One year later they founded the School of American Ballet and, in 1946, Ballet Society. Mr. Kirstein has been the general director of the New York City Ballet since its birth in 1948. He is the author of many important books on the dance, among them *Three Pamphlets Collected*, *Dance: A Short History of Theatrical Dancing*, and *Movement and Metaphor: Four Centuries of Ballet*.

LEWIS LLOYD

Lewis Lloyd was manager of Merce Cunningham and Dance Company from 1962 to 1968. Following his work with Cunningham he was general manager of the Brooklyn Academy of Music, program director for the Performing Arts for the New York State Council On The Arts, and then administrative manager of the WGBH Educational Foundation in Boston.

GORDON MUMMA

Gordon Mumma joined John Cage and David Tudor as one of the Cunningham Company's permanent composer/musicians in 1966. His *Mesa* (1966) was the music for Mr. Cunningham's *Place* (1966), and his *Telepos* (1972) accompanies *TV Rerun* (1972). Mr. Mumma was a member of the Sonic Arts Union and was a founder of the Once Festival in Ann Arbor. He has de-signed electronic music equipment not only for the Cunningham Company but for his own music and for the Expo '70 in Osaka. Mumma has been lecturer in music and dramatic arts at the University of Illinois, Ferienkurse für Neue Musik in Darmstadt, and the Cursos Latinoamericanos de Música Contemporánea (Uruguay, Argentina, and Dominican Republic). From 1975 to 1995 he was professor of music at the University of California (Santa Cruz and San Diego). His major book is *Cybersonic Arts: Adventures in American New Music*, edited with commentary by Michelle Fillion and foreword by Christian Wolff, was published in 2015. In 2019 he received the SEAMUS lifetime Achievement Award for contributions to electro-acoustic music.

RICHARD NELSON

Richard Nelson became company lighting designer in 1968, having toured as its technician between 1959 and 1962. His early work with Cunningham, Erick Hawkins, Aileen Pasloff, and James Waring preceeded assignments with Robert Wilson, Experiments in Art and Technology, Netherlands Dance Theater, the Boston Ballet, Lincoln Center Repertory Theater, the Louis Falco Company, and many Broadway shows including *All Over* and *The Magic Show*. In 1985 Nelson won the Tony Award for Best Lighting Design for Stephen Sondheim's *Sunday in the Park with George*.

PAULINE OLIVEROS (1932–2016)

The prominent American composer Pauline Oliveros is professor of music at the University of California at San Diego in La Jolla. She has worked in a variety of advanced musical forms of which her score for Cunningham's *Canfield* (1969), *In Memoriam: Nikola Tesla, Cosmic Engineer* is a prime example. She has long been Interested in the relationship between music and extrasensory perception. In 1974 she conducted two evenings of Sonic Meditations in New York City. She was the 2009 recipient of the William Schuman Award from Columbia University. In 2012 she received the John Cage Award from the Foundation for Contemporary Arts.

YVONNE RAINER

Yvonne Rainer, one of the founders of the Judson Dance Theater (1962), made a transition to filmmaking following a fifteen-year career as a choreographer/dancer (1960–1975). After making seven experimental feature-length films—*Lives of Performers* (1972), *Privilege* (1990), and *MURDER and murder* (1996), among others—she returned to dance in 2000 via a commission from the Baryshnikov Dance Foundation (*After Many a Summer Dies the Swan*). Since then she has made six dances, including *AG Indexical*, *With a Little Help From H. M.*, *Assisted Living: Do You*

Have Any Money? and *The Concept of Dust: Continuous Project— Altered Annually*. Her dances and films have been seen throughout the U.S. and Europe. Museum retrospectives of her work, including drawings, photos, films, notebooks, and memorabilia, have been presented at Kunsthaus Bregenz and Museum Ludwig, Cologne (2012); the Getty Research Institute, Los Angeles (2014); Jeu de Paume, École des Beaux Artes, La Ferme du Buisson, Paris, and Raven Row, London (2014). A memoir—*Feelings Are Facts: a Life*—was published by MIT Press in 2006. A selection of her poetry was published in 2011 by Paul Chan's Badlands Unlimited. Other writings have been collected in *Yvonne Rainer: Work: 1961– 73* (1974); *The Films of Y. R.* (1989); *A Woman Who . . . Essays, Interviews, Scripts* (1999); and *Moving and Being Moved* (2017). She is a recipient of two Guggenheim Fellowships, a MacArthur Fellowship, and a U.S.A. Fellowship.

ROBERT RAUSCHENBERG (1925–2008)

Robert Rauschenberg had a close and intricate relationship with the work of Merce Cunningham from 1954 to 1964. In 1961 he became the Cunningham Company's stage manager, lighting designer, and designer of its decor and costumes. He remained with the company through the world tour of 1964. His work in the theater has included many of his own pieces, and he was the moving force behind such major events as the First New York Theater Rally (1965) and the Nine Evenings of Art and Technology (1966). In the following list, those dances for which he designed costumes are marked *C* and those for which he designed decor are marked *D*: 1954—*Minutiae* (D); 1956—*Suite for Five in Space and Time* (C); 1957—*Labyrinthian Dances* (C), *Springweather and People* (C), *Changeling* (C); 1958—*Antic Meet* (D & C), *Summerspace* (D & C); 1959—*From the Poems of White Stone* (C), *Gambit for Dancers and Orchestra* (C), *Rune* (C); 1960—*Crises* (C), *Waka* (C), *Hands Birds, Music Walk with Dancers* (C); 1961—*Aeon* (D & C); 1963—*Field Dances* (C), *Night Wandering* (C; the original production, 1958, had costumes by Nicola Cernovlch), *Story* (D & C); 1964—*Paired* (C), *Winterbranch* (D & C; and its very special lighting).

VIOLA FARBER SLAYTON (1931–1998)

Viola Farber Slayton was a principal dancer of the Merce Cunningham Dance Company from 1953–1965, performing in twenty-six of Cunningham's works. After leaving Cunningham she formed her own company and has toured extensively in the United States and abroad. She was married to the former Cunningham dancer Jeff Slayton. She was artistic director of Centre National de Danse Contemporiane in Angers 1981 to 1983, and was also director of the Sarah Lawrence College Dance Department from 1988 to 1998.

MICHAEL SNELL

Despite the helpfulness of Michael Snell's article on the relationship of Cunningham's 1970 *Second Hand* to Erik Satie's 1919 *Socrate* (part of an article that appeared in the 1971 *Ballet Review* 3, no. 6) nothing else by Michael Snell seems extant. His biographical note at the end of that publication says, quite unhelpfully, "Michael Snell is a skin-diver who has followed the dance scene for some time." The article quoted in these pages is excerpted from Snell's longer, surprisingly snarky article, "Cunningham and the Critics," and is used here without permission as Mr. Snell has proven impossible to locate.

PAUL TAYLOR (1930–2018)

Paul Taylor, before six years as a soloist with Martha Graham, was a member of the Cunningham Company at Black Mountain College in 1953 and during the company's first New York season in the winter of 1953–54. He formed his own company immediately thereafter and has since performed the world over as one of the leading figures of the American modern dance.

DAVID TUDOR (1926–1996)

The pianist and composer David Tudor worked with the Merce Cunningham Dance Company since its formation in 1953. As a pianist and exponent of experimental contemporary music in the 1950s, his position was unparalleled, and compositions were sent to him from around the globe for their first performances. As an innovator of techniques for the production of live electronic music he expanded the limits of virtuosity in the medium. His *Bandoneon!* (1966) was the score for Mr. Cunningham's *Rainforest* (1968), and has since been frequently performed as a concert piece separate from the dance.

CHRISTIAN WOLFF

The composer Christian Wolff is also a classics scholar whose specialty is Euripides. He taught classics at Harvard, then from 1971 to 1999 he taught both music and classics at Dartmouth College. His work is equally well known and influential in Europe, Japan and the U.S. Many of Mr. Cunningham's dances have used Mr. Wolff's music, including *Untitled Solo* (*For Piano I*), *Lavish Escapade* (*For Piano II*), *Changeling* (*Suite*), *Rune* (*Music For Merce Cunningham*), *Tread* (*For 1, 2 or 3 People*), *Borst Park* (*Burdocks*), and *Loose Time* (*Moving Spaces*). *For 1, 2 or 3 People* and *Burdocks* are both central works and widely performed in concert. Starting in the later 1990s and until the dissolution of the Merce Cunningham dance company Mr. Wolff was, with Takehisa Kosugi, David Behrman, and John King, a member of the company's music committee and frequent performer on piano and percussion.

NOTES ON TEXT

PAGE 8

Martin Duberman, *Black Mountain: An Exploration in Community* (New York: Anchor Press/Doubleday, 1973).

PAGE 42–57

A small portion of this text appeared in "Essays, Stories, and Remarks about Merce Cunningham," *Dance Perspectives* 34 (Summer 1968). Copyright 1968 by Dance Perspectives Foundation and used with their permission.

PAGE 144–145

This article also appears in Yvonne Rainer, *Yvonne Rainer: Work 1961–73* (Halifax: The Press of Nova Scotia College of Art and Design; New York: New York University Press, 1974).

PAGE 210–211

Lincoln Kirstein, largely responsible for whatever classic ballet tradition America can call its own, held views on modern dance that were well known. Basically, he didn't believe there was a future in it. This text is excerpted from a 1971 correspondence between us.

PAGE 231

Jasper Johns in conversation with David Vaughan, "The Fabric of Friendship," page 141 of the remarkable book *Dancers on a Plane Cage, Cunningham, Johns*, which essentially served as the catalog for a 1989 exhibition presented by the Anthony d'Offay Gallery, London.

PAGE 266–268

Portions of the text appeared in somewhat different form in "Cunningham and the Critics," *Ballet Review* 3, no. 6 (1971).

PAGE 294–303

Gordon Mumma's 1975 contribution in these pages can now be found in his recent book, *Cybersonic Arts: Adventures in American New Music*, ed. Michelle Fillion (Urbana: University of Illinois Press, 2015).

PAGE 360–361

Reprinted from Edwin Denby, *Looking at the Dance* (New York: Horizon Press, 1949). Copyright 1949 by Edwin Denby. Used by permission of Horizon Press.

DANCERS PICTURED

ANTIC MEET

MERCE CUNNIUNGHAM

VALDA SETTERFIELD

SANDRA NEELS

CAROLYN BROWN

SUSANA HAYMAN-CHAFFEY

MEL WONG

ASSEMBLAGE

MERCE CUNNINGHAM

CAROLYN BROWN

MEG HARPER

SANDRA NEELS

CHASE ROBINSON

JEFF SLAYTON

MEL WONG

VALDA SETTERFIELD

SUSANA HAYMAN-CHAFFEY

BORST PARK

SANDRA NEELS

MERCE CUNNINGHAM

CANFIELD

MERCE CUNNINGHAM

CAROLYN BROWN

MEG HARPER

SANDRA NEELS

JEFF SLAYTON

VALDA SETTERFIELD

CHASE ROBINSON

VALDA SETTERFIELD

SUSANA HAYMAN-CHAFFEY

MEL WONG

CRISES

MERCE CUNNINGHAM

VIOLA FARBER SLAYTON

CAROLYN BROWN

SUSANA HAYMAN-CHAFFEY

HOW TO PASS, KICK, FALL AND RUN

MERCE CUNNINGHAM

CHASE ROBINSON

CAROLYN BROWN

JEFF SLAYTON

SANDRA NEELS

VALDA SETTERFIELD

NIGHT WANDERING

MERCE CUNNINGHAM

CAROLYN BROWN

PLACE

MERCE CUNNINGHAM

CAROLYN BROWN

MEG HARPER

JEFF SLAYTON

MEL WONG

SANDREA NEELS

CHASE ROBINSON

VALDA SETTERFIELD

SCRAMBLE

MERCE CUNNUNGHAM

CAROLYN BROWN

SANDRA NEELS

SUSANA HAYMAN-CHAFFEY

JEFF SLAYTON

CHASE ROBINSON

VALDA SETTERFIELD

RAINFOREST

MERCE CUNNINGHAM

BARBARA DILLY LLOYD

MEG HARPER

CHASE ROBINSON

CAROLYN BROWN

JEFF SLAYTON

MEL WONG

SECOND HAND

MERCE CUNNINGHAM

CAROLYN BROWN

ULYSSES DOVE

MEG HARPER

DOUGLAS DUNN

SUSANA HAYMAN-CHAFFEY

YSEULT RIOPELLE

ED HENKEL

SANDRA NEELS

CHASE ROBINSON

VALDA SETTERFIELD

MEL WONG

SIGNALS

SUSANA HAYMAN-CHAFFEY

MEL WONG

MERCE CUNNINGHAM

DOUGLAS DUNN

VALDA SETTERFIELD

LOUISE BURNS

TREAD

SANDRA NEELS

JEFF SLAYTON

DOUGLAS DUNN

MEL WONG

MERCE CUNNINGHAM

CAROLYN BROWN

MEG HARPER

SUSANA HAYMAN-CHAFFEY

CAROLYN BROIWN

WALKAROUND TIME

MERCE CUNNINGHAM

SUSANA HAYMAN-CHAFFEY

SANDRA NEELS

CAROLYN BROWN

WINTERBRANCH

MERCE CUNNINGHAM

CAROLYN BROWN

SANDRA NEELS

JEFF SLAYTON

VALDA SETTERFIELD

ACKNOWLEDGMENTS

Neither the original 1975 edition nor the subsequent 1986 Limelight Edition of *Merce Cunningham* contained an acknowledgments page—an omission I redress now, starting with the most overdue: Thank you to Barbara Newman, my closest friend in high school, author of *Striking a Balance: Dancers Talk About Dancing*. She requested I promise to see the work of Merce Cunningham if the opportunity ever arose. I agreed, but in the late 1950s this was easier said than done. It took five years and an oceanic crossing. Staying with my aunt in London in 1964, feasting on theater, I learned the Cunningham Company was there. "Oh!" I said to myself, "I'm supposed to see that." Somewhat dutifully I did. At the next day's matinee of *Coriolanus* I found myself distracted. Leaving at first intermission, I ran several blocks to the Phoenix Theater where Cunningham was in residence and snuck in, seeing every succeeding performance possible. This book would not exist had Barbara not exacted that promise from me.

Thank you to that dear man Leo Castelli, who gave me an exhibition at his West Broadway Gallery coinciding, more or less, with the publication of *Merce Cunningham*. He had no need. Ditto to Cornell Capa, who repeated the kindness later that same year at the institution he had founded the year before, the International Center of Photography. These exhibits were important to me not because of prestige of association but because the photographs could be seen properly. Neither edition of *Merce Cunningham* had been well printed.

Which leads me to a hearty thank you to Yolanda Cuomo, whose instincts and craft as a book designer have proven invaluable in *John Cage Was* (2014), *Greece 66* (2018), and now *Redux*. The thanks extend to Yo's wonderful team, Bonnie Briant, Bobbie Richardson, Jonno Rattman, and to Morgan Sloan, who uncannily did what was needed before I had to ask. I look forward to working again with Daniel Frank at Meridian Printing, who so beautifully realized *John Cage Was*.

Finally, thank you to Melissa Harris, who first connected me with Yo, and to Carolyn Brown and Alison Granucci, whose suggestions were helpful in bringing *Merce Cunningham: Redux* to fruition.

Merce Cunningham: Redux

Copyright ©1975 James Klosty
Introduction © 1986 James Klosty
Foreword © 2019 James Klosty
All other text © attributed authors

Published in the United States by powerHouse Books,
a division of powerHouse Cultural Entertainment, Inc.
32 Adams Street, Brooklyn, NY 11201-1021
e-mail: info@powerHouseBooks.com
website: www.powerHouseBooks.com

Third edition, 2019

Library of Congress Control Number: 2019948421

ISBN 978-1-57687-942-9

First edition designed by Jeanette Young

DESIGNED BY YOLANDA CUOMO DESIGN, NYC
Associate Designer: Bonnie Briant
Junior Designer: Bobbie Richardson
Assistant Designer: Morgan Sloan

Separations by Thomas Palmer

Typeset in Helvetica Neue and printed on McCoy Matte
Printed by Meridian Printing, Rhode Island
Under the supervision of Daniel Frank

10 9 8 7 6 5 4 3 2 1

Printed and bound in the USA

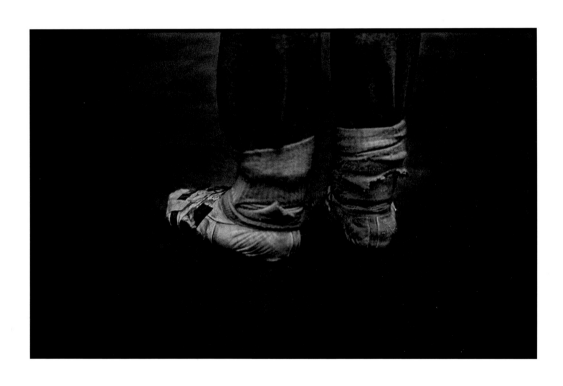

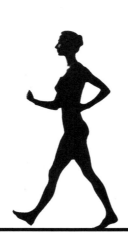

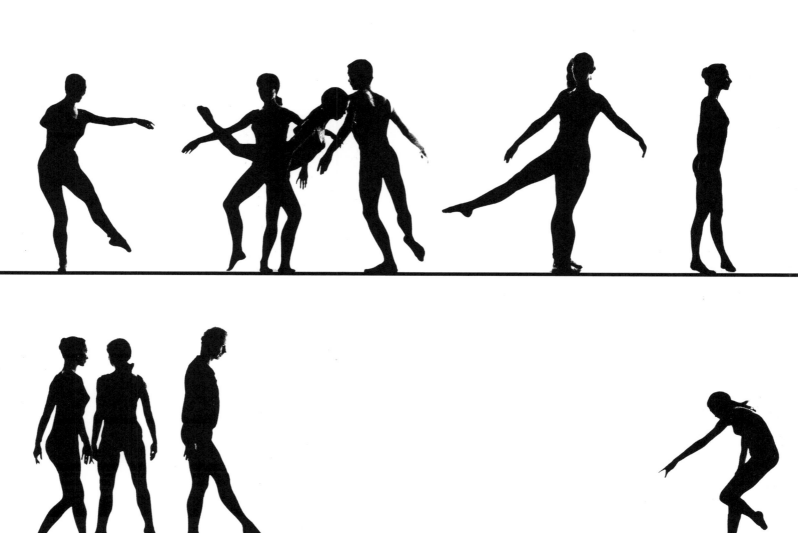

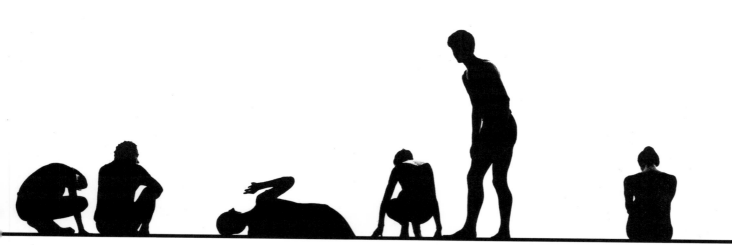